GNVQ Advanced

Business

SECOND EDITION

Roger Lewis • Roger Trevitt

STANLEY
THORNES

First published in 1994 by:
Stanley Thornes (Publishers) Ltd
Ellenborough House
Wellington Street
CHELTENHAM
GL50 1YD
UK

Reprinted 1994
Reprinted 1995
2nd Edition 1995

A catalogue record for this book is available from the British Library.
ISBN 0 7487 2203 3

The cover photograph is reproduced with the permission of the Telegraph Colour Library.

Typeset by Tech-Set, Tyne & Wear.
Printed and bound in Great Britain at The Bath Press, Avon.

Acknowledgements

The authors are grateful to all of those who have helped in this project. In particular we would like to thank:

- Margaret Chadwick of Lambeth College for contributing Chapter 4 on Information Technology and also for providing valuable assistance with research
- Liz Lewis for her many hours at the keyboard
- the Principal, our colleagues and students at Southwark College
- The following organisations for their especial help and co-operation: The Automobile Association and Sample Surveys Ltd; BTEC, RSA, City and Guilds and NCVQ; The Bank of England; British Rail and Barkers Advertising; The British Standards Institute; Lloyds Bank plc; Nestlé; The Toyota Motor Corporation; European Passenger Services, Bass Brewers.

GNVQ units on page iv are reproduced with the permission of NCVQ.

We would like also to aknowledge the support and encouragement that we have received throughout from the publishing team at Stanley Thornes.

Finally we wish to apologise to our families – again!

Roger Lewis
Roger Trevitt
June 1995

Contents

GNVQ Advanced Business: Summary of mandatory units

Unit 1 Business in the economy (advanced)

1.1 Analyse the forces of supply and demand on businesses
1.2 Analyse the operation of markets and their effects on businesses and communities
1.3 Examine the effects of government policies on markets

Unit 2 Business organisations and systems (advanced)

2.1 Investigate business organisations
2.2 Investigate administration systems
2.3 Analyse communication in a business organisation
2.4 Analyse information processing in a business organisation

Unit 3 Marketing (advanced)

3.1 Investigate the principles and functions of marketing in organisations
3.2 Propose and present product developments based on analysis of marketing research information
3.3 Evaluate marketing communications designed to influence a target audience
3.4 Evaluate sales methods and customer service to achieve customer satisfaction

Unit 4 Human resources (advanced)

4.1 Investigate human resourcing
4.2 Investigate job roles iand changing working conditions
4.3 Evaluate recruitment procedures, job applications and interviews

Unit 5 Production and employment in the economy (advanced)

5.1 Analyse production in businesses
5.2 Investigate and evaluate employment
5.3 Examine the competitiveness of UK industry

Unit 6 Financial transactions, costing and pricing (advanced)

6.1 Explain added value, distribution of added value and money cycle
6.2 Explain financial transactions and complete supporting documents
6.3 Calculate the cost of goods or services
6.4 Explain basic pricing decisions and breakeven

Unit 7 Financial forecasting and monitoring (advanced)

7.1 Explain sources of finance and financial requirements of business organisations
7.2 Produce and explain forecasts and a cash flow for a small business
7.3 Produce and explain profit and loss statements and balance sheets
7.4 Identify and explain data to monitor a business

Unit 8 Business planning (advanced)

8.1 Prepare work and collect data for a business plan
8.2 Produce and present a business plan
8.3 Plan for employment or self-employment

GNVQ Core skills: Summary of elements, level 3

Communication

3.1 Take part in discussions
3.2 Produce written material
3.3 Use images
3.4 Read and respond to written materials

Application of number

3.1 Collect and record data
3.2 Tackle problems
3.3 Interpret and present data

Information technology

3.1 Prepare information
3.2 Process information
3.3 Present information
3.4 Evaluate the use of information technology

Introduction

Welcome to your new course, the General National Vocational Qualification (GNVQ) Advanced level in Business. Starting a new course is fun, but it is never easy. This introduction will help to answer some of the questions you may have.

How does the course work?

The course is composed of **mandatory units, optional units** and **core skills units**. To begin with you will find it helpful to know the meaning of these terms.

Mandatory units

These cover the knowledge that is needed to understand how any business works. The mandatory units for Advanced Business are listed on page iv. You will need to study all eight units.

Optional units

These allow you to specialise in a particular subject or area of work. Depending on the awarding body for which you are entered, the optional units for Advanced Business include the following:

BTEC	C & G	RSA
Creative marketing communications	The European Union and local business	Quality, safety and the environment
Statistics for marketing	Developing human resources	Business law
Behaviour at work	Communications within business	Financial services
Financial services	Managing risk	Leadership and teamwork
Administrative operations	Legal obligations of business	Business and the European Union
Producer development and realisation	Business and the environment	Management information systems
Business and the law	International trade and finance	Industrial relations
Living and working in Europe		Conducting market research

You will need to choose four option units to study. (Note that your centre does not have to offer all of the options which are available. However, you should be able to take a combination of units which will help you to progress into higher education or business.)

Core skills units

These are the essential skills that you must possess to enable you to succeed in your future career. They are listed on page iv for level 3. You will need to develop these skills but they should not be thought of as 'subjects', but rather as tools which you will need in order to complete the mandatory and optional units.

Elements

Each unit is made up of a number of elements which tell you what you have to be able to do in order to gain the qualification.

What does an element look like?

Unit 4, for example, is composed of the following elements:

Unit 4 Human resources
- 4.1 Investigate human resourcing
- 4.2 Investigate job roles and changing working conditions
- 4.3 Evaluate recruitment procedures, job applications and interviews

What does an element consist of?

- **Performance criteria** These explain precisely what you have to do to be able to claim that you are competent, for example 'Identify job roles in business organisations'.
- **Range** This describes the limits or spread of knowledge you must achieve.
- **Evidence indicators** This is the work which you have done, for example reports, questionnaires, videos, photographs, etc., to show you have the skills knowledge and understanding needed in the unit.

How will the units be taught?

This is a matter for your centre to organise and it will vary from place to place. There may be sessions built around individual units or perhaps the course will be based on particular themes linking units. Perhaps an option will be combined with a mandatory unit, perhaps sessions will be set aside for a particular skill area such as IT. Your centre will decide how it can best offer the course to suit your needs.

What must I do to pass?

You must be able to demonstrate success in every performance criteria in each of the unit elements. In doing this you must also have shown that you are competent in the three core skills. You will need to achieve 15 units as follows:

- 8 mandatory units
- 4 optional units
- 3 core skills units.

How will I be assessed?

You will be assessed in two ways:

1 You must complete a portfolio of coursework. This will be built up as you go along. Your tutor will provide you with the necessary course documents and will review your progress regularly but you should make it your responsibility to keep your records up-to-date.

2 There is an external test which you must pass in 7 of the mandatory units. Unit 8, *Business Planning*, is not tested.

What grades are there?

If you achieve all competencies in all units then you will **pass** the award.

It is also possible to get the higher grades of **merit** and **distinction**. These can be achieved if you pass the external tests and your coursework is not just competent but shows that you have used a high degree of initiative and been effective in:

- planning and monitoring your work
- seeking out and using relevant information
- evaluating the outcome of your work so as to ensure that it meets the objectives you were given
- producing work of high quality.

Of course, some of your work may show these qualities and some may not. The merit and distinction grades are awarded where at least **one third** of the total evidence is of that standard.

How will this book help me to pass the course?

We have devoted 14 chapters of the book to Units 1 to 7. The last unit, Business planning, is covered in Chapter 15. This unit draws on much of the material covered earlier.

Each chapter has **activities** which will help you to develop and demonstrate your understanding, and there are also **assignments** at the end of each chapter which have been designed to cover every element. Some of the activities are short exercises which you can do in class, others will take several weeks of investigation. In total, the activities and assignments will provide a large amount of varied evidence for your portfolio by the end of the course.

To help you succeed in the external tests we have included a list of **key terms** and some short **review questions** at the end of each chapter. Make sure that you know and understand these.

Getting started

To succeed in this course you will need to take responsibility for your own actions. These introductory activities will help you to:

- be honest with yourself and recognise your strengths and weaknesses
- manage and develop yourself.

Activity

1 Team work

One of the skills you will need on the course is the ability to work with other people to complete a task. Throughout this book, you will find activities which will involve you working as part of a group or team. We use the terms 'On your own' and 'With your group' to show what is required. Many businesses want their staff to work in groups, because they believe this improves performance. For instance, some accountancy firms have taken their employees on a week's survival course to the mountains of North Wales. We cannot do this, so we will use our imagination instead.

The purpose of this activity is to examine how groups work, how you work within a group, and to help you to get to know your colleagues. Here are some descriptions of people you may find in your group:

Description	Characteristics
Information giver	Knows the information and is prepared to share it with the rest of the group
Questioner	Tries to find out more by asking 'Why?' or 'When?'
Joker	Good sense of humour, which helps in difficult situations
Clown	Far too chatty and always messing about
Shy	Might know all the answers, but is too afraid to speak
Silent	Never says a word
Hurt	Can find it difficult to accept criticism
Supporter/positive	Constructive and positive suggestions
Destructive/negative	Knocks every suggestion down and never puts anything in its place
Distracter	Never sticks to the subject
Bored	Never sees anything worthwhile: 'There no point in it'
Dominant	Always shouts down the less assertive members of the group; is frequently wrong
Aggressive	Over assertive and can become offensive
Reluctant	Unwilling and could be nervous about putting their views forward
Taker	Never contributes but always uses other people's views
Stirrer	Always tries to cause arguments
Initiator	Sparks off the group with useful suggestions
Practical	Keeps the group working and sticks to the tasks
Clarifier	Always asks for explanations
Summariser	Ties up or summarises what the group has achieved, can see the essential points

Divide your group into three teams.

a **Each team should choose 10 objects that it would wish to have on a desert island in order to survive.**

b **Once the group has chosen 10 objects, you should then use the checklist to identify yourself and other members of the group; you may fall into two or three categories. Remember tact and diplomacy are also essential!**
Decide, if this were for real, how the group should deal with difficult team members, and who should do it.

c **As a group discuss these questions:**
- **How were decisions made by the group?**
- **Did everyone participate?**
- **Did the group have a leader?**
- **Did the group have an identity or team spirit?**
- **Did the group achieve its objectives?**
- **How could the group improve?**
- **What qualities do you need to work in a group?**

d **Compare your team's responses with those of the other teams.**

2 **Problem solving**

The first stage in any problem-solving activity is to define the problem. When there is a problem it means that something has to be changed, for example long queues at the check-out of the supermarket, long delivery times, assignments are always given in late.

One approach, frequently used in industry as a starting point for solving problems, is called brainstorming. It is a useful method for generating ideas on how to approach tasks. It needs little skill and can produce instant results.

How to brainstorm

1 Get the team together.
2 Have ready a large sheet of paper, a flip chart or a board and a supply of pens, chalk, etc. to note down the suggestions.
3 Warm up with a 'silly' session to get people relaxed, for example 'How would you stop leaves falling off trees in autumn'.
4 Ensure that everyone in the team knows the purpose of the brainstorming session, i.e. the 'problem'. Every person should write down the problem.
5 The purpose of brainstorming is for the participants to produce as many suggestions as possible for solving the problem.
6 No one should criticise any suggestion or person, just try to keep the flow of suggestions going.
7 One person should write down every suggestion that is made. The team can look at them later.
8 Try to get as many ideas as possible.
9 Try to build on each other's ideas.
10 Make sure that everyone can read all the suggestions that have been made.
11 Only stop when everyone has dried up or run out of ideas.
12 Try to put the ideas into groups or categories.
13 Choose the five best ideas and try to explore them further.
14 Go for it!

The group should divide into teams of 4–6 people maximum.

a To warm up, brainstorm 'Five ways to stop leaves falling off trees in autumn'.
b This is for real. Brainstorm 'Five ways to reduce queues at the check-out of the local supermarket'.
c All teams should compare solutions and choose the best.

3 Where do you live?

On many occasions in this book we will use statistics about:

- standard industries
- standard occupations
- standard areas/regions.

These classifications are used by the UK government and the Statistical Office of the European Union, based in Luxembourg, as the basis for presenting many statistical series. For instance the standard regions which are used are: Wales, Scotland, North, North West, Yorkshire and Humberside, East Midlands, West Midlands, South West, East Anglia, South East and Northern Ireland. The United Kingdom consists of Great Britain plus Northern Ireland.

a Put your town and region on a copy of the map of the United Kingdom overleaf.
b Label the member states of the European Union on a copy of the map overleaf. You will need this information for Unit 5, Production and employment in the economy.
c Label the capital cities of the member states on the map.
d The Maastricht Treaty was in the news throughout 1993; label Maastricht too.

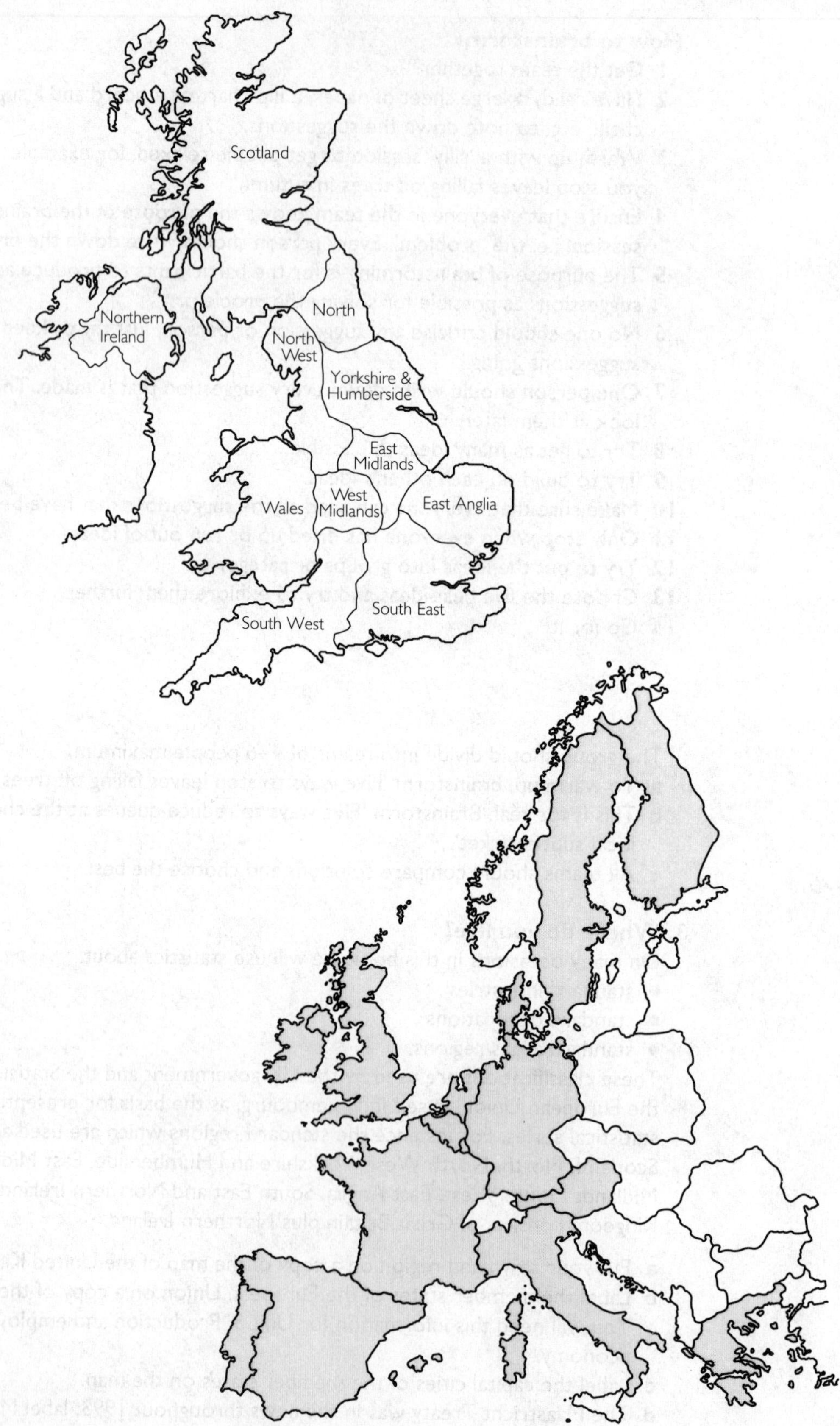
Scotland
Northern Ireland
North
North West
Yorkshire & Humberside
East Midlands
West Midlands
East Anglia
Wales
South West
South East

4 Finding information: 1

A major key to your success will be your ability to find information quickly. Your centre and local libraries will be your most important resources here; it is essential that you get to know them as quickly as possible.

The group should form four or five teams to find out the answers to these questions (there are a lot of them!).

a What is the Dewey Decimal System?

b What is classified under numbers 528, 523, 650 in the library?

c Find the *Annual Abstract of Statistics*. Find out the total UK labour force for each of the last five years.

d Find the *Monthly Digest of Statistics*. Find out the number of people employed per month for the last five months.

e Find *Social Trends*. Find out the projected population for the UK in the year 2000.

f Find the *Employment Gazette*. Find out the current employment for your town/local authority area.

g Write down the main information contained in each of these publications.

h Which newspapers and business periodicals does your library stock which could be useful in this course? Check the titles of publications against the mandatory units.

j Find the following information and say *where* you found it:

- **i** How far is it by road from Birmingham to Glasgow?
- **ii** Who is the heaviest man in the world?
- **iii** What is the highest mountain in each of England, Scotland and Wales?
- **iv** Name a town in North Humberside.
- **v** Find the telephone number of:
  - the local Inspector of Taxes
  - the local careers office
  - the local job centre.
- **vi** In what country would you find the Victoria Falls?
- **vii** Which underground line runs to Heathrow Airport?
- **viii** Where is Prestwick Airport?
- **ix** Where is Shannon Airport?
- **x** What is the current exchange rate for Spanish pesetas?
- **xi** Who was the King of England during the Second World War?
- **xii** What is the name of your local MP?
- **xiii** What is the name of your local MEP?
- **xiv** What are the names of the local constituencies?

5 Finding information: 2

Find the Standard Occupational Classification. This is a way of classifying the types of jobs in the UK. You will find the full list of occupations in Part A of the *New Earnings Survey 1994*. This is useful because it will enable you to be precise about how you describe occupations.

There are nine major groups of occupations:

Major group	Sub major group
1 Managers and administrators	Corporate managers Managers in agriculture/services
2 Professional occupations	Science and engineering Health professionals Teaching professionals Other professionals
3 Associate professionals and technical occupations	Science and engineering Health professionals Other associates
4 Clerical and secretarial occupations	Clerical occupations Secretarial occupations
5 Craft and related occupations	Skilled construction Skilled engineering Other skilled trades
6 Personal and protective services occupations	Protective services Personal services
7 Sales occupations	Buyers, brokers and sales reps Other sales occupations
8 Plant and machine operatives	Industrial plant and machine operatives Drivers and mobile machine operators
9 Other occupations	Agriculture, forestry, fishing Other elementary occupations

How are the following jobs/occupations classified?

hospital porter
motor mechanic
sales assistant
security guard
marketing manager
judge
printer
tobacco process operative
computer analyst
vet
college principal
teacher
engine driver
telephone fitter
police officer
playgroup leader

Socio-economic groups

Socio-economic groups are frequently used to target people for marketing purposes, for example: Who reads the *Sun*? Who watches *Neighbours*? The answers will determine what is advertised in the *Sun* and what adverts appear during *Home and Away*. Although many characteristics can be used to classify people, such as education, age, sex, number of people in the household, or income, occupation is most frequently used to indicate which social class people belong to.

Occupation	Social Group	Social Class
Professional Managers	A	Upper Middle
Middle Managers	B	Middle Class
Clerical/Office	C1	Lower Middle Class
Skilled Manual	C2	Skilled Working Class
Manual	D	Working Class
Students	E	

You will need this information for Unit 3, Marketing.

Activity

My skills

One of the questions often asked at interviews is 'What are your strengths and weaknesses?' Make a list of what *you* consider to be your main strengths and weaknesses. Some examples might be:

Strengths	**Weaknesses**
Kind	Give up too soon
Honest	Sulky
Reliable	Can't take criticism
Sociable	Never meet deadlines
Hard working	Sloppy
Ambitious	Untidy
Friendly	Could work harder
Conscientious	Careless
Determined	Always late
Organised	Disorganised

Once you have created your lists you need to create an action plan headed 'How I can improve', for example:

How I can improve

1 Weaknesses to be eliminated: 'Never meet deadlines'

Action plan

Do

- Keep a diary or year plan. Be aware of all work – be aware of all deadlines.
- Identify immediately the main implications, for example:
  What do I need?
  Where will I get it?
  When can I go there?
  Do I have to make an appointment?
  How long will it take?
- Allocate enough time and draw up a plan. Perhaps I can leave it for three weeks, perhaps I need to write a letter now. Be realistic, remember there are other things to do as well and allow for unforeseen problems!

Don't leave everything until the night before.

You should now complete the rest of your action plan. This will be an ongoing process. You will find a similar questionnaire in Chapter 15, Business planning, at the end of the book.

Presenting information

One key to your success is being able to present information effectively using the appropriate method. Sometimes it is important to use a computer, on other occasions it is sufficient, or even preferable, to work by hand.

You will need to use computers during the course. Remember Information Technology is one of the core skills. We do not attempt to teach you IT skills in this book, though many of the activities are designed to develop them. Here are some hints on general presentation.

The main applications that you will use will be word processing, databases, spreadsheets and desktop publishing. You may also use specialised packages, perhaps for accounting or design. There are many different products available but in general they will work in much the same way and give equally good results. Whatever package you use **do save your work regularly and keep back up copies** (these words are written with feeling!). It may be that 'it wasn't my fault – the network crashed!' but if you have lost an afternoon's work that is no consolation, you have still lost it!

Here are some of the types of **graphs** and **charts** which are available from standard spreadsheet packages. They are each based on the information given in the preceding table:

Car sales 1993

	Sales (millions)
Rest of year	1.34
August	0.4

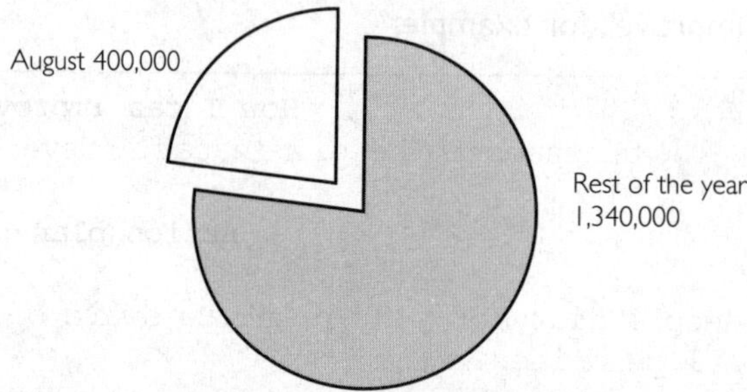

Source: Society of Motor Manufacturers and Traders

Figure A The pie chart shows car sales for August as a proportion of the year. Pie charts show the size of slices of the pie (the total).

Bread sales

Year	1980	1981	1982	1983	1984	1985	1986	1987	1988	1989	1990
Expenditure (£m)	1,509	1,512	1,497	1,494	1,507	1,542	1,551	1,539	1,564	1,526	1,461

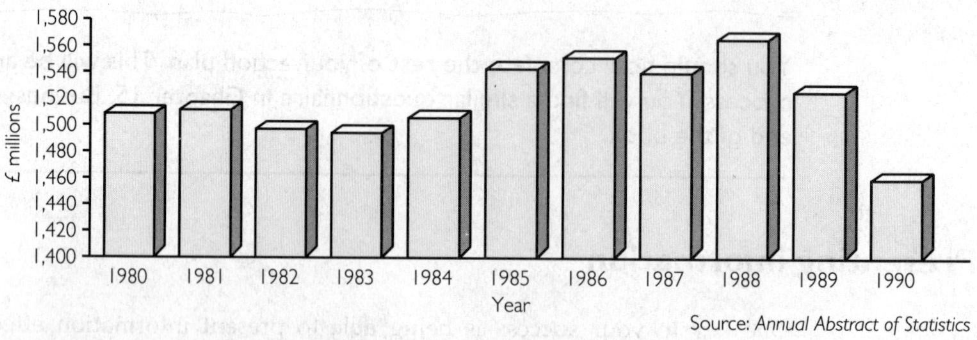

Source: *Annual Abstract of Statistics*

Figure B The vertical bar chart (also called a column chart). This shows yearly totals for consumer expenditure on bread. One year can be compared with the next.

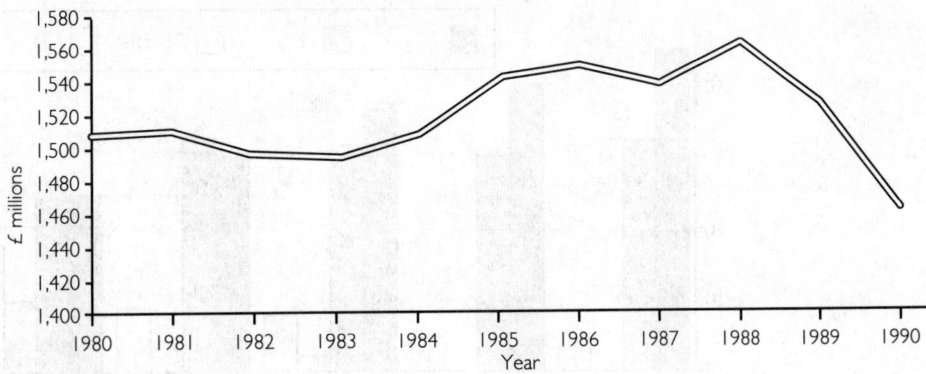

Figure C The line graph shows the same information as Figure B. Both bar and line graphs can be used to show trends.

Cost of running a PC for one year

	£
On all year	56.50
On office hours only	15.15
Automatic monitor switch-off	8.81
Ultimate power-saving PC	1.88

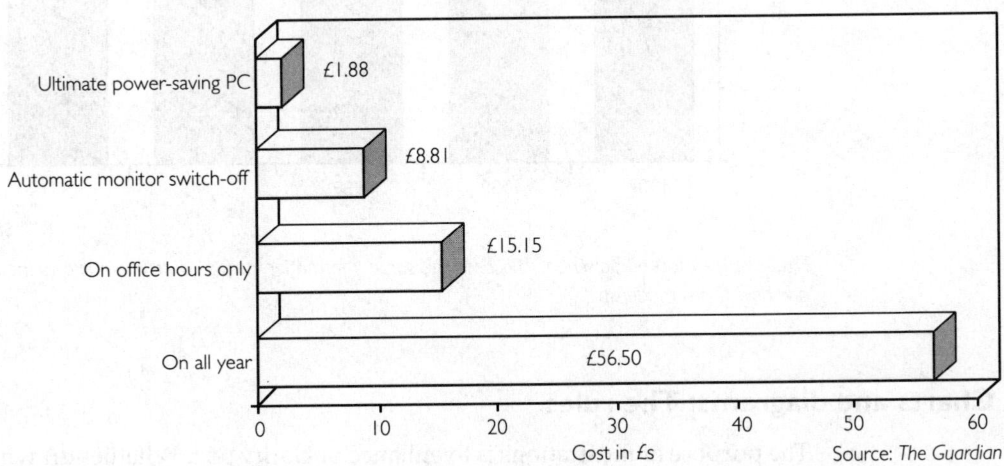

Figure D The horizontal bar chart. This is an alternative to a vertical bar chart. The example is in 3-D which merely makes it look better. In this case the items plotted do not show a trend but are different alternatives being compared. This information could not be shown on a line graph.

Revenue from singles in £ millions

	1987	1988	1989	1990	1991	1992
7"	45	40	38	30	25	15
12"	32	30	32	33	24	19
Cassette	0	0	2	4	10	16
CD	3	5	8	9	18	32
Total	80	75	80	76	77	82

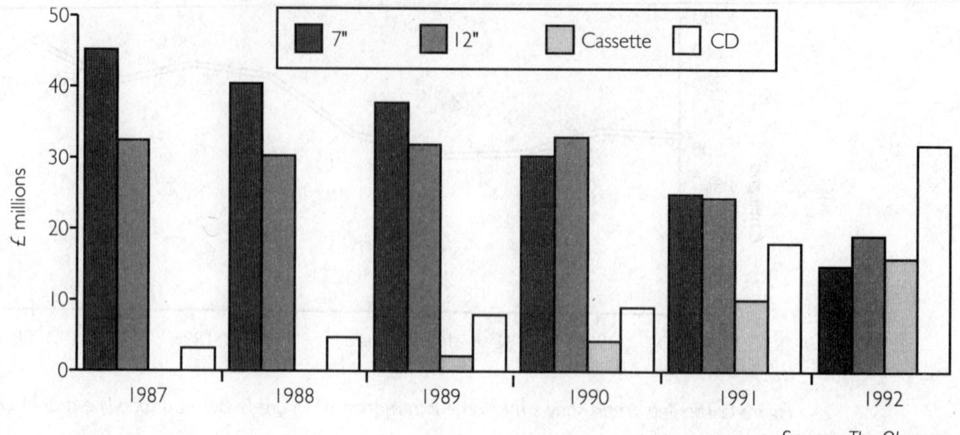

Figure E The multiple bar chart. This breaks down the total sales for each year into its component parts. These are compared with each other. They can also be compared over time.

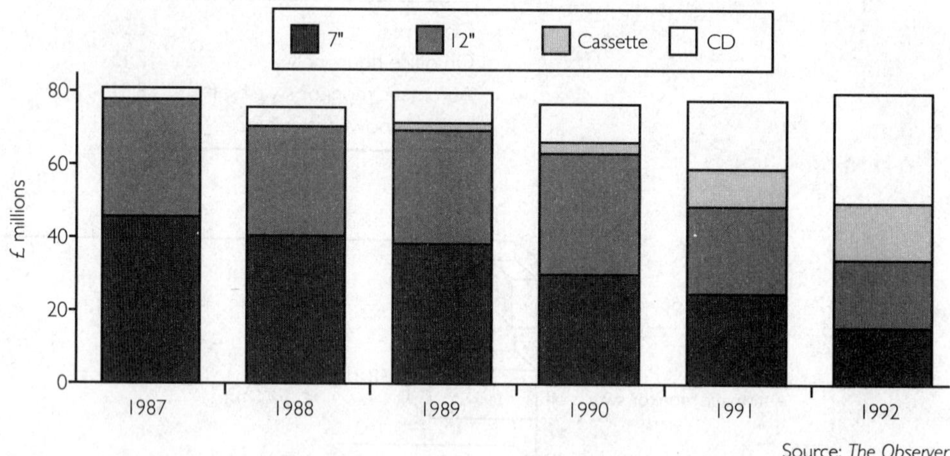

Figure F The stacked bar chart. This uses the same information as for Figure E but shows the total for each year and how this is made up.

Charts and diagrams: The rules

The purpose of illustrations is to enhance or clarify text. Whether drawn manually or by computer they should be clear, simple and useful:

1 There must be a title.
2 The source of the data must be given.
3 The vertical (or y) axis should show the dependent variable, for example sales, costs or production levels.
4 The horizontal (or x) axis will then show the independent variable, for example months, weeks, places.
5 Keep scales simple, use units of 10, 100 or 1,000 wherever possible. A computer will scale automatically, though you can alter this.
6 Use a key to show different data.
7 Use shading or colours to distinguish between different parts.
8 Label each axis, make sure the units are correct.

Line graphs
Good for showing historical data, but do not put more than five lines on the same graph.

Pie charts
Excellent for showing the relative proportions of data , but do not show totals.

Bar charts
Bars can be vertical, horizontal, adjacent or separate. Individual totals can be shown.

Component or stacked bar chart
Totals can be directly compared, but parts can be more difficult to distinguish.

Activities

1 Now it is your turn

Insolvency occurs when someone is unable to pay their debts. Look at the figures below:

Insolvencies for companies and individuals England and Wales (seasonally adjusted). The figures are rounded.

Year	**1992**	**1992**	**1992**	**1992**	**1993**
Quarter	Jan–Mar	Apr–Jun	Jul–Sept	Oct–Dec	Jan–Mar
Companies	5,800	5,900	700	6,000	5,700
Individual	8,800	8,800	9,300	9,800	10,200
Totals	?	?	?	?	?

a Complete the totals.
b Draw a single line graph to show the three sets of figures. The *y* axis should go up in thousands.
c What trend does the graph show? What do you think was the trend after March 1993?
d Draw a stacked bar chart to show how the totals were made up for the period above.
e Use the figures for sales of singles (Figure E) to draw two more different types of chart.

2 Keeping up-to-date

It is very important that you keep up with current events during your studies; you can do this by looking regularly at the newspapers and listening to the news. This activity will encourage you to build up a database of information, up-to-the-minute facts and figures, that you will find useful as reference material throughout the course. It will also encourage you to keep up with what is happening in the economy. This activity links directly with the assignment at the end of Chapter 14.

Background information

The share prices of the larger public limited companies are listed on the financial pages of daily newspapers. *The Guardian, The Independent* and *The Times* are suitable. Below is a sample of prices at the time of writing:

Sainsbury J	420p	Food retailing
Cadbury Schweppes	438p	Food manufacturing
Hi-Tec Sports	22p	Sports and leisure
Millwall Football Club	2.25p	Sports and leisure

On the same pages you will find the FTSE 100 (footsie) which shows how the top 100 companies are performing on the market, the foreign exchange rates showing the value of the £ sterling and the rate of interest. These matters will be explained in the course of the book; the purpose of this activity is to become familiar with the financial pages and to be aware of what is happening to the business world.

Activity

a Look through the share price listings and choose a company operating in an area of business which you find interesting. It is more useful if each member of the class chooses different companies in different sectors of business, for example, food retailing.

b Write to the company secretary (your library or a telephone directory will have the address) and ask for a copy of the latest report and accounts. Again don't worry if for the moment you cannot understand much of this. It will be very useful later.

c On the same day each week read the following from the newspapers:

- **i** the share price (in pence) of the company
- **ii** the FTSE 100
- **iii** exchange rate of the £ against: US dollar ($); French franc (f); German deutschmark (DM)
- **iv** rate of interest (base rate).

d Open up a spreadsheet file called 'share' and set up the template shown below. Enter your weekly readings onto this. Remember to save it after each each new entry.

	A	B	C	D	E	F
1	Date	Week 1	Week 2	Week 3	Week 4	etc.
2	Company name					
3	Share price (p)					
4	FTSE 100					
5	Exchange rate					
6	US $					
7	F Franc					
8	D Mark					
9	Rate of interest					

If it is not possible to get access to a computer yet, draw the table on paper and transfer the information at a later stage.

e Keep a brief weekly diary of the main events that have happened in business world – you will need to read the newspapers and listen to the news regularly. If the company you are following or its area of business is mentioned then make a note of this.

Supplementary activity

You could take it in turns, one student per week, to give the class a five minute summary of 'Business this week'. Alternatively you could produce a weekly newsletter.

f At various stages in the year you will find it useful to print out graphs to show what is happening to the economy. This will be quite simple if the data is on a spreadsheet. By referring to your weekly diary you should be able to explain why prices have risen or fallen sharply at a particular point.
For example if your company was North Bank plc then you might find this situation:

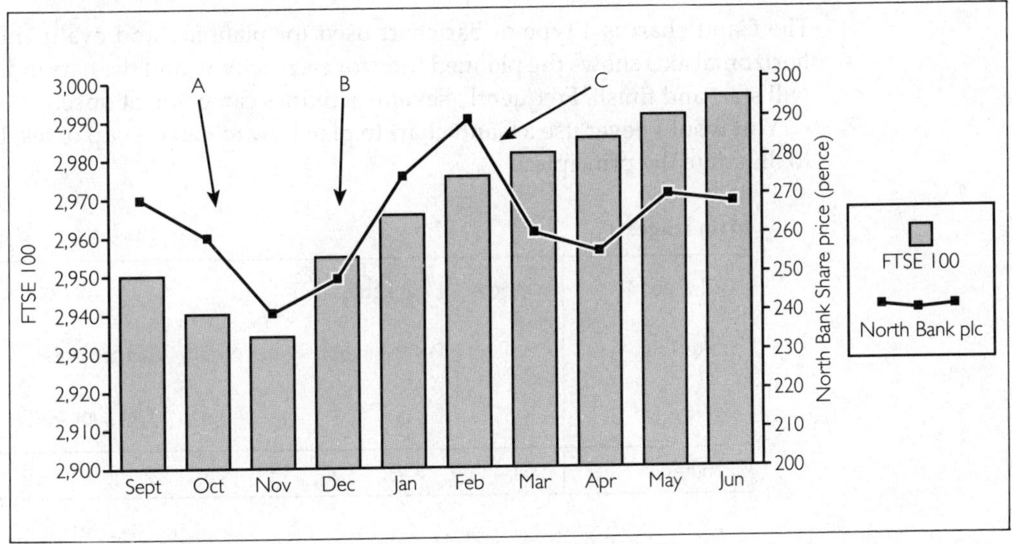

Figure G FTSE 100 and Share price of North Bank plc compared

At A: Business confidence is very low as a result of uncertain trade conditions and rumours of a general election. North Bank plc's share price is going down but so are prices generally as shown by the FTSE 100.
At B: Confidence has picked up throughout the economy as a result of measures announced by the Chancellor in the government's budget statement at the end of November. Prices generally, including those of North Bank, are rising.
At C: Footsie continues to rise but North Bank's price dips. This is because of unexpectedly poor profits announced at the end of the firm's financial year in March. (Note: The graph here is a 'combination chart', i.e. it has two vertical scales. This is a standard spreadsheet function.)
You can of course adapt this activity and keep other information too. The database that you build up will provide a valuable resource for studies across all units. In the past few years there have been stock market crashes, problems with the exchange rate ('black Wednesday') and dramatic changes in the interest rate. No doubt similar events will be repeated, and you will be able to record them as they happen.

g If you bought 200 shares in your company on the day you began this activity and sold them at the end of the year how much better or worse off would you be?

Are you a good organiser?

We have already mentioned the need to plan your time. Often there will be deadlines for you to work to. You will need to plan in order to meet these. Where a project is complex, and perhaps several people are involved, it may be difficult to see the best way to proceed. One tool you may find useful here is the Gantt chart.

The Gantt chart
This chart was originally used by the US Navy when it first developed the Polaris submarine, and it has since been associated with complex projects where timing and sequencing of stages is critical; in construction work for instance. You may come across computer programs capable of working out this 'critical path'.

The Gantt chart is a type of bar chart used for planning and evaluating projects. The horizontal axis shows the planned time for each activity and the bars indicate where this will start and finish. Frequently several activities can go on at once.

You would never use a Gantt chart to plan how to make a cup of tea, but it will serve to illustrate the principle:

Main stages

Boil water	Fill kettle		Heat kettle							
Make Tea			Put tea in pot		Pour water		Let tea brew			
Serve							Get cups out			Pour tea
Minutes	1	2	3	4	5	6	7	8	9	10

In Chapter 15 we will ask you to use a Gantt chart to plan the stages in setting up a business, but in the meantime you could find the technique a useful way of planning some of your assignments.

Activity

Assume that towards the end of the course you are asked to set up a display to show the excellent work that your group has done. It will be held in the reception area of your building where soft drinks and biscuits are to be made available for guests. Staff, students and other trainees will be invited, the primary purpose being to create interest and publicise the course for prospective students. You will work as a group and the event is to be held in one month's time.

Organise the event using a Gantt chart.

Hint: Proceed by

1 listing what needs to be done such as booking the hall, getting display boards, producing invitations, sending them out, ordering the food, and so on.

2 putting the tasks in sequence.

The secret of success

You will need to work hard, you expect that, but you can make your life a little easier. You will get good advice from your tutor so here are just a few brief pointers.

Buy a number of files or folders. What you will need rather depends on how your course is structured, but it may be sensible to have one file per unit. You will obtain a great deal of material and make a lot of notes during the course; all of this can become difficult to manage unless you have a system.

You will need to obtain relevant materials, try to keep up-to-date, but remember that collecting information is not an end in itself; it is what you do with it that is important. Where you use source material always quote the source and the date. Notice that at the beginning of each chapter we suggest items that it will be helpful for you to obtain.

Start off with the right equipment, this includes a set of floppy disks. One isn't enough – you will need to back up all of your files. Don't learn the hard way.

Finally believe in yourself and enjoy it. Good luck!

1 Government and business in the UK economy

What is covered in this chapter

- Production
- Decisions and choices – the problem of scarcity
- Economic systems
- How the UK economy works
- Government intervention in the economy
- Ways in which governments can influence markets
  - Regulation
  - Fiscal policy
  - Government and unemployment

These are the resources that you will need for your Business in the Economy file:

- a map of the UK
- a map of Europe
- *Annual Abstract of Statistics*
- regional data
- *Employment Gazette*
- newspaper articles
- the Budget speech
- *Monthly Digest of Statistics.*

Introduction

Walk along any high street and you will see signs of economic activity and government intervention. Are the shops busy? Do people look as if they are buying anything? Does the refuse collection vehicle display the name of the local authority or the name of a private contractor? Should there be smoke coming from that chimney? What about the smell of car exhausts? We tackle these and many other questions about economic activity in Chapter 1 – Government and Business in the UK economy.

All of the activity that you see in a typical high street is geared towards producing goods and services, those things that people need and want and are therefore prepared to pay for.

Goods are tangible objects such as cars, shoes, dishes and chairs. Services are intangible. They consist of acts which are done for us by, for example, doctors, bank managers and entertainers. This activity in which money changes hands is called economic activity.

Production

The industrial sectors

The economic activity needed to produce the goods and services we use takes place in what can be roughly divided into three industrial sectors:

- the **primary sector** produces goods from natural resources;
- the **secondary sector** produces goods, which have been manufactured or constructed;
- the **tertiary sector** produces services for people and industry.

The primary sector

The activities in the primary sector, sometimes called extractive industries, include:

- agriculture, forestry, fishing
- mining, oil extraction and quarrying.

These all involve taking directly from natural resources and such industries therefore need to be located where these resources exist.

The secondary sector

This includes the manufacturing and construction industries using the products extracted from nature. Manufacturing consists of the following classifications:

- metals, other minerals and mineral products
- chemicals and man-made fibres
- engineering and allied industries
- food, drink and tobacco
- textiles, footwear, clothing and leather
- other manufacturing.

Construction consists of:

- building and civil engineering.

Production industries is a term used to include those industries in the primary and secondary sectors of production:

Agriculture, forestry and fishing	Coal, oil and natural gas	Electricity, gas and water supply	Manufacturing industry

The tertiary sector

This consists of those industries which provide services and includes:

- wholesale and retail distribution
- hotels and catering
- transport
- post and telecommunications
- banking, insurance and finance
- public administration
- education
- medical, other health services, veterinary
- other services.

Activity

Discuss the following in a group.

1 Identify some of the business organisations in your local area which fall under each of the three sectors:
   - primary
   - secondary
   - tertiary.

2 Into which sector do most businesses fit?

3 What do you conclude about your area?

4 Do you feel that the economic activity of your area is typical of the rest of the UK?

5 In which sector do you feel you will eventually work?
   Is this any different from the others in your group?

6 Into which of the industrial sectors do you think the following fit?
   Lorry driver, professional golfer, computer programmer, coal miner, priest, bank manager, potter, assembly-line worker, plasterer, civil engineer, stock broker, secretary, farmer.

Effective demand

No goods or services will be produced unless they are needed or wanted or, as economists say, unless there is a demand for them. However, merely because we want something, it does not necessarily mean that there is an effective demand for the product. Effective demand exists only if we are willing and able to pay the asking price for goods or services. There are many things we aspire to, but if we cannot afford to pay there is no effective demand.

Robert Heilbroner (*The Worldly Philosophers*) put this idea neatly: 'wants are always as large as dreams ... demand is as small as a person's pocketbook'.

Goods and services are provided both for individuals and for industry. They may be categorised as consumer goods or industrial goods.

Consumer goods

These goods are bought by private consumers and households for their own use. They can be:

- convenience goods which are:
  - bought regularly at daily or weekly intervals;
  - staple goods, such as milk and bread;
  - impulse purchases which are bought on the spur of the moment (you often see these placed at check-out points);
  - often low-value items;
  - often bought without much time or effort spent on the decision to purchase.

  Convenience goods are sometimes called fast-moving consumer goods (FMCG) because so many purchases are made that stock turns over very quickly.
- shopping goods which are:
  - bought less often, for example, shoes, clothes, hair dryers and the major durable goods;
  - require more time and care before a decision is made to purchase, for example, prices and quality may be compared at a number of outlets;
  - generally of a higher price;
  - either necessities or luxuries.

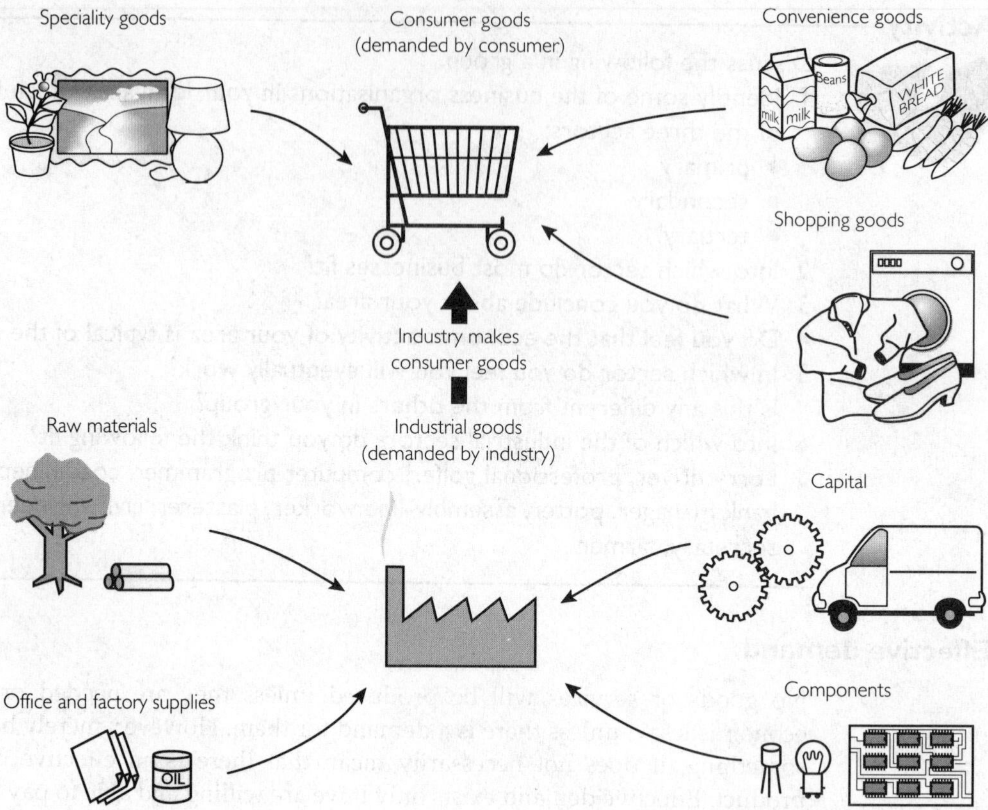

Figure 1.1 Industrial and consumer goods

- speciality goods which are:
  - items bought to emphasise a person's individuality;
  - given considerable thought and effort before being purchased;
  - items in the home, such as potted plants and prints, and personal items, such as clothes and make-up;
  - dependent on style, image and labelling rather than being price sensitive.

Industrial goods

Goods purchased by organisations in all sectors of the economy – primary, secondary and tertiary – are called industrial goods. They can be subdivided into three categories:

- capital goods and equipment – the building and machinery used to make goods or provide a service;
- raw materials, parts and components – for example, iron ore and limestone are raw materials bought and used in making steel; fruit and sugar are used in jam making; batteries, tyres and wheels are parts used in car manufacturing; and radios and computers may be assembled from compoents bought from other companies;
- office and factory supplies – these are often small items which are purchased frequently. The market for these can be very large and highly competitive, for example, computer accessories.

Notice that demand ultimately comes from the consumer. Industrial goods are needed because they help to make a product that the consumer demands. For example, sheet steel may be required by a car manufacturer, but only because consumers want cars.

Activity

Using the classifications discussed on pages 21 and 22, put these products into the appropriate category:

	Consumer	Industrial
A fridge bought by a family		
A fridge bought by a company		
A new factory		
A silk shirt labelled Giorgio Armani		
500 reams of perforated computer paper		
A railway magazine – it's your hobby		
A tin of beans		
A new video		

The chain of distribution

There can be no effective demand if goods and services are not made available to locations where customers are able to buy them. A whole network of organisations may be needed to supply a product to the market where this demand exists.

Do you sometimes have cereals, such as corn flakes, for breakfast? Figure 1.2 shows a typical **supply chain** for a cereal.

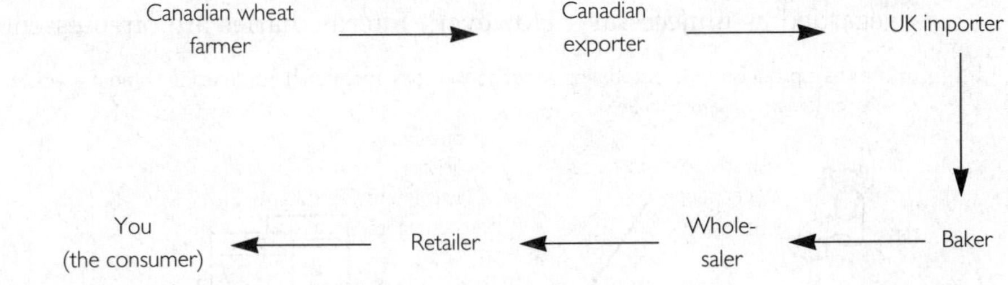

Figure 1.2

Activities

1 Look at the supply chain in Figure 1.2 and see if you can identify:
   a Where the primary, secondary and tertiary industrial sectors are involved.
   b The different goods and services that are involved.
   c What part you play in this chain.
2 Now draw out supply chains for:
   a a traditional English breakfast
   b a continental breakfast.

The more often a product changes hands the more expensive it becomes because everyone in the chain needs to be paid. The chain of distribution may have four main elements:

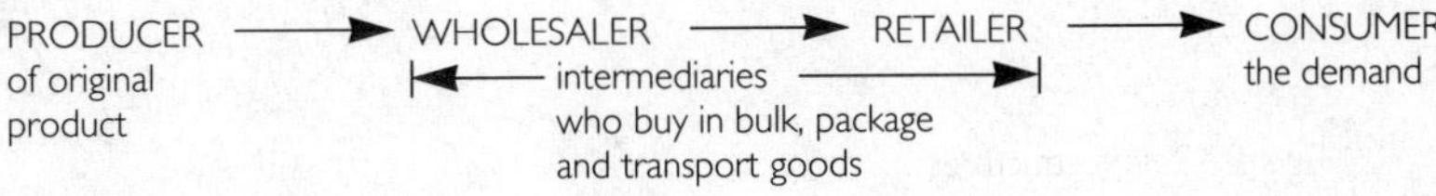

In all cases the producer and consumer are vital; someone must produce the product and someone must demand it. Whether intermediaries are used depends upon the nature of the product, where it is made, and how it is to be made available to the consumer. Examples of different chains of distribution are:

1 Producer ——► Consumer

This is known as direct selling. Examples would include the local baker, doctors, dentists and hairdressers: and large engineering projects such as the international rail terminal at Waterloo where Bovis Construction, the contractors, worked directly for British Rail, the customer.

2 Producer ——► Retailer ——► Consumer

Examples are clothing and footwear manufacturers who deal directly with large retailers. The F11 Group, for example, produces Lotus shoes for Marks & Spencer; car manufacturers, such as Ford, supply their agents who sell to the public; large supermarket chains, such as Tesco and Sainsbury, buy direct from the farms and factories which produce and manufacture goods to their specifications.

3 Producer ——► Wholesaler ——► Retailer ——► Consumer

When there is a large number of small retailers, the producer will usually deal with a wholesaler who buys in bulk, stores the products and sells them on to the retailer in smaller quantities. A small grocer will usually go to the wholesaler, perhaps a 'cash and carry' to collect stock. This may be done fairly regularly to avoid the grocer having to devote space to storage.

The services provided by these intermediaries, often called middlemen, are sometimes regarded as unnecessary. However, intermediaries are often essential in creating an

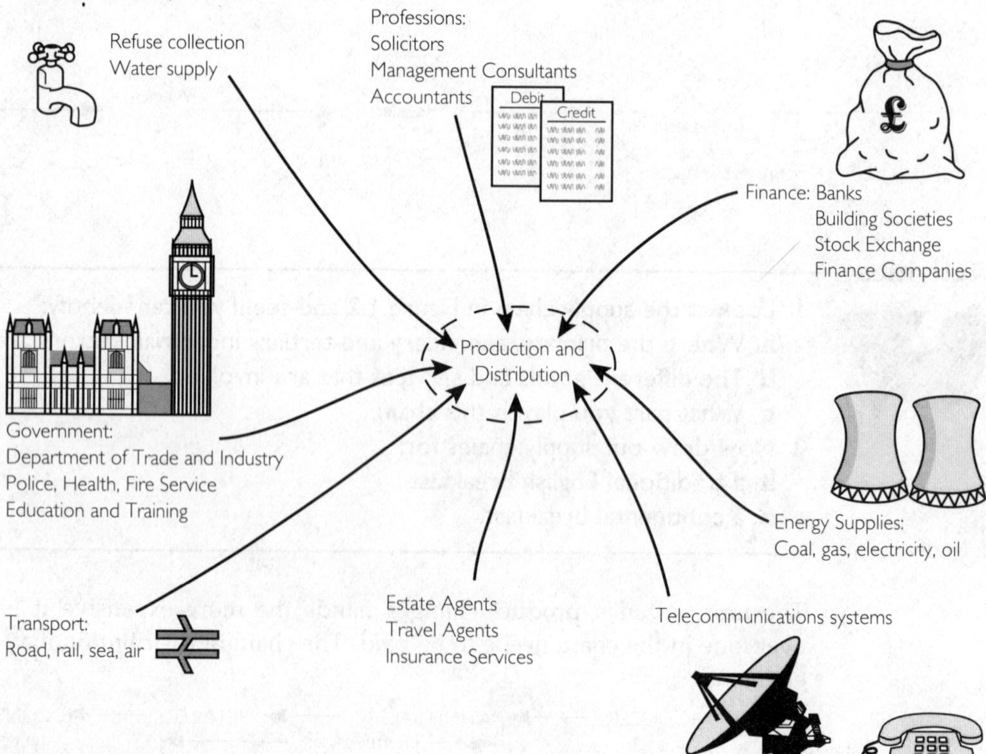

Figure 1.3 Infrastructures

effective demand. For example, if we have to travel to Tokyo for a stereo, or to Canada for breakfast cereals, we may decide we do not want them after all. In economic terms anyone adding value is said to be productive.

Trends in the industrial sectors

Employment

The broad trends in **employment** in the three industrial sectors in the UK are a reflection of changes in the wants of the consumer and the ways of satisfying these wants.

Employment has generally declined in the primary sector, because these industries have become more efficient. For example in agriculture, modern machinery means that one worker can now produce as much as several farmhands did previously.

The same trend is shown in the manufacturing sector and especially in textiles, shipbuilding, clothing and footwear, and leather goods. This is because many goods are now imported whilst mass production methods require fewer workers. It is expected that the only way for these industries to survive in the European Union (EU) is for them to concentrate on specialist, high-quality, higher-priced markets and products. One exception has been the 15 per cent increase in employment in office machines, a trend which can also be seen in other European countries.

The numbers employed in the tertiary sector have generally increased with the trend towards the provision of services. Jobs in the service sector are usually thought of as being more attractive than those in the production industries. This could be one reason why employment in production has declined. These **industry trends** are expected to continue.

Trends in employment can be summarised as:

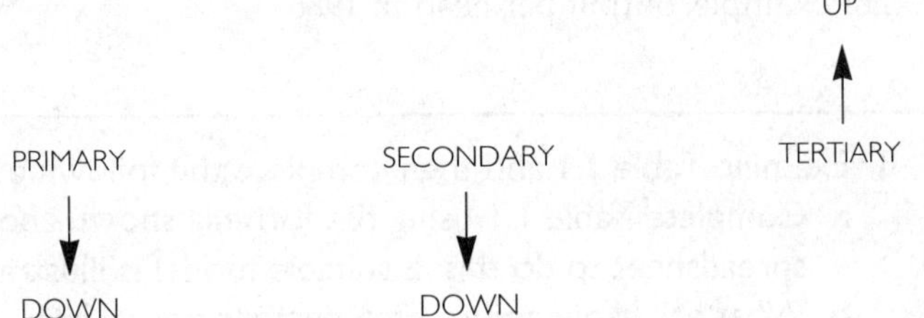

Output

Trends in **output** in a selection of UK industries, using 1985 as the base year are shown in Figure 1.4.

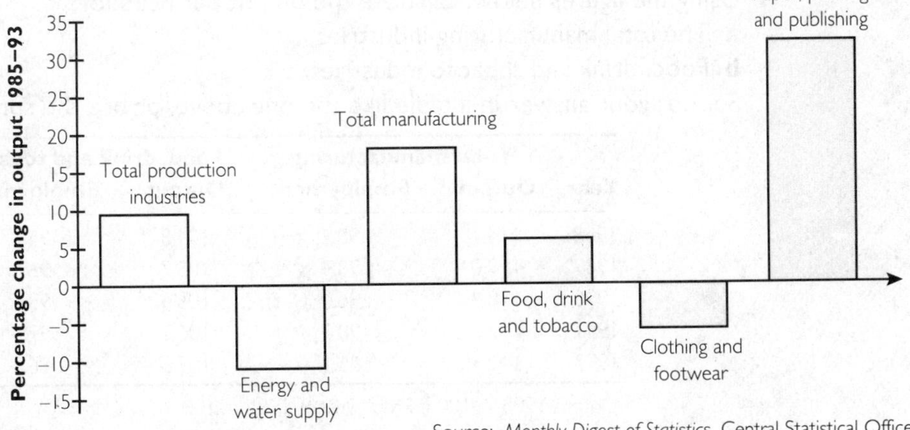

Figure 1.4 Trends in output for selected industries 1985–93

Relationship between output and employment

Figure 1.5 shows that the overall level of output in manufacturing in the UK has gone up, despite the falling number of people employed in this sector. This has been possible because productivity has increased. Since fewer people are now capable of producing more output, it is unlikely that employment in manufacturing will rise again.

Table 1.1 shows the trend in output and employment as index numbers for the clothing and footwear industries.

Table 1.1 Output, employment and productivity – the UK clothing and footwear industry 1985–92

Year	Output	Employment	Output per head
1985	100.0	100.0	100.0
1986	100.7	100.1	100.5
1987	103.7	99.3	?
1988	102.0	100.0	?
1989	98.3	95.5	?
1990	95.7	88.7	?
1992	87.8	75.8	?

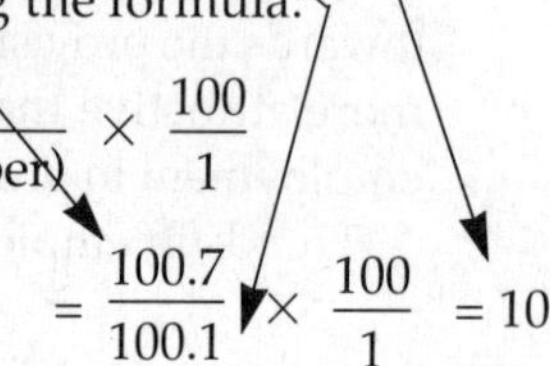

Productivity, or output per head, is calculated using the formula:

$$\text{Output per head} = \frac{\text{Output (as an index number)}}{\text{Employment (as an index number)}} \times \frac{100}{1}$$

For example, output per head in 1986 $= \dfrac{100.7}{100.1} \times \dfrac{100}{1} = 100.5$

Activities

1 Examine Table 1.1 and then complete the following tasks.

a Complete Table 1.1 using the formula shown above. (If you prefer to set up a spreadsheet to do this, a suitable model is illustrated on page 27.)

b What has happened to employment since 1985?

c What has happened to output since 1985?

d What has happened to output per head since 1985?

e In view of your answers to b and c how do you explain your answer to d?

f If you have used a spreadsheet, produce a graph to show these trends.

2 Using the figures below, calculate the output per head for:

a The total manufacturing industries

b Food, drink and tobacco industries.

Set out your answer in a table like the one above, or use the spreadsheet model.

	Total manufacturing		Food, drink and tobacco	
Year	Output	Employment	Output	Employment
1988	114.1	98.2	104.8	95.0
1989	119.0	98.4	105.7	96.6
1990	118.4	96.4	106.4	93.4
1991	112.2	90.0	106.2	92.7
1992	111.3	85.1	107.8	86.5

Output 1985 = 100 Employment 1985 = 100

Source: Department of Employment

c What conclusions do you reach?

3 Obtain a copy of the *Monthly Digest of Statistics* from your library.

a Repeat the calculations for two of the industries found in your area.

b Share the results with your group. What are your overall conclusions?

Suggested spreadsheet model:

	A	B	C	D
1				
2				
3	Year	Output	Employment	Output per head
4				=B4/C4*100
5				=B5/C5*100
6				=B6/C6*100
7				=B7/C7*100
8				=B8/C8*100
9				=B9/C9*100
10				=B10/C10*100
11				=B11/C11*100

To use this model:

a Log onto your spreadsheet.

b Set up the formulae in column D.

c Enter data in columns A, B and C.

d You can draw graphs to illustrate the data using the graphics facility.

Location of industry

Knowing where and why industries are located in a particular place will help a business tackle a number of problems, particularly those in marketing and distribution because the centres of industry are also the centres of population.

Factors affecting the **location of industry** are as follows:

1 Markets: services, and producers of high-weight, low-cost and fragile products, tend to locate near the market. Examples might be hairdressers, soft drinks distribution depots and potteries.

2 Labour: the type, quality, cost and availability are all relevant. Industries have different requirements which will affect their location.

3 Industrial areas: existing industrial areas tend to attract a range of new businesses. For example, sandwich bars grow up near offices, ancilliary industries associated with the oil industry appear around Aberdeen in Scotland; and the Channel Tunnel will attract business to the Ashford/Folkestone area of Kent. There are also external economies to be gained such as education and training facilities.

4 Environment: 'green field' sites have attracted Japanese car manufacturers. The area around Guildford in Surrey has attracted electronics companies. When exact location is not important, environment may be the deciding factor. Notice that advertisements for areas such as Milton Keynes stress this.

5 Land and premises costs: high costs tend to push businesses out of city centres. New buildings can be equipped more easily for modern technology.

6 Government grants and subsidies: these are given in some areas to help with relocation and premises costs. This is often an attempt to take work to the workers. The government itself has 'decentralised' by moving departments out of London to areas in Scotland and Wales.

7 Power: this is now of less importance than it used to be in choosing a location because electricity and gas are easily distributed.
8 Natural resources: climate, soils, and the water supply may be vital. Certain industries can only be located where natural resources exist. Examples are mineral water suppliers which need the natural springs and farmers who need the land.
9 Transport: weight-gaining processes, for example, brewing, tend to be located near the market; weight-losing processes are found near the source of raw materials, for example fish fingers at Grimsby.

Activities

1 Use the list above to help you identify reasons for the location of the following industries:
   Computer-related industries at Milton Keynes (high-tech/sunrise industries)
   Wembley Stadium (leisure industry)
   Pilkington's Glass, St Helens (manufacturing)
   Your local travel agent
   Your local baker
   The cider industry based around Somerset or Hereford
   Reeds Paper Mill at Aylesford in the Medway valley, Kent
   Nissan Cars, Sunderland
   The newspaper industry now relocated at Wapping in the London Docklands
   Sellafield nuclear reprocessing plant in Cumbria
   The pottery industry based around Stoke-on-Trent, Staffordshire
   Government departments: DVLA (Driving Vehicle Licensing Authority), Swansea; Inland Revenue dealing with income tax for London, at Livingston in Scotland.

   In each case, assign a score of one to five to indicate the importance of each of the nine factors. (One represents not at all important, five represents extremely important.)
2 Use the *Yellow Pages* or a *Thomson's Directory* and a local map (or your general knowledge) to look at the location of the following in your area:
   Travel agents
   Banks
   Light industries
   Hypermarkets
   Builders merchants.

   What are the requirements that determine the location of each?
   Note: You will need to consider location of a business in your business plan (Chapter 15).

Decisions and choices – the problem of scarcity

Having looked at the types of industrial activity and the reasons for choosing a location, we need to examine the economic system that has created this structure. The basic problem in economics is one of scarcity. There are not enough resources to go round, so decisions have to be made as to how they are to be allocated.

Opportunity cost

Every decision made by a business or a government is the result of having chosen a particular course of action from a number of options. A choice has to be made because the resources available are scarce and have to be used in the most efficient way.

If you have £10 and the choice facing you is either a night out or a new book then the economist would say that the cost of the night out is the new book which you have not bought. This technique, which involves expressing the cost of one option in terms of the one given up or foregone, is known as opportunity cost. Whenever we make a decision there is an opportunity cost.

Suppose the choice facing you is between a night out, or staying in to complete your coursework. You decide on the night out. Let us work out the opportunity cost. As a result of not completing the coursework, you fail to complete the course and are unable to get a job which pays well. Let's say you earn £2,000 a year less, which over your working life is about £80,000. An expensive night out!

Activity

What is the opportunity cost of:

a Not crossing the road at a zebra crossing?
b Not giving up smoking?
c Building a by-pass around a small country town?

No country has enough resources to produce all it wants, therefore people have to choose between options. Resources are limited and people's demands are virtually unlimited. Hence decisions have to be made about:

- What to produce – should it be food, clothing, coal or steel?
- How much to produce – should it be 50 million loaves of bread, 10,000 tons of coal, or some of each? The combinations which are possible are sometimes shown on a **production possibility curve**, as in Figure 1.5.

In this example, at point C on the curve resources are used entirely to produce coal;
at B the resources are used exclusively for making bread;
at A both bread and coal are produced.

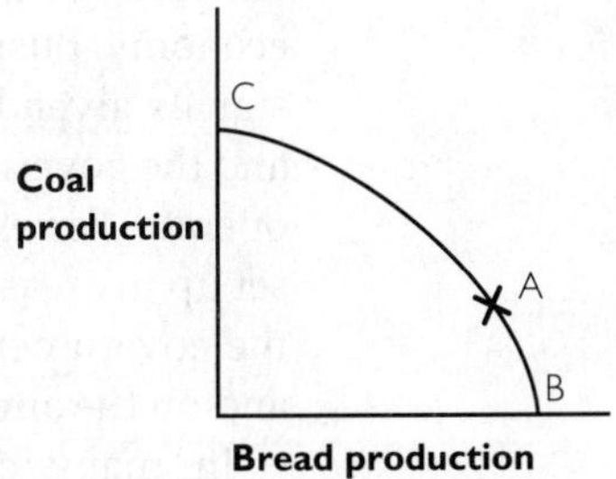

Figure 1.5

- For whom to produce – should goods and services be available to everyone or only those who can pay?
- Where to produce – should all heavy industry be located in the South West?

Each country has its own way of tackling these problems.

Economic systems

Economies can be divided under three main headings:

- **centrally planned**, or command, economies
- **free enterprise**, or market, economies
- **mixed economies.**

The centrally planned, or command, economy

Here every economic decision is made by the government. Prices are fixed and the supply of goods and services is controlled. Decisions about what, where and how much to produce are all made centrally. There are no market forces involved.

Twenty years ago the USSR and other countries in Eastern Europe could have served as examples of the centrally planned economy. However, with the fall of communism these countries are now moving towards capitalism. Almost for the first time they are experiencing inflation and unemployment.

The free enterprise, or market, economy

Here the government is not involved in economic activity. Prices are determined entirely by the market forces of supply and demand. All decisions are made by businesses and consumers. Land and capital resources are privately owned and there is no public ownership. The economy of Britain up to the early nineteenth century was largely free enterprise or *laissez-faire*. The government saw its job as one of keeping law and order at home and conducting relationships with foreign powers. Industry and commerce were a matter for private individuals. The state became involved with the business world as it became clear that the operation of the free market alone could not cure the enormous social problems brought by growing industrialisation.

The mixed economy

Here the decisions about what, how much, for whom and where to produce are split between the government (the public sector) and the private sector. The UK is a mixed economy. Businesses decide how much and what to produce on the basis of the market signals given by consumers. There is both private and public ownership of resources and the government may intervene when it believes that the market system has failed to operate. For example, it provides training for the unemployed, grants for businesses to set up in areas of high unemployment and social security benefits. In a mixed economy the government also sets targets for the economy as a whole, for example, on inflation and on the amount of money in circulation.

In many countries, industries such as coal, the railways, shipbuilding, steel, electricity, gas and water were nationalised or taken into state ownership. There were a number of reasons for this. Some industries were not profitable, and so were maintained by the state as they were felt to be of national importance, for example, steel. Others such as electricity and gas were seen as vital services which were natural monopolies. Since there was no competition in these industries it was not felt to be desirable for them to be in the hands of private business that tends to be more interested in profits than the good of society.

elfare State' is another sign of government intervention. It provides nefits for private individuals, the most notable being the National

UK has tried to move back towards a more free enterprise economy **on** programme. This has meant that many areas of business previously ave passed into the private sector. Other European countries have not, ne UK's example. The German government, for example, has shares in man companies, whilst the French government controls 30 per cent of uring industry and most of its banking. There are signs, however, of a h attitude. In June 1993 the French government announced its intention rge part of its state holdings in an attempt to raise money.

---

instorm the advantages and disadvantages of each type of economic e point of view of:

mer, a consumer, a factory worker, a civil servant, a pensioner.

---

ny works

see the economy in terms of households and businesses – that is, those the goods and services and those who produce them.

to produce goods and services a business will need resources. These are its are called factors of production. Figure 1.6 shows some of the inputs and volved in a production process.

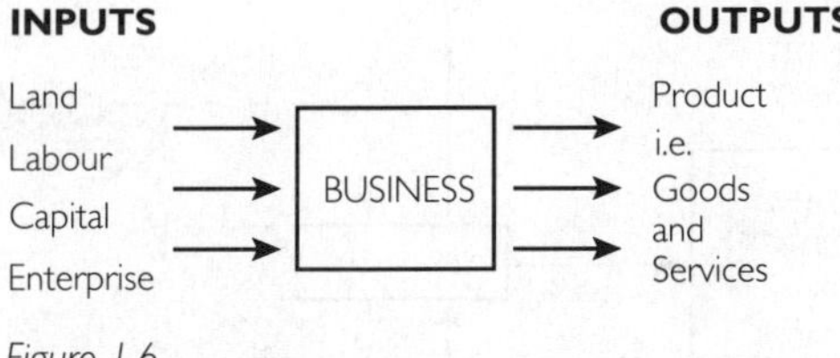

Figure 1.6

nd includes the factory site, natural deposits and minerals. Many home owners nly own the top three feet of the land their houses are built on. The reward for land is rent.

Labour is all the people in the business. The reward for labour is wages or salaries.

Capital is any buildings, property, machines, raw materials and some finished goods which a business may use to produce its output. The reward for capital is interest.

Enterprise is the owner's talent in setting up the business. The reward for enterprise is profit.

These inputs may be specific which means that they cannot easily be used instead of another, or non-specific when they can be easily substituted. In order to get its inputs or resources, a business will have to pay, so it will incur costs.

The simplest way of showing the economy is to think of it as a flow of goods and services moving between households and businesses, as shown in Figure 1.7.

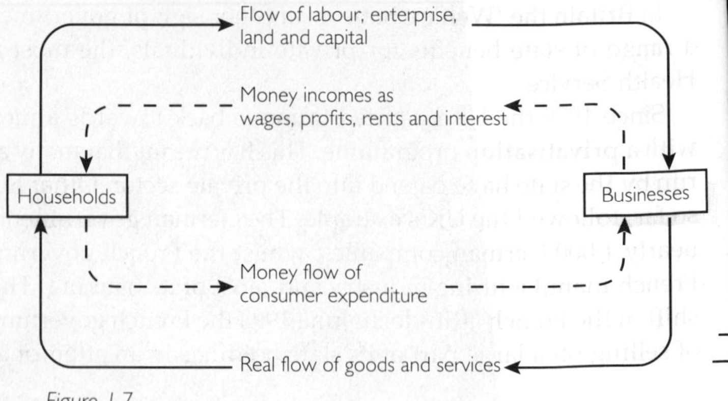

Figure 1.7

Circular flows in the economy

Workers offer their labour services to businesses which employ them. This i of people/labour. In return they are paid an income, their wages in mon **money flow**.

Businesses use the labour and other inputs or factors of production to c and services. This is the real flow of output.

Consumers spend their income on buying these goods/services. This i expenditure (see Table 2.3 on page 74 for a summary of consumer expenditur money flow.

This **circular flow** approach can be extended by including those items wh transactions between households and businesses. These are called leakage injections to the system. Both the government and other countries are invol process (Figure 1.8).

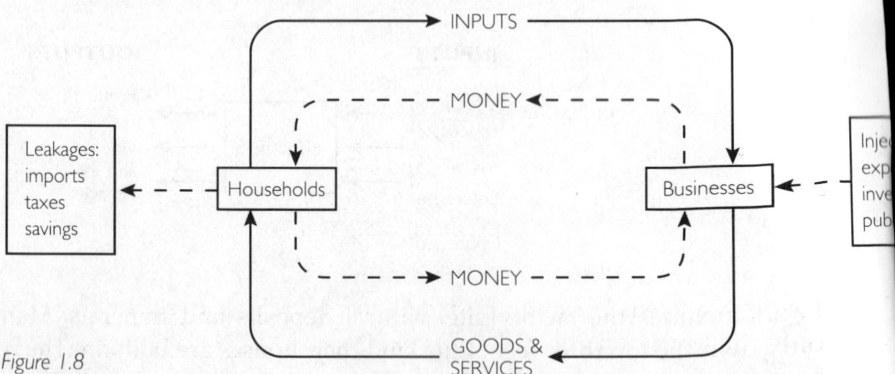

Figure 1.8

Leakages include:

- imports (what we buy from other countries) because money flows out of th
- taxes – the money is not available for consumer spending on goods and ser
- savings – because the money is not part of consumer expenditure.

Injections include:

- exports – a business receives income when it sells goods to other countries;
- investment – producers of heavy equipment used to manufacture cars, for e will receive income from car manufacturers who buy their products;
- government spending – the government buys goods or services from busine for example, when it builds a road or a hospital.

National income is found by adding together all the incomes received by labour plus the incomes received by the other inputs used by business.

INPUTS
labour receives wages
landowners receive rent
capital owners receive interest.

National product or **national output** is the money value of all the goods/services produced.
National expenditure is the money value of all spending in the economy.
These figures provide the basis for our diagnosis of the health of the economy.
They can give answers about the:

- rate of growth
- level of productivity
- wealth of the nation.

Activity

In the library locate the *Annual Abstract of Statistics*.

Find out the size of the UK national income. If the figures were out by just plus or minus 1 per cent what would the new figures be?

What determines the size of national income?

The size of national income is largely determined by:

- the level of technology and the amount of equipment used to produce goods and services;
- the amount of resources available for use;
- the size and quality of the workforce;
- government policies and actions designed to promote growth.

When governments and economists talk of growth they mean a real increase in the wealth of the economy.

Government intervention in the economy

The amount and direction of government intervention in the economy of a country is closely related to the political philosophy of the party in power: Very broadly, the Labour party favours selective intervention to deal with specific problems whilst the Conservative party particularly since 1979 favours a minimalist approach with minimum intervention. The Labour party recently abandoned 'Clause 4' of its constitution. It is no longer committed to the public/common ownership of industries.

Traditionally the main aims of the government's economic management have been to influence conditions in the whole economy, for example:

- to even out the trade cycle
- to avoid inflation
- to reduce unemployment
- to promote economic growth
- to achieve a positive balance of payments
- to control the exchange rate.

However, the supply side approach (see page 427) adopted by the Conservatives concentrates on making business more profitable so that businesses will want to produce more, take on more workers, grow and export.

The trade cycle – boom and slump

Societies where a free market exists have tended to experience economic growth so that over the years living standards have risen. This growth however has not been steady. It has been observed that economies experience fluctuations known as cycles when periods of boom are followed by periods of slump.

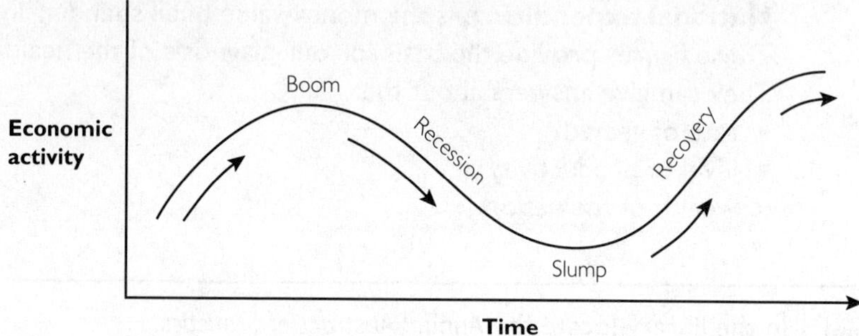

Figure 1.9 The trade cycle

Four stages to a trade cycle can be identified (Figure 1.9):

- In a boom demand is high, production and sales are high and there is low unemployment. Increased confidence leads to investment in industry and this in turn creates further demand. New businesses will start up creating further employment. There are ceilings to booms.
- As demand falls off relative to supply a recession sets in and the economy drifts towards a slump.
- In a slump or depression, demand is low, as are sales and production, and unemployment high. Confidence is low and there is little investment in industry. Many businesses will fail. There are floors to depressions.
- When a depression has bottomed out, there will eventually be an upturn in activity known as a recovery. This will lead towards the next boom.

Inflation

A rise in the price level is referred to as inflation. Businesses are directly affected in two ways by the level and rate of change in prices in the economy. As buyers of raw materials they are concerned about the prices of their supplies. As sellers of goods and services, they are concerned about retail prices. Two indices exist to measure these changes:

- the Index Numbers of Wholesale Prices measure changes in the prices of raw materials relevant to particular industries in the Standard Industrial Classification (SIC);
- the Retail Prices Index (RPI) measures changes in the price of goods and services provided by retailers. The RPI is calculated monthly.

A business will need to use this information as a guide price against which to compare its own retail and wholesale prices. It may ask, for example, 'Have these prices changed in line with the general trend?' or 'Are we charging more or less than our competitors?'.

Depending on the answers to these types of questions a business can:

- switch its source of supply from high to low price suppliers;
- switch its manufacturing from high to low price areas or even countries if it is a multinational enterprise;
- change the raw materials and ingredients it uses, and then market the products as new and improved;
- consider using more labour- or capital-intensive methods of production depending on the costs;
- change its marketing and promotion strategy, possibly to reposition the product and become more aggressive;
- try to improve productivity by using raw materials more efficiently.

Linde, the German chemicals giant, has moved production over the border into the Czech Republic where labour costs are a tenth of those in Germany. The countries of Eastern Europe currently have tens of millions of people willing to work for wages far lower than those in the West.

Alan Sugar has announced that his new Amstrad Pen Pad will be produced in China because of the low wage costs there.

Activities

Find the General Index of Retail Prices (RPI) in the *Monthly Digest of Statistics*.

1 Copy and complete the table below showing the General Index of Retail Prices with up-to-date figures. Plot the data on a graph leaving space for the next six months.

General Index of Retail Prices

(Jan. 1987 = 100)

1994	May	144.7
	June	144.7
	July	144.0
	Aug.	144.7
	Sept.	145.0
	Oct.	145.2
	Nov.	145.3
	Dec.	146.0

2 Write a brief note explaining what has happened to retail prices since May 1993.

Inflation in the UK was under control in February 1995 at 2.6 per cent. At one time it was rising at 10 per cent a year. This affected everyone, for example:

- savers saw the value of their savings fall as interest rates did not keep pace with inflation;
- businesses could not predict the prices of raw materials or finished goods so it was difficult to plan ahead;
- borrowers of money were better off because they paid back less in real terms than they borrowed;
- people on pensions and other fixed incomes were worse off;
- exporting became difficult as UK goods were relatively expensive compared with similar goods from other countries.

The Government has made curing inflation its top priority.

Unemployment

In recent years unemployment has been a problem across the EU. The **types of unemployment** can be classified as follows:

- Structural or technological unemployment is caused by changes in either the demand or supply of a product, for example:

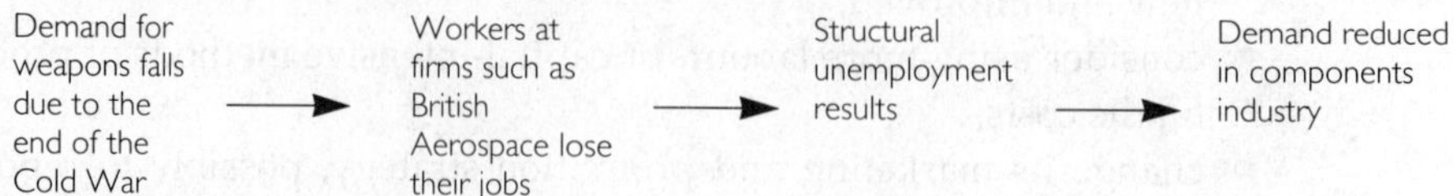

Capital investment, for example, causes:

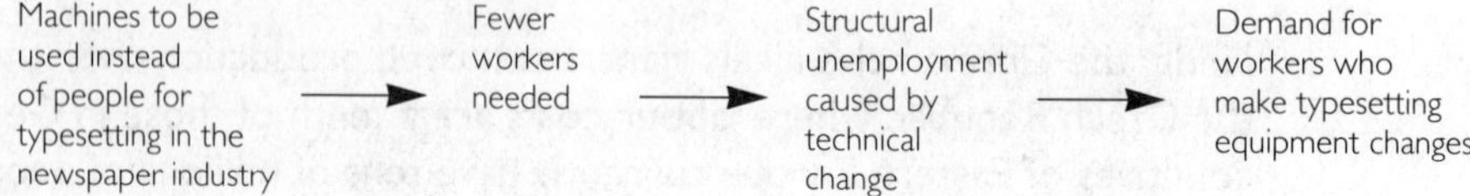

- Frictional or search unemployment refers to people who are unemployed and are searching for new jobs, either through choice, or because they have been made redundant. The time that people are out of work lengthens during a recession because there are more seeking jobs than there are vacancies available (see Chapter 10 on duration of unemployment). When governments from 1946 onwards spoke of full employment as their aim they meant unemployment not higher than 3 per cent. This acknowledges that at any time there will always be people in transition between jobs.
- Seasonal unemployment – some occupations are directly linked to the weather, for example Blackpool Pleasure Beach virtually closes from the end of October each year. People who are employed for the summer months then sign on as unemployed. Statisticians go to considerable lengths to even out the seasonal effects so that the underlying trends can be detected.
- Demand deficiency unemployment – caused by a general lack of demand in the economy, i.e. during a recession people have less money to spend on everything. For example, people will only buy new washing machines if it is uneconomic/not worthwhile repairing the old one. Most businesses will suffer and unemployment can occur anywhere in the economy.

The Phillips curve – relating unemployment and inflation

Professor Phillips observed a relationship between unemployment and inflation which he believed showed a link between the two. This relationship is plotted on a curve known as the Phillips curve (Figure 1.10).

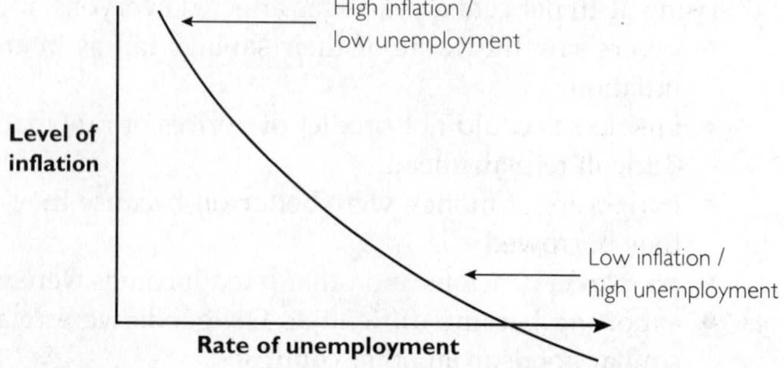

Figure 1.10 The Phillips curve

The theory is that high unemployment is linked with low inflation. This is partly because competition for jobs will keep down wage levels, which are an important cause of inflation. Similarly, low unemployment is linked with high inflation, as industry is forced to pay more to attract scarce labour.

If this relationship holds then, the theory goes, it is possible for governments to at least try to control unemployment through control of inflation. It is not possible to have the ideal position of both low inflation and low unemployment, but there could be some optimum trade-off position where both inflation and unemployment are at 'acceptable' levels.

Recent evidence suggests, however, that the relationship is more complex than this.

Balance of payments

Trade is a vital element in the economy of the UK. The nation cannot produce all that it needs, and must therefore import. However it must export goods and services of sufficient value to pay for these imports.

The **balance of payments** is the record of the value of all UK exports and imports. It is split into three parts:

1. Current account:
   - visible trade – **exports** and imports of goods such as machinery, equipment, chemicals and food, accounting for approximately 65 per cent of foreign trade;
   - invisible trade – exports and imports of services such as insurance, tourism and banking services, accounting for approximately 35 per cent of foreign trade.
2. Capital account:
   - short period inflow/outflow of capital;
   - long period inflow/outflow of capital.
3. Official finance:
   - foreign currency
   - changes in reserves.

When the value of exports is greater than that of imports there is a surplus. When the value of imports is greater than that of exports there is a deficit (Figure 1.11).

Over recent years the pattern has been for the UK to make a deficit on the balance of trade (trade in visibles), but to aim to make up for this by a surplus on invisibles. It is important to be clear that invisibles are exported when foreign countries buy UK services and imported when the UK buys foreign services. A British tourist visiting Spain, for example, will spend money (earned in Britain) on Spanish goods and services and therefore contributes to invisible imports. Similarly, overseas visitors to Britain help invisible exports.

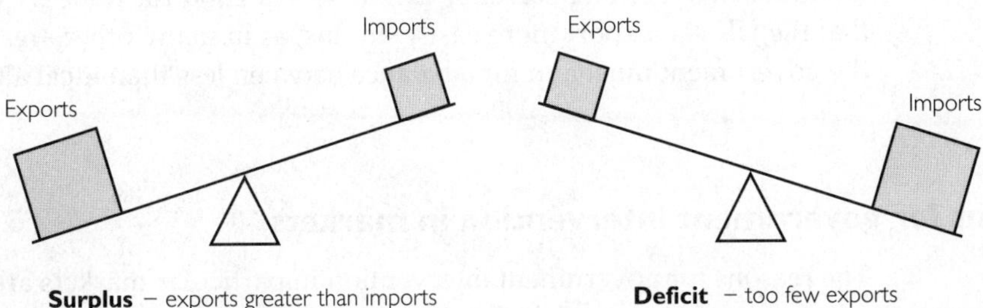

Figure 1.11 Surplus or deficit

One reason why recent governments have made inflation public enemy number one is that rising prices at home make UK goods more expensive to overseas buyers. We become uncompetitive in world markets.

The exchange rate

The exchange rate can also influence the level of trade between countries. For example, to buy German goods an importer in the UK will need to obtain deutsche marks (DM) by buying them with pounds sterling (probably through a bank) on the foreign exchange market. The more expensive the deutsche marks, the more expensive will be the goods. This might well affect the decision to buy.

The value of one currency against another is determined ultimately by the market place. If a currency is in demand then it will be strong, that is expensive, in terms of other currencies. If it is not in demand it will be weak. Left to themselves exchange rates tend to fluctuate as the demand for currencies changes. This in itself is not good for trade as it means that prices are uncertain and planning ahead is difficult.

The European Monetary System (EMS) is designed to control these fluctuations and allow stability of currencies within the EU. The UK joined the system fully in October 1990 by becoming part of the Exchange Rate Mechanism (ERM) which is a way of linking the currencies of EU members within specified bands. These bands were set so that most currencies had to keep within 2.25 per cent either side of its central rate. However, pressures on exchange rates across Europe forced a dramatic widening of these bands in August 1993 to 15 per cent either way, which cast doubt over the whole future of exchange rate policy, and the possibility of a single European currency.

When the UK entered the ERM in 1990, sterling was set at £1 equals DM2.93 (deutsche mark) and was allowed to fluctuate within 6 per cent of this. Where the currency value looked set to rise too high then the Bank of England and other EU central banks would sell pounds to reduce sterling's value. Where the value fell too low these banks would create a demand for sterling by buying it on the foreign exchange markets. This would raise the price.

Although the system did stabilise the value of the pound, many people argued that the original rate of entry was too high. Ultimately the markets too decided that this rate was unrealistic and continued to sell sterling despite the attempts of the Bank of England to bid the price up. In 1992, as the result of Black Wednesday, the UK left the ERM and the pound settled at a lower rate. In April 1995 the weaker pound sterling was worth DM2.22.

The result was that fewer German goods could be bought for a pound because British industry got fewer DM per pound. Such movements should reduce imports from Germany, because German goods become more expensive. On the other hand, Germany has to pay only DM2.22 to get goods which previously cost DM2.93. UK exports to Germany should rise as they have become cheaper.

Notice that a strong currency is not always good for trade. A weaker pound means that the UK can export more easily. In this, as in many other areas of economic policy, the government must aim for a balance between less than ideal alternatives.

Reasons for government intervention in markets

The reasons for government intervention in particular markets are different from those which are used to explain intervention in the whole economy. Here are some of the reasons why the government has intervened in particular markets.

Stimulate and encourage competition

The aim of competition policy is to increase competition to achieve better use of the country's scarce resources. There are four main principles underlying this philosophy:

1 Monopolies (situations where one company has more than a 25% share of a specific market) are presumed to be against the public interest because they limit consumer choice, result in higher production costs and have the opportunity to charge higher prices and restrict output;
2 Any merger or take-over which could lead to a monopoly should therefore be stopped;
3 Any agreements between companies which, for instance, try to fix prices, divide up the market, prevent new businesses from entering the market, prevent the introduction of new products which could harm profits or tie distributors to producers, should be banned as they are Restrictive Trade Practices eligible for investigation by the Monopolies and Mergers Commission (MMC);
4 Competition can make better use of scarce resources and could be more efficient.

Consumer protection

Even though some people could be employers or suppliers, we are all consumers. Are consumers getting a fair deal? Here are some issues to discuss with your group.

- 'The contents of this box may settle during transport'. Does this mean you are not getting the full amount?
- How much extra space is there in your box of cereals or frozen gateau?
- How thick is the glass jar of your chocolate and hazelnut spread?
- Does the jar of cosmetics look like this? Does it have a double shell?

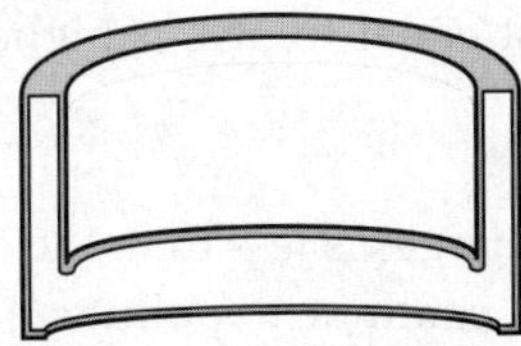

- How often have you seen notices in newspapers saying 'please return product Y9504 which could damage your health'?
- Do drug companies market new drugs too quickly, without enough testing, for example, thalidomide?
- Should there be more stringent controls on advertisers?
- Should children's toys be advertised to look as though they are life size?
- Why doesn't a hamburger look like it does on the photograph?

The legal system has been very concerned to protect the consumer against a whole range of possible abuse.

Environmental protection

The government emphasised its concern about **environmental protection** in 1970 when it set up the Royal Commission on Environmental Pollution. The commission has written 16 reports, including one on the quality of the UK's water. It has been mainly concerned with decreasing pollution which is not only an external cost to business but is also a social cost, meaning that it adversely affects society as a whole and not necessarily just the producer of the pollution. For example, car exhaust fumes affect children; emissions from power stations affect everyone and even fall in Norway as acid rain.

Several key questions need to be asked in any study of environmental protection:

- How much pollution are we willing to tolerate?
- Are we willing to pay to eliminate the pollution?
- Who should pay, the producer, and therefore ultimately the consumer, or the government?
- What are the costs and benefits of decreasing pollution?

The commission has used the best practicable method (BPM) to examine pollution control. This takes into account the type of pollution for example smoke or effluent, the method and cost of production and of controlling pollution.

The EU uses a similar concept to assess:

- Has everything practical been done?
- Has the best available pollution control technology been used?
- Is the cost excessive?

A judgement has to be made as to what is the best practicable method.

Reducing pollution

Pollution is viewed as a market failure in that the market mechanism has failed to stop producers from polluting the environment. It is therefore argued that a system of controls and charges is the best way of reducing the problem.

A business that, for example, discharges waste into a river would be charged according to the amount of pollution. There would, therefore, be a big cost saving to be made if a company cut down its pollution. However, it is essential that the level of charges is at least equal to, if not higher than, the cost of equipment to clean up the waste.

For example:

- if the level of charges is less than the cost of putting in pollution control equipment – companies will continue to pollute;
- if the level of charges is greater than the cost of pollution control equipment – pollution will reduce.

A business will be directly affected by any controls introduced to reduce pollution

- costs will rise
- **prices** may rise
- demand could decrease if the company does not possess a 'green and clean' image.

A quick walk through your local supermarket will reveal the extent to which 'environmentally friendly' is seen to be a selling point. Even unlikely products are affected, for example, petrol being sold from filling stations painted green by BP, whilst a new Ford car is marketed as being 'in harmony' with its surroundings.

Activities

1 How well is your school, college or home protecting the environment? Carry out a simple environmental audit to find out. Here is a sample checklist to get you going; you will probably think of other questions.

Are we wasting resources?

- What energy source is used e.g. gas, water?
- Is it being used efficiently (e.g. are windows left open, lights always on)?
- Can savings be made?
- How much waste is there?
- How is waste disposed of?
- Can anything be recycled?
- Are resources being used efficiently?
- Could fewer or cheaper resources be used?
- What measures are needed to improve?
- How much will they cost?

Social interests

Our society is continually changing. People are living longer. Unemployment can be found almost everywhere. Family life is changing. There are more single parent families. Social issues affect us all. Although many of these changes are welcome, for example, the improvement in living standards, there are others which can cause concern. The government intervenes to try and solve some of these problems.

- The UK mixed market economy has not provided enough public goods (sometimes called merit goods or social goods). These are goods which are provided by the state for everyone to use, for example, education, housing and health.
- When the profit motive is more important, particular groups become more vulnerable, for example, children need to be protected against violence on television (the 9pm watershed after which time children are supposed to be in bed!) and in the cinema (the certificate system). Equal Opportunities legislation has been introduced.
- As new materials and production methods are introduced workers need to be protected. Health and Safety legislation has been needed.
- The nation's health is getting worse. It is alleged that we eat too much fat and smoke too much. The government spends about £10 m per year on anti-smoking advertisements, but it makes about £7,000 m in tax on tobacco products. Should it do anything about this?

Activity

Your class should split into groups to discuss a social issue, try and say how it has been caused and how the government intervenes or could intervene.

Ways in which governments can influence markets

Regulation

This refers to the way in which the government or a regulatory body has the power to control the way particular companies or industries operate. The most familiar regulatory bodies are those concerned with the regulation of the now privatised utilities. These bodies are independent of the government. Their main functions to date have been to control prices and protect consumers' interests. OFGAS controls gas prices,

OFWAT controls water prices, while OFTEL controls telecommunications and sets maximum and minimum prices. The purpose of the latter is to make sure for example that BT does not set prices so low that new businesses cannot enter the industry (predatory pricing). Financial services are regulated by the Securities and Investment Board (SIB) (which wants to withdraw from direct regulation) and the Bank of England. OFSTED is concerned with the education curriculum. (Perhaps there could be a regulatory body for carpenters called OFCUT or one for students called OFHOME!! You can probably think of others.)

How much power do regulators have? *The Times* (January 1995) reported that Professor Littlechild, the Director General of OFER, the electricity regulator, had delayed publication of the prospectus for the government's £4 billion power privatisation following a recent large increase in wholesale electricity prices (the price at which the generators or makers of electricity sell to very large users such as ICI). He threatened to take action against either PowerGen or National Power if they did not comply. They could be referred to the MMC if they abused their positions.

Some critics have argued that regulators have too much power. They have made policy, not just enforced it, and regulation has become personalised. A former chairman of the Prudential Corporation, the UK's largest life insurers, said 'heavier regulation imposes a severe burden on life insurance companies. I spent too much of my time on regulatory matters'.

Activity

Find out which water, gas and electricity area you live in (check the bills). Could you get these services from an alternative company? Anglian Water claims to compete. Who might it compete with? Do these private utility companies have regional monopolies? Why do we need a regulator?

Self-regulation

Self-regulation occurs when an industry regulates itself without external intervention from the government or a formal regulatory body. Can people who work in an industry take an objective view if for example another person or business in the industry breaks the rules. Can they act as judge and jury?

This quotation from the *Financial Times* appears to suggest that they cannot. 'The system of self-regulation at Lloyd's of London was largely to blame for disastrous losses and its tight financial situation, a House of Commons inquiry was told. Lloyds names (the people who have traditionally used their cash and assets to support Lloyds) wanted a stronger independent system of regulation.'

Deregulation

This refers to situations where the government removes existing controls or regulations in a market in order to introduce or promote competition. It applies particularly to industries which have been privatised or commercialised. The growth of private courier and parcel services alongside the Royal Mail is a good example (the government attempted to privatise this service but failed due to public opposition). The deregulation of broadcasting and TV services has enabled companies such as Nynex to lay optical fibre TV and telephone cables under every pavement in some boroughs. Perhaps the best example of deregulation is the growth in public bus services run by private companies. For example, in the London borough of Bromley there used to be only red London Transport and Greenline buses but now there are also Blue and Yellow buses for new companies operating new routes. There are, however, few examples of buses directly competing on the same route.

Activity

Who gains and who loses when industries are deregulated? Look at the question from the point of view of the existing and new businesses, workers and customers. In the case of bus services, would more people travel?

Government franchising as a means of regulation

Although the term franchise normally applies to situations where one company allows another to use its name and business methods, in this case it refers to the position where the government sells the right to operate a particular service to a private company, for example, TV and radio stations. The method allows the government to specify the service standards required and to decide which company can operate the franchise.

A good example of the way the government is using franchising as a means of control and regulation is shown by the privatisation of British Rail. In January 1995 the Franchising Director of the BR privatisation programme announced the names of the first four franchises. These were Great Western, South West, Gatwick Express and London, Tilbury and Southend.

'This is the first time that there will be guaranteed minimum service standards' said the Transport Minister.

Opponents of the scheme said

'there will be fewer trains, more crowding, higher fares and no new investment'

'minimum service standards means cutting out early morning trains'

'there could be up to 20% less trains on the Great Western; services to Bristol, Truro in Cornwall and Carmarthen have been cut'

'it is like the George Orwell book *1984* – less means better!'

Companies wishing to operate these services must apply by tender for the privilege of doing so. This system is very similar to the way in which the regional commercial TV companies and local radio stations operate. When new TV contracts were awarded recently, Thames TV lost to Carlton Television the right to weekday broadcasting in the London area.

Statutory intervention

Statutory intervention refers to regulations, rules and laws approved by parliament. This type of intervention can have many purposes including: protecting the interests of consumers, making sure that trading is honest and fair, promoting competition, protecting the environment, protecting workers and promoting equality of opportunity. The majority of statutory measures will have some kind of impact on the market for products and/or factors of production.

Consumer protection

The Sale and supply of Goods Act 1994

This Act amended both the Sale of Goods Act 1979 and the Supply of Goods and Services Act 1982. It applies to all goods including food, regardless of where they are bought, for example, at shops, market stalls, door-to-door sales, home party sales, or catalogue mail order.

According to the Act the seller must ensure that goods are:

- of satisfactory quality: this term has replaced 'merchantable quality' used in the previous act. Satisfactory quality is defined as the standard that a reasonable person would regard as satisfactory, taking account of any description of the goods, the price if relevant and all other relevant circumstances. The quality of goods includes their state and condition plus fitness for purpose, appearance and finish, freedom from minor defects and safety and durability. Are you a reasonable person? What do you think is satisfactory?
- reasonably fit for any particular purpose, i.e. they must be able to do what the seller claims they can do, for example, an electric toaster should be able to toast four slices in one minute if this is how it was described.

The Act can be enforced as soon as a contract has been made between the buyer and seller, i.e. when the buyer has made an offer and the seller has accepted. A valid contract can be written or verbal. If the contract has been broken buyers can either get their money back or have the goods replaced. They do not have to accept a credit note.

However, consumers are not entitled to anything if they did not see obvious faults at the time of purchase, or were told about faults but chose to ignore them, or ignored any advice which was given.

Office of Fair Trading (OFT)

The OFT is responsible for the administration of UK competition policy, controlling monopolies and mergers and consumer protection. For example, it can investigate consumer complaints about untruthful trade descriptions, and about short measure being served in garages and pubs.

Kite marks and safety standards

Marks such as the British Standards Institution (BSI) Kite Mark, the BSI Safety Mark, the British Electrotechnical Approvals Board (BEAB), and British Gas Seal of Service all show that the products have been tested and approved for use.

Trading Standards Departments

Trading Standards Officers work for the local authority and have the responsibility for investigating consumer complaints against businesses, for example, poor and dirty food in restaurants, 'short' measures on petrol pumps, unsafe toys, etc. They have the power to take the business to court in order to pursue a case and prevent a re-occurrence of the problem.

Some EU directives on consumer protection

Table 1.2 Some EU directives on consumer protection.

Directive	Purpose
Misleading advertisements	Designed to protect consumers against misleading advertisements
Product liability	Makes manufacturers and importers liable for any injuries caused by defective products
Doorstep selling	People have a 7 day cooling off period in which to change their mind if they have been sold something in their own home
Consumer credit	Protects consumers when they have signed credit agreements
Toy safety	States that only safe toys can be sold in the EU
Price indication	All selling prices must be clearly displayed, e.g. in Public Houses
Unfair contract terms	To eliminate unfair terms in contracts
Package travel	Protection for people on package holidays if the travel company becomes bankrupt

Environmental protection

EU environmental policy

The EU environmental policy has these aims:

- to preserve, protect and improve the quality of the environment
- to help protect human health
- to help conserve natural resources.

There are over 300 EU directives which are designed to achieve these aims, for example on air and water pollution, the dumping of waste, controlling dangerous chemicals and protection of the natural heritage. The EU wants to make sure that all competition is free and fair so standards have been set to ensure manufacturers and suppliers can compete on an equal footing. For instance, car and lorry exhaust emissions are tightly controlled and all new models must meet these standards.

LAWS AND ECONOMIC INSTRUMENTS

International, European and UK laws on the environment all have an impact on business, and it makes business sense to keep abreast of developments, anticipate changes and keep within the expected guidelines.

On an international level, there are agreements to reduce the use of substances whose environmental impact is globally damaging. CFCs, for example, are being phased out by the end of 1994 because they destroy the ozone layer and by the end of 1993 are unlikely to be available. Many businesses are affected by international controls: if you're one of them you should be acting now!

In the European Union, over 350 pieces of environmental legislation have been published. The trend is towards a programme of sustainable economic activity requiring the voluntary commitment of all members of society. An ecolabelling scheme for consumer goods, for example, will allow customers to choose products which are less damaging to the environment. The scheme is voluntary, but gives a marketing advantage to those products carrying the ecolabel. Within Europe, different countries have their own legislation. If you've done business with Germany, for example, you'll know that this can be quite demanding.

In the UK, Her majesty's Inspectorate of Pollution (HMIP), local authorities and the National Rivers Authority (NRA) are the main players in controlling those industrial processes that most pollute the environment. These two bodies are due to combine with waste regulation authorities to form the Environment Agency. Integrated Pollution Control – treating the land, water and air as part of a whole to be policed together – is a fundamental principle and covers the most polluting industrial processes. For industry, Best Available Techniques not Entailing Excessive Cost (BATNEEC) is the pragmatic measure you may need to match up to. A second level of controls covering releases to air only, are regulated by local authorities on similar principles. These apply to a far greater range of companies – your company could be one of them. You should also be aware of the 'duty to care' regulations which make you responsible for the ultimate disposal of all waste: it doesn't stop being your concern when your disposal contractor drives it away from your premises.

Economic instruments are likely to become more important in the UK and Europe. As an example, to encourage the recycling of packaging there could be raw material and product taxes, waste collection and disposal charges, and a take-back duty on suppliers.

Source: DTI, *The environment: a business guide*

Equal opportunities legislation

Equal opportunities legislation is discussed in detail in Chapter 7. Discrimination still exists, in society, at work, in school or college, in the street, at sports grounds. It comes about because of people's attitudes which develop over many years. They are not helped by what we see, read or hear. We still get images of women or black people which are disparaging or stereotypical.

There are still only a small proportion of businesses which take an active approach to promoting equal opportunities policies in the workplace.

Activity

Although there are laws dealing with specific offences there is no obligation for a business to be an equal opportunities employer.

Look through the job advertisements of the newspapers. Note down those organisations which advertise that they are equal opportunities employers.

Classify these by type of organisation, nature of business and public or private sector. Are there any particular types of organisation which tend to advertise in this way? Why do you think this is?

A business could be affected by:

- the need to put in ramps for wheelchair users
- the need to design access-friendly buildings
- the need to introduce equal opportunities into job adverts, recruitment, promotion and training
- equal pay for equal work would directly influence the wages paid to men and women.

Research shows that employers see disabled employees as average or better than average in performance, attendance, job stability and safety. Yet although firms with over 20 employees are required to employ 3 per cent registered disabled people, fewer than one quarter do so (source: *Computer Weekly*, December 1992).

Activity

For this activity you should work in groups of five or six. Discuss each of the issues in the list and come to a positive conclusion about what you would do. Compare your conclusions with those of other groups.

a One of your colleagues is always telling racist jokes.
b The males in your group always get to the computers first.
c A girl in your group is constantly being harassed by a senior male colleague.
d You find racist graffiti in the toilets.
e One of your colleagues is very slow and quiet and is always being laughed at.
f Do you see discrimination around you? Where – on television, in films or in newspapers and books?

Health and safety legislation

Although today workers at their workplace are relatively well protected by legislation, this has not always been the case. Before the nineteenth century, employers were unconcerned about either the health or safety of their workforce. However, with the growth of trade unions, and with help from a small but important group of philanthropic individuals, conditions gradually changed. Pressure was put on successive governments to bring in legislation which would improve working conditions.

The Health and Safety at Work Act (HASAWA) 1974

This Act gives rights and responsibilities to employers and employees. Employers must provide:

- A safe and healthy workplace.
- Proper safety procedures – including fire drills, fire notices and exits.
- Safe machinery and equipment, which is properly guarded.
- Trained safety staff.
- A written local health and safety policy which is available to all employees.

Employees must:

- Act so as to protect themselves and others.
- Follow health and safety procedures.
- Not misuse health and safety material and equipment, for example, it is a criminal offence to play with a fire extinguisher, cause a false alarm, or write on/change safety signs.

The Act applies to all workplaces. Both employees and students have a responsibility to obey the Act.

The Control of Substances Hazardous to Health Regulations (COSHH) 1988

These regulations lay down the ways in which hazardous substances, for example, cleaning and decorating materials, can be controlled. They also say how people can be protected from them. All employees have the right to be told about the risks in their workplace, and what precautions should be taken.

As a result of HASAWA and COSHH:

- there are increased powers for the outside inspectors and for Health and Safety Officers at the workplace;
- the total responsibility for health and safety now lies directly with employers, managers and workers;
- considerable emphasis has been placed on the need to prevent accidents;
- greater importance has been attached to the training of the whole workforce;
- the need to prevent accidents happening to anyone at the workplace, including visitors, contractors and suppliers, has been recognised.

1992 Health and Safety Legislation – the 'Six Pack'

Since January 1993, new health and safety at work legislation has come into force. Known familiarly as the 'Six Pack', this legislation has been brought in to fulfil European Union Directives. The Six Pack is composed of:

1. Management of Health and Safety at Work Regulations 1992. The main purpose is to improve health and safety management by introducing proper systems for co-ordinating, control and monitoring.
2. Provision and Use of Work Equipment Regulations 1992. The main purpose is to bring together and clarify the many regulations that deal with equipment.

3 Manual Handling Operations Regulations 1992. The main purpose is to lay down proper procedures for manual handling, for example, carrying heavy loads which is a major cause of industrial accidents.
4 Workplace (Health, Safety and Welfare) Regulations 1992. The main purpose is to tidy up and clarify previous legislation covering working environment, safety, facilities and 'housekeeping'.
5 Personal Protective Equipment at Work (PPE) Regulations 1992. The main purpose is to tidy up and clarify previous legislation. It covers the use, type and storage of PPE.
6 Health and Safety (Display Screen Equipment) Regulations 1992. The main purpose is the laying down of rules and regulations for the health and safety of employees who continually use display screen equipment (DSE). For further information see Chapter 4 and Appendix 1.

In addition, the Construction (Design and Management) Regulations have to be implemented by 1994.

What has health and safety legislation achieved?

The statistics on health and safety cover those areas which are the concern of the Health and Safety Executive (HSE). They do not cover, for example, the King's Cross tube station disaster, or the sinking of the *Herald of Free Enterprise*.

The general relationship between fatalities – deaths – and accidents for the whole economy, looks like this:

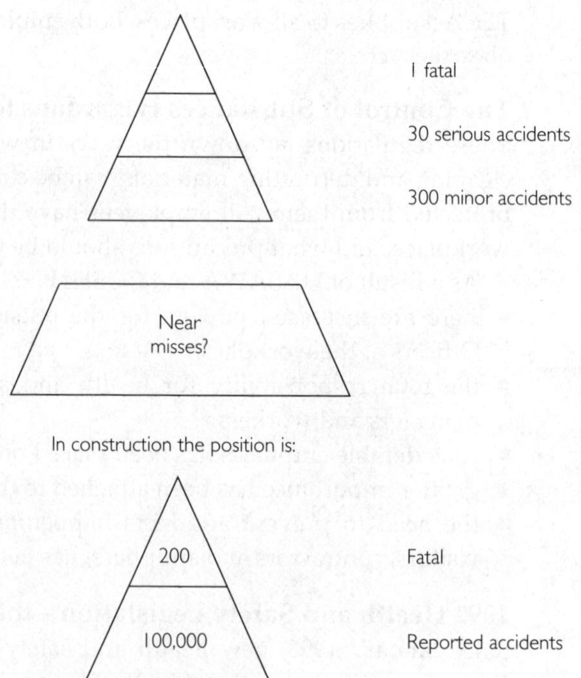

On average:

- one construction worker is killed every three days;
- 60 construction workers are reported injured every day;
- 12 members of the public are killed by construction work every year.

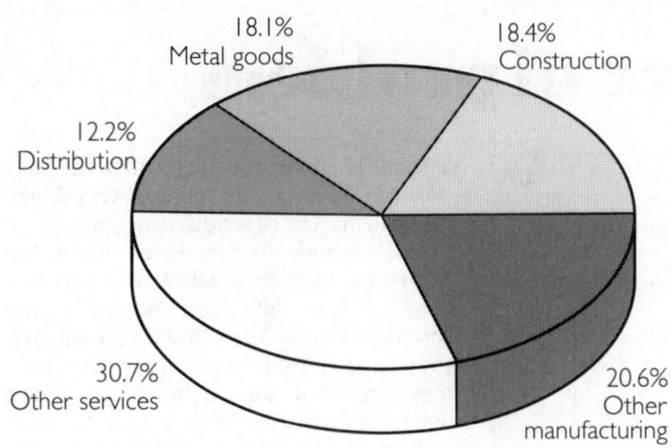

Figure 1.12 The distribution of non-fatal injuries

Despite these figures, there is major concern that there is still considerable under-reporting of accidents in the construction industry (information from HSE).

The distribution of non-fatal major injury accidents is shown in Figure 1.12.

Has health and safety legislation been a success?

The answer is generally a qualified 'Yes'! However, it is exceptionally difficult to compare accident statistics over a period of years. The definition of non-fatal major injury was introduced in 1981 and radically changed again in 1986. We can, however, compare the figures for fatalities, which cannot be under-recorded or hidden. The rate of deaths per 100,000 employees in all industries has been falling steadily:

1971	1975	1976	1985	1986	1987
4.3	3.7	3.4	1.9	1.7	1.6

But as the Health and Safety Executive says, 'The overall fatal injury rate is reducing steadily, but this reflects the shift to employment in service industries and probably a shift from heavier to lighter industry.'

Activities

1 Look at the local Health and Safety Policy Statement for your organisation. Now write a short article which summarises its main features.
2 Look at the accident book for your organisation. Make a chart which shows the main causes and number of accidents. Try to find out what was done to prevent a re-occurrence of any accidents.
3 Choose another organisation and repeat 2. Compare the two charts. What conclusions can be made?
4 Use the annual report published by the Health and Safety Commission to find the national figures on injuries and accidents for your industry. Choose one other industry and compare its health and safety record with your own.

Case study

Safety in the construction industry

The article on the following page looks at the results of a large number of 'blitz' visits made to building sites by Health and Safety Inspectors.

Blitz hinted at size of problem

In 1986 the Health and Safety Commission decided to take firm action in reducing the number of major accidents and fatalities in the construction industry. About half the fatalities were known to occur on small sites (less than ten workmen) so an eighteen month programme of enforcement-led activity ("blitzes") was set up, aimed principally at smaller sites.

In total, 8,272 visits were made, predominantly to "small" sites, and over 10,000 contractors were seen between May 1987 and September 1988. Overall the standard of health and safety found was reported to be "poor" and it was necessary to issue 2,046 Prohibition Notices (approximately one in four, although some sites were given more than one) and 96 Improvement Notices.

A variety of problems required enforcement notices as shown in Table 1.

The majority of action taken did indeed involve smaller sites, however this reflects the greater number of small sites visited. In fact, only a quarter to a third of small sites warranted action as opposed to over half of larger sites. There is therefore no justification in targeting a certain size of site in future, says HSE.

NATURE OF PROBLEM	% OF TOTAL
Defective scaffold (inc cradles)	28
Roofwork (poor or no edge protection)	18
Ladders (poor use/defective)	10
Fragile roof/rooflights	2
Other unsafe place of work	10
Unsafe access (excl ladders)	4
Excavations (poor support)	2
Dangerous electrics (excl underground cables)	5
Dangerous lifting plant	3
Other dangerous plant	2
Non-use of protective equipment	3
Other	13
TOTAL	100

Table 1. Matters on site requiring enforcement action

Health and safety awareness

Inspectors looked at the knowledge of agents, foremen and supervisors in charge of sites. One third were found to have an inadequate level of knowledge about "basic health and safety requirements" (where the person in charge could be found that is—on 19 per cent of sites the agent or supervisor was unavailable or non-existent!). Not surprisingly, half the sites where knowledge was "poor or very poor" also had matters of serious concern.

HSE found that publicity about the campaign had been effective (over one third of the sites had heard of the campaign) but it is doubtful if awareness of the campaign led to much, if any, improvement on site. It thus seems that publicity must be combined with action to raise awareness of health and safety (and the HSE's role) to a level where companies make the effort to improve health and safety.

The future of the blitz

It is unlikely that blitzes on such a large scale will be organised again as they are very costly. However, "mini" blitzes carried out in certain areas or aimed at certain types of contractors, for example roofing specialists, are a real possibility.

Although the blitz had some immediate effects it is doubtful whether there will be any long term improvements in safety standards. However, it will certainly have raised awareness of health and safety matters and is thus one step on the long road to safer working practices. ■

Source: *Health & Safety at Work*, November 1989

Activity

a Summarise the article given in the case study above. What does it tell you about the following:

- the safety record of the construction industry,
- the causes of the construction industry's poor safety performance record,
- possible approaches to solving the problems.

b What would the industry gain if it had a better safety record?

Legislation to control monopoly

Competition policy

Recent government policy towards competition has focused on two principles:

- that competition results in greater efficiency and a more effective allocation of resources. This has been the spur behind privatisation;
- that any barrier which prevents or reduces competition should be eliminated.

Competition policy in the EU and the UK starts with the assumption that competition should be encouraged because it is good for the economy and stimulates economic growth.

The legislation

The main legislation has been:

- Monopolies and Restrictive Practices Act 1948
- Restrictive Trade Practices Act 1956
- Monopolies and Mergers Act 1965
- Fair Trading Act 1973
- Competition Act 1980.

Case study

The Monopolies and Mergers Commission report and its effect on the brewing industry

In 1989 the MMC produced its report on the brewery industry. Its major findings were:

- beer prices had increased by more than the rate of inflation;
- national brewers were also major pub owners and this reduced consumer choice;
- there were entry barriers preventing new brewers from coming into the market;
- pub tenants were not able to bargain with the strong breweries.

The MMC proposed that:

- each brewer would have to sell off 50 per cent of any pubs it owned above 2,000, for example, if a brewer owned 3,000 pubs, it would have to sell 500;
- tenants should be able to sell a guest beer, for example, a Courage pub could sell a beer belonging to a competitor such as Bass;
- tenants should have greater security.

The result was that:

- the big brewers have created new companies which then bought the pubs;
- the big brewers swapped beer and pubs;
- brewery mergers increased, therefore reducing choice for the consumer. A number of companies including Boddingtons stopped brewing.

The legislation did not have the intended effect of increasing competition and giving the customer a better deal.

In January 1993 package tour operator Airtours launched a take-over bid for rival company Owners Abroad. The battle was about market share in an industry dominated by four major players. In fact the bid failed, but there was sufficient action for Professor Sir Bryan Carsberg at the Monopolies and Mergers Commission to show an interest.

David Crossland, Chairman of Airtours, was confident that the deal would not be stopped by the Office of Fair Trading as long as package tours within the UK were also taken into account. This is what happened when Thomson Holidays took over Horizon in 1989 to raise its share of the overseas market to nearly 40 per cent. After adding in the UK package market the MMC allowed the take-over to go through as Thomsons then had less than 25 per cent of the total.

Figure 1.13 shows market share of the foreign package tour market at the time of the Airtours bid.

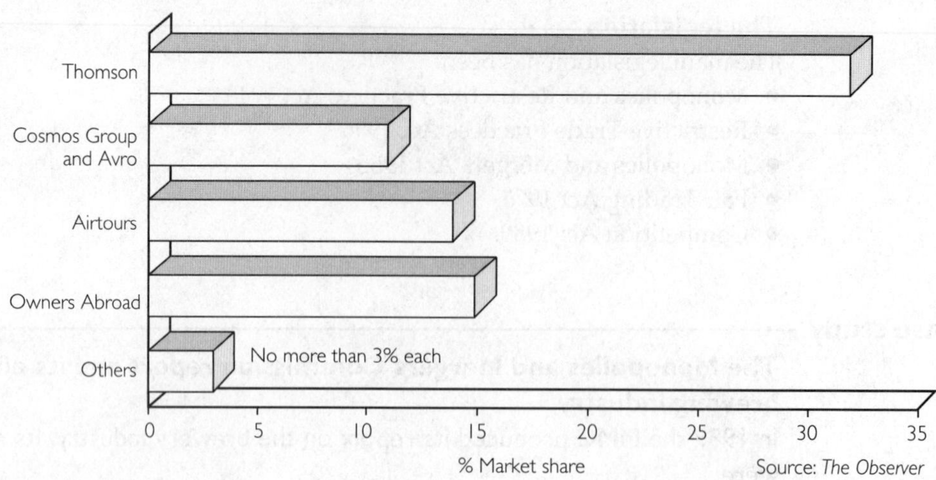

Figure 1.13 Market share of overseas package holidays

Activity

You are a journalist for the monthly trade paper *World of Travel* at the time of these events. Write a short piece to explain what is happening in the industry. You will need to explain clearly who is involved, what is happening and what the motives are behind the proposed deal. Explain also the role of the MMC and why it may become involved in this case.

Fiscal policy

Fiscal policy refers to the way in which government spends and raises money. It involves decisions about government expenditure, **taxation** and borrowing. The annual Budget statement which is presented to the House of Commons by the Chancellor of the Exchequer sets out the way in which the Treasury intends to raise the money that the various government departments will spend in the forthcoming financial year.

The 1993 Budget presented on l6 March 1993 was the last of the traditional spring budgets; it is now presented in November. In 1993, the then Chancellor, Norman Lamont, set out his plans as follows:

> 'This budget...gives priority to programmes that would help to promote growth and the long term performance of the economy...unemployment...cannot be reduced simply by stimulating demand. A deep-seated problem needs more fundamental solutions. It requires more flexible markets not just for labour but for goods and services. and it requires support given by governments to be directed less at propping up declining industries and more at helping the unemployed rejoin the workforce...we must continue to resist the job destroying measures coming from Brussels...that is why this government will never sign the Social Chapter.'

(The Social Chapter is part of the Maastricht Treaty and is explained in Appendix 3.)

This statement represented the government supply side view on how the economy should be managed (see page 427). One aspect that caused a great deal of comment was the Chancellor's prediction that the government might need to borrow £50 billion to balance the budget. Where planned expenditure exceeds planned income then the shortfall needs to be borrowed. This is called the public sector borrowing requirement (PSBR). The Chancellor was unwilling to increase taxation to raise funds because he felt this would stop the recovery from recession.

Where a PSBR exists there is a deficit budget:

Expenditure by government departments	=	Revenue from taxation	+	PSBR (deficit)

Alternatives are: a balanced budget where expenditure equals revenue or surplus budget where revenue exceeds expenditure.

Activity

Obtain information about the latest Budget.

1 Who was the Chancellor of the Exchequer at the time?
2 What happened to:
 a income tax?
 b corporation tax (paid by companies)?
 c value added tax (VAT)?
3 Was there any attempt to help small businesses?
4 What was the main aim of the Chancellor?
5 Who benefited and who lost out? Why do you think this was?
6 What did the Shadow Chancellor say on behalf of the Opposition?
7 Draw two pie charts to show:
 a where the money will go to
 b where it will come from.

Government expenditure

The size and direction of government public expenditure reflects its political views. The aims will be:

- To provide public services such as law and order and defence, which are unlikely to be provided in a free market economy.
- To subsidise essential needs, for example, many groups need state benefits to support them. Essential services such as health and education (merit goods) have traditionally been provided free. However, some schools and hospitals are now opting out of the state system.
- To provide local authorities with revenue to spend in addition to the money they raise through the council tax. This is gradually decreasing as council services such as refuse collection and education are financed in other ways.

Figure 1.14 shows government expenditure as a percentage of GDP (gross domestic product). This is the value of the total goods and services produced in the UK. The predicted fall in spending is in line with the government's intention to cut back the £50 billion PSBR.

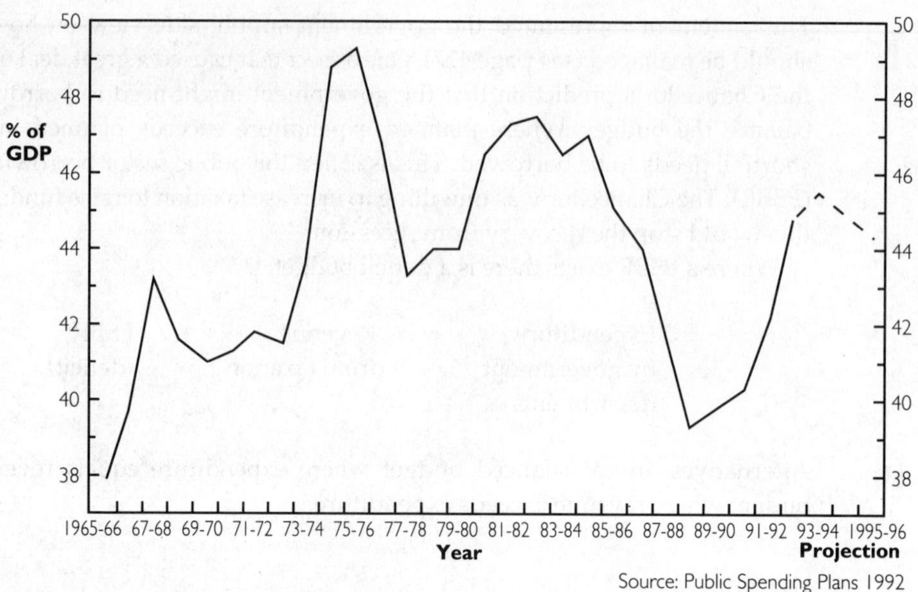

Figure 1.14 Government expenditure as a percentage of GDP (excluding privatisation proceeds)

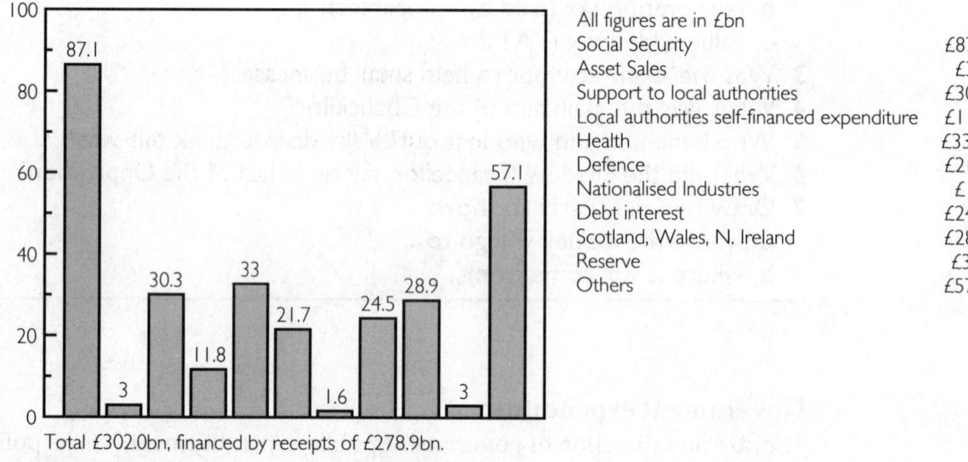

Source: The 1994 Autumn Budget Statement

Figure 1.15 Government expenditure 1994–5

Pensions and benefits

Pensions and benefits are a major part of government expenditure. They are directed at helping such groups as the unemployed, people with young families, people over retirement age and people on low incomes. The amount and type of benefits that are paid tend to reflect the political philosophy of the party in power. This area of state spending is likely to increase as the proportion of people over 65 rises.

The overall purpose of providing state-funded benefits is to try and reduce the level of poverty in society. There are still many families who cannot afford to pay for their essential needs – food, shelter and clothing – without some form of support.

The maintenance or otherwise of the National Health Service (NHS) can also be seen as a social and political aim of government policy. A number of former NHS hospitals have now contracted out of the state system, as part of the privatisation programme, to form hospital trusts. An example is Guy's Hospital in London.

A business could be affected by:

- a change in the employer's contribution to National Insurance;
- a change in the retirement age. It is estimated that a reduction in the male retirement age to 60 would cost business £500 million, whereas a rise in the retirement age of women to 65 could save money. The compromise solution would be for both men and women to retire at 63.

Both these measures would affect the conditions of supply. They could affect price depending upon whether the costs could be passed to the consumer.

Activity

British prime ministers

Clement Attlee	Lab	1945–51
Sir Winston Churchill	Con	1951–55
Sir Anthony Eden	Con	1955–57
Harold Macmillan	Con	1957–63
Sir Alex Douglas-Home	Con	1963–64
Harold Wilson	Lab	1964–70
Edward Heath	Con	1970–74
Harold Wilson	Lab	1974–76
James Callaghan	Lab	1976–79
Margaret Thatcher	Con	1979–92
John Major	Con	1992–

1 **Use Figures 1.14 and 1.15 and the list of prime ministers to find out if there is a relationship between the party in power and the amount of government expenditure. If there is a relationship, what are the reasons for this?**

2 **Money values have changed since 1945. How is it that we can usefully compare public expenditure over so long a period?**

Taxation

Taxation is the means by which government expenditure is financed. The main taxes are:

- Income tax – charged on incomes earned by individuals as employees through the Pay As You Earn (PAYE) system and on earnings from self-employment. Possible effects of a decrease in income tax are:
  - people have more money to spend
  - consumer expenditure rises
  - business sells more.

- Corporation tax – charged on profits earned by companies. Most large businesses employ accountants to find ways of minimising the amount of corporation tax they need to pay.
  An increase in corporation tax is likely to decrease retained profits which could lead to a rise in product prices
- Value added tax (VAT) – charged on the value added by each business in the supply chain as the product changes hands. Domestic fuel bills were zero-rated until it was announced in the 1993 Budget that they would be subject to VAT. It is now 8% (it was claimed as a green tax, see below). Consumers pay VAT when they buy certain goods and services. Adding VAT to a product increases the price the consumer has to pay which could lead to a fall in demand for that product.
  The Chancellor claimed that a fall in demand was the intended effect of adding VAT to fuel, i.e. that the tax was a green tax designed to save fuel, rather than to raise revenue.
- Local taxes – paid by businesses and residents to the local authority. There are seven rates for individuals paying council tax; business rates differ between areas. A business will need to consider rates when deciding on a location.
- Excise duties – the responsibility of Customs and Excise. They are charged on wines, spirits and tobacco. Increasing excise duties on tobacco could lead to:
  - a fall in demand
  - businesses could diversify, for example, British American Tobacco (BAT) could take over non-tobacco companies.
- Inheritance tax – charged on money and assets above a certain amount.
- Capital gains tax – charged when assets, for example a second home, are sold.

Purposes of taxation

The government uses taxation as a means of raising money for its public spending programme. However, it can also use it as a means of increasing or decreasing the amount of money people have to spend so as to stimulate or depress the economy. Its uses are therefore:

- to gain income to finance expenditure;
- to change the way income is distributed, the 'Robin Hood effect';
- to encourage or deter spending on particular items;
- to help manage the economy through the Budget.

Remember that taxation is a **leakage** from the flow of income whereas public expenditure is an **injection**.

Activity

1 Your group should split to investigate the current rates of:

- income tax
- corporation tax
- council tax
- business rate
- VAT.

When you have collected the information keep a record; this may be useful for your business plan.

2 Do you think these rates are sensible? A change in the basic rate of income tax by a penny in the pound, for example, would raise/lose £1,400 million for the government.

Monetary policy

Monetary policy can influence markets by controlling inflation through

- the price of money
- the level of economic activity – this affects the amount of money in the economy.

The theory is that there is a link between inflation and the money supply, in that if money is spent faster than goods are produced then prices will rise. This can happen if too much money is available in the economy. The difficulty is that the money supply is not easy to calculate: it is not simply a matter of counting the notes and coins that have been printed. Cash can be spent many times as it circulates through the economy – the faster it circulates the greater the money supply. There is also the growing use of credit where money can be spent in advance of earnings without the need for immediate access to cash.

Monetary policy uses two basic weapons to restrict money supply:

- the interest rate
- the lending policies of the banks and financial institutions.

An increase in the **interest rate** will make credit more expensive and therefore acts as a disincentive for people to borrow. Almost every business and consumer is affected. Companies that borrow money have to pay interest to the institution that lends it. Lenders of money receive interest.

With high rates of interest, companies will find it more expensive to borrow money and will be reluctant to finance investment in new machinery and equipment unless they can find alternative methods such as:

- issuing shares to the public;
- making sufficient profits which can be ploughed back into the company;
- taking over another business which has cash and/or assets that can be used.

Consumers will also be affected, particularly those with mortgages. During the recession of the early 1990s, the housing market was badly affected by high interest rates. Customers who have to pay more in interest will cut back in their spending on other goods and services. This is the opportunity cost – to buy one item we give up the opportunity of buying another.

After Britain left the ERM in 1993 it was easier to set interest rates independently of those set, for example, in Germany. Within a few months, interest rates were much lower.

Banks and other financial institutions create money by their lending. The government can place limitations upon the types and amount of lending. Where it wishes to stimulate the economy it can relax these controls.

The government can bring these monetary policies into effect through the Bank of England which acts as banker to the government. Since the major banks have accounts with the Bank of England they are compelled to react when it changes interest rates. Other institutions such as building societies are competing for the same customers as the banks. If, for example, the banks raise interest rates then customers will transfer their savings away from building societies unless they do the same. This in turn, means that the building societies must charge more for their loans.

Activity

Study the following data on interest rates taken from the *Monthly Digest of Statistics*:

1990	June	15%
	July	15%
	Aug.	15%
	Sept.	15%
	Oct.	14%
	Nov.	14%
	Dec.	14%
1991	Jan.	14%
	Feb.	13%
	Mar.	12.5%

1994	June	5.25%
	July	5.25%
	Aug.	5.25%
	Sept.	5.75%
	Oct.	5.75%
	Nov.	5.75%
	Dec.	6.25%

1 Bring the data up-to-date and comment on the trends.
2 Plot the data on a graph, leaving room to put in more data for the next six months.
3 A colleague has said 'but our organisation isn't affected by the rate of interest'. Write down all the points you would make to say 'Sorry, you are wrong'.

Activity

Which of the following would benefit from high interest rates and which would benefit from low interest rates?

a An old age pensioner living on capital.
b A single parent relying on state benefits.
c Tec-Neke Ltd who manufacture trainers; they have just taken out a large bank loan.
d An estate agent.

In each case explain your answer.

Government and unemployment

Unemployment has been a problem to successive governments. The theories as to how it should be dealt with have changed over the years; both fiscal and monetary policies have been tried.

The Keynsian approach

In the terrible unemployment of the 1930s one person in four was often unemployed. As a result of this, governments in Britain after the war determined to guarantee full employment as part of their policies. The approach was to fund public works programmes through the annual Budget, and reduce taxes to stimulate demand in the economy. This policy was based upon the theories of John Maynard Keynes who had advised the US government to spend its way out of the 1930s depression.

Injections of money into public sector projects such as building new roads, schools or hospitals would create a **multiplier** effect which would ripple through the economy like a stone thrown into a pond (Figure 1.16).

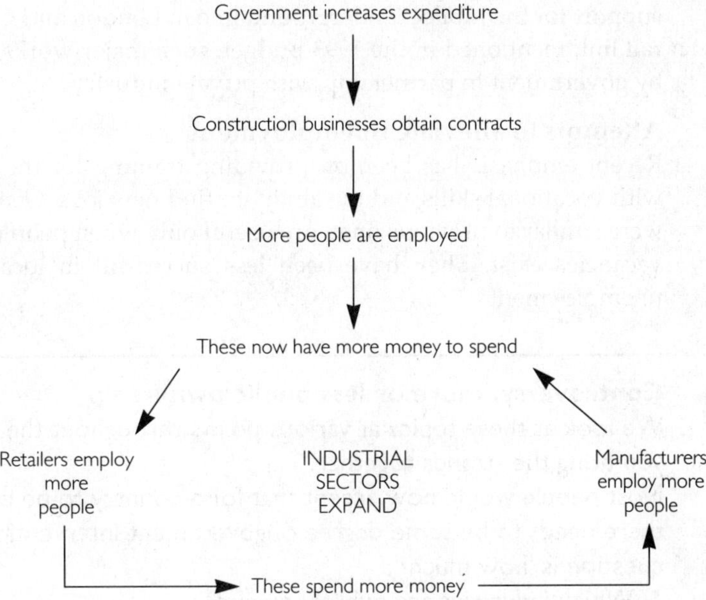
Government increases expenditure
Construction businesses obtain contracts
More people are employed
These now have more money to spend
Retailers employ more people
INDUSTRIAL SECTORS EXPAND
Manufacturers employ more people
These spend more money

Figure 1.16 The multiplier effect

The overall result would be reduced unemployment which would create more consumer demand as a result of increased spending. The theory suggested that the government would get its money back as the newly-employed workers would increase government income from taxation.

During the 1970s it became clear that this Keynsian approach brought its own problems. Increased demand tended to cause inflation, inefficient industries were artificially supported and imports rose causing balance of payments problems. Finally, unemployment still persisted.

Monetarism

Since 1979 Conservative governments, especially those of Margaret Thatcher, have believed that it was better not to intervene in the economy in the way described above. Instead they would rely on market forces to set wages and to determine which goods and services are necessary and which industries are efficient.

The monetarist theories of writers such as Milton Friedman have been influential. The argument is broadly that using public expenditure to stimulate demand will reduce unemployment only in the short term; in the long term it will increase wage costs as employers compete for workers. This leads to inflation as spending power increases faster than the supply of products available.

There was much talk in the 1980s of making industry more efficient; it must become leaner and fitter by slimming down. Only in this way, it was argued, could the UK compete in world markets and generate real jobs.

The belief that the economy works most efficiently with a minimum of government interference has meant that governments attempted to cut back on public expenditure programmes. They preferred to rely on supply and demand in the labour market to reduce unemployment.

There is now sufficient evidence to suggest that full employment is no longer regarded as a realistic aim of economic policy. Although the government declared support for the Jubilee Underground line in London and Crossrail, a new cross London rail link mentioned in the 1993 Budget, such major works are increasingly undertaken by government in partnership with private industry.

Attempts to alleviate unemployment

Recent emphasis has been on providing training for the unemployed to equip them with vocational skills and the ability to find new jobs. Generally, these schemes, which were similar to previous ones, are useful only when people are strongly motivated and vacancies exist. They have been less successful in local areas with high levels of unemployment.

Activities

Controversy: more or less public ownership

We look at these topics at various points throughout the book; this activity will help you bring the strands together.

Most people would now accept that for a country to be economically successful there needs to be some degree of government intervention and that the real question is 'how much?'.

1 Which industries are publicly owned?
2 Should there be more or less public ownership?
3 What are the advantages and disadvantages of public ownership?
4 Which industries have been recently privatised?
5 What are the advantages and disadvantages of privatisation?
6 What criteria would you use to decide if an industry is successful?
7 Which industries should be publicly owned?
8 Are you for or against public ownership?

Present your findings as a set of notes. Use your notes to discuss the issues in class.

Regional policy

In a free market economy, differences between regions should disappear because businesses would move from one region to another as opportunities presented themselves. In practice, this does not happen and the government has had to intervene to redress the balance between regions.

There have been two aspects to **regional policy**:

- taking work to the workers which involves the mobility of capital;
- taking workers to the work which requires a mobile labour force.

Taking work to the workers

This has taken two forms. First, the government has given incentives to businesses to start up or expand in areas of high unemployment or industrial decline. The types of incentive have included subsidised factories, tax relief on the purchase of capital equipment, free rent, subsidies to employ labour and general improvements to the area such as new road networks. Second, the government has restricted or controlled development in areas with high employment, by using building and planning controls.

The ability of companies to move depends on the mobility of capital: some businesses need to be located in specific areas because of the nature of the product or method of production. Other footloose companies are more mobile and can move to take advantage of government inducements. The advances in information and

communications technology have allowed many high-tech firms, the so-called sun-rise industries, to establish themselves by using government grants.

Taking workers to the work

In this case the government has given grants, help with removal costs, and information and training to workers to move form one area to another. When unemployment is generally low, this approach can be useful. During a recession, when unemployment is high everywhere (see Chapter 10 for regional unemployment) there is little opportunity for workers to move. Moving house has been particularly difficult since 1990 due to the negative equity gap cause by the fall in house prices. People who had been encouraged to buy their own houses bought them with large mortgages when prices were high. When house prices fell, people were still left with large mortgages, except now the mortgage values were bigger than the value of the property.

Despite many years of government intervention, regional differences still persist. It has been particularly unfortunate that regional help has gone mainly to manufacturing businesses which have suffered badly during the 1980s. In June 1993 the government redistributed government help to favour the South of England.

Poorer regions

The UK's membership of the EU has generated extra funds for the regions in industrial decline. The European Regional Development Fund, the European Coal and Steel Community and the European Investment Bank have all contributed financial help with large infrastructure developments, for example, roads and bridges such as the Humber bridge.

A decision to move by a business will depend upon its assessment of its own private costs and benefits. Government intervention tries to include social costs and benefits in its calculations of where to give regional assistance.

A business could be both directly and indirectly affected by government intervention in the regions. For example:

- a new or expanding business could have lower costs for labour, machinery, materials, finance and premises;
- an existing business could benefit from the multiplier effect of a new infrastructure project.

Review questions

1 Explain what has happened to the secondary sector of the economy.
2 What is productivity per head? How has it changed in the last three years?
3 Explain the supply chain for fish fingers.
4 What location factors would most influence an electronic manufacturer?
5 What are the characteristics of a free market economy?
6 What are the main reasons for government intervention?
7 What effect would leakages have on the national income?
8 Explain why India has a lower national income than the UK.
9 How might a wholesaler be affected by a rise in interest rates?
10 Why might a business gain from a cut in income tax?
11 What is the purpose of the Monopolies and Mergers Commission?

12 The makers of matches claimed an agreement was fair because its removal would injure the public. Is this an acceptable reason?
13 What are the main ways in which governments can influence markets?
14 Why might a business be tempted to move to an area of high unemployment?
15 What is deregulation?
16 How does the government try to protect the environment?
17 What is the ERM?
18 If the pound is strong, is this good or bad for the UK, and why?

Key terms

Primary sector
Secondary sector
Tertiary sector
Production industries
Supply chain
Industry trends
Employment
Output
Productivity
Location of industry
Production possibility
Economic system
Centrally planned
Free enterprise
Mixed economy
Money flows

Circular flow
National income
National product/output
National expenditure
Leakages
Injections
Government intervention
Objectives
Multiplier
Government policy
Monetary policy
Interest rates
Prices, inflation
Fiscal policy
Expenditure
Taxation

Business policy
Competition policy
Regulation
Deregulation
Consumer protection
Public spending
Health and safety
Balance of payments
Environmental protection
Types of unemployment
Monopolies and Mergers Commission
Social interests
Pensions and benefits
Regional policy

Assignment 1
Deep flan

This assignment develops knowledge and understanding of the following element:

1.3 Examine the effects of government on markets

It supports development of the following core skills:

Communication 3.2, 3.3, 3.4
Application of number 3.1, 3.2, 3.3
Information technology 3.1, 3.2, 3.3, 3.4

FLAN NEWS

Deep Flan Convenience Foods

It is rumoured that Deep Flan are thinking of opening a factory – we don't know where yet, but it will be good news wherever they go. They employ 300 at their current site and expect to employ another 250. The new factory will concentrate on their new Sweet 'n' Savoury range of Deep Flans. Geared to the European market they will appeal to a wide range of customers. Aimed specially at 20–30-year-olds, they conform to the new standards set for food labelling and contain no artificial ingredients. On sale throughout the UK, they will also be sold in GB and Del Haze stores in Belgium. Those Belgians have a treat ahead! Start with passion fruit and salmon.

Press cutting, June 1995

DEEP FLAN CONVENIENCE FOODS

Memorandum

To: Assistant — Re: New Statistics
From: Marketing Director — Today's date

Sorry about this, but I will be away for the next four weeks. We still need more information before we can make a decision about setting up our new 'Savoury Flan' production factory. At the moment the choice is between Bristol, Newcastle, Oldham and Tunbridge Wells.

I'd like you to do some research and write a report for me. We need information about:

- The reasons why the government might intervene in our industry.
- What food regulation might apply, for example on labelling.
- What would happen if the government put VAT on our flans.
- Interest rates – remember we need to borrow about £100,000.
- Prices – we need the retail prices and the wholesale prices for our foods that apply to us. You had better check out catering as well. (It is competitive.)
- Unemployment/employment – get the local figures for your top three choices.
- Premises costs, etc. – can you please find out if there is any regional or European help available (put this in an appendix) and what the business rates are.
- Social cost and benefits – Yes! I know we don't usually consider them, but one of our big shareholders wants us to have a more caring image. So try and say something for each place.
- Whether there is any government help available. Is the government likely to try and influence our decision, e.g. on where we locate.

I want your report in four weeks covering all the points with a recommendation for where we should go. Say why you have made your choice.

Remember it's your report and has to be on my desk in four weeks' time. I am seeing the director at 11 a.m. on Friday.

PS How will all these things affect us?

PPS Produce some charts on the computer, please – you're better than me!!

2 Business conduct and performance

What is covered in this chapter

- Business and the market
  - Demand for goods and services
  - The supply of goods and services
  - Supply and demand in the market place – the equilibrium price
- Markets
- The role of profit or loss
  - Business conduct in different markets
- The social costs and social benefits of market operations

These are the resources that you will need for your Business in the Economy file:

- articles on prices, profits and markets
- information from the Office of Fair Trading, for example *Square Deal*
- reports from the Monopolies and Mergers Commission
- *Who Owns Whom*
- *Monthly Digest of Statistics.*

Business and the market

In Chapter 1 we saw that business exists to supply the goods and services demanded by society and that government as well as private business are concerned with this provision. In this chapter we will look at the ways in which the market for goods and services works and how this affects the actions of business organisations.

All organisations will need to make policy decisions about how their business is structured and operated.

Business policy is concerned with objectives, structure, production methods, costs, pricing and performance. For instance, a decision to provide only high-quality goods would increase costs and probably lead to higher prices whilst to heavily advertise the product could mean that the business will need to expand production to cope with the anticipated extra demand.

Activity

Assume that businesses A, B and C all sell footwear:

- A is a stall in a street market
- B is a specialist footwear shop
- C is a mail order catalogue company.

For each of these explain:

1 What is the nature of the market they serve, i.e. who will their customers be, and who won't they be?

2 The type and quality of footwear they will provide.

3 The level of service that they provide: after sales, delivery, local supply, convenience, choice.

Now copy and fill in the chart:

	Customers	Product type/quality	Service
Stall			
Specialist			
Mail order			

Do you think there is a relationship between the type of market and the way in which the business chooses to supply that market?

Demand for goods and services

The **effective demand** for a **product** or service is the quantity that consumers are willing and able to buy at a particular price at a particular time. Companies need to know the effective demand in order to estimate their sales. For example Columbia, which is the exclusive trademark of Sony Music Entertainment Inc., could obtain information about the effective demand for the tapes and compact discs of its artists such as Bruce Springsteen by conducting a market research survey.

To find out how much customers are prepared to pay, market research is carried out. As part of this, individuals may be asked specific questions such as 'How many tapes would you buy at a price of £7.99?' The results for each individual are then tabulated to produce an individual demand schedule. Table 2.1 shows two demand schedules, one for person A and one for person B.

Table 2.1 Summary of tapes demanded by two people at a particular price

Person A Quantity demanded	Person B Quantity demanded	Price (£)
65	25	1.99
60	18	2.99
45	13	3.99
27	10	4.99
17	7	5.99
8	5	6.99
2	3	7.99
1	2	8.99
1	1	9.99

A graph can be drawn to show this information. Price is shown on the vertical (or y) axis, and the quantity demanded on the horizontal (or x) axis. The result is a **demand curve** which slopes downwards from left to right. Figure 2.1 shows the demand curve for person A and Figure 2.2 that for person B.

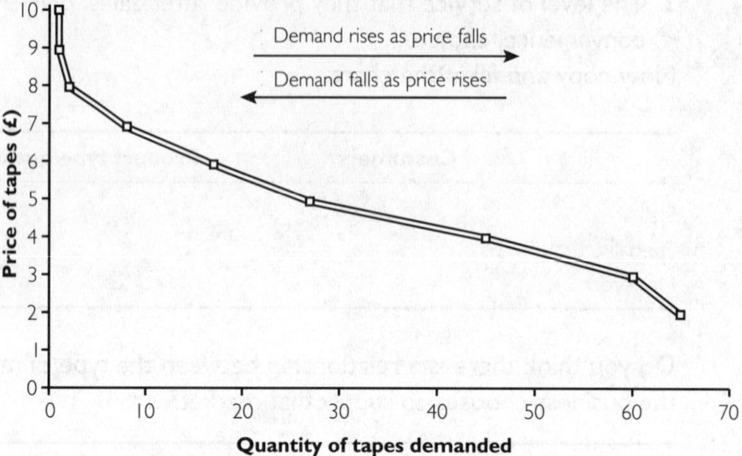

Figure 2.1 Demand curve for person A

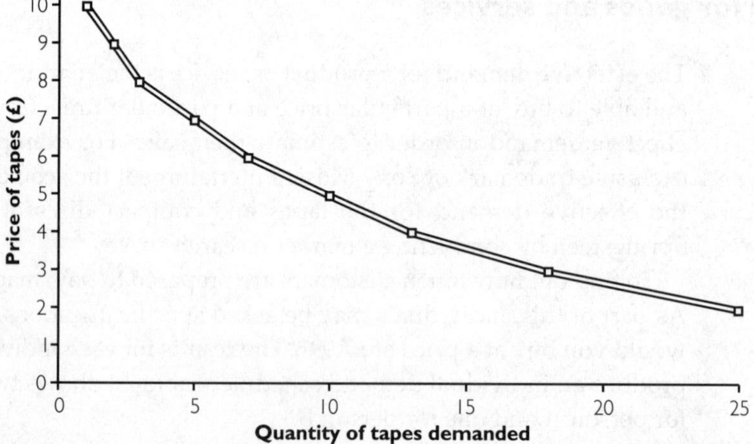

Figure 2.2 Demand curve for person B

Using a spreadsheet to plot demand curves

You can enter the figures from the table onto the worksheet in a spreadsheet package. The demand curve can be produced by highlighting the two columns of figures for quantity and price, and choosing the appropriate graph or chart command. Remember that this is an x–y graph and the x value is quantity.

When economists originally drew demand diagrams they did not put the dependent variable (quantity demanded) on the vertical axis, but instead placed it on the horizontal axis. Because of this mathematicians always claim that economics diagrams are the wrong way round.

In using a software package to draw graphs it is important to list quantity before price, as in Table 2.1. If this is not done price may be shown on the x axis.

Market demand

When the demand schedules for all individuals are totalled, then the total **market demand** curve can be constructed. If there were only two people in the market then the market demand schedule would be as in Table 2.2, which generates the market demand curve of Figure 2.3.

Table 2.2 Summary of tapes demanded by two people at a particular price

Person A Tapes demanded	Person B Tapes demanded	Market demand Tapes demanded	Price (£)
65	25	90	1.99
60	18	78	2.99
45	13	58	3.99
27	10	37	4.99
17	7	24	5.99
8	5	13	6.99
2	3	5	7.99
1	2	3	8.99
1	1	2	9.99

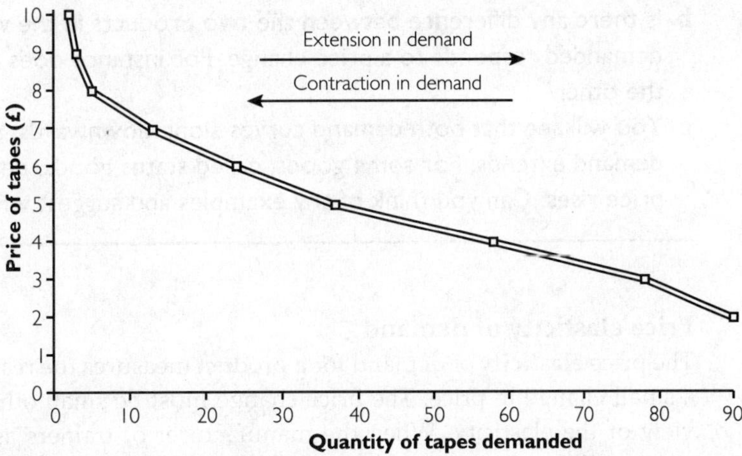

Figure 2.3 Market demand curve

Laws of demand

Organisations need to be able to predict how the demand for their product will change as a result of changes in price. Generally, the relationship between price and demand is straightforward and can be summarised in the **laws of demand**:

- as price rises, demand contracts or falls – this is called a **contraction of demand**.
- as price falls, demand extends or rises – this is called an **extension of demand**.
- when price is high, demand is low.
- when price is low, demand is high.

The terms 'contraction' and 'extension' of demand should only be used to describe the response of demand to a change in price. This is shown by a movement *along* the same demand curve. For instance on the market demand curve in Figure 2.3, a movement from left to right is an extension, whilst that from right to left is a contraction.

Activity

a Below is the demand schedule for salt. Draw the demand curve.

Quantity demanded	Price(p)
300	45
299	50
298	55
297	60
296	65

Here is the demand schedule for camcorders. Draw the demand curve.

Quantity demanded	Price(p)
3,000	450
2,500	500
1,900	550
1,000	600
500	650

What can you say about the way in which demand reacts to a price change in each case?

b Is there any difference between the two products in the way in which quantity demanded responds to a price change. For instance does one respond more than the other?

c You will see that both demand curves slope downwards, showing that as price falls demand extends. For some goods, called status goods, demand actually expands as price rises. Can you think of any examples and suggest why this happens?

Price elasticity of demand

The price **elasticity** of demand for a product measures the responsiveness in demand to a small change in price. The price change must be small otherwise we get a distorted view of the elasticity. When the manufacturer of trainers asks the question 'By how much will the sales of my trainers rise or fall if I lowered the price by £3?' the question is about the elasticity of demand.

The formula is:

$$\text{Elasticity of demand} = \frac{\text{Percentage change in quantity demanded}}{\text{Percentage change in price}}$$

If the answer to this calculation is greater than one then demand is **elastic**. If it is one then it is unitary. If it is less than one it is **inelastic**.

Elastic demand

When the demand for a product is elastic it means that a change in price gives rise to a more than proportionate change in demand (see Figure 2.4). So, for example, a 10 per cent fall in price will cause a larger than 10 per cent rise in demand, and conversely a 10 per cent rise in price will cause a more than 10 per cent cut in demand.

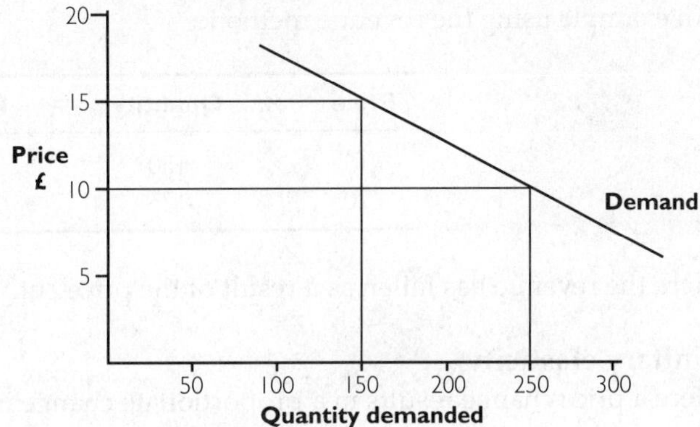

Figure 2.4 Elastic demand

An alternative way of looking at elasticity is to measure the change in revenue received by the manufacturer, for example:

Price	×	Quantity	=	Revenue
£15	×	150		£2,250
£10	×	250		£2,500

It is characteristic of elastic demand that revenue rises as a result of a cut in price, and falls as a result of an increase in price. This is the reason why British Rail, for example, charges lower prices in off-peak periods. BR would certainly not do this if it cost money. This policy encourages a significant number of people to travel by rail when they would not otherwise do so – the extra passengers more than offset the price cut.

In the 1980s the now defunct Greater London Council under Ken Livingstone reduced fares on public transport in a campaign called 'Fares fair'. The object was to make public transport available at a price which could be afforded even by the less well off. In fact, the elasticity of demand was such that revenue from transport rose.

Inelastic demand

When the demand for a product is inelastic it means that a small change in price will cause a smaller change in demand (see Figure 2.5). Here increased prices will cause increased revenue because demand falls very little. Reduced prices will cause reduced revenue because demand increases very little.

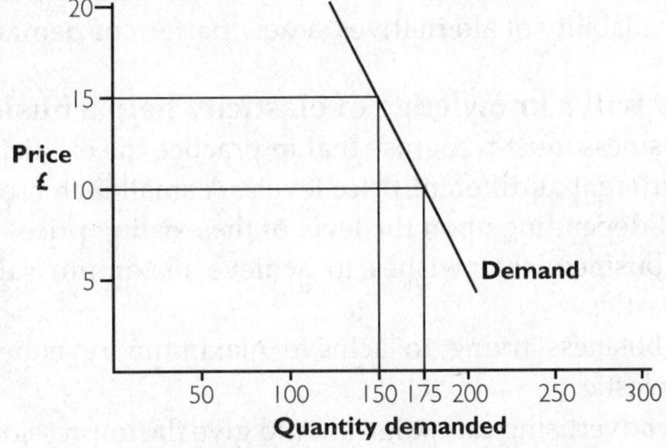

Figure 2.5 Inelastic demand

An example using the revenue method:

Price	×	Quantity	=	Revenue
£15	×	150		£2,250
£10	×	175		£1,750

Here the revenue has fallen as a result of the price cut.

Unitary elasticity

Here a price change results in a proportionate change in demand. Revenue is constant.

Price	×	Quantity	=	Revenue
£10	×	210		£2,100
£15	×	140		£2,100

What affects price elasticity of demand?

Elasticity of demand for a product will be different at different points along the demand curve. For example, 5p added to the price of a loaf of bread costing 75p will have a different effect from adding 5p to the cost of the same loaf priced at 35p. Factors affecting elasticity include:

- The number of **substitutes** for the product. That is, other similar products which the customer can purchase as an alternative.
  When there are a large number of close substitutes, demand is likely to be elastic. For example, if the six leading brands of training shoes are substitutes then the demand for any one of them is likely to be sensitive to price changes. Demand for goods which have few close substitutes is likely to be inelastic.
- Amount of consumer income spent on a product. The higher the proportion of consumer income spent on a product, the more inelastic is likely to be the demand. Goods which are purchased regularly or repeatedly for example, necessities, tend to be inelastic. Goods which are purchased less often tend to be more elastic
- Price. Very expensive goods tend to be inelastic with respect to price rises; a few extra pounds will not really matter if the product already costs £7,000. Conversely, many cheap items are inelastic with respect to price cuts, where a few pence will not make much difference.
- Time. Many items are bought as a result of habit so that in the short run price changes will be of little importance. However, once consumers have been able to assess the availability of alternatives, a new **pattern of demand** could emerge.

How will a knowledge of elasticity help a business?

A business must recognise that in practice the elasticity of demand for its products will be different at different price levels. A small increase or decrease may have a different effect depending upon the level of the existing price:

- a business that wishes to achieve maximum sales may cut prices if demand is elastic;
- a business trying to achieve maximum revenue may raise prices if demand is inelastic;
- an advertising campaign should give the impression that there is no substitute for the product, for example – Coke 'the real thing';

- a product will need to be repositioned in the market if consumers see it as inferior, that is if they buy less of it when their income rises. A champagne which formerly cost £9 a bottle was repositioned in April 1993 by the simple process of putting the price up to £18. Consumers now believe that at that price it must be good! This is called premium pricing;
- the Chancellor of the Exchequer has consistently raised taxes on items with inelastic demand; cigarettes, for example.

Activities

1 The Park Mini Market sells a range of fresh fruit, groceries and canned goods. There are no local competitors although there is a large supermarket on the by-pass to which there is an infrequent bus service but which has a large car park. June who owns the shop needs to charge higher prices than the supermarket to make a living, but realises that there is a limit.

June notices that:

- people spend relatively small amounts at a time
- few items are purchased at any time
- there are no competitors close by and therefore no close substitutes.

a How will a knowledge of elasticity of demand help her set her prices?
b Will there be a difference between products such as matches, cat food, giant packs of washing powder?

2 The partners in Pot Pourri (the business in Chapter 15) used elasticity to determine the price of dinner sets. Their market research into the effective demand for dinner sets shows:

Price	Quantity demanded	Total revenue
60	77	
80	69	
100	63	
120	55	
140	50	
160	43	
180	36	

a Copy and complete the table.
b Draw the demand curve and say what price would maximise their revenue.

Conditions of demand

In drawing a demand curve we are looking at the relationship between demand and price only. However there are other, external factors (Social, Legal, Economic, Political, Technological – SLEPT), called the **conditions of demand** over which the organisation has little control. These affect the demand for the organisation's product at a given price. Should they change, the demand at a particular price will no longer be the same – the demand curve will shift sideways. This is called a change in demand.

Changes in demand may be caused by:

- Changes in tastes, habits, customs and fashion. Each consumer has a particular set of preferences. These may depend on their age, personality, social and economic background, religion, etc. For instance, tastes in music vary between individuals and could influence their willingness to pay high prices. Companies try to change consumer preferences in favour of their own products by advertising and promotional campaigns which are aimed at particular segments or sections of the market. For example, in the case of Bruce Springsteen CDs and tapes, they are aimed at those identified as potential fans – probably the 'thirty somethings'.
- Changes in price of competitors' goods. We have seen that some goods, for instance Tetley and Typhoo tea, are substitutes; other goods are **complements**. This means that they are demanded jointly, for example, flour and fat to make pastry, sand and cement to make concrete. Here is a possible sequence of events for changes in the price of substitutes and complements:

Change in the price of a substitute

Price of Tetley tea rises with that of Typhoo unchanged → Demand for Tetley tea falls → Demand for Typhoo tea rises

Change in the price of a complement

Price of flour rises with price of fat unchanged → Demand for flour falls → Demand for fat falls

This relationship that exists between different goods is known as the **cross elasticity of demand** and is defined as:

$$\frac{\text{Percentage change in quantity demanded of product A}}{\text{Percentage change in price of product B}}$$

The manufacturer of Adidas trainers (product A) will need to know how the demand for its products is affected by a change in price of Nike trainers (product B), the competitor. If the demand for Adidas rises as a result of a rise in price of Nike, then Adidas and Nike are substitutes. This means that people will switch from one brand to the other; this is highly likely. However, if the demand for Adidas falls as a result of a rise in price of Nike, then the goods are complements, which is not likely. Complements exist where goods tend to be consumed together, as for example trainers and white shoe laces.

Where there is competition amongst a few firms, each manufacturer will need to be aware of its competitors' pricing strategies. Each will try to keep the loyalty of its customers.

- Income may change as a result of growing unemployment or increases in real wages. The effect of changes in income on demand is not as simple as it first appears. In general we can say that:
  - the higher the income the greater the quantity demanded of all goods;
  - the lower the income the less the quantity demanded of all goods.

However, for some goods it is the proportion of income spent on that product which matters most.

Income elasticity of demand measures the way in which demand for a product changes as a result of changes in consumers' income. The formula is:

$$\text{Income elasticity} = \frac{\text{Percentage change in quantity demanded}}{\text{Percentage change in income}}$$

Income elasticity can be negative or positive.

Negative income elasticity means that as real income rises, people will actually buy less of the product. Goods in this category are called **inferior goods**. Examples include bread, potatoes, flour, jam, certain canned foods and cheaper, economy products. People switch their expenditure as they become better off. They buy fewer potatoes and more meat. As real incomes rise producers of inferior goods will need to change the image of the product or find new ways of using it, such as potato croquettes, tinned potatoes or potato waffles.

Positive income elasticity means that people buy more of a product as income rises. The goods in this case are called **normal goods**. Examples include alcoholic drinks, cars and petrol, consumer goods such as CD players, fruit, nuts, coffee, cream, entertainment, holidays and meals away from home.

The graphs in Figure 2.6 show positive and negative income elasticity. Notice that income is on the vertical axis and quantity demanded on the horizontal axis:

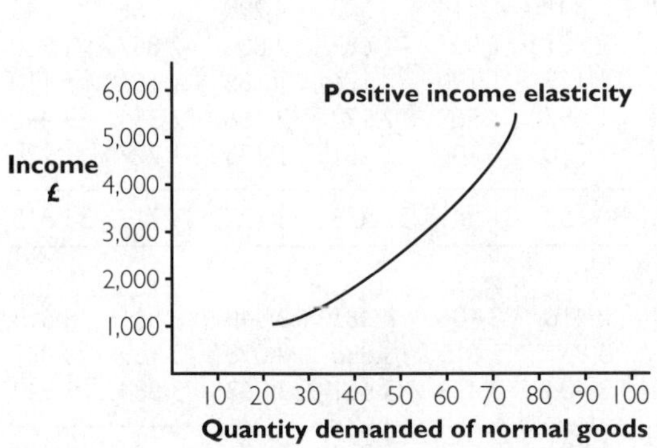

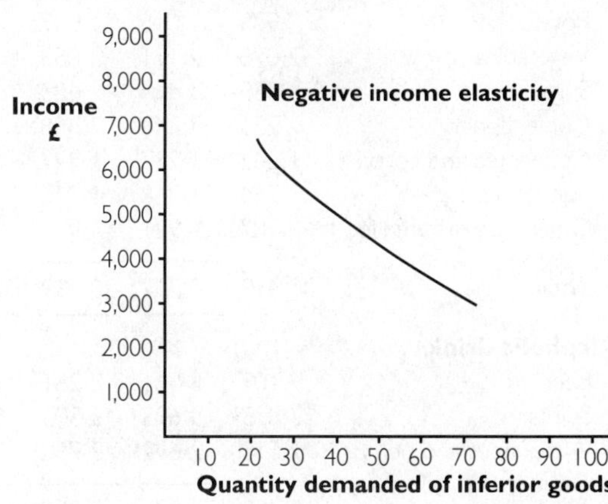

Figure 2.6 Positive and negative income elasticity

- Population – the number and type of buyers. The distribution, size and age of the population will all affect demand. A rise in the birth rate, for example, will increase the demand for baby products. People living longer will increase the demand for products and services for the elderly. Retirement homes are a good example.
  Marketing campaigns are frequently aimed at quite specific sections of the market, for instance the current fashion among TV advertising is to appeal to the 'twenty-something' audience with adverts for jeans, trainers and beer.
- Utility. This is the satisfaction which a consumer obtains from using a product or service. Most consumers will attempt to spend their income to achieve the highest level of satisfaction. They try to maximise their utility.
- Physical environment. Both climate and landscape can influence demand. A deluge of rain, for example, after a long spell of dry weather will immediately trigger a demand for umbrellas. Equally quickly, street vendors will appear to supply them. Other examples include the demand for clothing and drinks.

Activity

Look at the table for consumers' expenditure (Table 2.3). This shows where the major changes in demand have occurred.

Table 2.3 Consumers' expenditure at 1985 market prices: classified by function (figures in £million)

	1980	1981	1982	1983	1984	1985	1986	1987	1988	1989	1990
Food (household expenditure):											
Bread	1 509	1 512	1 497	1 494	1 507	1 542	1 551	1 539	1 564	1 526	1 460
Cakes and biscuits	394	1 405	1 441	1 455	1 426	1 420	1 457	1 509	1 576	1 574	1 570
Other cereals	1 189	1 198	1 171	1 189	1 218	1 203	1 312	1 386	1 451	1 513	1 560
Meat and bacon	8 592	8 354	8 472	8 079	7 791	7 898	7 974	8 151	8 292	8 390	7 980
Fish	1 000	1 023	1 024	1 057	1 034	1 055	1 092	1 043	1 136	1 228	1 160
Milk, cheese and eggs	4 639	4 527	4 455	4 522	4 433	4 385	4 365	4 378	4 375	4 310	4 240
Oils and fats	1 179	1 139	1 095	1 103	1 051	1 041	1 056	1 048	1 035	1 016	960
Fruit	1 839	1 800	1 705	1 798	1 696	1 666	1 871	2 030	2 108	2 247	2 320
Potatoes	975	1 015	1 037	1 115	1 111	1 211	1 113	1 175	1 168	1 183	1 203
Vegetables	2 076	2 111	2 053	2 270	2 229	2 328	2 574	2 610	2 795	2 880	2 885
Sugar	439	434	403	384	359	331	314	303	290	266	245
Confectionery	2 251	2 343	2 488	2 535	2 633	2 691	2 597	2 683	2 808	2 847	2 920
Coffee, tea and cocoa	1 262	1 237	1 222	1 270	1 200	1 179	1 190	1 176	1 188	1 156	1 110
Soft drinks	1 254	1 268	1 346	1 545	1 608	1 697	1 969	2 172	2 166	2 354	2 446
Other manufactured food	907	921	921	985	980	1 010	1 106	1 155	1 175	1 227	1 226
Total	30 419	30 217	30 299	30 801	30 276	30 657	31 541	32 358	33 127	33 717	33 315
Alcoholic drink:											
Beer	9 109	8 561	8 261	8 412	8 447	8 416	8 406	8 483	8 540	8 531	8 515
Spirits	3 923	3 693	3 503	3 597	3 641	3 831	3 815	3 880	4 098	3 969	3 897
Wine, cider and perry	2 515	2 692	2 780	3 050	3 275	3 404	3 478	3 661	3 763	3 884	3 942
Total	15 408	14 875	14 503	15 059	15 363	15 651	15 699	16 024	16 401	16 384	16 354
Tobacco:											
Cigarettes	7 768	7 109	6 525	6 480	6 259	6 112	5 940	5 902	5 935	5 970	6 035
Other	1 045	1 059	1 014	976	942	894	873	861	845	1 827	825
Total	8 806	8 167	7 541	7 456	7 201	7 006	6 813	6 763	6 780	6 797	6 860
Clothing and footwear:											
Men's and boys' wear	3 094	3 035	3 202	3 456	3 790	4 153	4 578	4 718	4 841	4 864	4 734
Women's, girls' and infants' wear	6 519	6 564	6 669	7 096	7 324	7 986	8 751	9 312	9 794	9 766	9 856
Footwear	2 293	2 195	2 358	2 519	2 644	2 772	2 893	2 902	2 889	2 889	2 879
Total	11 903	11 788	12 227	13 071	13 758	14 911	16 222	16 932	17 524	17 519	17 469
Fuel and power:											
Electricity	4 809	4 728	4 618	4 628	4 681	4 860	5 082	4 978	5 171	5 027	4 982
Gas	3 534	3 704	3 712	3 788	3 817	4 046	4 276	4 403	4 485	4 166	4 306
Coal and coke	1 058	1 042	1 023	955	786	1 006	851	774	757	681	591
Other	836	754	685	545	539	600	586	626	557	583	617
Total	10 282	10 246	10 047	9 916	9 823	10 512	10 795	10 781	10 970	10 457	10 496

Table 2.3 Consumers' expenditure at 1985 market prices: classified by function *continued*

	1980	1981	1982	1983	1984	1985	1986	1987	1988	1989	1990
Recreation, entertainment and education:											
Radio, television and other durable goods	1 485	1 668	1 975	2 402	2 764	2 944	3 466	4 126	4 815	5 347	5 398
TV and video hire charges, licence fees and repairs	1 886	1 995	2 122	2 448	2 522	2 552	2 735	2 581	2 705	2 732	2 678
Sports goods, toys, games and camping equipment	1 548	1 510	1 576	1 712	1 839	2 007	2 250	2 383	2 517	2 673	2 784
Other recreational goods	3 062	2 917	3 058	3 105	3 193	3 392	3 745	4 230	4 771	5 183	5 231
Betting and gaming	2 228	2 102	2 078	2 050	2 082	2 118	2 157	2 284	2 308	2 369	2 354
Other recreational and entertainment services	2 501	2 351	2 146	2 137	2 193	2 313	2 433	2 620	2 873	3 024	3 064
Books	923	909	846	788	737	739	824	879	941	952	1 008
Newspapers and magazines	2 303	2 451	2 347	2 269	2 292	2 299	2 345	2 387	2 328	2 351	2 350
Education	1 778	1 883	1 740	1 636	1 623	1 638	1 640	1 652	1 671	1 851	2 006
Total	17 082	17 225	17 595	18 547	19 245	20 002	21 595	23 142	24 929	26 482	26 873
Other goods and services:											
Pharmaceutical products and medical equipment	932	917	953	1 021	1 150	1 190	1 285	1 250	1 339	1 329	1 361
NHS payments and other medical expenses	992	1 103	1 237	1 349	1 314	1 405	1 590	1 763	1 899	1 957	2 127
Toilet articles, perfumery	1 954	2 054	2 176	2 269	2 434	2 497	2 744	3 119	3 375	3 337	3 292
Hairdressing and beauty care	1 206	1 169	1 120	1 171	1 209	1 283	1 348	1 397	1 401	1 389	1 361
Jewellery, silverware, watches and clocks	1 302	1 367	1 499	1 392	1 496	1 497	1 582	1 759	1 940	2 207	2 273
Other goods	1 927	1 839	1 908	1 947	1 942	1 972	2 082	2 205	2 610	2 646	2 744
Catering (meals and accommodation)	12 904	12 261	12 002	12 710	13 311	13 876	15 205	16 087	18 674	19 904	20 511
Administrative costs of life assurance and pension schemes	2 491	2 630	2 864	3 245	3 584	3 806	4 200	4 526	5 433	5 741	6 523
Other services	3 049	3 095	3 275	3 765	4 012	4 395	5 027	5 885	6 464	7 114	7 260
Total	26 691	26 425	27 080	28 869	30 452	31 921	35 063	37 991	43 135	45 624	47 452

Source: *Annual Abstract of Statistics*, HMSO

a **Which three items have shown the biggest fall in demand? Give reasons why each has fallen.**

b **Which three items have shown the biggest rise in demand? Give reasons why each of these has risen.**

c **Produce a short report (with diagrams) outlining the major changes that have taken place. Update the figures. Have the trends continued?**

How do changes in conditions affect the demand curve?

Whereas a change in price leads to a movement *along* the demand curve, changes in the conditions of demand will lead to a *shift* in the whole demand curve. A shift to the right is called an **increase in demand** (represented in Figure 2.7 by a move from D_0 to D_1). This shows that at every price more is now demanded.

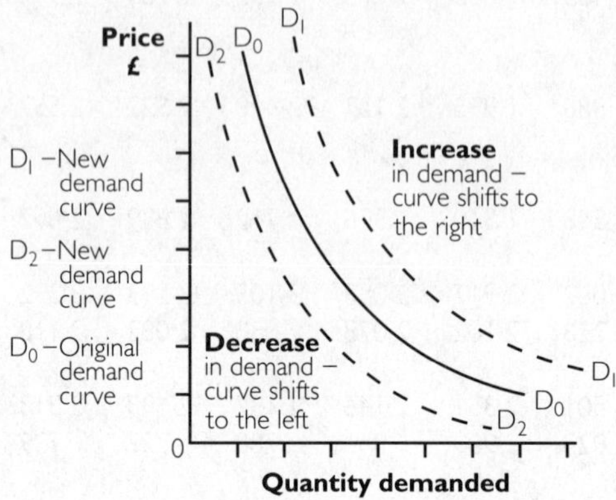

Figure 2.7 Shifts in the demand curve

A shift of the whole demand curve to the left is called a **decrease in demand** (shown in Figure 2.7 as a move from D_0 to D_2). Hence at every price less is now demanded.

Activity

1 Examples of the changes in the conditions of demand may be:
- an ageing population leading to a change in demand for nursing homes. Demand for places at £300 per week has changed;
- a change in lifestyles has shifted demand for health products. Now more people are prepared to pay for these at existing prices;
- demand for cosmetics which have been tested on animals has altered as a result of public awareness. As a result demand has changed at existing prices.

a Which way will the demand curve shift in each case?

b Can you give other examples of how conditions of demand have changed for products?

2 Working with three or four people carry out an investigation into the demand for petrol by students. You should conduct a sample survey, using the most appropriate method from those given in Chapter 5. Each member of the group should question about 20 people. Do not fill in all the questionnaires yourself.

a From the information that you collect:
- construct an individual demand curve
- construct a 'market' demand curve (you will need to combine your results with those of other members of your group)
- find out the factors which affect the demand for petrol. (Hint: Use the five factors listed under 'conditions of demand' earlier (SLEPT). Use a four-star rating system to discover the importance of each factor for each consumer.)

b Present your findings as a written and oral report using suitable tables, charts and diagrams. You must present the final report using an overhead projector.

c Make a recommendation as to the highest possible price for petrol in the market segment you have investigated.

d What factors will cause the following changes in the demand for petrol:
- extension
- contraction
- shift to the right (increase)
- shift to the left (decrease).

e What use is all of this information to the oil companies who supply petrol?

3 Draw the diagrams for each of the following tasks:

a How would the demand for butter be influenced by a change in price of margarine?

b How would the demand for bread be affected by the publication of a report called *Wholemeal Bread Can Kill*?

c Would the demand for cars be influenced by a change in interest rates?

4 In June 1993 it was announced that research showed that five cups of instant coffee per day reduced the likelihood of a heart attack. This was a complete reversal of advice previously given by doctors. How could this affect the demand for:
- instant coffee?
- real coffee?
- tea?
- biscuits?

Your answer needs to refer to shifts in demand, substitutes and complements.

The supply of goods and services

The supply of goods is the amount which producers and sellers are prepared to offer for sale in the market at a particular price over a specified period of time. The supplies of several firms can be added together to give the market supply curve for an area or for the whole country. This is done in the same way that demand from individual consumers is added to give market demand.

Notice that supply must be distinguished from resources. Trees in a forest are resources, but they only become part of the market supply when the price of timber rises sufficiently to make it worthwhile to fell the trees.

How does price influence supply?

The *supply schedule* is a way of writing down the amount of a product which businesses are prepared to market at a particular price. A supply schedule is shown in Table 2.4. The supply curve of Figure 2.8 is based on these figures. It shows how supply is affected by price.

Table 2.4 Supply schedule

Price(£)	Quantity supplied
0.99	50
1.99	120
2.99	190
3.99	280
4.99	390
5.99	520
6.99	700

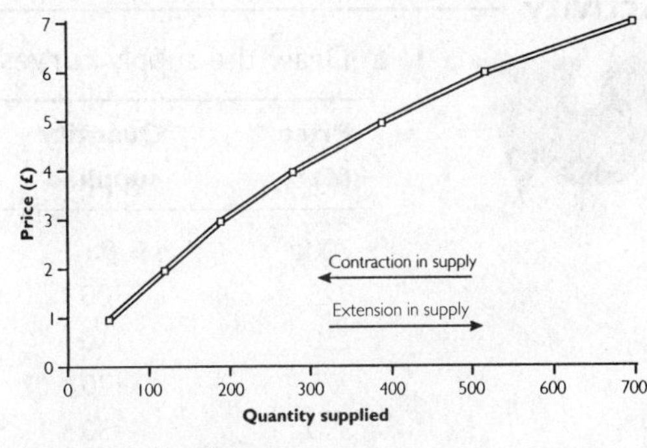

Figure 2.8 Supply curve

The supply curve in Figure 2.8 is upward sloping. This shows that:

- producers are willing to supply more when the price is high: the profit motive;
- when the price of the product rises supply tends to rise – or *extend*;
- when price falls, supply falls – or *contracts*.

An extension or contraction of supply is caused by changes in price and is shown by the movement along the supply curve.

Elasticity of supply reflects the way the supply of a product reacts to a change in the price. It is defined as:

$$\text{Elasticity of supply} = \frac{\text{Percentage change in quantity supplied}}{\text{Percentage change in price of product}}$$

As with elasticity of demand, where the answer is one or over the supply is elastic. Where the answer is less than one the supply is inelastic. When the answer is one, elasticity is unitary.

Speed of response to change

The speed with which supply can respond to changes in price is important when considering the elasticity of supply. A business may be prepared to supply an increased amount of a product as the price rises, but there may be difficulties in doing this quickly. It is possible to talk about what will happen in the short run and the long run. In the short run, for instance, supply of a product may be inelastic; in the long run it may be elastic.

The **short run** is a period of time within which the business is unable to alter the amount of resources it uses. Inputs or factors of production which cannot be altered are called **fixed** and include: heavy machinery, buildings, land, specialist staff and certain raw materials. The length of time varies between industries and depends upon the type of product and method of production. A substantial increase in demand for paper, for example, could be met by building a new factory for pulping wood. It may also be necessary to plant more trees.

A **variable** factor of production is one that can be varied or altered in the short run. An example would be overtime worked by employees, or the amount of raw materials such as clay in a pottery.

The **long run**, or long term, is the time in which any input can be varied. A new blast furnace, for instance can be built or a new car factory constructed. This period depends on the type of product and method of production. Industries which require a large amount of complex machinery and equipment will take longer to set up than simpler, less capital intensive operations.

Activity

1 a Draw the supply curves for these three supply schedules:

Price (£)	Quantity supplied	Price (£)	Quantity supplied	Price (£)	Quantity supplied
200	95	9	1100	75	1500
225	100	10	1500	100	2000
250	110	11	2200	125	2500
275	120	12	2700	150	3000
300	130	13	3500	175	3500

b What is the relationship between price and the quantity supplied in each case?
c Is there any difference between the three products in the way in which quantity supplied responds to a price change? Which is the most elastic? Which is the most inelastic? Which one has unitary elasticity?

2 How might major expenditure on health and safety by a leisure company affect the supply of its leisure centre services?

The conditions of supply

What else apart from price influences the amounts supplied? The supply curve shows what will happen to supply as price changes under the present conditions of supply. The decision on how much to supply is made by the management of an organisation. It will consider internal factors such as the costs of production and external factors such as the number of competitors. Together these are known as the conditions of supply.

Changes in:

- technology
- costs of production
- expectations, and
- world events

all affect supply, and may be inter-related.

- Changes in technology. New production methods using computer-controlled systems and new materials can shift the supply curve by reducing costs. Improvements in silicon chip technology, for example, have increased the supply of microcomputers.
- Changes in the costs of production. These can occur because of changes in the price of the inputs used by an organisation. The cost statements shown in Chapter 12 give a detailed breakdown of production costs. Broadly, raw material and labour costs when added to factory overheads such as rent and rates give the manufacturing cost. To this is added administration, such as secretarial support; finance, such as interest charges; and sales and distribution to give the total cost. Price changes in raw materials, parts and components may lead management to use inferior substitutes, thus creating problems with quality.
- Changes in the suppliers' expectations. The fear of a boom or slump, whether real or imagined, may either lead organisations into new markets or force them to contract out of existing ones.
- World events. Supply may be determined not only by the actions of suppliers reacting to market forces, but by world events affecting the supply of resources. These include:
  - political factors – the price of oil may rise because of war in the Middle East;
  - natural causes – earthquake, flood and drought may affect the supply of goods, especially agricultural goods.

How do changes in the conditions of supply affect the supply curve?

Changes in the conditions of supply will lead to a shift in the whole supply curve. It will shift to the right if more is supplied at a given price – this is an *increase in supply*. It will shift to the left if less is produced at a given price – this is a *decrease in supply*.

For example, a fall in costs due to a reduction in interest rates will encourage more production at a given price as it will now be more profitable. As a result more will be supplied at that price; supply will increase. If, on the other hand, raw materials such as hardwoods become more difficult to find, and consequently more expensive, then supply at each price will be reduced; supply will decrease (Figure 2.9).

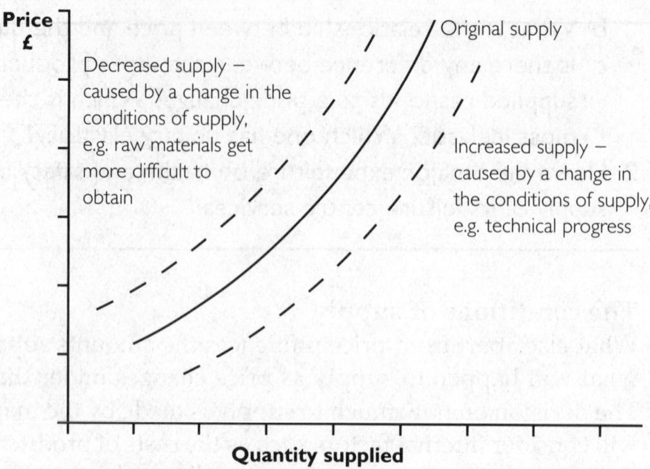

Figure 2.9 Increase and decrease in supply

Activity

A fishy story

A potato shortage is squeezing the profits of Britain's 9000 fish and chip shops and forcing up prices. The shortage is due to the wet and cold winter. Many growers are holding back supplies because they think that demand will stay high. (How could this affect prices?) The secretary of the National Association of Fish Fryers said, 'The market is very competitive and shops are not willing to pass on the extra costs to their customers. Instead they are having to ... 'How do you think the sentence finished? In the same week it was reported that 'Storms drive up the price of fish'. How might this affect prices in the short term and in the longer term? How will fish and chip shops respond?

Supply and demand in the market place – the equilibrium price

A free market is one in which prices are determined solely by the interaction of supply and demand. Prices are freely negotiated between the buyers and sellers of a product. There is no outside interference in the trading process. For instance there is no government setting minimum or maximum prices for political reasons.

To illustrate how the process works, economists start by drawing supply and demand curves on the same diagram. At the beginning of trading the price could either be:

- below the level where supply equals demand, or
- above the level where supply equals demand.

The position where supply equals demand is called the equilibrium.
Figure 2.10 shows the equilibrium price on the vertical axis at P_e, and the equilibrium quantity at Q_e on the horizontal axis. Once equilibrium has been achieved there is no reason why price should change. Both buyers and sellers are satisfied; the object of trading is to reach this mutually agreed price.

How is the equilibrium price achieved?

When the initial price is above the equilibrium at P_a the supply is much greater than the demand. The excess supply will push prices down. The falling price will cause demand to extend and supply to contract. Trading and bargaining will continue until the point where the buyers are willing to buy the product and sellers are still willing to sell. This is the equilibrium price and the market is now stable or in balance.

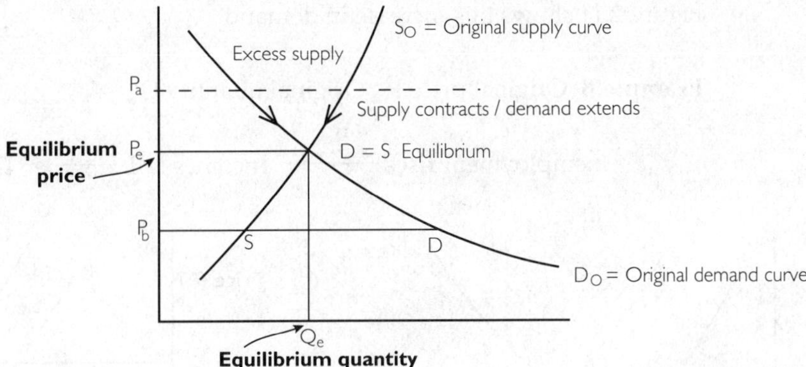

Figure 2.10 The equilibrium price

A good example of this activity is a street market at 5.30 p.m. on a Saturday. Unsold stocks of perishable goods will have 'reduced' price tags. The price cutting will continue until the surplus stock is sold or destroyed. A buyer's market exists where there is excess supply.

Perhaps the most obvious example of the determination of equilibrium price in the business world is found in the markets in the City of London. The price of foreign currency is fixed on the foreign exchange market, the price of stocks and shares is fixed on the stock market and the price of goods such as tea, tobacco and copper is fixed on the commodity markets. In each case buyers and sellers bargain to fix the equilibrium price. These markets are governed by the laws of supply and demand.

What causes a change in equilibrium price?

A change in any of the conditions of supply or demand will cause a movement in price to a new equilibrium.

- The social environment could change. For example, as consumers become more health conscious there could be an increase in demand for polyunsaturates; this will increase the price.
- The legal environment: for example, new laws controlling car exhaust emission could increase production costs.
- The economic environment might change. For example, a rise in unemployment would reduce incomes and decrease demand.
- The political environment might mean that there is an embargo on goods from certain countries. This would decrease their supplies and tempt UK companies into providing alternatives.
- Technology continually changes. A new, more cost-effective method of production could increase supply.

In each case either the demand or supply curve will shift. Remember:

- an extension or contraction of supply or demand is caused by a change in price;
- an increase or a decrease in supply or demand causes a change in price.

Example A Original price P_o, Original quantity Q_o

Interest rate falls ⟶ Consumer income rises ⟶ Demand increases

Figure 2.11 shows this increase in demand.

Example B Original price P_o, Original quantity Q_o

Unemployment rises ⟶ Incomes fall ⟶ Demand decreases

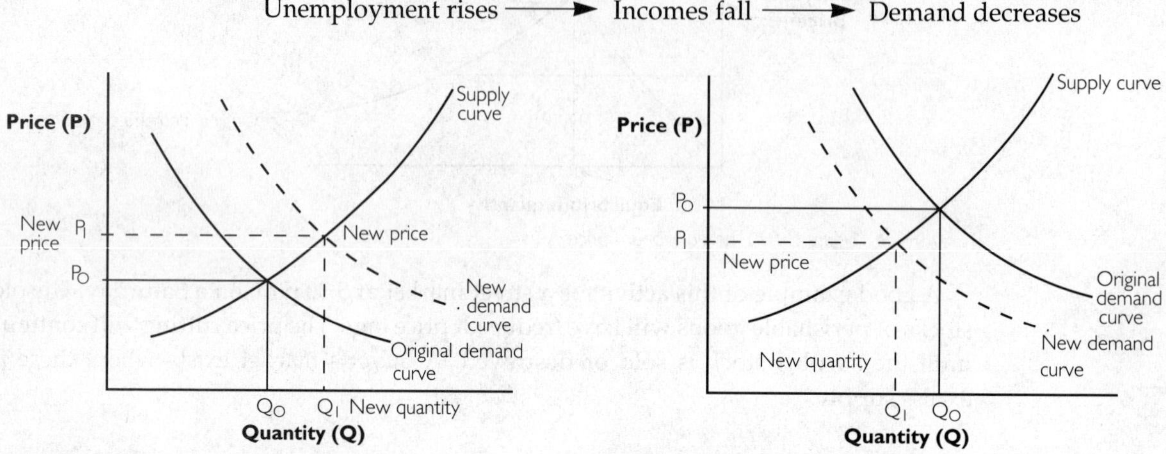

Figure 2.11 An increase in demand

Figure 2.12 A decrease in demand

Activity

Quantity demanded	Price(£)	Quantity supplied
2,000	10	650
1,850	20	800
1,620	30	980
1,420	40	1,200
1,330	50	1,330
1,110	60	1,540
970	70	1,680
810	80	1,750
620	90	1,930

a Draw the supply and demand curve on the same graph.
b Show and read off the equilibrium price and quantity.
c How is the equilibrium price achieved if the initial price is below the equilibrium at £30?

Factors which determine price

In setting a price a business must be aware of a number of factors.

External factors

These are the features of the market place outside the business. If the business enters the market it will seek to influence some of these, whilst others cannot be changed. When setting a price the business will need information about:

Supply and demand: where there are no controls on the market, price is determined by the forces of supply and demand. Paintings by Picasso, Cup Final tickets and vintage cars all fetch high prices because they are in short supply relative to demand. A business must understand the demand for its product and whether it is price elastic. It must also be aware of its production capacity, i.e. its ability to supply.

The effect of competition is to increase supply and reduce prices. The first calculators sold for over £100, many times the cost of production, because the supplier had a monopoly. Some years later, despite inflation, they are now available for a few pounds. This is the result of competition from new manufacturers attracted by the promise of high profits.

Market controls: sometimes market forces are regarded as undesirable and controls are introduced by government, often for social reasons. A business must be aware of controls in its own industry.

Legislation: Resale Price Maintenance (RPM) allowed manufacturers to set the price at which retailers must sell. This had the effect of keeping prices artificially high as it disallowed price competition. In 1964 RPM was ended except where it could be shown to be in the public interest. Most manufacturers can now recommend a price but cannot enforce it. The price competition which resulted in the grocery trade led to the rise of the supermarket chains and the decline of the more expensive local shopkeeper.

RPM was retained in the book trade and there is a current debate about this. Some argue that allowing price competition will result in shops stocking only big sellers like Danielle Steel, and that consumer choice will be reduced rather than improved.

Price fixing controls: many of the privatised public utilities such as British Gas, the regional water and electricity supply companies and British Telecom (BT) were regarded as 'natural monopolies'. The government aim is to promote competition and choice in the market, but meanwhile various watchdog bodies, such as OFGAS, OFWAT, OFFER and OFTEL, have been set up to regulate these industries and protect the public interest. Part of this regulation includes price controls set by parliament. Competing companies such as Mercury are aware of the restrictions placed upon BT.

BT is obliged to:

- keep price increases at the retail price index minus 7.5 per cent
- raise rentals by no more than 2 per cent above inflation.

BT claims that it makes a loss on rentals as a result.

Illegal controls: in most cases a free market is considered desirable as it gives the consumer choice. However, it does not suit all firms. In some industries firms meet to form cartels – groups of businesses who illegally fix prices and share the market. Cartels have recently been found in the cement industry in Europe (1994) as well as among airlines (see page 101).

Environmental considerations

The tax system is not only a means by which the government can raise funds, it also allows it to influence the price of goods and therefore the demand for them.

- **Pollution:** the government imposed 8% VAT on household fuel for the first time in the November 1993 Budget. It was claimed that this was a 'green tax', designed to make people use fuel more efficiently and so help reduce global warming from CO_2 emissions. This is important for firms in the heating and insulation industry. The tax system is also used to make ordinary 4 star petrol dearer, and less attractive, then unleaded. (Recent research actually suggests that in some respects leaded petrol is the more dangerous.)

- **Health and safety:** the government has stated that price rises are the most effective way of discouraging smoking. In successive budgets, tax on tobacco has been increased. To a lesser extent this also applies to alcohol.

Legislation to promote health and safety and to reduce pollution will generally increase business costs and therefore prices. The relatively slow pace at which the government is bringing in measures to control global warming is partly due to a fear that the cost to UK business will make it uncompetitive in world markets.

It could be argued that a fit workforce will eventually save costs by: less absence, fewer claims for compensation, reduced recruitment and training costs and more efficient working, but this is a long-term gain.

EU regulations, particularly on food preparation, have certainly increased costs. It is not always certain that there are benefits to offset these.

Internal factors – business aims and strategies

In the long term a business may work towards the following objectives (see page 125):

- profit maximisation
- enlarging market share
- return on investment (to reward shareholders)
- establishing a reputation, perhaps for quality, for instance Rolls Royce, or value for money; for example John Lewis 'Never knowingly undersold'.

Any pricing strategy must be consistent with the aims of the business.

Business aim	Strategy that may be used
Position a product in the market	Charge what the market will bear: possibly a different price for different customers (price discrimination). Premium pricing (perceived value pricing): putting a high price on a product to give the impression that it is high quality. Some products are in demand because they are expensive. This is used where the demand is inelastic.
Pricing a new product (pioneer pricing)	Penetration pricing: a low price is charged in order to get into the market. The price will increase when the product is established. The risk is that low price requires high sales volume in order to generate profit. Skimming (creaming) the market: a new product may bear a high price when it is first introduced. It may have a novelty or scarcity value, and the supplier may have little direct competition; perhaps it is protected by a patent. As with premium pricing, the high price may give extra appeal. Gradually the price will be reduced as competiition appears.
Promoting a product	Promotional special offers on existing products. Introductory offers on new products. The aim is to make people aware of the product and tempt them to try it. The offer will be for a limited period only.
Increasing market share	Destruction (or destroyer) pricing: very low prices, often below cost, to force out competition. This may lead to price wars. Expansion pricing (economies of scale leading to lower price).
Maximising sales in a market	Loss leaders: very low prices on selected products, sometimes below cost. The idea is to attract customers in the hope that they will also buy other items which are profitable.

Case studies

Have a look at these case studies.

In a television advertisement for Tesco, Hugh Laurie's voice-over announced 'We actually lose money on these items but we hope that you'll stay and buy some other things too'.

At the time that Bulmers were first asked to distribute Red Stripe lager it had a small loyal market mainly among people from the Caribbean (where it was brewed). After Bob Geldof was caught on film drinking it during the Band Aid concert Bulmers decided to forget the existing customers, change the image, increase the price and promote it as a 'premium' beer.

During 1994 the price of *The Times* newspaper was reduced to 20p. *The Daily Telegraph* responded by coming down to 35p.

At Christmas 1994 the price of Christmas turkeys was down to 34p per pound – less than cat food. It cost the supermarkets more than this to buy them.

'The right pricing policy is to ask yourself the question 'What will customers be prepared to pay for this product or service?' It is not always the best policy to pitch your price below the competition, especially if your product has some technical advantage.'

(Source: Geoff Wood, *Marketing*, Employment Department booklet).

Thomson Holidays have expanded over the years by taking over other businesses in the industry. It has been said that they are too powerful, but they argue that they act in the consumer's interest by keeping prices low. Currently package holidays are cheaper than they were some years ago.

Exporters entering new export markets may receive government subsidies to help them keep prices down. The former Eastern block countries were able to sell cheap cars to the West using these means.

The Scottish-based coach company Stagecoach has been expanding its operations into England since the government's deregulation of bus services. In Darlington it took over by running a free bus service which put the local company Darlington Transport out of business.

The cross-channel ferry companies periodically offer day trips for £1, often in conjunction with a newspaper such as *The Sun* or *The Daily Mail*. The Channel Tunnel car-carrying service (Le Shuttle) is beginning to do the same.

Activity

For each of the examples explain:

- the aims of the business
- the pricing strategy that is being used to achieve these aims
- collect any current examples that you come across.

Case study

European Passenger Services – just the ticket

EPS runs its high-speed 'Eurostar' rail service from mainland Britain to the continent via the Channel Tunnel. The company carried its first fare-paying passengers in November 1994 when it opened the route from Waterloo International Terminal in Central London to Brussels-Midi and Gare du Nord in Paris.

The full service will also include:

- beyond London daytime trains – from various UK cities to Paris and Brussels
- night trains from London and various UK regions to cities on the continent.

Other factors:

- duty-free goods, currently available on ferries and airlines until 1999, are not available on Eurostar or any other Channel Tunnel services
- the completion of high-speed links in Belgium and on the section between London and the Tunnel will eventually reduce travelling time even more.

The journey

PRICING POLICY

The fares structure is attractive to both business and leisure customers. Principal competitors are the airlines.

Discounts are offered at off-peak times and are available to senior citizens and young people.

Night services will also aim to compete primarily with air travel, combined with overnight accommodation and so it will be essential to take account of equivalent air fares and hotel rates.

Fares will be adjusted to take account of any changes in general price levels and market conditions including airline deregulation.

Source: EPS International Train Service Fact Sheets no 31

Just the ticket

Eurostar

Return fares to Paris and Brussels

	Paris	**Brussels**
Travel time: From Waterloo	3 hours	3 hours
Discovery Gold First class tickets Meal served at seat Flexible reservation	£195.00	£195.00
Discovery Standard accommodation Flexible reservation	£155.00	£155.00
Discovery Special Must be booked 14 days in advance Standard accommodation Not possible to change ticket	£95.00	£95.00

British Airways [3]		Paris	Brussels
	Approximate travel time: From central London including transfer time to and from the airports	3 hours	3 hours
	Club Europe Business class Includes meal & drinks/champagne Fully flexible	£245.00	£304.00
	World offer [1] Standard accommodation Restricted availability Includes meal	£83.00	£93.00
	APEX Must be booked in advance Standard accommodation Includes meal and drinks	£112.00	£132.00 [2]

[1] *Only available until Nov 2nd.*
[2] *PEX fare – no advance booking, not flexible*
[3] *All airfares will include £5 departure tax from November*

Tunnel dearer than airlines

Transport Correspondent

THE cheapest rail fares for the first commercial passenger services through the Channel Tunnel will be more expensive than those being offered by airlines services. The cheapest return fare is £95 compared with British Airways' £83 deal, and British Midland's £81.

At the business end of the market fares are much more competitive with Eurostar significantly cheaper.

European Passenger Services pledged that the price structure would last only for the launch period. In the New Year a 'new and wider' fares tariff will be announced.

British Airways said it was 'looking at the overall market' and was more interested in the longer term fare levels due to be announced in January.

Source: Adapted from *The Guardian*

Forecast customer mix for intercapital Eurostar trains:

INTER-CAPITAL DAYTIME TRAINS

Business	18%
Independent leisure	64%
Inclusive tour	18%

Source: EPS International Train Service Fact Sheets no 28

Activities

1 Identify the internal and external factors which will have been considered when pricing the Eurostar service.
2 Explain the different pricing strategies used by EPS and the purpose of each. (You should mention the purpose of the 'launch' period.) Illustrate your answers using the information provided and any more that you can obtain.

3 Explain which market sector, business or leisure, you feel would be most price elastic.
4 EPS is a government-owned company which will eventually be privatised. What do you think will be its long-term objectives and how might these be different if it remained in the public sector? What part can pricing policy play in achieving these objectives?
5 The cross-channel ferries are not regarded as major competitors. To what extent do they sell a different product?

(You may be able to obtain updated figures including profit information by contacting EPS at Waterloo.)

The market for goods and services

We have seen that businesses compete within the market place to sell their products. We will now look at these markets in more detail.

Case study

The market for trainers

Do you wear trainers? Why do you wear them? In 1992 over 65 million pairs were sold of which 18 per cent were bought for sports and 82 per cent for casual wear or leisure use. The market is dominated by the big brand names:

- Adidas: started in 1920 by Adi Dassler
- Nike: named after the Greek goddess of victory
- Reebok: started in 1895 in Bolton
- Hi-Tec: started in 1974
- Puma
- Dunlop.

These six companies control some 70 per cent of the total market for trainers (Figure 2.13).

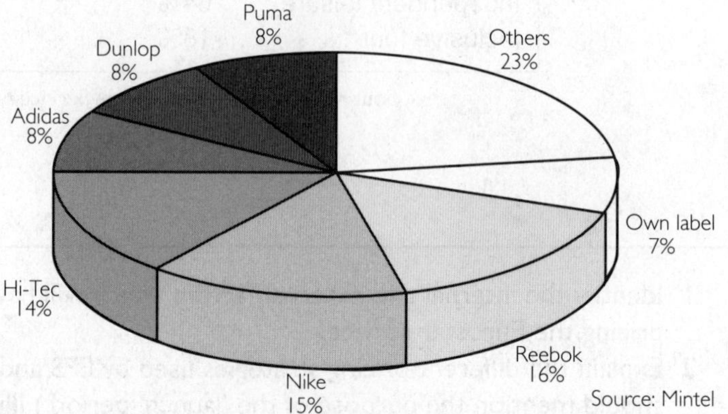

Figure 2.13 Sports footwear: UK market share

How is the UK demand for trainers calculated?

We need to know:

- The value of sales from UK manufacturers.
- The value of imports. This has never been less than 80 per cent of the total demand.

UK demand is then the value of UK sales plus the value of imports minus the value of exports. This market is worth about £200 million a year.

Activity

a Using the information about the value of the total market for trainers given in the Case Study above, calculate the actual sales of each company from the official figures.

b Ask ten people which trainers they wear and why. Include all of the pairs that they own.

c Combine your results with the rest of your group. On the basis of your survey complete a table like the one below.

	A	B	C	D	E
1	Sports footwear market survey				
2				For	Other
3	Company	No of pairs	% market share	sport	use
4	Reebok		=B4/B12*100		
5	Nike				
6	Hi-Tec				
7	Adidas				
8	Puma				
9	Dunlop				
10	Own label				
11	Others				
12	TOTAL	=sum(B4:B11)	=sum(C4:C11)	=sum(D4:D11)	=sum(E4:E11)
13					
14			% used for sport	=D12/B12*100	

This data can be recorded conveniently on a spreadsheet; some sample formulae are given to show how percentages and totals can be calculated. You can complete formulae for column C either by entering the formula or using the copy command. Remember to check that the total of column C is 100 per cent. (It may give an error reading until some data is entered.)

d Produce a pie chart to show the results of your survey. Charts of your results can be produced on the spreadsheet. How do your results compare with the pie chart in Figure 2.13? Can you explain why there may be differences?

e Calculate the percentage of people in the sample who actually use the trainers for sport.

You will need to do some market research for your business plan (Chapter 15).

In July 1993 it was announced that Nike had lost £500m and Reebok £300m in stock market valuation in anticipation of profits decreasing. The reason for this is thought to be the rise in demand for Doc Martens boots (worn unlaced). Trainers are reverting to being worn for sports.

Markets

Originally the term *market* was only used to describe a place or building where people, the buyers (who create the demand) and sellers (who provide the supply), met to buy and sell goods. Today the term market is used in three distinct ways:

1. As a quantitative description of the number of customers, for example the size of the market for trainers, i.e. the size of the demand for a particular product or commodity.
2. The business or trade for a particular product, for example the money market, the market for wheat, the antiques market. Today there are markets for every conceivable product and factor of production (see page 484 for a discussion of the labour market).

Product market for goods and services	Factor market
There are markets for manufactured, semi-manufactured and primary goods and commercial, personal and financial services.	There are markets for labour (e.g. doctors and football players), land (e.g. in urban and rural areas) and capital (e.g. the money and capital markets).

3. The market system/market mechanism/market process which describes the interaction or trading process between buyers who are looking for maximum satisfaction and sellers who are trying to make the most profit.

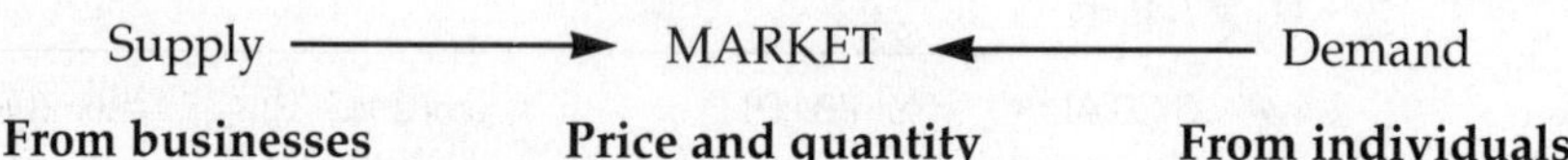

Markets can be local (for example, when fish are caught and sold locally at the harbour), regional, national or international (citrus fruits, wheat), depending on the type of product, the number of sellers or suppliers and the number of buyers or demanders. With the increasing influence of the Single European Market (SEM) the market for many products is becoming European.

How the market system can help allocate resources

One of the main functions of a market is to allocate and distribute resources. We can see how the market process works by using a real example, which shows how a change in the conditions of demand for one product can affect the position in other markets. Later in the book you will find other examples, such as in the markets for skilled and unskilled labour.

Salmon and oyster farming

On the west coast of Scotland, oysters and salmon are farmed in the clear waters of the Scottish lochs. The markets for oysters and for salmon are in equilibrium, with demand equal to supply. However, suppose there is a decrease in demand for oysters and an increase in demand for salmon because people's tastes have changed. What will happen in each market? Table 2.5 shows the effects of the changes.

Table 2.5 Effects of changes in the oysters and salmon markets

	Oysters market	Salmon market
The effect on prices	There is a decrease in demand, but the supply is fixed. There will be an excess supply and prices will need to fall if producers are to get rid of their surplus stocks	There is an increase in demand but the supply is fixed (it takes three years before salmon reach a commercial size). There will be excess demand and the price will rise
The effect on profits	Profits in this market will fall as prices and demand fall	Profits in this market will rise, as prices and demand rise
The effect on investment and employment	Producers will have to reduce their costs. High-cost suppliers are likely to go out of business. Workers will be made redundant	Supply will expand in response to the higher profits. This will induce businesses to invest more. More workers will be employed
The long-term effect	Businesses are likely to leave the industry. Suppliers of oysters have started farming salmon	Businesses are likely to enter the industry

How will these changes in the markets for oysters and salmon affect the factor markets?

As profits in each market change, banks and other financial institutions will be reluctant to lend money for further investment to oyster farmers. Because financial institutions need to lend in order to make money to satisfy their shareholders, they will lend to salmon farmers who are making extra profits.

On page 477 we show how these changes in the product markets can affect the position in the labour market.

Activity

1 Explain what could happen to prices, demand, supply and profits in the tea and coffee markets if there is a rise in demand for coffee and a fall in demand for tea.
2 Explain what might happen to prices, demand, supply and profits in the markets for apples and bananas if there is a fall in demand for apples.
3 What will happen to the demand for workers:
- in oyster and salmon farms
- on tea and coffee plantations
- on banana plantations and apple orchards?

The role of profit or loss

Profit is the reward for the risks which people take when they use their capital to finance business. Because the future is uncertain, people do not know in advance whether a business will succeed and so hopefully make a profit, or fail and make a loss. People therefore need an incentive or inducement before they are willing to take risks and invest their capital by becoming owners or shareholders. In a market economy, the incentive is profit. Generally the bigger the risk, the higher the reward. What type of person are you? Are you a risk taker, or do you go for the safe investment with a lower reward?

Insurable and non-insurable risks

Risks which can be predicted and measured can be insured against. The number of fires each year can be calculated, as can the amount of expected damage they can cause. What cannot be foreseen is where the fire is going to happen. It is not possible to insure against risks which cannot be predicted or quantitatively measured, for example, the profit or loss caused by the success or failure of a business.

Insurable risks	Non-insurable risk
Fire	Making a loss as a result
Theft	of bad judgement about
Death	expected demand for the product

Businesses make profits when the sales revenue earned from selling products is greater than the total cost involved in producing and distributing the goods.

What does the amount of profit depend on?

The amount of profit earned by the business depends on:

- the size of the profit margin or mark-up on costs that it uses to arrive at the selling price; the higher the percentage mark-up, the larger the profit (see Chapter 14 for a fuller explanation).
- the cost involved in producing and distributing the product. Generally when costs rise, either profits will fall (that is, profit margins are squeezed), or the business will have to work harder to maintain the same level of profit. For example, when the price of diesel fuel went up as a result of the tax imposed at the 1994 Budget, business costs increased but businesses found it very difficult to increase prices. The result was a general downturn in profits.
- the amount of revenue made from selling the goods or service; generally the higher the amount of sales revenue, the larger the amount of profit.

Why does the level of profits change?

The best way to find out why the level of profit changes is to look at the reasons why some companies made large profits in 1994 and others did less well. Who were the winners and who were the losers? Table 2.6 shows some examples.

Table 2.6 Winning and losing companies in 1994

Company	Sector	Country	Reason for success/failure
Winners			
Nokia	Engineering	Finland	Massive sales of mobile phones
Petroleos	Oil	Spain	Good conditions created by government
British Steel	Metals	UK	Very good exports
Heineken	Drinks	Netherlands	Better bottling plant/production
Tesco	Retail	UK	Highly competitive pricing policy; low price, high volume
BOC (Oxygen)	Chemicals	UK	Rising demand due to industrial upswing
Losers			
Eurotunnel	Transport	France	Tunnel opened very late!
Kingfisher (Woolworths)	Retail	UK	Weak sales at Comet
Benetton	Retail	Italy	Continuing political problems
Cable and Wireless	Utilities	UK	BT winning the competitive battle

Activity

Look at the winners and losers in Table 2.6. Was the success or failure due to a change in margins, costs or sales volume/sales price?

What happens when profits rise or fall?

Every business needs finance if it is going to expand. Profit is the main source of internal finance available for ploughing back into the business. Almost 65 per cent of all new business investment is financed from internally generated funds. Businesses succeed by successfully anticipating and meeting customer demands. This success leads to increased sales and the reward is increased profits. One success leads to another and several things could happen:

1 The business is able to invest more of its own money so it does not need to borrow as much and its debt is reduced.
2 By investing more it is able to expand, sell more and make more profit.
3 Because the business is making more profit, outside investors such as banks become more willing to lend to or invest in the business.
4 Other businesses may become envious of the profits being earned and either decide to enter the industry themselves (become a new entrant) or to take over the business earning the profit.

The level of profit can act as a magnet or deterrent to new capital; it can be a positive or negative signal to new investors. It has been suggested that over the last 20 years the amount of profit made by different sectors of industry and by individual businesses has been so low that it has been the major cause of low investment in UK industry. Decreasing profits mean that businesses are less willing to borrow money to put into new investments, that is they are less willing to take risks. Dividends and returns to shareholders (owners) may be cut, so making it more difficult to attract new investment.

When there is a recession or when the 'feel-good' factor is missing:

- people are less optimistic about the future so they become unwilling to spend, move house, invest, or take risks with hard earned savings
- businesses are forced to close loss-making operations, and make workers redundant. When a business closes its high cost operations or stops making or selling unprofitable products to concentrate on its 'core' business the process is called restructuring or rationalisation.

The only businesses which survive and attract funds are those which make money. Remember high profits attract funds so the business can expand.

Activity

Bare necessities: clothing, food and music

Study each of the four newspaper headlines and the accompanying information, then answer the question below.

Teflon-coated trousers: out of the frying pan into the non-stick trousers

The Times reported that the chemical firms Ciba and Du Pont, who own the Teflon trademark, had developed a process for sticking Teflon to fabric to form an invisible non-stick protective shield. 'We have thrown everything at them, curry, wine, sauce; nothing sticks and nothing stains', says a spokesperson from Farah who make the new trousers. 'They are waterproof, stainproof and breathable'.

Gore Tex are currently the leading makers of waterproof, breathable clothing.

Credit Lyonnaise to sell Adidas stake

The European reported that the French bank Credit Lyonnaise, which made a record loss of over £800 m in 1993, was selling its 19 per cent shareholding in Adidas International Holding. This company owns most of the German sports and leisurewear giant Adidas.

Northern foods profits down 26%

Following a 26 per cent cut in profits, factory closures and job losses are likely. The foods and dairy manufacturer, which supplies Marks and Spencer, Sainsbury's, Tesco and Asda, blamed the fall on rising milk costs and intense pressure on its selling prices from retailers.

Music and rentals help Thorn EMI profits rise 27%

The popularity of the latest releases by the *Rolling Stones* and *Pink Floyd,* and a double album of early *Beatles* work for the BBC, has boosted profits for Thorn EMI and its retail music outlet HMV. 'This will allow us to pay more to our shareholders', said the chairman.

In each of the cases outlined above, what is likely to be the effect on:

a profit
b prices
c workers
d competitors
e shareholders?

Structure, conduct and performance of markets

When looking at the UK economy it is useful to be able to notice the different ways in which markets can be organised, how different business organisatións perform within these markets and whether there is a particular benefit for customers or business in each. This is called the structure, conduct and performance approach. It can be seen that these three aspects are inter-related: **market structure** influences prices and the type of competition. Companies can compete by cutting prices, improving quality, or introducing new designs, such as putting more air into the soles of trainers! The way in which a business *conducts* its sales, product, and price policies will affect the *performance* of the business.

Structure of the market

Market structure refers to the way in which the market is organised. We will ask four basic questions:

- How many sellers supply the market?
- How many buyers demand the product?
- How do similar products compete? – a brand image.
- How easily can new firms enter the market?

The *number of sellers* is usually regarded as a key factor when describing a market. The standard method of classifying markets by the number of suppliers is:

- Monopoly – one supplier
- Duopoly – two suppliers
- Oligopoly – few suppliers
- Competitive – many suppliers.

Monopoly: theoretically, a monopoly is a market where there is only one supplier. In law, a monopoly is a company that has more than 25 per cent of the market. Monopolies can occur for many reasons. One is because a company possesses a unique design or product which is protected by a patent. To obtain a patent a company must register the design or product with the UK or/and European Patent Office. The holder of the patent gets the exclusive right to make, use and sell the invention for 20 years. This gives time for the inventor to get a reasonable return or profit on the original **research and development** costs. In 1980 the US allowed new types of life which had been created in the laboratory to be patented. This decision is popularly called the Frankenstein Law.

Natural monopolies can arise if a business owns the sole rights to sources of raw materials, for example bauxite or mineral water. An area may possess a unique combination of the qualities needed to produce a particular product, for example the Perigord area of France is famous for truffles and Roquefort cheese. Before privatisation services such as gas and electricity were regarded as natural monopolies. Local monopolies can occur when there is only one shop or pub in a village.

Whenever there are barriers which prevent new firms from entering the market a monopoly is likely to exist and persist. There are a number of monopolies in the UK, for example:

- 56 per cent of the market for corn flakes is controlled by Kellogg's.
- 70 per cent of the market for baked beans is held by Heinz.
- 63 per cent of the market for sugar is held by Tate & Lyle.
- 70 per cent of the frozen vegetables market is held by Unilever.

Duopoly: A duopoly is a special form of oligopoly, when only two firms dominate the market. Duopolies exist in the markets for biscuits, coffee, corned beef, tinned fruit and tobacco.

Activity

Find the names of the duopolists for the products listed on page 95.

Case study

Detergents

The market for soap, washing powder, detergents and toothpaste is dominated by two companies. Look at almost any packet of branded detergent, for example Persil, Daz, Ariel, Radion, Bold. Find the name of the company which makes it. It will either be Unilever or Procter & Gamble.

Each company produces an almost identical range of products. Recent fashions have led to concentrated powders, refill bags, biological, non-biological, all-in-one powder and fabric conditioner and a powder especially for coloured clothes. There appears, however, to be little price competition. The terms 'leader' and 'follower' are often used to describe the actions of duopolists. The leader will develop a new concept, for example all-in-one powders, which will be followed by the other. The positions may change and leap frogging can occur, particularly if one powder contains an ingedient which is alleged to destroy clothes!

Dirty play in war of the washing powders

RIVAL cleaning conglomerates Unilever and Procter & Gamble are locked in a bitter battle over whether or not a new washing powder rots your clothes.

Senior executives from the Anglo-Dutch Unilever were reduced to waving women's underwear at a press conference yesterday to refute claims from their American-owned rival that new, improved Omo powder damaged clothes after just 24 washes.

Between them, Unilever and Procter & Gamble sell 90 per cent of the soap powders and liquids in Europe, amounting to some £6 billion a year.

Unilever has seen its share of the soap market decline under an onslaught from Procter & Gamble. New Omo was its secret weapon. But a Procter & Gamble executive was quoted as saying that after 24 washes, fabric showed signs of damage.

Unilever immediately called a press conference at which a scientist held up an item of underwear which had been washed 380 times and challenged: 'Can you see any holes?' The allegations, said Unilever, were 'totally unfounded' and lawyers are being consulted.

Unilever's new powder will be released here next week under the name Persil Power. A spokeswoman said: 'This new product involves five years of research and 34 different patents. I suppose it is not surprising that competitors are trying in a rather desperate way to challenge that.' A spokeswoman for Procter and Gamble today said: 'Our concern is to protect users of P&G products and the safety of their garments. P&G brands could be blamed for damage which may have been caused by earlier use of a product.

'We have therefore run tests on the new Lever products, bought from stores, based on standard industry test protocols which have been used for more than 25 years.

'P&G would have preferred to wait until full independent test results were available before this issue was brought to public attention. However newspaper articles, and Lever's own press conference, have raised questions which we can not ignore.'

Source: *Evening Standard*, May 1994

Oligopoly: if three to five major companies dominate a market, as is the case with trainers, this would normally be regarded as an oligopolistic market.

There many examples of oligopoly markets which are concentrated on a few large companies. Concentration ratios are used to measure the market power they possess. Three and five firm concentration ratios are used. An example of a three firm concentration ratio is given by:

$$\frac{\text{Proportion/share of the market held by the top three firms}}{\text{Total market size}}$$

Market size can be measured using either employment or sales. Here are some three-firm ratios:

- Three firms control: 100% of the baked beans market
  90% of the frozen fish market
  80% of the market for crisps
  95% of the market for wallpaper

The concentration ratio for baked beans means that every baked bean eaten in the UK is made by one of just three companies. From the earlier case study we can see that six firms control the market for trainers.

Competition: a competitive market exists when there are many firms in the market. Generally they will be fairly small with little power or control over what they can do. Competition can be divided into two types: imperfect and perfect.

Perfect competition is a market where there are many small firms each of which sells an identical product but is unable to affect either the price at which it sells, or the quantity. This type of competition is rarely found in practice, although the film *Trading Places* which dealt with the market for frozen concentrated orange juice is a good example.

The key difference with **imperfect competition** is that the goods provided by each supplier are not identical. Every firm will try to distinguish its product from others. **Product differentiation** can be achieved by packaging, brand name or **quality**. Each business is trying to achieve a monopoly for its product. A glance at *Yellow Pages* will reveal lists of plumbers, hairdressers, electricians, grocers, etc., all of whom are offering the same service. How do you choose? What criteria do you use?

Activities

1 **Look through the *Yellow Pages* and try to identify some examples of each type of market structure. Note that any monopoly is likely to be local. (Hint: Count the number of firms listed under each classification.)**

2 **The industrial editor of your local newspaper has asked you to write a feature on competition in your local area. Use your information to write the article. You should mention the following terms: monopoly, duopoly, oligopoly, competitive.**

How many buyers demand the product? This is the second criterion in looking at the structure of a market. It is about the amount of bargaining power which the buyer possesses.

The number of buyers is important in determining prices. When faced with a large powerful supplier, buyers could decide to combine together themselves. A number of situations are possible all of which will affect price in a different way:

- one buyer and one seller
- one buyer and many sellers.

For each selling situation there is a corresponding buying classification, for instance there may be one, two, few or many buyers.

Activities

1 Who has the power when Marks & Spencer negotiates with a large number of suppliers?
2 Why have independent grocers combined together to form Spar and Mace?
3 Who has the power when Tesco negotiates with Unilever (Birds Eye) over supplies of frozen vegetables?

Product differentiation and branding is the third of the characteristics used to describe the structure of a market. It refers to the attempts made by one business to distinguish its products from those of its competitors.

Are all detergents the same? Why do we think they are different? Why do we buy one brand of trainers as opposed to another? The answer is because the suppliers have convinced the consumer that the products are different. Brand names, packaging and advertising are all used to differentiate one product from another. Advertising is the main element in the price of a packet of detergent. Unilever spends £130 million and Procter & Gamble Ltd £80 million a year on advertising. The purpose of product differentiation through advertising is to make the consumer believe that one product cannot be substituted for another. Brand loyalty should reduce the elasticity of demand and move the demand curve to the right.

Activities

1 Sunkissed Bread has a large advertising campaign. Use supply and demand analysis to show the likely change in demand for Sunkissed and its main rival Brother's Pride.
2 What features do plumbers in your area use to differentiate their services?
3 Why does the Royal Mail do so little advertising?
4 What is the market structure of high street banking? Why does it advertise?

Entry conditions governing the ease or difficulty with which new business can enter the market will have an important influence on whether a particular market structure is temporary or permanent. It may be that there is a lack of knowledge of the real earnings in the industry so that new firms are not attracted.

Where a new business does wish to gain a foothold in a market there may be difficulties.

- It may lack the necessary finance. The high cost of the initial investment needed to begin production in, for instance, the car industry will deter newcomers. Where patents or copyrights exist these will prevent new entrants from using existing technology. An existing business, however, may consider it worthwhile to raise the finance and develop new technologies if it believes the profits are worth the risk.

- Whether companies will enter a market depends on the behaviour of the existing firms. If they expect new competitors they will pursue policies which deter them. A monopolist which behaves as if it is going to last forever by charging high prices and paying insufficient attention to its customer base could attract newcomers and lose its monopoly position. Smiths crisps dominated the market until Golden Wonder entered 30 years ago.
- When a high level of advertising expenditure is needed, for example with detergents, this will deter new entrants.
- When the minimum size of operations is very large, i.e. there are large **economies of scale**, newcomers are less likely. A new company is unlikely to be able to mass produce bread but may well start on a small scale with a range of speciality loaves.

In the UK brewing industry, all of these **barriers to entry** can be seen operating:

- The tied house system stops newcomers from distributing their products.
- The licensing process prevents newcomers from acquiring premises, because every public house must be licensed by the local magistrates.
- Heavy advertising costs prevent newcomers from achieving volume sales.

The net result is that new entrants have had to develop or import **speciality goods** which cater for minority tastes.

With the Single European Market, some of our views about the structure of markets may have to change. Sales by foreign owned companies are likely to rise and change market shares. The opportunities for entering new markets will increase, as will the possibilities for product diversification, so **conglomerates** are likely to become more important.

Business conduct in different markets

Businesses will behave differently within the different markets that exist. A monopolist is able to alter either the price of the product or the amount produced, but not both. When the price is raised the monopolist has to adjust the output to the new level of demand. Generally the monopolist has more flexibility to alter prices, but must be aware of the possibility of new business coming into the market. To understand the monopolist's pricing policy we must distinguish between a permanent monopoly, where the prospect of new competition is remote and a temporary monopoly where new competition is a strong possibility. The monopoly which regards itself as permanent could either 'play safe' and charge reasonable prices or charge high prices and risk adverse consumer reaction or indeed government reaction. The temporary monopoly would have less freedom to manipulate prices.

The government has recently set guidelines through the 'watchdog bodies' on the amount by which the newly privatised gas, telephone and electricity prices could rise.

The prices that oligopolists charge depend upon the strength and size of the competitors, and the size and strength of the market. If one company is much larger than the others it can fix the price levels for the industry as a whole allowing other companies to follow. In the supply of petrol for instance, Shell or Esso will normally take the lead.

Depending upon the price which has been set, high and low cost companies will have more or less difficulty in being able to compete. Frequently, however, oligopolists do not compete on price but prefer non-price competition such as special offers. Newspapers will have bingo competitions, Burger King and McDonalds have scratch card competitions, Pizzaland offers 'buy one pizza get another for a penny'.

In a duopoly, there could be cut-throat competition if each firm attempted to undercut the other's price. It is in these conditions that a **cartel** may be formed as an alternative.

Activity

Company A	Company B: Raises price	Keeps price the same	Lowers price	Keeps present products	Develops new products
Raises price					
Keeps price the same					
Lowers price					

Copy and complete the chart to show what company B might do when company A makes the first move. Terms you could use are: increase, decrease, same, more than.

Price discrimination

This refers to a situation where a business is able to charge different prices in different markets, that is, to discriminate between markets. For this to work the markets need to be distinct and separate with no transferability between them. Good examples of **price discrimination** include:

- peak and off-peak rail travel
- home and export sales
- midweek and 'weekend' pricing.

What these have in common is that the elasticity of demand for the products is quite different for each market. Where demand is inelastic the business is able to put up prices without losing revenue because demand will fall very little at the higher price. This is peak period pricing. At off-peak times prices are reduced to attract more customers and increase revenue. British Rail pricing reflects the elasticity and inelasticity of demand for rail travel. High prices are charged during the morning 'peak' and between 4 p.m. and 6 p.m. on weekdays. Companies practise price discrimination to maximise revenue and increase profits.

Different pricing strategies are discussed in detail on pages 84 and 285.

Activity

Give three other examples of price discrimination. Explain why each occurs.

Cartels

Aggressive competition can be very painful to businesses. A price war, for instance, where one business attempts to undercut the others can be very damaging to profits. Sometimes business, rather than competing will share out the market. A **cartel** is an arrangement or agreement between companies within the same market to act together. There are two types of cartel:

- the price fixing cartel
- the market sharing cartel.

In the price fixing cartel the members charge higher prices than they would if they were competing. It may include credit arrangements and discounts to disguise the fact that a cartel exists. For instance, some companies may charge higher prices but allow large discounts to bring the real price down to that of companies with lower prices. The net effect is that the prices are the same. The symptoms of this type of cartel can be:

- a common set of prices which are quoted by a number of companies;
- prices which tend to move together.

In the market sharing cartel, companies agree to split the market. A major feature of this might be bid rigging. If, for example, a new college corporation wants a company to provide maintenance of its equipment it will ask a company to tender (quote a price) for doing the work. Various companies will be asked to bid for the contract. However, if there is a cartel:

- some companies will not bid when they are expected to – bid suppression;
- some companies deliberately put in very high bids – complementary bidding;
- companies take turns to put in the lowest bids as different jobs come up. In this way they all have the opportunity to share in the market.

Case study

Sky Wars

The airlines on major routes have traditionally joined in price-fixing agreements to share out business. In early 1992, however, American Airlines sent shudders through the industry by changing its fares structure and cutting costs. As a result they reported bookings up by 46 per cent.

Different companies have different ideas on this depending upon their strength, ability to compete and how they see the market. Many Europeans, such as the French, prefer high fares and low volume, believing that there is only so much trade to go round. To them a cut in fares will mean a cut in revenue. Others such as US Air, Delta, Britain's BA and Singapore Airlines are more optimistic; they are prepared to follow American Airlines and go for an 'open skies' policy. They believe that low fares will encourage mass travel as the web of cartel agreements is replaced with competition.

All of this will involve huge expenditure for new aircraft to replace ageing fleets. If competition prevails the passenger should win the 'sky wars' as fares come down, especially on transatlantic routes which will be a major battleground.

Activities

Discuss with your colleagues the following points.

1 What do the American and French attitudes assume about the elasticity of demand for air travel?

2 What factors do you think affect the elasticity of supply of air travel:
- in the short run?
- in the long run?

How shops compete

Shops compete on quality, variety, convenience, after-sales service and price. For example, turkeys were sold at 34p a pound during Christmas 1994; a spokesperson for a leading supermarket said, 'Yes, we are selling turkeys at a loss, but we hope that people will come in and fill their trolley with high priced premium items with a high profit margin, such as double cream with brandy'. Did you buy any?

Tesco vs Sainsbury

This was meant to be a year of serene triumphalism for Sainsbury, the leading supermarket chain, which in the summer marked the 125th anniversary of its founding with a self-congratulatory book called The Best Butter In The World. Another 12 months of superstore openings, sucking customers away from town centres, and of celebrity recipe TV commercials successfully pushing selected product lines.

But 1994 has turned out to be, if not exactly *horribilis*, then certainly pretty *putridis*. Profit growth has slowed, depressing shares. And whenever the flogging of food has been in the news – notably over the introduction of its mock-Coke own-brand cola – the Sainsbury image has suffered. Small wonder that one recent interviewer found the billionaire chairman, David Sainsbury, on grumpy form, testily insisting that a standard loaf could be bought in his shops for 25p.

His mood will not have been improved by last week's incident in which 353 store managers – responding robotically to computerised instructions from the firm's London HQ – removed a 20-page Tesco supplement containing money-off vouchers from every copy of Radio Times on their shelves. Later countermanded as 'an error of judgment', the order wasted hundreds of employee hours, alienated customers, and generated such sarky headlines as 'Good magazines weigh less at Sainsbury'.

Although this bizarre episode was a rare instance of hand-to-hand fighting, the enemy retail giants are increasingly seen in direct confrontation – as with Tesco's victory in the takeover battle for the Scottish chain William Low. Tesco's strategic switch to competing on price has escalated the 'store wars', ending a period of hugely profitable coexistence.

Rivalry is sharpened by the clear-cut contrast between the two chairmen: Sainsbury is an art-lover, a David Owen fan and the scion of a business dynasty; whereas Tesco's Sir Ian MacLaurin is sporty, Tory-voting and self-made. Last weekend, MacLaurin turned the screw in a 'Dear David' letter requesting an assurance that the Radio Times affair 'would not be repeated'. He got it.

So before consuming his Christmas pud à la Julie Walters, David Sainsbury will be sitting down to another traditional recipe (unlikely to become a TV ad, sadly, although Graham Taylor or Norman Lamont would voice it very nicely) – for kebabbed scapegoat.

Take one Sainsbury's junior marketing executive or magazine buyer. Tenderise for several hours with mallet. Rub in salt. Remove guts for garters. Dice into cubes, and turn slowly on a spit over a high heat. Serve with humble pie. Delicious!

Source: *The Sunday Times*

Activity

Packing them in: how major supermarkets compete

Carry out a mini-survey of supermarkets in your area. You should compare choice, availability of goods, prices, signs, width of aisles, general environment, special facilities, for example baby changing and access for the disabled, image and parking facilities.

How radio competes

Figure 2.14 shows the changes in average weekly audience for various radio stations. For example, Radio 3 has lost 568,000 listeners, while Classic FM has gained 298,000.

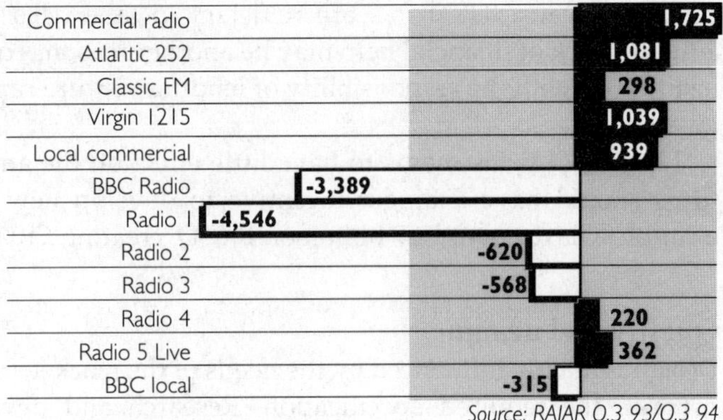

Figure 2.14 Changes in weekly audience figures (in thousands) for various radio stations

Source: *The Guardian*, October 1994

Activities

Radio Gaga

1. Why is Radio 1 losing millions of listeners? Has Chris Evans helped?
2. Why are market share and audience figures so important to radio stations?
3. Carry out a survey of your group. What station do you listen to? Have you changed stations?
4. What section of the market does each station appeal to?

Business performance in different markets

Different aspects of performance in the various markets can usefully be discussed under the headings:

- Research and development
- Quality and design
- Profitability
- How do companies grow?
- Rationalisation
- Market failure.

Research and development

In theory, the modern tendency for output to be concentrated in a few large companies should help **research and development** (R&D). These companies have: large financial resources; greater ability to take risks; a protected market, with barriers to entry; and an incentive to improve profits and introduce new products. So there should be a close relationship between the level of concentration and the amount of R&D. Industries where there are many small producers will find it difficult to raise enough finance for large-scale R&D.

A distinction needs to be made between invention, which refers to the discovery or production of some new or improved machine or process, and innovation, which is the commercial introduction and development of an invention. Inventions can come from very small firms, but successful innovation needs the resources of a large enterprise. The UK has a reputation for being good at invention and poor at innovation, possibly because UK firms are reluctant to take risks with new and untried ideas, although lack of financial help may be another reason. Today there are several financial institutions with the responsibility of lending venture capital to help inventors develop ideas.

The size of firms seems to have little effect on the amount of R&D, although large firms should have a bigger incentive to develop new processes and products. For example, Glaxo spent £2.7 billion on R & D, creating £10.8 billion of added value.

Quality and design

Design is mainly influenced by the needs of the market and the ability of the business to produce the required specification. Research and development is essential if new designs are to be created and marketed successfully. Conflict can occur if continuous design changes are required to maintain demand at the existing level, as these result in higher costs of production. **Production methods** have to be sufficiently flexible to cope with design changes. This is particularly important in markets which are sensitive to changes in tastes and fashion, for example trainers, food and clothing.

In this context a design change can mean introducing: a new product such as Mars ice cream, or blue Smarties; changing ingredients, for example, salmon and broccoli flans; changing flavours, for example, prawn cocktail crisps; and changing packaging like Sainsbury's lemon washing-up liquid bottle.

Closely connected with these changes in design is the need to maintain or improve **quality**. Does your car have a six-year anti-corrosion warranty? Can it go 12,000 miles between services? These features demonstrate how much the quality of cars has improved, in terms of performance and reliability. Commitment to quality is essential if a business is to retain its competitive edge in today's markets.

In many markets, but particularly in oligopolies and duopolies, design and quality improvements have largely replaced price cutting as the main means of competition between firms. There is now a much greater emphasis on non-price competition. Shell and Esso adverts for example, say very little about price, or indeed about petrol, but a great deal about what can be bought in forecourt shops.

In the US, price cutting is still seen as the key method of competition.

Profitability

There appears to be a closer relationship between the type of market structure and profitability. Generally, the higher the level of concentration, the higher is the level of profit. In other words, when a business has a high degree of monopoly power, it should anticipate higher profits because of the greater control it has over the market. Where there is little likelihood of new firms entering the market then, as we have seen, government may attempt to encourage competition.

Traditionally, for the economy as a whole, the UK has a very low rate of profitability when measured as the rate of return on capital employed.

How do companies grow?

Companies can grow because of internal reasons such as:

- using profits to build up the business;
- making full use of managerial skill and enterprise;
- taking calculated risks which pay off.

External growth however can be equally, if not more, effective. **Take-overs** and **mergers** can provide a quick if sometimes painful route to becoming a 'big business'. During the 1980s there were some spectacular acquisitions, for example Isosceles plc purchased Gateway for £2,250m and Habitat Mothercare plc paid £1,500m for British Home Stores (now BHS with a new logo and image but no food section).

We have already seen that as part of competition policy the government is concerned with the power of monopolies. The trend for one company to take-over or merge with another is something that the Office of Fair Trading must watch.

When two organisations which operate at the same stage of the supply chain join together this is called a *horizontal merger*.

	COMPANIES		
Supplier	A	B	C
Manufacturers	X	Y	Z
Distributors	H	J	K

For example, A merges with B, or J with K, or X with Z.

If the two manufactures X and Z merged, the benefits would be:

- a larger share of the manufacturing market.
- more control over suppliers and distributors.

Economies of scale would result due to their ability to buy in bulk, and to make more efficient use of labour and materials. Examples of such **integration** include United Biscuits which owns McVities and Crawfords biscuits and KP snacks (makers of nuts, crisps, Skips and Hula Hoops).

Mergers between companies at different stages of the supply chain are called *vertical integration*. For example, Y could take over B to secure its source of raw materials. This is called *backward integration*. If Y took over J to secure distribution outlets for its products, this would be *forward integration*. Brewery groups, for example, are manufacturers who may also own hop gardens to control supplies of raw materials, and pubs which are the retail outlets. BP, the largest company in the UK with sales of £25,900m, is *vertically integrated*, having oil and gas exploration, refineries and petrol stations.

Lateral integration occurs when a company takes over another company in a related industry. For example, BAT the tobacco and cigarette group, has largely taken over companies which make or sell fast-moving **consumer goods**. A **conglomerate** is a merged company which has diversified across a range of activities. Hanson, the UK's seventh largest company with sales of £7,500m is a conglomerate.

Organisations diversify because:

- They want to spread their risks by operating in more than one market.
- They believe that there are better prospects in other markets.
- They can use their expertise and technology more efficiently.
- They are finding it difficult to survive in their existing market and need to diversify geographically, or by widening their product range. For example, Ovaltine has brought out a new range of Ovaltine Lite. Nike is putting air into squash and badminton shoes and Reebok has brought out football boots. McDonalds is selling pizza!

Case study

Philip Morris, Marlboro man and king-sized operator

In 1847 Philip Morris founded a small tobacconist's shop in Bond Street in the West End of London. By 1992, the US-based Philip Morris was the world's largest consumer packaged goods company. Sales were $59 billion, it had 170,000 employees and boasted more than 3,000 products.

The company has used the huge profits from its tobacco products, especially the Marlboro brand, to fund diversification into other areas. Although the new food side to the company is contributing more and more, the sales of tobacco have actually increased, even within the declining US market. This has been achieved by aggressive advertising to build the brand and by price cutting to defend Marlboro against inroads made by cheaper rivals. Overseas, markets in Eastern Europe are providing new opportunities.

In 1993 Philip Morris owned companies including: Miller (US brewers), General Foods (main brand Maxwell House), Kraft (cheese and dairy products), Jacobs Suchard (Swiss chocolate), Freia Marabou (Scandinavia's largest chocolate manufacturer) and Terry's of York (chocolate again). In total, acquisitions have so far cost Philip Morris around $30 billion and the trend is set to continue. Figure 2.15 gives a breakdown of the group's projected profit.

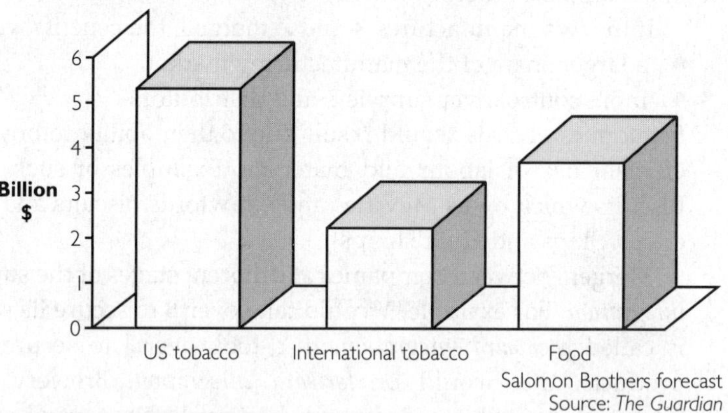

Figure 2.15 Philip Morris projected profits 1993

Activities

1 Suggest reasons why Burton Group plc purchased Debenhams.
2 Suggest reasons why Rowntrees merged with Nestlé.

Rationalisation

When the business becomes so big that it cannot be managed effectively it might need to sell off or close down parts which are unprofitable and are no longer seen as part of the core business. For example, the British Shoe Corporation sold off part of its manufacturing business and Ward White sold off its shoe interests to Boots plc (the chemists). Cadbury Schweppes sold off Typhoo Tea and Smash ('For Mash get Smash') instant mashed potatoes to focus on its core business of confectionery and soft drinks. Sometimes the existing management will purchase the business as a management buy-out.

Market failure

Market failure occurs when the forces of supply and demand do not result in a 'satisfactory' price or output. It is the government which usually decides what is 'fair' or 'satisfactory'. As we saw in the last chapter, government can intervene in the market to try and bring about a fairer allocation of resources by:

- taxing goods which it considers harmful or undesirable, in an attempt to reduce consumption. These are called indirect taxes and affect the supply of the product (see Figure 2.19 on page 111);
- suggesting guideline price rises. For example, gas and electricity price rises have been limited by the 'watchdog' bodies appointed when the industries were privatised;
- setting targets for production. For example, within the EU the Common Agricultural Policy has encouraged the production of dairy products. Minimum prices were set which were above the equilibrium. Farmers were given milk quotas which determined the amount of milk that they could produce (these quotas were valuable in themselves and were bought and sold). Fields of the yellow flowered oil-seed-rape plant can be seen everywhere, because the EU has subsidised its production. A subsidy has the effect of reducing the costs of production and will shift the supply curve to the right.

The effect of a subsidy is shown in Figure 2.20 on page 112.

Social costs and social benefits of market operations

The key questions which must be asked when assessing the performance of various market structures are:

- Does the consumer win or lose?
- Are the 'right' goods being produced?
- Can everyone afford them?
- Does everyone get a 'fair deal'?

Externalities are the social benefits or social costs which affect society as a whole.

Some projects confer social benefits on a wide range of people in addition to the immediate users. For example, the new HIB vaccine for meningitis should protect the child who is vaccinated but will also reduce the risk to others who might have caught the disease. The vaccination scheme has been actively encouraged by the government which spent £1.5 million promoting the programme.

Social costs include the waste, noise and pollution which are produced by industry and car users. Whenever social costs exist the market has failed to operate.

Cost benefit analysis

Cost benefit analysis (CBA) is a technique for analysing all the costs and benefits which arise from a particular project or situation. It can be used to assess the implications of controlling pollution and has been used to assess whether major projects such as the Jubilee Underground line extension in London should be built.

Costs are classified as social or economic. Social costs are the intangible, adverse side effects on the society such as increased noise or loss of an attractive view. Economic costs are the financial costs involved in the project, for example, the construction costs.

Social benefits are the intangible advantages or gains to the area or society, for example, an area may be cleaner or more attractive. Economic benefits are the tangible financial gains to the area or society, for example, the revenue obtained from the road bridge over the River Severn.

For CBA to help us with decision making, all costs and benefits should have a monetary value put on them. The proper decision or best practicable economic option is where the overall benefits are greater than the overall costs.

Case study

The Jubilee Underground line extension

The project has been designed to improve the links between the London Docklands development and central London and is being built with a mixture of private and public sector money. It is an excellent example of how cost benefit analysis can be used to help make decisions.

After much consultation a report entitled 'Jubilee Line Extension – Environmental Statement' was published in March 1990 for London Underground Ltd. One of the **objectives** was: 'To construct and operate the line with the minimum of disturbance to local infrastructure, communities and the environment.'

The report examines social costs and benefits, and identifies a range of impacts both during construction and during operation. Here are some of the activities involved:

- site preparation and construction
- demolition of buildings
- piling and excavation
- tunnelling
- transport of materials
- removal of waste and spoil
- operation of the line and the stations.

The whole project was put in doubt when Olympia and York, builders of Canary Wharf in the Docklands, and the main financial backer was hit by the slump in property prices. However, the decision to go ahead was made in March 1993. Figure 2.16 shows the work sites and the proposed new Southwark station.

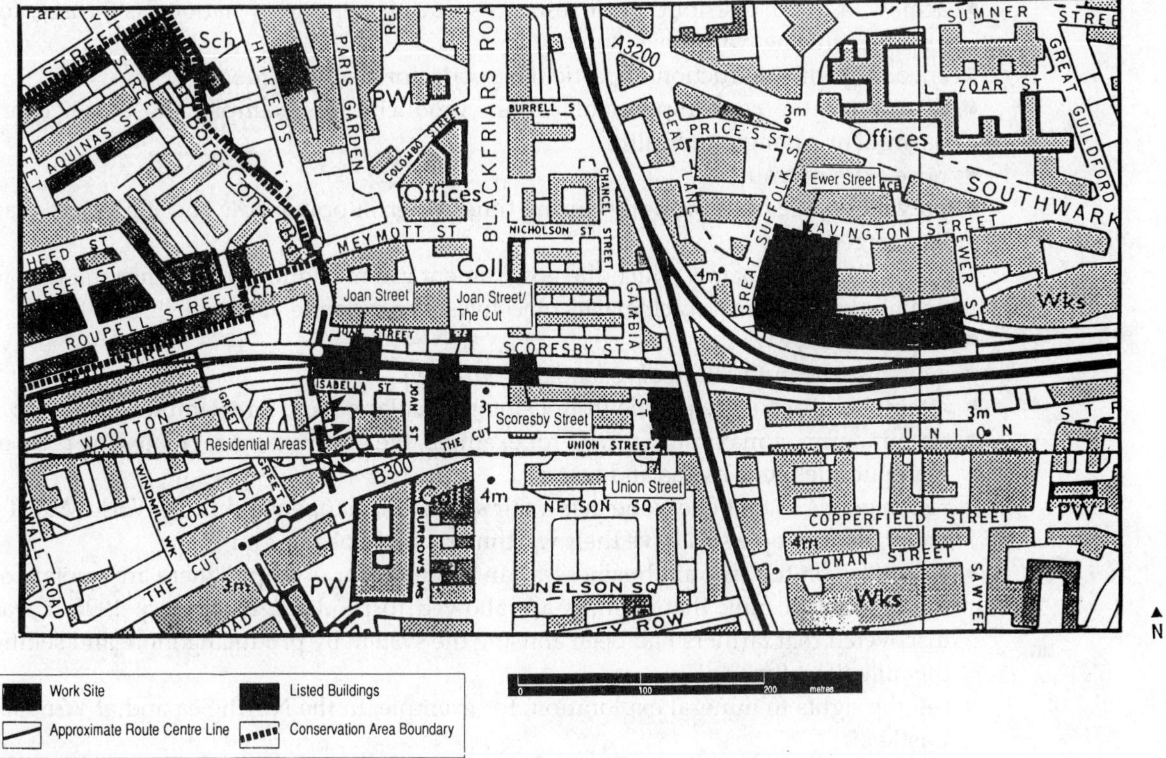

Figure 2.16 Work sites at the proposed new Southwark Station

Activities

1 Identify the different groups who could be affected by the project. There could be beneficial or adverse effects.
2 Identify the social costs involved in the project.
3 Identify the social benefits of the completed project.
4 How do you think the college shown at the junction of The Cut and Blackfriars Road will be affected?

In the consultation and planning stages of a project pressure groups will form. In this case they would represent the views of groups of people who will be affected in some way by construction or by the completed line. The aim of these groups is to influence important decisions.

5 Assume that you belong to a pressure group which is attempting to gain wider support for its views over the Jubilee line development. Write a press release designed to represent your views to the newspapers. You may be either for or against the project.

Effect of government intervention in the markets for goods and services

In addition to the reasons we have already looked at, there are other occasions on which the government may intervene in the operation of specific markets. For instance it may wish to:

- achieve a fairer distribution of resources during periods of national shortage, for example, during wartime;
- encourage the production of particular goods, for example, foods;
- discourage the consumption of certain products, for example, those which are harmful or a danger to health;
- raise extra revenue;
- prevent people from profiting during times when supply is low and high prices can be charged.

There are many measures which the government can introduce to influence the way in which markets operate to achieve its objectives. For example, it can:

- impose taxes;
- subsidise the production of essential products;
- attempt to discourage people from using particular goods, for example, cigarettes;
- set minimum or maximum prices, for example, the government regulates the price of many utilities such as gas and water;
- ration goods so that everyone gets a fair share (this happened during World War II – many older people still have their wartime ration books),
- fix quotas on the amount businesses can produce, for example, there are quotas for the amount of milk that farmers are allowed to produce. In January 1995 it was discovered that farmers had been abusing the system by producing more and selling the milk illegally;
- sell the rights to mineral exploration, for example, in the North Sea and at Windsor Castle.

Each of these measures will have different effects in the market place. Whenever the government intervenes in the market place then supply, demand or price could be affected. Here are some examples of how the measures might work.

Example 1: Government sets a minimum price above the possible equilibrium

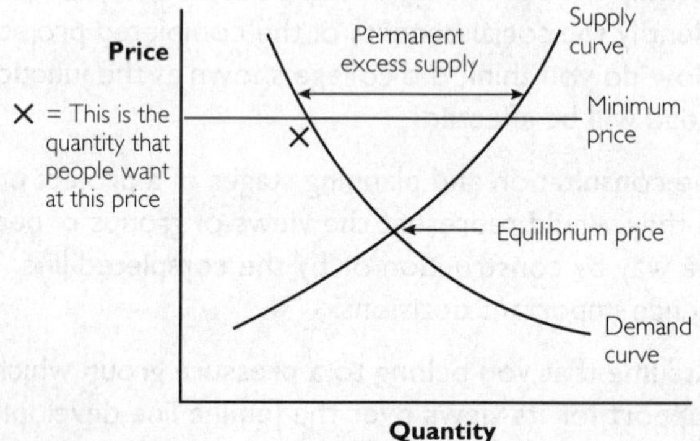

Figure 2.17

Note: the price cannot fall, therefore supply will always be greater than the demand. There is a permanent excess supply. This has happened with the Common Agriculture Policy of the EU and has been the cause of the 'butter mountains' and 'wine lakes'. The price has been set too high and people are unwilling to buy the goods. Try to work out the price at which they could be sold. In order to get rid of the excess stocks, both the EU and USA have sole their surplus product to developing countries at very low prices.

Example 2: Government sets a maximum price below equilibrium

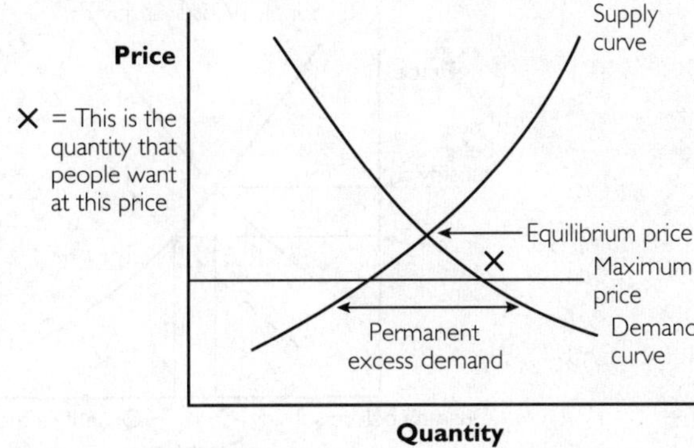

Figure 2.18

Note: the price cannot rise, therefore the demand will always be greater than the supply. There is a permanent excess demand. This frequently happens when both the public and private sector fix a maximum price for events where only a limited supply of tickets is available. Because there is a very large demand, people are willing to pay inflated prices. Ticket touts can always be seen outside any large event. Have you ever bought from or sold a ticket to a tout? A similar situation has arisen in the market for private sector rented accommodation where maximum rents were fixed resulting in a shortage of private sector property and inflated but illegal rents. The government took action in the 1994 Budget to prevent this happening.

Example 3: Government imposes a tax on the supplier

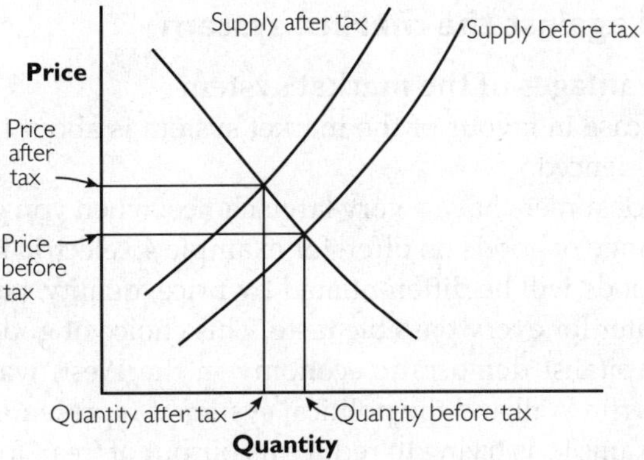

Figure 2.19

Note: a tax is equivalent to an increase in production costs and will have the effect of shifting the supply curve to the left. Less will be supplied at a higher price. Part of the tax is paid for by the customer. The amount that the customer pays largely depends on the elasticity of demand and supply.

Example 4: Government subsidises the supplier

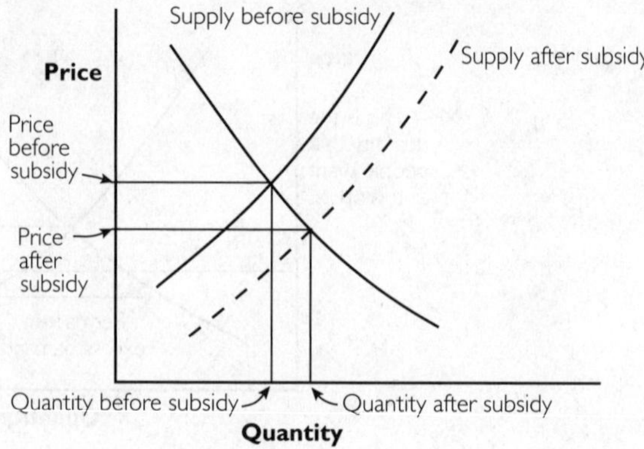

Figure 2.20

Note: a subsidy is equivalent to a decrease in production costs and will have the effect of shifting the supply curve to the right. The EU has subsidised the production of many agricultural products, for example, oil seed rape (the fields of yellow flowers which can be seen in the summer). The result of this policy has been a large increase in supply. The opportunity cost is the loss of production of other commodities.

Activity

Describe what could happen to supply, demand or price if the government:
a taxes petrol or beer or tobacco
b increases income tax
c gives a subsidy to farmers if they plant more wheat
d insists that all cars are produced to higher safety standards.

The case for and against the market system

Advantages of the market system

The case in favour of the market system is about the advantages or benefits which are experienced.

1 Consumers have a very large choice; when you go into any shop there will be a huge range of goods on offer, for example 45 electric kettles (see the Argos catalogue). The goods will be differentiated by price, quality, packaging, style and image. They will cater for every possible taste. This choice of goods, which is typical of any advanced capitalist democratic economy in the West, was one of the main reasons why the Berlin Wall and the political system it represented was torn down. Today Poland, for example, is trying to reduce its output of 'real' food and boost its production of sliced white bread and processed cheese, while the West is marketing organic real products. Why do you think that Poland is trying to copy the West although the West is now trying to use less processed food?

2 The quality of goods for sale is high because only those goods which consumers are willing and able to buy will continue to be sold. Businesses which sell poor quality goods will eventually fail, for example home delivery pizza companies will only succeed if they can get repeat business; people will not re-order a bad pizza.

3 Goods should be produced at the lowest possible cost and therefore at the best, or optimum, level of efficiency. This is because only those companies which operate at the maximum level of efficiency will succeed, make a profit and stay in business.
4 Because the system encourages competition, prices will be kept low and new products will be developed although some will fail because consumers do not want them. Do you remember Betamax video tapes which for a time rivalled VHS in popularity?
5 The government is not involved in any of the decisions about production or consumption.
6 The individual consumer plays the key role in determining what is to be produced. The consumer is said to be king with consumer sovereignty. Consumers decide what, where, when, or how many items are to be produced, by being prepared to pay for the goods they want. If they are not willing to pay, then the goods will not be made.
7 Resources are used in the best possible way. They will not be wasted, so there will be **technical efficiency** and they will only be used to produce those goods with the highest added value; this means that there will be **economic efficiency**.
8 The economy should grow because businesses will want to produce more.

Activity

What do the following extracts have to say about the success or failure of the market system?

Jail and the market don't mix

The private sector approach to prison management is wrong; what is needed is leadership not management. Prisons are not good candidates for privatisation. A prison is not an economic entity which can and should be replaced by market disciplines. It exists to hold, punish and reform prisoners. The state has decided to send people to prison and it should implement that decision.

(Adapted from *The Times*)

Market logic reigns at the end of Peru's cocaine trail

Some mountain villages in Peru exist entirely on their earnings from the cultivation of coca, the raw material of cocaine. 'If we could get a decent price for our maize we would stop growing coca tomorrow', said one farmer, 'but the fact is we get £400 a month for coca', that is 10 times as much as any alternative.

(Adapted from *The Guardian*)

Market failure in a cup of instant coffee

All too often these days we face the choice of a bland, standard, idiot-proof, long-life, add-boiled-water-and-stir drink, or nothing at all. When you are in the restaurant car on the train from Paddington to Cardiff and passing Swindon at 100 mph, you do not have the option of buying your mid-morning coffee elsewhere.

Is the spread of the dreaded Maxpak a rare anomaly, or does it represent something more general about the way markets really work?

(Adapted from *The Sunday Times*)

Activity

The efficiency of the market system

The efficiency of the market system describes the extent to which the market:

a recognises and provides consumers with the goods and services they want;
b uses resources in the most effective way, by producing at the optimum or most efficient, least cost level.

Here are eight criteria that can be used to decide whether a particular market structure is efficient. What are the social costs and benefits in each case?

1 Are the goods and services produced in the most efficient way?

2 Are the goods and services distributed in the most efficient way?
3 Do consumers get a wide variety of goods i.e. do they get a choice?
4 Are the goods of the highest possible quality?
5 Are methods of production and new materials developed?
6 Do new businesses with new ideas have the opportunity to enter the industry?
7 Are prices reasonable and satisfactory to the buyer and seller?
8 Is the level of profit acceptable?

	Efficient production	**Efficient distribution**	**Variety**	**Quality**	**New methods**	**New businesses**	**Prices**	**Profits**
Monopoly								
Duopoly								
Oligopoly								
Competition								

Copy and complete the chart. You might find it easier to work with a particular industry, for example music (competitive) or breweries (oligopolistic plus many small independent brewers) or detergents (duopoly). You can obtain company reports by ringing *The Financial Times* company report service.

Review questions

1 What is needed for demand to be effective?
2 Name the laws of demand.
3 If the price of pencils fell, what would happen to the demand for pens?
4 How could a rise in income affect the demand for cabbage?
5 How might a fall in income affect the demand for colour TVs?
6 What could increase the demand for a product?
7 What is the difference between a contraction in demand and a decrease in demand? Draw an example of each.
8 Why do holiday companies charge more for summer holidays?
9 If demand for product X rises as a result of a fall in price of Y, what can you conclude?
10 What are the differences between monopoly and competition?
11 What are the conditions of supply and demand?
12 Why might a monopolist charge different prices in different markets?
13 Give three reasons why a business might wish to rationalise its production.
14 Could new firms easily enter the steel industry? If not, why not?
15 Suggest two ways by which a business could grow.
16 Why might a manufacturer buy out a retailer?
17 Name three symptoms of cartels.
18 Give three disadvantages of large companies.
19 Why do small firms still exist?

Key terms

Effective demand
Demand curve
Market demand
Laws of demand
Conditions of demand
Substitutes
Complements
Normal goods
Inferior goods
Utility
Increase in demand
Decrease in demand
Contraction of demand
Extension of demand
Elasticity
Elastic demand
Inelastic demand
Cross elasticity of demand
Income elasticity of demand
Pattern of demand
Quality
Market failure
Opportunity cost
Fixed cost
Short run
Long run
Economies of scale
Internal economies
External economies
Diseconomies of scale
Supply curve
Influences on supply
Equilibrium price
Market structure
Monopoly
Duopoly
Oligopoly
Competition
Mergers
Take overs
Conglomerates
Integration
Product differentiation
Barriers to entry
Business conduct
Price discrimination
Cartels
Research and development
Efficiency
Externalities
Market system
Social costs
Social benefits

Assignment 2 Identikit

This assignment develops knowledge and understanding of the following elements:

1.1 Analyse the forces of supply and demand on business
1.2 Analyse the operation of markets and their effects on businesses and communities

It supports development of the following core skills:

Communication 3.1, 3.2, 3.3, 3.4
Application of number 3.1, 3.2, 3.3
Information technology 3.1, 3.2, 3.3

You work in the marketing division of Bearings, a medium-sized manufacturer and retailer of men's, women's and children's clothing. This is an industry which is led by market demand, and styles and fashions are continually changing.

Over the last 20 years there has been a fundamental change in the way men, women and children dress. Styles have become more casual, with a greater emphasis on co-ordinated clothes.

Men's outerwear can be divided into coats, jackets, knitted items, suits, jeans and trousers. Women's outerwear consists of coats, jackets, suits, knitted items, jeans, trousers, skirts and dresses.

Bearings is trying to break into the market with a new range of clothes for men and women called 'Identikit'. They wish to know what would be the best price and quality range to target. It is suggested that you examine either the market for menswear or womenswear.

You will need to use your library to find some of the information. You will also need to devise a questionnaire and interview a sample of people.

Your tasks

1 Find out:

a the current male or female population nationally and locally in the following age ranges:
15–19
20–24
25–34
35–44
45–55
55+

b the forecast for the population nationally in each age group.

2 Examine the employment and earnings trends for males and females in your area and nationally.

3 The consumer profile. Investigate where people buy their outerwear. Create a matrix like this:

Age of customer	Price of clothes		
	Low	Middle	High
16–25	Top Shop Top Man		
26–40			
40+			

4 Average spend. Find out how much people have spent on outerwear in the last six months and what they bought. Try to do this by age group.

5 Retail competition. List the ways in which the retailers of womenswear/menswear compete.

6 Comment on the design and quality of the clothing in each of the price categories: low, middle and high.

7 List the possible causes of changes in the demand for and supply of outerwear.

8 How might customers and competitors affect the demand, supply and price of outerwear?

9 Write the final report using the structure, conduct and performance approach. Make a recommendation as to what price level you would charge for the Identikit range.

UNIT 2 BUSINESS ORGANISATIONS AND SYSTEMS

3 Administration and communication systems

What is covered in this chapter

- Business organisations and types of ownership
- The structure of organisations
- The purpose of administration
- Administration systems
- Statutory and legal requirements
- Communications at work
- The suitability of administration systems

These are the resources that you will need for your Business Organisations and Systems file:

- business documents, for example, invoices, order forms, quotations, etc.
- employee handbooks
- company memos, reports, newsletters, notices
- Inland Revenue literature
- guides to Social Security benefits.

Business organisations and types of ownership

The mixed economy of the UK has a range of organisations providing goods and services:

PRIVATE SECTOR
SOLE TRADERS
PARTNERSHIPS
LIMITED LIABILITY COMPANIES:
a Private limited companies
b Public limited companies
FRANCHISE
CO-OPERATIVE
SOCIAL (NON PROFIT-MAKING) ORGANISATIONS

PUBLIC SECTOR
CENTRAL GOVERNMENT CONTROL:
a Government departments
b Public corporations
LOCAL AUTHORITY CONTROL

PRIVATISATION
organisations transfer to the private sector

Anyone wishing to set up in business will need to begin by deciding, not only which good or services to provide, but also which form of business organisation is the most appropriate. The main features of private sector organisations are described below. The various accounting requirements for each type are considered in detail in Chapter 14.

Sole traders

A **sole trader** is a business that has one owner. It can trade under the owner's name or under a business name. For example, Joan Willis – Greengrocer, could trade as The Southern Fruit Centre if she wished. The business name does not have to be registered but care must be taken not to use a name that is already registered as the property of another business. There are other restrictions; words such as 'Royal', 'Authority' and 'International' cannot be used without proper entitlement. If a business name is used then the owner's name should also appear on the business stationery.

Many small business such as local shopkeepers, window cleaners and market traders operate as sole traders.

The advantages are:

- The business is simple to set up and there are no legal fees.
- There are fewer regulations concerning accounts than with other organisations.
- The owner has freedom to make decisions and there is no need to consult anyone else.
- The owner can enjoy all of the profits.

The disadvantages are:

- The owner may have limited funds and may find it difficult to borrow.
- Where money is borrowed it may be necessary to name personal property as security for the loan.
- The owner must usually rely upon his or her expertise, as skilled employees are expensive.
- Long hours may have to be worked to make ends meet, or keep the business expanding.
- The owner cannot afford to be ill for any length of time.
- Any losses must be borne entirely by the owner.
- The owner has personal responsibility for all of the debts of the business, and has unlimited liability. This means that if there is insufficient money in the business to pay creditors then the owner's private property may be sold off to raise funds.

In summary, the sole trader organisation is simple and offers freedom, but it demands commitment and entails risk to one's private property, or personal wealth.

Partnerships

A **partnership** must have at least two owners and can, in most cases, have up to a maximum of 20. There are some exceptions to this, such as firms of accountants, solicitors and Stock Exchange members for which there is no legal limit. The business (or firm as it is sometimes called) is jointly owned by the partners.

The partnership is often used as a form of organisation by professional people such as doctors, dentists and solicitors who find they can offer a wider service by operating together with colleagues who have different specialisms. A surgery, for example, may be run by three doctors who are all partners in the practice. A group of friends could set up a partnership to run a small business.

Partnerships may trade under the names of the partners or under a business name, though the choice of name is subject to the same restrictions that apply to sole traders. Jones, Jones and Medwin – Estate Agents may trade as Pembroke Properties. Again, the partners' real names must appear on the firm's stationery.

As there is more than one owner the partners often employ a solicitor to draw up a partnership agreement at the outset. This sets out such matters as how much capital is invested by each partner, how profits will be shared (one partner may work longer hours or be more senior than another) and whether any partner will receive preferential drawings in the form of a salary. Such an agreement will help resolve any arguments later on.

In the absence of a partnership agreement the Partnership Act 1890 is used to settle disputes.

The advantages are:

- More capital is available than for a sole trader.
- It may be easier to borrow money as more owners means that more security is available than for a sole trader.
- There are few regulations though the Partnership Act does apply.
- A wider degree of expertise is available to the business than to a sole trader; indeed partnerships may be formed by people in a similar line of business because they have a range of expertise between them.
- Responsibilities of running the business and responsibilities for any losses are shared between partners.

The disadvantages are:

- There is a need to consult with partners when making decisions, so there is less freedom than with a sole trader.
- Profits are shared.
- As with sole traders, partners are personally responsible for business debts (though the responsibility is shared). As a rule partners have unlimited liability for the debts of the business, although limited liability status may be extended to a 'sleeping partner' who invests money in the business but takes no part in management decisions. Where this arrangement exists there must always be at least one partner with unlimited liability for business debts.

Limited liability companies

A **limited company** is owned by its shareholders. There must be at least two shareholders but there is no legal maximum. In several very important respects a limited company is very different from the other forms of business organisation mentioned above.

All limited companies must be registered with the Registrar of Companies at Companies House to whom financial information must be sent each year. This information is available for inspection by any member of the public.

If someone wished to take either a sole trader or a partnership to court then they would be suing the owners of these businesses. A limited company on the other hand is a separate legal entity. That is, the company exists in law separately from its owners. The company itself is sued rather than the shareholders, so that their personal assets are not at risk.

Whilst sole traders and partners both own and control their respective businesses, a company is not necessarily run by all of its shareholders. Instead a board of directors is elected by the shareholders to run the company on their behalf. In a small company the shareholders may also be the directors. A large company, however, may have thousands of shareholders. These people have bought shares as an investment and most have neither the desire nor the ability to run the company. In any case there would be far too many of them to make this possible. The election of directors with special expertise is usually the solution.

If a company gets into financial difficulties and goes into liquidation the shareholders stand to lose, at most, only the amount they have invested in the business. Their liability is limited to this amount. Even if there are unpaid debts after the business has been broken up, the shareholders will not be called upon to forfeit their personal assets in repayment.

Limited liability was introduced in the mid-nineteenth century at a time of great industrial development when shareholding had a particularly bad press.

Several unscrupulous companies had gone out of business leaving huge debts to be paid out of the private possessions of the shareholders. Some of these people had invested their life savings and not only lost their money, but their homes. Limited liability was designed to protect shareholders from this unreasonable risk, but the underlying motive was to ensure that large projects, such as the building of the railways, could continue to raise capital. The government realised that the general public would not continue to invest in companies if they stood to lose their private possessions when things went wrong. Limited liability was introduced to reassure the investing public.

Limited liability gives the shareholders a distinct advantage over the unlimited liability of the sole trader and partnership. From the point of view of those dealing with a company, however, there is the risk that if the business fails they may not get paid. For this reason a private limited company must display the words Limited or Ltd in its name whilst a public limited company must display the letters plc.

Private limited companies (Ltd)

These may not offer their shares to the general public. They tend to be smaller than public limited companies (plcs) although many have substantially more share capital than some of the smaller plcs. Private limited companies are formed by many small to medium-sized businesses. Specific examples might be a local garage, or a farm. This is also the form of organisation used by most of the clubs in the football league.

Public limited companies (plcs)

These may offer their shares to the general public, often through the Stock Exchange. It is the share prices of these companies that are displayed in the daily press. Most of the larger companies are public limited companies. They include household names such as Sainsbury's, Marks & Spencer, ICI, the high street banks, some football clubs such as Tottenham Hotspur, as well as the newly privatised businesses such as British Airways and BT.

Some companies start as private limited companies and become plcs to raise money for expansion. This is the route taken by companies such as Amstrad and Manchester United. A minimum of £50,000 in share capital is required before a company can go public, though most have considerably more than this.

The advantages of forming a limited company are:

- Shareholders have limited liability.
- The sale of shares enables larger sums of money to be raised.
- Whilst the company has this money permanently, the individual owners can recoup their money by selling their shares to others.
- Directors may be brought in as experts in certain fields.

The disadvantages are:

- There are a number of legal requirements to fulfil in setting up a company.
- Regulations mean that a company is more expensive to set up than a sole trader or partnership, although the cost may be as little as £100, and some already registered companies can be bought off the peg.
- The accounting of a company is less private than for other forms of organisation. Companies are governed by the Companies Act 1985 which states that financial records must be audited and made available to the Registrar of Companies at Companies House.
- Directors need to report back to the shareholders at the annual general meeting (AGM) where unpopular decisions and poor results must be explained.

Co-operative

A co-operative is a business owned and operated by its members. Each member of the co-operative can:

- vote at meetings
- take part in making decisions
- receive a share of the profits.

There are two types of co-operative. The retail co-operative (familiarly known as the Co-op) is nominally owned by its customers or members, each of whom receives a share of the profits, called a dividend (the *divi*'), based on the amount of purchases they make. The second type is the producers' or workers' co-operative in which the workers own and manage the business. These co-operatives can be found in primary (e.g. farming) and secondary (e.g. making motorcycles) sectors of the economy. In the Mondragon district in Spain there is a workers' co-operative with nearly 25,000 workers who produce a wide range of goods and services for sale throughout the country.

Holding companies

Where plcs have developed different areas of activity for which they set up new companies or have acquired other companies in take-overs on the Stock Market, they become holding companies, whilst the companies they own are called subsidiaries. An example is the Kingfisher group which owns retail outlets such as Comet and Woolworths. It is Kingfisher that is quoted on the Stock Market.

> Newspapers continually report on take-overs, often involving well-known names. In June 1993 the tour operator Airtours took over the Cardiff based rival tour operator, Aspro, to increase their market share.
>
> Look at *Who owns Whom* in your library. You will see that many household names are part of a larger group.

Activity

Which businesses are owned by:
Storehouse plc (general retailers)?
Allied-Domecq plc (spirits, wines and ales)?

Multinationals

Some organisations spread their operations across the world to get the benefits of cheaper supplies and labour, and wider markets. Motor manufacturers such as Ford and Nissan enter new markets and switch production to take advantage of the cost of inputs, whilst Philip Morris, manufacturers of Marlboro cigarettes have diversified into a variety of new products, including chocolates, at a time when Western governments have begun to discourage the consumption of tobacco.

Social (non profit-making) organisations

Non-profit-making organisations may range from small local clubs and societies to large organisations with huge annual turnovers such as the Co-operative Society, the trades unions, the Automobile Association and some building societies. What these have in common is that they plough back any surplus they make to benefit their members in the future. In this respect, although they may make money on the year's activities it is not a profit, because no owner is entitled to take the money.

Certain of these organisations exist in what is known as the voluntary sector. Such organisations are often registered charities and include well-known names such as Oxfam, Greenpeace and the National Trust.

As Table 3.1 shows, some charities raise considerable sums of money – often with the help of donations from large companies seeking to build a positive public image.

Table 3.1 Charities and donors

Top ten fund-raising charities in 1991 (£ millions)	Voluntary income	Total income	Top ten corporate givers in 1991 (£ millions)	
National Trust	63.0	116.6	British Telecom	14.5
Oxfam	51.5	69.2	BP	14.1
RNLI	46.6	54.2	NatWest	11.7
Imp. Cancer Res. Fund	44.1	49.8	British Gas	10.0
Cancer Res. Campaign	40.2	47.3	Barclays	8.6
Save the Children	38.7	56.3	Shell UK	6.4
Salvation Army	35.2	72.1	Grand Metropolitan	6.0
British Red Cross	32.6	68.4	Glaxo Holdings	6.0
Help the Aged	31.6	35.4	TSB Group	5.5
Barnardos	31.5	71.6	Marks & Spencer	5.5

Source: *The Guardian*

Central government control

Government departments and their areas of responsibility are shown below:

Department	Responsibility
Treasury	Economic policy
Home office	Police, prisons*, law and order
Foreign office	Relationships with other countries
Defence	Armed forces
Department of Trade and Industry	Government promotion of business
Social security	Benefits
Health	Hospitals* Nursing homes* Medical/dental practices*
Education	Schools*
Transport	Roads
Agriculture	Farming and food production
Employment	
Welsh Office	
Scottish Office	
Northern Ireland	

* These services, or parts of them, may also be privately run.

Public corporations

Public corporations have tended to be in heavy industry, energy supply and communications. Such industries have been government controlled because they fell into one of the following categories:

- they are of strategic importance to the country;
- they are unattractive to the private sector because enormous capital investment is required and profits will take years to come through;
- they may be natural monopolies which could be exploited by private owners concerned with profit;
- they may be essential services which should be run for the benefit of the community.

Public corporations are set up by an Act of Parliament. Government provides the capital through the Treasury and a chairperson is appointed who is responsible to Parliament. Any profits are ploughed back into the industry or taken by the government. Any shortfall is made up by the Treasury. Generally these industries have been expected to at least break-even.

Since the Second World War the attitudes of different political parties have caused various industries to be 'nationalised' and 'de-nationalised' in line with government policy. Shipbuilding for example has moved several times between the public and private sectors.

The Conservative government under Margaret Thatcher began the process of 'privatisation' under which many of the public corporations were sold off to the public sector where they now operate as plcs. Remaining public corporations currently include British Rail, the Post Office and the BBC.

Local authority control

With the introduction of 'privatisation' by the government, the responsibilities of local government have declined. Local authorities have been forced to privatise many of their traditional services by a process, called Compulsory Competitive Tendering (CCT). This means that private companies can bid or tender to provide, for example, school meals and household refuse collection. In 1993–4 the items of expenditure and income for the London Borough of Bromley were as follows:

Service	Expenditure (£m)	Income (£m)
Development & Building control	3.8	1.5
Education*	117.8	28.3
Libraries	6.2	0.5
Leisure	12.4	3.0
Environmental health & Trading standards	2.3	0.1
Housing**	7.1	8.6
Housing benefits	34.6	33.0
Social services	40.1	7.0
Highways & Engineering services	17.6	3.5
Refuse collection & Disposal	5.2	1.0
Central & Judicial services	17.6	11.3
Provision for inflation & interest earnings	5.4	4.0
Contribution to capital fund	5.0	–
Levying authorities' charges	3.6	–
Bromley's Expenditure	278.7	101.8
Less Income		
Revenue Support Grant	–	68.8
Business Rate	–	62.3
Bromley's Net Requirement	278.7	232.9
Precepts		
Metropolitan Police	16.1	–
London Fire & Civil Defence Authority	2.2	–
TOTAL	**297.0**	**232.9**

Notes: *Some schools are 'opting out' of local authority control.
**The income generated is partly from the sale of 'council' houses.

Business objectives

Before we investigate the various administrative systems that can exist in businesses we need to look at how a business sets its goals and the type of business goals it may pursue. We have already seen that different businesses may have a variety of different goals.

Cyert and March in *A behavioural theory of the firm* suggest that:

- The managers of the business will have their own personal goals such as trying to gain the biggest salary, controlling a large budget or being responsible for a large staff.
- Managers take pride in working for the business and in running and managing their own departments.
- This pride can cause a conflict of interest between managers, each of whom tries to push the interests of his or her department at the expense of others.
- There are various groups who have a stake in the business, for example, shareholders, employees or customers. These groups, however, do not usually take an active part in the way a business is run because they have been compensated for not interfering. (Do you have an account with a building society? Do you as a shareholder attend its Annual General Meeting?)
- The managers of the business determine its goals by a process of bargaining, for example, Cabinet Ministers, Heads of Department, Section Leaders and Course Tutors in a college all fight to get as large a share of the budget as possible.

Qualitative objectives

Look at the mission statement or objectives for your organisation. Does it say:
'Our staff are here to help'
'We provide the best quality service'
'We aim to serve the community'
'Service with a smile'
'The best after-sales service for miles.'
These goals are chosen because they are inoffensive and will be acceptable to everyone. They help to unite the staff.

Quantitative objectives

Quantitative goals are targets which can be aimed at, for example, £250,000 a year profit; or 500 units sold, or 24,000 produced; or a market share of 21 per cent. Cyert and March suggest that a business will have five quantitative goals:

1 Production
2 Stock
3 Sales
4 Market share
5 Profits.

Production

The goals of the production department are:

- to run the equipment at the most efficient level, so avoiding breakdowns and the need for continuous maintenance. (Scottie, the engineer in *Startrek*, was always objecting to Captain Kirk pushing his engine too hard!)
- to achieve high-volume production runs which require only minimum changes to machine settings. (The author has personal experience of machine supervisors who hated 'stop-start' production, primarily because the workforce was on an output bonus and always blamed the supervisor if output was low.)
- to maintain output levels regardless of sales volume. (What would happen to the stock of finished goods?)

Remember that you will have to do a business plan in Chapter 15. You will need to take care to match production with sales.

Stock

Most store/stock managers have a morbid fear of running out of either the components and raw materials needed by the business, or the finished goods. The result is that they treat the stock as their own personal possessions. Have you ever tried getting Pritt Stick in your organisation? The main benefit of this approach is that:

- the sales department knows it has stock available and can guarantee delivery;
- the production department knows there will be no hold-ups in production because of a shortage of components.

Sales

Depending on the organisation and whether it is selling goods or services, both sales revenue and sales volume can be relevant.

The local library or careers centre will measure its success in terms of volume (no pun intended), i.e. the number of people who use the service, whereas for a manufacturing business volume might only be achievable with a price cut and a consequent loss in revenue. There can be conflict within a business if it tries to achieve maximum volume and maximum sales simultaneously. W.J. Baumol in *Business Behaviour, Value and Growth* has suggested that managers aim to maximise the sales revenue of the business whilst at the same time making just enough profit to satisfy the shareholders. He believes the reason for this is that most managers get rewarded on the sales they make rather than the profits. What effect would a profit-sharing scheme have on this approach?

Market share

This is closely related to the businesses desire to achieve sales revenue or volume. The market share is the fraction or part of the market which a business controls. Generally, a bigger share of the market gives more power and influence to a business. If the business abuses this power by acting against the public interest, for example by charging high prices, it could be investigated by the Monopolies and Mergers Commission.

Profits

Traditionally, it has been assumed that all firms attempt to make the most profit they can, i.e. to maximise their profits. They, therefore, adopt pricing and production strategies which specifically aim to achieve this goal. For example, production/sales could be restricted to force up prices. More recently, it has been suggested that instead of maximising profits, businesses try to achieve satisfactory or secure profits. This is particularly true during a recession.

Profits are defined as the reward for taking risks, therefore high profits imply that high risk strategies have been adopted. Satisfactory profits on the other hand, indicate a more cautious approach has been taken. This could be more appropriate when conditions in the marketplace are uncertain and businesses only have a sketchy knowledge of all that is happening in the external environment.

Growth

Many managers in business are motivated by their desire for more money, status, power and prestige. In most cases the only way these ambitions can be realised is if the business grows. Growth therefore becomes a major goal of the management. They can achieve this by increasing the overall size of the business by merging or joining with other firms, or by buying them out through a take-over. Once one company takes over a competing company, it gains a greater share of the market and increases its overall strength and bargaining power.

Survival

While GEC and BAe think in billions, at the other extreme some businesses think only of surviving. J.K. Galbraith in his book *The New Industrial State* says that survival is the main objective of every business. This is particularly relevant during a recession – in the first six months of 1993 some 32,500 businesses failed, a rise of 6 per cent over the same period in 1992.

When managers are concerned with survival they tend to be very cautious and reluctant to take any risks, this can mean that profits stay very low and the policy is self-defeating.

Public service

Many non-profit making organisations exist only to provide a public service and their sole purpose for raising money is to help them carry out their activities. They are not interested in profit making but in providing a service to the community. Examples are The National Trust, local authorities and charities such as Oxfam.

Sources of departmental conflict

Sales maximisation

The marketing department want any order, however small or unusual	BUT	The production department want long runs and dislike one-off jobs, refusing small orders

Profit maximisation

To achieve this production may have to be cut back to keep up prices	BUT	Production and stock control would fight any decision to reduce output; this is seen as a loss of power and status

Activity

What purposes might these organisations have?

Marks & Spencer	A local hairdresser	Shell Petroleum
The Police Force	ICI	Your organisation
The local council	The RSPCA	A local sports club
J Sainsbury		

The structure of organisations

Organisations will develop different organisational structures. The way in which they develop depends upon a variety of factors including:
- the products and services produced;
- the objectives and goals of the organisation;
- the geographical area served;
- the size and complexity of the organisation;
- the method of production;
- the activities performed.

We can identify a number of types of organisational structure. These include:
- hierarchical structures including line and staff functions;
- matrix or project-based structures;
- flat structures;
- divisional or departmental structures;
- centralised or decentralised structures.

Hierarchical organisations

Two friends may set up a small business and work together on an equal footing, perhaps as a partnership, or as a private limited company. However, as the organisation expands and takes on employees there will be a clear need to establish who is in charge, who gives orders and who carries them out. A structure is necessary and it will almost certainly show that there are different levels of authority. Such a structure is called a **hierarchy**.

We will see that there are a number of different structures which an organisation can develop but unless they are very small or very democratic (some co-operatives, for instance) they will have hierarchies within them.

Hierarchical organisations are those where the whole structure conforms to a triangle shape. It is narrower at the top where the ultimate power lies (with, say, one chief executive) and broadens out towards the base (with, say, 1,000 shop workers at the bottom). In the hierarchical organisation there is a clear line of authority from the top of the organisation to the bottom (see Figure 3.1).

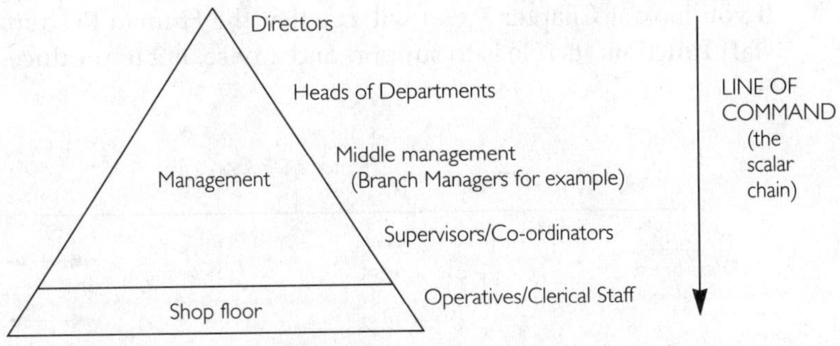

Figure 3.1 The hierarchical structure

Line and staff functions within hierarchies

According to Joan Woodward in *Industrial Organisation Theory and Practice*, the structure of an organisation is determined by the activities and functions needed to achieve its goals. These functions are divided into **line** (or **task**) **functions**. These are functions which an organisation specifically carries out to achieve its main goals and objectives. For example, in a company making hi-fi equipment the main tasks would be to produce, market and sell the equipment; its structure should enable these goals to be achieved. There are three essential tasks, so it would make sense for the company to set up three specialised departments or sections to be responsible for these (see Figure 3.2).

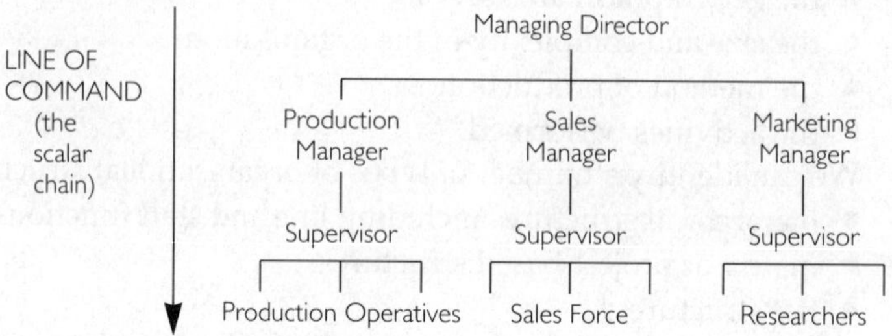

Figure 3.2 Line departments

Those departments concerned solely with the main tasks of the organisation are called **line departments**. A distinct chain of command, called the scalar chain, runs in a line from the top of the organisation down through each department to the shop floor.

Each line department is managed by a line manager. In Figure 3.2 the Production Manager is the Supervisor's line manager. Notice that each employee has only one line manager; this is called **unity of command**. One line manager, on the other hand has authority over a number of employees; the manager has a **span of control**.

Staff (or element) functions are those which support the main activities of the organisation. The hi-fi company may, for example, decide that it needs a specialised department to look after finance and accounts. This function may well help the business to operate more effectively, indeed it may be essential. However its role is to support the main functions (the line functions) of producing and selling. It is not in the line of command but works across the organisation to give help and advice at various points, perhaps with drawing up departmental budgets and monitoring these. The finance department is a staff function (see Figure 3.3). It is important to realise that the Accountant has no authority over the Production Manager. The relationship is a staff relationship, that is between people, not between a superior and a subordinate. If there is a problem then the matter will be reported to the line manager who has authority. If you look at Chapter 7 you will see that the Human Resources Department is also a **staff function**. Its role is to support and advise, not to produce.

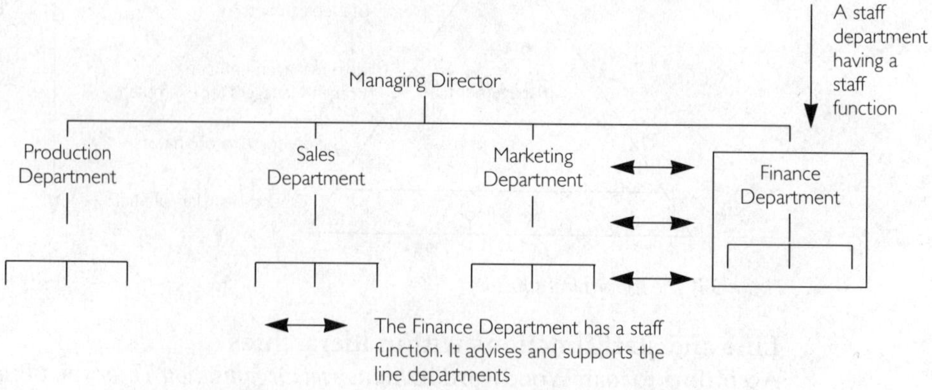

A staff department having a staff function
Managing Director
Production Department
Sales Department
Marketing Department
Finance Department
The Finance Department has a staff function. It advises and supports the line departments

Figure 3.3 Line and staff departments

Warning! Do not confuse line functions with line relationships. Line managers, and therefore line relationships, exist wherever there is a distinct chain of command. This can of course happen within all departments. The Human Resources Manager, for instance, may be the line manager for the Staff Welfare Officer and the Finance Manager may be the line manager for the Accountant; these still remain staff functions.

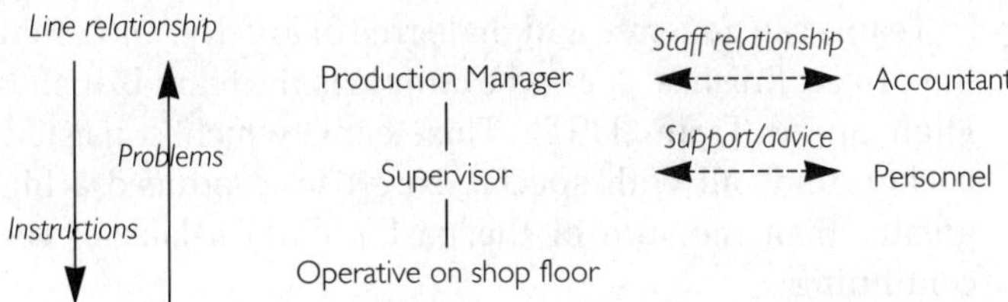

Where support services are organised so as to provide support across the whole organisation this is called a functional relationship. An example might be the Personnel/Human Resources Department or the Media Resources Department in a school or college; both service the whole organisation.

Advantages and disadvantages of hierarchical organisations

Advantages	**Disadvantages**
Clear management structure	Many layers of communication
Clear lines of responsibility and control	Many layers of authority and decision making
Functions are clear and distinct	Cross-departmental communication can be difficult

Matrix (or project-based) organisations

This is a team system which brings together people from different skill areas to handle a specific project, and see it through to its conclusion. If they are to succeed, these teams need to be able to work closely together (see Figure 3.4).

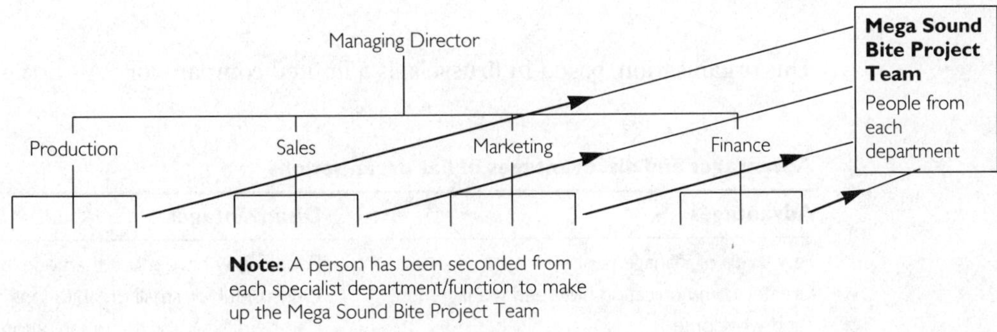

Figure 3.4 A project organisation chart for the hi-fi company

Glaxo, British Telecom and British Aerospace all use multi-skill project teams, particularly for developing new products and services. The method overcomes most of the disadvantages of the line, and line and staff types of organisation when specific projects can be identified, because:

- communication within the team is easier;
- specialists can contribute new ideas and see problems in a different way;
- a close team can be dynamic and enthusiastic, leading to a high level of motivation.

Teams can generate a high degree of loyalty, and often regret having to split up when the project finishes. A good example is the team British Rail put together to develop the High Speed Train (HST). This team, which consisted of people from a variety of backgrounds all with special expertise, produced a high level of synergy (the whole greater than the sum of the parts). Only a lack of cash prevented the project from continuing.

Flat organisations

Flat organisations are those which have a relatively few or even just one level of management. They are frequently found in the service sector of the economy. They tend to be smaller and less complex than hierarchical organisations.
Many partnerships, co-operatives and some private limited companies have a flat structure with all the management at the same level.

The structure shown in Figure 3.5 is for Communication Systems SA. This is a public relations company with international clients or customers. These clients are the 'accounts' shown in the chart.

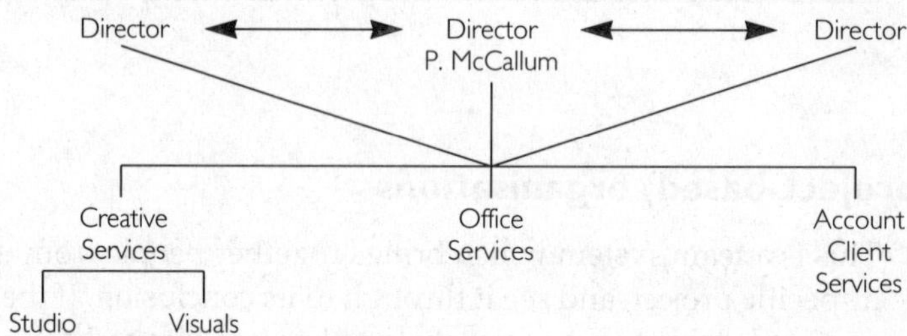

Figure 3.5 Organisation chart for Communication Systems SA

This organisation, based in Brussels, is a limited company or SA – Societé Anonyme.

Advantages and disadvantages of flat organisations

Advantages	Disadvantages
Few levels of management	People may have more than one 'boss'
Greater communication between management and workforce	Only useful for small organisations
	Can be difficult for the organisation to grow
Better team spirit	

Divisional and departmental structures

Very large companies are often organised into divisions or departments each of which is responsible for separate product areas or geographical areas.

A good example, shown in Figure 3.6, is for ICI's Polyurethane Division. Four levels of management are shown (the hierarchy), although lower levels – not shown on the chart – also exist. Each Managing Director is responsible for a division. The main reason for the structure is to simplify an otherwise complicated system of management. Whilst each division works within guidelines set by the main ICI Board, it is largely autonomous and accountable for its own costs and profits.

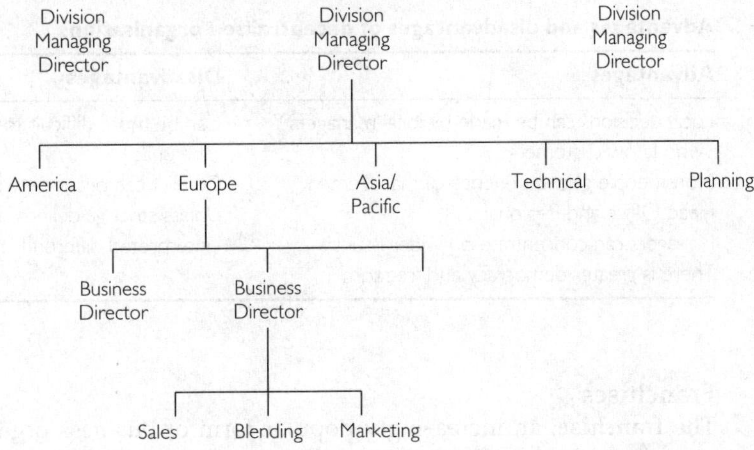

Figure 3.6 ICI's divisional structure

Colleges and schools are often organised into departments with the Head of Department being responsible for the staff, curriculum, budget and student performance. Each department will work within guidelines laid down by the Principal or Head Teacher.

Centralised and decentralised organisations

A **centralised** organisation is one in which the majority of the power, authority, responsibility and decision making is concentrated with a few senior managers. This can help speed up the decision-making process, particularly when business conditions are changing quickly, as fewer people are involved and less consultation is needed. Senior managers will have a bird's eye or overall view of the whole enterprise, enabling them to take immediate action to achieve their goals.

Some functions (such as purchasing) are best controlled from the centre, as large discounts can be obtained from bulk buying. Whilst High Street banks, for instance, often have to refer to Head Office when they provide or call in large loans.

Centralisation works well in small to medium enterprises, but can become cumbersome and inefficient in larger organisations when control and communication become difficult

A **decentralised** organisation is one where the authority and responsibility for specific decisions has been delegated (given) to lower levels of management. This type of structure is frequently found in large retail companies such as Sainsbury's. Each store will have its own Manager who is responsible to a Regional Manager or Director. The Store Manager will be responsible for sales, profits, the ordering of stock, store lay-out, and the hiring and firing of staff.

Advantages and disadvantages of centralised organisations

Advantages	Disadvantages
Decisions can be taken quickly and easily – specialist facilities can be developed and used by the whole organisation, e.g. personnel Specialist staff can be used Larger scale discounts can be obtained for buying in bulk	Little opportunity for local decision making Few opportunities available to gain decision-making experience 'All power corrupts and absolute power corrupts absolutely'

Advantages and disadvantages of decentralised organisations

Advantages	Disadvantages
Local decisions can be made by local managers who know customers More people gain experience of management Head Office and Regional Managers can concentrate on wider issues There is greater democracy and freedom	Can be more difficult to supervise and control all the units Conflict can occur between the separate parts Unless strict guidelines laid down, policies can be interpreted differently by individual managers

Franchises

The **franchise**, an increasingly popular form of business organisation, is a particular example of decentralisation. Here the parent company called the franchisor will sell the right to use its name to an independent operator called the franchisee. The operator will buy an agreed amount of stock from the parent company, pay a percentage of annual profits over and agree to provide a certain standard of service. In return there will be help in setting up, the benefit of national promotion and a ready-made image. Examples of franchises include Bodyshop, Wimpy and BSM (British School of Motoring).

Activity

You have been asked to prepare notes for a short talk which you have to give to a group of new trainees/students who have joined your organisation. Your talk should cover the following points

a The number of people the organisation employs.
b If it is a school or college you could also indicate the number of students.
c The legal form of the organisation, for example plc, partnership, etc.
d Which sector of the economy it is in.
e The organisation chart.
f The structure of the organisation, for example, hierarchical, flat, decentralised, etc.
g Advantages and disadvantages of this type of structure.
h Identify where you might find staff functions, line functions, staff relationships, line relationships.
i Say why the organisation has this particular type of structure – what internal/external factors have affected the structure.

Organisational cultures

Alongside this formal method of classifying organisations there are a number of terms which can be used to describe the style or culture of organisation.

Style of organisation	Characteristics
Formal	Organised by established rules norms, conventions and procedures which are rigidly adhered to
Informal	Loosely organised and does not stick to rigid rules and procedures
Bureaucratic	An organisation in which the actions and decision making can be impeded by unnecessary and over enthusiastic official procedures 'Jobs worth rules!'
Mechanistic	A bureaucratic organisation which changes very little if at all
Autocratic	An organisation in which all power and authority for the decision making rests with one individual
Organic	An organisation which is able to adapt and change in response to outside forces

The purpose of administration

Every business needs to be organised in order to achieve the objectives we have looked at. Try to imagine what would happen in your organisation if there were no systems for:

- recruiting new students or employees
- dealing with customers
- dealing with suppliers
- entering students for examinations.
- paying wages and handling cash.

The purpose of the administrative system in a business is to create an ordered routine which enables the business to function smoothly. It brings together the various parts of the business so that they all work together towards the same goals.

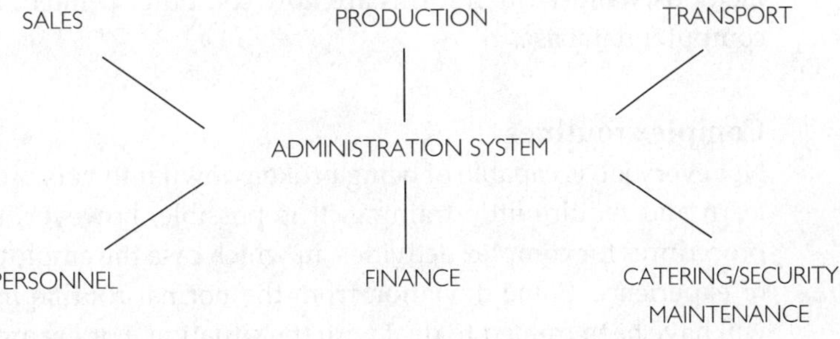

Activity

The qualities of a good administrator

An administrator is a person who helps to direct, control or manage the affairs of the business. A college, for example, may have a Chief Administration Officer, or CAO, a Deputy Administration Officer, a few Office Managers, and many Administration Officers and Assistants, all working at different levels of administration.

a On your own, choose five qualities which you think are needed by a good administrator. Write down why you think they are important. List them in order of importance.

Here are some to start you off, you will probably think of others: methodical, caring, conscientious, quiet, bossy, strong willed, likes order, enjoys routine.

b With your group, compare your list with that of your colleagues. What conclusions can you draw?

c Arrange for an administrator in your organisation to visit your group. Prepare questions to find out what they do, and whether they agree with your list of qualities.

Routines

A routine is a standard method for carrying out a task, for example when checking a sales invoice, or completing an order form. The best approach is to follow the same sequence each time because it is very easy to make a mistake if the task is attempted haphazardly in a different order each time. For a routine to work successfully the task must stay the same so that standard rules and procedures can be followed. When procedures are continually changed the routine is broken and errors can occur.

Before a routine can be established each job will need to be broken down into individual steps or stages. Although this helps to improve efficiency, because people can learn the job quickly, it can lead to boredom and loss of concentration if the job becomes too repetitive. Junior staff are often given routine tasks after only a short training session, for example, simple sorting and filing, routine calculations on invoices or order forms, filling shelves or stacking boxes.

Many routine functions have now been automated, which means people have been replaced by machines. For instance manual handling has been replaced by mechanical methods, hand-written forms are now computer printed, and filing may be done on a computer database.

Complex routines

Not every job is capable of being broken down into very simple steps, which are easy to learn and require little training. It is possible, however, to make standard rules and procedures for complex activities, in which case the employee will need special training or experience. Some deviation from the normal routine may occur, but the employee will have been trained to deal with the situation. For example, administration assistants who are responsible for checking and authorising expense claims will usually only be able to authorise claims up to a set limit, above which they may have to contact a supervisor.

Non-routine activities

These are activities which occur less often but which nevertheless should be anticipated. The business will still need rules for dealing with these events. People working in a non-routine job will need to know the limits or parameters within which they can operate, yet still be able to use their skill and initiative in dealing with situations, for example, salespeople.

Table 3.2 Examples of routine and non-routine functions in a supermarket

Routine	Non-routine
Completing regular order forms	Ordering seasonal goods, using set pr
Taking delivery of stock	Contacting supplier if the stock is dam
Carrying out normal health and safety checks	Dealing with an emergency, e.g. a cust... ...ips and breaks an ankle
Maintaining security of the stock	Dealing with a shoplifter
Allocating work when all staff are present	Coping with staff absence
Dealing with customer enquiries in your own section	Dealing with enquiries in another section
Restocking the vegetable freezer	Restocking when the freezer has broken down
Using a bar code reader at the cashpoint	Dealing with a difficult customer when the scanner does not work

Activities

1 Divide into groups and discuss the best way to deal with the non-routine examples given in Table 3.2.

2 For your organisation, make a list of routine and non-routine tasks carried out by the administrator. Who is responsible for each task?

The ideal administration system

What would an ideal administration system be like?

- Each section or department, such as Sales or Finance, would have clearly defined and specific objectives which were known and agreed by all staff. An example would be, 'all orders must be despatched within 48 hours of receipt'. To achieve this the organisation would need good communication between management and workers, and a system to enable the objective to be achieved.
- There would be effective methods and procedures of working. Preferably these should be written down. Many administration problems are caused by a lack of written instructions, which are particularly noticeable if staff are continuously changing and new employees have to be trained orally.
- There would be proper procedures for controlling and monitoring work. This aspect of administration requires a high level of supervision and well-motivated staff. Jobs will need to be properly structured to avoid 'bottlenecks' and possible over- or under-loading of some staff. When a business is changing it is important that individual workloads are kept under constant review.

Delegation

In every large organisation it will be necessary for managers to give the responsibility for much of the administration to their subordinates. This process of delegation needs clear lines of communication and authority as shown in the organisation chart below:

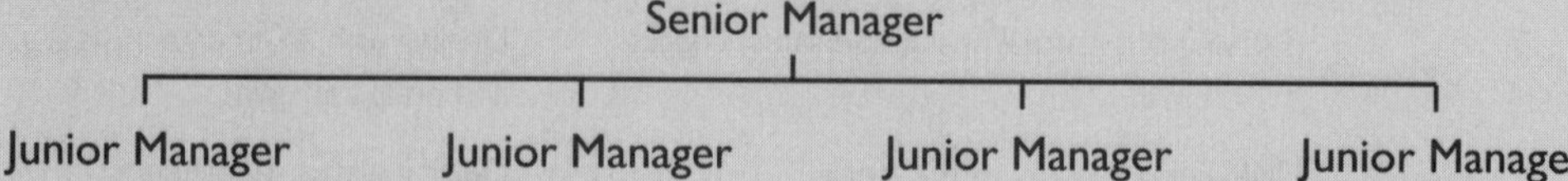

For this policy to work successfully, it will be necessary for the Junior Managers to be properly trained to handle the extra work and responsibility, and to know exactly the limits within which they can operate. For example, a Sales Manager must know what discounts and/or price cuts would be allowed to be given in any negotiations with buyers.

The Senior Manager is always accountable for whatever a subordinate does, and should accept full responsibility for any mistakes made. He or she also has to make sure that all delegated tasks are properly carried out. When the subordinate is fully trained, competent and trustworthy this is relatively straightforward. However, if this is not the case a manager may be very reluctant to delegate work.

There are many reasons why managers do not delegate, for instance, they may not trust the subordinate, or they believe the subordinate could become too powerful or successful and eventually take over their job, or they may feel it is quicker to do the job themselves.

At the other end of the scale, some managers delegate too much and could find themselves losing touch with the job and not knowing what is going on.

Activity

Chris works as a manager with the Hurstfield Local Authority. She gets into work at 7.30 a.m. every morning (but does not have to arrive until 9 a.m.). Most of this time is spent trying to work out what she will do today. Whenever she is asked a question the answer is always the same 'Go away, I haven't got time'. She feels overworked, can never make a decision, and is obsessed with the detail of the job. Chris started very well but now she 'cannot see the wood for the trees' and is working continuously, whilst everyone else in the office seems to be sitting around doing nothing. Morale and job satisfaction in the office are very low.

One Friday she gets home and decides that the situation has to change. She rings you up and says 'Tell me what the problem is and how I can change it.'

Write down five changes Chris could make to improve everyone's life.

- The administration would have sufficient resources to achieve its objectives. Although every department in a business will always claim that it does not have enough resources it is important that the administration function does have the staff, materials and equipment that it needs to meet deadlines and perform efficiently. Much will depend on the importance which is given to administration within the business. In some production orientated companies, administration is seen as a peripheral or incidental activity, and can be under-resourced. At the other extreme, administration can assume too big a role and the business can become bureaucratic with too many unnecessary procedures.
- There will be proper controls and methods for supporting the people and resources in the business. In many organisations the administrative staff are called support staff because a major responsibility of administration is to support the work of other functional departments, such as Production and Transport.

The Company Secretary

In some businesses the administration is run by the Company Secretary. All limited companies must by law have a named Company Secretary who may also be responsible for:

- providing secretarial facilities to the directors, governors and executives;
- dealing with any legal issues, for example, a change of use of the premises;
- dealing with financial issues in the business, for example handling mergers or take-overs;
- taking responsibility for administration including the storage, retrieval and provision of information;
- administering the services of the business such as security and maintenance;
- overseeing the final accounts of the business.

- Recording and monitoring the performance of the business. The administration section of every department will be responsible for collecting, analysing and providing essential management information.

College Management Information System (CMIS)

The CMIS is a fully computerised software package which has been specially designed to help college management make decisions. When all the relevant data has been inputted it is capable of providing a wide range of management information.

The system is divided into several modules each of which has a special function, for example, Accounting Records, Student Records, etc. These can be accessed to provide answers to a variety of questions such as, How many students are aged between 16 and 19? How many students live in postal area SE11? etc. The answers or reports are given in *tabular* or *graphical* formats.

The system is quick and efficient and can help management divide its student population into segments which can be specifically targeted with advertising to help recruitment.

Activity

Find out if your organisation has a management information system. Invite someone from the Administration department to talk to your group about the system in use. Write up the talk as a short article which explains how it works.

Administration systems

The administrative system of a business is based on its offices. In a small organisation this might literally be one room with a small number of people. Whereas in a large organisation there could be many administrative offices each with a specialist responsibility and function. For example, the sales office services, or administers, the work of the sales department and the finance office administers the financial affairs of the business.

Generally, the larger the organisation, the more specialised its office workers become, and the more complex is the administrative system. For instance, a local office of the Department of Social Security (DSS) could have one person dealing only with clients with surnames A to F, and at the Thames Water Authority, there could be one person dealing with post codes BR1 to BR7.

Any business can be regarded as an open system that links with the outside environment, takes in inputs and converts them into outputs.

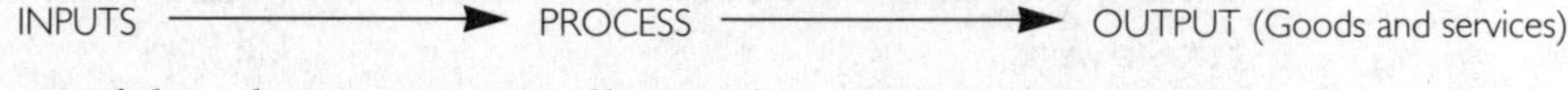

Every part of the administration will contribute to this process:

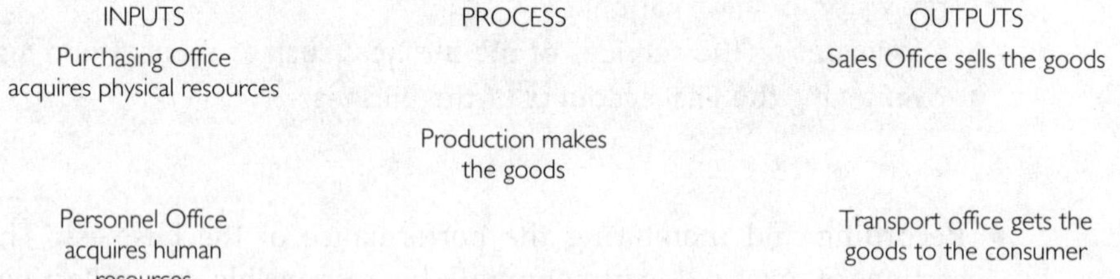

Each office is in effect a sub-system of the organisation's administrative system.

This organisation has seven offices each of which is dedicated to a specific department/function.

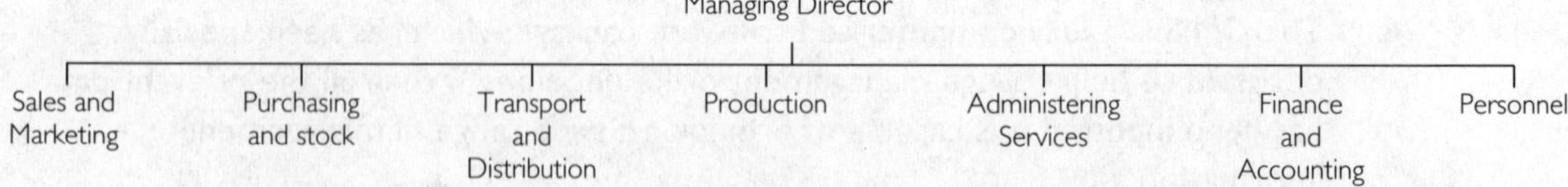

Before we look at their administrative responsibilities we will first look at the functions performed by any office. Whatever the style of office, they all have the same purpose – to give a service. They may;

- Receive information by fax, telephone, letters of enquiry, quotations, invoices, etc.
- Store information on computer disk, on file or in account books.
- Analyse information, for example, in accounts, sales figures, costings, personal data.
- Supply information to enquiries, customers, suppliers, distributors and management.

This is shown in Figure 3.7.

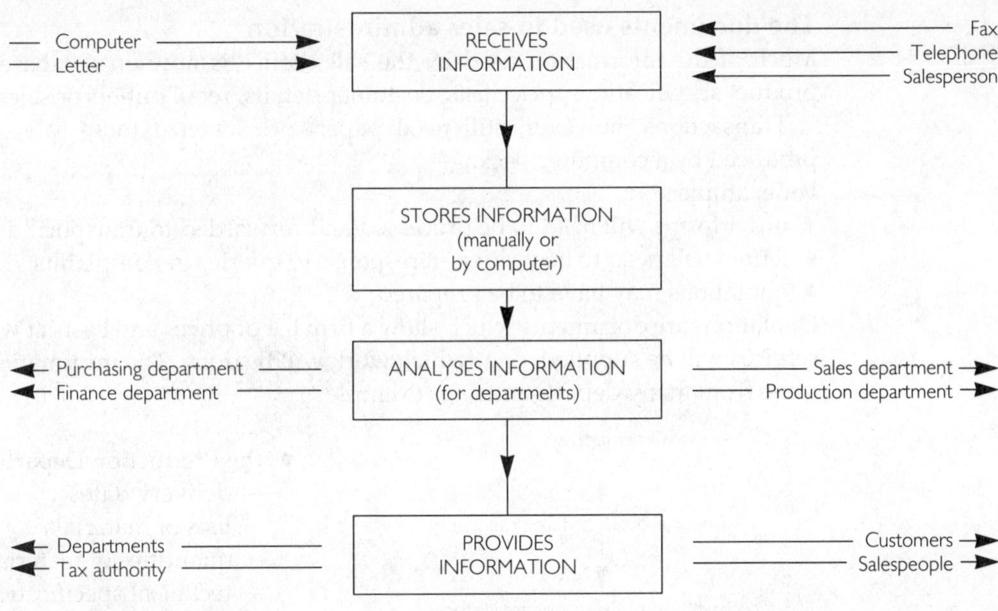

Figure 3.7 The office

Sales and marketing department

A typical sales and marketing office might be responsible for:

- processing all sales information
- marketing research – data collection, analysis and presentation
- customer care and service, dealing with customer complaints and problems
- sales promotion and advertising
- preparing sales budgets and forecasts
- providing support services to sales staff, credit clearance and credit control
- sales administration, for example, processing orders and preparing quotations and invoices.

In order to fulfil these responsibilities, the Sales Department will have to work closely with the Finance, Purchasing, Production and Transport departments. There needs to be a mechanism for investigating and correcting failures in the administration system so that if a breakdown in communication/administration occurs, for example, insufficient material is available for a special order, then it can be corrected.

A business which has sales and/or market share as its prime objective would give top priority to the work of this office, so improving the customer's impression of the business.

Sales department information

Information for the sales department comes from:

- internal records and databases
- existing and potential customers
- enquiries and requests for prices
- sales staff
- market research
- publicity and promotion campaigns.

The documents used in sales administration

Much of the information used by the sales office is now on databases, for example, product specifications, price lists, customer details, retail outlets or sales data, etc.

Transactions, however, still need paperwork, even if these sales documents are produced by a computer package.

For example:

- order forms will need to be processed and forwarded to transport/distribution;
- letters will need to be written in response to queries or complaints;
- quotations may have to be prepared.

Quotations are documents which show a firm list of prices and costs at which goods and services will be supplied, or at which work will be done. The information for them will come from many departments, for example:

Order received
Check all details and file order
Check with stores that goods are in stock
Inform Production if goods have to be made
Inform Customer of delivery time
Inform Despatch to deliver goods
Inform Accounts to prepare invoice

A typical administration system for processing orders

- the Production Department provides
  - delivery dates
  - lists of materials
  - quantities of materials
  - technical specifications
- the Distribution Department provides
  - methods of delivery
  - delivery schedules
  - storage
- the Accounts Department provides
  - standard prices
  - standard costs
  - methods of payment
  - credit clearance
  - customer accounts

The way in which documents are used for accountancy is explained in Chapter 11.

Case study

Mail order catalogue selling

Mail order companies such as Freeman's, based at Clapham in London, Grattan, based at Bradford West Yorkshire and Family Album, located in Manchester, all rely on having efficient and cost-effective systems for selling and distributing their goods. These systems are fully computerised but each company takes great care to ensure that customers deal with real people whenever they place an order or make an enquiry.

There are four parts to the sales administration process which directly meet customers' needs:

- **Ordering** Most orders are taken directly by phone and keyed directly into the computer. Information about stock availability and advice about deliveries can be given immediately because the computer system is linked with the stock and storage sections. Ordering is quick and easy.

Order received
Stock checked
Availability confirmed
Delivery confirmed

No written confirmation of a telephone order is necessary.

- **Delivery** Once customers have ordered goods, they want them as quickly as possible. Mail order companies do not normally use their own transport, but instead use external carriers such as the Royal Mail or White Arrow, a specialist transport company. This is because the maintenance and upkeep of vehicles could be very expensive. However, the companies are increasingly using their own couriers to deliver goods. The normal delivery time is about seven days and is free. However, if the customer is willing to pay extra, delivery can be reduced to 48 hours. Goods can be returned or exchanged in the same way.
- **Payment** Home catalogue shopping has specialised in flexible methods of payment, ranging from full payment on delivery to 50 week instalments which are interest free. The companies rely on their agents to collect and forward the money. Mail order companies need to be able to control their cash flow and monitor debt repayments very carefully.
- **Storage and warehousing** The administration of this section requires a system that will minimise the costs of storage, update stock records, provide information to answer telephone queries, and show when goods need to be re-ordered. All information is stored on computer and is immediately available to management as part of the management information system.

Activity

On your own, investigate the sales administration processes used in your organisation. Write a short report which shows the sequence of activities and includes the documents that are used. Compare this with another organisation with which you are familiar (your work experience organisation perhaps). Can you say why there are differences? Does it matter if goods or services are sold?

Purchasing and stock department

The main purpose of the purchasing department is to buy the goods needed by a business:

- at the right time
- at the right price
- at the right quality, and
- in the right amount.

A typical purchasing department could look like this:

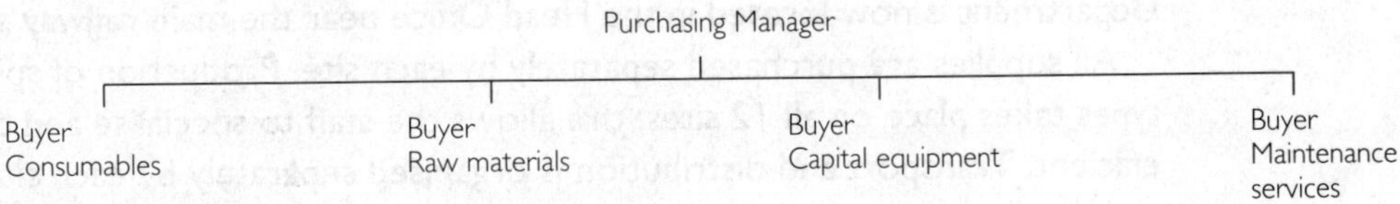

Centralised or decentralised purchasing

Centralised purchasing occurs when one specialist department does the buying for the whole organisation. Decentralised purchasing involves branches/subsidiaries also being given the responsibility for purchasing.

Advantages	Disadvantages
Bulk purchases can be made with large discounts	Branches or subsidiaries cannot make their own arrangements
Better stock control and monitoring	Possible delays in the internal administration process
Less duplication and wasted effort	Subsidiaries or branches may resent total 'head office' control
One buyer can build close relationship with suppliers	
Specialists can develop complete product knowledge	Subsidiaries cannot develop their own expertise
Stock records can be centralised to give a better service	

Which purchasing system is chosen will depend upon the size of the company. Small, single-site businesses would normally opt for a centralised system. Large companies may also adopt a centralised approach when internal distribution systems are good or the company wants to retain control or promote a 'company image'. All McDonald franchises, for example, must buy from central stores.

Finding suppliers

Every business must ensure that it gets value for money when it buys its supplies. To do this it must have an up-to-date and accurate database of possible suppliers. Existing suppliers should already have a 'vendor rating'. This means they will have been classified according to various criteria, for example, reliability, price competitiveness, quality, service. New suppliers will need to be vetted before any order is placed, for example: Are they capable of doing the work? How long has the company been registered (check with Companies House)? Do they have adequate insurance? Who is the insurer (check with the insurance company)? Do they belong to the authorised trade association (check again)? Can they provide a banker's reference, i.e. are they creditworthy because complex legal proceedings may be necessary to claim back money if a supplier stops trading?

Case study

Coventry Chemicals

Coventry Chemicals began nearly 90 years ago producing patent medicines; their most famous product was the 'Coventry Cough Cure' which it was claimed could cure anything from gout to toothache. It began in a small factory in the centre of Coventry but expanded very quickly. Today it has 12 sites spread across Coventry. The Personnel Department is now located in the Head Office near the main railway station.

All supplies are purchased separately by each site. Production of specific product types takes place on all 12 sites; this allows the staff to specialise and become more efficient. Transport and distribution is organised separately by each site. All research and development takes place in one building outside the city centre. The Sales Department is located in the Head Office; it has few links with any other department.

At a recent meeting the Customer Care Department reported:

- That there had been an increasing number of complaints from customers saying that on some days they could get three or even four small deliveries.

- Suppliers were grumbling that they were being asked to supply small amounts of office stationery to separate sites.
- The sales department had agreed to sell something which the company did not make. It was also noted that the Hayley Street site were still buying new filing cabinets, whilst at the same time the Michael Road branch were throwing away cabinets which were perfectly good.

Activities

1 The Administration section, in which you work, has been asked to investigate the situation described in the case study above. Write a brief Memorandum to your section head, Carol Peters, giving:
  a The main advantages and disadvantages of centralisation.
  b Some suggestions for re-organising Coventry Chemicals which would solve some of its problems.

2 Investigate your own organisation to find out which functions are administered centrally and which are decentralised. Write out your findings as a 250 word article suitable for an organisation newsletter. Explain why this situation has come about. Do you think any changes should be made?

Transport and distribution

The transport department will have to organise the way that goods are sent to the wholesaler, retailer or customer. The decisions it makes about the type of transport to use will depend on the weight, volume and value of its goods. For example, bulky, low-value products can be sent by rail or canal, whereas high-value, high-priced items could be air freighted. Other considerations are, the speed of delivery, insurance and whether an outside carrier should be used.

The administration system required to distribute and transport goods and services will need to achieve two key objectives. First that the right goods are delivered to the right people at the right time and in perfect condition. Secondly, that total transport costs are kept to a minimum.

Let us suppose that a clothing company intends to open a new warehouse, with the intention of achieving the lowest possible transport costs. What information will it need to enable it to make a decision?

It will need to know how much it is likely to deliver to each area, and the transport costs which are involved.

Location	Number of items delivered	Transport cost per item per mile	Total transport cost (Col 2 x Col 3) in £
Belfast	276,000	20p	55,200
Cardiff	137,000	20p	27,400
Norwich	111,080	20p	22,216
Southampton	154,675	20p	30,935
Hull	132,540	20p	26,508

The *optimum* or best location is that which saves the company the most money. In this example the best place would be Belfast, because if the company builds the warehouse there it would save £55,200 in transport costs. If the business set up in Norwich it would only save £22,216.

Activities

1 Can you work out how much it would cost to transport the items to each place if the warehouse was built in your area? (Hint: You will have to work out how far it is to each town.)

2 You work as an assistant in the Work Study department of Coventry Chemicals.

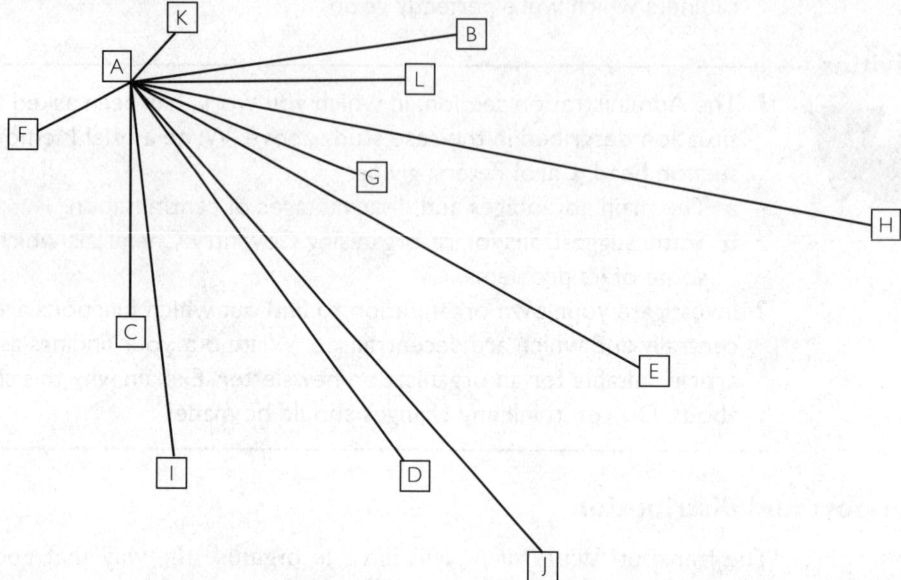

Figure 3.8 Diagram showing the Coventry Chemicals sites. Drawn to scale of 0.5 cm = 1 mile.

Coventry Chemicals is located at 12 sites across Coventry (see Figure 3.8). At present, all stores are kept at site A. The cost of delivery is 40 pence per mile. Here are the deliveries made each week.

A	B	C	D	E	F	G	H	I	J	K	L
7	15	14	10	4	9	20	12	9	11	14	6

MEMORANDUM

To: GNVQ Trainee
From: Leila Matthew
Re: New Location of Stores

Welcome back from holiday! You will see from the attached map and figures that we have been working. Can you carry on with the rest of the work for me please. You will need to:

1 Work out the present cost of deliveries. I have drawn in the current method, for example, a van will go from site A to site D and return. This process is repeated for each site.

2 The plan is drawn to scale so you will have to measure each trip separately. For example, site B is 4.5 cm or 9 miles away. Therefore the cost is 15 trips x 9 miles = 135 miles
135 miles x 40 pence = £54 x 2 (for the return trip) = £108

There must be a better route than this. Remember if you want to distinguish yourself around here you have to do things on your own! Can you please suggest some alternatives by the time I return in two weeks.

Production department

The structure of a typical production department is shown below:

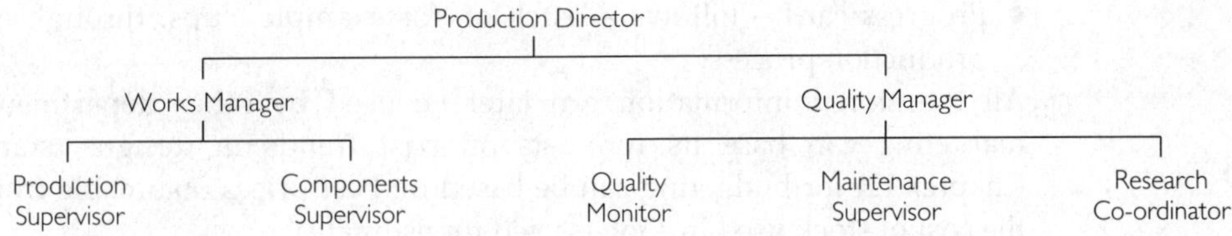

Case study

Rookery

At the Rookery Porcelain Factory, the Production Director is responsible for the Works Manager and the Quality Manager. The factory produces technical porcelain, used as an electrical insulator on high voltage wires and railway lines; tableware for restaurants, private use and hotels; and 'sculptures' including vases and pots.

The Works Manager is responsible for ensuring that:

- all goods are manufactured to the pre-determined specification and design. To do this the Manager must liaise closely with the Marketing Department to ensure that market trends are matched by the production facilities. There has recently been a shift from traditional to modern design.
- production capacity is planned to meet the forecasted demand. Some flexibility in the use of equipment is possible between the 'technical' and 'tableware' production.
- individual production lines for plates, cups, saucers, etc. are operating efficiently.
- sufficient stocks of raw materials and finished goods are available to meet demand.

The Quality Manager is responsible for:

- research – including finding new uses for existing products and developing new designs to meet changing market demands.
- quality control – which involves random sampling of items as they move on conveyor belts from the kilns to the 'decoration' stage.
- maintenance – all machinery maintenance is carried out by a team of engineers capable and willing to handle any maintenance task.

Rookery have devised a series of systems to ensure that the Production Department meets its targets:

1. Routine preventive maintenance checks on all equipment on a daily basis.
2. Weekly meetings between the marketing and production departments.
3. Quality monitoring checks, for manufacturing faults, glaze and decoration.
4. Liaison between production and the purchasing section.
5. Computer recording of all output.
6. Automated control of all raw materials including kaolin (the china clay) and glazes.
7. Automated handling of raw materials.
8. Computer database records of all stocks.
9. Computer Aided Design (CAD) software with 3-D object imaging processes. Objects can be 'flipped' and 'rotated' on screen.

Documents used to provide a permanent record

Although all records are stored on disk, staff still want hard copy and a written record. They use the following:

- Order form – records orders for raw materials from suppliers.
- Delivery note – confirms delivery of raw materials from suppliers.
- Requisition note – used internally to obtain goods from the stores.
- Progress card – follows a batch of, for example, cups, through each stage of the production process.

All the stored information can later be used by other departments, for example, marketing can base its forecasts on past trends in designs, standard costs (see Chapter 12) for budgeting can be based on best prices obtainable from suppliers, and the cost of stock used in a job is used for estimates.

Administering services

The type of services provided within a business can include security, catering and maintenance. For each of these the business can either choose to provide the services itself, that is, use in-house staff, or use an external company (contracting out).

Security

Many organisations now have static or mobile guards to protect their staff, premises, equipment, materials and cash. For example, shops have guards to prevent shoplifting, building sites have security to protect materials and equipment, and colleges and offices use guards to prevent unauthorised people from entering the premises.

Using in-house staff

The major advantage to an organisation of providing its own security system is the greater amount of control which it has over the staff. For instance staff can be required to patrol all areas, check fire exits or even act as a reception point.

There are four main disadvantages to employing in-house staff for security:

- when security guards are ill no cover may be available;
- if their performance is below the standards defined in the original job specification, unless guards are on fixed-term contracts it may be difficult to dismiss them;
- management time is needed to supervise the security staff;
- it costs more to employ in-house guards than it does to use an outside company/ contractor, especially where 24-hour security can be obtained for about £140 per day.

Catering

With catering the same choice exists – that is, whether to provide the facilities in-house or use outside caterers. More businesses now recognise the advantages which can be gained from having good canteen facilities on the premises – both staff morale and motivation can be increased.

Advantages of in-house catering	Disadvantages of in-house catering
Greater control over staff	Requires trained personnel
Greater control over facilities	Needs administration
Greater control over menus	Sometimes given a low priority
Possibility of profit	Can be a major source of complaints
	Staff absence can cause problems
	Can be very expensive and might need to be subsidised to keep prices low

Activities

1 On your own, find out if your organisation provides its own catering or uses an outside company. Can you say why this decision was made? Can you extend the list of advantages and disadvantages given above?
2 With your colleagues, compare two organisations, one doing its own catering, the other using a catering contractor. What are the administrative differences? Who takes the risks? Who bears the losses? Who makes the profits? Who employs the staff? Who makes the decisions?

Choosing an outside contractor/company

Many organisations now use outside companies to provide the catering, security, maintenance and payrolling facilities which they need. This situation has come about because the government has privatised many of these services. Schools and colleges, for example, no longer have to use the services formerly provided by the Local Authority. They are now free to choose whatever company they want, providing they have the funds available.

There are three stages in choosing an outside company or contractor:

- Stage 1 – prepare a specification which details what is required. This should include, for example, the level and type of service that is required, the minimum standards that should be achieved, the hours of duty, holiday times and place of work.
- Stage 2 – advertise that a contract is available for a limited time and invite tenders from companies. Newspapers and magazines, such as the *Contracts Journal*, would be suitable publications in which to advertise. Contracts above a certain amount have to be advertised throughout the Single European Market, thus giving all European companies a chance to compete.
- Stage 3 – evaluate the tenders, using the criteria of value for money. This will normally mean that the most expensive tenders are rejected. The choice will therefore be between the three or four lowest price tenders.

Finance and accounting department

This chart shows the structure of a typical accounts department:

The Accounts Department is normally responsible for:

- keeping the account books up-to-date;
- providing costings for departments, products, or processes;
- budgeting and control of finance;
- cash flow, i.e. ensuring that the business has sufficient cash to meet its outgoings;
- analysing and providing financial information to management;
- making and recording payments to suppliers;
- paying staff wages and salaries;
- preparing the annual accounts.

For each of these functions the business will have to set up administrative systems which can:

- collect
- analyse, and
- provide information required by law, for example, the end of year accounts or VAT returns.

There are two requirements for the administration system needed for financial accounting. The system must be able to:

- record information. The records can be kept manually in books of accounts, stored in a database or in a computerised accounts software package. Legally they must be available for inspection by the Inland Revenue and by the company auditors at any time.
- report on the financial health of the business at the end of the year. The Companies Acts lay down specific rules and regulations which must be followed by all limited companies when they prepare their annual accounts (see Chapter 14 for further information on this). The accounts must be prepared so that they give a 'true and fair view' of the business. This means that they should be as objective as possible and capable of being externally checked and verified.

The administration system needed for management accounting needs to be able to:

- collect
- store
- analyse, and
- provide financial information which is used internally by management.

The management accounting information system is used for:

PLANNING DECISION MAKING and CONTROL.

It is concerned with future financial events. The Management Accountant will need to be able to answer questions such as, When will the money be available to renew the roof at the Sandfields site? Can we proceed with the introduction of both the new product ranges?

The Chief Accountant who is usually on the management board will have to work closely with department heads when preparing budgets and monitoring financial progress.

Activities

1 **On your own, draw a chart which shows the responsibilities of people working in the Finance/Accounting department of your organisation. Find out what jobs they do.**

2 **With your group, compare your findings with those of your colleagues. Give reasons why they may be different. Do the jobs and responsibilities depend on the type of organisation?**

Personnel department

The main function of a personnel department is to recruit, select, train, and develop staff. The purpose of personnel administration, is to provide and develop systems to carry out these functions and to maintain accurate personnel records as required by law.

Many records are now stored on computer and personnel departments have to be very aware of what they can and cannot do with the information under the Data Protection Act 1984 (see Chapter 4 for details of this Act). However, all personnel records must be kept safe, secure and confidential.

It is a legal duty for every business which has employees to have personnel records which show the tax that must be paid, the employees' and the employer's National Insurance Contributions (NICs) and the Statutory Sick Pay (SSP) or Statutory Maternity Pay (SMP) which is received by employees. Additionally an accident book must be permanently available, for recording all accidents.

Personnel records

Like any office in the organisation the Personnel Department will:

- receive information from internal and external sources, for example, the Inland Revenue;
- store information;
- supply information to internal and external users, for example, management or the Department of Social Security (DSS) which uses the data on sick pay.

Information received by Personnel

The information which the Personnel Department receives will come mainly from three sources:

- its own employees;
- Government departments (which provide information about tax, National Insurance, sick pay and maternity pay);
- the Health and Safety Executive (HSE).

Information held by Personnel

The personnel records which are kept by the Personnel Department must cater for the needs and activities of the business. They can include application forms, pay details, records of training, sick pay, and absence and holiday entitlement. Equally important is the need to keep records which can provide management with information for planning and decision making.

The storage and retrieval system used for records which is adopted by a business will depend upon:

- the size of the business, for example, a small company will have little need for a complex computer package, but could use a 'stand alone' computer or even a manual filing system;
- whether speed is important, for example, in a large organisation with many employees, a manual filing system could be very slow and cumbersome; a specially designed computer package, however, could be very efficient.

Although every business has its own special requirements, they are all faced with the same choice – to adopt a manual or computer record system. There are many advantages for a business if it introduces a computerised personnel system. These include:

- confidentiality – all personnel packages have a facility called 'password protection' this means that only people who know the password to enter the system will be able to access it. In this way sensitive personal information can be kept secure and secret;

- the high quality of the analysis which a computer can carry out – very large databases can be interrogated quickly and easily. For example, a specific question such as, 'How many people have worked in the company for more than 15 years?' can be answered almost immediately, whereas with a manual system, finding this information could be a very long and tedious task;
- the specific payroll facility included in many packages – allowing the computer to calculate all the details needed to pay employees their wages or salaries. Additionally, some are able to output a computerised pay slip. In a large company with hundreds of employees this process, which used to be done manually, can now be completed by a few staff in a fraction of the time. This in turn has resulted in considerable cost reduction.

Information supplied by Personnel

Personnel data is an essential ingredient of a business management information system. It can be used within the business, for example:

- to forecast the demand for labour (see the section on Manpower Planning in the Human Resources unit);
- to monitor and control sickness and absence;
- to improve recruitment advertising and selection.

Statutory and legal requirements

All employers have certain statutory or compulsory legal duties which they must carry out. Every business will need to organise its Personnel Department so that it is capable of administering these mandatory requirements.

Statutory Sick Pay (SSP)

Employers have to pay a minimum amount of sick pay to most employees who are aged 16 plus if they have been off sick for more than four consecutive days. This Statutory Sick Pay (SSP) is paid by the employer as normal pay. Records of SSP and sickness absence must be kept available for inspection by the Department of Social Security inspectors. The records show:

- the dates on which the employee was absent owing to sickness for four consecutive days,
- the days when SSP was not paid during this time,
- the dates of the 'qualifying days', i.e. those days when the employee was supposed to be working; for most employees these would be Monday to Friday.

Any absence of less than four consecutive days is not eligible for SSP. The first three days of sickness absence, called 'waiting days', do not qualify for SSP. SSP is only payable for the first 28 weeks that an employee is absent through sickness.

An example of how the SSP system works

Janice Danny was off sick from Monday 1 November to Sunday 7 November. The normal working week, the qualifying days, are Monday to Friday. No SSP is paid for the first three 'waiting days' Monday, Tuesday or Wednesday. SSP will only be paid for Thursday and Friday.

Activities

1 Create a check-list to provide a routine for working out the number of days SSP an employee is entitled too. The first question is done for you. Use the example given on page 150 to help you.

Has the employee been off work on sickness absence for more than four consecutive days?	
NO	YES

2 As an administrator in the personnel section of your organisation you are expected to know everything. What answers would you give to these questions?

a Can I have Jane Wilson's phone number, I need to ring her and she's off sick?

b My uncle has died and I need time off to go to the funeral. Am I entitled to compassionate leave?

£250m 'mistakes' in health payments

by LUKE BLAIR, Political Staff

A HUGE increase in errors over sick and maternity payments could involve more than £250 million.

As Social Security Secretary Peter Lilley faces an unprecedented squeeze on his budget, MPs are alarmed that "year after year" over a quarter of sick and maternity payments appear to be wrong.

An investigation by a Commons watchdog committee was told that 24,000 cases were suspected of errors two years ago.

A year later, the figure had nearly trebled to 70,000 and further checks revealed "consistent" mistakes in 25-30 per cent of payments.

With more than £1 billion claimed back by employers for statutory sick or maternity pay in 1991-92, the blunders could involve more than £250 million.

Despite the scale of the problem, the most senior civil servant in the Social Security Department has admitted it is "not cost-effective" to investigate many cases.

Sir Michael Partridge told MPs on the Public Accounts Committee that one probe had recovered only £4,500 — but cost £24,000 in staff time.

"Frankly, that is not a value for money exercise," he told the committee.

MPs were shocked that no checks had been made of the numbers entitled to claim sick pay for 19 years, while there were no details at all on the number of pregnant mothers failing to receive maternity pay to which they were entitled.

MPs have also demanded close monitoring of schemes set up to improve the situation.

Part of the problem has been employers, who are required to keep records of sick and maternity payments and submit annual returns to the Inland Revenue, so Social Security officials are trying to make the system easier to understand.

"We consider it essential that the department should be able to demonstrate adequate stewardship and clear accountability," the committee said.

Source: *Evening Standard*, 23 June 1993

3 As a group, discuss the article above. What does it tell you about administrators and administration systems?

Statutory Maternity Pay (SMP)

The employer will pay Statutory Maternity Pay (SMP) to those employees who are off work to have a baby. Only those women who have been continuously employed by the same employer for at least 26 weeks are able to receive SMP. An employee must provide the employer with a Maternity Certificate (Form MAT.B1) before any SMP can be paid.

As with SSP, the employer will need a system for administering SMP. A record will need to be kept which shows:

- the dates of absence, and
- the amount of maternity pay.

A pre-printed form (Form SMP.2) is available from the Department of Social Security which employers can use to record this information.

Activities

1 Obtain copies of both forms mentioned above and use them to write a short note which explains the employee's right to claim SMP.

2 Investigate how your organisation administers SMP. Write an article with a maximum of 200 words which explains to employees how their claims for maternity pay are dealt with.

Employment law

An important aspect of the work of the Personnel Department, is the necessity to keep abreast of changes in employment law. Although we examine this in detail in Chapters 7 and 8 we are concerned here with the administration of the employees' statutory rights.

Every employing organisation will need someone who is an expert in employment law, as personnel issues can be very sensitive. If a business makes a mistake, it could result in a lengthy and costly legal case and possible adverse publicity.

Although most statutory rights begin when an employee starts work, some of them only apply if an employee has been with the business for several years and/or works for more than 16 hours a week. For example, most employees need to have been with the same employer for two years before they can claim for unfair dismissal.

Employees' statutory rights – an 11 point check-list

Generally, employees have the statutory right:

1. For a detailed pay statement which shows how their money has been earned and what deductions the employer has made.
2. Not to be discriminated against on the grounds of race, gender or marital status.
3. To equal pay for work of equal value.
4. To at least one week's notice of dismissal if they have worked for two months.
5. To SMP.
6. To SSP.
7. To a safe and healthy workplace under the Health and Safety at Work legislation.
8. To redundancy payments if they have worked for the business for at least two years. (Redundancy means that the employee's contract of employment is terminated because the job no longer exists.)
9. To complain to an Industrial Tribunal if they think they have been unfairly dismissed after working for the same business for at least two years.
10. To the same conditions of employment if the ownership of the business changes, for example, if the business which they work for is taken over by another company.
11. To belong to a trade union (but if you worked at GCHQ, a government establishment at Cheltenham, you would not have this right).

These statutory rights are not affected even though the employee may have signed a contract of employment. This is the meaning of the words 'Your statutory rights are not affected' that are seen on many products.

Activity

If you have a job this activity is specially for you.

Using the check-list find out if you have these rights where you work.

Taxation

When employees earn more than the basic tax allowance the employer will have to deduct income tax, i.e. employees pay income tax as they earn. This is known as the Pay As You Earn (PAYE) system.

In order to comply with Inland Revenue requirements an employer will have to keep these official records for each employee:

- the amount of tax deducted from the employee;
- the total tax paid by the employee;
- the employee's and employer's National Insurance contributions;
- the amount of SSP paid to the employee;
- the amount of SMP paid to the employee.

These records can be kept on paper or on computer. Form P11, the 'deductions working sheet' is the official paper document given out by the Inland Revenue for use in a business. You will find an example of form P11 in G. Clarke and R. Lewis, *GNVQ Intermediate Business* (Stanley Thornes, 1993).

If the business uses a computerised system for calculating pay, income tax, SSP, SMP and National Insurance it will need to apply to the Department of Social Security before these software records can be used.

Communications at work

In this section we examine the communication system of the business. Figure 3.9 shows the five types of communication.

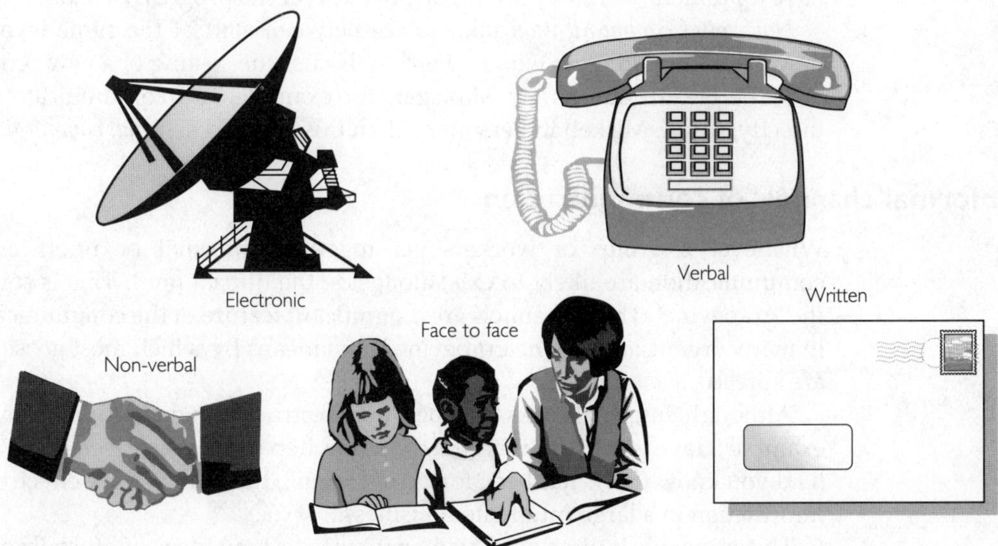

Figure 3.9 Types of communications

Every organisation will need to be able to communicate effectively with staff at all levels for it to function smoothly and efficiently. A properly structured communication system will require clear and well-defined channels of communication, which are used by everyone in the business. For example, a manager must first communicate with supervisors, then supervisors must communicate directly with operatives, and vice versa.

Formal channels of communication

Formal channels of communication are shown by the lines on an organisation chart. Look at this chart for the Expresso Vending Machine Co. Ltd:

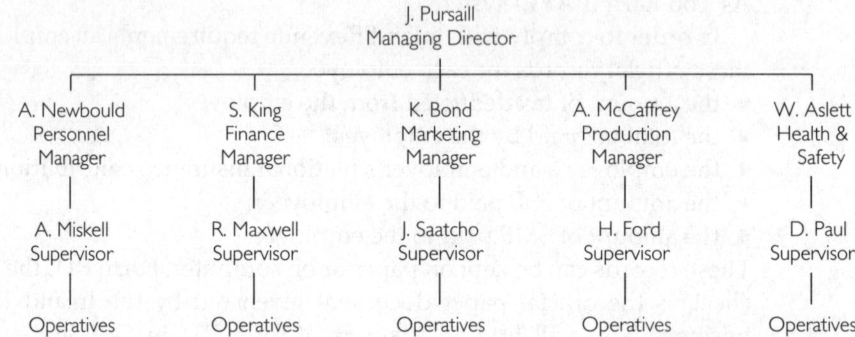

In the Expresso Co. the Managing Director communicates directly with the five managers on a daily basis. They have a formal team meeting once a week to discuss company policy. The managers have the delegated authority to run their own departments. They communicate with their staff through the supervisors, such as D. Paul. It is the supervisors who deal with the operatives. This process is called *vertical downwards communication* and usually involves managers giving oral or written instructions/orders to their subordinates.

Operatives can only communicate upwards through their supervisors, for example, production operatives will have to go through H. Ford who is the person who contacts the departmental manager. Staff in this business only go to see their supervisor if they have a problem, or if they are reporting back on the progress of a job.

Horizontal communication takes place between staff at the same level, for example R. Maxwell would meet with H. Ford to discuss the costing of a new product.

If the Health and Safety Manager, for example, can communicate with any staff directly, say A. Miskell in Personnel, then this is called *diagonal communication.*

Informal channels of communication

Whenever a group of workers get together, informal or unofficial channels of communication are likely to exist alongside the official ones. This is sometimes called the 'grapevine'. These channels are a significant feature of the communications network in many organisations. The grapevine is the means by which most gossip and rumours are spread.

Although informal links can be very destructive when rumours are untrue, for example 'Have you heard that X in the stores department has been made redundant!' or 'Did you know that Y has been forced to resign!', they can be very effective in spreading information in a large multi-sited business.

The grapevine is often used by managers to test out ideas unofficially or, for example, to find out what staff really think about the organisation.

Activity

For each relationship give three examples of business communication that might occur:

Supervisor → Manager
Manager → Supervisor
Supervisor → Supervisor
Supervisor → Operative.

Who communicates?

Everyone in a business communicates:

- workers will communicate with supervisors and each other;
- managers must communicate with their staff;
- employers will need to communicate with the workforce and with external groups;
- unions must communicate with their members;
- management must communicate with the unions.

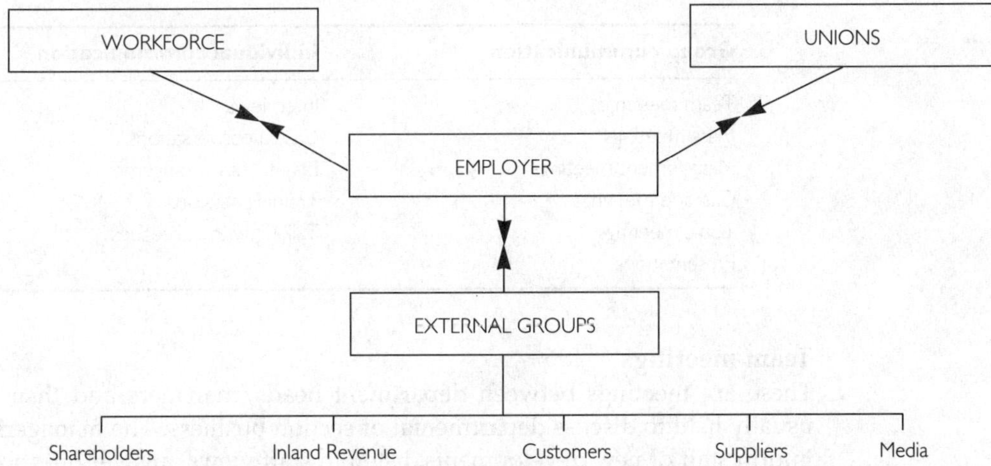

Different types of communication will be required for each group or audience. Methods which are suitable for internal users are unlikely to be appropriate for external ones. Memos, for example, are only used internally. Whatever method is chosen will depend upon:

- the size and type of workforce and its location, for example, people may be spread over several buildings or floors;
- what is being communicated, for example, complex instructions will require a different approach from a simple announcement.

Generally, a mix of methods is likely to be the most useful.

What needs to be communicated?

- Shareholders want information about the financial performance of the business.
- Employees require information about the terms and conditions of work.
- The Inland Revenue need details about employee taxation.
- Customers need product advice and information.
- Suppliers need orders.
- The media wants news about people and products.

Information needed by employees:
- Health and safety requirements of their job and workplace.
- Terms and conditions of employment, for example, hours of work, rates of pay, holiday pay, period of notice needed in order to leave the employer.
- Job description which sets out the requirements of the job.
- Disciplinary procedures.

This information is best given to employees in a company handbook when they join the company.

Face-to-face and verbal methods of communication

Face-to-face communication is the direct and immediate person-to-person contact where the communicators can see each other. It will involve both verbal and non-verbal communication. With face-to-face communication there should be opportunities for dialogue, discussion, questions and answers.

These are the main types of face-to-face communication:

Group communication	Individual communication
Team meetings	Interviews
Mass meetings	Casual conversations
Management meetings	Day-to-day arrangements
Cascade meetings	Training sessions
Topic meetings	Talking with colleagues
Presentations	

Team meetings

These are meetings between department heads/managers and their staff. They are usually held to discuss departmental or section business. The managers will be able to inform staff of new developments, listen to staff views, answer questions and provide feedback. They can be very helpful if the group is fairly small and people are willing to participate. These meetings can be formal, with a chairperson to control and direct the meeting and a secretary to write notes, or informal with no written record.

Mass meetings

When, for example, the principal of a school or college meets with all the staff, or when top management meet all the workforce, this is called a mass meeting. It may be used, to inform staff of new targets and developments. In an emergency, it could be the quickest way of contacting all staff. These meetings can be impersonal if little time has been set aside for questions and answers and can be difficult to control if they have not been properly organised.

Management meetings

The management group of most organisations will meet regularly to discuss policy, review targets and performance, decide priorities and take decisions which will affect the whole business. These meetings between managers help to establish a team spirit amongst members of the group.

Cascade meetings

These meetings often follow management meetings. The cascade principle works like this:

1 Personnel, Finance, Marketing and Production (A. Newbould, S. King etc.) Managers attend a management meeting.
2 Each manager meets their supervisors to inform them of the outcome of the meeting and what they need to do to implement the decisions.
3 Supervisors meet with operatives to tell them what they need to do.

Topic meetings

These are special meetings called to examine specific issues or topics, for example, sales targets, quality control, or wastage on the production line. Attendance will be by invitation only, i.e. not everyone will need to attend. Everyone invited should participate if these meetings are to be successful and achieve their intended objectives.

Presentations

Presentations are a popular method for communicating with sales staff. When new or updated products are introduced the Sales Manager may make a presentation to demonstrate the features of a new range by using a variety of audio visual techniques, for example, films and videos.

Making a presentation

1 Collect the information – make sure it is accurate and up-to-date.
2 Obtain the evidence – you must be able to support any arguments you make.
3 Prepare all the materials you will need, for example, notes, pictures, videos.
4 Try to think of what questions you might be asked – then find the answers.
5 Try to think of where people could disagree with you – then find the answers.
6 Make your presentation clear, interesting and simple – would you like to listen to yourself?
7 Look at your audience and do not be afraid to smile – use positive body language.
8 Use visual aids like the projector; use big writing on transparencies with few words.
9 Always be positive.
10 Be prepared for questions – they show people have listened to you.

Individual communication

Individual communication can either be totally informal, for example, talking with friends, or formal, for example, at an interview. The business will only need administrative systems for the communication which directly affects its activities, for example, recruitment and selection interviews, disciplinary and grievance hearings, appraisal interviews, and equal opportunities issues.

It is now possible to bring people together for a meeting using telecommunication, computer and satellite link-ups. This facility is called **video conferencing**.

What are the barriers to good communication?

Communication can break down because either the sender or the recipient of the information has failed to convey the meaning and/or importance of the message.

Sender breakdowns

The sender of the information could be at fault because:

- the language could be too difficult or complex;
- there could be too much information, so that the recipient misses the key points;
- the sender may be using threatening verbal or body language, for example, shouting or being aggressive, so that the recipient does not listen;
- the sender may be afraid of giving direct orders, so the recipient does not recognise what is required;
- the sender could be 'talking down' to the recipient, so the latter is unwilling to listen.

Method breakdowns

When the information is very detailed or complicated, then written instructions are better than verbal messages which can be misinterpreted.

Recipient breakdowns

The recipients of the information could be at fault because:

- they may deliberately choose to misinterpret the message because of their attitude, for example, subordinates might not want to be bothered to wear safety helmets because the weather is hot;
- they do not listen because they do not want to hear the information, for example, people do not like to hear bad news.

Activities

1 List the main advantages and disadvantages of using verbal methods of communication.
2 Say briefly which is the most suitable method of communication, giving your reasons, in each of the following situations:
  - a Explaining how a new machine operates.
  - b Telling employees about the new sales targets.
  - c Giving the results of last week's record output.
  - d Telling staff the names of the new people who have joined the organisation.
  - e Keeping a permanent record of an interview.
  - f Proposing a new method of working.

Special needs in communication

A significant number of people either cannot see or cannot hear, whilst an even larger number have visual or hearing difficulties. Perhaps you are one of these people or perhaps you have a friend who is visually or hearing impaired. If this were written in Braille your fingers would be interpreting a series of raised dots on this line. (Get a friend to write backwards very heavily with a ball point pen. Now turn over the page and try using your fingers to find out what the message is.) Do you find that you need extra light to read? Does this help? Is this worse?

Activity

How well do organisations cater for people with special needs?

1 Carry out a survey of your organisation to find out how well it caters for people with seeing or hearing difficulties. You should examine:
   - the signs
   - the leaflets and publicity materials
   - whether audio and/or visual warnings are given in an emergency

- whether facilities exist for people with visual or hearing difficulties (e.g. computers with voice recognition or touch screens, audio loop system); you should list what these are.

2 In your home, examine the size of the print on packets and tins.
3 In the street, examine how people with special needs are helped to cross the road or catch a particular bus.

In each case rate each feature out of 10; give 10 points for excellent and 0 for very poor. When you have finished your survey write or tape a short report indicating any problems and giving suggestions for improvements. You could contact the Royal National Institute for the Blind and the Royal National Institute For the Deaf, which are both in London, to find out what special equipment exists.

Non-verbal communication

More commonly known as body language, non-verbal communication (NVC) refers to the way people communicate without the use of words.

Good communicators know:

- how to use body language to project themselves;
- how to interpret the NVC signals given out by others.

Body language can either be used consciously, for example, people deliberately shrug their shoulders, car drivers give V signs, football players often fake injury; or unconsciously, for example, people twist their hair or fiddle with their ears.

Learning body language is the same as learning any language, it will enable you to understand and communicate much more easily with people.

Types of body language

Eye contact Do you look at people directly? Do you look away when talking to your friends, work colleagues, junior staff or senior staff? How do these people look at you? There are many reasons why people do not look at each other, for example:

- they may be shy or insecure,
- they may be telling lies, for example, 'Sorry I'm late for work, but the bus broke down.'

Body contact Do you shake hands when you meet people? Do you greet people with a kiss on each cheek? Is your handshake wet and limp, which indicates a lack of interest in the meeting, or firm and positive? Do you touch people when you are talking? These are all examples of body contact.

Facial movements When we smile, we use 15 facial muscles. The human face can change its expression more than any other creature. We can show anger, pleasure, grief, happiness, sadness, disappointment, love or compassion. How do we use these expressions?

Between friends

Smile	Smile
Sadness	Shared sadness
Disappointment	Sympathy

At work

Senior	Junior
Sees disappointment so may deliberately make things worse or try to lessen the blow	Shows disappointment but would do better to try to show no emotion

Activity

The group should divide into pairs. Person A, without using any words, should try to show these emotions – hatred, anger, fear, hope, love, joy, pleasure, disappointment. Person B must try and guess what emotion is being shown.

Persons A and B should then swop roles.

Head movements

Nodding the head usually indicates that a person agrees or says 'Yes'; shaking the head usually means 'No, I do not agree'. Do these movements mean the same in every country?

Gestures

These are movements of the head, hands or body which are made to express or emphasise an idea. For example, people:

- point their fingers when arguing,
- shake their fists when annoyed,
- shrug to say 'I don't know/care'.

Activity

The board meeting

Chair: Enters looking angry.
'Good morning. I have a very pleasant (shakes fist, looks annoyed) announcement to make. We have an extra £0.5 million available'.

Managers: Look annoyed, disgusted, upset.

Manager 1: Seething with anger.
'I'm delighted. (Points finger at others.) This is just what we wanted to introduce the new product.'

Manager 2: Looks appalled and shakes head.
'This is excellent news. We'll run the new advertising campaign immediately.' (Clenches fist, grits teeth.)

Manager 3: Shows no emotion or reaction. Keeps voice very quiet and flat, sounds bored.
'This is fantastic, the best news I've heard for a long time. (Sighs and yawns.) 'We can begin the new R and D programme tomorrow.' (Sighs again and drops shoulders.)

Manager 4: Looks down at the table and never raises eyes. Appears shy and retiring.
'Utterly brilliant. This means two more staff. I'll get on to it now.' Looks dissatisfied and unable to do anything.

Manager 5: Smiles and looks happy and delighted.
'I'm appalled. We cannot afford this. (Nods head.) In finance we have been against this decision.' Looks around smiling at everyone.

Six people should act out this scene whilst other colleagues act as observers. Actors and observers should then reverse roles.

a Was the activity confusing?
b Was it difficult to combine contradictory signals, i.e. speech and body language?
c Which is more important – speech or body language?

Dress

The way people dress is an important signal about how they feel and behave. Their clothes are an extension of their personality. The confident person will wear bold and striking colours and patterns. The shy personality will tend towards muted, neutral shades. By the same token, people judge us by how we are dressed. If you want to be taken seriously in business you will wear a suit. Our appearance gives other people that important first impression.

Posture

The way people stand or sit, give out different signals. For example, if someone sits forward in a chair, it generally means they are interested in the conversation. If they lean back and fiddle with their hands, this can be interpreted as 'I'm bored'.

Someone who stands up straight is assumed to be honest and positive, whereas a person who slouches and leans forward is thought to be the opposite. If a person stands close to you when talking, the impression is one of sincerity.

Activities

1 Look at the five pictures (Figure 3.10). Can you say what body language is being used? What emotions are each person showing? What might they be doing? What jobs might these people have? Give reasons for your answers and discuss these with the rest of your group.

Figure 3.10 What body language is being used?

2 Now look at the two pictures of the groups (Figure 3.11) and repeat the first activity.

Figure 3.11 What non-verbal communication is being used here?

Case study

Written communication

IDENTIKIT PLC

The case study materials consist of:

- a letter
- a **fax** transmission
- an internal **memo**
- the consultant's **report** with these headings:
  Terms of Reference
  Procedure
  Findings
  Conclusions
  Recommendations.

Study the materials.

1 The letter
Why has this method of communication been chosen?
What style and tone has been used, for example, friendly, formal, informal?
Why has this approach been used?

THE LETTER

People World Wide

30 May 199-

Mr Kit Identi
Managing Director
IDENTIKIT PLC
Cloth Hall
Lincoln

Dear Mr Identi

Personnel Policy

I am now able to confirm that I will be able to come on Wednesday 3 June. I am enclosing the first draft of my report for you and your colleagues to look at prior to my visit. You will see that I have made a number of suggestions about the way in which IDENTIKIT could advertise new posts. These will involve the company spending more money but I know you want the best people and they do not come cheap.

Yours sincerely

Kathy Martins
Personnel Consultant

Personna House • Covingham • Phone 0189 33245 • Fax 0189 33246

The letter shown here has all the key features:

- Company name
- Date
- Name and address of the recipient
- Name and address of the sender
- Position of the recipient (Managing Director)
- Position of the sender (Personnel Consultant)
- Telephone number of the sender
- Salutation: here it is 'Dear Mr'
- Complimentary close: here it is 'Yours sincerely'.

Ms Martins has already met Mr Identi so the style and tone of this letter is different from that which would be written as a letter of introduction. This would be more formal and less familiar. Different salutations and closes, for example, 'Yours faithfully', would be used.

Key features of a formal letter

The letter could be the only contact that a person has with a business. It should, therefore, be seen as an integral part of the promotional strategy of the company.

2 The fax
Why has a fax been used?
What style has been used?

3 The internal memo
Why has this method been chosen?
What style and tone have been used? Remember it is from the Managing Director.
Why has this approach been used?

4 The report – this is an example of one type of report.
What style has been used?
Why is the numbering so precise?
What is Ms Martins saying to IDENTIKIT PLC?
Why do you think a consultant was brought in?

5 What other communication might have taken place? When might this have happened?

THE FAX

FAX TRANSMISSION

From:	Kathy Martins	Personnel Consultant
Questions?	Call 018933245	People World Wide
	Fax 018933246	Personna House, Covingham
To:	Kit Identi	Managing Director
Company:	Identikit PLC	Tel: 01463 565656/Fax: 565655
Address:	Cloth Hall	Lincoln
Date:	2 June 199-	
Time:	21:53	Pages: 1 (including this one)

I confirm that I will be able to attend the meeting on Wednesday 3 June.

If there are any problems please contact me.

Key features of a fax

All the essential parts of a fax are shown here, namely:

- Two telephone numbers
- Two fax numbers
- Two addresses
- Date and time
- The number of pages (in case some are not received)
- Name and position of who is to receive the fax
- Name and position of the sender of the fax
- Company names.

THE MEMO

IDENTIKIT
Memo

To: All Senior Managers
From: Kit Identi
Re: Recruitment Advertising

Date: 4 May 199-

I have arranged for Kathy Martins the Personnel Consultant to visit us sometime in the next two weeks. Probably on the 7 May.

These are the Terms of Reference Ms Martins will be working to:
- To examine the present system of recruitment of senior managers.
- To suggest changes to the system.

Please give her your full co-operation, I know you will!

Ms Martins will be sending around a questionnaire, complete it as quickly as you can. She wants to interview Ben and Sylvana 'in depth'!!! These are Ms Martins' words. I will ask her to report as quickly as possible.

Key features of a memo

- TO... This can be a named person or it can show the position of the person, for example, Principal, Marketing Director, etc.
- FROM... Again this can be a named person as in this example, or it can show the position the person holds.

  The form of address used depends on the status of the sender and recipient and the nature of the contents, for instance, whether it is formal or informal. Sometimes the mood or attitude of the sender will influence the tone and style of a memo, for example, the sender may want to demonstrate authority. The formal approach is frequently used when the recipient has done something wrong.
- DATE... Always include the date; remember this is a written record and memos are often used to confirm or deny an event or action has occurred.
- RE ... or reference. This should briefly show the subject matter of the memo.
- CONTENT, STYLE and TONE ... Most organisations will have a particular 'house style' which will be used in all their correspondence. This is intended to create and/or enhance their image. Normally, memos should be kept brief and to the point. Memos are normally only used within a company; they are an internal method of communication.

THE FORMAL REPORT

To: Kit Identi, Managing Director
From: K. Martins

Report on recruitment policy at Identikit PLC

1.0 Terms of Reference

This section should show the limits of the report and the precise areas which it should cover, for example:
Following the meeting held on the 7 May these Terms of Reference were agreed:

1.1 To examine the present system of recruitment of senior managers.

1.2 To suggest changes to the system.

2.0 Procedure

This section should show how the information was collected, for example:

2.1 A survey was conducted of all job adverts which had been placed in the last two years, and who was subsequently recruited.

2.2 A questionnaire was given to all senior managers, to find out their opinions on the present recruitment system. This had 20 open-ended questions which gave an opportunity for everyone to make a contribution.

2.3 The Personnel Manager and Deputy Manager were interviewed in depth, as a follow-up to the questionnaire.

3.0 Findings

This section should give the main findings of the report as a series of numbered headings, for example:

3.1 Survey of Advertisements

Advertisements had only been placed in the two local evening newspapers 'The Star' and 'The Echo'; these had produced only a small response.

3.1.1 Advertisements 1991-1992

Only 20% of these advertisements had produced a successful response.

3.1.2 Advertisements 1992-1993

These were marginally more successful with a response rate of 25%.

3.2 Questionnaire Results

All questionnaires were returned, fully completed. The general feeling was that in order to attract more candidates it was necessary to advertise more widely.

3.2.1 National Newspaper Advertising

All managers felt that it was necessary to advertise in the national press, particularly when there was a special feature on the clothing industry. There was no agreement on what newspapers should be used.

3.2.2 Magazine Advertising

All managers suggested that the company should advertise in the trade magazine 'COVER UP', which is published every two weeks.

3.3 Interviews
The two interviews with the Personnel Managers confirmed the general findings.

4.0 Conclusions
This section should sum up the major findings of the report, for example:
Because vacancies have only been advertised locally, Identikit PLC have only been able to attract a small number of applicants for any post. Most of the people who applied appeared to be well-intentioned but unsuitable.

5.0 Recommendations
This section should contain the main and subsidiary recommendations which can be made as a result of the investigation which has been carried out, for example:
5.1 Identikit PLC should advertise its senior management posts in national newspapers.
5.2 Identikit PLC should advertise in the trade publication 'COVER UP'.
5.3 Identikit PLC should set aside a budget to cover the increased cost this policy will incur.
5.4 Identikit PLC must ensure that a standard format is used for all its advertisements.

Activities

1 Earlier today you met briefly with the Deputy Manager – Marketing in the corridor, 'a corridor meeting'. You think you agreed to produce the figures for the last two years on the company's exports to Cyprus in five (or was it nine?) working days. Write the memo confirming what you think was agreed.

2 You receive this memo from your section head. However, you do not think you agreed to attend the meeting, and in fact cannot attend at the time. Write a memo in reply.

MEMO

To: GNVQ student Date: Today's date
From: A. Driver
Subject: Meeting with new Trainees

Thank you for agreeing to attend the meeting with new trainees on the 23rd. Your session provisionally called 'How to claim sick pay' will be at 11 a.m. in the staff rest room.

I know that you will be a great success, I am relying on you to be there.

Many thanks
AD

INFORMING EMPLOYEES

YOUR EMPLOYEE HANDBOOK: WHAT'S IN IT FOR YOU

It tells you how the business is run.
What rules and regulations we have.
What the arrangements are for:
holidays, pay, pensions, etc.
How to complain if you have a problem with
racial or sexual harassment.
What the disciplinary and grievance procedures are.

KEEP IN TOUCH

Welcome to the first edition of our newsletter 'Informing Employees'

METHODS

Newsletters and house journals
such as those produced by BP, Sainsbury's and Grand Metropolitan usually appear regularly with information and news about the organisation and more chatty personal, social and sporty items. There could be a 'Who is Who' section, or even an interview with one of the managers. Maybe a crossword. The purpose of the newsletter is to tell employees what is going on in their organisation before they find out from somewhere else.

Notices
These can be useful if they are well-designed and eye-catching. But make sure you use the correct noticeboard. If there are too many notices on the same board none of them get read!

Bulletins
These are used for giving news or information within the business. They need to be restricted to really important events because if they appear too often they will not be read. They must be kept short.

Keeping employees informed: open channels of communication

Written communication between management and employees

We have already seen how meetings can be used to inform workers. There are occasions, however, when the written word can be more effective, for instance when a permanent record is required or detailed technical information has to be communicated. With the widespread use of word processing and desk-top publishing software packages many schools, colleges, companies and charities now produce their own **newsletters** and **journals.** With open channels of communication, there is no restriction on who sees or receives information. A restricted channel of communication refers to situations where particular information goes only to specified named people, 'for your eyes only'. This ensures that information is kept secure and confidential.

Activities

1 On your own, prepare one item for your organisation newsletter.
2 With your group, produce a newsletter for your organisation. This must be word processed and include graphics.

STAFF MEETING

Purpose: To discuss the ***Christmas Party***
Place: Staff Dining Room
When: 3 October 199–
Time: 5.30 p.m.

Notices are intended to inform, instruct, persuade, entertain or warn. They should be clear, direct, and simple and contain all the essential information. People are very quick to put up notices but very reluctant to take them down. This notice should be taken down on 4 October.

Activity

'Know what I mean, Harry?'
Copy and complete the chart showing the effectiveness of various types of communication method.

Effectiveness criteria	Letter	Fax	E-mail	Telephone	Personal meeting
Ease of use					
Ease of access					
Cost					
Speed					
Security					
Permanent record					
Personal interaction					
Impact on users					
Interaction between organisations					
Whether formal or informal					

The sales campaign: communicating with the customer

The purpose of a sales campaign is to expand the sales of the product. Most campaigns will use a mix of advertising and promotional methods to get the intended message across to the customers. There are two basic types of campaign:

- the hard sell, which uses a direct, positive, aggressive, insistent approach to advertising, for example: Buy Bland X, Buy Bland X, Buy Bland X;
- the soft sell approach, which uses indirect suggestion and inducements; this can be more informative, factual and less emotional.

Whatever the approach, all the materials produced, such as brochures, leaflets, advertisements and flyers, must be clear, direct and simple. They should all have the same style so that customers immediately recognise the product. Look at the GNVQ logo on the front cover of this book. It is used by the publishers for all its GNVQ titles. The size, style of font and spacing are all important. Which do you prefer: HELVETICA, Courier or Times New Roman? Do you like the text tight or loose ?

Activity

Look at the promotional materials produced by your centre. What type of approach is used? Are the materials (for example letterheads, departmental/centre leaflets, adverts, invitations to meetings, compliment slips) consistent in style? Do they look professional? Do they communicate the message clearly? How do they compare with the competition? Are they honest and truthful?

Can you do better? Produce your own one-page advertisement for this course.

The suitability of administration systems

Now that we have looked at the way in which business administration and communication systems work we need to examine how effective and efficient they are.

The efficiency of the administration system can be improved if the office environment in which people work is carefully designed to achieve the maximum output at the lowest cost. Many questions need to be considered, for example, with regard to office layout:

- Is the lighting adequate?
- Is the heating level satisfactory?
- Is ventilation satisfactory?
- Is there excessive noise?
- Are the work surfaces at the correct height?
- Is there enough room for people to work?
- Is the work arrangement suitable?
- Can the work flow properly?

Each of these factors will affect the way people work. The problems arise because different people have different needs. People with weak eyesight for example usually require more light than those with almost perfect vision. People with asthma need a different level of humidity. The design and layout of the office must be flexible enough to give people the conditions they need to be able to work at the optimum or best level of efficiency.

Activity

On your own, study the article *Desks out the door* (Figure 3.12).

a Do you think that this is an appropriate solution to the problem?
b What is meant by 'environmental control'?
c How do you think the staff in the new office will feel?
d Would you like to work here?
e Would this arrangement work in your organisation?
f Would this arrangement work in all offices ?

In your group, compare your views/answers with those of your colleagues. Why are there differences?

DESKS OUT THE DOOR

A new concept for workplaces could revolutionise our daily lives

Jane Bird writes

Later this year 750 staff of the customer services division of a computer company will move into smart refurbished headquarters in Basingstoke, Hampshire.

They will occupy a space that housed 500 people before it was burnt down in March last year. But the 50 per cent increase in capacity does not mean more desks crammed together. In fact, the new building is more spacious.

The gains have been made by abolishing the idea that everyone has a desk. Nigel Dowler, the intelligent building services marketing manager for Digital Equipment, says: "The previous building was half-occupied most of the time because the majority of staff spent a lot of time away from the office visiting customers."

Instead of personal desks, the £30 million showpiece office comprises working modules for different types of activity. Staff book the modules for the days they work. They might choose a compact workstation checking electronic mail, or an area with desk space for writing reports, while conference rooms can be reserved for meetings. The building is being wired with a computer network to monitor who is at a particular desk so that telephone calls can be correctly routed. "A single network will handle data, voice, security, access, heating, ventilation and air-conditioning – processes traditionally managed separately, each with its own control system," Mr Dowler says.

Every desk will have a computer point into which equipment from different suppliers can be linked. Space sharing is the key feature of the office of the future, says Mr Dowler, who has just launched the company's consultancy service, which advises on building design.

Environmental control is also essential. The spread of desktop PC's and terminals, especially those with colour screens, requires buildings to have better ventilation.

"In the old days, computers were hidden in air-conditioned rooms in the bowels of a building. But now vastly more heat-dissipating units are being spread around offices and entire buildings have to be environmentally controlled," Mr Dowler says.

Increased mobility is another feature of the modern workforce. Radio telephones are beginning to offer services such as telepoint, which enable staff to carry cordless handsets. But how will staff feel about no longer having their own desks?

Mr Dowler believes they will accept the change if their company involves them in the analysis of how much time they need to spend in the office.

To encourage acceptance of the new office, Digital Equipment has installed leisure areas, comfortable chairs, and showers for lunchtime joggers.

"The current collapse in the commercial property market presents a great opportunity for companies to acquire premises for bargain prices and fit them up for long-term use," Mr Dowler says.

Source: *The Times*, 30 May 1991

Figure 3.12

Document design

Documents or forms provide a permanent visual written record of the activities of the business. Many documents such as student registers and those used for accounting purposes, must be kept by law. Although they are a major means of communication and information they can also be used to monitor and control activities and provide a check against possible mistakes. Good clear documents are essential if a business is to succeed in achieving its objectives. Documents must be well-designed and clearly laid out, they must be easily understood and user-friendly, and when necessary available in several languages. Each section of the document should follow a logical sequence.

Activity

Below is the first draft of an order form by the partners of Pot Pourri, the new business in Chapter 15. You have been asked to design it.
What information has been omitted? (You will find an example of a well-designed order form in G. Clarke and R. Lewis, *GNVQ Intermediate Business* (Stanley Thornes, 1993).)
If you prefer, you can design an order form for your business as part of your business plan.

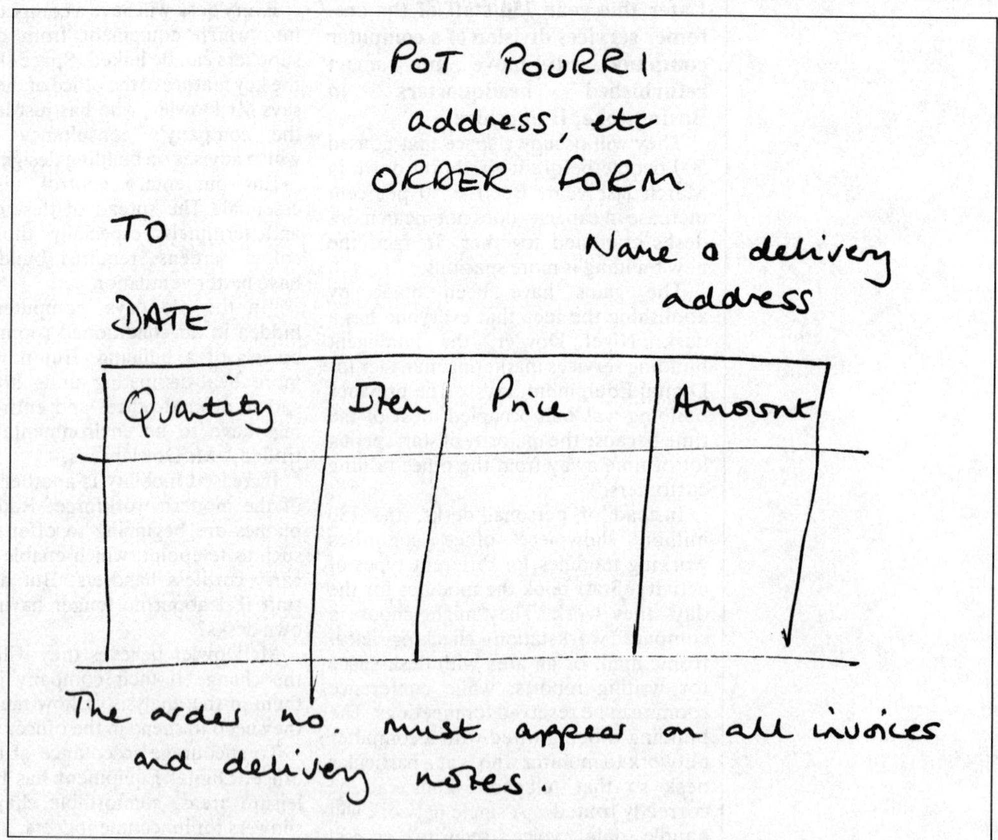

POT POURRI
address, etc
ORDER FORM

TO

Name & delivery address

DATE

Quantity	Item	Price	Amount

The order no. must appear on all invoices and delivery notes.

Document procedures

Documents are an essential part of the administration process and are the main way in which the business keeps track of raw materials, stock, finished goods and people! We can see this in action if we examine the following:

A day in the life of a student application form

Step 1 Potential student fills in form.
Step 2 The form is sent to the institution.
Step 3 The form is received by the institution and the key details such as name, address, telephone number, are either recorded manually in a 'logging in' book or put onto computer. A reference number will be added to make the person/form easier to track.
Step 4 The form is sent to the tutor of the course which the person applied for.
Step 5 The tutor records the details and notes the reference number.
Step 6 An acknowledgement is sent and the person will later be called for interview.

Although it is useful to set out document flows in this way, there are techniques which are more formal and precise. These can be used to work out the most efficient method for completing a particular activity. Once this has been established it will become a 'standard method of working'. Many organisations have rule books which contain these standard methods; these are used for training new employees.

Method charts

Method charts are a visual means of describing a particular activity. These are the standard symbols which are used:

Operation – any task such as form filling, entering data

Delay – for example, a person might go to a filing cabinet to retrieve a form

Movement for example, a document could be passed from one person/department to another

Stored – for example, documents could be filed

Checking – for example, checking totals, finding tax codes for an employee

Using these symbols we can be more precise about the activities:

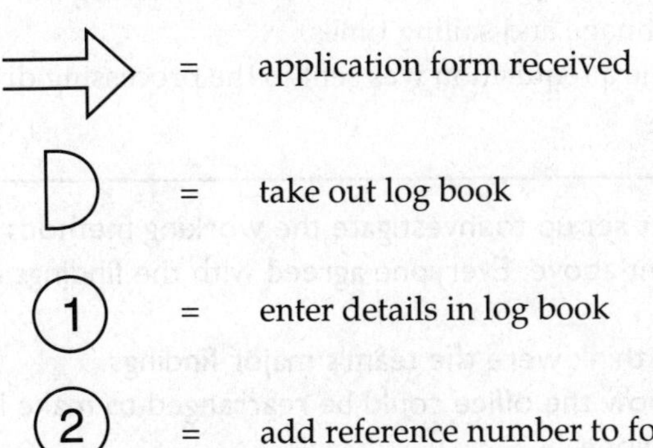

□	=	check all details are accurate
D	=	collect acknowledgement letters from cabinet
③	=	complete letter adding reference number
▽	=	store log book in cabinet
⇨	=	send form to tutor
④	=	start on next form

Activities

1 Look carefully at the sequence of activities. Can you suggest any improvements? Pay special attention to the D symbols. When should the form be sent to the tutor?

2 Examine the sequence of activities for any operation with which you are familiar, for example, at work or at home (making a slice of toast). Set out the activities using the symbols and suggest some improvements.

3 Set out the activities involved in 'A day in the life of a student application form' (page 173) for your particular school/college.

String or network diagrams

A string diagram shows all the movements made by people at their workplace. At one time the author worked in the export department of a large shipping company. A work study was carried out to examine the flow of work within the office. Figure 3.13 (opposite) is a plan of the office showing the movements of people and documents.

This is some of the work that was done in the department:

1 Export order forms were collected from the current orders outstanding area.
2 Orders were checked against available stock.
3 If stock was available, the form went to the next stage – finding out which ships were available (including tonnage and sailing times).
4 If no stock was available a requisition was sent to the processing division.

Activity

A method study team was set up to investigate the working methods and processes of the shipping department above. Everyone agreed with the findings of the method study team.

a Write down what you think were the team's major findings.

b Draw a plan showing how the office could be rearranged to make life easier and more efficient for everyone.

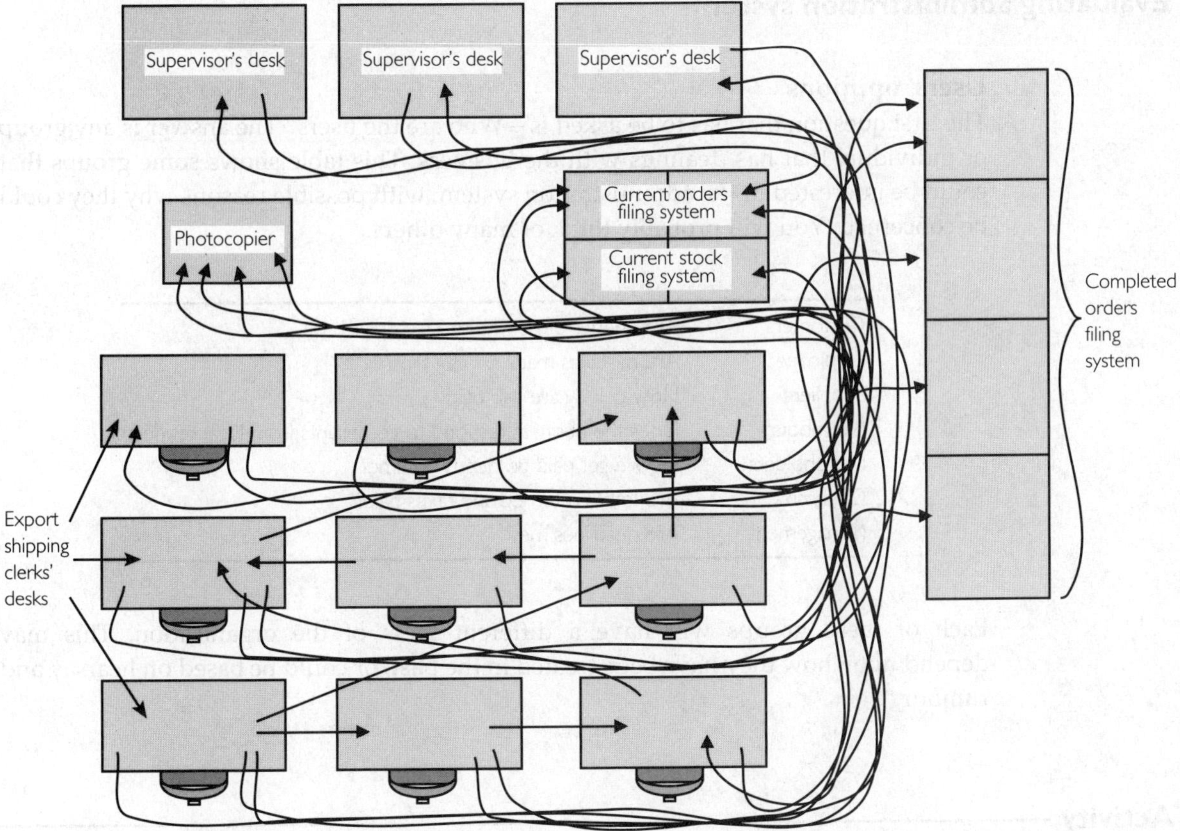

Figure 3.13 String diagram showing movements in an export shipping department

Parkinson's Laws and the Peter Principle

C. Northcote Parkinson is famous for Parkinson's Laws which were published in 1958. These are:

1 **Work expands to fill the time available**
Parkinson said that there was no relationship between the number of administration staff and the amount of work that they did, i.e. a large administration staff will always find work to do regardless of the size of the business. Have you ever been to meetings which lasted three hours, when the work could have been completed in an hour?

2 **Expenditure rises to meet income**
Businesses, and indeed individuals, will always find ways of spending their money!

3 **The time spent on an agenda item will be in inverse proportion to the amount of money involved**
This is because high-spending projects tend to be very complex, and most people who attend meetings do not have the knowledge to challenge the proposal. Have you ever been to meetings where most of the time seems to be spent on the petty items?

L. J. Peter is best known as the originator of the Peter Principle which states:
In a hierarchy every employee tends to rise to the level of his incompetence.
This means that in organisations where there are many levels of management people get promoted until they eventually occupy jobs at which they are no good. (What does this tell you about the way managers are appointed in large businesses?)

Evaluating administration systems

Users' opinions

The first question that has to be asked is – Who are the users? The answer is any group or individual that has dealings with the business. This table shows some groups that could be interested in the administration system, with possible reasons why they could be concerned. You will probably think of many others.

Customers	Are queries dealt with satisfactorily?
Employees	Are mistakes made on pay slips?
Suppliers	How quickly are bills paid?
Neighbours	Does the business respond to complaints from local residents?
Shareholders	Do we get paid dividends on time?
Government	Are forms returned and taxes paid?
Management	Are deadlines met?

Each of these groups will have a different view of the organisation. This may depend upon how they have been treated in the past, or could be based on hearsay and rumour.

Activity

Your group should work in teams of four or five people to survey people's opinions of the administration system of an organisation with which you are familiar. If you work in the administration section of your business join a group from another department/business and try to be objective! You will find it easier if you prepare a set of questions in advance – in a matrix with space to write people's responses, for example.
This activity requires great tact. Take care when you present your results.

Work study

Work study is the process of examining tasks and activities performed at the workplace with the purpose of increasing efficiency and productivity.

Although originally only used for factory-type activities it is now applied to a wide range of manual and non-manual work. For example, it can be used to examine and make improvements in the way:

- an office is organised
- administration is carried out
- goods are handled and transported
- labour is organised and scheduled
- materials are selected and used
- goods are displayed and shelves are stocked
- supermarket check-out points are arranged and operated

In order to make improvements to any system it is first necessary to investigate how the work is done at present. Once this process is complete proposals for change can be made.

These are the steps required before a recommendation can be made:

Step 1 Select a job. Two criteria are used to do this, the amount of benefit that can be expected and the cost involved.

Step 2 Observe and record the activity using flow charts or string diagrams to show the movement of people and/or materials. Observation can take days or even weeks because it has to be accurate and complete.

Step 3 Examine and analyse. Once the observation has been completed it needs to be analysed so that an alternative can be found which improves on the existing method. Here are some examples of possible improvements: there is less waste, fewer hold-ups, less stress or absenteeism, shelves are continually stocked, queues are shorter.

Step 4 Implementation. This can be the most difficult part of a work study. Full consultation will need to take place if any changes which are made are going to be successfully implemented.

Work study has sometimes been called time and motion study, however this term has gone out of fashion.

Managing change

Successful organisations are always changing in response to outside pressures in the market place. In order to cope with these changes the business will need to have an effective administration and communication system. A good indicator of the success of the business is the extent to which it can implement change without disrupting its normal operations or aggravating its workforce.

There are many reasons why organisations may need to change. Market demand could rise or fall necessitating a change in production methods. Changes in the labour market, for example, a shortage of skilled labour, may mean that production will need to become more automated. The Single European Market will affect the way in which many businesses will operate, for example, new materials may have to be used, or new products developed. Perhaps the most significant change which has occurred in the last ten years has been the increasing use made of information processing in all parts of the business. This has affected every aspect of the business such as the number of people needed to do clerical jobs, the way the job is carried out, the way information is recorded and stored, etc.

Activity

As a group brainstorm the way information processing has affected business. Prioritise your final list and say why you have made these decisions.

Before any change is made many people will have to be consulted. Figure 3.14 gives an extract from an Advisory Conciliation and Arbitration Service (ACAS) publication.

Management of change

What is meant by the management of change?
Management of change is the careful consideration, during the planning stage, of all the factors involved in or affected by the proposed change. It also involves taking all the steps necessary to ensure smooth implementation. However, despite planning, the implementation of change may be adversely affected by events external to the organisation which it could not have foreseen or over which it had no control.

What factors must be taken into account?
The following factors should be examined in an integrated way, taking care that action in one area does not have an adverse effect elsewhere:

- strategic factors: is the change in line with the organisation's overall strategic plan?
- financial factors: is the change financially sound and in line with the business circumstances of the organisation?
- organisational factors: does the change require alterations in, for example structure, culture, pay and grading, recruitment selection, training or communications?
- industrial relations factors: does the change have the support of recognised trade unions?
- work structure and job design factors: how can the jobs affected directly or indirectly by the change be best designed to ensure that there is no loss of job satisfaction?
- human factors: does the organisation have the commitment of senior managers and all other employees affected and do employees have the necessary skills and competencies required by the change?

What other steps are necessary for successful change?

- appoint someone with accepted status and influence to be responsible for the change
- try to create a climate of openness and trust

Source: *The ACAS Employment Handbook*

Figure 3.14 Advice from ACAS

In Chapter 4 we look in detail at the way information technology has revolutionised the way that businesses operate.

Review questions

1. What business objectives would be most suitable for a local hairdresser?
2. When should written instructions be used?
3. List the advantages and disadvantages of sole traders, partnerships and limited companies.
4. Would a business use a mass meeting to communicate information?
5. What statutory payments have to be made to employees?
6. List the advantages and disadvantages of flat and matrix organisations.
7. What criteria would you use to assess the efficiency of an administration system?
8. How could a salesperson benefit from using body language?
9. How might a breakdown in communication occur?

10 How could a breakdown in communication be solved?

11 Explain the importance of sales administration.

12 Lesley has just set up a small word processing business. What administration is needed?

13 You are about to go on holiday for two weeks. What administrative arrangements would you make?

14 Taibach Engineering is undecided about whether to have a centralised or decentralised purchasing policy. What would you advise?

15 What conditions are necessary for delegation to work successfully?

16 When might a manager have a face-to-face meeting with an employee?

17 Chris, who runs a mobile disco, asks your advice on whether to have a computerised accounts package to keep the accounts. What would your advice be?

18 What administration links exist between Purchasing, Production, Storage and Sales?

Key terms

Business objectives
Production
Stock
Sales
Market share
Profits
Growth
Survival
Service
Liability
Delegation
Purpose of administration
Administration systems
Sales documents
Orders
Centralised
Decentralised
Transport
Production
Services
Franchise
Catering
Co-operative
Personnel
Verbal communication
Non-verbal communication
Meetings
Written communication
Sole traders
Partnership
Private company
Public company
Flat organisation
Hierarchical organisation
Matrix organisation
Public ownership
Body language
Method charts
String diagrams
Work study
Open communication
Restricted communication
Statutory rights
Employee rights
Formal communication
Informal communication
Channels of communication

Assignment 3
The quality organisation

This assignment develops knowledge and understanding of the following elements

2.1 Investigate business organisations
2.2 Investigate administration systems

It supports development of the following core skills:
Communication 3.1, 3.2, 3.3, 3.4
Application of number 3.1
Information technology 3.1, 3.2, 3.3, 3.4

For this assignment the members of the group should initially work individually. You should each choose two businesses, one of which should be a plc (preferably one you are familiar with, such as a high street store).

Your tasks

1 Obtain the company report for your chosen plc. You could do this by writing to the company secretary or public relations department.
2 Describe the ownership of the two businesses. What effect do the owners have on each company?
3 Identify the aims and purpose of each business. For the plc, you will find these in the company report. For other types of business, you may have to ask the owners.
4 Draw an organisation chart for each business. Why do they differ? What are the advantages and disadvantages of each? Identify the key people managing the major sections.
5 Work with two or three colleagues and compare and contrast the businesses you have each chosen. (It helps if the businesses are in the same sector, for example, hotels, food stores etc.)

Note: You could adopt one of these businesses as we suggested in the Introduction. For example, you could also look at its marketing policy, the supply and demand for the products, its human resources policy and its balance sheet.

6 Your organisation has made the decision to produce a quality manual. This is a very big and complex task which can take an enormous amount of time and effort. Your group has been chosen to help write the background information which will form part of the final 'Quality Manual'.

The basic purpose of the documentation is to demonstrate that the organisation has quality procedures for dealing with its customers.

Produce a procedure manual which either:

- details the processes involved for students to obtain and be informed of their examination results, or
- details the procedures used by the business to deal with customer complaints.

The manual should show:

a The main stages of the process.
b The forms and documents which are used at each stage.
c The records which are kept, how they are used, and whether they are manual or computer based.
d The various checks which are made to ensure that each stage has been carried out, for example, acknowledgement slips or a person's initials.
e What things can go wrong and how they are dealt with.

f Which staff are involved at each stage and who is responsible for the process.

The manual should be consistent in style and format with other similar documents and manuals that could be used by the organisation. Remember it is a document which itemises procedures, so it has to be clear and accurate. It should make cross-references to other procedures and systems used within the organisation, for example, student registers, student application forms, and examination entry forms.

Put in an appendix to the manual which shows:

a The type of business (for example, plc)
b The structure of the process
c Strengths and weaknesses of the present structure
d User's opinions of the system.

If you think the system could be improved you will have to decide how this can be done.

4 Communications and electronic information processing systems

What is covered in this chapter

- Communications systems – the telecommunications link
- Types of communication using new technology:
  - Telephone
  - Fax
  - WANs
  - LANs
- Security and networks
- Electronic information processing systems
  - The purpose of information processing
  - Types of computer
  - Hardware and software
  - The computer system – the hardware
  - The computer programmes – the software
- The effects of using IT
  - The Data Protection Act

These are the resources that you will need for your Business Organisations and Systems file:

- up-to-date computer magazines
- summary of the Data Protection Act
- relevant newspaper articles
- access to a personal computer.

'Information provision is a multi-faceted activity driven by very heavy demands. Increasing competition drives the need to make better and faster business decisions'.

Mike Fisher, Information Services Director, Bass Brewers

In Chapter 3 we looked at the various forms of business communication. In this chapter we will concentrate on the technology that enables businesses to communicate more quickly and effectively.

Communications systems – the telecommunications link

In the past the telephone and postal services were the usual means of communications. Now that micro-computers are part of the office environment computers can send messages to one another. The receiving computer may be in another building, in another town or even in another country. The main transmission media for messages by fax, telephone or computer are the same. They are:

- cables, which may be copper wire or fibre optic
- microwaves, sent by repeater stations or satellite.

Together these media form the telecommunications link. A single message may use a variety of these media.

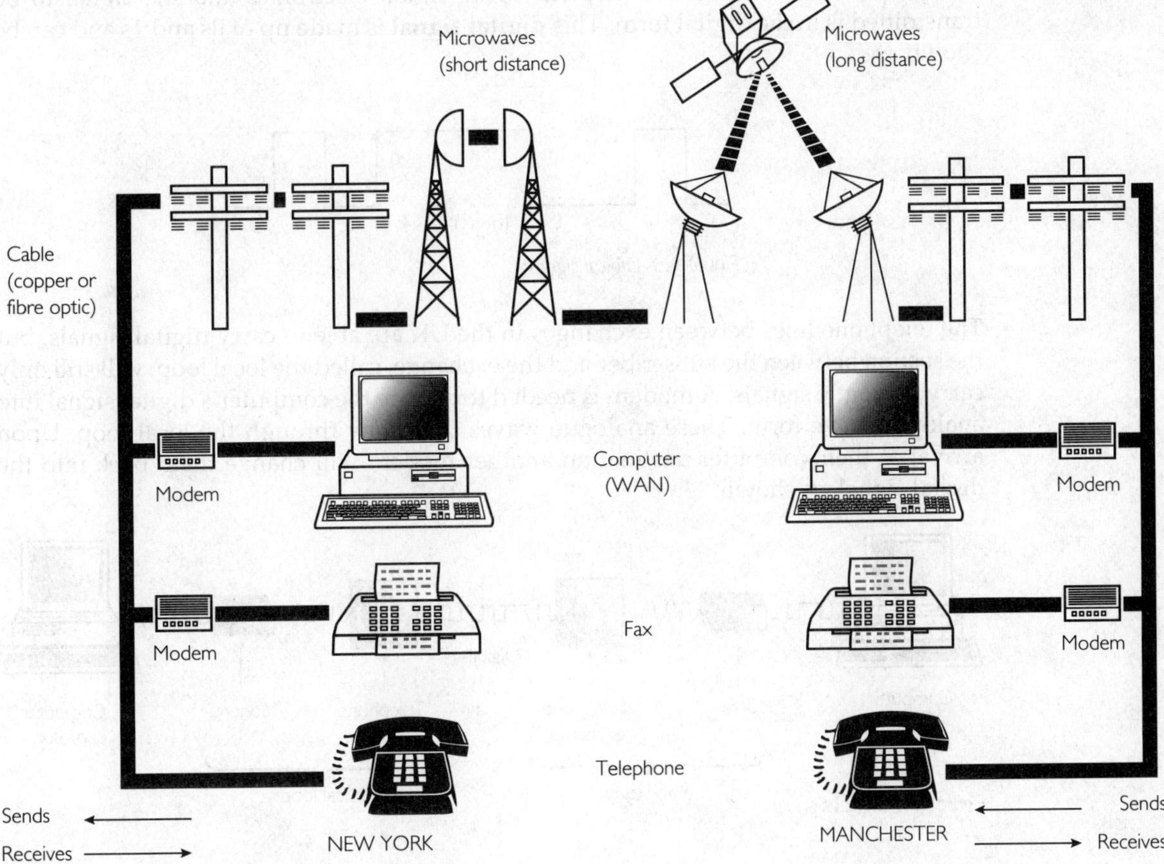

Figure 4.1 The telecommunications link

In the next pages we will look at:

- modems and why they are needed
- microwaves
- fibre optic cable and its advantages.

Modems

A modem (MOdulator/DEModulator) is a device which will change a digital signal into an analogue signal and vice versa. Modems can be built into computers and fax machines or connected to them separately.

Modems are necessary because telephone lines were originally for speech (voice) transmission and were not designed for use by computers. The electrical wave which travelled along these telephone lines would be a copy of the speech wave. These waves are called **analogue waves** and can be shown as:

Figure 4.2 Analogue waves

Computers and fax machines depend upon digital electronics and the signal to be transmitted is in the digital form. This **digital signal** is made up of 0s and 1s and can be shown as:

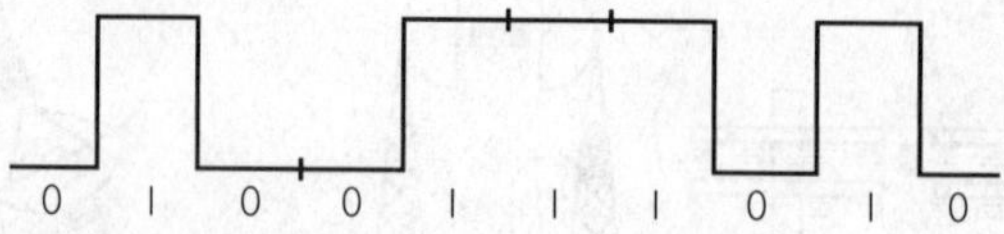

Figure 4.3 Digital signals

The telephone lines between exchanges in the UK are able to carry digital signals, but the section between the subscriber and the exchange, called the local loop, will still only carry analogue signals. A modem is needed to change the computer's digital signal into analogue wave form. These analogue waves then flow through the local loop. Upon arrival at their computer destination another modem will change them back into the digital signal, as shown:

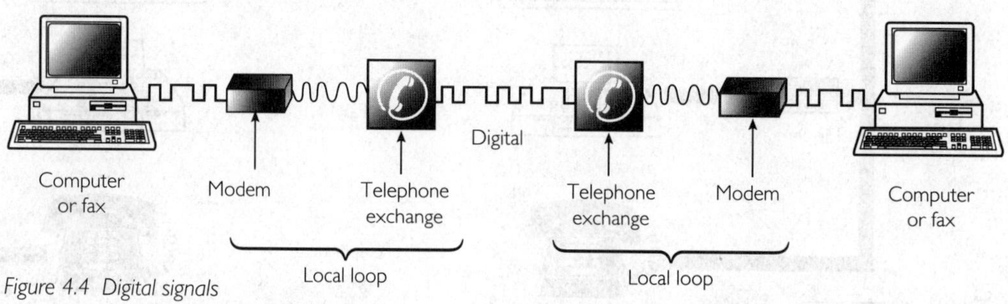

Figure 4.4 Digital signals

Modems over the years have got faster and smaller. The first pocket-sized, portable modem was on the market in the late 1980s and today modems the size of credit cards are available for slipping into a specially designed socket in a portable computer.

Bits and speed

Each 0 and 1 in the computer's digital system is called a binary digit or a bit. It is generally accepted that 10 bits represent one character; this means that to send the word 'Bat' from one computer to another 30 bits will be transmitted. The speed at which these bits are transmitted is measured in bits per second (bps). Obviously the faster that data (in the form of bits) is transmitted over the telephone lines, the less time spent 'on the phone', and the cheaper the phone bill .

Modem speeds have increased from a pedestrian 200 bps available in 1989 to 70 times faster today. This enables fast and cheap transmission of large files.

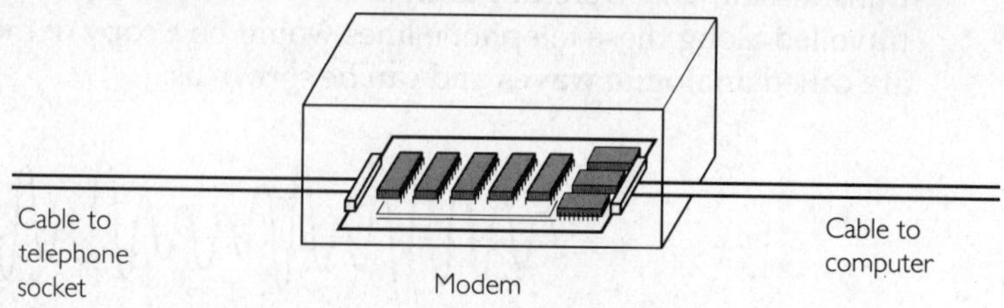

Figure 4.5

Activity

A 400-page (single-sided) document is to be sent from a computer in the UK to a receiving computer in the USA. The document is single-line spaced with 60 lines to the page and 90 characters on each line.

a What is the total number of characters to be sent?

b How many bits will be sent?

c The UK company is currently using a modem which has a transmission speed of 2400 bps. Cost of telephone calls to USA in business hours is £1.70 per minute.
- How long will it take to send the document?
- How much will it cost?

d The UK company are deciding whether to buy another, faster modem. The model they are interested in has a transmission speed of 9600bps.
- How long will it take to send the document?
- How much will it cost?

What are microwaves?

Microwaves are very short radio waves. They can be transmitted for short distances over land from one repeater station to another. Mercury has 2,700 miles of microwave links.

For long distances, a satellite link is needed to receive, boost and retransmit microwaves.

Features and fortunes of some communication satellites

Satellite	Date launched	Features
Echo 1 and Echo 2	1960	Looked like huge tinfoil balloons; signals from the satellite earth station simply bounced off them and reflected back down to another satellite earth station. Hit by thousands of tiny meteorites and became too badly pitted to be of any use
Telstar	1962	The first live transatlantic broadcast. It was rather disappointing with pictures so fuzzy and lined that it was only just possible for viewers to make out a face
Early Bird (renamed Intelsat I)	1965	First geo-stationary satellite to cover the Atlantic region. Handled 240 two-way phone calls simultaneously on one TV broadcast. Intelsat I was small enough to fit in a car boot
Intelsat II to V launched in this period		
Intelsat VI	1990	As tall as a double-decker bus, it can handle 44,000 two-way phone calls and three TV broadcasts at the same time

Glossary of terms

Geo-stationary orbit	The satellite orbits the earth at the same speed as the earth rotates. The satellite appears to be stationary from the earth
Intelsat	The International Telecommunications Satellite Organisation was set up in 1965 to manage the new satellite communications system. BT is a founder member of this organisation and is its second largest shareholder

Case study

Mercury Communications and fibre optic cables

Mercury (a subsidiary of Cable & Wireless) was granted a fixed network licence in 1982.

Mercury's network is entirely digital; the first of its kind in Europe. They have laid 4,950 miles of fibre optic cable, including main routes between exchanges and local fibre optic schemes in several UK cities.

In the City of London Mercury laid 500 km of fibre optic cable in the redundant pipes of the old London Hydraulic Power Company. They bought London Hydraulic in 1985 specifically for this purpose. These nineteenth-century pipes now form part of the telecommunications network for carrying nearly a third of the City of London's business traffic.

Mercury chose fibre optic cable because 'their capacity, or bandwidth, is theoretically limitless. In practice, this means that the carrying capacity of a cable is not limited by the cable itself, but by the electronics connected to it. Increasing the capacity of a route therefore becomes a relatively simple matter of replacing this equipment, rather than the cable'.

The telephone system today

Since 1984, when British Telecom was privatised, businesses wishing to install a new telephone system have a choice of licensed operators. Mercury began in the business market, but now also has 600,000 residential customers. It handles 400,000 more signed up by cable TV companies who have been allowed to offer telephone services since 1991.

Two new companies are Energis, owned by the regional electricity companies, and Ionica, a new telecom company.

The US company American Telephone and Telegraph has recently been granted a telephone operator's licence. It is expected to concentrate on the business market.

Mobile phone companies include Vodaphone, Cellnet (60% owned by BT), Mercury One-2-One and Orange.

Types of communication using new technology

As we have seen, the telephone system is now the basis of world-wide communication. Businesses use the system by means of:

- telephone
- fax machine
- computers linked into wide area networks or WANs.

Telephone systems

Modern switchboards are computerised. This allows:

- automatic redialling
- logging of calls made
- playing music to waiting callers
- automatic queuing systems.

Portable (mobile) phones are becoming more popular. They allow people travelling to keep in touch with their base. Paging systems are an alternative. These give out a bleep to tell the carrier to call their office.

Phone answering machines can tape callers' messages. It is now possible to play these messages back from a distance by calling the number and typing in a pre-set code.

The fax machine

Fax machines are now essential office equipment. They are used to transmit and receive copies of documents.

The sending fax machine scans a sheet of paper and converts it into digital signals. A modem (this is built into the fax machine) is used to transmit these along the telephone line. At the receiving end a thermal printer builds up a pattern of black and white on heat-sensitive paper according to the 0s and 1s in the digital signal.

If businesses use the ordinary telephone line (PSTN) for transmission they run the risk of:

- part of the document being illegible if there is a few seconds' interference on the line
- slower transmitting speed if the line is noisy.

Some businesses use private lines to overcome these transmission risks.

The fax, short for facsimile, machine has been around a long time; the original idea was conceived by a Scottish crofter in the nineteenth century. Fax machines came into widespread use in the late 1970s when international standards were set. Before this time their use was restricted because machines could only communicate with those made by the same manufacturer.

WANS – wide area networks

WANs are formed by computers linked via the telephone line; the computers may be in separate buildings, or, as is often the case, in separate parts of the world. WANs may be used for internal communication (between parts of an organisation) or external communication with other businesses. As well as the computer, the following equipment is required:

- a modem
- a telephone socket
- communications software that allows the computer to communicate with the modem.

The computers (either sender or receiver) may be very large mainframes, mini-computers or micro-(desk-top) computers.

How a WAN can benefit a business is shown in the following sharply contrasting case studies.

Case study 1

International Labour Reports (ILR) is a magazine which reports on labour news from all over the world. The ILR office is situated in a rural corner of South Yorkshire.

ILR subscribed to a commercial system (called Geonet) which provided a means for ILR to communicate with other groups around the world. (This is a similar service to Telecom Gold which is run by BT.) ILR chose Geonet because it included many other radical groups around the world who could exchange relevant information with ILR.

The Geonet system provided the following two services.

- Electronic mail transmission. This meant that ILR acquired an electronic mailbox and messages could be transmitted to this mailbox at any time by other subscribers to Geonet.
- Bulletin boards. These were notices for anyone in the Geonet system to read. In the Geonet system bulletin boards existed for different areas of interest, for example green issues, labour movement, Central American news and so on.

Writers contributing to the ILR magazine can send an article down the telephone line from anywhere in the world to the ILR office where it is stored on hard disk. Editors edit the material as it stands on the screen; typesetting instructions are inserted and then sent to the printers in Manchester.

Celia Mather, editor of ILR says: 'Electronic communications has proved to be invaluable to ILR. We can gather news right up to deadlines, incorporating it swiftly into existing articles.'

Case study 2

J. Sainsbury uses a large mainframe computer situated at its head office in London. In 1982 trials took place at Sainsbury's supermarkets in Putney and Wandsworth using ICL System 25 mini-computers. After further trials all branches now have their own mini-computers. These branch computers are linked by the public telephone line to head office.

These computer connections have many uses within Sainsbury's. These include:

- improved stock control enabling Sainsbury's to operate a 'de-stocking' programme – not holding more supplies on the shelves or in the warehouse than is necessary to meet customer demand. Branch requirements are relayed via the mainframe at head office to a network of over 20 depots across the country
- a simplified and streamlined ordering system by enabling head office and the depots to establish instantaneous data links. At 4.00 p.m. each day each branch is ready for the computer centre at head office to 'poll' the confirmed branch orders for that day. This is an automatic procedure
- 'messaging' – by having a direct link with the mainframe at head office this allows the passing of messages between head office, the five area offices and the branches
- text retrieval – instruction manuals and training programmes are sent from head office to the branches.

Activity

a Read through the case studies for ILR and J. Sainsbury. Using two columns draw up a list of the uses of electronic communications for each business. If there are uses which are common to both write them across both columns.

b Keith Adams, head of information technology at W. H. Smith News sees the purpose of IT investment as 'getting the right product to the right place at the right time'. How do ILR and Sainsburys achieve this?

Electronic mail (E-mail)

E-mail is the transfer of text (for example letters, memos and reports) between computer users. Such reports are confidential (in this respect E-mail is different from a bulletin board which is a general notice board). Communication may be one-to-one, a person sending a private message to another person, or one-to-many, in which one person sends a message to many people connected to the network.

Some organisations belong to public E-mail services. BT provides Telecom Gold, a subscription service through which each user acquires an electronic mailbox. (In the ILR case study on page 188, the organisation subscribed to Geonet for E-mail services.)

EDI (Electronic Data Interchange)

EDI is a form of electronic mail which allows the passing of orders, invoices and other trade transactions directly between company computers. It avoids the problems of traditional paper-based communication systems in which documents are printed out by the sender, posted and keyed in again by the receiving company.

Users include retailers such as Marks and Spencer who use the Tradanet system. Each user of the service is given a postbox and a mailbox. They can post outgoing trading information to other companies via their postbox and collect incoming information from their mailbox. The Tradanet computer acts as a clearing house by sorting all mail in the post boxes and sending it to the correct mail box. The trading data received by companies is fed directly into their computer systems, thus avoiding the need to re-key it. Lloyds Insurance market (London) has its own EDI system, Limnet.

BACS (Banks Automated Clearance System) is an example of EDI. BACS is used by the clearing banks to sort cheques. This works by reading data from the cheques by magnetic ink character recognition. The system is also used in paying salaries directly to employees' bank accounts using a tape or disk prepared by the employer.

Internet (the Net) – the information superhighway

What is the Net?

The Internet is a vast international network of networks. It enables computers to share information (obtained from organisations such as libraries, universities and research laboratories) and communicate directly, sending and receiving E-mail world-wide.

How to join the Net

Connecting to the Internet can be achieved in one of three ways. The appropriateness of each method of access depends upon the size of the organisation wishing to join.

- Direct connection – this type of link is used by larger institutions, corporations and government agencies. It involves setting up an Internet connection (gateway) and paying to have a full-time link with the network. Computers connected in this way are part of the Net. (See Figure 4.6.)

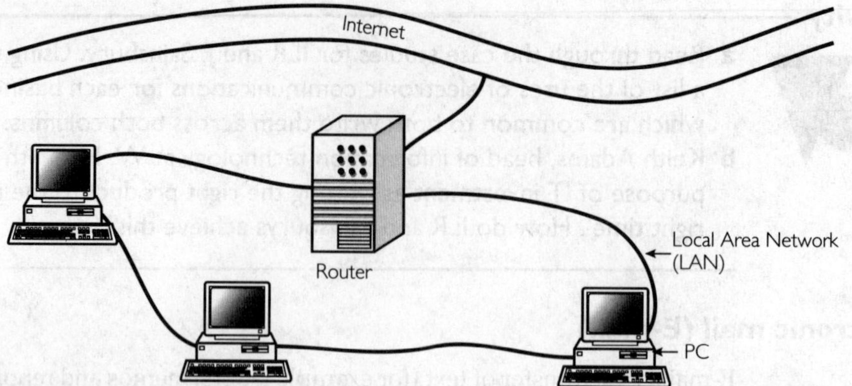

Figure 4.6 A direct Internet connection

- Service providers – these are organisations that allow smaller organisations to use their computers to access the Internet. In the smaller organisations the link is established by calling the service whenever the Internet needs to be accessed. (See Figure 4.7.)

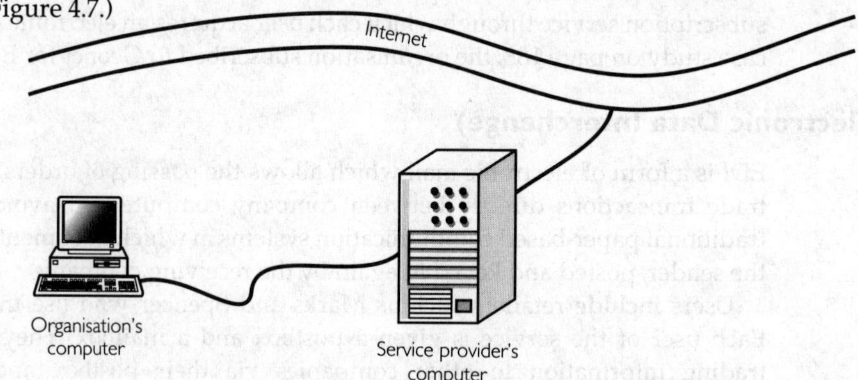

Figure 4.7 Connecting to the Internet using a service provider

- Commercial on-line services – these provide Internet gateways although in some instances these gateways provide only limited access to the Net. Commercial on-line services include: CompuServe, Delphi and Demon. Connections to the Internet are also charged at the local telephone call rate.

What are the Internet services?

The internet services include:

- E-mail
- UseNet, a collection of bulletin boards set up by subject matter
- Talk, like the telephone except that you have to type everything out
- Tools, called Archie, Veronica and Jughead, used for searching the huge libraries of information on the Net
- The World Wide Web, a more advanced information-retrieval system that organises its contents by subject matter
- Gopher, for tunnelling from one place on the Net to another
- WAIS (Wide Area Information Service) carries out a general search for keywords. This usually identifies relevant databases around the world. Further searches will turn up a list of relevant documents.

In November 1994 Bill Gates of Microsoft offered £10,000 for information leading to the information hacker who is distributing the latest Windows 95 system free to the world via the Net.

The importance of bandwidth

Bandwidth is a measure of the carrying capacity of the different telephone links. Fibre optic cable is attractive as a telephone link because of its large bandwidth. Another important consideration is the bandwidth of signal(s) being carried.

Telephone speech (voice)
Music ↓ increasing bandwidth
Television pictures (video)

When a business installs a new telecommunications system it must ensure that there is sufficient bandwidth available in the telephone links to carry the signals they wish to send.

ISDN – WANs without modems

In 1990 British Telecom introduced a telecommunications link which would not only carry voice and data, but also had the capacity to carry video pictures. This link is called **ISDN (Integrated Services Digital Network)** and it is able to carry digital signals using the existing public telephone lines right to the customer's wall socket. There is no need for a modem. ISDN achieves this digital connection by using what BT call 'a smart interface' at the user's end and 'additional intelligence' built into the existing telephone exchanges.

Despite all this wizardry ISDN was slow to take off and acquired some alternative explanations of the acronym: 'It Still Does Nothing' and 'I Still Don't kNow' to name but two. However, due to much careful marketing and profile-raising ISDN is now available to 90 per cent of the UK, 20 years after the technology was first developed.

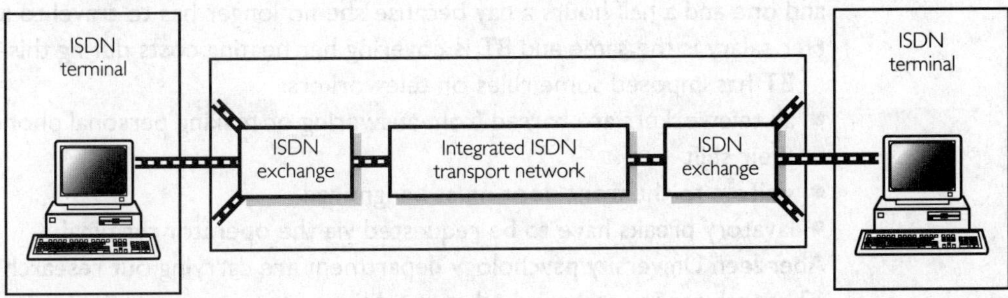

Figure 4.8 The 'digital bit-pipe' – no modem is needed with ISDN

ISDN can carry more information; it can carry it faster and with fewer errors than public telephone lines. In fact ISDN has a huge bandwidth (2 million bits) and because of this it is capable of supporting simultaneous voice and data connections. For example, this would enable two people, one in Glasgow and the other in Bristol, to discuss monthly sales figures on the telephone while both view the relevant spreadsheet on their individual PC screens in their own offices. The bandwidth can also support simultaneous transmission of voice and video.

If a business needs to send large amounts of information or have simultaneous voice/data and voice/video links British Telecom will install the ISDN link, consisting of a slim white box with two telephone sockets at a cost of around £400 (conventional telephone connection costs around £300).

In April 1992 BT and IBM unveiled what they claimed to be 'the world's first PC video phone' – at last the phone with a TV picture which has been mooted for so many years; almost a futuristic dream (or nightmare!). This time, though, the video pictures will appear on the PC screens. The availability of the system depends upon connections to ISDN. The cost of upgrading a PC to incorporate a videophone is estimated to be about £4,000.

ISDN allows:

- teleworking
- video conferencing.

Case study

In June 1992 BT launched a one-year teleworking trial involving home-based directory enquiry operators in Scotland. Ten telephone enquiry operators from the Inverness exchange were relocated to work from home for one year.

The key to the service was ISDN. Each operator was given a desk unit which consisted of a PC videophone and a call management console. The ISDN connection allows the operator to process work normally and to have a slow-scan video communication with the operator centre in Inverness (desk-top conferencing).

BT says the equipment costs are about £17,000 per operator. Hidden costs are the ISDN line connection (£400), two and a half days training per operator and the unspecified cost of developing specialised software to run the system.

Teleworking operators deal with about 400 calls on an 8-hour shift. They use the videophone to talk with their supervisor and other teleworkers. There is also a link to the restroom at the Inverness exchange to allow them to chat with other operators during breaks.

Shona McGougan, an operator who works from home, says she saves £50 a month and one and a half hours a day because she no longer has to travel to and from work. Her salary is the same and BT is covering her heating costs during this trial period.

BT has imposed some rules on teleworkers:

- all teleworkers are barred from answering or making personal phone calls during their shift
- visitors to the front door must be ignored
- lavatory breaks have to be requested via the operator terminal.

Aberdeen University psychology department are carrying out research into the 12-month trial to assess whether conditions prove too stressful for lone workers. 'I am enjoying it so far' says Ms McGougan. 'I do not really miss the office environment because I can chat via the videophone'.

Activity

a Make a list of the advantages and the disadvantages of teleworking for:
- BT
- the teleworker.

b What other jobs do you feel could be carried out through full-time teleworking? You may wish to refer to Chapter 8, page 361.

Video conferencing

People at different locations may be linked by both sound and vision so that they can hold meetings. It may be necessary to meet in specially equipped rooms, although it is possible to hire mobile transmitter vans which allow conferences to take place from the firms' own premises. The participants may be linked by satellite or by ISDN.

Video conferences are a convenient and cheap way of meeting as there is a considerable saving in accommodation, travelling and time. A one-hour conference with a location in the USA is currently available for around £100.

On the downside, conference participants claim that it is difficult to pick up cues such as body language and asides, so discussion is often at a formal, exploratory level. There is also a time lag for the satellite bounce (watch Peter Snow speaking to Washington on *Newsnight*). Big deals are not usually closed in this way.

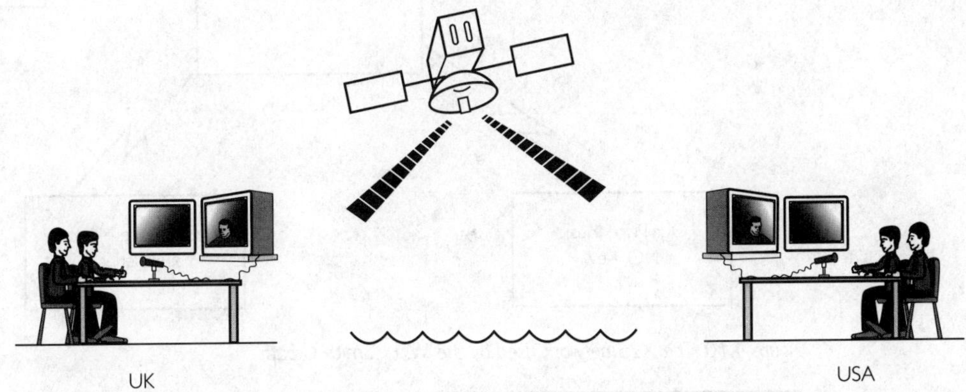

Figure 4.9 Video conferencing

X25 – packet switching

Another method of sending data over a WAN is called packet-switching. Here the digital signal is divided into packets of digital signals each labelled with its source and destination. X25 provides a standard for using these switched data networks.

Case study

An example of an X25 network being used in a company to link company divisions is found in the W. H. Smith Group. Here the corporation is divided into separate, virtually autonomous divisions which include:
W. H. Smith Retail with its 500 high street stores
Our Price Music and video with 300 shops
W. H. Smith News with 70 IT development staff based at Swindon,
90 depots around the country and
its financial centre in Bradford.
Communications depend upon an X25 network which is run from Newbury.

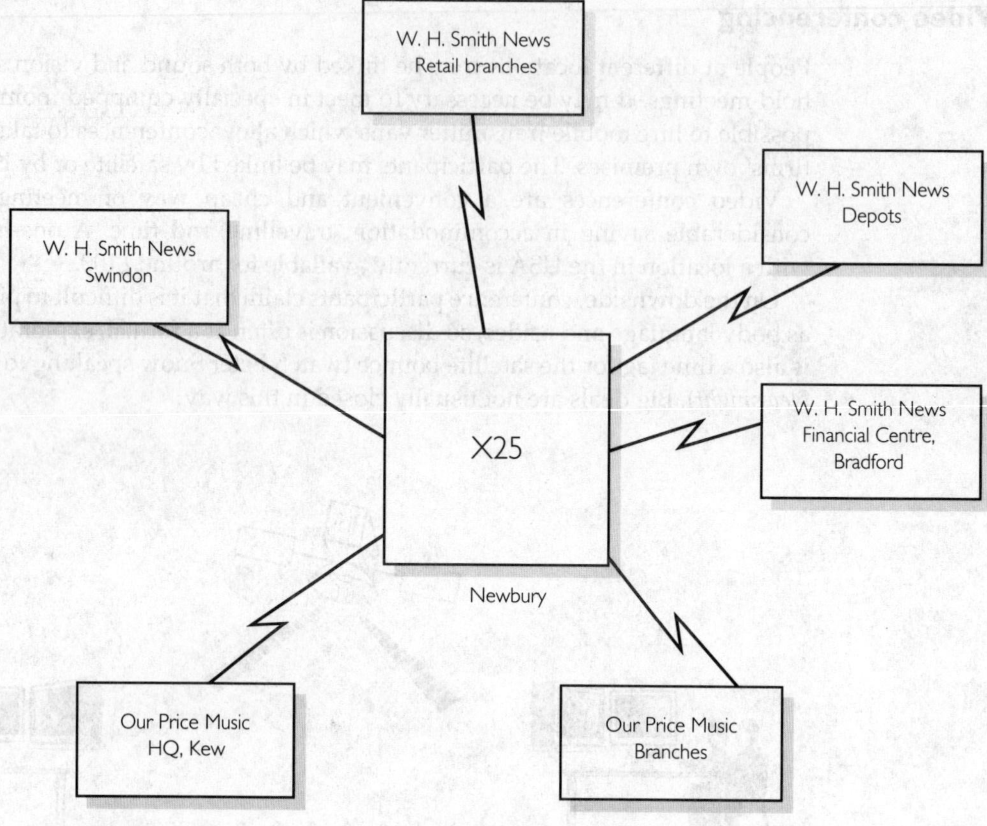

Figure 4.10 The X25 network used by the W. H. Smith Group

Viewdata

Viewdata is a two-way communication system. The PC user can request pages of information from a remote computer database. The link between the PC user and the computer database is the telephone line and again a modem is needed.

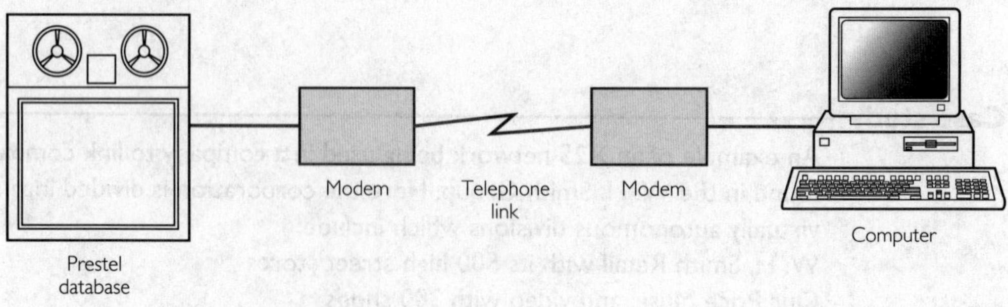

Figure 4.11

The public viewdata service, Prestel, was launched in 1978. The user is able to access particular databases to obtain different types of information, for example:

Company information	To call up a complete company financial report and credit option the Infocheck Credit Database would be accessed at the cost of £3.95 per minute (Infocheck has full reports on more than 380,000 companies in the UK)
Market research information	To search for all mentions of a company in the UK quality press over the past 3 months, the FT Profile Database would be accessed at the cost of £5.65 per minute

It is significant that BT's advice to customers is 'Use a fast modem if you can'. Do you remember why?

Local area networks (LANs)

The methods of linking computers described so far are examples of WANs. All have involved sending data over a wide geographical area using telecommunication links such as telephone or ISDN lines.

When computers are linked together without using telecommunications links this is called a **local area network** or **LAN**. The computers which are linked are geographically close, usually in the same building. Communication is internal, within the organisation.

LAN business is booming. Businesses are keen to install **PC** (personal computer) networks and Microsoft (the software giant) estimated that around 70 per cent of all PCs were networked in 1995, compared with 30 per cent in 1992.

It had been felt that with the introduction of the stand-alone PC the exchange and sharing of information ceased. Networking not only restores this sharing but organises and manages it better. **E-mail** (electronic mail) provides one means of organising and managing information flow.

E-mail may be supplied on a LAN so that 'mail' can be exchanged among the users of the network. One potential application which has sparked great interest is workflow automation. Here, existing business processes that involve circulating paper or forms among employees are replaced by electronic forms following pre-programmed rules and carried by E-mail.

In the example shown on the following page, an employee, Bill, fills out an electronic expense form that is automatically routed to his manager, Susan, for approval. After this, the form goes directly to accounting, or if the amount is greater than £500, Susan's boss, Farooq, must add his digital signature. The approved form is forwarded automatically to accounts payable. At steps along the way information about the transaction is sent to other software packages, such as a spreadsheet and the finance department's database.

Activity

1 List any other office processes which you feel could be carried out by using this workflow application of E-mail. Why did you chose those particular processes?

2 What is the difference between E-mail and bulletin boards? Which is a 'restricted' and which an 'open' form of communication?

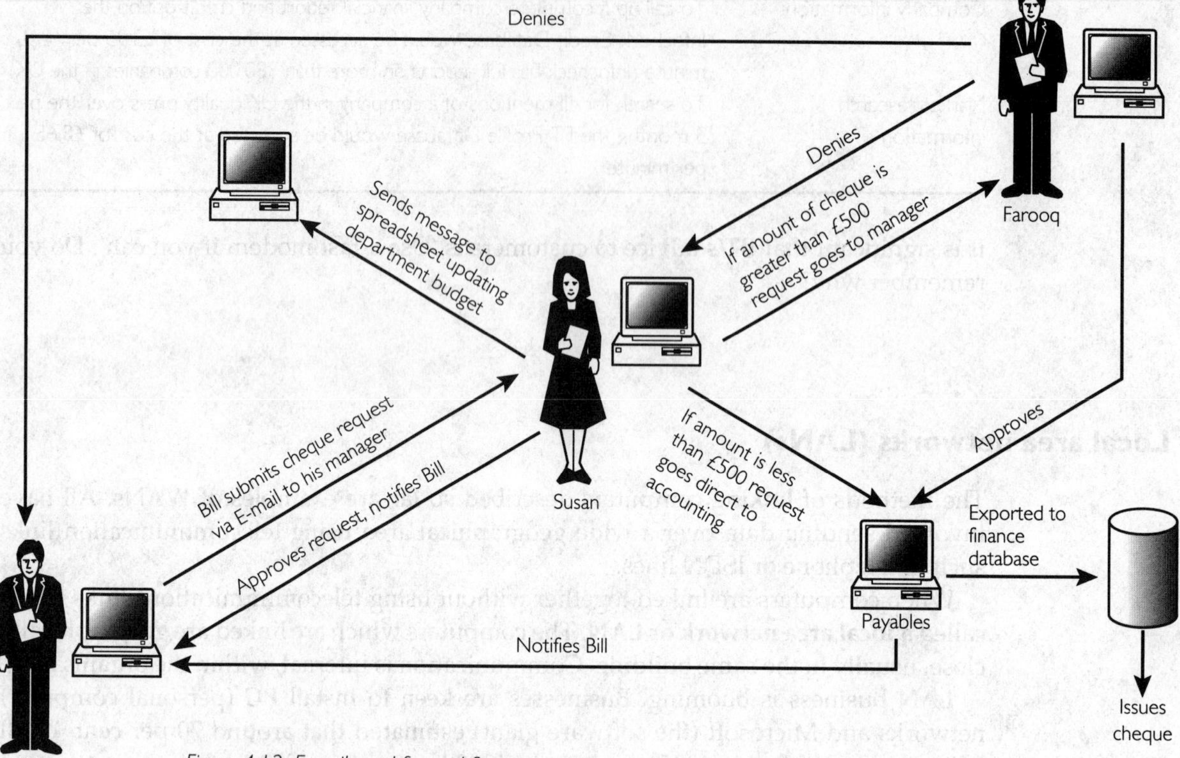

Figure 4.12 E-mail used for workflow automation

LAN network types

LANs can be used either with or without a file-server (or client-server).

File-server A file-server is a powerful PC with a large capacity hard disk (permanent data store) which is reserved for use as a file-server. This means that it cannot be used as a network workstation.

The file-server:

- provides storage space on the hard disk for the software programs
- provides storage space on the hard disk for centrally stored files
- provides files and software upon request to the LAN workstations (users)
- receives, temporarily stores files to be printed, establishes a print queue.

Novell is an established server-based operating system and is suitable for over ten users.

Computers in LANs may be linked in bus, ring or star networks.

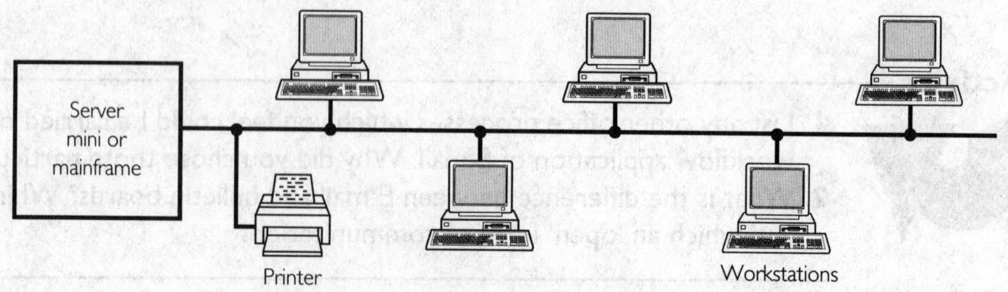

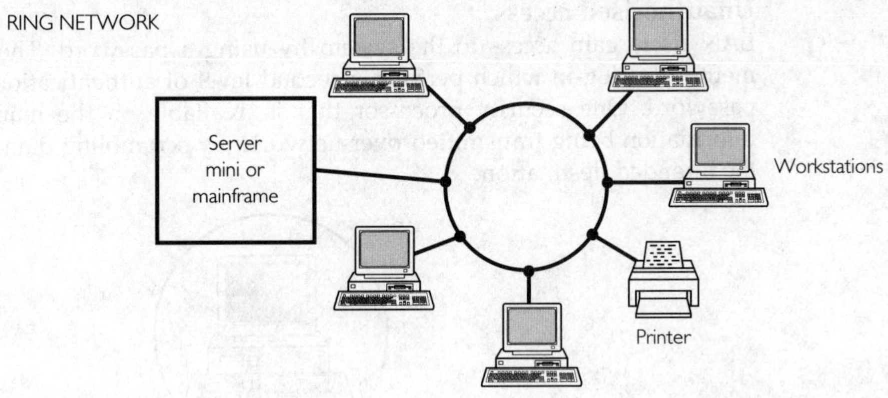

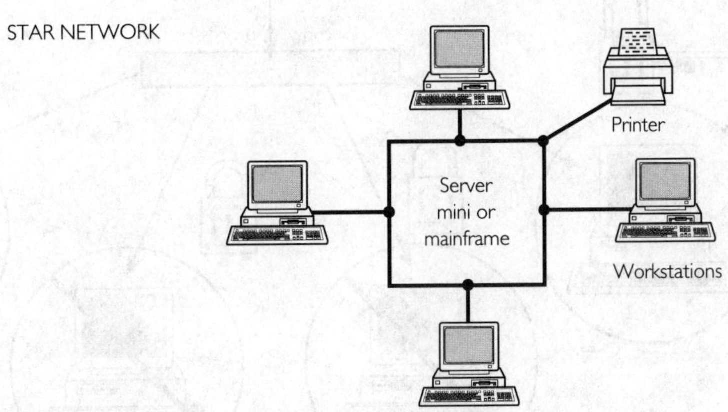

Figure 4.13 LAN topology – types of LAN

Where a LAN has no file-server each workstation has a hard disk and users can decide which files stored on the hard disk can be made available to other LAN users. The files which can be accessed by other LAN users are called 'public' files. This is called peer-to-peer networking.

The software available for this type of network is Windows for Work Groups and LANtastic. This network system is suitable for up to ten users.

Activity

Look at the network system used at your place of work or study:

- **Does it use a file-server or a peer-to-peer system?**
- **Why do you think this is?**
- **Which network software is used (e.g. Novell)?**

Security and networks

Security is a key issue with PC networks. Examples of threats to security are:

- unauthorised access to information on the LAN by people within the organisation
- viruses: programs that 'infect' and destroy data
- hackers armed with modems breaking into the WAN.

Unauthorised access

LAN users gain access to the system by using a password. There are sophisticated methods of log-in which perform a second level of authentication beyond the simple password. One security processor that is available on the market aims to protect information being transmitted over networks by scrambling data to all outlets except the intended destination.

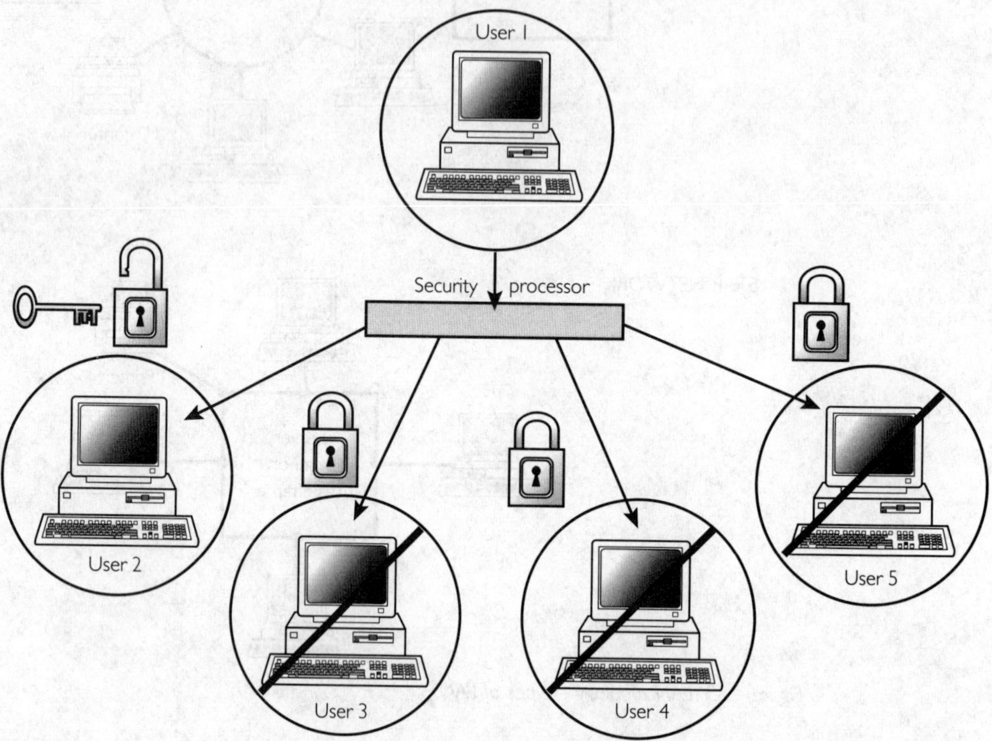

Figure 4.14 The security processor allows data to pass from User 1 to User 2 only

In Figure 4.14 User 1 wants to send sensitive payroll data to her assistant, User 2. No one else in the group has reason to see it. The message is broadcast through the security processor which is programmed to *pass* data to User 2 and *jam* data to all others.

Viruses

According to Alan Solomon, of Dr Solomon's Anti-virus Tool Kit fame, about 20 viruses account for 95 per cent of virus-attack reports. All the popular virus kits can recognise and deal with common viruses. However, network PCs are more vulnerable and E-mail is a possible vehicle for virus propagation. It is possible to implement virus scanning systems at various points of the network, although most users currently do not.

Hackers

Illegal entry into computer systems is a crime under the Computer Misuse Act 1990 which states that a person is guilty of an offence if:

a he [sic] causes a computer to perform any function with intent to secure access to any program or data held in any computer;
b the access he intends to secure is unauthorised; and
c he knows at the time when he causes the computer to perform the function that this is the case.

Case studies

FT computer hacker

In 1993 Paul Bedworth, a computer hacker, gained access to the *Financial Times*, EC headquarters and clearing banks. The FT was said to have lost £20,000 when the system which compiles the FTSE 100 share index was tampered with.

There was no doubt that Paul Bedworth was a hacker. At his trial, his defence was that he was an obsessive person besotted by computers. Although the judge stated that 'pathological obsession' was no defence the jury found him innocent. There has been little public sympathy for the victims of this particular hacking, despite the evident financial loss and disruption.

Paul Bedworth is now studying artificial intelligence at Edinburgh University. He now says that hacking is 'silly' and that he has given it up.

A month later two older hackers each received the maximum prison sentence of six months. The judge described hacking as 'intellectual joy riding'.

BT employee saw password on office noticeboard

It was claimed that a British Telecom employee copied information held on its customer service files after seeing the database number pinned on the office wall. There were fears that the secret telephone numbers of high-ranking public figures, military installations and the offices of MI5 were involved. BT was at pains to deny that the system had been entered by a hacker from outside. They did, however, admit that it was difficult to stop someone inside who had the password from taking files.

On a separate occasion it was alleged that disks containing the whole BT telephone directory, including ex-directory numbers, have been on sale for around £30 at car boot sales.

Computer fraud on the increase

A survey of over 1000 companies by the Audit Commission has shown that since 1991 there has been a 38 per cent rise in computer fraud, an eightfold increase in the use of illicit software and a fivefold rise in virus infections. In one case a firm spent £50,000 checking 450 machines and 4,000 disks in an attempt to track down a virus.

Management do not appear to understand the risks. The survey showed that 60 per cent of organisations had no security training and over 80 per cent did not analyse risks.

Fraud included staff stopping action for payments against friends and relatives.

Source: Audit Commission Report *Opportunity Makes a Thief*, HMSO, November 1994

Activities

1. In the light of the Computer Misuse Act 1990, quoted on page 198, what do you think about the jury's decision in the Paul Bedworth case?
2. Suggest ways in which BT could prevent a recurrence of its internal information leaks.
3. Draw up a list of possible threats to security of data held on computer. For each threat suggest how the problem may be prevented.

Review questions

1 What type of signal does a computer use? What changes it into an analogue signal?
2 Why is optical fibre used as a transmission medium? Why is this important?
3 How do microwaves differ from ordinary radio waves?
4 How does a computer hacker operate?
5 Why do microwaves need satellites?
6 What does the term viewdata mean?
7 What do the abbreviations WAN and LAN mean?
8 What do the initials ISDN stand for?
9 List three advantages that ISDN has compared with existing telephone lines.
10 What is video conferencing?
11 What is meant by teleworking?
12 Explain in one sentence the use of a fax machine.
13 What services does electronic mail offer when used on a LAN?
14 Name one public E-mail service.
15 What is the purpose of a file-server in a LAN?
16 List three threats to computer security.
17 Are LANs used for internal or external communication?
18 Is E-mail a restricted or an open channel of communication?

Key terms

Modem
Bandwidth
Digital
Analogue
Fibre optics
Microwaves
Satellite
Electronic mail (E-mail)
ISDN
Teleworking
WAN
LAN
File-server
Security
X25
Facsimile (fax)
Mini-computer
Mainframe
PC
Internet
Electronic Data Interchange (EDI)
Bulletin boards
Teleconferencing
Internal and external communication

Assignment 4.1 Computer communications systems in the workplace

This assignment develops knowledge and understanding of the following elements:

2.2 Investigate administration systems
2.3 Analyse communication in a business organisation

It supports development of the following core skills:

Communication 3.1, 3.2
Information technology 3.1, 3.4

This assignment will require you to look at your organisation with a view to identifying:

- the uses of electronic communication systems
- the perceptions of the users about these systems
- possible improvements to the systems.

You may work with a partner. You should clearly identify your individual roles and keep a record of each partner's contribution to the assignment. It will be necessary to arrange interviews and to prepare interview questions in advance. It will also be necessary to find convenient times for surveying the rooms.

Your tasks

1 In your place of work or study carry out a survey looking at the different ways in which electronic communications systems are used. Organise your findings into:

Location	Equipment type	Function	User (internal/external)
e.g. room C2	4 PCs (LAN network)	Registry	J Wong

2 Arrange to interview two members of staff, one teaching and one non-teaching, who use computers in their work.
   a Identify how computer communications systems have affected the efficiency of their work. In what ways has job satisfaction changed?
   b Ask what security problems exist, what measures are taken to deal with these and with what success? Do they feel security measures limit the effectiveness of the system?

3 Referring to this chapter, suggest ways in which you feel that the existing computer systems could be improved to bring about a system in line with staff requirements. For the purposes of this task assume that expense is no object! Mention any possible negative effects of these changes.

Presentation

Present your findings in a word-processed informal report using the headings: introduction, information and conclusion. The room survey should be attached as an appendix and presented in tabular form.

Electronic information processing systems

The purpose of information processing

Stock control, payroll, personnel records and invoice systems all involve **information processing**. This involves processing the raw facts (the **data**) and producing **information**. This information may include:

- order levels for stock control
- total wages on the payroll
- commission earned by a sales representative
- statistical information graphically displayed for personnel.

The processing used to be carried out manually but now more and more manual systems are being replaced by computer systems. This is known as electronic information processing – it uses information technology.

In looking at information processing systems, manual and electronic, we need to consider:

- the collection of the data to be processed
- the tasks which are being carried out by the processing system
- the devices and media used to enter, store and output the data
- the use of the processed data (the information).

It is the tasks, and the devices and media stages which are replaced by computers when changing from a manual to computerised system.

Data and information

Data has no meaning, for example 111148 appear to be random numbers. Information has meaning; 111148 is a date of birth; information processing puts data into context to give it meaning.

Some examples of information processing systems are shown below. More detail about the devices and media will be provided later in this section.

Information processing system for payroll

Collection	Tasks	Devices and Media	Use
Time sheet	Updating Calculating	Keyboard to disk (in) Printer and VDU (out)	Payslips Payroll

Information processing system for a library

Collection	Tasks	Devices and Media	Use
Membership form Book details	Updating Cataloguing Calculating	Keyboard to disc (in) Bar-code scanner (in) VDU and printer (out)	Membership monitoring Book monitoring Book usage Reminder letters Overdue fines

Information processing at work

Case study

Equal opportunity monitoring of staff

This document was produced by the personnel department of a London borough to explain how equal opportunities data relating to staff will be collected, secured and utilised:

Data collection

All data collected will be based on the individual employee completing a self-assessment form. Once data has been collected on existing staff, maintenance of the system will require information only on new starters through the recruitment procedure. The details required to be completed will be agreed with the trade unions in advance. Completed forms from individuals will be sent directly to the personnel department. Information on their ethnic origin will be given by employees on a voluntary basis.

Data security
All data will be securely stored in the micro-computer with encrypted individual code word access to authorised individuals only. No equal opportunities data will appear on the main viewing screen without a special password and individuals with such authority will be limited to personnel staff. Access for this group of staff is required for editing purposes only. The system is located within the personnel section which has an on-going responsibility to ensure absolute confidentiality of all personal information.

Data use
No analysis on the ethnic origin of staff will be undertaken without prior agreement of the employees' panel, including analysis requested by central government. Data will only be analysed on the specific instructions of the head of personnel or head of policy and planning. Each request for data analysis will be recorded in the ledger and signed for as a record of an approved transaction. All analyses will use anonymous data to show trends within the organisation. No individuals names will appear on any analyses.

Activity

Read the case study about ethnic monitoring carefully:

a Fill in the stages of this data processing system under the headings: Collection, Tasks, Devices and media, Use.

b You have been given the job of carrying out this equal opportunities monitoring. Your tasks are:
- Design the self-assessment form to collect the data (*Hint:* look at any organisation's application form).
- Write a reassuring memo to staff who may feel threatened by this monitoring.

Batch and real time processing

The manner in which information is processed within a business is determined by the needs of that particular organisation. There are two systems of processing information.

Batch processing

With **batch processing** all the transactions for a period of time are collected into a batch. This data is then inputted into the computer. The accounts department may collect invoices, batch them and enter them into the computerised accounts at regular intervals; twice a week perhaps.

Real time processing

With **real time processing** the user can obtain instant, up-to-date information from the system. Any input takes effect immediately. Such systems are used by:
- travel agents making airline ticket reservations
- stockbrokers buying and selling shares
- the holder of a bank account, querying the bank balance and making withdrawals of cash from a 'hole in the wall' dispenser.

Activity

Batch processing may be described as a time-driven system, whereas real time processing may be described as event-driven.

Explain the difference between a time-driven and an event-driven system. Use examples other than those given above.

Types of computer

It is becoming increasingly common for information to be processed by computer.

The traditional way of differentiating between computers is to divide them into three categories:

- **mainframe**
- **mini**
- **micro-computers.**

Mainframes are large, central computers developed in the late 1950s and 1960s to meet the accounting and information needs of large organisations. The largest mainframe can handle thousands of terminals and has huge permanent storage. IBM was the market leader in mainframe production.

Mini-computers are between the mainframe and the micro in terms of size, power, memory and price. A typical mini might have between 5 and 50 different users.

Micro-computers, also called personal computers or PCs, first appeared in the mid 1970s. They are called micro-computers because the part that processes information is contained on one integrated circuit, called the microchip. Most microcomputers are used by one person at a time.

Since the 1980s the distinction between mainframe and mini-computers, as multi-user computers, and micro-computers as single-user computers, has become blurred, for example:

- many micro-computers are more powerful than earlier mainframes
- powerful micro-computers can be linked to remote terminals
- new mini-computers use microprocessors.

It makes more sense now to distinguish between the machines by the function they are designed to perform, for example:

- distributed computing systems, in which communications between linked computers and shared access to files is made easier
- centralised computing systems, in which access is made by several users to one central computer
- stand alone computers.

Distributed computing systems

Here the user has computing power and access to central resources such as databases and printers. A local area network set up with E-mail services and resource-sharing is a distributed computing system. A powerful PC would meet these needs.

Centralised computing systems

This system is designed to be used by several users simultaneously. This may be for a whole organisation or for a department within an organisation. In this system the programs, data and processing capabilities are kept under central control. Users gain access to these systems by remote terminals. Most mainframe and mini-computer systems would meet these needs. A powerful PC could also be used.

Case study

Dustbin efficiency sweeps away the mainframe
In 1993 Brent Council in North London set up an Executive Information System to assess the quality of their dustbin collection service. The system enables managers to extract detailed statistical information and display this as easy-to-read graphs and tables. Brent's system has a network of 40 PCs using Windows 3.1. The previous network used an IBM-compatible mainframe. What does this tell us about modern PCs?

Hardware and software

Hardware – this is the physical equipment which makes up a computer system. The most important part of this is the central processing unit (CPU). The devices which are attached to this are called **peripherals**. These can be classified as:

- input devices, such as the keyboard, the mouse, the scanners
- output devices, such as the monitor or visual display unit (VDU) and the printer.

The disk drive is both an input and output device.

Software – this refers to the programmes which run on the computer.

- Systems software looks after the operation of the hardware. This includes operating systems such as MS-DOS (Microsoft disk operating system), OS/2 WARP (as advertised by IBM as an example of multi-tasking – 'Did you see the hourglass?') and Unix. Systems software enables the computer to run applications software.
- Graphical User Interface (GUI). 'Environments' such as Microsoft Windows are increasingly being used as an interface between the systems software and the user. These allow programmes to be run by clicking on icons (pictures) rather than by typing code.
- Applications software refers to the programs which we use to perform tasks. These include word processing packages, database management systems, spreadsheets, graphics packages and so on.

The computer system – the hardware

In Chapter 3 we saw that business administration involves the receiving, processing, storing and communicating of information.

All computer systems have four main stages of operation.

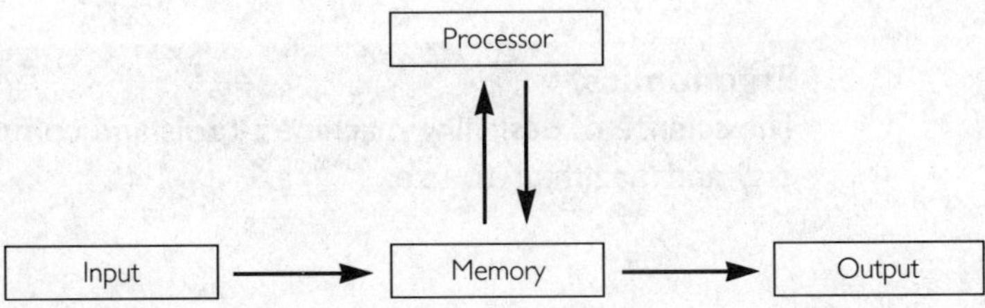

Figure 4.15 The four stages of computer operation

These are:

- input – device for inputting instructions and data into computer memory
- computer memory – the internal memory of the computer; also called RAM
- processor – carries out the user's instructions upon the data
- output – device for showing the result.

Computer systems either complement or replace existing manual systems. In the office a simplified comparison between manual and computer systems is:

Function	Manual	Computer system
Receiving information	In-tray	Input devices
Holding information temporarily	Working surface	Computer Memory
Processing information	Desk calculator	Processor
Sending information	Out-tray	Output devices
Storing information permanently	Filing cabinet	Disk and tape storage

Computer input devices

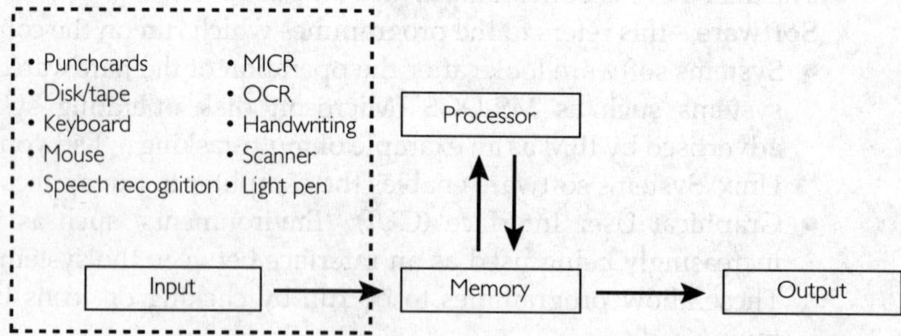

Figure 4.16

Input devices turn data into bits which the processor can deal with. Inputting is very important because this is the point where human contact is necessary. This contact causes different concerns to the employee and the employer. The issues are:

- human errors may occur in inputting – information inaccurately inputted and not detected can result in incorrect information being stored (GIGO = garbage in garbage out!)
- speed of inputting can translate into cash savings for the company
- the health of the person carrying out the inputting can be seriously affected.

Ergonomics
The science of designing machines, tools and computers so that people find them easy and 'healthful' to use.

We will look at input devices from the point of view of ergonomic factors, as well as their appropriateness for the job.

Punch cards

Punch cards were prepared by punching holes on card or paper; a hole meant '1', no hole '0'. A separate machine was needed to read this information into the computer. This was once the main input method but is now rarely used.

Disk and tape

Magnetic disks and tapes can store information permanently. These media may then be used to input information into the computer. Preparation of this information (called data preparation) is carried out using a keyboard and is either key-to-tape or key-to-disk. For example, in a payroll system the following data preparation steps may be carried out:

1 the clerk keys in details from paper documents. These details are stored on magnetic tape
2 a verifier (a piece of data preparation equipment) checks that the data on the tape correspond to the data keyed in
3 errors are reported and corrected
4 the tape is placed in the computer's magnetic tape reader and the data inputted to the computer's memory.

If a disk were used the process would be identical except that the information keyed in would be stored to a disk and these data would be read into the computer using a disk-drive.

Keyboard

The keyboard is used to input data either directly into the computer's memory or indirectly via tape and disk. Whichever method is used the keyboard is the first point of input.

The usual keyboard design is the QWERTY keyboard which is 120 years old and was designed to slow down typists who went too quickly for the original manual typewriters. It has been found that long periods of using a keyboard can cause **repetitive strain injury (RSI)**, a muscle and tendon disorder causing pain in the hands and arms. Apple and several small companies have produced alternative keyboards with the keys arranged in a dish around each separate, outward-pointing hand. This helps to relax the shoulder and arm muscles.

The keys on the keyboard may be tailored to particular applications so that each key will represent a particular item. For example in a hamburger restaurant, one key may represent a cheeseburger sale. Such keyboards, called concept keyboards, are also used for educational purposes.

Case study

Keyboard strain secretary wins case

Denise Burgess, who had worked for Autoglass for three years, was dismissed from her £12,000 per year job after developing RSI. She was awarded £5,500 for unfair dismissal by an industrial tribunal. This was the first time an RSI sufferer had been awarded compensation for unfair dismissal.

'When it was at its worst I could not comb my hair or brush my teeth.' said Mrs Burgess. 'I still have to be careful. I can't carry heavy shopping, but I'm getting better.'

As a result of the case the *Financial Times* improved severance pay for nine journalists dismissed after developing RSI.

Source: *Times Newspapers*, January 1992

Some word processing packages, such as IBM Multimate, count the number of keystrokes to determine the most/least efficient typists. Similarly supermarket checkouts record the items scanned by each operator per minute. Work-related upper limb disorders (including RSI) are increased by the need to reach ever faster targets.

The EU Directive 90/270 on the minimum safety and health requirements for work with display screen equipment states that: 'No quantitative or qualitative checking facility may be used without the knowledge of the workers.' This is designed to help the users of equipment. However, where organisations operate a bonus system, with some actually using league tables of inputting performance, knowing that checking is taking place does not help.

Mouse

This device contains a roller-ball which, when moved on a table-top, relays signals that move a pointer on the screen. Long periods of use with the mouse can cause as much pain as the keyboard. In response to this Microsoft have mapped the hand movements used to navigate a mouse. Their new Microsoft Mouse, version 2, is longer and sleeker. It has a hump and longer buttons, and was designed with the aid of ergonomic experts.

A recent development for portable computers is the roller-ball which is built-on to the keyboard. Here the ball is held in one place and rotated using the palm of the hand.

Speech recognition

Speech recognition systems convert speech into digital code. This has been an area where there has been much work but until recently little progress. Most speech, for example, contains redundant information (such as coughs) and the packages have to disregard this. Some systems have drawbacks:

- conversation uses around 10,000 words, but many systems use only about 1,000. This is enough for specific tasks, such as ordering an airline ticket
- in some systems the speaker must speak slowly leaving a pause between each word
- the recognition may be restricted to one specialist language, such as air traffic control.

Recent developments include:

- Phillips Dictation systems is launching a model (1995) which recognises 50,000 words in continuous speech
- both Apple and Microsoft have kits which enable users to issue commands such as 'open file' or 'delete' to their computers
- the US West telephone company allows Voice Dialling in Colorado. (Voice recognition is particularly helpful for users with physical disabilities.)

By using AI (artificial intelligence) techniques speech recognition is becoming practical and affordable. Users include pathologists who now dictate their reports straight to text while doing their job, instead of making notes to be typed up later. It is also used by journalists suffering from bad cases of RSI.

Magnetic ink character recognition (MICR)

MICR is used by banks to process large numbers of cheques quickly. The special symbols in magnetic ink on the bottom of each cheque are read using a MICR reader, either directly into the computer's memory for processing or on to magnetic tape for later input into the computer.

Optical character recognition (OCR)

OCR depends on printing information in a special typeface so that it can be read into the computer. These special characters can then be read from individual forms into the computer. OCR is used:

- to read gas and electricity bills
- in the issue of insurance renewal notices
- in capturing data from cash registers, accounting machines and adding machines.

Handwriting recognition

This logical development from OCR suffers from many of the same problems as speech recognition. There are no systems which can reliably recognise everyone's scribble. However, if a handwriting recognition system is trained by its user, and if characters are entered one at a time into boxes, then even the cheaper systems can attain reasonable levels of accuracy. Amstrad's electronic organiser Pen Pad PDA 600 relies on the machine recognising the user's handwriting. Each letter has to be written carefully in a separate box on the screen and the penpad has to be trained with samples of characters it cannot initially make out.

EPOS – Electronic Point of Sale

In retailing organisations computerised tills are used to record information about the goods sold. In supermarkets the laser beam scanning of bar codes is widely used. The scanners input data into the computer to process, improving speed of throughput of customers, stock control and reordering procedures.

Scanners

A scanner can read printed text and graphics into the computer. It may be hand-held so that it is manually passed over the material or it may be a desk-top machine. Scanners are much used for production of marketing material.

Light pen

This uses a light-sensitive stylus to enable the user to select items from menus and draw on the screen. The pen may be used for monitoring and adjusting industrial processes, for example regulating the temperature of an incinerator unit. When using this pen the user touches the screen at intervals and thus does not suffer from the muscular pain which sustained use would cause.

Activity

You are a manager of a large mail-order company. Orders are currently input using a standard QWERTY keyboard. Recently, one of your employees who suffered from RSI was dismissed by your company. At an industrial tribunal she received a large financial settlement and the company got a lot of bad press. The senior managers are keen to project a more 'caring' image.

You have been given the job of investigating ways in which work patterns, conditions and equipment could be changed to reduce the likelihood of RSI. A meeting is arranged with the union representative and you both 'brainstorm' as many ideas as you can, bearing in mind certain conditions which cannot change such as:

- the inputting is carried out in a large, busy, open-plan office
- many of the customers do not complete the order forms accurately and some forms are almost illegible.

However, money is available and the company is keen to invest in new equipment.

Now write out a list of your ideas.

Computer memory

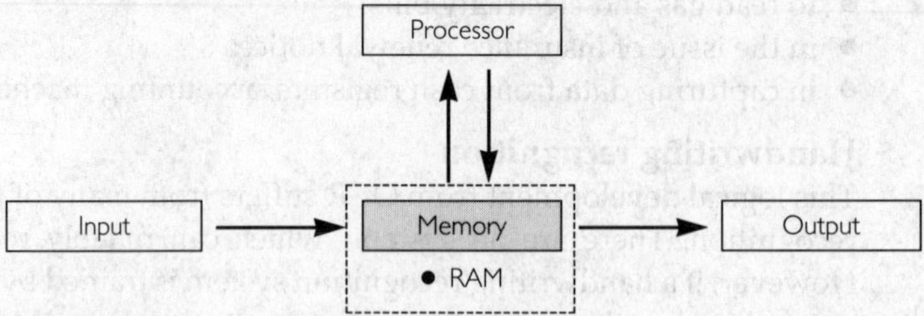

Figure 4.17

After data have been entered they are stored in the computer memory before being processed. After processing the data are returned to the computer memory. The memory capacity is measured in bytes; one byte represents one character (there are ten bits in a byte). This means that a computer memory of 2 megabytes can store 2 million bytes which is 2 million characters.

In PCs this memory is called **Random Access Memory**, or **RAM**, and consists of silicon memory chips in which the data are stored as electrical charge. This storage is temporary. If the computer is disconnected from its electrical supply all the data will be lost.

Computer processor

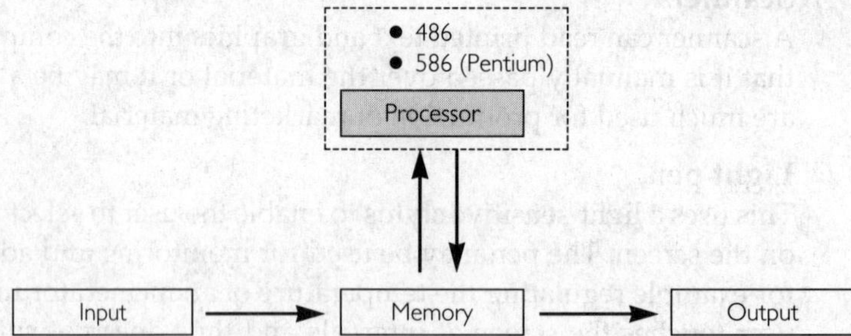

Figure 4.18

The **central processing unit (CPU)** interprets and processes information and instructions. It is made up of:

- the control unit which makes the program run in the correct sequence
- the arithmetic logic unit which carries out arithmetic and logical operations (comparisons).

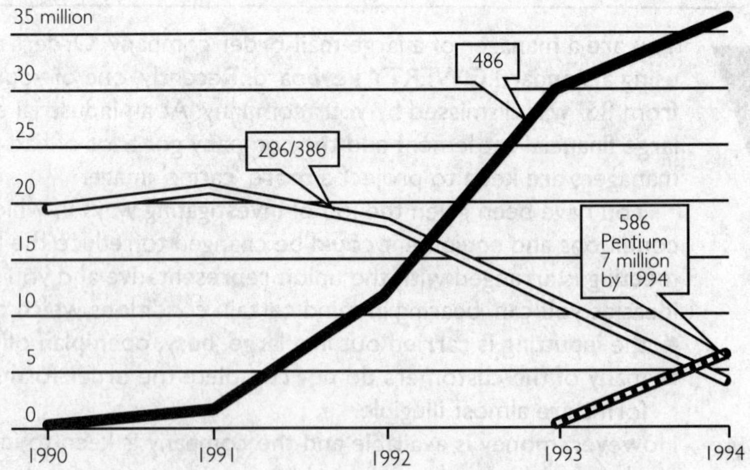

Figure 4.19 PC sales by processor

When both of these are contained on one integrated circuit the CPU is called a microprocessor or chip. Intel, the large American chip manufacturing company introduced its 8086 series of silicon chips in 1978. Since then a succession of increasingly powerful chips have been introduced: the 80286, 80386, 80486. They launched the 80586 (called 'Pentium' for copyright reasons) in summer 1993, and its power and speed were expected to leave the others at the starting post.

Intel's domination of the microprocessor market is now under threat from competitors such as Texas Instruments and Advanced Micro Devices (AMD). To survive Intel has had to accelerate its development of silicon chips to deliver a new generation every 18 months. In 1992 Intel spent $850 million on research and development to get to the market place with faster microprocessors.

Pentium panic

A fault was discovered in Intel's pentium chip at a time when sales were running at seven million a year. There was an inaccuracy in the fifth place of decimals. For ordinary users this was unlikely to cause a problem, but in areas where accuracy is critical such as in medicine, scientific research and space flight there could have been major difficulties. Intel agreed to withdraw affected machines and fit an accurate chip free of charge (November 1994).

Computer output devices

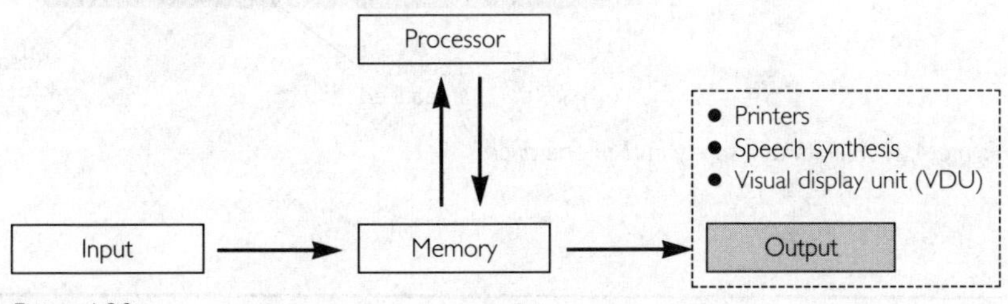

Figure 4.20

As with input devices output devices are a point of contact with the user. This means that the same issues of economics and ergonomics are evident.

Printers

Printers can be divided into two main categories:

- impact printers which involve the printer head actually hitting the paper. Examples are daisy-wheel and dot matrix printers. These printers are noisy and require a printer hood to reduce the noise level; they are used where carbon copies are needed, for example to produce invoices
- non-impact printers include the ink-jet and bubble-jet where the ink is sprayed on to the paper. Laser printers attract ink powder to an electrostatically charged page. These printers are quiet and of high quality.

Speech synthesis

This is much easier to achieve than speech recognition; virtually any PC can be equipped to read text with a minimum of errors. Systems are already in use which quote stock prices and bank balances.

One expert said that 'Speech synthesis is like squeezing toothpaste out of the tube, and speech recognition is like trying to squeeze it back again' (quoted in *The Guardian* 22 April 1993).

Visual display unit

The VDU or monitor produces an on-screen display for the user. The EU directive of 29 May 1990 on the minimum safety and health requirements for work with display screen equipment came into effect in the UK on 1 January 1993.

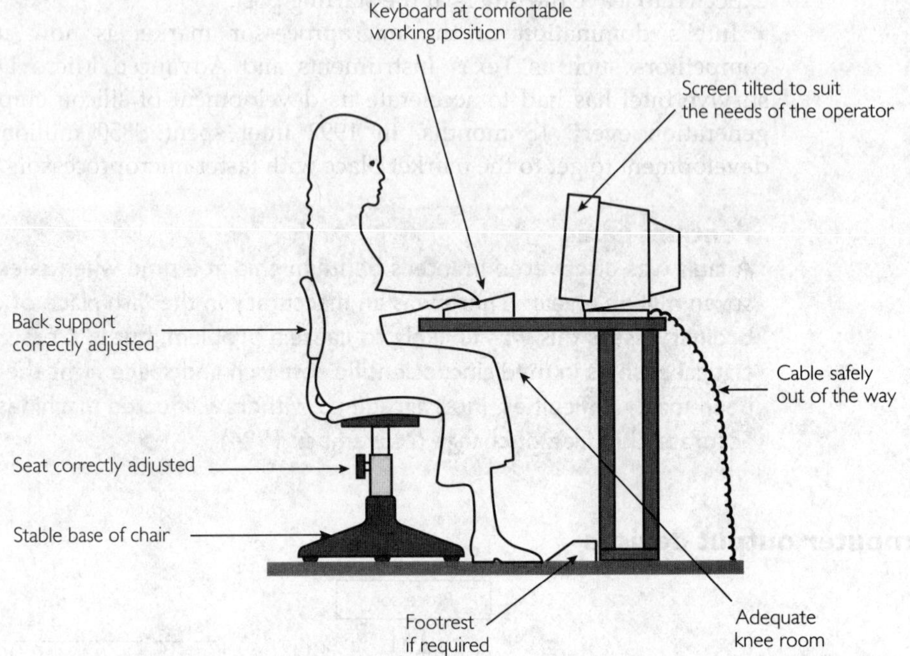

Figure 4.21 Health and safety in IT in operation

Activities

1 Safety and health requirements for work with display screen equipment

The EU Directive 90/270 which came into effect on 1 January 1993 contains the following Articles under the section headed Employers' Obligations:

Article 4
Workstations put into service for the first time

Employers must take the appropriate steps to ensure that workstations first put into service after 31 December 1992 meet the minimum requirements laid down in the Annex

Article 5
Workstations already put into service

Employers must take the appropriate steps to ensure that workstations already put into service on or before 31 December 1992 are adapted to comply with the minimum requirements laid down in the Annex not later than four years after that date

The list of minimum requirements for Articles 4 and 5 is included in the Annex.

Read carefully the minimum requirements laid down in sections 1 and 2 of the Annex (to be found in Appendix 1 of this book). Assess the facilities of your computer room in light of these requirements and prepare a written account. Your account should take the form of a list of the items not complied with, together with your comments on each one.

Remember these points:

- decide how you will organise your work on paper first
- carry out your research and note your results on paper
- decide how you wish your final account to look
- word process your work remembering to proof-read carefully
- format your document to make it look as professional as possible.

2 Protection of workers' eyes and eyesight

> **Article 9**
> **Protection of workers' eyes and eyesight**
>
> 1 Workers shall be entitled to an appropriate eye and eyesight test carried out by a person with the necessary capabilities:
> - before commencing display screen work
> - at regular intervals thereafter
> - if they experience visual difficulties which may be due to display screen work.
>
> 2 Workers shall be entitled to an ophthalmologic examination if the results of the test referred to in paragraph 1 show that this is necessary.
>
> 3 If the results of the test referred to in paragraph 1 or of the examination referred to in paragraph 2 show that it is necessary and if normal corrective appliances cannot be used, workers must be provided with special corrective appliances appropriate for the work concerned.
>
> 4 Measures taken pursuant to the Article may in no circumstances involve workers in additional financial cost.
>
> 5 Protection of workers' eyes and eyesight may be provided as part of a national health system.

You are a union representative in the offices of Hackney & Fields and have been asked by some of the secretarial staff about the new EU Health and Safety requirements for VDU users and eye tests.

Questions include:

'I understand that eye tests will be necessary. How often will these be?'
'What if the tests show that I have a problem?'
'What will all of this cost me?'

Draw up a notice for display in the computer room to explain the provisions of Article 9 in clear, simple language. Make sure that you deal with the concerns expressed above. If you feel that there are areas of the EU directive that are difficult to interpret, quote the actual EU directive.

Permanent storage

The computer memory, the RAM, is only for temporary storage. Disks and tape provide a means of permanent magnetic storage.

Disks

There are two types of disks: floppy and hard.

Floppy disks are portable and cheap. Physical size and capacity are given below.

Size of disk	Density	Capacity
3.5 inch	HD (High density)	1.44 MB
3.5 inch	DD (Double density)	720 KB
5.25 inch	Quad density	1.2 MB
5.25 inch	Double density	360 KB

Hard disks are fixed within the computer chassis. A standard desk-top computer will have a storage capacity of around 200 megabytes.

Tapes are used as a back-up for all the data stored on a hard disk. A file-server for a LAN will have, in addition to the 500 megabyte hard disk, a 500 megabyte tape back-up facility. Multiple back-up copies can be taken at regular intervals, for example twice weekly. Sometimes copies are stored at remote locations as a precaution against losing information in fires, etc. These precautionary measures are costly but necessary.

A recent development in disc storage is the **CD-ROM**. This system uses small, plastic-encased discs similar to the compact discs (CDs) used for playing music. These allow data to be more tightly packed than is possible on the conventional system, so that up to 650 megabytes can be held on a single disc. Again, like the music CDs, the data is retrieved by the use of a special disc-drive which uses a laser beam instead of the usual magnetic read/write heads. Searches are made as in a conventional database.

The fact that CDs can store a vast amount of data makes them ideal as a way of storing reference material. Encyclopedias, atlases and clip art are available to computer uses in this form. Some of the national newspapers also make their back editions available in this form every six months.

Activities

1 Check whether there is a CD-ROM available in your centre library, and in your local library.
  - **a If so, what material is held in this way?**
  - **b What are the advantages from the point of view of the library?**
  - **c See if you can find out the cost of a disc.**

2 Look at advertisements for stand-alone PCs. What size of hard disc is currently available? How does this compare with the storage capacity of a CD-ROM?

The computer program – the software

The most popular software applications are:

- word processing: word processors have replaced typewriters in the modern office. Professional appearance is possible for letters, memoranda and reports, often incorporating graphics such as charts and clip art. Advantages are on-screen editing, formatting and spell-checking. Time saving devices include pre-set style sheets, glossaries or phrases and macros (preset routines). Mailmerge which allows relevant names and addresses to be added to standard letters is a time-saving facility (and is also responsible for the junk mail we receive). Examples are Word for Windows, Wordperfect, Amipro and Wordstar.

- database management system: this is an electronic filing system. It may contain files on different areas of work such as stock, staff or students. Each file consists of a number of records (see Figure 4.22); for instance in the student database each student will be a record. In turn each record is made up of fields such as surname, age or date of birth. The database can be rapidly sorted and searched, so that relevant reports such as mailing lists or staff rotas can be printed. Examples are Access, Superbase and Dataease.

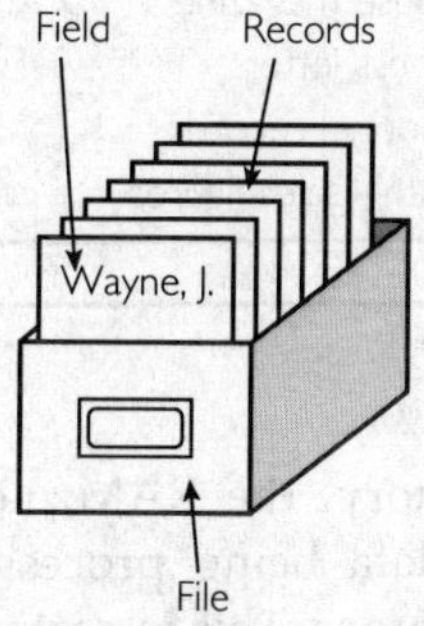

Figure 4.22 Structure of the file

- spreadsheet: this package is used for numerical work and is particularly important in accounting. Cells can be programmed to perform rapid calculations and charts can be generated to illustrate the results. Spreadsheet models are shown later in Chapters 12 and 13. Examples are Excel, Lotus 123 and Supercalc.
- desktop publishing: this allows for the design of high-quality materials such as in-house magazines and manuals. The package can import text from wordprocessing packages and combine this with graphics and designs. It is possible to manipulate the images so as to make up a page of professional appearance. Increasingly, wordprocessing packages are allowing for this type of document production. An example is Pagemaker.
- integrated packages (multi-purpose systems): some software packages combine the functions described above. The advantage is that data can be easily transferred from one application to another. Examples are Works and Framework.
- suites of packages: it is important for any company to standardise its set of office applications. There should be a standard word processor, spreadsheet, database and graphics package. It makes sense for businesses to buy suites of packages and increasingly software manufacturers are combining their packages in this way. Two of the major suites of packages currently available are Lotus SmartSuite, which contains Ami Pro, Lotus 123, Freelance Graphics, Organiser and Approach, and Microsoft Office Pro, which contains Word, Excel, Access, Powerpoint and Mail.

Specialised packages

- Accounting packages: accounting is one of the main functions for which information technology is used. Integrated accounting packages allow data from a single entry to be automatically transferred to different sections of the accounting system. There are significant improvements in time and accuracy. These packages are specialised databases; they allow for efficient inputting, rapid searching and accurate reporting. Examples include Pegasus and Sage Sterling.
- Computer-aided design (CAD): these packages are used in place of technical drawing at the design stage in engineering. Images can be created to scale in 3-D. An example is Autocad.

Activity

Complete the following table.

Job	Program	Suitable package
Preparing purchase ledger (suppliers' accounts)	?	?
Designing in-house magazine	?	?
Producing business letters	?	?
Amending personnel records	?	?
Displaying monthly sales figures	?	?

The computer memory, the RAM, needs to be large enough to store parts of the program and the data being processed. Over the years computer programs have become larger and larger. This is particularly the case with the packages which use the Windows environment. All Windows software will need at least 4 megabytes (4 million bytes) of RAM available.

Graphical user interface, Windows and usability

Graphical user interface (GUI) is the design for that part of the program that interacts with the user. GUI involves using a mouse to:

- click on pictorial representations of computer functions called icons;
- click on certain keywords to obtain pull-down menus and dialogue boxes.

The GUI was originated at Xerox Corporation's Palo Alto Research Center (PARC), in the USA, in the early 1970s. In 1984 Apple released the Macintosh which was the first affordable machine to use GUI.

In 1991, Microsoft had phenomenal success with Microsoft Windows 3 which provided the features of a graphical user interface and makes these features available for a range of different packages such as Word for Windows, Excel, Pagemaker and Access. This success was followed in 1992 by the launch of Windows 3.1 which provided even more GUI features.

The common lay-out format for each different program and the use of GUI features improves the usability of the program:

- in economic terms this can result in a cash saving for the employer as users can work more quickly, make less errors, require less training
- in ergonomic terms the software package is more user-friendly, causing less stress.

The EU Directive 90/270 on the minimum safety and health requirements for work with display screen equipment supports the development of GUI software. It states that: 'Software must be easy to use, where appropriate adaptable to the operator's level of knowledge or experience' (See Appendix 1).

The effects of using information technology (IT)

Business computers have been available for over 40 years and most organisations now use them. This trend is unlikely to be reversed but firms wishing to install information technology should be aware of what it is that they hope to achieve, what the implications are and whether they will get value for money.

Studies in recent years for example show that:

- IT does not seem to be linked to overall productivity increases
- 70% of users declared that their systems were not repaying the investment made in them
- only 31% of companies report that IT has been very successful
- 20% of money spent on IT is wasted and 30–40% of expenditure gives no measurable benefit

(Source: quoted by Dan Remenyi *Information Management Case Studies* - Pitman)

The need for an IT strategy

A business should have an IT strategy. Many organisations have acquired computers on an ad hoc basis in the past, different departments having chosen different systems as the need arose. Such a business may find it impossible to transfer data from one part of the organisation to another because the different systems cannot be linked.

Evaluation of systems

Computer manufacturers are continually developing faster systems and business is urged to continually upgrade to these. (Remember the advertising for the 'Pentium' chip which suggested that everything else was now out of date?) However, studies show that software, rather than hardware, should be the most important factor when deciding to increase use of computers in a company. For instance, if the need is to upgrade the accounting system it will be the available software which is important.

Three sets of criteria may be used to evaluate any office application:

- How powerful and easy to use is it? Graphical user interfaces such as Microsoft Windows (the market leader) and IBM's OS/2 (in second place) do appear to improve productivity especially where new users are concerned. Most new software uses GUIs.
- How well do applications work together? It is vital that duplication of data-entry is avoided. Where data exists within the organisation it should be possible for it to be used wherever it is needed. This is only possible if the computers used within different parts of the organisation are able to 'talk' to each other. Compatible software needs to be used across the organisation. (Can you use your discs in all of the computer rooms at school/college?)
- How functional is the application? Do the software applications do what they are meant to do? If the system is adequate there is no point in spending money on a new one just because it exists.

Costs

Information technology is important where it enables a business to achieve its goals. However, cost is always important and evidence seems to show that IT is more expensive than firms realise. According to KPMG Management Consultants (1992) 'hidden' support costs can be five times the amount estimated. This includes help from other staff and time spent on security and back-up procedures. They believe the cost of owning a PC can be up to £6,000 pa.

Other costs can include:

- staff training
- introducing health and safety measures
- the need to maintain efficient security
- the requirement to have effective contingency procedures.

Computer systems are capable of failure and disasters can occur. A dramatic example was the failure of the new computer at London Ambulance Service. As a result ambulances failed to respond to emergency cases.

Two recent trends in keeping down IT costs are:

- **Downsizing** – When we look at Human Resources Management (Unit 4) we will see that downsizing means laying off employees. However, in IT it simply means using smaller systems, such as a mini-computer instead of a mainframe, or a PC instead of a mini. This is possible as the hardware becomes more powerful.
- **Outsourcing** – This again is a term used in Human Resources Management; it refers to the growing trend of buying-in services rather than employing them full-time. In IT outsourcing of staff and equipment is becoming more popular as a way of cutting costs. It is usual, for instance, to have a maintenance contract rather than to employ specialist maintenance staff within the organisation. Similarly systems analysts are bought in to adapt applications to the business' needs. (A college management information system will have been set up with such advice.)

Benefits

Benefits to a business from information technology are difficult to measure. However, broadly benefits can come under the following headings:

- **Efficiency systems** – these systems enable the business to gain the same or better results form fewer resources. This may mean a reduction in staff (and therefore cost) needed for a given level of operations because of the speed with which operations can be performed. An experienced word processing operator can call up and edit a document whereas a typist would start again. The accountant can produce complex financial calculations rapidly using a spreadsheet; if required, figures can be graphed instantly. A database search can be conducted in a fraction of the time that it would take to sort through the manual records.
- **Effectiveness systems** – these systems allow managers to make better decisions so that the organisation benefits. Management information systems, for example, aim to allow managers access to better quality (accurate and up-to-date) information.
- **Empowering/exploiting systems** – these change the way in which a firm does business. Using IT may enable a firm to operate in a way that was not previously possible. Real-time systems which allow Sainsburys to reorder stock from the electronic point of sale (EPOS), or the Tribute ticketing system used for booking railway tickets within Britain and to European destinations are examples. Ultimately the benefits to the firm will come through efficiency.

IT and the employee

Where an organisation is introducing IT for the first time new software should be introduced in stages and with full consultation, so that users have the chance to adapt to the new system and gain some appreciation of what the computers can do.

To the extent that IT allows a job to be performed more effectively such a system may lead to increased job satisfaction. The ability to communicate instantly and in detail provides opportunities for business that would otherwise be lost. Potentially IT allows for high quality presentation, though relevance and quality remain the responsibility of the user.

Efficiency may mean that less people are required and that staff are made redundant. Remember that whilst a reduction in staff is of benefit to an organisation ('right-sizing' to use Human Resources jargon) it does not benefit the employee. The loss of jobs in middle-management in particular has been attributed to the increased use of IT within organisations.

Whilst the introduction of IT requires training for new skills, some employees may be de-skilled. For example double-entry book-keeping can be performed effectively by an accurate data inputter and an accounting package – little knowledge is needed and the books will always balance. Where work is reduced to simply keying-in data there can be a loss of job satisfaction and a risk of repetitive strain injury.

Stress can occur with the increased rate of work and the monitoring of staff performance by speed or accuracy of which some packages are capable. Certainly computerised systems are capable of turning out more information which may add to the workload of managers.

Case studies

The need for information technology

Cygna insurance is based in Philadelphia and has 500 offices worldwide. Externally it uses over 35,000 different forms representing tens of millions of sheets of paper. There is a vast cost, not only in paper, but in storage and in replacing forms as they become obsolete. This runs to millions of dollars a year.

Moving the forms into electronic format would save on paper and warehousing. There would be an additional saving because the electronic data would be in a format which could be processed by computer rather than needing to be retyped, as under the existing paper-based system.

Management Information Systems (MIS) at Bass Brewers

At Bass, as with many other organisations, management falls into three broad categories.

- Strategic – concerning the direction of the business (such as increasing market share)
- Tactical – setting up budgets, putting operations in place
- Operational – running the business on a day-to-day basis.

The managers need a variety of information about customers, suppliers, products, prices, discounts, invoices and so on. In a competitive market this information needs to be of high quality and it needs to be up to date. It can take the form of text, numbers and increasingly graphics, video and voice. The key is information technology.

Gathering information This is now almost completely electronic. Internal data comes from transaction processing systems such as EPOS (electronic point of sale) tills in pubs, accounting systems and so on. External data comes from EDI. E-mail is used to deliver text and high-quality graphics are moved over LANs.

Much information is gathered by people in the course of their daily jobs. Stores records and bar sales, captured electronically, provide important management data.

Use of information by management Information is one of the tools that management use; the other is people. Questions that need answering are: What is cashflow like? What is the period profit? Are we up to budget? How are sales? How many customers have we gained/lost? What do Sainsburys want tomorrow? Answers to these and many more questions are the basis for management decisions.

Equipment used Bass use 8 large IBM AS400 computers. Connected to these by a WAN are 104 LANs, 120 file servers and around 3,500 PCs which use Windows. The data collected through the system is processed and turned into information in the form of various management reports.

Source: Bass Brewers

Cost effectiveness of computers at Sefton Meadow Seafoods

Sefton Meadow Seafoods is a Liverpool-based packing company. They use a LAN of eight PCs and a fileserver with 8 Mb of RAM and a 500 Mb hard disc. The company uses Datafile accounting packages.

The package has proved cost effective with the following benefits:

- 35 per cent reduction in accounting fees. The auditors took a third of the time to go through the books
- customer debts are dealt with effectively as the company always has up-to-date knowledge
- disc space is needed but is very cheap – 500 Mb costs around £150
- the computer has paid for itself – accounting staff have been halved!
- cash is now managed better so the overdraft is reduced with a saving on interest charges.

Source: adapted from *PC User*

Activities

Effects of information technology

1 The usual reason for the introduction of computers to the administration system is to increase efficiency. Identify ways in which this happened in the case of Sefton Seafoods. How could it help in the case of Cygna?

2 How will the management information system be of benefit to Bass?

3 Are the effects of introducing IT always beneficial:

   a to the company?

   b to the employees?

Give reasons and examples.

4 Unlike the Internet a management information system will have restricted access. What measures might Bass take to ensure the security of their information? What are the possible consequences if this information fell into the wrong hands?

5 What type of computer do you think each of the following is:

   a IBM AS400 (Bass)

   b the fileserver (Sefton Meadow Seafoods)?

6 What benefits will EDI have for Bass?

7 Microsoft use the word 'intuitive' when advertising Windows software on television. What are they trying to say about Windows?

The Data Protection Act 1984

With the development of computer databases a great deal of private information has been amassed on individuals by organisations such as hospitals, insurance companies and banks. The speed with which computers can search and sort data allied to the fact that the data can be accessed from great distances via modem has meant that it is increasingly easy for this information to be passed on. It was recognised that there was a need to protect the rights of those about whom data is held.

The **Data Protection Act 1984** only applies to automatically processed information. This is usually information which is processed on a computer. It does not cover information which is held or processed manually, for example, ordinary paper files.

Appendix 2 contains:

- unfamiliar word or phrases which are used in the Act
- the eight data protection principles
- data which is exempt from the Act
- the powers of the Data Protection Registrar
- individual rights.

Activity

You have been asked for advice about several incidents regarding data protection. Read Appendix 2 carefully and then suggest appropriate action:

a 'I've just been refused a bank loan; they say I've got a criminal record. This is completely untrue. There must be some mistake.'

b 'I'm fed up with junk mail. I joined the AA recently; I didn't tick the box about not being on a mailing list because I know they're not allowed to pass on information, That's what data protection is all about.'

c 'At work they're started to collect information for equal opportunities monitoring. There was no mention of data protection on the self-assessment form we were asked to complete. When I asked at personnel they said this was similar to payroll data and they didn't need to register. What *should* they be doing?'

d 'I'm really upset. When I joined a snooker club I filled in an application form which included a question about marital status. At the time I didn't object to this question but now the whole club seem to know about me. I thought this information would be confidential.'

Key terms

Data processing
Data
Information
Batch processing
Real time processing
Input devices
RSI
RAM
GUI
Icon
Windows
Bytes
CPU
Printer
VDU
Permanent storage
Floppy disk
Hard disk
CD-ROM
EC Directive 90/270
Data Protection Act
Spreadsheet
Word processor
Database
Desk-top publishing
Hardware
Software
Input
Output
Processing
Memory
CAD
Applications software
Systems software
Management information systems (MIS)

Review questions

1 What is the difference between data and information?
2 Batch processing is time-driven. What does this mean?
3 Give one example of batch processing.
4 Real time processing is event-driven. What does this mean?
5 Give one example of real time processing.
6 What do the initials RSI stand for?
7 What happens to the computer memory (RAM) when the electrical supply is disconnected?
8 Name a major manufacturer of microprocessors (the silicon chip).
9 What is the connection between GUI and usability?
10 Which recent directive has been concerned with VDU users?
11 What is the difference between impact and non-impact printers?
12 Give an example of an impact printer and one example of a non-impact printer.
13 How many megabytes will a $3\frac{1}{2}$ inch high density floppy disk store?
14 How many kilobytes will a double density disk store?
15 How much information is a CD-ROM able to store?
16 In which year did the Data Protection Act become law?
17 Name five input devices.
18 Name three output devices.

Assignment 4.2
Is IT working?

This assignment develops knowledge and understanding of the following elements:
2.4 Analyse information processing in a business organisation.

It supports development of the following core skills:
Communication 3.1, 3.2
Information technology 3.1, 3.2, 3.3, 3.4

You are required to act upon the following memo. You may use your college/school, work experience placement or any other suitable local organisation.

Your organisation

To: A Student

From: Senior management team

The senior management team wish you to carry out a survey into the effectiveness of electronic information processing within the organisation. Specifically we want you to:

1 Identify those sections within the organisation where you would find the following: number processing, text processing, record-keeping concerning personal details (for example of employees or customers), use of graphics.

Discover which hardware is available in each section and which software is used by/for each of the functions. Please indicate its particular use (writing newsletters etc.)

This information can be presented in the form of a table.

2 Please comment on the compatibility (or otherwise) of software between sections. If you can, discover whether there is any overall company policy about buying new hardware and software.

3 Are we registered with the Data Protection Registrar? If so, why is it necessary?

Would you briefly summarise rights of individuals under the Data Protection Act. Do we inform individuals of their rights? If so please give details; if not do they know them?

Are there any costs to the organisation in complying with the Act? Again give details.

4 We need to know how information technology is affecting the organisation.
Would you interview two managers in different sections to find out how they feel IT benefits the business and its employees. Specific examples would be helpful.
Do they see any disadvantages either to employees or to the business?

5 Please provide a brief conclusion giving any suggestions for improvements.

Notes
Our managers are busy so please make arrangements for interviews in advance.
Use appropriate software for the report, please proof-read carefully and spell-check. Make sure you keep a copy on disk.
A sheet of contents will be helpful, so you will need to provide page numbers. For reference purposes would you put your name and your filename in the footer?
If you attach appendices make sure that you refer to them in the report.

UNIT 3 MARKETING

5 Market research and forecasting

What is covered in this chapter

- What is marketing?
- Market research
  - Methods of collecting data
- Sampling
- Consumer characteristics
- Forecasting

These are the resources that you will need for your Marketing file:

- questionnaires
- company reports
- published forecasts
- marketing magazines
- statistical publication
- Euromonitor.

What is marketing?

The dictionary definition of **marketing** is 'the business of selling goods including advertising, packaging, etc.' The 'etc.' is important because it is what marketing is about; the identification and satisfaction of customers' needs and wants. Advertising and packaging are only a small part of this process.

The Chartered Institute of Marketing defines marketing as 'the management process responsible for identifying, anticipating and satisfying customer requirements profitably'. For Nestlé, for example, it is finding out what consumers want and giving them a reason for buying a particular product. This is done by a process called branding which endeavours to give a product distinction from other products and make people want to buy it. Branding gives a product unique appeal, with a name, a pack design and a 'personality'.

Activity

1 Carry out a small survey in your class or in your local supermarket. Find as many products as you can in the Nestlé range. (*Hint:* They range from confectionery, coffee, mineral water and tinned spaghetti – to pet food!)
2 Choose five of the products; say what 'personality' you think they have. Have Nestlé succeeded?

Marketing aims and objectives

One marketing **aim** could be 'to increase sales'; one marketing **objective** could be 'to increase sales by 8 per cent over the next two years'.

Objectives must be precise and quantified to show the time span within which they are to be achieved. They should be attainable, realistic targets, which motivate the business and serve as the basis for its planning and decision making.

Every business will have its own marketing objectives which depend on its needs and wants and those of its existing and potential customers. Lloyds Bank plc, for example, might wish to increase or decrease loans and deposits, or sell more financial products, such as mortgages and investment schemes. A betting shop might wish to spread its risks and improve its image. A college might wish to attract more adult students onto GNVQ Advanced level courses. An English Riviera resort, such as Torbay, might wish to sell more holidays during September and October to extend the holiday season.

When we look at a range of businesses, several common objectives emerge.

Objectives

1 To increase sales revenue (for example, by 19 per cent over two years) – whilst physical sales are important in many businesses, it is the sales revenue which matters most. There is little point in chasing every sale, however small, if it involves increasing costs by a disproportionate amount, although a business may sometimes do this to keep 'goodwill', or if it believes there could be long-term gains.

2 To increase market share (for example, by 4 per cent over the next 18 months) – the market share is the proportion or percentage of the market served by a particular brand or business. Being Number One adds sales and status to a brand – the implication is it must be good. However, being Number Two in the market can also be turned into a classic selling point, as the famous slogan 'We are Number Two. We try harder!', demonstrates.

3 To maintain/improve product and business image. What image or mental picture do you have of politicians, used car salespeople ('remarketing'!), Marks & Spencer? Companies spend millions on promoting and protecting their images. Banks, for instance, rely entirely on public confidence in order to operate. Companies are very concerned to protect their image. For example, when jars of baby food were found to have been tampered with while on supermarket shelves, the manufacturers, Heinz, put plastic tamper-proof seals around the lids. Marketing departments have now made these seals a selling point 'Double wrapped for perfect freshness'. Some companies, for example, ICI, Hanson and Cadbury's, tend to use corporate advertising to promote their image, whilst other companies, for example, Nestlé concentrate on brand or product promotion. Note that 'improving the brand image' is an aim; it could become an objective if it could be related to a quantified improvement in, for example, sales volume or value.

Activity

A company's image depends to some extent on the relationship between price and quality. The diagram shows one way these could be related. Can you name some retail outlets which come into each category?

		Quality	
Price	High	'Cowboy'	'Premium'
	Low	'Economic'	'Bargain'
		Low	High

4 To give quality assurance – Total Quality Management (TQM) is now recognised as vital, if a business wants to increase its sales and meet its customers' demands. Quality systems began as a method for controlling production. Today these systems are applied to all aspects of the business and marketing is no exception.

The first aim of many businesses is to provide 'quality goods' and a 'quality service'. Quality standards have been developed, which when achieved by a business, show that it is practising quality approved system. ISO 9000 is the international standard. In order to achieve TQM the business will have to make sure:

- that management and workforce are fully committed and focused on quality;
- that everything a business does is done for the customer;
- that everyone is seen and treated as a customer, both externally (buyers of products) and internally (the person who works next to you). In practice, this would mean, for example, handling internal and external phone calls in exactly the same way;
- it knows its customers' problems and needs. This means creating a customer care service which works on the principle of once a customer, always a customer.

Marketing objectives provide a vision of what the business intends to achieve in the medium to long term. They are the key to its survival.

Maslow's Hierarchy of Needs has many applications, for instance in Personnel (see Chapter 7) where it is about motivation and in Marketing where it is about satisfying consumers' needs.

These needs are expressed through our demand for food, shelter, clothing, music, education, holidays, status symbols such as 'flash cars', mobile phones and designer suits. Can you think of other examples in each category?

These needs are continually changing, as people grow older, change jobs, change homes or have children. Marketing too, needs to be dynamic to keep pace with these changes. To get the data it needs a business will have to carry out market research. It will need to find out what consumers and other businesses need, in its local, regional, national and international markets.

Gathering market information

Organisations require data and statistics for many purposes including:

- having a permanent record in order to make comparisons with past events, for example, are sales this week better or worse than this time last year?
- possessing the background information to help solve problems;
- making comparisons with competitors, for example, has our share of the market gone up or down? have we met our targets?
- providing a foundation and guide for decision making, for example, on the appropriate volume of sales in targeted sections of the market;
- planning for the future as the more information a company possesses the easier it is for it to achieve its objectives;
- for use as a management tool to control its budgets, for example, comparing the difference between planned and actual promotional expenditure;
- making forecasts and estimates;
- assisting quality control. Statistical techniques can provide a powerful tool for controlling and monitoring production quality. This is important for customer satisfaction and reduces complaints.

Most companies, however small, have an **information need**.

Sources of information

Every business now has almost instant access to a vast amount of data. Much of the general information is free, although more specialised sources can be expensive especially for private subscribers.

Within the business, every department and section will have its own records which are an invaluable source of marketing management information. These are discussed further in the section on Business documents. Here are some of the more important sources of internal data that can be used to complement the external secondary material.

- **Sales department:** sales targets, sales invoices, *promotion* details, orders
- **Finance department:** invoices and *prices*, standard costs, customer accounts
- **Personnel department:** job descriptions, time sheets
- **Production department:** *product* records, quality data
- **Transport department:** delivery times, delivery routes, *place* and suppliers, customer details, distribution data.

All this information will be needed by the marketing department to analyse past trends and make forecasts. We have highlighted the four 'Ps' Price, Product, Promotion and Place. You will see in the next chapter how these are used to formulate marketing plans.

The main written sources of external information published by the government are shown in Table 5.1. Most of these would be available in any library but a business could obtain the more specialist publications direct from the Department of Trade and Industry (DTI); the Central Statistical Office (CSO) also publishes a guide to sources of information. You should copy and complete the table yourself. Much of this material is now available on disk.

Table 5.1 Sources of information

Information needed / **Publication**	Annual Abstract of Statistics	Monthly Digest of Statistics	Business Monitors	Employment Gazette	Family Expenditure Survey	Census of: Population Distribution Production	Social Trends	Eurostat
Education						✓		
Labour/Wages	✓	✓		✓			✓	
Trade	✓	✓						
Finance	✓					✓		
Production	✓	✓				✓		
Population	✓					✓	✓	
Retail prices				✓	✓			
Wholesale prices								
Market share			✓					
Consumer spending					✓			
Sales forecasts			✓					
Financial statistics	✓		✓					

Additionally, a wide range of information is provided by both national and international institutions, for example, the World Bank, European Union, UNESCO, banks, trade unions, trade associations, the CBI and Chambers of Commerce.

Market research

Have you ever been stopped on the street by people who say they are doing market research when in fact they are either trying to sell you something (usually financial services!) or raising money for some cause or other. Have you been interviewed for an opinion poll and been asked whom you would vote for? The people who are asking these questions are market researchers or interviewers and are working for a market research company.

Although the image of these opinion polls was dented in the General Election of 1992 (they were wrong by 8 per cent, or the difference between a Labour and Conservative government) they are still used.

What is market research?

Market research has been defined as 'systematic problem analysis, model building and fact finding for the purposes of improved decision making in the marketing of goods and services'. Put simply it means getting the information for identifying the customers' needs and wants and spotting market opportunities and trends.

Researching customers

To meet its customers' needs and therefore improve its chances of survival, a business must provide customers with what they want, when they want it, at the right price and quality. To do this it will need to know:

- how many customers there are;
- how much they are willing to pay, including their buying habits and patterns of spending;
- what their needs, desires, expectations, likes and dislikes, attitudes and prejudices are;
- how it can best inform, persuade and convince customers to purchase the product;
- what motivates customers and what attracts them to particular brands, for example, it could be the quality, design, colour, safety, or guarantees given with the product.

To achieve maximum sales, an organisation will need to use its **market research** data to target its customers. This process is allied to **market segmentation** and means sub-dividing the total market into segments or sections. This can be done, for example, on the basis of age, income, geographical area (local, regional or national) and/or lifestyle. Marketing activity can then be directed and focused towards the chosen groups.

A new furniture store, for example, might concentrate on people in their twenties, setting up home for the first time. Banks target 18-year-olds at the beginning of the new academic year. This extract from the 'Bianco' press release (Nestlé, white chocolate) shows how segmentation is used in practice.

> 'The advertising strategy aims to establish the brand positioning as playful, carefree spontaneity. The target audience is all chocolate lovers – primarily women aged 20-35 but not excluding men. The "core" age will be 25 years old'.

Researching competitors

The main reason for a business researching competitors' products is so that it can develop and market its own brands more successfully. It will need to find out:

- whether competitors have similar products;
- what their prices are;
- how they will react to a new competitor, for example, will they cut prices, or offer discounts. Following the launch of Yorkie by Rowntree Mackintosh in 1977, Cadbury reacted by redesigning and re-launching their Cadbury's Dairy Milk range in a new chunky form;
- how they produce, sell and distribute their products.

Look at these four points with respect to the rivalry between Cadbury's and Nestlé. How do you think they apply?

The answers to these and other questions about competitors can help a new business to gain a foothold in its chosen market and keep an existing business ahead of the competition.

How market research is carried out

These are the stages required for carrying out a market research investigation.

Stage 1

Define the terms of reference and decide what information needs to be collected. If it is a problem which is being investigated, be absolutely certain that you know what the real problem is. Always try to narrow the problem down, which makes it easier to investigate. Look for symptoms in the business such as:

- unsatisfactory quality,
- a high level of complaints, or
- a poor delivery record.

Once the problem is isolated and defined, any solution will usually require the company to move from its present unsatisfactory position to a new satisfactory method of operation.

Stage 2

Plan the investigation. Some of the criteria that will need to be considered at this stage are:

- the deadline for completion,
- the complexity of the issues (more complex issues take longer to investigate),
- the costs which are involved,
- whether the survey is to be local, regional or national,
- the extent to which the survey can be computerised.

If complicated issues are being investigated it is best to have properly trained interviewers, even though this can be expensive. Future problems can also be avoided if proper planning is undertaken at this stage.

Stage 3

Collect the data. A sample will probably need to be selected. The type of sample will depend upon the requirements of the investigation. A national sample will be more expensive than if the survey is localised. The collection method chosen will largely depend on the time and costs involved, and the response rate which is required. Additionally, if a questionnaire is to be given out, it will need to be drafted and piloted before it is given to the public. Finally, considerable care should be taken when framing the questions to be asked.

Stage 4

Organise the data. Once the data has been collected, it needs to be coded, counted and classified. Computers are now frequently used to do this.

Stage 5

Analyse the data. A range of statistical techniques will need to be used to analyse and interpret the data. For instance, if a mail order company is experiencing difficulties with deliveries and has received a number of complaints, once it has received the survey data it will need to calculate:

- historical trends so as to establish patterns of events,
- average delivery times,
- variability or variation from the average.

Stage 6

Presenting the information. Effective presentation is the key to persuading people to accept the results of an inquiry, however pleasant or unpleasant these may be for the audience. A range of techniques is now available to present results.

Stage 7

Drawing conclusions and giving recommendations. When these are required, propose some options, evaluate each one and make a recommendation.

Finally, thoroughly check your report or presentation before it is submitted.

Types of market research information

Market research can be conducted into the whole range of marketing activities carried out by the business.

Sales research	**Advertising research**
Market share	Assessment of adverts
Channels of distribution	Media studies
Distribution costs	Recall studies
Test markets	Cost effectiveness
Export markets	Export requirements
Product research	**Forecasting**
New products	Short and long term
Packaging and design	Sales trends
Competitors' products	Profit comparisons
Product testing	Customer behaviour
Product substitutes	Export opportunities

Primary and secondary research

Broadly, there are two ways in which the information can be acquired: by **primary** or first-hand research or by **secondary** or second-hand research.

Primary research

This may be either the company's own personal research, or it could be research carried out by a specialist market research agency on the company's behalf. It may involve direct contact with possible consumers and competitors. Using an agency can be much cheaper than if the business does everything itself.

The information obtained is called *primary data*. It is collected for a specific purpose, will be original and will be up-to-date. It can be used to provide answers to problems or to establish a database for future operations.

Secondary research

This uses published or secondary data which has been collected by others for their own purpose. Great care needs to be taken when using secondary sources and research.

Always bear in mind that the data has been collected and analysed for some other purpose and this may have affected the data analysis and presentation.

When using material published by someone else, a company should ask:

- Which organisation collected the information?
- Is the source reliable?
- What purpose did the collectors wish to achieve? For example, statistics about smoking prepared by a tobacco company, or statistics about railway travel prepared by a road haulage pressure group are likely to be biased in their favour.
- When were the figures collected?
- What do they include/exclude?
- What do the definitions mean?
- Are the data accurate?
- Is the organisation politically neutral?

Methods of collecting data

There are four basic methods which can be used for collecting information:

- questionnaires
- telephone interviews
- face-to-face interviews
- direct observation.

The choice of method will be determined by many factors. For example, if a wide area has to be covered it may be more appropriate to use postal questionnaires because these can be cheaper than using interviewers. When the type of information required is complex or difficult, trained interviewers could give a better result. In practice it is a matter of balancing the cost and effort involved against the rate of response. Higher response rates are usually more expensive to obtain.

Below is summary of the advantages and disadvantages of each method of collecting market research data.

Method	Advantages	Disadvantages
Telephone survey – a structured set of questions is recommended	Easy to carry out; fast and convenient; flexible; satisfactory response rate; people may be more willing to respond over the phone	Can be expensive, depends on time and distance; respondents have little time to answer; body language cannot be seen; can be biased
Postal survey – a clear, detailed questionnaire is needed	Costs can be controlled; people have time to respond; any area can be covered; people may be more truthful, particularly if the reply is anonymous	Very low response rate, i.e. the number of replies; questions cannot be explained or answers verified
Face-to-face interviews – a personal interview between the interviewer and respondent	High response rate; flexible and easily controlled; extra questions can be asked; answers can be clarified; body language can be seen	Very expensive; needs trained interviewers; can take considerable time; can be biased unless people are carefully selected
Observation – direct observation of a task or activity	Very accurate and can be easily controlled, e.g. accompanied shopping to find out what and how consumers buy	Very expensive and time-consuming; needs full co-operation from the people being observed

Interviews

A **structured** interview is a formal interview during which the interviewer will ask a set number of prepared questions usually based on a questionnaire. Most street interviews are structured.

In **unstructured** interviews, the interviewer will try to guide the interviewee by prompting and asking leading questions which encourage replies. They tend to be expensive because more time is involved, but a good response rate is expected. They are often used in social surveys where an informal approach is required.

Questionnaires

A **questionnaire** is a set of printed questions which is given to a number of people in order to collect statistical information. Questionnaires can be used at college, in the home, at the local shopping centre, or on an aeroplane when you return from holiday. They can be completed by the respondent (the person completing the questionnaire) or an interviewer can write down the answers which the respondent gives.

The purpose of a questionnaire is twofold:

- to gather general information about the respondent such as age and occupation. This will later be used to determine what market segment or category people belong to.
- to collect the specific data required for the investigation. Whenever possible a trial or pilot survey should be carried out first to ensure that the final questionnaire works and will achieve its purpose.

Types of questions

Dichotomous – these are close-ended questions with only two possible choices, for example, yes or no; agree or disagree; true or false. They are good for providing **quantitative information**.

Multiple choice – these are also close-ended because a definite answer has to be given. However, in this case there are more than two choices.

Open-ended – these are questions which do not have a predetermined answer. They are often used by retailers to find out customers' opinions. Although they are good for gathering **qualitative information**, they can be difficult to interpret. For example, 'What do you think of the shop in general?' or 'How were you treated by the sales people?' could produce the reply 'Very nicely'. But what does 'nicely' mean?

Scaled or rated questions – these give the respondent a fixed range of possible replies. For example:

Q8. I would now like you to give your opinion of how you would expect AA staff to deal with breakdowns. Below is a list of things that have been said about AA staff.

First of all please give your opinion of the service you would expect from AA TELEPHONE STAFF whom you would ring in the event of a breakdown. Please give your answer by ticking the relevant box using the scale 1 to 10 shown below where 10 is the most positive answer and 1 is the most negative answer.

	10	9	8	7	6	5	4	3	2	1	
H. Efficient	☐	☐	☐	☐	☐	☐	☐	☐	☐	☐	Inefficient
I. Courteous/Polite	☐	☐	☐	☐	☐	☐	☐	☐	☐	☐	Rude/Abusive
J. Helpful	☐	☐	☐	☐	☐	☐	☐	☐	☐	☐	Unhelpful
K. Professional	☐	☐	☐	☐	☐	☐	☐	☐	☐	☐	Unprofessional
L. Warm/Friendly	☐	☐	☐	☐	☐	☐	☐	☐	☐	☐	Cold/Unfriendly
M. Respectful	☐	☐	☐	☐	☐	☐	☐	☐	☐	☐	Patronising/Condescending
N. Reassuring/Calming	☐	☐	☐	☐	☐	☐	☐	☐	☐	☐	Brisk/Abrupt
O. Concerned/Interested	☐	☐	☐	☐	☐	☐	☐	☐	☐	☐	Unconcerned/Disinterested

Figure 5.1 An example of a rated question from an AA questionnaire

Some basic rules on how to construct a questionnaire

GIVE AN EXPLANATION OF THE QUESTIONNAIRE HERE AT THE BEGINNING

1. Every question should be essential. Beware of the temptation to ask too many questions.
2. Questions must not be ambiguous. There must be only one interpretation possible.
3. It should be easy for people to understand the question, for example, 'Do you walk to school?' is better than 'Do you perambulate to school?'
4. Every question should be precise because vague questions will only confuse people.
5. Questions must not be biased or break the equal opportunities laws. An 'ethnic monitoring' question can be asked, when the respondent decides the group to which he or she belongs.
6. Questions should be short, because asking and answering questions costs time and money.
7. Questions should not embarrass people by being too personal or complicated, for example, 'If you had £5 and had already spent 85p on butter, £1.75 on cheese, would you buy a Crispy Cake for £3.50?'
8. Questions should be carefully laid out using lots of space.
9. Questions should be arranged in a logical order and follow on naturally.
10. Wherever possible provide 'tick boxes' or a rating system to allow people to answer quickly and easily, for example, 'What is your attendance on the GNVQ course?' could be rated as:

    Excellent ☐ Very good ☐ Satisfactory ☐ Fair ☐

    Poor ☐ Don't know ☐ Don't care ☐.
11. All questions and answers should be coded to allow for simple computer input. The results and analysis of the data can then be done quickly.

SAY 'THANK YOU' AT THE END OF THE QUESTIONNAIRE.

Activity

The Principal of your college/school has asked your group to carry out a market research survey to find out what students think of the institution and its courses.

a Construct a questionnaire which covers college/school facilities, cleanliness, atmosphere, library, the quality of the courses, details of the respondent and suggestions for improvement.

b Pilot, test and refine your questionnaire by trying it out on a few people before you carry out your full survey.

(Do not carry out the full survey.)

Sampling

A sample survey is a way of collecting primary information from a small part of the total number of individuals or items that could be investigated, for example, a spoonful of rice from a saucepan is a sample. The total is normally referred to as the **population** or universe. For example, in a car factory, the population is the total number of cars produced; in a bakery, it is the total number of loaves of bread which are baked; in a hairdressers, it is every client.

The sample which is chosen should be representative, i.e. typical of the whole population. It is a cross-section. The purpose of sampling is to find out and make estimates about the population which are based on the results of the sample. Ideally a sample should be as large as possible and/or practicable, because a bigger sample will give more accurate results about the population.

The benefits of sampling a population compared to investigating every item – a census, for example, the Census of Population that counts everyone in the UK every 10 years – are that:

- the costs are lower;
- inputting and analysis of the data is quicker (most of the 1991 census results are now available);
- greater flexibility and control are possible.

Bias in sampling

Bias refers to any influence which makes the results obtained from the sample differ significantly from the actual or true results for the population. Bias can occur because:

- the list of items from which the sample is selected is inaccurate or incomplete, for example, on the electoral register people may have moved elsewhere;
- the sample is unrepresentative, or untypical, for example, items could be selected because they are convenient or easy to reach, like always asking your friends or family, or always going to the local shop, when you are asked to find people to answer a questionnaire.

The sampling frame

The **sampling frame** is the information required before a sample can be chosen. It is normally a numbered list of all the items in the population, for example, the chassis numbers of cars on a production line, the batch numbers on canned drinks, the bar codes now found on most products. Creating the database for a sampling frame can be a very expensive process, particularly if a very large number of items or individuals is involved. For example, listing all the people in the UK would be a very tedious and costly process, although some 40 million people are on a database which shows their credit rating.

Random sampling

A **random sample** is one in which every item which can be chosen has an equal chance of being selected. For this to be achieved a complete sampling frame must exist with every item identified and numbered. Each item can be selected either by:

- sampling without replacement which means once an item has been chosen, it cannot be chosen again, such as numbers in the National Lottery, or
- sampling with replacement which means an item can be selected more than once.

There are several ways in which this can be done. When the numbers are fairly small, each individual can be allocated a number, and the sample can be picked out of a box or hat, such as a raffle. Alternatively, random number tables can be used to give random numbers which show the items to be selected.

Random number tables

These are published lists of random numbers. Here is part of a random number table:

07 51 34 87 92 47 31 48 36 60 68 90 70 53 36 82 57 99 79 23 03 00 12 29

The numbers show which items should be selected for investigation. The sample is chosen by taking numbers which correspond to the size of the population. For example, if the population has between 10 and 99 items only two-digit numbers should be chosen from the table.

Activity

Example of simple random sampling

A GNVQ Advanced group consists of 75 students. You are required to select 20 at random. Using the random number table above, the individuals selected would be numbers 07, 51, 34, 47, 31, 48, 36, 60, 68, 70, 53, 57, and so on until we had chosen 20. Note that numbers 87, 92, 90, 82, 99 were ignored, as we only required 20 students out of the population of 75.

Electronic selection

Most scientific calculators will now generate random numbers. ERNIE is the Electronic Random Number Indicator Equipment used to select the winners of Premium Bonds.

Activity

Use your calculator to produce random numbers. Now select five people from your group.

With random sampling, the selection of items should be unbiased and free from personal prejudice. Random sampling works better if the population or group is homogeneous or broadly similar, this means that any item that is chosen would be representative.

Stratified sampling

A stratum (the singular of strata) is a segment or group of items with a set of common characteristics such as age, sex, income group, etc. A stratified sample is one where items are specifically chosen from each strata to represent the population. It is a useful method only when the population or universe can be divided into strata or bands. The members of each stratum will need to be known before the sample can be chosen. Each strata should be homogeneous, or broadly similar, so that any item could be chosen.

Simple random sampling can then be used to select items, so that the sample should reflect or be representative of the whole population. A complete sampling frame is required and it must have enough information to distinguish between the strata. Without a database, creating such a detailed list can be a very expensive process. Generally, a stratified sample will give a more accurate picture of the population than a simple random sample.

Activity

Example of stratified sampling

Suppose we wish to test the weight of cans coming off a production line, which are produced in these proportions:

	X Population	Y Sample
Chilli beans	50	5
Garlic beans	80	8
Paprika beans	150	15
Curry beans	120	12
	400	40

Column X is the total amount produced of each product.

Column Y is the sample size required.

The company usually samples 10 per cent. Therefore a total sample of 40 items must be selected. For a representative sample 10 per cent of each product should be chosen. For example, with curry beans, 10 per cent of the total production is required; 10 per cent of 120 equals 12.

The government statistical service uses stratified sampling to collect much of its information because it is cheaper and can give very reliable results. Here is an example of the strata it works from to gather data about businesses. The 'chance of selection' refers to the likelihood or probability of a business being chosen.

Strata businesses with	Chance of selection
500 employees or more	Certain
200–499 employees	1 in 2
100–199 employees	1 in 12
50–99 employees	1 in 16
11–49 employees	1 in 48
10 and fewer employees	None

Systematic sampling

In this method the first item is selected at random. Subsequent items are then selected systematically, for example, every ninth item is chosen until the total number is achieved. The method is simple to organise and relatively cheap. Its use is recommended when the population is known to be homogenous so that it does not matter which items are chosen. A complete sampling frame is only required if a desk-based selection is to be made. In a street, however, every ninth person is easy to choose.

Multi-stage sampling

This method avoids the need for a complete listing of all items, so a full sampling frame is not required. It is simple to organise and relatively cheap to implement. Groups are sampled in stages.

Example of multi-stage sampling

A company has been asked to survey students in the European Union.

- **Stage 1** – choose a country. Each country would be given a number and then chosen at random. The sampling frame would be countries.
- **Stage 2** – the UK has been chosen, so the next stage is to assign numbers to counties and choose a county. The sampling frame is counties.
- **Stage 3** – your county has been selected. For this stage each GNVQ centre (the information needed for the sampling frame) would be assigned a number and one centre chosen by simple random sampling.
- **Stage 4** – your centre has been chosen. Students of GNVQ Advanced Business at the centre are now allocated numbers. A sampling frame of students is needed, for example, the register. You have been chosen to represent the views of students in Europe.

Cluster sampling

Ideally, the population should be divided into specific groups or clusters. Clusters are then chosen at random. Every item in the cluster is included in the sample. There should be minimum variation between clusters and maximum variation within a cluster. Therefore any cluster could be chosen. A complete sampling frame is not required, but a list of clusters is needed. Once a cluster is chosen, a list of all items within it must be available.

Cluster sampling is easy to administer and carry out, providing the chosen items are close together, for example, housing estates or courses at a college. The results can lack precision and could be biased if the chosen cluster is unrepresentative of the population.

Quota sampling

Quota sampling is a non-random way of sampling. It is often used by interviewers in the street. Audience research surveys carried out on behalf of TV companies frequently use this method. Interviewers are given the responsibility of deciding who is to be included in the sample. The size of each quota, should reflect the population in general. So the sample should contain the same proportion of people with a particular characteristic as are found in the population.

With the broadcasting survey the population is divided into socio-economic categories. So if 5 per cent of the population are in the AB category, then 5 per cent of the sample should come from this group.

Every interviewer has a quota or percentage to interview from each category. The system is cheap and convenient to carry out, but basic information about the population is needed. It is difficult to control, as the choice of who to interview is entirely at the discretion of interviewers. It is the interviewer's choice as to which category a person belongs. How can you tell?

Opinion polls

Political opinion polls use a quota sample. First, 100 constituencies are chosen at random. Secondly, 15 people in each constituency are selected on a quota basis.

Gender	Class	Age
7 males	ABC	4 age groups are used
8 females	C2	
	DE	

Is the quota representative? Should the quota be changed?

Media polls

These tend to attract only those people interested in a topic. The results are likely to be negative, because these are the people who feel most strongly about an issue, for example, they will phone to say they are against fox-hunting, the route of the Channel Tunnel Rail Link, or a new airport runway at Stansted. Newspaper polls tend to be biased towards a particular class, for example, *Sun* readers are mostly C2 and *Financial Times* readers are mostly A/Bs.

Cross-tabulation

There is now so much data held on people that market research companies can now cross-refer the types of people who watch, for example, particular TV programmes with what they eat and drink, with how they live, with what they read. This process, called *data fusion*, is part of the £2 billion TV advertising market.

Activities

1 a Choose 20 people at your workplace, school or college using each of these methods:
- random sampling
- systematic sampling
- stratified sampling
- quota sampling.

b Construct a short questionnaire which will enable you to obtain their views on the canteen facilities.

c Compare the findings from each sampling method. Give the advantages and disadvantages of each method.

d Are there any differences/similarities in the results obtained by each method. Can you say why?

e Write a memo to your Head of Department explaining your findings.

2 Which would be the best sampling method for a small retailer to use to obtain customers views on the level of service? Give reasons for your choice.

3 Which would be the best method for a large nationwide mail order company to use? Give reasons for your choice.

4 A retailer has carried out a survey of customers each Monday morning for the last three weeks. The results of the sample do not reflect the sales of the shop for the whole week. Can you suggest what is wrong with the sample, and how it could be improved?

5 You should have already constructed and piloted a questionnaire about your centre (see page 233). Carry out the survey of your institution. Write up your findings and send these to your Marketing Manager.

Test marketing

In business, it is often the case that companies do not have sufficient time or money to perform rigorous statistical analysis. Therefore, before a product is launched nationally, manufacturers will often first test the reaction of consumers in a specific region. This may well include a full press and TV campaign with promotional back-up, such as free samples. For example, the launch of Guinness's Draught Bitter in cans in the LWT area, involved giving out free samples at London mainline BR stations.

The data which a company obtains in this way will enable it to decide whether it is worthwhile to go for a total nation-wide launch. The test area should ideally be a microcosm of the nation as a whole.

Test town operation – a field trial

This is a miniature version of a test market in which a product whose qualities in use have already been verified through blind placement tests (for example, asking consumers if they prefer A or B without the consumer knowing which is the new product – the Pepsi challenge) is marketed in a limited way so that actual movement through the shops can be audited. Consumers may also be asked to return pre-paid cards giving their views on the product.

The results from these cards would not be read as if they were representative of all consumers in the test town – the universe – but rather as an indication to be used to form a judgement. Therefore, if a few hundred returned cards show a consistent result, this would be sufficient justification to proceed with a wider launch. It is all a question of reconciling what is required with what is practical.

Great care needs to be exercised when interpreting the results of a test market operation, in case they are biased. In the Guinness example the following questions, amongst others, should be considered:

- Was the weather very hot?
- Was the competition advertising its products at the time?
- Are London commuters typical of the population as a whole?

Case study

Yorkie – consumer research

The development of Yorkie, by Nestlé, demonstrates how all the aspects of marketing can be brought together to achieve a successful product.

Sophisticated techniques were used to select the market opportunity. A wholly integrated approach was taken towards the design and presentation of the product and a range of selling and promotional methods were used for its launch.

Yorkie was a deliberately and scientifically conceived and planned entry into the highly competitive chocolate bar market. It was designed to compete with Cadbury's Dairy Milk.

Some research was already available showing people's attitudes to existing brands and their reasons for changing. This was backed up with large-scale qualitative research to find out more about people's motivation, needs and satisfactions in the market for chocolate.

Five new products or concepts were originally created for initial market testing. Each of these had its own name, packaging style, pack design and advertising approach, expressed both visually and verbally.

The five concepts were each tested on four groups of consumers who looked at every aspect of the product. The results of these tests were then evaluated. One concept came out top, that of a thick milk chocolate block to be eaten as sustaining food, in the context of vigorous open air activity; it was called 'Rations'.

The consumer test panels had two criticisms. First, they did not like the name Rations and its implications of wartime austerity, and secondly the image of utility without the enjoyment. New names and new presentations were tried, each of which was subjected to consumer research by the group discussion method. Simultaneously, changes were made in the chocolate moulds to give a more chunky appearance.

By this process of creative invention, research, consequent modification and innovation, the product, its name, package, design and advertising proposition and expression were integrally developed in relation to each other and were mutually supportive of the basic opportunity.

The market opportunity was defined as a gap for a solid, thick block of chocolate – more satisfying as something to eat than existing, thinner blocks – presented with nourishing, sustaining associations. It was also presented as something enjoyable and not merely utilitarian. All these specifications were derived from knowledge and observation of the market and from detailed and repeated use of consumer research.

Source: Information kindly provided by Nestlé

Consumer characteristics – the target audience

Population

Before any market research survey can be undertaken, a business will need to have as much information about its customers (the sampling frame), as possible because the size, gender and age structure of the population are all important in determining the level of demand for a product and the amount of consumer expenditure. For example, the size and composition of a family will influence the type of goods and services which it purchases.

Activity

a Obtain the figures for the age/gender structure of the UK population.
b Plot this data on a suitable chart.
c Obtain these figures for your local area. The 1991 Census of Population data should be available.
d Plot this data on a chart.

Businesses will also need to know the location of the population in order to market their products. People who live in different areas such as rural or urban, inner city or suburban, have particular lifestyles. Shops in urban and rural areas have to provide different goods and services.

The density of the population, i.e. the number of people per square kilometre is needed to determine the number of potential consumers in an area, and to enable a business to plan its distribution.

The socio-economic structure of an area (which is based largely on educational background), must also be determined because particular products sell better in some areas than in others.

Population figures are shown (in 000s) in Figure 5.2.

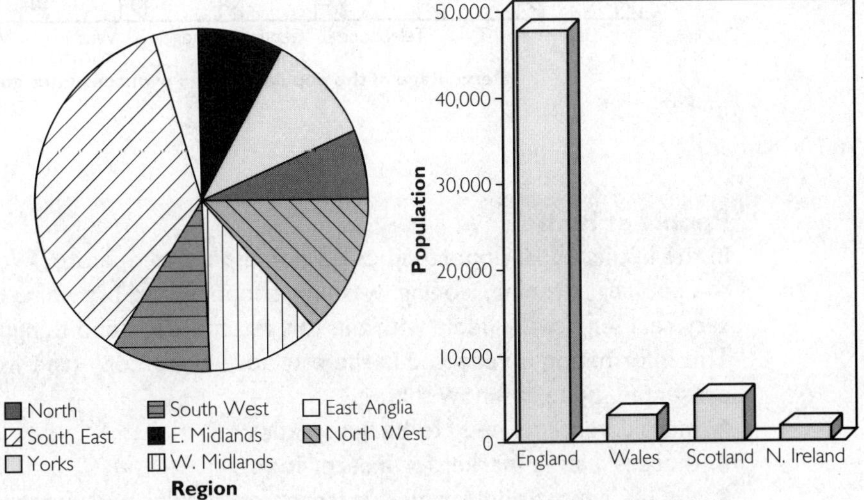

Figure 5.2 Regional population

Activity

a Obtain the figures showing the location of the population in your local area.
b Prepare a set of notes which could be used by a local business, for example, a bakery or double glazing company, to target its consumers.

Lifestyles

The *Family Expenditure Survey*, *Social Trends* and *Regional Trends* are an excellent source of marketing information on consumers. They can be used to find out what is in the average home, how people spend their leisure time, and who does the jobs in the home. These **sources of information** can be used by a business when planning its advertising and other promotion. They are the basis for dividing the population into market segments, i.e. groups of people with common characteristics. Look at Figure 5.3. What does it tell us about living standards and lifestyles in the UK today?

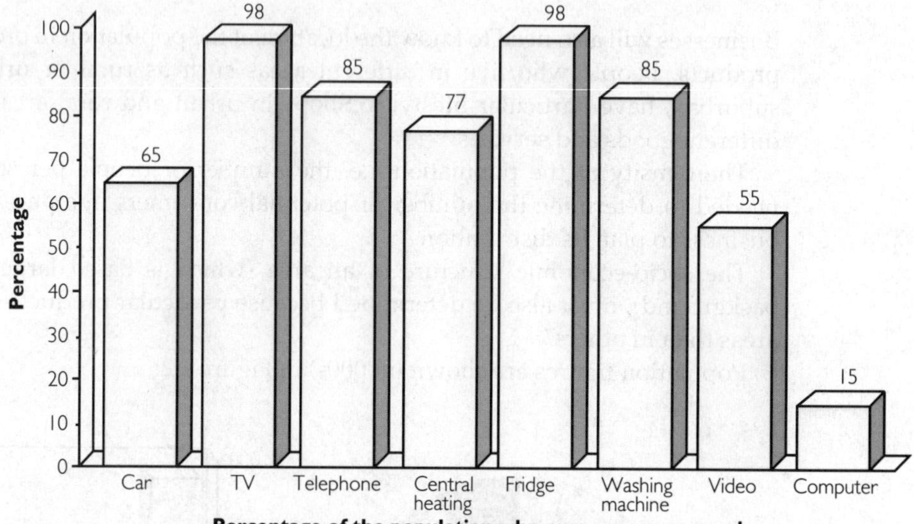

Figure 5.3

People at home

In the home, equal opportunities do not appear to operate. Women normally do the cooking, cleaning, ironing, washing, shopping and providing the home taxi service. Men usually fiddle with the car, attempt to mend things and do the garden. This information is reflected in the way advertising copy (the words) is written and presented. Did you know that:

- most detergents need to be automatic;
- there is a large market for freezer food;
- the UK's most popular meal is frozen oven chips with frozen beefburgers, and one frozen vegetable – guess which one!
- most decisions about shopping are made by women, therefore the advertisers appeal to women?

On the other hand, only a small percentage of people have a microwave, double glazing or an electric lawn mower. Should these products be advertised on TV? Currently, they are heavily advertised in the local and national press (because it is cheaper) and double glazing is also marketed over the telephone.

On average, people watch TV for between three and four hours every day. Some 17 million people will watch *Coronation Street* at 7.30 p.m. This is prime time television and is very expensive for advertisers, but the audience is huge.

Activity

A consumer profile

Your group is a market segment. What are its characteristics? To find out you will need to research yourselves.

a Devise a questionnaire which covers:

- What consumer durables people have at home.
- How they spend their free time.
- How they spend their money.
- What appeals to them, for example, sunshine, grass, etc.

These questions will help you create an advertisement. Once the questionnaires have been completed, work out what percentage of the group, for example, watches Brookside, or has a vacuum cleaner.

The same questionnaire can be used to survey other market segments (groups) at your work/study place.

b Use the information you have collected to suggest:

- Five products that could be promoted (advertised) to the group.
- The emotions/feelings that the advertisers should try to use.

c You have been given 15 seconds of advertising time on TV. Sketch five pictures (the storyboard) which show how you would advertise the product.

d Write the script or 'voice over' that would be used.

e How you would advertise the product, for example, what personality would the product have?

Help wildlife – buy HAPPY!

f With the SEM (Single European Market) companies will need to tailor their products to the needs of specific groups of people in specific areas. Should companies produce large volumes of BLAND X to get as large a market as possible at the lowest cost? Or should they customise their products by varying the ingredients and design? Remember that companies advertising in more than one country will need to be sensitive to ethnic differences.

Targeting the consumers

Stats, lies and stereotypes

The 1991 census is advertisers' latest crib for targeting consumer groups. Alexander Garrett reports

Over the next few weeks, householders will be rushing to discover – with varying degrees of indignation – the council tax band their home is in. What few realise is that there are other, more arcane systems for classifying where they live, which directly affect their choices as a consumer.

This month, the 1991 census results are dispatched to market analysis firms – companies that process the raw data on our sex, incomes, occupations and method of commuting to work, and then put a label on the neighbourhood where we live.

The results will be seized upon by advertisers intent on targeting 'upwardly mobile young families' and 'affluent households', while steering a wide berth around 'crowded council neighbourhoods' and 'low status areas with flats'.

So depending on where you live, you may or may not receive that coveted invitation to become an American Express Card member. More importantly, if your neighbourhood is regarded by the marketing people as Britain's answer to the Bronx, that upmarket supermarket will be located elsewhere. On the plus side, if yours is designated an area of young families, you can count on an endless stream of cheap nappy offers.

Matching addresses to life-styles and social ambition is known as 'geodemographics'. This links your post-code to one of the (somewhat larger) enumeration districts used in compiling the census, and thereby draws conclusions about your likely spending habits.

For the past 10 years, marketing analysts have been using the results of the 1981 census. So what has changed since then? 'Those figures are only going to be seriously out of date in areas where there has been a real change in the housing stock,' argues Greg Ward, sales and marketing director of the company Pinpoint. He points to areas such as Milton Keynes where swathes of new housing have sprung up, or Docklands, where yesterday's crumbling warehouse has become today's yuppie apartment block.

And Greg Bradford, managing director of rival CACI, says: 'We're going to see how patterns of affluence and poverty have changed over the past 10 years. We have many companies waiting anxiously for the release of this data.'

Already some statistics have been publicised. Cleveland and Bedfordshire, for example, have most children in percentage terms, whilst Sussex and the Isle of Wight have most pensioners. Wiltshire has the most employment while Surrey has most cars.

The census also included new questions on ethnic background and long-term illness. So we now know that Leicestershire has the most Indians, West Yorkshire the most Pakistanis and inner London the most Caribbeans. West Glamorgan, on the other hand, has the greatest incidence of people with long-term ailments. The first of these will certainly be a boon to those in the fledgling ethnic marketing business, which sells products such as hair and skin treatments to the nation's black consumers.

Marketing people of every persuasion will be less interested in headline statistics, however, than the practical business of allocating resources for maximum effect.

Census data has traditionally been used to select recipients in direct mail campaigns, to identify the best locations for stores and to find the optimum sites for advertising posters. According to Bradford, the uses are becoming increasingly sophisticated. 'For retailers, it is not just a question of where to site stores. I might want to have a different product mix in each store, according to the make-up of the local population.'

A less positive use of 'geodemographics' is the way banks, building societies and retailers identify those branches they should close down.

TYPE A

'Rural.' Very high proportion of the population employed in agriculture. Tendency towards large houses. Many non-working women; high multiple car ownership (necessary in rural areas). Relatively few children.

TYPE B

'Armed forces.' Predominantly members of H.M. armed forces. Large numbers of young children and adults 20-34. Many housewives at home, high incidence of families moved within the previous year.

TYPE C

'Upwardly mobile young families.' Clear age profile of adults aged 25-44 years with children 0-15 years. Many women work, more full-time than part-time. Predominantly owner occupiers in fairly large houses (5/6 rooms).

TYPE D
'Affluent households.' Older profile than type C; adults 35-54 with older children, mainly teenage. Mostly owner occupied houses with 6, 7 or more rooms. Multiple car owners. Mainly employed in finance, services and public admin.

TYPE E
'Older people in small houses.' One quarter are over 65. Council housing, few cars, most dwellings are small. Those inhabitants who do work tend to travel to work by bus or on foot.

TYPE F
'Suburban middle-aged or older.' Not quite as old a profile as type E, but nearly half are over 45. Predominantly owner occupied, in contrast to type E, and houses are larger (4-7+ rooms).

One new area where the census will be deployed is in buying television airtime for advertisers. Agencies have depended on information from BARB – the Broadcasters Audience Research Board – which has a panel of 4,500 couch potatoes recording every zap of their viewing habits in special diaries. The results – as well as providing weekly television ratings – give some insight into who watches what.

But a new system called Viewpoint, developed by Pinpoint in conjunction with BARB, links the BARB panel directly with the census results, via the postcodes of the panellists. According to Ward, advertisers will now be able to buy a commercial in a particular programme knowing precisely the households that will be watching. For example, analysis of a typical Wednesday evening in August shows that among Type A households – farmers and other rural dwellers – *Home and Away* was easily the most popular programme on ITV, outdoing even *News at Ten*. Quite why this tale of 'everyday' life in Australia should appeal to the country set is a mystery; but for purveyors of fertilisers, Range Rovers and Barbour jackets, it is clearly the place to book airtime. Type Cs – 'upwardly mobile young families' – showed a distinct indisposition to watch anything on ITV on the evening in question – maybe because they were all washing nappies – but did tune in to *Brookside* on Channel 4.

Type Ds – 'affluent households' – shot through the roof when superchef Anton Mosimann came on, while Type Es – 'older people in small houses' – watched lots but showed a curious ambivalence towards the *Golden Girls*.

The advantage of this to advertisers, claims Ward, is that the census-based 'neighbourhood types' are a more useful barometer than the more straightforward 'social class'. 'For example,' he points out, 'a C2 often has more disposable income than a C1.' Another potential benefit is that consumers can be reached initially through television, then followed up with direct mail or leaflet drops – all based on neighbourhood definitions.

But how accurate are these methods? After all, even the basic census data is in some doubt, with claims at one stage that the Office of Population Censuses and Surveys 'lost' up to 800,000 people, possibly because of non-registration for poll tax. And the BARB panel seems a small sample from which to predict the viewing habits of 56 million people. 'It's as accurate as the rest of the BARB figures,' argues Ford. 'This data doesn't necessarily say anything about you as an individual, but it does say that in your neighbourhood there is a high proportion of people with particular traits. If an advertiser wants to reach those people, he is going to get more of them in one programme than in another.

The greatest danger – perhaps outweighing privacy considerations – for the householder is that their choice of consumer goodies will be restricted because they live in too poor an area. But who knows? By 2001, perhaps enough citizens will be sufficiently clued-up to exaggerate on their census form and get that new Harrods food hall built down the road after all.

TYPE G
'Working people with families.' Predominantly middle-aged parents with teenaged children, many housewives working part-time. Mix of council tenants and owner occupiers.

TYPE I
'Low status areas with flats.' Many young adults, many immigrants, high unemployment. High incidence of students, full-time working women, house-moving. Poor amenities.

TYPE K
'Poor multi-ethnic areas.' Many children and young adults. Very high incidence of immigrants, predominantly from the Indian sub-continent. High unemployment; mixed housing tenure.

TYPE H
'Poor urban areas.' Many young adults, plus some retired people, some children thus rather a mixed age profile. Some incidence of people born in the Indian sub-continent. High owner occupiers.

TYPE J
'Inner city bedsits.' Many young adults, few children. Volatile in terms of house-moving. Many students (relatively) and many full-time working women. High incidence of single people living alone.

TYPE L
'Crowded council neighbourhoods.' Many children, equally spread by age band. High unemployment. Overcrowding, few cars. Mainly council housing, typically 2-4 rooms. Employed in utilities; manufacturing, construction.

Activity

Look at the article 'Stats, lies and stereotypes' from *The Observer*.

a Do you find the categories useful? How do you think they are used by advertisers?
b Do you agree with the way the market has been segmented?
c Which segment are you in?
d What is geodemographics?
e Discuss the article with your colleagues and form a conclusion.

Buyer behaviour

When we examine the demand for a product, we talk about 'effective demand', i.e. the consumer's willingness and ability to pay for a product, at a particular price, at a particular time. However, when does willingness become a purchase or sale, and why and how does it happen?

The retail environment

Every day the consumer is bombarded with information about products, on TV, on the radio, in the press, in shop windows and doorways.

Have you ever walked past a baker's shop where the bread is baked on the premises and displayed in the window? The smell of the fresh bread comes out of the doorway, and there is a special offer for 'Hot, Freshly Baked Bread'. Have you been tempted to go in and buy some?

Everywhere, the consumer is tempted into buying. The fresh food at the supermarket is placed near to the entrance, as are the perfumes in a department store (they make people feel good when they enter). Goods are displayed and promoted so as to appeal to the emotions and senses. If the consumer is just about to purchase, any of these signals could trigger an actual sale.

Personality

What motivates the consumer to buy one product and not another is the satisfaction that can be expected from its use. This expectation is related to the consumer's need for the product, which can be real or imagined. This need is in turn a reflection of the consumer's personality, background, education, culture, age, gender, friends and family.

For example, one consumer could buy Nike trainers, another Adidas, another Dunlop Green Flash (this person is not fashion conscious!). Each company will have a share of the market. The size of the market for trainers refers to the actual number of trainers which are bought and not to the size of the population.

When market size is greater than population, it means that people purchase a product, for example, bread, many times.

When market size is less than population, it means the percentage of people buying the product is less than the population.

To increase market size, a business can either:

- persuade more people to buy the product;
- persuade the same people to buy more of the product.

Consumer trends

Look at the table showing consumer expenditure on pages 74–5.

A variety of trends can be seen, for example:

Expenditure	Trend
Newspapers and magazines	Small rise
Bread	Decrease
Beer	Decrease
Wine, etc.	Increase

These differences reflect the effect of changes in income, unemployment, relative prices and social conditions on the demand for goods. Further changes in these variables can be expected over the next three years as the UK economy reacts to closer membership of the SEM. The anticipated changes in fiscal and monetary policy which were signposted in the 1994 Budget by the Chancellor, Kenneth Clarke, will also affect retail sales.

What affects consumer spending?

Consumer spending or retail sales depend upon:

- the size of the population – the number of possible buyers;
- personal disposable income – which measures the consumers' ability to pay;
- relative prices – which are a measure of how changes in the price of particular goods, for example, 'household items' relate to the Retail Price Index (RPI);
- rate of savings – which measures the consumers' willingness to buy (If they save, then they are not willing to buy. Effective demand requires consumers to be able and willing to purchase.);
- unemployment rate – which measures the health of the UK economy;
- past trends – which measure the actual market size.

The demand for a single product may be largely affected by just one of these variables, in which case we can find a relationship using the 'line of best fit' (see page 251). Alternatively, many factors could be relevant, so that multiple regression techniques will need to be used.

Many empirical market research studies have been done which confirm the key relationships we looked at in Chapter 2. Generally:

- Retail sales rise when income rises (they are positively correlated). The regression line would slope upwards to the right providing the demand is normal.
- Retail sales rise when population rises (note that, for example, car driving/ownership is restricted).
- Retail sales fall when unemployment rises.
- Retail sales fall when savings rise.
- Retail sales fall when RPI rises.

A business would need to confirm if and/or how each of these affects the demand for its products.

Elasticity

Elasticity plays an important part in the forecasting process, for example:

- Retail sales of durable goods such as furniture tend to be very responsive to changes in income (they are income elastic). As Santi and Ewa, who own a furniture shop in Madrid, told the author, 'during a recession, people don't replace furniture, they keep their old furniture until it falls apart. When the economy improves, sales start to pick up fairly quickly.'

- Retail sales of non-durable goods, for example, food and clothing tend to be less responsive to changes in income (they are income inelastic). Is this because they are needs? Can you think of other examples?

Activity

How economic factors affect consumption

Copy and complete the matrix. We have filled in four cells to start you off! A – sign shows a negative relationship, for example, as unemployment rises, furniture sales fall. A + sign indicates a positive relationship, for example, when incomes rise, people buy more furniture and vice versa. Give reasons for your choice in each case. You can extend this activity by including social factors.

	Factors		
Product	**Unemployment**	**Income per head**	**Savings**
Furniture	–	+	
Clothing			
Footwear			
Eating out	–		
Food	+		
Petrol			
Camcorders			
Holidays			
Entertainment			
DIY			

Forecasting – using marketing research information

Accurate **forecasting** of the potential demand for products or services is the basis of all planning for any business. Estimates of costs and resources cannot be made until a reliable calculation is available for the likely level of sales.

Two sets of information are needed:

- the business will need forecasts about its external environment, such as the expected rate of economic growth and inflation in the UK; these are available from government sources. (The Annual Budget Statement published in November of each year will have this information.)
- forecasts of the total market, which the business would estimate using historical figures. The business can then use its own predicted market share to derive its sales forecast.

Time series analysis

A time series shows historical data which can be used and analysed to predict future trends. Most of the tables and charts in this book are time series, for example, the figures on consumption on page 74–5.

Finding a trend using moving averages

The first step in analysing a time series is to isolate and define the underlying trend. Here are the weekly sales figures for the Arigato Shikako TV Co.

Week	1	2	3	4	5	6	7	8	9	10	11	12	13	14	15
Sales	260	290	340	270	300	370	280	320	400	290	330	440	300	350	490

Figure 5.5 shows the graph of these figures.

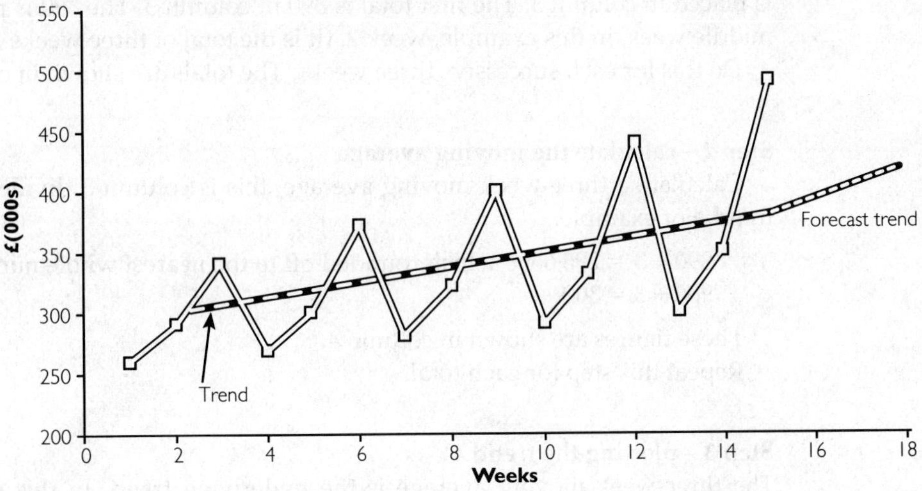

Figure 5.4 Weekly sales of TVs

We can see from the graph that sales of TVs peak every three weeks. We must take a three-week moving average to smooth out these peaks and find the underlying trend.

Week	Sales	Three-week moving total	Three-week moving average or trend
1	260		
2	290	890	297
3	340	900	300
4	270	910	303
5	300	940	313
6	370	950	316
7	280	970	323
8	320	1000	333
9	400	1010	336
10	290	1020	340
11	330	1060	353
12	440	1070	356
13	300	1090	363
14	350	1140	380
15	490		
Column 1	Column 2	Column 3	Column 4 (Column 3 ÷ 3)

Step 1 – calculate the moving total

Calculate a three-week moving total using the sales figures in column 2.

$260 + 290 + 340 = 890$
Week 1 + Week 2 + Week 3
$290 + 340 + 270 = 900$
Week 2 + Week 3 + Week 4
$340 + 270 + 300 = 910$

The total 'moves' by deleting the first week and adding the subsequent week. The total is placed in column 3. The first total is 890 in column 3. The 890 is placed opposite the middle week, in this example, week 2. (It is the total of three weeks.)

Do this for each successive three weeks. The totals are shown in column 3.

Step 2 – calculate the moving average

Calculate a three-week moving average, this is column 3 divided by 3, to find the trend. For example:

890 ÷ 3 = 296.6666 which rounded off to the nearest whole number is 297;
900 ÷ 3 = 300.

These figures are shown in column 4.

Repeat this step for each total.

Step 3 – plotting the trend

The three-week moving average is the underlying trend. In this example there is a definite upward trend in the sales of TVs, although the fluctuations are increasing. The trend line is now plotted on the graph. This business will have to take immediate action to find out why sales are varying so wildly.

Step 4 – Making the forecast

To make the forecast the trend line must be extended to the right. This process, called *extrapolation*, will give an estimate of the trend for the next few weeks. (Although a longer forecast can be made, the business will need to be certain that the same conditions of demand and supply will exist for the expected duration.)

Activity

a Look at the table for consumer expenditure on page 74. Choose one item from each category then:
- Plot the data on a graph.
- Calculate the trend.
- Forecast the next three years.

b What assumptions have you made?

c Can you see any relationships between the products?

Correlation and regression analysis

If a relationship exists between two variables, for example, advertising expenditure and sales, or number of ice creams sold and the temperature, it can be used to make forecasts about future demand.

The accuracy of the forecast will depend upon how close the relationship is. The closer the relationship or the higher is the **correlation**, the better will be the prediction. We will use a scattergraph to see if two variables are related.

The following table shows the figures for advertising expenditure at a local cinema and the size of the audience. The x-axis (horizontal) is used to show the independent variable, in this case, advertising.

The *y*-axis (vertical) shows the dependent variable, cinema tickets. The number of tickets sold depends on the amount of advertising.

Advertising expenditure (independent variable)	**Cinema tickets sold (dependent variable)**
6	34
13	56
21	67
29	78
38	89
47	98
50	108
62	120

A scattergraph (also called a scattergram or scatter diagram) is a graph of '*x*', the independent variable shown on the horizontal axis, and '*y*' the dependent variable shown on the vertical axis.

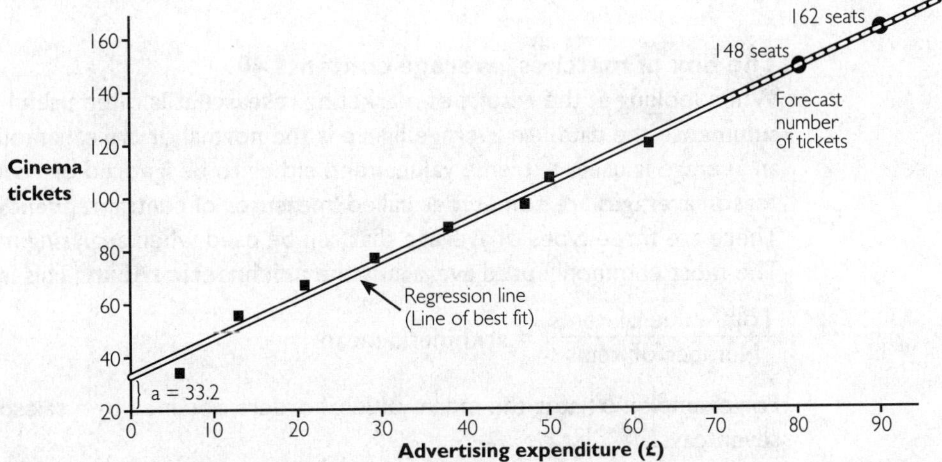

Figure 5.5 Forecasting using a regression line

Looking at the scattergraph in Figure 5.5, we can see that there appears to be a very close relationship, between the variables; namely, when advertising rises, the audiences go up. This is called **positive correlation**. The line slopes upwards to the right. Correlation is positive if both variables rise together (sales rise when advertising rises). The straight line is called the **regression line** or the 'line of best fit'.

This line was fitted and drawn using 'Freelance Graphics', a Lotus package. Other packages will do the same. The computer does the calculations so the line does not have to be a hand drawn guess.

We can now extend the line to predict what will happen to sales at higher levels of advertising expenditure. This forecast is also shown in Figure 5.5.

Now look at the scattergraph showing the relationship between the sales of beer and lager (Figure 5.6). In this example the sales of beer have fallen whilst that of lager have risen. The line slopes downwards to the right. **Negative correlation** is the result of one variable rising as the other falls.

In Figure 5.7 there appears to be no relationship, therefore we cannot use a regression line for forecasting in this case.

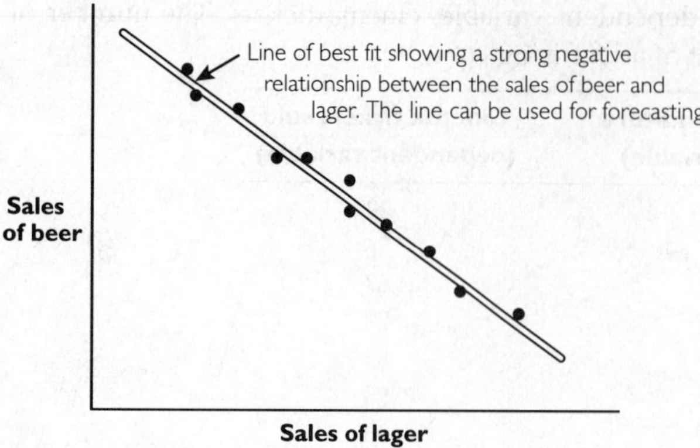

Figure 5.6 Negative correlation

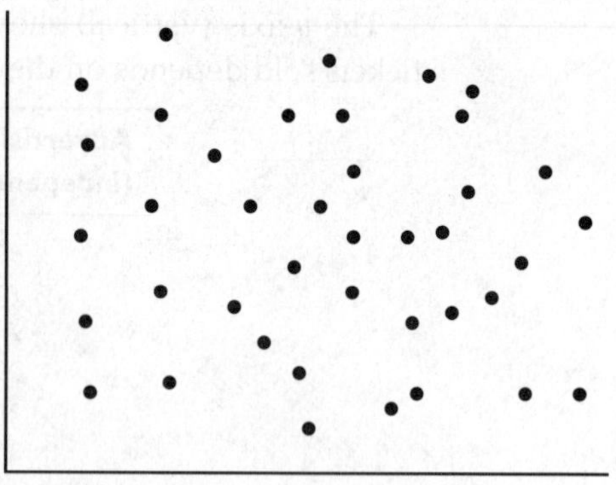

Figure 5.7 Scattergraph showing no relationship between variables

The box of matches, average contents 40

When looking at the results of marketing research it is often useful to be able to summarise the data. An average figure is the normal or typical amount. Whenever an average is used, extreme values tend either to be ignored or reduced; for this reason averages are sometimes called 'measures of central tendency'.

There are three types of average that can be used when analysing marketing data. The most commonly used average is the **arithmetic mean**. This is calculated by:

$$\frac{\text{Total value of items}}{\text{Number of items}} = \text{arithmetic mean}$$

For example: What is the mean value of orders obtained by a salesperson over seven days?

£158 £168 £158 £150 £153 £155 £136

$$\frac{\text{Total value of items}}{\text{Number of items}} \; \frac{1078}{7} = £154$$

Note that the arithmetic mean uses all the data, it is affected by extreme values and is only approximation: £154 was not sold on any day.

Mode: this is the number, value or item which occurs most often in the population. It is the most fashionable or popular (in the early sixties Mods were young people who dressed in fashionable clothes) so in the examples above the mode is £158; it is the modal value. The mode is not affected by extreme values.

Median: When all the items are placed in ascending or descending order the median is the middle value of the sequence, for example:

£136 £150 £153 **£155** £158 £158 £168

£155 is the median value. Because it is the middle value it tells us that 50% of orders are greater than £155 and 50% are less. It is not affected by extremes.

Activities

1 a Draw a scattergraph to show this data:

Price (£)	Demand for computers
800	633
1,100	450
1,000	570
850	620
950	590
1,200	399
900	610
1,050	520

b Either draw a freehand 'line of best fit' or input the data onto the computer and generate the line.

c Estimate the demand for computers when the price is £1,400.

d What can you say about the demand curve for computers?

2 a Draw a scattergraph to show the sales of CDs and bicycles:

Sales of CDs (£)	Sales of bicycles (£)
170	50
110	100
175	350
100	250
150	200
130	300
120	150
160	325
140	75

b Draw a 'line of best fit'.

c Estimate the sales of CDs when the demand for bicycles is 125. Can you do this? Should you do this?

Qualitative methods of forecasting

Client and customer surveys

With this method, a business will survey its buyers to find out what they expect to be ordering over the next 12 to 18 months. Although the method is also popular with both the CBI and government departments, which publish regular reports on buyers' expectations, it does have problems:

- buyers may be reluctant to reveal their intentions;
- buyers might not know their future demands.

Useful information on the level of future orders and the level of current stocks is available, however, from the Business Monitor series published by HMSO and the Central Statistical Office.

Sales staff surveys

Although this method appears sensible, in practice, as any photocopier sales representative will tell you, there are problems. The sales representative said:

> 'Whenever the sales management team are carrying out a survey to try and estimate next year's sales say you don't know, or say you have several leads but can't be certain. When our company did a staff survey and found sales were expected to be pretty buoyant, they tried to change the commission we got on sales. We will never tell them anything again.'

Do you think this situation is representative of that in other companies?

The Delphi method

This method is named after a famous oracle who lived at Delphi, a city in Ancient Greece. It involves asking a group of experts to look into the future to predict major trends. For example, it is suggested that books and literacy will become more important as computers demand high levels of reading skills. Experts, however, can be expensive, and it could be cheaper for the business to join a trade or research association which specialises in its products, from which it can get its information.

Managerial expertise

Whatever research data is collected, it will be necessary for the management team to use its knowledge and expertise to analyse it. Professional judgement can still be better than computer diagnosis.

Two methods of forecasting are sometimes used:

- The 'top down' method in which the Senior Management Team will set central guideline targets which individual departments will then use to make their own estimates.
- With the 'bottom up' approach, the departments will forecast their own targets which are then aggregated to form the basis of the corporate goals.

Problems with forecasts

The accuracy of any forecast depends upon many factors such as:

- How much data do we have? Generally the more data a business possesses the more reliable will be the forecast, for example, a bigger sample is more reliable than a small sample.
- Will the external environment remain stable? Will there be significant changes in the social, economic or technical environment? For example, will the cost and source of raw materials remain the same.
- Will the internal environment remain stable? Will the business keep the same objectives or pursue the same policies?
- Is the data representative or biased?

WHY DO YOU NEED FIGURES?

If you are lost during a country drive you will want to consult a map to find out where you are and this will tell you in which direction you should go in order to reach your destination. In the same way in business you need a continuous assessment of the environment in which you operate and your position in it. Information on which to base this assessment can come from discussion with acquaintances, from salesmen and trade journals, but it is more realistic and firmly based if it contains a fair sprinkling of reliable statistical information relevant to *your* situation. Having assessed the present (or, more correctly, the immediate past—because all statistics are to some extent out of date) you reach the real purpose of the exercise—where can you go next? The largest companies have departments whose sole job it is carefully to work out forecasts of sales for the next year, the next five years, or even longer (they find, incidentally, that the discipline of doing these forecasts provides just as many benefits, if not more, than the forecasts themselves).

In a small or medium size firm you may not have the time, money or staff to do this sort of thing formally. But you are making decisions all the time which affect the progress of your firm and these decisions usually have behind them the thought, however unconscious, that you are trying to take your company in this or that direction. Most of your problems differ in degree, rather than in kind, from those of large firms. Like them you will benefit from planning ahead with the help of statistics, even if your calculations are restricted to the back of an envelope.

CRYSTAL BALL GAZING

Many businessmen are extremely sceptical about forecasting the future of their firms in a world full of changing conditions. But it is this very uncertainty that makes forecasts, or a range of forecasts, necessary. The alert firm will work out alternative contingency plans to take advantage of opportunities which often become apparent during the forecasting exercise. Anyone questioning the validity of planning ahead should ask himself whether his present position could have been stronger had he made decisions five years ago on the basis of all the information available at that time. And can he really be content if he is selling the same range of products to the same markets five years hence? Planning ahead in a systematic way should occupy a reasonable portion of any chief executive's working hours, and this does not mean planning just for next week, next month or even next year, and plans should not be abandoned just because they look foolish after they are a few months old. Try to pin down the cause of mistakes and revise at least once a year to take advantage of the flow of new information—some of it statistical—from government sources.

Source: *Profit from facts*, HMSO

Activity

a As a group, brainstorm some of the changes taking place in society which could have an influence on a demand forecast for your organisation/college or school. For example, more leisure time, changes in local authority control, etc. Say what effect each could have.

b The group should then arrange a meeting with the Head of Department to compare expectations.

Case study

In almost every developed economy, two special factors have a very important influence on the demand for many products. These are new car sales (registrations), and new house building (housing starts) and housing sales.

New car sales

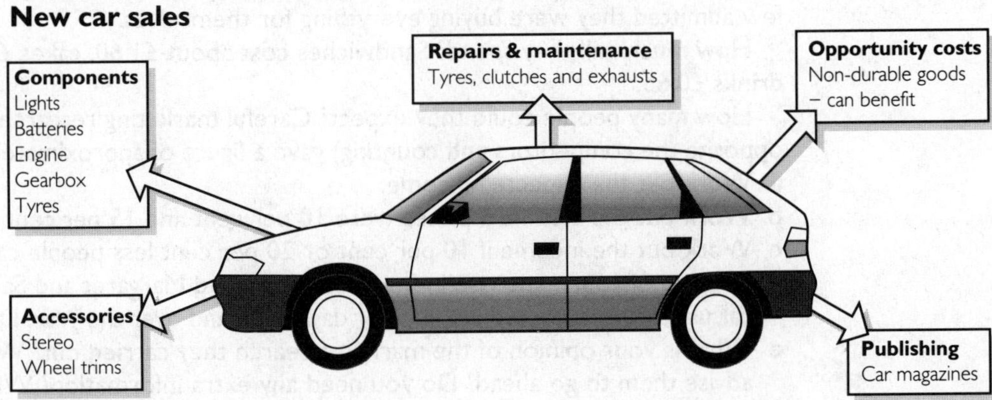

Figure 5.8 Multiplier effect of new car sales

The sales of new cars tend to fall during a recession (and push the economy further into decline because of the reverse multiplier effect). The money which is not spent, i.e. that which is saved, is then used to purchase other items. For example, you may postpone buying a new car and buy a cheap holiday instead. This is sometimes called the 'knickerbocker glory' effect and refers to a situation where people compensate for not being able to get what they want by treating themselves to something special and cheap. (In the recession of the nineties sales of chocolate bars rose as people perceived buying chocolate as a way of treating themselves cheaply.)

House purchases

Here again there is a far-reaching multiplier effect locally, regionally and nationally. Some products are directly affected, for example, raw materials and components. Furniture and household appliance sales are affected, but what happens to repairs, maintenance or DIY products?

Activities

1 Produce a diagram similar to that shown for car sales, which shows the possible impact of house starts/purchases on various groups in the economy.

2 Add two more columns to the Activity on page 248 showing 'car sales' and 'house purchases' and then put in the relationships giving reasons for your choice.

3 **Jubilee Sandwich Bar, Blackfriars Road**

Margaret and Sarah are hoping to open a sandwich bar. To do this they will need to estimate the potential market for their services. They have decided to do some market research to find out who their customers are; this should give them the answers the need to make a sales forecast.

Look at the map on page 109. Blackfriars Road is on the south side of the River Thames; the river flows just 100 metres to the north. There are a large number of offices in the area, including the headquarters of Sainsbury's and IPC Magazines. The Daily Express, Conoco and Network South East are in Blackfriars Road. Southwark College is in The Cut and Unilever is next to the Thames. The market would be office workers, Monday to Friday only.

How often would people buy? Margaret and Sarah believe that the early morning and lunch time would be the busiest. There are queues at all the existing sandwich bars at this time, despite the fact that the market is highly competitive.

How many sandwiches, cakes, etc. will people buy? Their research shows that one person would normally buy, on average, 2.5 sandwiches, 2 cakes and 2 drinks. Most of the people who were asked said 'I am buying these for my friend'; very few admitted they were buying everything for themselves.

How much will they spend? Sandwiches cost about £1.60, cakes £0.90 and drinks £0.65.

How many people could they expect? Careful marketing research (standing opposite the competitors and counting) gave a figure of approximately 400 per day.

a Work out the expected income.

b Work out the income if prices were 10 per cent and 15 per cent less.

c Work out the income if 10 per cent or 20 per cent less people came in.

d Because of your expertise in forecasting demand Margaret and Sarah ask you to calculate their expected income per day/week, and over the year. Do this for them.

e What is your opinion of the market research they carried out? Would you advise them to go ahead? Do you need any extra information? What effect might the Jubilee Line have on future sales?

Review questions

1. When would a business use secondary information? Does its use have any disadvantages?
2. When would a business use closed questions and/or open questions?
3. Why and when would a business use quota sampling?
4. What are the main objectives of telephone interviewing?
5. What are the main methods of collecting primary data? Why would a business use face-to-face interviews?
6. What marketing information would a business need to estimate the market for microwave cookers, videos and electric irons?
7. What methods can be used to forecast demand?
8. What criteria would you use to choose a sample?
9. An hotel interviews all its guests in January? Why might this survey give a one-sided result?
10. What is the difference between qualitative and quantitative research?
11. What are the main reasons why people buy flowers and BMW cars?
12. How can the level of income affect demand?
13. What is meant by a market segment? What market segment should a window cleaner aim for?
14. What are the main sources of marketing information?
15. What market research should a small local hairdressers carry out?
16. What needs do people have? What need is fulfilled by a silk shirt or blouse?
17. When might a business use unstructured interviews?
18. What are the major problems involved in forecasting? How could these be minimised?
19. Why would a company use a sample survey in preference to a census?
20. An average family has 1.7 children: what does this mean?

Key terms

Marketing
Aims and objectives
Information need
Sources of information
Market research
Market segmentation
Primary research
Secondary research
Interviews
Structured
Unstructured
Questionnaires
Population
Sampling
Bias
Sampling frame
Random sampling
Stratified sampling
Systematic sampling
Multi-stage sampling
Cluster sampling
Quota sampling
Opinion polls
Test marketing
Lifestyles
Buyer behaviour
Consumer trends
Consumer spending
Forecasting
Time series analysis
Correlation
Regression
Regression line
Qualitative research
Quantitative research
Averages

Assignment 5
The future for trainers

This assignment develops knowledge and understanding of the following elements:

3.1 Investigate the principles and functions of marketing in organisations

3.2 Propose and present product developments based on analysis of marketing research information

It supports development of the following core skills:

Communication 3.1, 3.2, 3.3, 3.4

Application of numbers 3.1, 3.2, 3.3

Information technology 3.1, 3.2, 3.3

You work as a marketing assistant in the marketing department of either Nike, Adidas or Hi-Tec. (All three companies will need to be researched by the group.) Today, the department receives the following memo:

MEMORANDUM

To: Marketing Department Date: Today's date

From: A. Kotler Re: Sales forecast

We have been asked to prepare a short-term prediction of consumer demand for trainers for the next three years. Can you please prepare a report in our standard format.

1. Please use the figures for 'footwear' in the UK national accounts to predict consumer spending on 'all footwear' for the next three years. You should provide a graph of past data and the trend. (You can get the figures from the Annual Abstract of Statistics.) State what assumptions you have made and why, for example, about population changes and the amount of participation in all sports, etc. (PS I like graphs.)

2. Can you carry out some market research to find out our customer profile? A simple questionnaire would be suitable. This is your chance to try out those different types of question you were telling me about! We want to know about:
   - use of product related to age/gender
   - how much people spend on one pair of trainers
   - how much they spend each year
   - which brand of trainers they usually buy – you will need this to calculate market share
   - what people like about the product
   - what changes people would like
   - what people think about our promotion and advertising, etc.

   Try and get people to rate trainers in order of preference.

3. Find out what type of shops people use to buy trainers. This will help our promotion campaign. Try something like this; it's not quite right and will need working on!!

	Name of outlet		
Age	Low price	Middle price	High price
1-15			
16-24			
25-34			
35-44			
45+			

Here are the national figures showing the retail market share:

Specialist multiple shoe shops	32%
Specialist independents	20%
Sports shops	7%
Mail order	4%
Market stalls	6%
Clothing shops	6%
Variety stores	5%
Others, department stores, etc.	20%

Please write a short memo saying how your local data compares.

4. Out of the total spent on all footwear about £600 million a year is spent on trainers. Please estimate expenditure for the next three years. (The proportion of the total has been rising at about 5 per cent per year.)

5. Estimate the market size for our trainers. If you make assumptions, please say why and how we can achieve your targets.

6. Make a presentation based on your market research which includes people's views on our trainers, for example quality, price, possible changes in style, etc.

6 Marketing activities

What is covered in this chapter

- Introduction
- The marketing mix
- Product
- Promotion
- Price
- Place or distribution
- Marketing strategy
- Marketing plan
- Advertising standards
- The selling process

These are the resources that you will need for your Marketing file:

- advertisements
- questionnaires
- logos
- mission statements
- packaging
- promotional materials
- price lists
- marketing magazines.

Many organisations provide free literature on their marketing as part of their public relations function.

Introduction

Having looked at market research and forecasting in the last chapter, we now examine the way in which a business will use the information that it collects to inform and direct its marketing activities in order to achieve its **goals**.

Business attitudes to marketing – customer focus

According to P. Kotler in *Marketing Management* it is only in the last 30 years that marketing has become an important business activity. Before 1960, he maintains, companies were mainly concerned with engineering and production. Even today there are still companies that do not give enough attention to marketing their products. Two different approaches are usually adopted by such companies:

- the product approach – when the business is exclusively concerned with manufacturing quality and efficiency, typified by the attitude – 'We don't need marketing, our product will sell itself.'
- the technology approach – these businesses are characterised by technological innovation. The Spectrum computer and the Sinclair C5 battery-powered car (now used as children's pedal cars at Camber Sands), were both invented by Sir Clive Sinclair. Whatever happened to them? Was enough attention paid to marketing?

When the business puts the customer first it is customer-orientated; it responds to consumer demands for new products and it is dynamic and responsive to the needs of the market. Really successful companies fall into this category.

The structure of the business tends to reflect these attitudes. Some managers and some departments will have more power than others. This can be due to the personality of individuals or to the importance or weight given to the function. However, this balance should vary as corporate goals vary.

With incorporation and the need for many colleges to increase student numbers, greater emphasis has been given to the marketing function. Can you say what is happening in your organisation?

The hierarchical structure of many companies actually prevents the business from meeting customer needs because they concentrate too much on departmental objectives. They need to think horizontally instead of vertically and see the flow of goods to the consumer as a continuous process:

Purchasing → Research → Production → Sales Marketing

This could be achieved by having, for example, Brand Directors, Innovation Managers and Brand Development Managers, who can take a wider view of the business and follow the product through from the development stage to its final destination.

Marketing objectives

Post Office Counters Ltd in its 'Mission and Vision' has these objectives:

- to 'meet the needs of our customers in the community'
- to be the 'leading provider of benefits distribution, postal services, banking and bill payment facilities'
- to 'deliver these services with integrity, efficiency and in a professional way'.

For Tesco it is 'offering the customers the best value for money and the most competitive prices'.

Activity

a On your own, investigate the marketing objectives of your organisation. Compare these with the objectives of another business in a different industrial sector.

b Can you say why there are differences? Are there differences, for instance, between charitable and commercial organisations?

The marketing mix

The **marketing mix** refers to the way in which the four key parts of a company's marketing policy are combined to achieve its objectives. The four elements, sometimes called the 'Four Ps' are:

- PRODUCT
- PROMOTION
- PRICE
- PLACE.

The marketing department will be largely responsible for ensuring that the Four Ps are used in the most effective way. The following case study shows how the marketing mix was used in a shirt making company.

Case study

Springfield Shirts

In 1992 at the height of the recession, Jay and Sam Springfield, the joint managing directors of Springfield Shirts, were forced to re-evaluate the marketing strategy of the company. They had four decisions to make, and asked themselves these questions:

1 What products should we sell? Prior to 1992 they had adopted a low volume/high price strategy which had worked well when people had money to spend. In 1992, however, sales had dropped dramatically. They decided to change their approach and concentrate instead on low-quality, high-volume items, particularly children's T-shirts in a limited range of bright, luminous colours.

2 What price should we charge? Once the initial decision had been made they decided to sell at a basic trade price of 50p per T-shirt. (The trade price is that at which the wholesaler would buy the shirts.) Discounts would be given for advance orders, which would enable them to forecast production requirements.

3 What promotion should we use? This was decided as being through the trade and by 'word of mouth'.

4 How should we distribute the goods? The conclusion was that traders would come to the company to collect and pay cash with order.

Today the shirts can be seen in street markets, outside railway stations, and at Sunday markets. They retail for '£3 each, any colour any size'. The Springfields look forward to all shops being open on Sundays.

Activity

This activity should be carried out as a group discussion.

a How did a knowledge of the marketing mix help the Springfields grow?

b Why do you think they made these decisions?

c Do you agree with the decisions they made?

d Do you think the new policy succeeded?

Product

The term **product** refers to the output of any business. This can either be tangible things, the physical goods, which you can touch, see or smell, such as a dishwasher or cod and chips; or the intangible services, such as dentistry or banking. Consumers buy particular products because they expect to get satisfaction or benefits from using them. This satisfaction can be obtained from any aspect of the product. For example, it could be the brand name of the dishwasher, the flavour or the 'packaging' of the cod and chips, or the reputation of the dentist. Whatever the reason, it is all part of the product.

Product development

Why does a business develop new products? The simple answer is that because the market is continually changing the business must develop new products to keep ahead of its competitors. The Chairman of Unilever said recently:

'In the battle for competitive edge we define the need, create the brand and move it around the world at the marketing equivalent of the speed of light. Innovation is moving so fast that you need to be scouting ahead and creating markets.'

The creation of markets is very effective. Instead of being consumer driven, i.e. responding to consumer needs, companies are now telling and showing customers what they need.

How do market changes affect the business?

Whenever there are changes in the market place the business should respond. For example, as the location and age structure of the population change, this creates new opportunities for product development so retirement homes are built to cater for the increase in the ageing population.

TV companies are also well aware of these changes as they re-run *Thunderbirds, The Man From UNCLE,* and *Startrek*, first shown 20 years ago, to new audiences.

People's preferences change; for example, the growth in demand for Flora margarine stems from a need for products which are high in polyunsaturates and low in saturates. This is a social trend towards more healthy living.

The growth in demand for convenience foods, for example, Menu Masters, arises from changes in lifestyles and social conditions. The demand for labour-saving devices has also increased for the same reasons.

Computer games, videos and camcorders are all examples of products that have been created in response to changes in leisure habits.

For a business to achieve its objectives, it must increase or at least maintain its share of these changing markets. To be at the leading competitive edge of innovation, it will need to take risks by developing new products and improving existing ones. For example, Unilever tries to launch one new product every month. Henkel Cosmetics launched the first 'two in one toothpaste', which combines a toothpaste with a mouthwash, in July 1993.

Companies making trainers introduce new designs and materials to keep ahead of their competitors. The Single European Market gives UK business an unprecedented opportunity to enter new markets with products specifically tailored for European tastes.

How does a business develop new products?

Market research

We have already seen that a business will need to carry out market research before it develops, launches and markets a new product.

Here is a review of questions which the business will have to consider:

- What are the gaps in the market?
- What are the gaps in the product range?
- What new technology is available? For example, the non-stick coatings on pots and pans was developed for the US Space Programme.
- How big is the market?
- What should be the market segment?
- What is the competition doing?
- What price should the product be?
- How should we advertise?
- What should our message be? For example, Highlands Airways – we aim for the top!
- How should we sell it?
- What sales can we expect?
- What profit can we expect?

Activity

Here is your opportunity to begin developing your ideas for new products or designs. You should be leading consumers into believing they need what you are going to give them, for example, pineapple crisps.

As a group, brainstorm as many ideas as you can for a new convenience food which the consumer 'cannot do without'! Decide on a name for it. Does it already exist? Choose five options for further exploration along the lines suggested above.

What are we selling?

This is a key question, the answer to which will determine the thrust and direction of the business. Look at these examples:

- Does Hovis sell bread, or nostalgia and memories of the good old days?
- Is Peugeot selling cars or adventure?
- Are P&O Ferries selling the trip from Dover to Calais or a cruise?
- Is Laura Ashley selling a lifestyle?
- Does a sports club sell the sport or the social life?

The Laura Ashley decision to produce and market a 'lifestyle' took it from being a small, single-product business, to the corporation it is today. Biba, famous in the 1960s, began as a small, single outlet, selling very trendy women's fashion, in Kensington, London. It grew quickly by diversifying the product range and then collapsed. Be warned – every company must take care to protect its core or main business!

The 1993 Planet Reebok Campaign for Reebok trainers under the slogan 'Live life to the fullest with Reebok', was intended to:

- make Reebok the world leader in trainers (currently it is second to Nike).
- keep people buying brand name trainers.

Do you buy brand names?

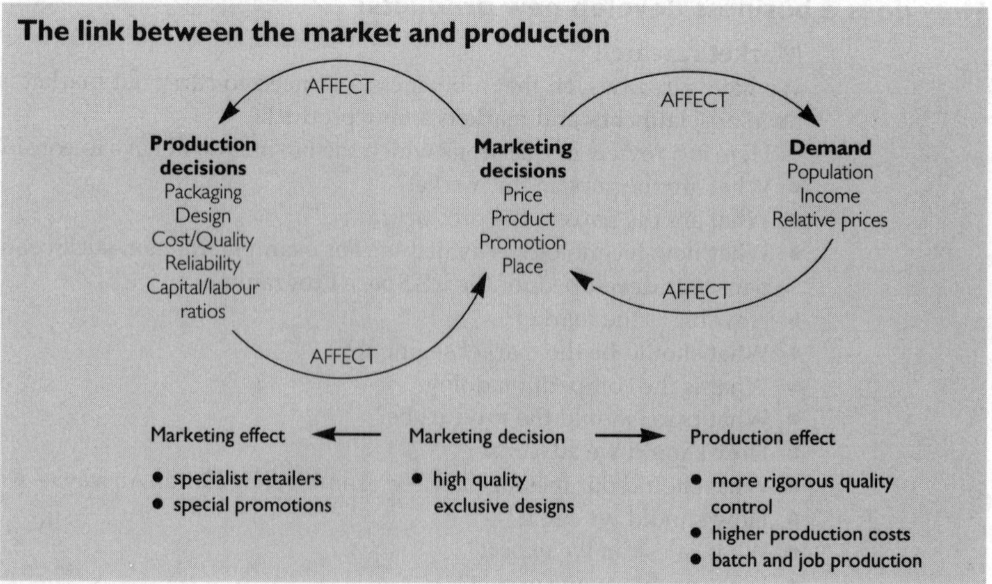

Case study

Unilever

Unilever is one of the world's biggest multinational companies with production units and sales throughout the world. It has a total turnover of approximately £25 billion. Its headquarters is in Blackfriars on the south bank of the Thames (see the map on page 100). Here are some of the brands it owns:

- Persil
- Sunsilk
- Flora
- Jif
- Signal
- Delight
- Omo
- Pepsodent
- Oxo
- Surf
- Timotei
- Cup-A-Soup
- Shield
- Brut
- Menu-Masters
- Comfort
- Obsession
- Steak House
- Boursin
- Magnum
- Colmans.

Activity

Each member of the group chooses one of the products from the Unilever range (you can add the products of Walls and Birds Eye if there are not enough).

a Say what is being advertised and what is being sold.
b What market segment is being catered for?
c Where and when is the product advertised?
d The group should create a matrix showing each of these variables, for example:
- brand name
- what is being advertised
- type of product
- where advertised
- when advertised
- market segment.

Evaluating and assessing new products

The feasibility study

Once the business believes it has a sound idea it will need to carry out a **feasibility study** to find out if it is worth putting into production. It will need to look at:

- The costs and method of production – the decision to use 'flow', 'batch' or 'job' methods will directly affect the selling price and therefore its possible market.
- The potential size of the market and the volume of sales. This has to be large enough to justify the development costs, which in some cases can be considerable, for example, Cadbury's Wispa cost £11 million to develop. Do you prefer Aero?
- The new product's position within the existing product range. (The product range is sometimes referred to as the *product portfolio*.)
- Consumer reaction – if consumers react negatively at this stage it would be a sign that they did not like the product in its present form, and it probably needs radical alteration.

The £1.5 billion UK snack food market

The top three UK snack food companies are Dalgety (with 15.5 per cent of the market) who own Golden Wonder Crisps, NikNaks, Wotsits and Pots; United Biscuits, who own KP Foods (they have 38.4 per cent of the market) and therefore Roysters, Hula Hoops, McCoys and KP Nuts; and Walker Smiths (a Pepsico subsidiary with 36.2 per cent of the market), owners of Walkers Crisps, Smiths Crisps, Monster Munch and Quavers.

Source: *Marketing*

Product failure

For every new product that succeeds in the market there are probably 100 that fail either because the market research was inadequate, or production faults occurred which could not have been foreseen.

The Boston Box

The Boston Box, created by the Boston Consulting Group, classifies products according to their market share and potential for market growth. It is often used by management to help decide on the appropriate product range.

Market growth

		High	Low
Market share	High	Stars	Cash cows
	Low	Problem children	Dog

'Stars' are products with a large share of a market with a high growth rate. A 'problem child' is a product with a small share of a market with a large potential for growth. It will probably require intensive advertising. A 'dog' is a product which is probably making a loss and should be dropped from the product range. A 'cash cow' will be highly profitable, but will still need marketing to maintain its portion of the market.

Developing the product – the prototype

The purpose of the **prototype** or pilot stage is to find out if the product works, i.e. the prototype will be used to test consumer reaction. Several versions will initially be made and tested on consumer panels. These panels should be representative of the intended market segment.

For example, the Deep Flan Company has decided to produce a new sweet and savoury flan with pineapple and tuna. Several versions would be baked with variations in the amount and texture of the pineapple, from 'mush' to 'chunks', and of tuna. The balance of ingredients in the pastry base will be altered. The company's preference is for wholemeal pastry. The Marketing Department has discovered that this can be used to enhance the product's image of being 'healthy' with 'a home-baked taste'. A test panel of consumers will be asked to rate each flan by various characteristics and qualities. The winner or highest-rated version will go forward for test marketing in a selected area.

A critical factor at this stage is the cost of production, which will determine the texture and balance of ingredients – 'mush' is cheaper than 'chunks'.

Activity

The Board Game – Imagination Ltd

This activity, which covers several numeracy core skills, provides a starting point for Assignment 6.2 at the end of this chapter.

You work in the new product development section of Imagination Ltd. This is a large business which produces toys and board games. The market is very big but volatile. Very few games and toys either make or stay in the best seller lists very long. The game of 'Monopoly' is very much an exception. Only a small proportion of the new products shown at the annual Toy Fair, a yearly must for suppliers and buyers of toys, ever reach the shops.

As an ideas person you have the joint responsibility for developing products to the prototype stage.

On 3 January, the manager walks in saying 'OK that one's over, let's get on with the next one. In four weeks' time I want a new board game on my desk. These are the criteria I want you to work to. The game:

- must be playable by at least two people;
- must be attractive, easy to play and addictive;
- must have a box;
- must have a catchy name;
- must have instructions suitable for the target age group – in fact I want the complete game on my desk ready for playing;
- must encourage healthy eating amongst children (we have a strong possibility of a tie in promotion with the Deep Flan company). For example, you could land on the salad square and go forward two squares or land on the fatty sausage and go back two squares – I'll leave this to you. However, this is only a suggestion, and if you can come up with a better idea don't hesitate to try it out.'

a Make the game, including the box and all instructions.

b Write a set of notes that explain how the game would be produced. Include an estimate of the cost of materials. The card which is currently used costs £2 per square metre. You must try out different shapes for the box with an estimate of the costs for each option.

c What is the expected market for the game? Does it have any competitors?

The product lifecycle

This is a description of the life of a product, from its launch to final withdrawal from the market.

For every successful product in the market there are probably twice as many that have failed. Have you ever heard of Hula-Hoops (large plastic rings or hoops which children tried to keep swinging around their waists), Strand cigarettes with the slogan 'You are never alone with a Strand' or Watney's Red Barrel, a keg beer which was heavily promoted by the brewers Watney's, but still failed in the market. The Campaign For Real Ale (CAMRA) began as a result of brewers trying to introduce 'Eurofizz' to a public who did not want it. Every Marketing Manager will be aware that most products have a limited life span and that the public taste is very fickle.

The product lifecycle model (Figure 6.1) shows how products go through four stages during their life in the market place.

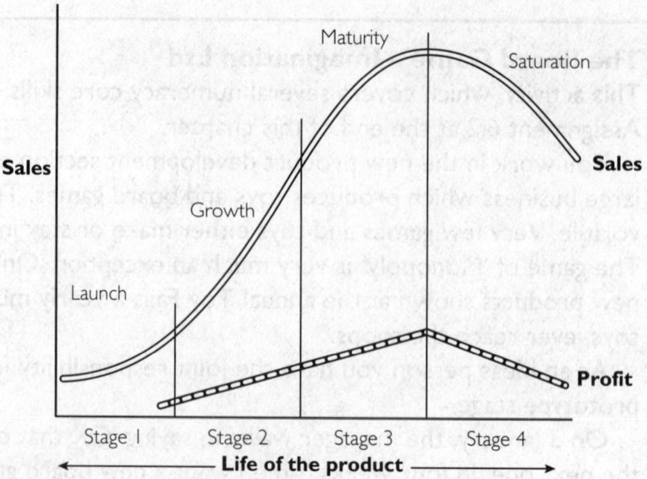

Figure 6.1 The product lifecycle model

Figure 6.1 is a model, no scales are shown on the axes because both the time and the amount of sales will vary with different products in different markets.

Stage 1 – introduction and launch

Introducing a new product into the market can be a very expensive process. During this stage, costs are likely to be very high and profits will tend to be low. This case study shows the investment costs involved with developing and launching Cadbury's Wispa.

Case study

The Wispa chocolate bar was Cadbury's answer to the original Aero which was made by Rowntrees. Demand for Aero had been increasing steadily and had reached the point when it was beginning to take a larger share of the market for pure chocolate products.

Cadbury's, therefore, undertook considerable market research with a wide variety of new products to find the one that people liked better than Aero. Hundreds of blind placement tests were carried out in the North East of England. The product that was eventually developed and launched took several years to perfect.

Nearly £10 million was spent on building a brand new factory, with new tools and equipment. When it was finally launched nationally Cadbury's knew that they were on to a winner. A further £5 million was spent on promoting and advertising the new bar using big name TV personalities, special offers and gifts.

Subsequently, Rowntrees developed the chunky Aero, a sure sign that sales of Wispa were beginning to bite into the sales of old style Aero. Which product do you prefer?

Stage 2 – growth and development

During this phase the product should be establishing itself in the market, sales and profits should be increasing and the initial investment should be paid for. If there is still little competition, profits could be at their highest.

Stage 3 – maturity and competition

This stage is characterised by an increase in competition which could lead to increased costs because of extra advertising and promotion. It was during this stage that new chunky Aero was developed. Sales of the product are still increasing but at an ever-decreasing rate. Price cuts, special offers and discounts may be given in an attempt to stimulate sales.

Stage 4 – saturation and decline

This stage is typified by declining sales and low profits. Even price cuts and advertising are not enough to tempt the consumer into purchasing. The business may attempt to re-launch the product in a different form. For example, the introduction of compact discs has meant that fifties and sixties music has been rediscovered. When record companies release 'Greatest Hits' and compilations, it generally means that the star or group is in **decline**. Some products may get an unexpected boost at this stage, for example, when *Lady Chatterley's Lover* was shown on TV in 1993, the book of the TV version went into the best seller lists!

Activities

1 At what stage of their lifecycle are these products?
Mars, Kit Kat, Wispa, Secret, Walls ice cream, Mars ice cream, Smiths Crisps, the Mini car, Radion, Persil, Horlicks, Diet drinks, LPs, compact discs, Doc Marten boots.

2 If you consider any of these products are in decline what would you do to revive them and why?

The product mix

The **product mix** refers to the range of products sold or produced by a business. A brewery, for instance, will make a range of beers of different strengths and quality. It will charge premium/high prices for its stronger brands. Most large companies, for example Unilever, will aim to have a range of products which cover as many market segments as possible. Schools and colleges do this by offering a variety of courses which appeal to a wide range of people.

In some cases this will be achieved by the development of new products or by differentiating existing ones. Car companies, for example, make four- or five-door cars, with or without metallic paint, sporty wheel trim, automatic gear box, sun roof, etc. – the so-called 'optional extras'. Special editions are sometimes made; in June 1993 Peugeot was advertising the 'Key Largo' and 'Key West' versions of its 106 range. Smarties, for example, are available in five standard packs – tubes, multipacks of three and five tubes (for supermarkets), cartons and mini-cartons. Each option requires a variation of the production process and will normally be offered at a different price.

Companies will also aim to have products which are at different stages of the product lifecycle.

Positioning the product

The position of a product refers to a specific quality or characteristic of the product which is most often stressed in its advertising and is best known to the customer – its 'personality'. In other words, what immediately springs to the customer's mind when the product is mentioned. What image do you have of a *Sun* reader as opposed to a *Daily Telegraph* reader, of a Rolls Royce as opposed to a Citröen 2CV?

Every business will attempt to achieve a unique position for itself, its products or its services, in the heart and mind of the consumer. It will do this by emphasising one or other of its main features – its **unique selling point (USP)**. (Note that you will have to identify a USP for the product in your business plan.) Peaudouce, the makers of nappies, claim that the unique patented 'multi-strand elasticated panel' in its new product give it a real USP over its competitors!

As you read the following list of features try to think of some product examples.

Key features used to position a product

Quality –	the best there is
Who makes it –	e.g. 'We are the largest/smallest company so we try harder'
Price –	e.g. 'Never knowingly undersold' or 'Best prices, best service'
Physical characteristics –	e.g. biggest, smallest, sweetest
Who uses it –	e.g. a famous personality, but beware the Nike trainers example where all three of its personalities failed in the Olympics
Benefits from use –	e.g. cures headaches fast
The location –	e.g. 1,000 car parking spaces on the doorstep
Value for money –	e.g. 'With Fairy Liquid you get this much more'
Image –	e.g. smart, attractive, friendly staff
Service –	e.g. 'The smiles are free' or 'We answer every call'

Extension strategies

These are the methods that are used to try and extend or prolong the life of a product. Two techniques are particularly important. The first is repositioning, which means changing the customer's view or image of the qualities and characteristics of the product. Here are some examples of **repositioning**; you will probably think of others.

Product	New position
Lucozade	A sporty image
Sherry	Drink it cold with ice
Chocolate	New chunky blocks
MFI	Upmarket
Horlicks	Drink it anytime even cold
British Home Stores	Now BHS with a new logo
British Telecom	Now BT with a new logo

Small changes to aspects of the product can have a dramatic effect on consumer demand. Examples include Ariel and Persil (changes to the accelerator), and blue Smarties (introducing a new colour). Companies may even change the name, Marathon, for example became Snickers though the ingredients stayed largely the same. Coca Cola and BP redesigned their logos. Have you noticed?

Activity

1 You work for a company which makes watches. Sales have recently been falling. The public image of the product is that the watches are only for very rich people. Yet they are not really very expensive.
Write a memo to your section head suggesting two ways in which the watches can be repositioned.

2 How might the makers of these products distinguish/differentiate them from their competitors: Computers? Calculators? Crisps? Carrier bags? Chips?

3 Copy and complete the matrix by giving a suitable extension strategy for each product. You will probably be able to think of other strategies which can be used.

Product	**Strategy**			
	Repackage	**New promotion**	**Redesign**	**Improve**
Butter				
Cider				
Men's suits				
Hats				
Bacon				
Cocoa				
Typewriters				
Fish				
Candles				

Promotion

Look at this cartoon of sandwich boards. What does it say about promotion?

The term **promotion** refers to those business activities which are intended to persuade the customer to buy or stock the product. The customer can be a manufacturer, wholesaler, retailer or consumer.

Packaging

Think of Toblerone and Smarties – these have all the qualities of good packaging. The key features of packaging are:

- instant recognition
- attractive
- eye catching
- persuasive
- protecting the product from damage during storage and transit
- functional and easy to open.

As Nestlé says 'a good consumer package protects the product it sells and sells the product it protects'.

Activities

1 Brainstorm the key features of packaging shown above and then apply them to your boxed board game.

2 The group should divide into four or five teams to examine the packaging of these products:
1 dozen eggs, a round box of cheese triangles, a carton of milk, a loaf of bread, a water melon.
Use the criteria above to rate the packaging out of 10. You must open each package and rate this feature!

Advertising and publicity

Advertising, in some form or other, has been in action for centuries. The red and white barber's pole is a reminder of the days when barbers doubled as dentists. The inn sign was important when customers could not read.

Advertising provides information to the buyer. It can be informative when it tells consumers about the product, what it does, how it works, what it costs and where it can be bought. It is persuasive when it is intended to tempt consumers to buy a particular product in preference to any other.

Why do firms advertise?

The main purposes of advertising are to:

- increase demand, i.e. shift the demand curve to the right, so that the business can sell more at any particular price;
- create or change the image, for example, Yoplait Yoghurts are in a package which conveys the image of a basket of fruit. Adverts such as 'nothing is like' or 'the biggest small car in its class' are intended to hit a competitor's product;
- create brand loyalty so that customers will continue to buy the product;
- raise the profit revenue by appealing to the emotions, for example, charities are now advertising heavily;
- maintain the present market share.

Advertising is the main means by which a business can tell the public about the product and what it can do.

Activity

Advertising the board game – Imagination Ltd

MEMORANDUM

To: New Product Development Section
From: The Chief Executive

Congratulations! Your idea for a new board game is excellent. Now it has to be marketed.

We have decided to allocate you – £500,000 – yes, £1/2 million. We're not talking £250 for a window cleaner here. You will, of course, be working with a few colleagues, but I want to see exactly what work you have done on this project. That's how you get a distinction in this business!

First the research. Find out:

- What can we get for our money?
- What media mix should we choose?
- How much will each cost?
- When should we advertise?
- If you choose TV, what programmes? What times?
- If you go for magazines, which ones and how much space will we get for our money?

Make sure you get your target market right. You have four weeks. The deadline is vital, and don't forget the executive summary with your recommendations. I don't want 15 comics in a folder – this has to go before the Board.

J W Spear and Sons the makers of the board game Scrabble spent £2 million on its latest TV and cinema advertising campaign, targeting 150 cinemas with 20-second commercials.

Advertising media

The advertising medium is the means by which information is communicated to the public. The message is the medium. The mass media are the means of communication which reach large numbers of people – TV, newspapers, radio and magazines are the primary mass media.

The choice of medium will depend upon the product and the marketing objectives, for example:

1 Television advertising is expensive but can be targeted at regions or specific groups according to education, age or lifestyle. Viewing panels are used to find out the

nature of the audience for any particular programme and time slot. A points rating system is used to price the TV advert – in this case points means pounds! Considerable information is available, for example, people who use olive oil also drink wine, read, like holidays abroad, own a car, use mayonnaise and, would you believe, watch Brookside! So if you watch it, you are likely to see adverts for these products. Specific programmes are used to advertise specific products. However, do you switch channels when the ads are on? The Broadcasters' Audience Research Board (BARB) has introduced a new electronic system for measuring audience appreciation of TV programmes, rather than just producing numbers of people watching.

2 Newspaper advertising is less expensive, but can again be used to target specific groups of people. *Sun* readers are in the C2 category, whilst the A and B groups read *The Times*. It can be very effective locally. The cost of advertising in newspapers depends mainly on the size of the readership and the size of the advertisement.

3 Magazines appeal to quite specific market segments, sports, leisure interests, railway magazines, etc. Nike and Adidas, for example, advertise regularly in sports magazines.

4 Posters are generally used to display very direct messages, for example, 'Vote for me!' Campaigns can be planned locally, regionally or nationally. They are frequently used to back up a TV campaign. Poster sizes vary from 2 to 50 square metres; the largest size gives a very large message! Nestlé use posters extensively for advertising Polo, Yorkie, Kit Kat and Aero.

5 Cinemas – unless you arrive late, you cannot escape from cinema advertising for gin, Bacardi, Martini, jeans and the local Chinese restaurant, which never looks like the one you use!

6 Radio – audiences or market segments, can be targeted locally or nationally. As with TV, specific programmes and stations attract different types of people. In London, for example, Capital Gold plays sixties and seventies music, whilst Capital FM plays contemporary music – each appeals to different markets. As with TV, advertising costs depend on the time of day and the size of the audience. For example, Capital FM which reaches 32 per cent of the adult audience in its transmission area, charges £1,800 for a 30-second commercial on a P1 or Prime Time slot (morning and evening rush hours). Capital Gold, with 20 per cent audience, charges £750 for the same time and slot.

7 Leaflets, flyers and handouts are cheap and cheerful. They can be delivered by hand or distributed as newspaper or magazine inserts. The flyer for this book went to a targeted market of schools and colleges.

The media mix

The **media mix** refers to the choice of medium used by a business to convey its advertising message. A typical large advertising campaign for a nationally distributed brand could be split:

5 per cent for posters
5 per cent for radio
10 per cent for cinema
20 per cent for newspaper and magazines
60 per cent for TV.

A small local business could distribute its budget between the local press and radio, plus leaflet distribution.

Case study

Publicity

Publicity is the technique, process or information used to attract attention to products or people. The Lloyds bank logo, for example, is used on the sales literature, bank statements, cheque books, letters to customers, branches, point of sale displays and in TV and newspaper advertisements. Why do you think the logo is so widely used?

Activity

These are the figures for the Sega 1991 advertising budget.
Total budget £6.25 million split between:

TV 57.6 per cent, Press 19.2 per cent, Cinema 9.6 per cent,
Radio 4.8 per cent, Posters 4.8 per cent, Market Research 4 per cent.

a Why do you think Sega split its budget in this way?

b Draw a pie chart to show the information.

Source: Figures supplied by Sega

How effective is advertising?

The evaluation of an advertisement should take place before and after the campaign.

Pre-campaign testing Adverts can be tested either before or after they have been produced. With radio and TV adverts, pre-production testing, although cheaper, can often be meaningless. Advertising agencies often use specially selected groups of people to assess advertisements for visual appeal, image, information, enjoyment, communication and the quality of the message. The client, which is the business selling the product, will also be closely involved. It may want a different image or more emphasis on one aspect of the product.

Post-campaign testing Once an advertisement has been seen or heard, the client will want to know how effective it has been. Sometimes this is straightforward, for example, 'This product is not for sale in any shops and is only available directly from the company', can be assessed by the number of orders/sales the client company receives. Recently, over 200 people were caught watching TV channels they were not entitled to use, when they replied to a free offer advertised by the TV station.

Newspaper adverts often carry code numbers which must be quoted in the reply so the advertiser can find out how effective an advert has been. Similarly, coupons to be returned are coded so that the advertising medium (a specific magazine, for example) can be identified.

How memorable are adverts?

Recall is a method used to test the effectiveness of advertising. In spontaneous recall, consumers are asked to name any advert which they have seen or heard in, say, the last 10 days. With prompted recall, consumers are asked to say whether they have seen or heard an advert named by the interviewer.

Activity

a Everyone in the group should watch commercial TV for a week noting the companies/products which are advertised. Each of you should then ask 10 people to name the adverts they remember seeing. (You can check these against your own list.) You can also use your list to prompt people into replying.
b The group should then compare results to produce a percentage response rate. Check the marketing magazines to see how your results compare with the 'official' figures.

If an advertiser has spent a large amount of money on a campaign, but the recall rate is very small, then this suggests the campaign has not been very effective. Perhaps the advertiser should consider changing its advertising agency.

What affect can advertising have on costs and prices?

For the economy as a whole, the quantitative importance of advertising is minimal. For some products, however, advertising costs are quite significant. Some 30 per cent of the retail price of a bottle of mineral water, for example, is marketing costs.

Some companies rely on advertising as their major source of revenue, for example, commercial radio and TV, and national and local newspapers. Free newspapers rely entirely on advertising for their existence. In many cases if the advertising input was removed, then either the price would rise substantially or the product could disappear. Conversely, the low level of advertising on supermarket 'own label' products does keep prices down. Nationally sold, branded products tend to have higher prices – customers pay for brand names. Look at the price difference between Heinz baked beans and a large supermarket's equivalent size, look-alike own-brand label tin of beans.

Activity

Imagination Ltd
Write a short press release informing the media of your new board game. (You should note that some journalists will use this material without making any changes so it needs to be good and accurate.)

Advertising budgets
Advertising budgets are split into two categories: 'above-the-line' expenditure which is advertising to consumers through the mass media, and 'below-the-line' expenditure through the retail and wholesale trade. The majority of a budget is spent on above-the-line promotion.

Public relations

Every organisation will have a file which contains a record of each time it has been mentioned in the media. The **public relations** or PR department of an organisation has the responsibility for getting this publicity. Pop groups, politicians, personalities, presenters and plcs could all have someone responsible for PR.

Public relations involves:

- keeping the media informed of new products or changes to existing products;
- providing press releases, stories, facts, lies, photos, secrets, etc., on behalf of the client, to the media;
- lobbying: persuading journalists, TV presenters, etc. to write or mention the client. For example, a travel article on Poland might say at the end, 'Our reporter, Holly Day, travelled to Poland courtesy of the Polish National Airline LOT', i.e. the trip was free in return for a free 'plug';
- organising functions and events where there will usually be a famous personality;
- community relations: for example, the local theatre could give away free tickets to the current pantomime to the winner of the 'Name everyone in the theatre last night competition!!' Blunders can be made if the business cannot deliver what it promises. Is any publicity good publicity?

Everyone's a winner

by SIMON TRUMP

DRINKS giant Coca-Cola was at the centre of a Hoover-style promotions blunder yesterday.

Its offer of thousands of pounds worth of computer games to customers who bought a specially coded bottle backfired after scores of drinkers claimed a prize.

The company had promised £260 Sega mega drives to those who found the letter M, G or B inside the cap.

But all three letters appeared in a wrongly stamped batch of bottles – making everyone appear a winner.

Staff told thousands of callers who jammed a hotline yesterday, expecting to claim their prize, that they would be getting a T-shirt instead. And the company will this week launch a national advertising campaign to apologise.

The blunder comes just a fortnight after three Hoover executives were sacked over a free flights fiasco.

A Coca-Cola spokesman said: "It is an unfortunate coincidence."

A spokesman for the Advertising Standards Authority said: "There has patently been no intention to mislead."

Source: *Today*, 19 April 1993

- organising a product launch, the purpose of which is to achieve as much free publicity as possible, by inviting the press, TV, radio, the local MP, etc. Almost anything can be launched, for example, a new album, the opening of a new creche, changing the use of a large hall into an open access study area, etc. Your new board game would be launched at the Toy Fair; new cars are unveiled at the Motor Show.

It is the ultimate aim of every PR person to get a mention on the TV news. Do not do as one enthusiastic student did when set the task 'try to get your organisation mentioned on the news'; he tried to rob the place!

Sponsorship

When Everton beat Manchester United in the 1995 FA Cup Final their sponsors NEC must have been delighted that their investment had paid off. Who sponsored Manchester United? **Sponsorship** can mean giving financial support to an organisation, an event, an activity, or a person. The main purposes of sponsorship are:

- To raise customer awareness of the organisation and its products.
- To raise the company profile.
- To create, enhance or change an image, for example, cigarette companies sponsor motor sports.
- To generate increased sales.
- To widen the audience which sees the company's logo. Companies now sponsor sports events (Kronenbourg 1664 sponsored the 1994 Tour De France and there was also a team sponsored by GB, the company featured in the assignment on page 63), plays, opera and pantomimes.

Cadbury's PANTOMIME SEASON IN ASSOCIATION WITH Save the Children

A successful sponsorship can generate millions of pounds of extra sales. When Andre Agassi won Wimbledon in 1992, the makers of his tennis racket, Donnay, estimated it was worth at least £100 million to the company. Local companies are increasingly prepared to sponsor local events.

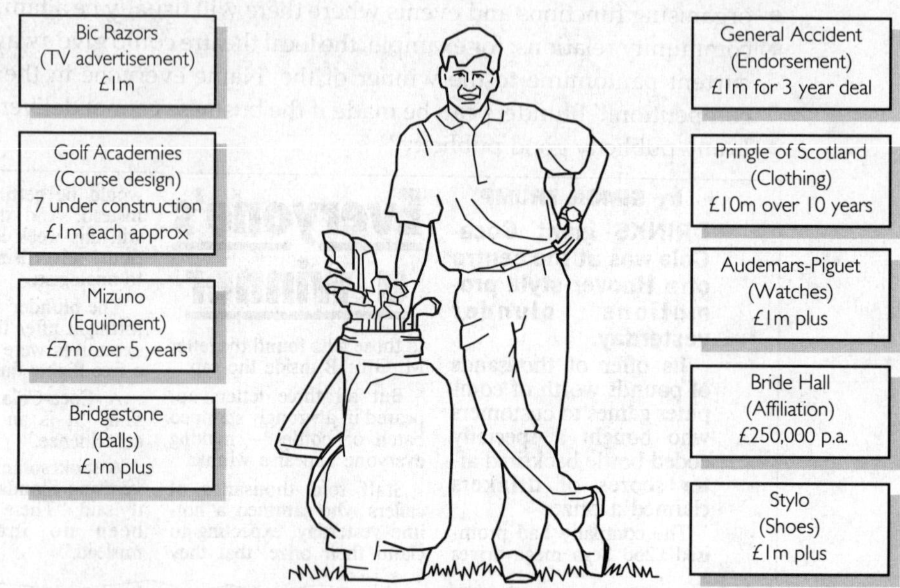

Nick Faldo – looking at a fortune

Activity

Imagination Ltd have decided to run a competition to find a sponsor.

Write a letter to Imagination Ltd, the maker of children's toys and board games, suggesting a suitable sponsorship giving reasons for your choice. Detail the other promotional activities it might undertake as part of its sponsorship programme.

Consumer sales inducements/promotion

Sales promotion refers to the techniques and methods used by a business to sell its products to either customers or other businesses.

Vouchers and coupons

These can be given to staff, customers and clients. Gift vouchers are a very efficient way of promoting sales as they cost the company very little. Boots and Marks & Spencer are the leaders in this field. Coupons are normally offered as '50p off your next purchase'.

The number of coupons issued each year averages 6 billion of which about 400 million are used or redeemed. So 5.6 billion are unused! Only a small percentage are redeemed against a specific product and this has been a major disadvantage. Analysis of coupon redemption has been difficult in the past but the new EPOS (Electronic Point Of Sale) checkouts with bar code readers will soon, however, be able to match a coupon against a specific sale.

Samples

Sachets of just about everything are now stuck to magazines, in order to tempt the consumer to buy the magazine and try the product.

Gifts

CDs, floppy discs, seed trays and a bait box (this was attached to a fishing magazine) were all available at the time of writing. We were told that the seed trays came separately from the magazine and had to be stuck on by the retailer!

Competitions

These are popular in newspapers and magazines. They are good for selling the paper and advertising the prize. In addition, the names and addresses of the entrants can be used as a potential customer database.

Discounts

Discounts such as multibuys, 'buy five and get the sixth one free', for example, are popular with supermarkets. The 13.5 per cent extra offer is the UK's attempt at bringing the 440 ml can into line with the standard EC 500 ml measure. You will probably be able to think of many others.

Why do companies offer these inducements? Do you buy products because there is a gift attached? Do you use the garage with the forecourt promotion? And, crucially, do you stay loyal to your usual brand or do you switch if the competitor has a special promotion? All these offers are about keeping customers loyal.

Consumer and trade marketing

The Whitbread Beer Company have 'axed the age old demarcation between the trade and consumer marketing functions'. This will mean that brands can be marketed with 'one voice across all outlets'.

Trade promotion

Point-of-sale displays

These are displays which are set up near the till or check-out point. Retailers will be supplied with brochures, mock-ups of the product, leaflets and shop window displays which can be used to focus the customer's attention on a particular product. They appear to be very popular in chemists.

Point-of-sale methods are increasing in importance, particularly in supermarkets, where evidence suggests that almost 30 per cent of purchases are the result of on-the-spot decisions. How often have you heard people say 'I only came in to buy three items and have ended up with a full trolley!'?

Supermarkets have spent millions researching their stores, store layout, shelf and aisle positions, and the location of items which tempt consumers to spend more money. Dalgety, the makers of Golden Wonder, have introduced a new point-of-sale stand which is able to display a mass of individually signposted snacks. The company claims that by taking the products out of boxes and off the floor, it will achieve what confectionery and soft drinks manufacturers have done for their products.

Activity

Check this out at your local supermarket:
- Are bread and milk furthest from the entrance?
- Are packet sauces next to the meat?
- Are biscuits next to the tea and coffee?
- Are fruit and vegetables near to the entrance?
- What is next to the check-out points?
- Which items are on the middle shelves?

Can you say why the products are in these positions?

Competitions

Many suppliers run competitions specially for retailers, as a **loyalty** incentive to get them to sell more of the product. The prize is usually the title Retailer of the Year and an off-season week in Tunisia.

Training

Many manufacturers and suppliers offer free training in product knowledge to retailers and stockists. This method of promotion helps everyone, including the consumer.

Discounts

Discounts are offered to retailers when they buy in bulk or order in advance. They are particularly important when a business is trying to launch a new product. Wholesalers and retailers have to be persuaded, or induced, to stock new and untried goods with uncertain profits. This is part of the 'below-the-line' promotional expenditure.

At the time of writing, Walls, who sell 70 per cent of the £800 million UK ice cream market, with 9 out of 10 of the best sellers, had just been referred to the Monopolies and Mergers Commission again (the last time was in 1979).

The complaint was that the freezer cabinets provided by Walls cannot be used by other ice-cream manufacturers. You will notice that the other makes are often sold in off licenses and other non-traditional outlets, as this was the only route open to them.

On average, some 60 per cent of a sales promotion campaign budget for a consumer product, such as bottled mineral water, would be spent on point-of-sale and retail promotions.

The overall objectives of sales promotion are:
- to encourage potential customers to buy the product;
- to promote and/or maintain customer loyalty;
- to persuade businesses to stock and sell the product.

Activity

The sales promotion budget for Sega was £2.25 million. This was split as follows:
- point of sale, 45 per cent;
- retailer promotions 25 per cent;
- joint promotions 21 per cent;
- Sega bus tour 9 per cent.

Draw the pie chart from this data and comment on the figures.

Direct marketing

Direct marketing is any form of sales, supply or promotion made directly to the consumer. Included in direct marketing are: direct mail, either off-screen or off-page mail order, tele-marketing, door-to-door distribution and direct reply advertising.

There are two main advantages of direct marketing.

- The market can be precisely targeted because the business contacts a known person directly.
- Costs can be controlled and the business will know exactly what it costs to generate sales.

These are important points because most advertising campaigns tend to be hit and miss affairs, and the businesses do not usually know who has responded.

Direct mail

Used extensively by charities, financial services and book clubs, **direct mail** can be very precise. As computer databases become more efficient, individuals can be contacted directly with personalised mail. Much of the mail received is unsolicited 'junk mail', i.e. it is not asked for, and the Data Protection Registrar is now getting an increasing number of complaints about some direct mail methods. Agencies sell lists of potential customers. These are gained from people who have, for example:

- returned 10 tokens from the *Echo* for a £1 day trip to France. The names and addresses of many *Echo* readers will, therefore, be known. Other market research will have confirmed what these people eat, drink and how they spend their leisure time. Companies which make these products will later buy these lists of names;
- given their names and addresses to the market researcher giving away cigarettes to people queuing for the Bruce Springsteen or Bon Jovi concerts at Milton Keynes;
- joined a book club.

Every time someone completes a questionnaire they add to the information stored on a database.

Mail order

Mail order companies all sell direct to the public through catalogues. Other companies use home parties to sell children's clothes, cosmetics, jewellery, etc. These are all precisely targeted because the people who run parties only ask people with similar interests.

Tele-marketing

Telephone marketing (**tele-marketing**) is increasing. It is cheap to set up, very persuasive on a one-to-one basis and the message can be varied.

Door-to-door distribution

In the case of **door-to-door distribution**, the salesperson will literally knock on every door trying to sell goods or services. Some companies leave an order form with a catalogue 'to be collected later'; in some cases the catalogue also has to be returned.

Direct reply advertising

With this method advertisements are placed in newspapers or on TV and customers have to reply direct to the advertiser.

Pyramid selling

Pyramid selling is found in all areas, from jewellery to burglar alarms. Here is an example to show how pyramid selling works.

The creator of the pyramid (it could be the manufacturer) advertises for distributors to sell its wonderful new range of products.

The first distributors will pay a reasonable price to the manufacturer for their stock.

In order for these distributors to make any money they will have to sell their stock of goods to more distributors at even higher prices.

At the bottom of the pyramid will be people who have bought stock at exorbitant prices which can only be sold at a loss.

Admen talk telephone numbers

WHEN Peter Wood, £ 6 million-a-year chief executive of Direct Line Insurance, posed for a picture in last week's *Observer*, it was fitting that he chose a telephone on racing tyres as his prop. The souped-up phone with its infuriating musical horn is the star of the company's TV commercial, arguably the most successful example of direct response television advertising, and a major contributor to Wood's wage packet.

DRTV – or 'Doctor TV', as it is known in the trade – is, according to ITV, one of the few growth areas in television advertising. The ITV Association estimates that 15 per cent of commercials screened today carry a telephone number, compared to 10 per cent two or three years ago. And Kate Hampton, the ITVA's business development manager adds: 'The people who are using direct response are coming back and spending more and more money with us.

The rationale is simple: when times are tough, the marketing department needs to demonstrate that the money it spends is working. Direct response is the easiest advertising to justify; you simply add up the new business generated over the telephone, subtract the costs of airtime, production and handling calls, and if you have made a profit then the argument is won.

Activity

1 Read the article 'Admen talk telephone numbers' and say what the advantages and disadvantages are for these groups:
consumers; television company; Marketing Manager; manufacturer; you.
2 Why do you think direct response off-screen TV advertising is increasing?

Brand names and logos

Brand names are an essential part of the way a product is packaged. Every company will want the consumer to ask for its product by name.

The purpose of branding is to differentiate products which are basically similar. It is, therefore, an important feature of the non-price competition which exists in duopolistic and oligopolistic industries. Each business is trying to establish its own 'niche' in the market. The companies making trainers concentrate entirely on using the brand name to sell the products. They will reinforce this by putting their names and logos on carrier bags, T-shirts and sweat-shirts which the consumer then pays for! The 16–20-year-old market are the major buyers of brand name products.

From the manufacturers' and retailers' viewpoint, branding is important because it helps to create consumer loyalty and increase sales. If consumers can be persuaded to only buy, for example, High Track trainers, the company has effectively achieved an inelastic demand for the product and can use this to adjust its prices accordingly. What can you say generally about the price of branded and non-branded goods?

Spot the difference . . . Nestlé has apparently "redesigned" the packing and logo of the UK's biggest chocolate brand Kit Kat. Not content with elbowing out the Rowntree's name, the Swiss company claims to have given the famous white on red logo "a crisper feel through a more refined oval". It is the first time the logo has been changed since the 50s and aims to give the £200m brand "even better shelf stand out".

Source: *Marketing*, 15 July 1993

Communications mix

The **communications mix** refers to the combination of promotion methods which a business will use to promote and sell its products. For example, a typical travel company would promote its product – the holiday – by a combination of:

- advertising through national newspapers and magazines;
- advertising in the trade press;
- public relations events and exhibitions such as the World Travel Market, which is for trade clients, and the Holiday Show, which is for the public;
- direct mail shots to former clients;
- 'free' trips for the media and travel agents.

Activities

1 Your Marketing Manager has asked you to prepare a set of notes showing the pros and cons of the different types of promotion. Prepare the notes as requested.

2 The total marketing budget for the Sega 1991 marketing campaign was £10 million, split as follows: advertising 63 per cent; sales promotion 22 per cent; public relations 7.5 per cent; sponsorship 2.5 per cent; contingency reserves (to cover unforeseen events) 5 per cent.
Why was the budget split in this way?
What would you have done?

3 On your own, carry out the task specified in the memo below:

> ***IMAGINATION LTD***
> ***Memorandum***
>
> To: GNVQ Student — Today's date
> From: R. Ling
>
> Promoting the board game
>
> Following your successful proposal for the media mix for the new board game, I would like you to complete the project by suggesting and creating the communications mix. There is an extra £0.5 million available. I want a full breakdown with costings, etc. Maximum four-page report please.

4 With your group, propose a communications mix for each of the situations below. Justify your choice in each case.

Situation	**Budget**		
	Low	Middle	High
A holiday cottage near Brecon A new children's ice cream A hotel in Bath A local typing agency			

The term 'budget' refers to the amount of money which can be allocated in each case. You have to decide which level is best. Always remember the more you spend here the less is available for spending elsewhere – that's 'opportunity cost'.

Price

The price at which a business sells it products is an integral part of the marketing mix. Ask yourself the questions: How much would you expect to pay for a new microwave oven? Would you buy one for £40 or does this sound too cheap, i.e. it cannot be any good for that price? Do you associate price with quality? What about a £20 Easter egg for a member of your family? Does this seem expensive? What about a present for your best friend which costs £60 at Harrods in London and £20 in your local high street? Do you link the price with the place where it is bought?

The seller of any product will have considered these and many other questions before deciding on the price at which to sell goods – 99p, £1.99, £2.99 all look and sound better than £1, £2 and £3.

Pricing policy

The **pricing policy** that a business adopts will depend upon many factors. For example:

- If the business is operating in a competitive market it could choose to keep its prices in line with its competitors, or try to undercut them.
- If the product is new and has only just been launched, a low introductory price could be chosen to tempt purchasers. The soft drink Gini was launched at 20p but is now the same price as other canned drinks. Marshall Cavendish, the publisher of weekly part-works such as *The Great Composers and their Music*, offered the first two weeks for the price of one, and a free binder!
- If the business decides to maximise profits this will have a different effect on price than if it decides to maximise its share of the market, i.e. the company's objectives are important.
- Costs of production, both fixed and variable, can be significant, if the business chooses to adopt a cost-based pricing system. Look at the prices in your local sandwich bar – do they vary with the type of filling?

We have already seen in the unit Business in the Economy, that economists see prices as being determined by the market forces of supply and demand. In the Financial units you will discover that accountants also have a role to play. In this section we will look at pricing as one vital part of the company's marketing mix.

Pricing Yorkie

When Yorkie was launched, it was critical that it offered competitive value, i.e. grams of chocolate per penny of price. Because Yorkie was thicker than competitors' chocolates, the surface area of the top of the pack was smaller, and the value for money appeared to be less good. However, it was a heavier block and although more expensive than the competition, gave better value for money.

Source: *Nestlé*

Pricing new products

When a business introduces a new product or re-launches an existing one, it has to make a decision about which price to choose.

Penetration pricing

In the case of **penetration pricing** prices are set very low so as to enable the company to gain a foothold in the market. Once this has been achieved prices may be progressively raised. Exporters have often used this method to gain a foothold in another market. A good example was the launch of the VTech 486Sx computer in the UK during 1993. The original market price of £999 including VAT generated a very large demand. During the next three months the price was progressively raised to £1,399.

Skimming pricing

With **skimming pricing** prices are initially set very high to take advantage of the public's desire for a new product or design. The term 'skim the cream' pricing is often used to describe this approach. Computer software packages, computer games and mobile telephones are excellent examples of this type of pricing. However, as consumers become more sophisticated they will often delay purchasing until the price comes down.

The Monopolies and Mergers Commission may intervene if it believes prices have been kept artificially high for too long, as happened with the makers of CDs.

Positioning pricing

With positioning pricing prices are set which reflect the consumer's view of the product, for example, good champagne is supposed to be expensive, therefore a cheap champagne will be associated with poor quality. If the business sets too low a price, consumers may not buy the product; it's all a matter of psychology! The lowest priced tender, for example, is often not accepted.

Products are often re-positioned at higher prices to change their image.

Cost-based pricing

Pricing methods which are based on the cost structure of the business are favoured by accountants because they are supposedly more accurate and reliable. The cost of production is used as a baseline figure and the price is then marked up by the required amount. For example, if a retailer buys a product for £35 and wants a return or profit of 20 per cent, it will add 20 per cent to the buying price to get the selling price of £42. This is the 'value added' to the product.

If the business is trying to maximise its profits, it should price the product so as to make marginal cost equal to marginal revenue. This is called **marginal cost pricing**. In order for this method to work successfully all costs need to be accurately accounted for, particularly those associated with a change in the level of output. In many firms this is a very difficult process, which is why the simpler mark-up procedure is used.

Demand-based pricing

Many businesses set their prices based on what they think the consumer is prepared to pay. There are many examples of where this technique is used, for example: consultants vary their fees according to the client; market traders will charge whatever they can get away with; jobbing gardeners will look first at the value of the property, then decide on a price; the local corner shop which buys its supplies 'cash and carry' will set the highest price it can, if the goods do not sell it will merely reduce the price.

Competitive pricing

This is a situation where the business sets a price roughly in line with its competitors. This process works reasonably well if the cost structures of the companies are roughly similar.

Discount pricing

In many competitive markets, for example office machinery or office consumables, the published list or catalogue price is only the starting point for bargaining. Buyers and Purchasing Officers in most businesses should be able to obtain the goods for less than the advertised price, particularly if they intend dealing with the supplier in future. Phrases such as 'We definitely want to buy from you, its only a question of price' will help get the deal you want.

Many firms can be forced into price cutting if they are short of cash or need to increase sales quickly.

Differential pricing

A business may sometimes charge different prices for the same product at different times, for example, peak and off-peak telephone calls, rail travel and holidays. Prices in this case will be based on the elasticity of demand for the product (see page 68 for an explanation of elasticity).

Activity

1 On your own, for each situation below say whether the price level will be 'low', 'middle', or 'high' in order for the business to achieve its objective. Give reasons for your answers.

2 With your group, compare your results with those of your colleagues. Do you agree?

	Prices		
Situation objective	**Low**	**Middle**	**High**
Revenue maximisation			
Short-term profits			
Long-term profits			
Profit maximisation			
Customer loyalty			
Market penetration			
Maintaining market share			
Repositioning a product			
Launching a new service			
Break even			
Eliminate competitors			
More business			
Public service			

Price setting and price structures

The process of setting or determining the price at which to sell goods or services varies from being relatively straightforward, for example, a window cleaner, to the highly complex situation found in, for example, an oil refinery where the problem is how to allocate costs for the range of products refined from the crude oil.

Whether the task is simple or complex, the business will have to consider these factors:

- Identify the customers. What can they afford/what are they willing to pay?
- Investigate competitors' prices, then decide whether to keep prices in line or undercut them.
  Calculate the costs and sales associated with possible price levels, keeping in mind the highest and lowest prices that could be charged, for example, a new business will have to be able to match the lowest price available unless it is offering something extra.
- Decide on a **price structure**, for example, will similar products all sell within a fixed price band. Some tins of paint, for example, sell at the same price regardless of the colour, even though different colours cost more to manufacture.

The prices of many electrical items are broadly in line with each other, as this list of prices shows. This is called **team pricing**. Check this out for yourself.

Cordless jug kettle	£19.99
Toaster	£19.99
Electric iron	£19.99
Hand blender	£19.99
Sandwich maker	£23.99
Electric carving knife	£16.99

Activity

a Each member of the group should choose a different product. On your own investigate the prices at which it is sold and present the results in a report. The report should cover:

- the type of price structure that exists and why;
- the number of brands on sale and whether they are made by the same company;
- the type of non-price competition.

b With your group, compare your findings with those of your colleagues and write a report which uses a range of examples of different price structures.

Place or distribution

Place or **distribution** refers to the ways in which the seller gets the right goods and services to the customer, either consumers or other businesses, on time, first time, every time.

Distribution is a customer service that should satisfy the actual and perceived needs of the buyer. If it does not, the producer will soon go out of business.

Have you had any of these experiences?

- The goods you ordered are not delivered on time.
- Your local shop stops selling your favourite brand.
- You are over-charged twice in the same shop.
- You are told 'Sorry, no, we've run out of ...'.

What have you done each time? Have you complained? Have you stopped using the shop without saying anything? Have you switched brands? Each decision we make will affect the place and distribution policies of the business.

Distribution channels

Remember that the channel of distribution (see page 23) is the method by which goods and services reach the customer:

The business will have to decide whether to deliver the goods directly to the customer, or use an intermediary such as a wholesaler, agent or retailer. The decision which is made will depend on the answers to these questions:

- Who are the customers and what are their needs?
- Where are they situated and what outlets are available?

We can compare the costs and benefits associated with each decision as follows:

Direct to customer	Using an intermediary
Gives the producer total control	Can be very expensive
Provides immediate customer service	Provides storage facilities
Can be very expensive if the producer has to run its own fleet of transport	Able to provide small quantities
Can be expensive if there are many customers with small orders, widely spread	May not give the image required by the manufacturer
Producer can give the image it wants	Can be important in large areas with few customers
Gives good customer feedback and response	More difficult to control
All stock is readily available, but costly to store	May only carry a few popular lines
Centralised storage can be inefficient particularly with bulky or heavy products	Intermediary or decentralised distribution is needed for high-weight, low-price goods
Will need to provide a range of customer services	Retailers can provide services such as free delivery and installation

The ultimate decision will depend upon whether the product is a physical good or a service.

Physical (product) distribution

Physical goods can either be provided direct to the final customer (direct sales) or through an intermediary (indirect sales). The grocery trade is a good example of how this distinction works. Most small retailers, for example, obtain their supplies through wholesalers because they are conveniently located and willing to sell small quantities. However, when goods are bought in this way they are expensive. Therefore, some retailers have combined together, for example, Mace, so that they can buy in bulk yet still retain the advantage of being close to their customers. The large supermarket chains are vertically integrated, which means they buy direct from the manufacturer and sell through their own outlets.

Activity

Compare the costs and benefits of each method of grocery distribution from the point of view of:

a a customer who is physically disabled
b a small shopkeeper
c a food manufacturer
d a wholesaler
e a student
f a large supermarket.

Service distribution

The main differences between the distribution of goods and services are that:

- services can only be provided direct to the customer. A dentist, for example, cannot work through an intermediary;
- because services are intangible, it means they cannot be stored and have to be provided on demand. This means that if you want to see a U2 concert you have to go

when they are performing. If you wish to go on holiday to the Gran Canaria Princess Hotel in Playa del Ingles during August, you can only go if there are vacancies.

Service industries, therefore, have to be able to spread the demand for their services. They do this by changing the Four Ps:

- Price – peak and off-peak pricing is a key feature of many service industries, for example, holidays are priced according to the season, rail travel and telephone call charges vary with the time of day. The purpose of these policies is to spread the demand.
- Product – administration systems have been devised which help to spread the loadings, for example, holidays and dentists have to be booked in advance and staff are specially trained to give advice and help.
- Place – services have to be provided where the customers are situated, for example, hairdressers, dentists and plumbers can be found in any reasonably populated area. The provision of services is decentralised and therefore expensive. Tour operators, for example, Airtours have therefore taken over travel agents.
- Promotion – special promotions advertise the benefits of using off-peak facilities, for example, no queues and no waiting at the restaurant (between 6 p.m. and 7 p.m.).

The Monopolies and Mergers Commission has investigated many cases of exclusive distribution agreements, between manufacturers and retailers, which act as a major barrier to the entry of new firms and products into an industry.

Many new businesses have been forced to seek alternative methods of distributing products when large firms have already tied up the existing market outlets. This can be a very expensive process.

Activity

Suggest, with reasons, suitable distribution channels for each of the following:

a launching Belgian chocolates in the UK market
b hand-made woollen socks
c a travel firm based in Solihull that sells coach holidays
d a manufacturer of equipment used in the steel industry.

Case study

Sales distribution and information technology

In Nestlé Grocery and Nestlé Food there are sales teams for each of the key areas: supermarket chains, the co-operative movement, and the wholesale and independent grocery trade.

Orders for the various divisions and areas are received and processed by sales office teams in Croydon, York, Chepstow and Warrington. Deliveries to the companies' customers are made in several ways. Large orders to major customers are often sent direct from factories. Smaller deliveries are handled through a national network of depots fitted with the most modern equipment, designed to hold and handle a wide range of different products and packs.

A fleet of trucking vehicles is used to carry goods from the factories to the depots.

Extensive use is made of computers. All sites have computers linked to the head office. Applications range from straightforward automation of clerical and secretarial work, stock control and invoicing, to order picking and load planning systems.

Marketing strategy

The **marketing strategy** of a business is the method by which it intends to achieve its objectives. All Four Ps will need to be considered to get the most suitable marketing mix. The business will need to know:

- Who its customers are and what they want from the product.
- Why and where they buy the product.
- How they like to buy and what they are prepared to pay.

This example shows what customers want when they buy a fridge. The information is based on a market research survey of buyers' expectations.

What people want when they buy a fridge

Product	Price	Place	Promotion
Good performance	Value for money	Customer care	Helpful literature
Good design	Discounts	Credit	Information
Reliability	Low prices	Free and easy parking	Truthful, with all facts
Safety	Stable prices	Free delivery	Modern premises
Quality	Competitive prices	Disposal of old machine	Friendly staff

Depending on the results of the market research the business can create or adjust its marketing mix.

Marketing plan

Planning is the process which, as Drucker has said in his book *Marketing Management*, 'makes the future happen'. The marketing plan is a part of the corporate plan which sets out the targets and objectives for the whole organisation. The corporate plan can consist of these elements:

Corporate plan

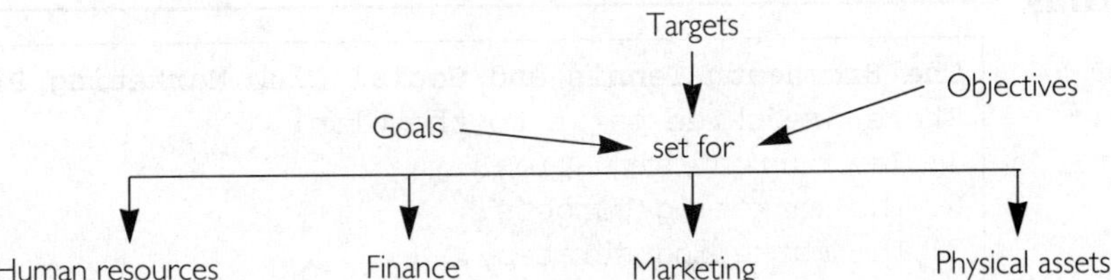

Plans can be constructed in two ways, either from the 'top down', in which case senior management will set the overall targets and departmental managers will have to work out how these can be achieved, or from the 'bottom up' when departments set out what they want to achieve and managers then derive the corporate targets.

The marketing planning process consists of the following stages:

- Corporate targets are determined for the organisation.
- The marketing department is given its objectives.
- The marketing department assesses what market opportunities exist and decides which are worth pursuing based on the likely costs and profits.
- Marketing strategies are formulated based on the marketing mix.
- Plans are constantly monitored and if necessary corrective action taken.

The purpose of a marketing plan is to:

- set out the present situation of the business;
- show the targets the business intends to achieve;
- state how the targets will be achieved.

Structure of a marketing plan

The structure of marketing plans can vary depending on the needs of the organisation and the purpose for which they are prepared. Here is an outline which will help you understand this structure:

1 Business goals	List here the specific short- and long-term goals of the business.
2 Present situation	Give here an analysis of the market and the customers. Identify the competitors. Identify the strengths, weaknesses, opportunities and threats which face the business, for example, what is the unique selling point? are all the resources needed already available?
3 Marketing targets	Identify and quantify targets, for example, sales of £15,000 in the first year.
4 Marketing mix	Give here the key features of the Product, Price, Promotion and Place.
5 Marketing strategy	Show how the Four Ps will be achieved by identifying, for example, a sales plan, an advertising plan. Go into detail, such as 10,000 leaflets will be printed at a cost of £49.
6 Summary and conclusions	Summarise the main features of the whole marketing campaign.

Now look at the case study which shows how this structure can be used to write a plan. (You will need to produce a marketing plan to accompany your business plan in Chapter 15.)

Case study

The Bromheath Tennis and Social Club Marketing Plan

There are three parts to the plan:

1. The current situation.
2. The marketing targets.
3. The marketing strategy.

THE CURRENT SITUATION

1. Although there has been an increase in playing members, fewer people are using the clubhouse facilities. A number of other clubs which had been 'inactive', have been revitalised as a result of being privatised.
2. Marketing assets – the club has four tennis courts, recently resurfaced, two playing fields and a clubhouse and bar. Bromheath runs six tennis teams, three football teams and two hockey teams. It has an excellent reputation for its sports. However, it is not known for its social life or club atmosphere. Our market research shows that members would welcome more social events. Club facilities are good but under-utilised. There are

two part-time cleaners, one full-time manager and a part-time assistant, who look after the grounds and the clubhouse. The staff are capable and would welcome more responsibility. The club is self-supporting and financially viable. Our USP is anyone can join, we welcome players of all ages and ability. Other clubs in the area tend to be more exclusive and only allow people of a certain standard to join.

3. Future developments –
   a) Competition is expected from a possible new David Lloyd indoor tennis complex.
   b) We intend targeting younger people as our policy of encouraging youngsters has worked very well.
   c) We intend introducing a new family membership scheme.

THE MARKETING TARGETS

1. A 15 per cent increase in membership.
2. To run at least one social event every two weeks.
3. To increase bar revenue by 10 per cent.

We consider these targets to be realistic and achievable. Please note that we have quantitative targets.

THE MARKETING STRATEGY

1. The manager will be given responsibility for publicising the club in order to obtain more members.
2. Special coaching will be arranged for all players.
3. A programme of special events has been arranged. This will include guest speakers from the world of tennis, quiz night, a barn dance, barbecues, a special junior night, a fireworks evening and special promotions night in the bar. All club facilities will be bookable for birthdays and special occasions. These events are all intended to increase the usage of the club during the week.
4. The club manager will be given a bonus for all sales above a certain minimum.
5. Promotions will be through the local paper and library. Also through the local radio station.

We believe that this strategy will enable us to achieve our planned targets. We will monitor the progress of this plan and if any variance occurs, we will take appropriate action, for example, lay on or run an extra event.

Activity

The above report was written by one of the members. Before it is submitted to the Bromheath Club executive committee for discussion, you are asked to look at it, and make any amendments you think are needed.

Write a brief report saying whether this plan appears viable/sensible (giving your reasons). Make any suggestions you think are necessary. Is there any extra information you require?

Assignment 6.1 Clean up the Act

Develops knowledge and understanding of the following element:
3.1 Investigate the principles and functions of marketing in organisations

It supports development of the following core skills:
Communication 3.1, 3.2, 3.3, 3.4
Application of number 3.1
Information technology 3.1, 3.2, 3.3

The Monopolies and Mergers Commission Report *Household Detergents* (1966) said that the market for household detergents was dominated by Unilever and Proctor and Gamble, who between them accounted for some 90 per cent of all sales.

Both companies advertise through national media, primarily commercial television. The Commission said that:

> 'manufacturers' selling costs account on average for nearly a quarter of what the customer pays for product, the greater part of this cost being expenditure on advertising, promotion, and market research'.

It concluded:

- that it is uneconomical to market two very similar products;
- that the companies use excessive advertising;
- that the customer pays the costs and gets few benefits.

Proctor and Gamble claimed 'that this is a high risk industry because the large outlay on advertising and promotion can be recouped only if maximum efficiency is maintained'.

On prices, the Commission found that there was little, if any, direct price competition, and that product differentiation was in quality, image, free gifts, customer inducements, etc., and that overall prices were 'unnecessarily high'. The two companies were again in the news in 1994.

Your tasks

On your own you must produce a report which covers:

1. What detergent products are now made by both companies.
2. The prices of comparable detergents at a range of outlets. Is there any price competition?
3. What sales promotion methods are used
4. What the marketing mix of each company is.
5. How effective you consider their marketing activities to be. You could carry out a survey of consumers. Do they use direct or indirect methods?
6. Which detergents were mentioned in the 1966 report. Which ones still exist and which have disappeared. What does this tell you about the product lifecycle?
7. Whether you think these companies advertise too heavily.
8. Whether the conclusions of a similar report would be any different today.

10,000 to go in efficiency drive at Procter & Gamble

Mark Tran in New York

PROCTER & Gamble, the Ariel washing powder-to-Pampers nappy conglomerate, is likely to cut its global workforce by up to 10,000, or 10 per cent, as a result of intense competition in its main markets.

The cutbacks follow a seven-month review of its operations and marks the first attempt by the company, based in Cincinnati, Ohio, to deal with the effects of the global economic slowdown.

Procter & Gamble employs 5,500 people in Britain, with manufacturing plants in Manchester, Essex and West Yorkshire. Its products range also includes Fairy Liquid and Vidal Sassoon shampoo.

A spokesman said it was too early to say how many jobs might be lost in Britain because "no final decisions have been made".

Procter & Gamble will soon begin offering voluntary severance and early retirement to hundreds of salaried workers, including some well-paid managers in sales, market research and other departments.

The company has grown dramatically in the last decade, making more than 40 acquisitions, penetrating 29 new countries and entering 20 new business categories.

As a result, the company said, it needed to reorganise to make sure that its management was efficient and costs were kept low.

"Streamlining our work by eliminating duplication and doing away with unnecessary activities will make it easier to run the business and lower our costs," Procter & Gamble said in a statement.

In December, the company hired the consultant Booz Allen & Hamilton to help employee task forces develop a cost-cutting plan. Most workers have been given job performance evaluations in the past few months, with the weaker performers being quietly encouraged to leave. But the company refused to comment on how many employees would be lost.

Procter & Gamble has said it intends to cut expenses from 14.5 per cent to 12 per cent of sales revenue over the next three years. Based on 1992 sales of $29.4 billion, that means reducing costs by about $750 million.

Source: *The Guardian*, June 1993

See also *Dirty play in war of the washing powders*, page 96.

Advertising standards

The Advertising Standards Authority (ASA) is a voluntary body which supervises all advertising, except that on radio and TV. Its role is to protect consumers' interests. It administers The British Code of Advertising Practice and the British Code of Sales Promotion Practice. These work on the assumption that all advertisements should be legal, decent, truthful and honest. Although the ASA tries to prevent the media from carrying objectionable advertisements it does not enforce the law.

The ASA monitors advertisements on a daily basis and can investigate written complaints from the general public. If it is unable to stop offensive advertisements appearing, it can as a last resort refer the advertiser to the Director General of the Office of Fair Trading using the Control of Misleading Advertisements Regulations. Most advertisers stop running their advertisements before this stage is reached.

Recently, the Authority took action about a Benetton advert showing a new-born baby.

Activity

Look at the article on the next page and answer the following questions:

a Do you think that consumers should be protected?

b Should the advertising industry be allowed to regulate itself?

Advertising code curbs campaigns aimed at children

THE advertising industry is to be required to take a more socially responsible stance in advertisements aimed at children. New rules published today will include a ban on alcohol advertisements in publications or on poster sites where more than 25 per cent of the potential audience is aged under 18.

From next month campaigns for slimming products directed at children or adolescents will be banned, as will any suggestion that it is desirable to be underweight. Crash diets may not be promoted unless it is made clear that they are to be used under direct medical supervision.

Caroline Crawford, a spokeswoman for the Advertising Standards Authority, which regulates all print and non-broadcast advertisements, said that the revised code was designed to reflect the public's growing awareness of social problems and health and environmental issues. "The old requirements for advertisements to be legal, decent, honest and truthful remain, but the industry itself now feels that there is a need to spell out more clearly some of its responsibilities, especially towards the more vulnerable members of society."

To protect children's health the code, which has not been revised since 1988, stipulates that advertisements should not encourage children to eat or drink just before bedtime or to replace main meals with snack foods. Promotions or competitions aimed at children should not require excessive purchases before a child can take part.

The new code, which comes into practice from February 1, contains stiffer guidelines and rules in a wide range of product areas. Celebrities will not be allowed to endorse medicines and claims such as "environmentally friendly" will no longer be acceptable without convincing proof that products cause no environmental damage. Advertisements for alcohol will have to include a warning on the dangers of drinking and driving. Car manufacturers will no longer be able to make claims for speed or acceleration the predominant message of advertisements.

Advertisers will also be urged to consider public sensitivities before using controversial material and should take care to avoid causing offence on the grounds of race, religion, sex or disability.

The new code has been approved, and in some cases instigated, by all the leading advertising trade bodies, including the Advertising Association and the Institute of Practitioners in Advertising.

Source: *The Times*, January 1995

The selling process

At the beginning of this unit we defined marketing as the management process or philosophy concerned with identifying, anticipating and satisfying customer requirements. The overall objective of any marketing is to make a sale. Selling is the end product of the marketing process; it is part of marketing. If the marketing activities of the organisation have been successful the product will be correctly priced, on sale through all the right places (channels) with all the added extras (value) required by customers. People should literally be queuing up to buy the product (selling timeshare apartments is exactly the opposite) so that no hard selling is needed. In these circumstances, the sales person will be able to provide information and advice, and discuss the product's benefits without having to continually 'make the sale'.

The family tree below shows the position of selling:

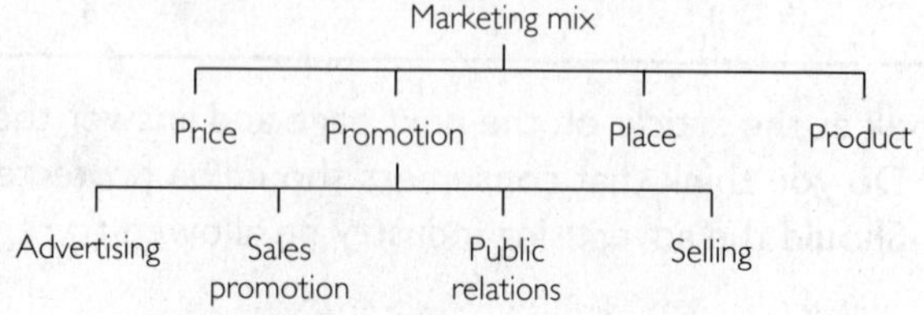

Activity

A job description for sales staff

Use the material in the Human Resources unit to write a person specification and a job description for a sales person. You should cover both the personal qualities required, e.g. self confidence, initiative, enthusiasm, good communicator etc., and the roles and responsibilities. Look at any advertisements for sales staff in the local and national press. Do the qualities and/or responsibilities depend on the type of business or situation, such as 'selling an existing product' 'selling an exciting new product', 'selling in an overseas market', 'telephone selling'?

Opening the sale

Wherever the sale is taking place, for example, in an office, on the door step, in a shop or on the factory floor, it is essential to be prepared. First impressions count. You must be able to state the product's benefits. You must know, for example, what the product does, how it works, its physical and aesthetic qualities, whether it is in stock, what the delivery date is, whether there is a charge and how it can be paid for. Ask the customer positive questions which require specific answers such as 'How can I help you?' rather than 'Can I help you?' or 'Do you like the blue ones?' rather than 'Do you see anything you like?' Find out what the customer wants.

Dealing with objections

Being able to deal with customer objections is the key to any successful sale. How does the salesperson do it? Here are some tips.

1 Anticipate what might go wrong or what questions the customer could ask and include possible answers in a description of the product's benefits.
2 Be pleased that the customer has asked questions.
3 Be willing to listen and respond.
4 Sympathise and understand but never agree.
5 Be prepared to ask more questions.
6 Once you have found out the reason for the objection, for example 'my friend bought one here recently and it fell apart after a week', you can then adopt a strategy to overcome it. For example, you could choose to ignore it or treat the experience as unfortunate or exceptional or ask what the specific problem was.

Closing the sale

Here are some of the ways which a salesperson in an electrical store could use to obtain an order.

Fear close

'I'm sorry, I do not think there will be any left if you come back later.'

'I'm sorry but we cannot keep the product at this very low price for more than two days.'

Alternative close

'Would you like the cordless model?'

Re-assurance close

'We have already sold 20 of these this week.'

The obvious 'Do you want me to pack this one for you?'

'We can of course arrange to take away your old machine.'

Activity

Divide into groups. Each group should choose a different product and go to a range of retailers to look at different sales methods and customer service, for example electrical goods in specialist retailers, department stores, catalogue shops, mail order. YOU DO NOT HAVE TO BUY ANYTHING.

Produce a *Consumers Guide to Good Retailers*; you can include suggestions for improvement!

Review questions

1. How might a marketing decision to sell low quality/high volumes, affect production costs?
2. What might push a business into developing new products?
3. What effect could the different stages of the product lifecycle have on business pricing?
4. How could a manufacturer of tents reposition its products in the market place?
5. Why is packaging important for the consumer, retailer and manufacturer?
6. What advertising media should be used by a small sandwich bar? Why?
7. What media mix would be most suitable for a college/school/your company? Why?
8. Why do nuclear reprocessing plants undertake public relations?
9. Suggest a suitable sponsorship for a shoe manufacturer – give your reasons.
10. What sales promotion would be most suitable for a health club and sauna?
11. What are the costs and benefits of direct marketing for the seller and buyer?
12. Suggest an appropriate communications mix for a small high street hairdressers.
13. Give your advice for a marketing mix for a car washing business.
14. When and why would a business adopt skimming pricing?
15. Why and when would an hotel use differential pricing?
16. Suggest appropriate distribution channels for 'home grown vegetables'. Give your reasons.
17. What are the key features of the Sale of Goods Act? Why are they necessary?
18. An advert says 'gold rings 18 carat', when they are copper. How could a customer complain?
19. List the possible stages of a marketing plan. Why are they needed?
20. How would you convince people to eat more fish?

Key terms

Marketing goals
Marketing mix
Product
Promotion
Price
Place
Market changes
Product development
Market research
The market and production
Evaluating products
Feasibility study
Prototype
Product lifecycle
Launch
Growth
Maturity
Saturation
Decline
Product mix
Positioning
Unique selling point (USP)
Extension strategies
Repositioning

Promotion
Packaging
Advertising
Advertising medium
Media mix
Advertising effectiveness
Public relations
Sponsorship
Sales promotion – consumers
Sales promotion – trade
Direct marketing
Indirect marketing
Mail order
Tele-marketing
Direct reply
Brand names
Communications mix
Pricing policy
Penetration pricing
Skimming pricing
Positioning pricing
Cost-based pricing
Marginal cost pricing
Demand-based pricing
Competitive pricing
Discount pricing
Differential pricing
Price setting/structures
Team pricing
Distribution channels
Product distribution
Service distribution
Marketing strategy
Marketing plan
Consumer protection
Sale of goods
Advertising standards
Trading standards
Selling

Assignment 6.2
The mobile disco 'Blue Rain'

This assignment develops knowledge and understanding of the following elements:

3.2 Propose and present product developments based on analysis of marketing research information
3.3 Evaluate marketing communications designed to influence a target audience
3.4 Evaluate sales methods and customer service to achieve customer satisfaction.

It supports development of the following core skills:

Communication 3.1, 3.2, 3.3, 3.4
Application of numbers 3.1, 3.3
Information technology 3.3, 3,4.

You have always wanted to be a disc jockey. You like all types of music and have an enormous knowledge of pop groups from 1959 to the present day. You would like to DJ part-time with the aim of eventually going into commercial radio.

Your idea is to get as much work as possible and get yourself known. You are confident and outgoing, with a good sense of humour. You have done some market research. The *Thomson Directory* and *Yellow Pages* were helpful in finding out how many other mobile discos were in the area (look under Discos: Mobile).

The target audience is likely to be 6–18-year-olds, probably students. You believe there is a market for birthdays, school/college functions, cubs, brownies, guides, etc. The venues are likely to be private homes, schools, colleges, church halls.

Your message is 'We only play what you like – classic hits sixties to nineties'. You will run speciality nights such as 'Paella Night' with Spanish music and food.

You must be prepared to play any reasonable request, from a wide range of music. The lighting must be dramatic!!

Your task

Write the marketing plan showing:

- the market research
- the current situation, including the competition
- the marketing targets
- the marketing mix, detailing the Four Ps – Price, Product, Promotion and Place; under Promotion you should look at:
  - advertising
  - publicity
  - public relations
  - sales promotion
  - direct and indirect selling and marketing
- the planned marketing strategy
- future plans you may have, for example, playing different music to appeal to a wider target audience.

Put in a brief appendix which shows the stock and equipment you will need, with a global estimate of the cost.

7 Human resources management

What is covered in this chapter

- The role of human resources/personnel management
- The responsibilities of HR management
- Human resources planning
- Employer responsibilities
  - Equal opportunities legislation
  - Contracts of employment
  - Health and safety
  - Payment of wages and salaries
  - Training and career development
- Employee responsibilities
- Procedures for resolving disputes
- Industrial relations – trade unions and staff organisations
- Improving employee performance

These are the resources you will need for your Human Resources file:

- health and safety policy statement
- contract of employment
- equal opportunities policy
- business mission statement or objectives
- newspaper cuttings on legal cases
- trade union rules and regulations
- copy of business disciplinary procedure
- copy of grievance procedure
- copy of appeals procedure
- the organisation's rules and regulations
- business annual report
- citizen's charters

The role of human resources/personnel management

People, or in management jargon, **human resources**, are the most important resource in any organisation and, not surprisingly, there is a direct connection between the quality of the workforce and commercial success:

To succeed, an organisation needs staff who are committed to meeting its aims and objectives, equipped to do so by adequate training and motivated by management to achieve their potential.

It is the role of human resources management to recruit, develop, and retain quality staff.

Within a small business, with perhaps one or two employees, responsibility for human resources will lie with the owner or with the partners, while small companies may have one person whose job it is to look after issues relating to staff. Large organisations with many employees, on the other hand, will have a whole section devoted to personnel.

Human resources v personnel

Originally personnel departments were set up to look after the welfare of employees and the day-to-day administration of policies affecting them. The term **human resource management** (HRM) first appeared in the 1980s. Personnel shifted from being a servicing department to one at the centre of business strategy, its role being to actively help the business pursue its goals by creating an appropriate workforce.

This advertisement shows what the job involves:

Resources Manager

to £28,000 plus benefits

Media Marketing is the UK's number one computer supplies distributor, serving companies such as IBM, 3M and Sony. We have built our success on people and we now need an accomplished HR professional to design and implement a Human Resources strategy.

Reporting to the MD, you will set up the complete HR function, providing an expert recruitment, selection and induction service; as well as designing and developing flexible and dynamic employment policies. Specifically, this will involve an advisory service to department managers; identifying and facilitating training – all-in-all establishing the credibility of HR as a vital and tangible commercial function.

You will be a graduate-calibre HR professional with at least 5 years' good FMCG experience – including 3 years' of providing employment policy support and a minimum 2 years' managing recruitment using assessment centre methodologies. Training experience would be a real advantage. Tenacious, resilient and business-minded, you will have the tact and judgement to establish your personal and professional credibility – plus the creativity and initiative to influence business performance.

In return we offer a good remuneration package and excellent prospects in a young, ambitious company.

The responsibilities of HR management

Figure 7.1 gives an idea of the range of functions which may come under human resources. In some cases these may not all apply. In a very large organisations it may be necessary to organise the various human resources functions into separate sections each with a manager.

Whilst managers throughout the organisation have a major part to play by identifying specific resource requirements, implementing policies and setting up systems which enable employees to perform, the Human Resources Section will be in a position to set up procedures and to advise on personnel issues; it is, as we noted in Chapter 3, a 'staff' function.

The Section will give practical help and advice to other managers throughout the organisation. Ultimately, the main aim is to make the most effective use of people.

One of the major reasons given for the success of the Japanese economy is the greater emphasis which Japanese companies place on developing their employees. Toyota put it this way:

> 'The key to maximising quality and productivity lies in tapping the innate judgement and creativity of employees in the workplace'

Source: *Toyota Motor Corporation Human Resource Information*, 1992

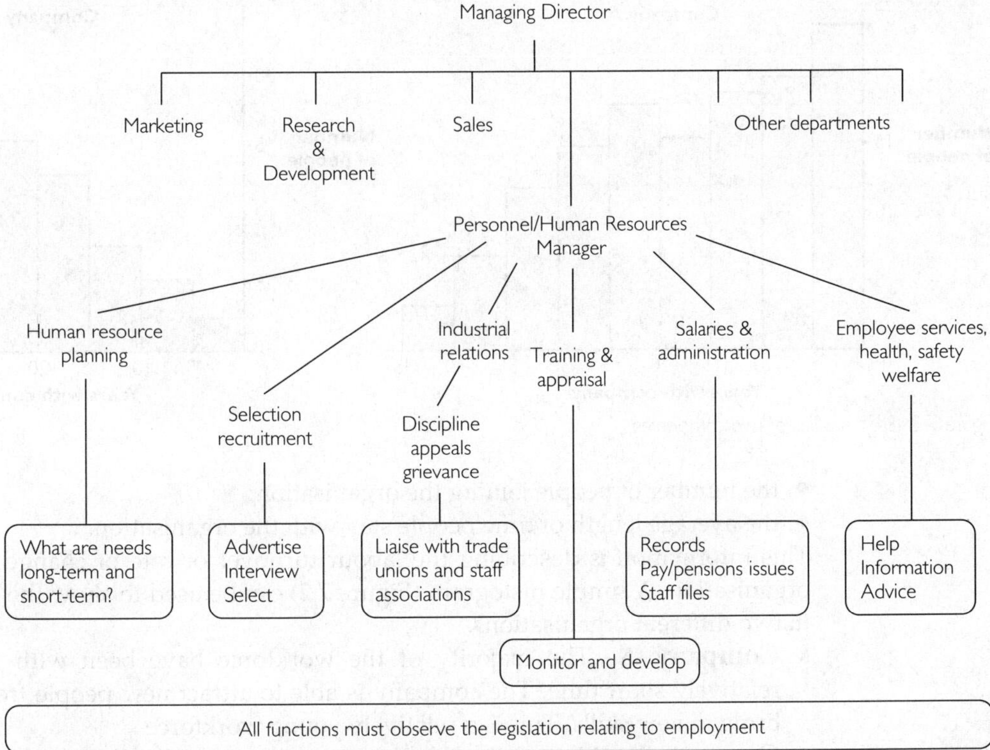

Figure 7.1 The responsibilities of the Personnel/Human Resources Department in a large company

In the 1980s the electronics company Amstrad was seeing a rapid rise in profits through computer sales based on a 'pile 'em high and sell 'em cheap' policy. Alan Sugar (AMSTRAD stands for AM Sugar Trading) felt that he did not need the usual 'paraphernalia of professional staff relations'. He would have nothing to do with trade unions and did not believe in personnel management. One head of an Amstrad subsidiary even had to pretend that his personnel manager did something else!

At this time Sugar still ran his operation as a sort of large-scale market stall. With increased growth, however, he came to recognise the importance of human resources management. Source: *Alan Sugar – The Amstrad Story*, David Thomas.

Human resources planning

Human resources or manpower planning is a technique for predicting or forecasting how many and what type of staff will be required at some specific date in the future. Statistical methods can be used to do this but prediction still remains an uncertain and expensive business.

In order to create a manpower or **staffing plan**, an organisation will need a large amount of data and information. Some of this will be available internally and some externally.

Internal information

Internal information should be available for:

- the number of people leaving the organisation (with reasons);
- the number of people known to be leaving, for example, through retirement;

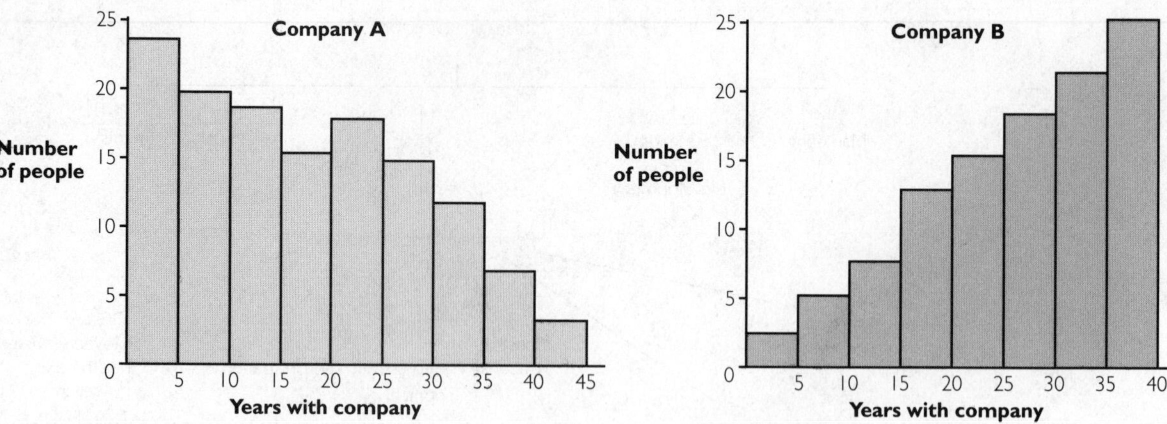

Figure 7.2 Staff profiles of two companies

- the number of people joining the organisation;
- the average length of time people stay with the organisation.

This information is describing the labour turnover or rate of change of labour in an organisation. A simple histogram (Figure 7.2) can be used to show the labour turnover in two different organisations.

- **Company A** The majority of the workforce have been with the company a relatively short time. The company is able to attract new people from outside who bring in new skills. This is a relatively young workforce
- **Company B** Most of the employees have been with the company for a very long time. Labour turnover is very low. It would appear to be a good employer. However, there are hidden problems. Why does nobody leave? Is it an easy job? Do the older employees have the necessary skills?

Some degree of labour turnover is both useful and desirable, because it brings in new staff. However, a high level of labour turnover can be very expensive, for example, there will be:

- training costs of new staff;
- recruitment and selection costs;
- efficiency costs – new staff tend to produce lower quality work;
- leaving costs;
- higher costs for existing staff who cover vacant posts.

At the same time, organisations will need to find out why there is a high rate of labour turnover, for example:

- Is motivation or morale low?
- Are working conditions poor?
- Are the pay structures unsuitable?
- Should incentives be given?
- Do recruitment and selection policies need to be changed?
- Should there be incentives based on length of stay with the organisation?

External information

Organisations are also affected by external factors which are largely outside of their control.

PEST analysis

In order to create a manpower plan, an organisation will have to take account of political, economic, social and technological factors.

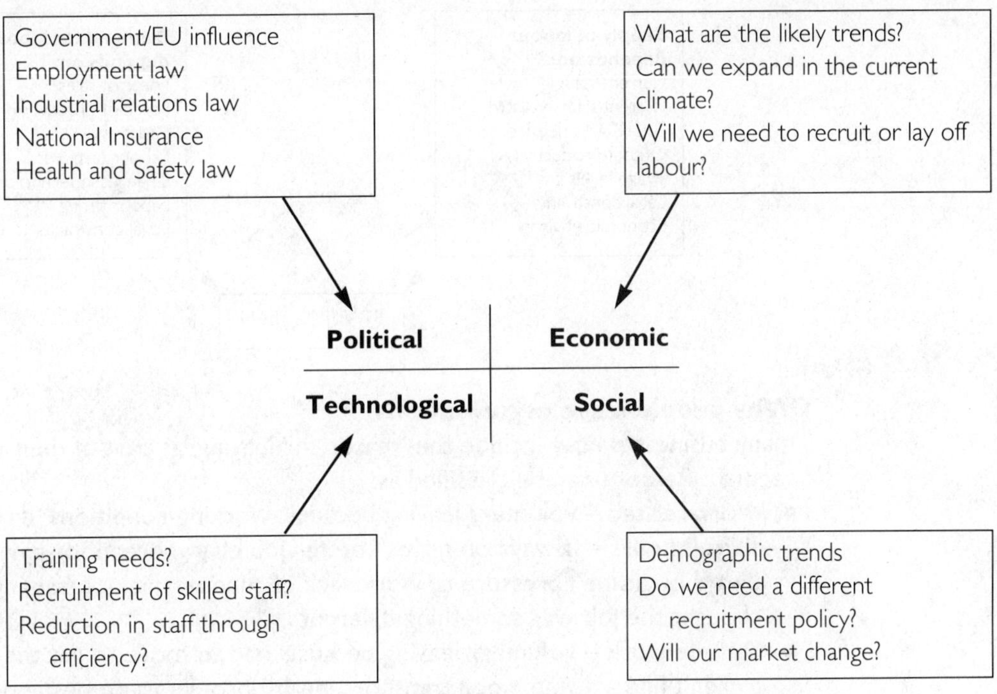

Figure 7.3 PEST analysis

The old-age problem
The reduction in the birth rate and improving nutrition, hygiene and healthcare have meant that the UK population is getting older. This trend will continue and is of great importance to employers who will need to plan for employment and re-training of older people when fewer younger recruits become available. The government is currently considering changes to retirement ages which will probably mean longer working lives for women. By 2029 one person in four will be over the present pension age.

Economic conditions

Changes in the economy will have a direct affect on the demand for products and a derived effect on business demands for labour.

Human Resource Managers who are planning staffing budgets will want to know/find out whether their businesses normally move in line with the general economic trends.

What information is needed for a staffing plan?

To create a staffing plan a business will need to use information to be able to forecast the supply and demand for labour:

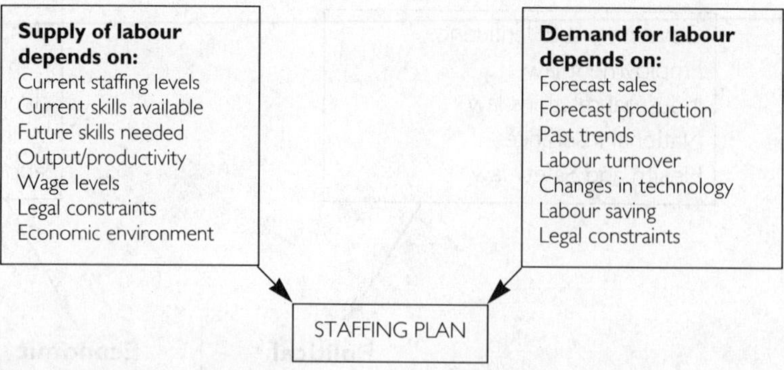

Supply of labour depends on:
Current staffing levels
Current skills available
Future skills needed
Output/productivity
Wage levels
Legal constraints
Economic environment
Demand for labour depends on:
Forecast sales
Forecast production
Past trends
Labour turnover
Changes in technology
Labour saving
Legal constraints
STAFFING PLAN

Why people leave organisations

Many businesses now include the 'reason for leaving' as part of their personnel records. Reasons can be classified as:

- Work-related – voluntary leaving because: working conditions 'dirty' or 'hard'; difficult hours – 'always on nights'; better job elsewhere; poor pay; 'Manager's always on at me'; pressure of work; lack of support; lack of training; disillusioned 'thought the job was something different'.
- Outside work – voluntary leaving because: had to move to get the job, but couldn't find a home; poor transport; health problems; domestic problems; 'had to think of the children's education'; took early retirement.
- Legal – involuntary leaving because: dismissed; made redundant.

Case study

Radiant Heat Ltd

Radiant Heat Ltd, based at Dudley in the Midlands, make a range of 'period style' gas and electric fires with flickering flame effects for either artificial coal or logs. Demand, although seasonal, has increased on average by 2 per cent per annum for each of the last three years. There has been a similar modest increase in the number of workers required.

At 2 p.m. on 30 November 1994 the senior managers met to discuss the implications of the government's Budget. Here are the notes of the meeting chaired by the Managing Director, Bill Long.

The MD began by saying that:

- making domestic fuel and power subject to 8 per cent VAT had done them no good at all - although they were pleased to see that the rise to 17.5 per cent had been abandoned
- they had to respond to the way the increase in families' fuel bills had reduced the demand for their fires.

Paula Long [Bill's niece] pointed out that gas and electricity represented about 12 per cent of the weekly expenditure of low-income families - even more for pensioners - and these groups would be hit very badly, although they might be helped by extra benefits.

Bob Tanner [the Marketing Director] said 'I'm supposed to be positive, so lets look on the bright side. The attempts at stimulating house building could help demand and simplifying the tax system for small businesses is bound to be good. We could always take on more long-term unemployed and get a subsidy for doing it.'

At this point Minati Das [Personnel Manager] objected strongly to the idea of sacking current employees in favour of employing new cheaper workers.

The meeting continued for another 20 minutes. Then the MD summed up.

'This is what we need to do:

Work out future demand
Work out what we expect our sales to be for the next three years.

Decide how this can be met
If we think sales will fall we can see if we can get by with the present staff. We can always stop recruiting. Could we move to smaller premises? Could we sell some of the machinery? Are we tied in to any long-term contracts with suppliers?

Assess whether we can cope with our present resources
If the worse happens, will we need to make people redundant?

Activity

a Identify the problems that may face Radiant Heat in terms of human resources (hint: do a PEST analysis):

b Are there grounds for optimism?

c
- Which external factors will affect the business? How can the business respond?
- Which factors are under the control of the business?

d What are the possible legal problems? (You need not go into details here.)

Employer responsibilities

An employer is responsible for maintaining the rights of employees. This means that the employer must:

- uphold legislation on equal opportunities in both the recruitment process and during employment
- abide by the contract of employment.

Additionally the employer is responsible for:

- health and safety of employees
- dealing with payments and related matters such as National Insurance Contributions (NIC), Pay as You Earn (PAYE) and pensions
- training and career development.

Equal opportunities legislation

The Disabled Persons (Employment) Acts 1944 and 1958

These place obligations on employers of 20 or more people to employ 3 per cent registered disabled people. It is not an offence to be below this quota and most firms do not meet it. The quota will be abandoned in 1996. Under the disability discrimination bill, disabled people will be given the right to 'non-discrimination' at work.

The Rehabilitation of Offenders Act 1974 (amended 1986)

Where a person is convicted of certain offences and has had a period free of convictions he or she is said to be rehabilitated; the conviction is 'spent'. This means that the conviction does not need to be declared on a job application form. The rehabilitation period varies depending upon the offence, for example, up to six months in prison has a rehabilitation period of seven years.

Certain professionals such as accountants and those working with people under 18 are never rehabilitated; this means that they must always declare their offences which may then affect the decisions to employ them.

The Sex Discrimination Acts 1975 and 1986, and the Race Relations Act 1976

The aim of these Acts is to avoid direct or indirect discrimination against candidates on grounds of race, sex or marital status. **Direct discrimination** is when people are excluded by reference to sex, race or marital status, for example, 'single men only need apply'. Most direct discrimination, however, is not so obvious but occurs when job stereotyping takes place. For instance, assumptions may be made that a new secretary will be a woman and the plumber will be a man.

Indirect discrimination occurs when certain attributes relating to race and sex are asked for which cannot be justified by the job. For example, 'UK qualifications only' will exclude all overseas applicants; 'must be 6 feet' will exclude most women.

Most sex discrimination cases are won by women, although the very first was won by a man who was told that a telephonist job was for women only. The law does acknowledge that some jobs such as acting, or social work with particular groups of people, do require people to be of a certain sex or race.

Equal Pay Act 1970

Women have the right to be paid equally to men for work of equal value – this is not necessarily the same job.

Men and women should get equal pay when the work they do is broadly similar or when their jobs have been graded as equal as part of a job evaluation programme. Therefore, if the value of the job done by a production supervisor is identical to that of a male canteen supervisor, they should receive equal pay. The main problem has been that there are very few occupations in which men and women do similar jobs. In most occupations either the majority of the workers are male or female. This has meant that in most cases there is still a wide gap in the wages of men and women.

There have been an increasing number of 'equal pay' cases heard by Industrial Tribunals. The pioneering case was brought by a cook at Cammel Laird shipyard who won the right to be paid the same as male painters.

Employment Act 1980

Maternity rights. Women may have time off for ante-natal care, and 18 weeks paid leave during confinement with Statutory Maternity Pay (SMP) being given. There is protection against dismissal when pregnant, for women with two years continuous service. Dismissal on the grounds of pregnancy is now treated as sex discrimination as it can only happen to women. This follows a number of cases in which women have received large compensation payments after being dismissed from the armed forces.

Case study

Brendan O'Connell, a male hospital orderly, was awarded £1,000 after a health authority was found guilty of sexual discrimination. The tribunal found that the interviewing panel had been influenced by the fact that there were no men's lavatory or changing facilities in the unit where the job was to be. Lynda Carr, director of the Equal Opportunities Commission's employment department commenting on the case said that 40 per cent of enquiries now came from men questioning employment practices in the service industries. She stressed that the Commission was dedicated to opposing sex discrimination against both men and women.

Source: *The Times*

Activity

a What kind of discrimination was at work in the case study above?
b Under which Act of Parliament was the offence committed?

The Equal Opportunities Commission (EOC) will investigate complaints of discrimination on the grounds of sex and/or marital status. It will also monitor business activities including job advertisements and will help with codes of practice. The Commission for Racial Equality (CRE) performs similar functions with regard to race.

Equal opportunities policy – an ethical consideration

Although all organisations must obey the relevant legislation, equal opportunities policies are not required by law. Some companies feel that they do not need a written policy because they believe that their good intentions are sufficient. The Halifax Building Society functioned for 130 years without a policy and the introduction of one did not make an immediate impact. However, the Equal Opportunities Manager feels that 'it formalised the fact that we want to develop fair employment practices' (*Best Companies for Women*, Scarlett McGwire).

The equal opportunities policy may go beyond the law and declare the intention to treat people equally regardless of age, sexual orientation and religion. The law does not deal with these matters.

The British Institute of Management reported in 1988 the results of a survey of 350 member organisations.

- Equal opportunities policy in place and senior executive with equal opportunities responsibility – 51%
- Commitment to equal opportunities at board level – 59%
- Commitment to equal opportunities in collective agreements – 28%
- Taking active steps to implement the policy – less than one-third.

What do these figures indicate?

The following is an extract from a college student handbook. This relates to equal opportunities with regard to race.

Anti-racist Code of Practice

The College is totally opposed to racism in all its forms. Racist behaviour, language and activities discriminate against and disadvantage black people and other ethnic minorities. Racism is also hurtful and damaging to individuals, the College and the community.

Racism may be obvious or more disguised. Obvious (overt) racist acts include assaults, threats, comments, 'jokes', name-calling, graffiti, wearing racist badges, bringing racist material into College and attempts to recruit students to racist groups.

Any such offence against the Code may lead to suspension and exclusion from the College under the Disciplinary Procedures.

Activity

The statement above represents part of an equal opportunities policy.

1 Obtain the equal opportunities policy for your organisation. Hold a discussion which covers the advantages and disadvantages of having such a policy, whether it is necessary, whether it needs updating, how it can be improved, and how it can be publicised.

Alternatively:

2 If your organisation does not have an equal opportunities policy then find out whether there are any plans to introduce one. Discover who will draw this up. Discuss whether in your opinion there is a need for such a policy – or is the law sufficient?

Contracts of employment

When a new member of staff is appointed a **contract of employment** is drawn up by the employer and signed by the employee. A 'contract' is a legal term meaning an agreement between parties or sides which can be enforced by law. The contract of employment exists to give both parties a degree of protection, certainty and security. It begins, when the employer makes an offer of work with payment of money and the employee accepts the offer at that rate and agrees to work. Each side or party is giving a benefit to the other: the employer is paying money, the employee is performing work. This benefit is legally called 'consideration'. The offer, acceptance and consideration are the three essential parts of any contract.

By law an employee who works for 16 hours or more a week must be given a contract of employment within 13 weeks of commencing employment. The Employment Protection (Consolidation) Act 1978 lays down minimum details which must be included. These are:

- the name of the employer and the employee;
- the date when employment began;
- the date on which the employee's period of continuous service began (this may be different from the above if a person transfers from one organisation to another and all service is taken to be continuous. This may happen to civil servants changing departments);
- pay scale, how payment will be made and at what intervals;
- hours of work;
- holiday entitlement;
- terms relating to notification of sickness and sick pay;
- pension arrangements;
- length of notice which an employee is entitled to receive and must give;
- job title;
- disciplinary rules – or where they may be found – appeals procedure and grievance procedure.

Other conditions which may be included are: the need for medical examinations, working from different locations, the right to search employees, the need for confidentiality and the need to obey certain specific rules of the organisation. These could be included in a separate staff handbook.

All of the above are called the **express terms**, that is, they are openly agreed. There are also unwritten **implied terms** in the contract. These are not set out in writing and not spoken of but are assumed to hold. For example, the employee has a duty of fidelity (trustworthiness) to the employer, and is expected to exercise due care. The employee in turn will expect to be supported, if in a managerial role, and will not be expected to do anything unlawful as part of the job.

Published information

Published information, such as the details specified in the job advert and job description, also form part of the express terms of the contract of employment. This is because they contain details of the offer made by the employer which was accepted by the employee, for example, if the phrase 'the person appointed can be expected to work weekends' appeared in the advert then the employee cannot complain when asked to work weekends.

> **Common law v Statute law**
> The implied terms are called 'common law duties' and are derived from legal decisions made by judges as distinct from statute law, which is the law made by Acts of Parliament.

Activities

1 Discuss with fellow students and your tutor a 'Course Study Contract' and then devise a contract between yourself and the centre where you are studying. Use the information above to give you the basic elements. State the duties placed on yourself and the centre

2 Decide what might happen in the following circumstances when the contract might have been broken (breached) by one party:

a You fail to provide assignments on time.
b You are absent for long periods, for example, weeks.
c Your lecturer turns up late.
d You fail the course.

> Remember, don't sign anything until you have read and understood it.

3 Sometimes people will voluntarily work without a written contract for a period to see whether a situation will be satisfactory. This may happen, for instance, with some sports coaches and managers in the music business. What advantages do you feel there are in having written contracts?

Health and safety

The Health and Safety at Work Act (HASAWA) 1974 made employers responsible, 'as far as is reasonably practicable', for the health, safety and welfare of all employees. The inspectors of the Health and Safety Executive have powers to enter premises, identify hazards and issue improvement notices.

The Act requires that all workplaces controlled by the employer must have a safe environment without risks to health. Specific areas which may be inspected are:

- plant and systems of work
- handling, storage and transportation procedures
- provision of information, instruction, training and supervision
- provision of adequate facilities and arrangements for the welfare of employees.

Provisions differ from industry to industry and employers must be aware of the specific regulations which apply. As with equal opportunities, a firm may go beyond the law and draw up its own code of practice, possibly in consultation with the trades union.

Recent European legislation also places obligations on employers. Articles 4 and 5 of EU Directive 90/270 relating to computer equipment are shown in Appendix 1 and discussed in detail in Chapter 4.

Practical health and safety measures

Accident reporting

Whenever there is an accident at the workplace the manager would normally be responsible for:

- entering the details in the accident book;
- completing the accident report form;
- investigating the cause of the accident and keeping a written record;
- publicising potential hazards;
- liaising with the union safety representatives
- convening the Health and Safety Committee. This committee is required by law and must include representatives of the unions and management.

The first aid box

A first aid box should be available. It should be made of suitable materials, easily identifiable (preferably with a white cross on a green background) and contain suitable first aid materials and nothing else. It should be checked regularly.

Activities

1 Check your organisation:
   a Where is the first aid box in your organisation?
   b Where is the accident book in your organisation?
   c Where 400 or more employees work in an organisation there should be a properly equipped and staffed first aid room. Does this apply to your organisation?

2 Below is the agenda that you have received for the second meeting of the Health and Safety Committee for your organisation. The minutes for the first meeting are attached. (These will be item 3 on the agenda and you will need them at the meeting.)
Hold this meeting, make sure you have all the information needed. You will need to take minutes that must be available for the next meeting in three months' time.

```
Own organisation
Health and Safety Committee
Date - 4 weeks from today
Agenda
1. Introduction
2. Apologies
3. Minutes of the last meeting (attached)
4. Matters arising
5. No smoking policy - should our organisation ban smoking on the
   premises?
6. Any other business (AOB)
7. Date of next meeting
Distribution:
Key Manager, Secretary, H&S reps (one for each unit), union reps,
management reps
```

```
Own Organisation
Health and Safety Committee
Minutes of the first meeting
 1. Key Manager welcomed everyone to the first meeting
 2. Apologies - none
 3. Minutes - agreed as amended
 4. Matters arising. The Chair regretted that there was
    insufficient information about:
    a) Possible hazards in the general office - action Group 1.
    b) Hazards in the computer area - action Group 2.
    c) Fire escapes and exits - action Group 3.
    Agreed Groups would prepare information for the next meeting.
 5. Alcoholic drink
    Agreed No one, including management, allowed to drink at any
           time between the start and the end of their working
           day.
```

6. Machine guards
Agreed A new guard would be fitted to the machine shop lathe number 3.
7. First aid boxes
Agreed These would be checked and refilled weekly by Bill Lisle.
8. Protective glasses
Agreed G Whitehouse would ensure these were available for all staff.
9. Photocopiers
Agreed Group 4 would check whether these were ozone friendly. They will also check whether there are any dangerous emissions and if so whether a suitable extraction fan should be fitted.
10. Next meeting - date agreed
11. Members present
Gillian, Lorraine, Pauline, Denise, Chris, Toyin, Claremont, Natasha, Rita, Delclam, Cathy, Ola, Andrea, Carol, Linda, Karen, Foday, Risi, Geoffrey, Meiron, Veronica, Adermi.

Remuneration – payment of wages and salaries

All employees are required to keep accurate pay records and a number of documents are provided for this purpose

Documents used in the payment of wages and salaries

STAGE	EMPLOYER'S JOB	DOCUMENT USED
1	Calculate GROSS PAY for the pay period (week or month)	Wages: Job card, time sheet, clock card Salaries: Annual salary divided by 12
2	Calculate deductions: a) Statutory deductions (required by law) i) Income Tax (PAYE)** @ 20%, 25% and 40% of taxable pay	INCOME TAX TABLES: A Free Pay B Taxable Pay Employee's P45 for tax code number
	ii) National Insurance based on % of Gross Pay	NATIONAL INSURANCE TABLES P11 TAX DEDUCTION CARD
	b) Voluntary deductions Pensions/superannuation AVCs (additional voluntary contributions) Trade union subscriptions SAYE (save as you earn) and others requested by the employee.....	
3	Calculate net pay NET PAY = GROSS PAY – DEDUCTIONS	PAY ADVICE or PAY SLIP to show Gross Pay, details of deductions and Net Pay

4	Compile a list of pay details of all employees	PAYROLL (this is all of the details from all payslips on One sheet)
5	Pay the employee and inform him/her by sending payslip	CASH (may be used for wages) CHEQUE (wages or salaries) Transfer direct to employee's bank account. by: BANK GIRO through BACS* (most usual method for salaries)
6	At intervals deductions sent to government departments responsible: Income Tax sent to Inland Revenue National Insurance to Department of Social Security	
7	At the end of the tax year each employee is informed of the tax paid during the year and annual pay	P60

*Bankers Automated Clearing Services
**Pay as you earn

Current rates of income tax, NIC and allowances are shown in Appendix 4.

Other employee rights

These include:

- Statutory Sick Pay (SSP). An employee is entitled to SSP if absent from work due to illness. Self-certification is accepted during the first week; thereafter a doctor's certificate is required (Employment Protection Consolidation Act 1978). Most organisations are no longer able to reclaim this from the government.
- All employees are entitled to time off work for public duties, without pay. These include service as a Justice of the Peace, as a governor of a school and jury service (Employment Protection Consolidation Act 1978).
- Where employers keep employee information on computer files, the employee may, under the Data Protection Act, be able to ask for details of this. Details of this Act are reproduced in Appendix 2 and discussed more fully in Chapter 4.

Training and career development

Staff **training** is essential if people are to continue to be efficient members of an organisation. It will:

- help employees achieve maximum efficiency in their current jobs;
- help the organisation meet its targets for developing and keeping people with the right skills to meet future needs;
- balance the needs of the individual with those of the organisation.

It is no longer true that a job is for life and workers may need to be trained several times during their careers. The nature of their jobs will almost certainly change over time and it is likely that workers will move to other jobs, either in different organisations or through promotion within the same organisation. It has often been the case that in harsh economic times training is one of the costs that can be cut immediately with no obvious short-term effects. This, however, is a short-sighted policy – with predicted shortages in skilled labour training should be seen as an investment.

Training should begin as soon as a new employee joins an organisation. It can take the form of:

- a general induction programme which introduces the member of staff to the organisation, its facilities, its people, rules and regulations;
- specialist health and safety training;
- specialist on-the-job training;
- off-the-job training.

Induction

Induction is an introduction to the organisation for new employees. It is designed to familiarise new recruits with the organisation, its rules, facilities, policies and key staff. Some organisations provide an induction pack which includes these details. An induction program may include:

- an introduction to the organisation;
- the policies of the organisation;
- specific rules and procedures including health and safety;
- benefits and terms of employment;
- job details;
- introduction to key staff;
- facilities available.

The programme may take the form of talks, discussion and familiarisation with the premises. The aim is to allow the employee to settle in quickly and work effectively and confidently from the start.

The induction period varies with the nature of the job. A Regional Health Officer with the Post Office, for instance, has a four-week induction which includes delivering mail. This is to give an insight into the fitness levels required for the various jobs within the organisation.

Health and safety training

It may be necessary for some jobs that specialist health and **safety training** is given. The specific type of training will depend upon the job. It may involve working with machinery, working with chemicals or working in dangerous situations, for example, at great heights. In some organisations safety matters may be dealt with in the induction programme.

On-the-job training

Many jobs require no prior experience. In the workplace the job will need to be explained and perhaps demonstrated. For instance a cashier will need to know how to work the till, and to understand standard procedures for accepting cheques, store and credit cards. A new Clerical Assistant will need to understand the filing system, the computer software and the various forms and documents associated with the job. The main way in which this is achieved is through on-the-job training (OJT).

Off-the-job training

Off-the-job training is literally any type of training that takes place away from the job. Employees may attend college or a training agency, or courses may be held in-house in specially equipped training rooms. An organisation may have its own trainers or increasingly specialist staff are 'bought-in' for short courses. The growth in conference facilities, often provided at hotels, means that staff may be sent for specialist one-day or residential courses, particularly in the managerial field.

Training techniques used include traditional methods such as lectures, videos and demonstrations. In addition, trainees are now more actively involved in training using methods such as:

- case studies involving role-play and discussion;
- simulations using state-of-the-art software, BR for example simulate the Channel Tunnel crossing;
- interactive video where the trainee, rather than passively watching, will be required to respond at various points. Depending upon the response the video will follow different sequences.

Games and outdoor pursuits may be used to develop qualities in staff such as team spirit, trust and initiative. These can bring benefits when transferred back to the work situation.

Training and equal opportunities

The author, Scarlett McGwire, researched a large range of companies in an attempt to find those which provide the best opportunities for women. Her findings, published in *Best Companies for Women* (Pandora 1992), include the following observations:

> 'The best companies provide training for their staff at all levels, throughout their careers, so employees are always encouraged to realise their potential. Sometimes women do not recognise the skills they have and lack of confidence in their own qualities can stand in the way of advancement. Many companies have arranged women-only courses to combat this'.

Companies found to have a good record include:

- Rank-Xerox and the Rover Group both of which run assertiveness courses which also cover career planning;
- ICL who allowed every woman in the company to go on a training course within an 18-month period. This was a result of union pressure because of the number of women in low-grade employment.

McGwire concludes that 'Any woman applying for any job at any age would do well to discover what their potential employer has to offer in terms of training, and indeed whether training is available for all staff at each and every level of that company.'

Activities

The training plan is a key part of the organisation's overall human resources plan. Preparing the plan will involve identifying training needs and suggesting the most appropriate types of training.

1 Prepare a training plan for each of the following organisations (the check-list on the next page may be helpful):
   - J Bolton Ltd, a toy manufacturer, that will introduce new production equipment shortly.
   - The Southfleet Council (a large local authority) which is updating its computer software to a 'Windows' environment.
   - Lightening Electrics who wish to encourage a greater number of women to become managers.

- A freelance accountant who wishes to learn an integrated accounting package.
- An advertising agency where 'too many stars' make it difficult to see projects through on deadline. Much time is wasted on arguments about which ideas should be used.

2 Prepare a personal training plan. This should:

a Identify your current skills and knowledge.

b Identify the skills and knowledge that you wish to acquire.

c Give the timescale for the achievement.

d Propose the method of achievement.

3 You have been asked to help with the preparation of induction for new recruits/students to your organisation. Write a brief set of notes explaining the key features of your organisation that a new person should know about.

Check-list for the preparation of a training plan for an organisation:

- What skills do employees possess?
- What skills will they need to possess?
- Is some form of appraisal or assessment needed to see if employees are suitable?
- Can people be trained in-house?
- Does the organisation have to go outside?
- What training is available?
- Who should be trained:
  all staff?
  key staff?
  all managers?
- Should everyone be given total quality management training? (This means meeting the customers' needs at the right price at the lowest cost, first time, every time.) (See page 334.)

Employee responsibilities

The employer has the right to expect the employee to work in a responsible manner. In practice this means that the employee should:

- comply with the (express and implied) terms of the contract of employment
- comply with the Health & Safety regulations (HASAWA also puts obligations on employees to work in a safe manner)
- work to achieve the objectives of the organisation
- behave responsibly towards customers
- meet quality standards.

Failure to work responsibly may lead to disciplinary action being taken.

Procedures for resolving disputes

Although employment law sets out the rights and responsibilities of employer and employee, an organisation will need to set up procedures to be used when either side has a complaint. An employer will use a **disciplinary procedure** against an employee. An employee should have recourse to a **grievance procedure** against the employer. Where the results of procedures are disputed then either side should be able to **appeal**.

Best practice

Here are some examples of 'best practice' found in industry:

- All rules and regulations should be in writing (express terms of a contract are ideally written down, but are legally binding even if verbally agreed).
  They should state to whom they apply.
  Administration should be simple and easily understood.
  Cases should be dealt with quickly.
- Type of disciplinary action should be described.
- The level of management allowed to make decisions should be specified.
- People should be told if complaints are made about them.
- Apart from summary dismissal for major offences no one should be dismissed for a first offence.
- All complaints should be fully investigated.

Disciplinary procedures

Suspension Where a serious alleged offence has taken place and it would be unwise for the organisation or the employee, if the employee were to stay at work, then the employee may be suspended. For instance if you are involved in a fight at work it would be unwise of the company to allow you to stay at work and probably unwise for you – the fight might erupt again. You would be suspended from work until the matter had been investigated. Sometimes soldiers and police officers involved in serious incidents may be suspended on full pay until investigations are completed.

Oral warning (first warning) This is given when an employee fails to meet the organisation's required standards of work or behaviour. A note would be made in the employee's file and the immediate line manager would be informed.

Formal warning This may be oral, but is more likely to be an oral and written warning. It should contain targets which the offender must achieve, and point out the consequences of failing to meet these. It should be confirmed in writing with copies for the employee, the employee's file and for management.

Final warning This would be an oral and written warning issued for a persistent offence when the employee has ignored or failed to achieve the required standards. It would state that the employee will be suspended or dismissed if specific targets are not met within an agreed time. There would be confirmation in writing, with copies, as for a formal warning.

Dismissal For a serious offence or when all forms of warning have failed, the employee may be dismissed. The period of notice is given by the contract of employment with that organisation. After the period of notice has been worked, the employee no longer works for the organisation.

Summary dismissal When the contract of employment has been seriously broken, for example, in the case of theft, there would be an investigation with the employee and a 'friend' present (the friend could be a lawyer or union representative). If found guilty, the worker could be dismissed immediately with no notice. Other reasons for summary dismissal are:

- assaulting other employees.
- deliberately breaking company rules.
- destroying company property.
- repeated insubordination (not obeying instructions).

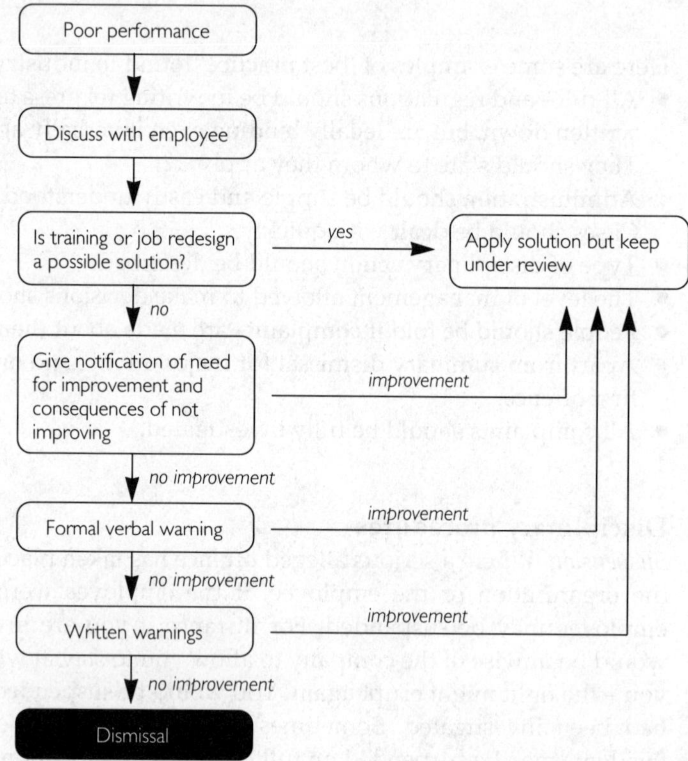

Figure 7.4 Example of the procedure that may be followed where an employee is seen to be incapable of performing the job satisfactorily

Activity

Obtain the disciplinary and grievance procedure for your organisation. Does it follow the outline given here? Is there anything missing or has anything been added?

Fair dismissal

An employee who is fairly dismissed has no grounds for complaint. An employee may be fairly dismissed for the following reasons:

Reason	Example
1 Lack of qualifications	Where a certain qualification is claimed but not actually held dismissal may occur if this is essential to the job. For instance auditing may only be carried out by professionally qualified accountants. However, if the job is being satisfactorily performed dismissal may not always be regarded as fair.
2 Lack of capability to do the job	A worker is no longer able to perform the job adequately; this may be through sickness or injury.
3 Conduct	Continued breach of contract, for instance violence or fighting in the workplace.
4 Where it would be breaking the law to continue with employment	A driver may lose his or her driving licence.
5 Redundancy	If the employer has not sufficient work for the employee then an employee may be made redundant. The employer must abide by any contractual agreements and will pay compensation to employees who have worked over 16 hours per week for at least two years for the same employer. The actual amount paid depends upon the length of service. During 1992–3, in London alone, some 400 people were made redundant every day as a result of the economic recession.
6 Other substantial reasons	Personality clashes which inhibit the working of the business.

Since the 1980s the government has encouraged people to use redundancy payments to set up small businesses. Where there is a strong trade union redundancy payments may be substantially above the minimum specified.

Activity

Which of the following examples are reasons for fair dismissal? Where you feel that a dismissal is fair, say to which of the six categories listed above it belongs.

a False information is given on an application form:
- a plumber claims to have a plumbing qualification
- a driver claims to have a clean driving licence
- a security guard says that s/he has no criminal record.

b An accountant has suffered from continuous illness.

c A production worker cannot do the job he or she was contracted for, even after thorough training and sufficient warnings have been given.

d A cashier becomes pregnant.

e A computer operator has not successfully completed a trial or probationary period of employment after full training and sufficient warnings have been given.

f A librarian refuses to work at weekends although this is part of the job description, and appeared in the original advert.

g A worker joins a trade union – the management does not approve.

h Breach of the rules:
- a driver is drunk on duty
- a nurse is found smoking in a sterile area.

i A cashier steals from the organisation.

j A member of the research staff tells competitors about new designs that the company has developed.

k A manager is made redundant after all possible alternatives have been explored.

l A solicitor has committed a serious criminal offence.

Unfair dismissal

The Employment Protection (Consolidation Act) 1978 identifies circumstances where it is unfair to dismiss an employee. These are:

- where an employee of more than two years' standing, becomes pregnant and is not taken on again after the baby is born;
- where a 'spent' conviction is the reason for dismissal;
- where an employee is dismissed for joining a trade union;
- where an employee elects to stay outside a trade union (with some exceptions, an employee cannot be sacked because they belong to or do not belong to a trade union);
- where a worker is dismissed because of sex or race;
- where the employer does not follow the agreed procedures, perhaps by not giving the required notice of termination or by not following the laid-down disciplinary procedure.

Constructive dismissal

This occurs when employees themselves end the contract because they believe that it has been broken by the employer. For instance, if an employer significantly changes the terms and conditions of employment without notice or agreement the employee may resign. Perhaps the employer begins to demand extra unpaid hours or jobs which were not originally required. In such circumstances employees may be able to claim constructive dismissal if they feel that they were unfairly forced to leave.

Appeals against disciplinary action

Appeals within the organisation

The ultimate disciplinary action is dismissal. However, an employee may wish to appeal against any of the whole range of measures which make up the disciplinary code. For instance,the employee may appeal against a letter of warning being placed on his or her file if he or she regards this as being unfair.

Whenever there is a disciplinary procedure in an organisation, there should also be a recognised, formal **appeals procedure**. This will give employees the opportunity to explain their version of what has happened whenever disciplinary action is being taken. It is the manager's role to inform the employees of this right to appeal. When employees are disciplined they should therefore be told:

- that they have the right to appeal;
- about the appeals procedure, that is, how they may appeal;
- about any support services that are available such as occupational health;
- about any action which will be taken and what this means.

Normally, any appeal must be within three working days of a warning being given.

An appeal is chaired by a Senior Manager, in a school this may be the Principal or Head Teacher. The employee can be represented and/or helped by either another employee, or by a union officer. This person can act in either a passive role, as an observer, or in an active role by providing evidence for the defence.

An appeal can force a review of disciplinary action but can never make it more severe. Where an appeal fails the disciplinary action stands; this may mean dismissal.

But what happens if the employee takes the matter further?

Appeals outside the organisation

Legal disputes between employers and employees over equal pay, sexual harassment, racial discrimination, redundancy pay and unfair dismissal are dealt with by **Industrial Tribunals**. These were set up in 1964 to provide a simple informal way of resolving conflicts which could not be solved inside the organisation. They consist of a Chairperson (who is a legal expert), one management representative, and one worker's representative.

There are a number of stages. Initially the case will go before the Advisory, Conciliatory and Arbitration Service. ACAS (which is discussed in more detail later) will examine the evidence and try to assist both parties to reach a settlement. It is for this reason that managers must keep detailed records of all disciplinary action taken against workers. It is equally important for workers to keep records.

If this attempt at settlement fails then the case goes to an industrial tribunal. At the tribunal, the employer has to prove the dismissal was fair, in other words, the employer attempts to prove innocence.

Since the introduction of the Employment Protection Act, industrial tribunals have considered thousands of complaints for unfair dismissal. There is no Legal Aid and only 1 per cent of appelants have had their jobs back.

No Legal Aid is available for those appealing to an industrial tribunal. However legal advice of up to two hours is available under the 'green form scheme' to those on low incomes. Legal advice can be expensive!

It takes about three months to get a hearing. Most cases are then dealt with in one day.

The average cost of a tribunal settlement is £1,200 whereas for a settlement by ACAS it is £200.

If you want to know more about industrial tribunals, Job Centres and DSS offices have an information booklet produced by the Employment Department. ACAS is at 27 Wilton Street, London SW1X 7AZ.

What types of decision can a tribunal make?

A Tribunal can either:

- decide in favour of the employee, i.e. agree that the employee was unfairly dismissed. In this case the complaint is upheld, or supported, against the employer; or,
- decide in favour of the employer, i.e. disagree that the employee was unfairly dismissed. In this case the employer's defence, that the dismissal was fair, is upheld.

Appeals against decisions: 'We'll take this one all the way if we have to!'

Once a Tribunal has finished its work, either party can appeal against its decision. These appeals are based on technical legal points. They are dealt with in the first place by the Employment Appeals Tribunal (EAT), which is chaired by a High Court Judge, assisted by two legal experts. Should either party still not accept the decision the action can be taken next to the Court of Appeal, then if necessary to the House of Lords and ultimately to the European Court of Justice (ECJ).

What ruling can a tribunal make?

If the employee has been unfairly dismissed, the tribunal has to consider an appropriate response. The three possibilities are that the employee can:

- Return to the original job under the same terms and conditions as existed before he or she was dismissed, including any compensation for loss of wages, pension etc. This is called **reinstatement**.
- Be given an alternative job equivalent to the original one. This is called **re-engagement**.
- Receive a financial settlement, called **compensation**.

There have been a number of cases where companies do not wish to take back a former employee or the employee does not wish to return. The tribunal will take account of these wishes. If an employee is judged to have been fairly dismissed, then the dismissal still remains in force.

Note: Under EU legislation in 1994, part-time workers have the same rights as full-time workers.

The appeals procedure

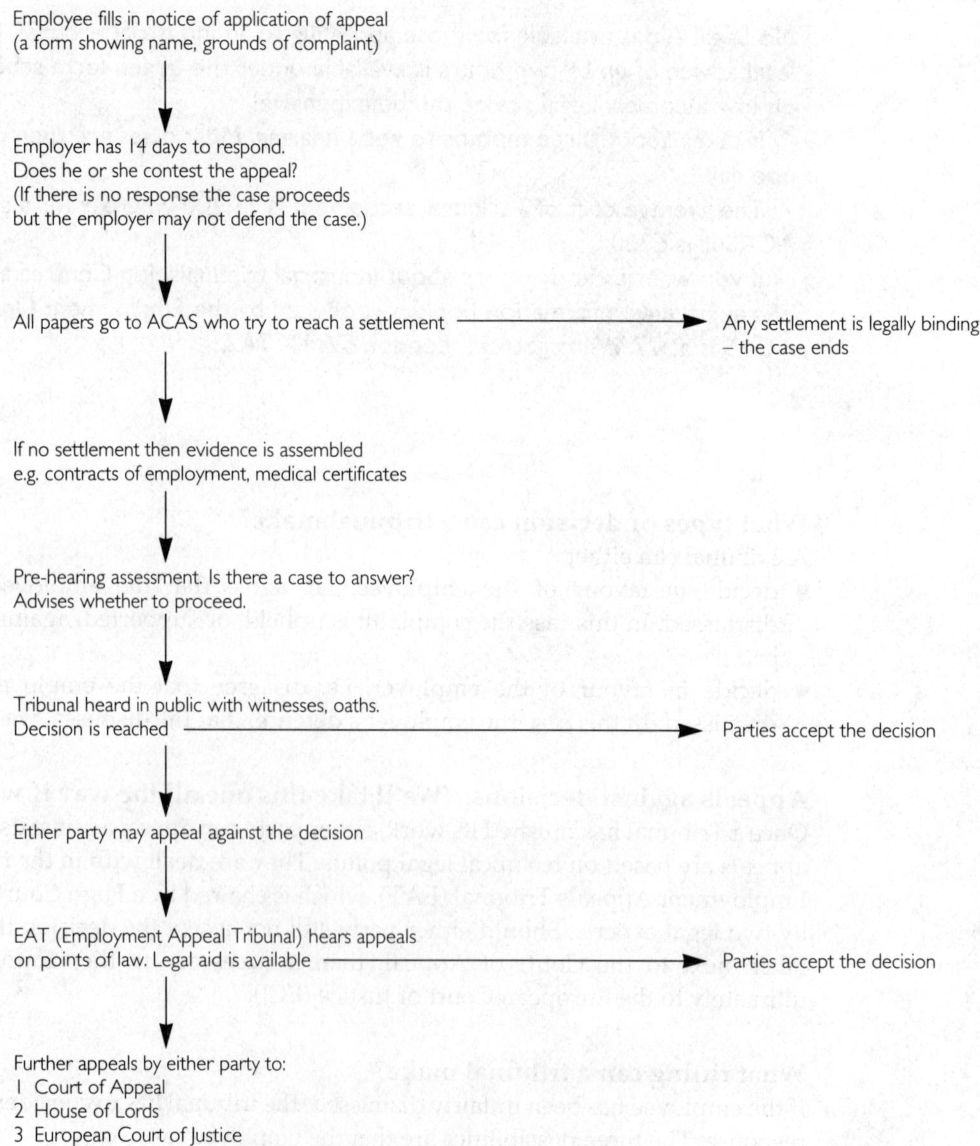
Employee fills in notice of application of appeal
(a form showing name, grounds of complaint)
Employer has 14 days to respond.
Does he or she contest the appeal?
(If there is no response the case proceeds
but the employer may not defend the case.)
All papers go to ACAS who try to reach a settlement
Any settlement is legally binding
– the case ends
If no settlement then evidence is assembled
e.g. contracts of employment, medical certificates
Pre-hearing assessment. Is there a case to answer?
Advises whether to proceed.
Tribunal heard in public with witnesses, oaths.
Decision is reached
Parties accept the decision
Either party may appeal against the decision
EAT (Employment Appeal Tribunal) hears appeals
on points of law. Legal aid is available
Parties accept the decision
Further appeals by either party to:
1 Court of Appeal
2 House of Lords
3 European Court of Justice

Case studies

In August 1992, BT engineer Michael Stoneham dropped his claim for unfair dismissal at the Industrial Tribunal in Chelsea. Mr Stoneham was dismissed after having 1,158 sick days over 16 years. He claimed these were due to a series of mishaps and that 'They had always wanted to get rid of me'. BT, who were awarded £200 costs, said that the case should never have been brought.

A computer engineer sacked for refusing to get his hair cut won his claim for unfair dismissal against his employer, On Line Software. Kevin Lloyd was awarded £4,351 for loss of earnings. However the Tribunal rejected a claim of sexual discrimination based on the fact that women are allowed to wear hair of any length. This, they ruled, was too simplistic.

Bridget Reynolds won her claim for sexual discrimination against the Mitsubishi Trust and Banking Corporation. She was sacked after having time off for a hysterectomy because the company felt that she would be unfit for work within a reasonable period of time and that there would be later complications. The Industrial Tribunal ruled that hysterectomy was 'as much a peculiarly female condition as pregnancy and is to be equated with it … We find that the applicant has been discriminated upon on the grounds of her sex.' Mrs Reynolds was awarded compensation but could not claim unfair dismissal as she had only 18 months of service.

Activity

A disciplinary interview

The Sanctions Department of a large retail store deals with queries from retail staff as to the credit-worthiness of customers who have accounts. The department – a staff function – is on the fourth floor.

Deanne, who is 17 years old, works in this department on Saturdays only. She has been with the company for six months. On at least five occasions she has been late starting work, and although she has given excuses, these have been very flimsy. On three occasions she has left work early. So far she has been given two verbal warnings about absenteeism and lateness. Deanne is very capable and an efficient worker when present; the firm does not really want to lose her.

On Saturday Deanne does not turn up. As there have been no phone calls or warnings the Sanctions Manager is in a very difficult position. The section is a member of staff short and the boss is now getting cross about the 'lenient' attitude towards Deanne. There has to be some firm action.

a The group should divide into fours. Each member of the group should take roles as follows:

- Deanne
- a representative from the staff association
- the Sanctions Manager
- a second member of management team.

None of you has taken part in a disciplinary interview before, but the firm produces practical guidelines for conducting such an interview as part of its disciplinary procedure. These are shown on page 326.

b Make careful notes of what you intend to say. Deanne and the member of the staff association should work together in this as should the two members of the management team. At this stage the pairs will work separately. However, agree on the following:

- Was written evidence available with dates/reasons/excuses?
- Have notes been made on the employee's file?

c One group should now run the interview in front of the class. It will be led by the Sanctions Manager while the other manager takes notes. The interview will follow the guidelines given below.

d The group should observe the interview and discuss the results. Points which may be considered are:

- What was the outcome?
- Was the interview stressful/friendly/formal/informal?
- How long was the interview?
- Are the parties 'satisfied' with the result?
- What could have been done differently
- Have the correct procedures been followed?
- Is the case likely to go further (to an Industrial Tribunal)?
- Are there any equal opportunities issues here?
- Was it fair?
- What power does the interview panel have at this stage?

Guidelines for disciplinary interviews

1 Introduce those present to the employee and explain why they are there.
2 Explain that the purpose of the interview is to consider whether disciplinary action should be taken in accordance with the organisation's disciplinary procedure.
3 Explain the format of the interview.
4 State precisely the nature of the complaint and outline the management's case by going through the evidence that has been gathered.
5 Give the employee an opportunity to respond, to state his or her case and present evidence.
6 Use the interview as an opportunity to gather all the facts and take note of any special circumstances.
7 If it is clear that there is an adequate explanation, no further disciplinary action will be necessary.
8 At the end of the interview summarise the main points made by both management and the employee and highlight any areas which need to be checked.
9 Do not hesitate to adjourn the interview if this is necessary to check information or to assist in the consideration of a disciplinary penalty.
10 Ensure that the employee is left in no doubt about the outcome of the meeting and the further action that may be taken.

Industrial relations – trade unions and staff organisations

The term **industrial relations** refers to the relationship between the organisation and its workforce. We will see in the discussion of business finance later that industrial relations cannot be objectively valued and entered on the business balance sheet as an asset, however their effect on the prospects of a business is crucial.

Good industrial relations are a priority for every business. They may be fostered by:

- positive consultation between management and the workforce; where they exist, this may take place through trade unions;
- employee participation in the management process.

Case study

Trade union development

A **trade union** is defined in law as 'an organisation...whose principal purposes include the regulation of relations between workers and employers or between workers and employers' associations.'

Many of the rights that employees currently enjoy have been won as a result of trade union pressure over the years. Trade unions aim to represent the interests of their members through:

- negotiating with employers to improve pay and conditions of their members. Where the conditions for a group of workers is set nationally in this way this is called 'collective bargaining';
- representing the interests of their members in disputes, perhaps by giving advice and legal support;
- providing education and training;
- acting as a pressure group on government to gain legislation and policies which will benefit their members.

The history of the union movement has been one of a struggle for recognition. For hundreds of years trade unions were forbidden by law as being 'in restraint of trade'. Nevertheless throughout the nineteenth century there was a gradual growth in the skilled unions.

After 1946 unions increased their membership and power and the Labour Relations Acts of the 1970s extended union rights to the extent of allowing 'closed shops' – a situation in which a worker must belong to a certain union in order to hold a job.

From 1946 to 1979 the union movement was at its strongest. Since 1979 the Conservative government especially under Mrs Thatcher has brought in legislation to reduce trade union power. In some ways the arguments about 'market forces' have been similar to those used in the nineteenth century. See Chapter 10 for a description of the legislation.

Trades unions at work

An employer does not have to recognise a **trade union** unless an agreement already exists for an organisation that is being taken over. However, in practice unions are frequently recognised for negotiating purposes; sometimes there are a number of them in one organisation. In schools for instance, teachers may belong to one of several unions, the NUT (National Union of Teachers) or the NAS/UWT for example, whilst the support staff may belong to UNISON.

Where there is more than one union in the organisation there will probably be a joint union committee which negotiates with the employer on issues common to all unions. General health and safety matters such as working temperatures or the discovery of asbestos might cause common concern.

Most, though not all, unions are affiliated to the **Trade Unions Congress (TUC)**, formed in 1868. This attempts to speak for the whole union movement especially in relation to government policies. However, it has powers only to persuade individual unions to act, although it can suspend members.

Structure of a trade union

We will assume that employees at ABC Ltd belong to two different unions (Union 1 and Union 2). Figure 7.5 shows how they would fit into the trade union structure.

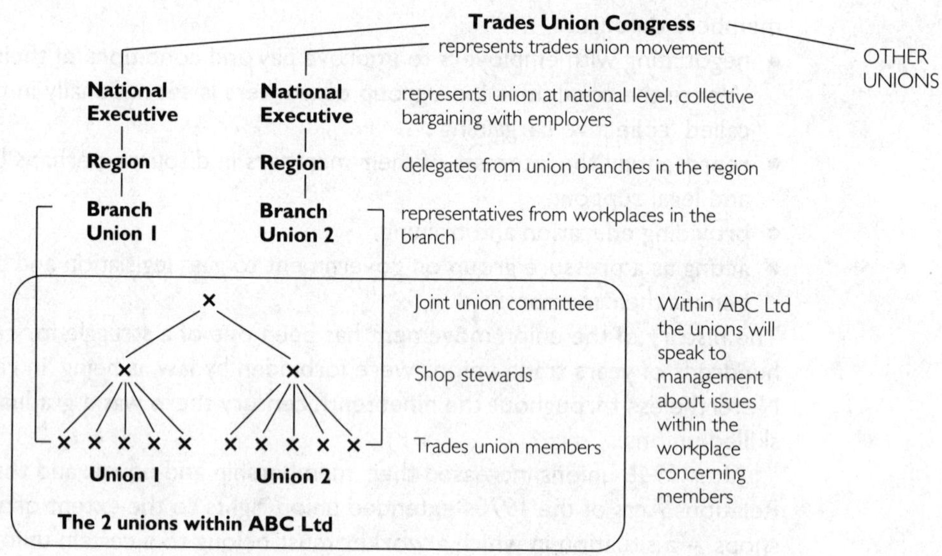

Figure 7.5 Example structure of a trade union

Employers' associations and the CBI

The employers' equivalent of a trade union is the **employers' association**. Employers in certain industries join together to express their collective views. Examples include:

- The National Farmers Union (NFU) – an employers' association despite its name!
- The Engineering Employers Federation
- The Institute of Directors.

Just as the TUC represents the trade union movement, so the employers' federations, as well as some individual companies, are represented by the **Confederation of British Industry (CBI).**

Works councils

By the end of 1996 British multinational firms operating in Europe will need to set up Works Councils for their employees in EU states. The directive applies to all companies with over 1000 employees and over 150 employees in at least two EU countries. The Councils will be entitled to meet central management once a year to receive a report outlining business prospects. The idea is to involve staff in consultation and decision-making. They will be informed about take-overs, shifts in production, changes in technology and other corporate decisions. The exact benefits are unclear, but are likely to include: quicker implementation of decisions, better communications and improved morale.

By early 1995 at least twenty-five companies had begun to push ahead with agreements, including: ICI, United Biscuits, Pilkington, BP, Cadbury Schweppes and Blue Circle. Although the Social Chapter of the Maastricht Treaty was not accepted by the British government, in practice it is likely that these firms will also set up Works Councils in the UK.

Consultation and negotiation

A complex range of relationships exists between employers, trade unions, management, workforce and the government. Discussions can take place between any of these on a number of levels.

Level	**Who will meet?**	**Type of issue (examples)**
Section or department within the organisation	Supervisor and shop steward (the union representative in the workplace)	An issue confined to a particular workplace or site. Perhaps: new office or works layout, new machinery, no heating, the disciplining of a worker or a complaint against a manager.
The organisation as a whole	Senior managers and union branch officials	Issues affecting the whole organisation. Perhaps: introduction of a new shift system, introduction of short-time working, or redundancies.
The industry as a whole	Employers' representatives from the whole industry meet officials from the national executive of the union. Remember that in some cases the government is the employer.	Issues affecting the whole industry such as privatisation, negotiations on pay and conditions for workers in the industry.
National issues which cut across industries	Employers' federations such as the CBI meet officials from the TUC (Trade union Congress) and government departments such as the DTI (Department of Trade and Industry)	National pay policies, for example, should there be voluntary 'pay restraint' in order to curb inflation? Regional policies for employment, training and regeneration of industry.

Case study

Toyota Motor Manufacturing UK

Toyota have signed a single union agreement with the Amalgamated Engineering and Electrical Union (AEEU). No other unions are recognised or represented. Both the company and the union recognise the need to have a positive relationship and have agreed jointly to:

- maintain a prosperous business operation;
- provide each member with a voice in the company's future;
- promote economy of operation, quality and quantity of output and a safe working environment;
- foster flexible working practices and effective team working;
- constantly seek improvements in quality, efficiency and the working environment;
- promote fair and equitable treatment of all members;
- resolve members' concerns through the management chain at the lowest possible level, and thereafter through procedures using a non-adversarial problem-solving approach – based on consensus rather than confrontation.

Activity

1 What would be the advantages of a single union agreement:
- to the union?
- to the company?

2 How is this different from a 'closed shop'?

3 How do you think that providing each member with a voice in the company's future will be implemented?

4 'A non-adversarial problem solving approach – based on consensus rather than confrontation' – what does this mean?

Consultation

Consultation is particularly important when an organisation proposes changes to existing working practices. Consultation:

- enables management to try out ideas in advance;
- allows for the full participation of all the key players;
- stimulates motivation and improves morale;
- can achieve co-operation and compliance, for example, if unions are represented on a committee and agree to a particular change, they cannot later say 'we were not consulted';
- should solve problems before they arise.

Industrial disputes and industrial action

Industrial disputes occur when the normal consultation procedures fail to produce an agreement or satisfactory solution. Disputes can arise over a failure to agree on matters such as:

- holiday entitlement
- payment and grading of staff
- conditions of work
- treatment of individual employees with which the union does not agree, for example, the circumstances under which an employee is dismissed may be seen as setting a precedent if it is accepted.

Industrial action is the way in which workers try to resolve disputes if all other procedures have failed and negotiations have broken down. Essentially this means that the workers will refuse to co-operate with the employer. There are various categories of non-co-operation.

Withdrawal of goodwill

This means that workers may:

- refuse to attend meetings which are called out of working hours;
- agree an 'overtime ban', that is refusing to work overtime (normally overtime is not included in the contract of employment but can be of benefit to the employer who gets flexibility of production from existing staff, and to the employee who is paid a higher rate for unsociable hours);
- refuse to cover for absent colleagues;
- work to rule which means that members follow exactly every rule and procedure laid down by the organisation. Many of these may be out of date and, if followed precisely, may lead to a slowing down in production or a deterioration of service.

Whenever there is an industrial dispute it is important that management behave reasonably so as not to encourage any further action such as a strike.

Strike action

A **strike** is a withdrawal of labour by the unionised workforce. This is the ultimate action that the workforce can take and is normally to support claims relating to pay, working conditions or terms of employment. **Strike action** is serious both for the management who lose production and the employees who lose pay. It is not undertaken lightly and is only used as a last resort when all means of reaching a settlement have been explored.

In order to enforce a strike, union members may 'picket' a workplace. This means that they attempt to persuade people from going in to work and 'breaking the strike'.

An official action is supported by the trade union. Sometimes the union will not support industrial action which then becomes unofficial. Those taking unofficial action are placing themselves in a vulnerable situation. As they have no union to support them against the employer they may be risking dismissal through breaking their contracts of employment.

Sometimes, as in the recent Timex dispute, the management will 'lock-out' the workforce during a dispute. This will prevent employees entering the premises until an agreement is reached.

ACAS

The Advisory, Conciliation and Arbitration Service, better known as **ACAS**, was set up in 1976 following the Employment Protection Act 1975. Its main purpose is to help improve industrial relations and therefore it includes representatives from both the unions (TUC) and the employers (CBI). ACAS covers a range of activities:

- providing advice on industrial relations;
- producing codes of practice, for example, designing disciplinary procedures;
- helping to resolve industrial disputes between employers and unions:
- resolving individual disputes over employment rights.

ACAS at work

In its **advisory** capacity ACAS also gives independent advice to trade union workers or employers on a range of industrial relations issues such as:

- whether a new payment scheme should be introduced;
- whether working hours should be changed;
- whether new redundancy procedures are appropriate.

Conciliation is the process of bringing together the various parties to a dispute to try and reach an amicable solution.

Arbitration means investigating, listening to, making suggestions and negotiating.

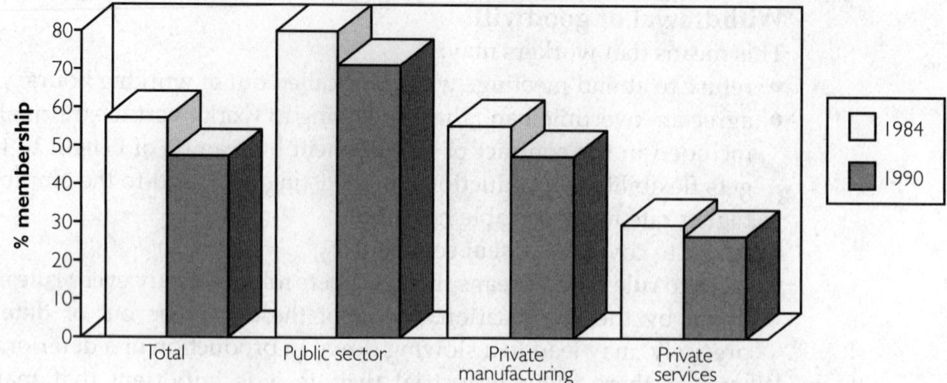

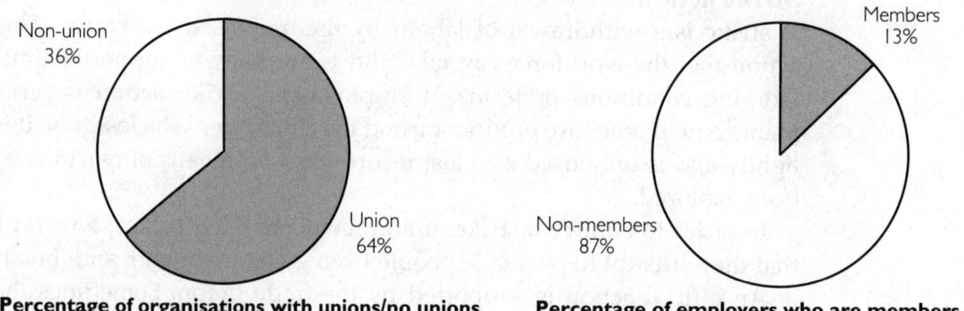

Percentage of organisations with unions/no unions in the workplace

Percentage of employers who are members of employers' association in 1990

Figure 7.6 The changing face of industrial relations in the UK

Figure 7.6 shows the results of a survey that was based on interviews with over 2,000 employers in the private and public sectors. Sponsored jointly by the Employment Department, ACAS, the Economic and Social Research Council and the Independent Policy Studies Institute the report produced in September 1992 concluded that:

- only a minority of employees are covered by collective bargaining as a result of the decline in union strength and the reduction in the representation of employers' associations;
- union membership has declined because of Conservative legislation and the dissatisfaction of workers;
- most changes have occurred in the private sector.

Activity

In this example the union and the employer are not talking to each other. 'Negotiations have broken down. We have tried everything but there is a complete deadlock...we can't even agree on talks about talks.' ACAS will act as the go-between to try and bring the sides 'to the table' so as to achieve an agreement acceptable to both parties.

Scenario

AYR-LOOMS LTD, a large clothing manufacturer, intends putting its staff on short-time working or possibly even on 'zero-hour' contracts (that is, they are only called in to work when they are needed). The problem is caused by a serious drop in demand due to recession. The company is hopeful that things will pick up with seasonal demand but if not will need to consider redundancies. All of the workforce are on full-time contracts, but as there is a fairly high turnover of staff at the company many have worked there for less than two years. The staff through their union intend to fight the proposals.

1 a Using all of the information that you have, including your knowledge of the law, prepare a case in favour of:
- the union
- the management.

b Suggest how ACAS could use its position and experience to solve the dispute.

c What do you feel the outcome would be?

2 Produce a brief summary of the findings of the Workplan Industrial Relations Survey. You should:

a summarise the information shown in the charts in Figure 7.6;

b consider to what extent the TUC and the employer's federations are representative of workers and employers;

c outline the law as it currently stands with regard to trade union membership and influence.

Improving employee performance

The efforts of human resources management are ultimately directed towards improving the performance of employees and thereby enabling the organisation to achieve its objectives. How can we measure this performance?

Performance through profitability

In Chapter 14 we will look in detail at measures of business financial performance. One measure of the performance of a business is to compare its profits with the profits over previous years and with profits of businesses in the same industry. These figures will give an indication of whether the organisation is performing adequately. Detailed breakdown of results by department will enable managers to pinpoint any problems more accurately. This is the purpose of budgetary control.

Performance through quality

Traditionally, quality control was found in manufacturing industry. Its function was to check that products were up to standard. Today quality control is found in all types of organisations, those providing services as well as those manufacturing goods. Quality is maintained by identifying problems and remedying them before the organisation's reputation is damaged in the market place.

Case study

A sweetener from Sugar

When Amstrad announced its new PC 2000 range of desk-top computers reaction was generally favourable with most reviewers agreeing with *PC User* magazine that the machine 'deserves to do well'. There was to be a problem, however. The design team used by Amstrad was too small for the ambitious task of creating a sophisticated machine to the required specifications in the time available. Although the machine worked well in tests a problem developed shortly after it went onto the market. A design fault had gone undetected.

In order to rescue the situation the company was forced to act quickly and expensively. All unsold machines were withdrawn and existing users' faulty machines were modified at a cost of £75 each to the company. As a gesture of goodwill a free one-year, on-site maintenance contract was thrown in.

'A dramatic gesture is now needed to overcome any suggestion that the company is failing in its duty to supply reliable products', said Alan Sugar. The fault had been one of quality control and it was costly.

Although the quality of output is not solely a matter of employee performance, an aware and well-motivated workforce can play an essential part in ensuring that production is up to standard.

Total Quality Management (TQM)

Rather than employing a section to identify poor service or faulty components before they reach the market, TQM aims to ensure that no products or services fall below standard in the first place. This is called ZD (zero defects). The idea is that where one department deals with another within the organisation the relationship is that of customer and supplier. In this way everyone is aware of quality and is responsible for providing it at all times.

Performance through productivity

In certain jobs, management are able to identify measures of productivity which would be reasonably expected from employees. In the retail travel industry, for example, sales of £250,000 per year per employee might be regarded as good in certain agencies. In manufacturing it is possible to calculate the number of units per hour that should reasonably be produced on the production line.

The introduction of new technology has also enabled management to monitor staff efficiency with some accuracy. The speed of data inputting can be recorded by the computer package, a method employed by, for example, some the mail order companies. Supermarkets such as Sainbury's similarly record the number of items per minute processed by their check-out staff.

Where such measurement is possible retraining needs can be identified for under-achievement, ergonomically designed workstations can be installed to improve performance and a system of rewards can be introduced as an incentive. For example, it is common for a salesforce to be paid commission for sales over a certain value, whilst in manufacturing bonus payments may be paid for production over an agreed minimum.

Performance-related pay

More and more employers are trying to link pay to **productivity**. Productivity-linked pay increases are generally acceptable to employers and government as they neither add to unit costs nor to inflation. A major difficulty with performance-related pay, however, is that productivity is not always easy to measure.

A system of rewards can be used as an incentive

The difficulties in measuring productivity

In some jobs it is not easy to measure productivity in the conventional way. The effectiveness of employees in certain jobs such as administration, occupational medicine and training may be difficult to assess. The productivity of whole areas of provision such as health, education, and the police also poses problems. In recent years, in its drive to get 'value for money', the government has attempted to apply the rules of the market place to these public services, often with difficulty. Some other examples of productivity measures are as follows:

- In 1993 schools 'league tables' were published for the first time. Schools were rated in terms of examination passes achieved by their students. This caused some controversy. The argument is that whilst examination success may indicate areas of excellence and areas in need of improvement, it does not necessarily reflect the abilities and efforts of the teachers who are working under different conditions in different schools.
- National Health Service hospitals are being encouraged to increase the 'throughput' of patients and to reduce waiting lists. There are problems here in that not all medical conditions are comparable and some are chronic (on-going).

Case study

The Sheehy Report – productivity of the police

In July 1993 Sir Patrick Sheehy announced his recommendations for the future of the police. Sir Patrick, chairman of BAT Industries, had been commissioned by the government to look into ways of making the police service more efficient. The main purpose of the Report was to suggest ways of getting 'value for money' by improving productivity. The recommendations suggested that:

- Pay for new entrants to the service should be reduced.
- Performance-related pay should be introduced.
- There should be fixed contracts of ten years initially to be reviewed thereafter every five years. The end of 'a job for life'.
- Retirement should be at 60 (rather than 55) to reduce pension costs.

In October 1993, the government decided to act on part of the report. There has been considerable controversy and opposition to some of the suggestions. Points that have been made by critics include the following:

- Performance should not be judged only on clear-up rates and response times to crimes. Such a policy would encourage officers to concentrate on the easier cases and would discourage thorough investigation of serious cases; those that may take a long time and require many officers.
- The low starting pay would be bad for motivation and affect the quality of recruits. A trainee traffic warden, for example, would earn considerably more.
- Short-term contracts would mean the 'end to policing as a vocation'. Since experienced officers are more expensive it would be possible to save money by replacing them with new recruits when their contracts were reviewed.

Activities

1 Obtain a copy of the Patients' Charter from your local hospital. How will the hospital's performance be measured?

2 How do you think police performance can best be assessed? What are the problems?

3 How do you think the performance of your college or school should be judged? Are there any difficulties in actually measuring this?

4 'The best team always wins' – John Sillett as manager of Coventry City. Why can league tables be misleading?

Appraisal

An increasingly important way of getting feedback on employee performance is through appraisal. The idea is to help the employee to become more effective.

Schemes are set up within the organisation so that employee performance can be evaluated through observation and discussion. Appraisal may be closed in which case the appraiser's report remains confidential. More usually the process is open, in which case the appraisee takes an active part in the review process and discusses the results.

The appraisal system usually consists of:

- Review – What is the appraisee's job and how it has it changed? How effectively is it being performed? What are the difficulties?
- Action – Sets out priorities for any development or training needs, agrees targets to be set, identifies any support that is needed.
- Monitoring – Are the targets achieved?

Appraisal may yet provide a basis for rewarding 'productivity' in those occupations where, as we have seen, the traditional bonus and commission schemes are difficult to apply.

Activity

Newbould Engineering

MEMORANDUM

To: All employees

From: R Martinez, Personnel Director

Performance Appraisal Scheme

We are setting up a Performance Appraisal Scheme. We would like you to help us by giving us your views – this is your chance.

Performance appraisal is basically a way of measuring and assessing the performance of all employees as objectively as possible. We intend to make this an open process. Our appraisal scheme is intended to

- evaluate your performance
- fix realistic targets and objectives for work
- help you to perform well
- monitor your progress.

The purpose of our scheme is to help you to help us. Without you we cannot achieve our goals.

A complete appraisal for one person will usually take three months with:

- a first meeting, generally with your immediate supervisor, to agree targets and objectives;
- a second meeting – a one-to-one appraisal;
- a third meeting, again one-to-one to see how things have gone.

We should all gain as:

- you can tell us about your needs
- we can organise the help and training that you want
- it should bring 'them' and 'us' together.

We know other companies have made mistakes and caused some resistance to appraisal, but your management are fully committed to the idea. We are talking to you now so as to avoid problems later. Everyone will be appraised, myself included. Objective standards will be set to avoid stereotyping and any bias (the 'he/she has never liked me' feeling). Appraisers will be told to use the whole of the five point rating scale, so if you're excellent, good, average, fair or poor, we'll record it.

TELL US WHAT YOU THINK!

1. Do you think that agreeing standards with the supervisor is necessary?
2. Who do you think should do the appraising?
3. Do you have any worries about our scheme?

4. Should we have a five-point scale? Can you suggest alternatives?
5. What performance features should we rate? (Your GNVQ list of skills will help you here.)
6. What ought to be the aims of our scheme?
7. What benefits do you think our organisation will gain?
8. How do you think you will benefit?

As an employee respond to this memo honestly and positively.

Motivation – ways of improving performance

As you read this ask yourself the question, Why am I doing this? Is it because:

- you have to, or
- you enjoy it?

The question 'What motivates staff?' is a crucial one for management to consider. We have already looked at different approaches to performance by various businesses. Over the years a number of management theories have been put forward in an attempt to explain the nature of motivation and suggest ways in which it may be improved.

Elton Mayo – the Hawthorne Experiment

Mayo conducted the so-called Hawthorn Experiments in the 1920s at the Hawthorne works of the American Western Electric Company in Chicago, where over 30,000 employees made telephone equipment.

He was asked to investigate why, despite improved facilities and benefits, there was much dissatisfaction and poor productivity. His experiments seemed to show that people respond positively if they are given recognition. It was this, rather than the physical working conditions that were important. He also emphasised the importance of group cohesion – feeling part of the team.

Abraham Maslow and the hierarchy of needs

Maslow developed his Theory of Human Motivation in 1943. He believed that motivation comes from a desire to satisfy needs. He placed these in a hierarchy with basic needs at the bottom and higher needs at the top.

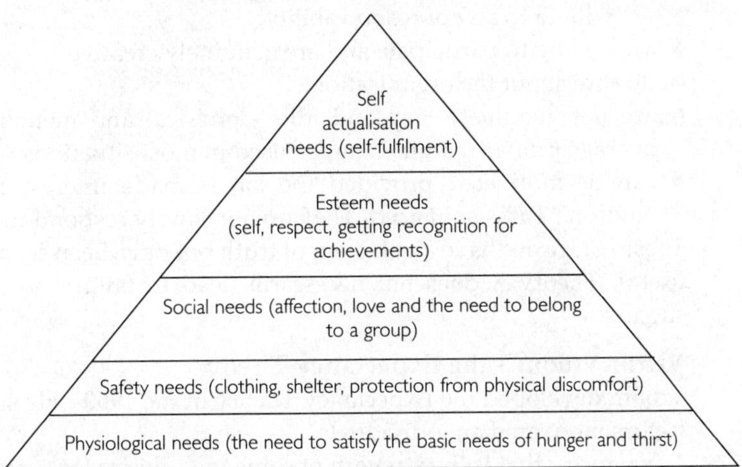

Maslow argued that people are interested in satisfying basic needs first and then, once these have been satisfied, become interested in higher needs. Someone who is well paid and quite comfortably off will therefore be better motivated by being offered more power than by being offered a little more money. (Why do rich men spend their time being directors of football clubs?) In practice, Maslow accepted that a variety of needs will exist at the same time, but that some are stronger than others.

Frederick Herzberg – motivators and hygiene factors

Herzberg's theories, produced in the 1950s, concern job satisfaction. From numerous interviews with accountants and engineers he concluded that two sets of factors are important:

- **hygiene factors** – these include reasonable pay, satisfactory conditions of work, benefits packages – and without these, people are dissatisfied, but they alone do not lead to job satisfaction;
- **motivators** – these include responsibility, challenge, self-improvement – these provide job satisfaction.

Hertzberg's theories gave rise to the notions of:

- job enrichment – this involves including motivators in the job, perhaps by giving employees more responsibility and involving them in decisions. Human resources managers call this 'empowerment'.
- job enlargement – this means broadening the job by putting together a number of similar functions. The worker may not need more skill but will have variety and a wider view of the work.

Douglas McGregor – Theory X and Theory Y

In his book *The Human Side of Enterprise* (1960) McGregor put forward two extreme views about the way in which organisations regard their employees.

According to **Theory X** (the traditional view) most people are idle and lazy, they

- want to be given orders;
- have no ambition;

- will not accept responsibility;
- do not like change;
- do not care about the organisation for which they work;
- only work because they have to;
- are only motivated by money.

Theory Y is much more hopeful and positive. It suggests that workers:

- are willing to accept responsibility;
- are willing to participate and are genuinely creative;
- do care about the organisation;
- are not genuinely lazy and idle – physical and mental effort is natural and the average human's brain is under-used in most situations;
- can be motivated provided the job is made interesting – 'enriched' – and the environment is enhanced. They do not simply respond to threats.

These categories have an element of truth but have been seen as too broad to be entirely useful. Theory X does not necessarily lead to failure nor does Theory Y guarantee success.

Victor Vroom – the Expectancy Theory

Vroom developed the Expectancy Theory in the 1960s. He suggested that two separate factors motivated an individual:

1 Valance – that is the strength of someone's desire for something.
2 Expectancy – the person's estimation of how likely it is that this can be achieved.

For example a sports car may be the reward for breaking the sales record. This may be a strong motivator for some people, but not if people feel that this is a trick to get everyone to work hard and that there is virtually no chance of winning.

Gaining employee co-operation

Human resource management has used the various theories on motivation to develop practical ways of encouraging employee co-operation. These include the following areas.

Involving employees in decisions

- Representation: employees may be represented on the board of directors. For instance colleges have a teacher representative on the board of governors.
- Consultation: changes affecting employees may be put into place only after consultation with trades unions, staff associations or representatives at works councils.
- Quality circles: employees are encouraged to work in teams to suggest solutions to problems and new ways of working.

Developing team spirit

- Team working: employees may be encouraged to develop loyalty to a team so that they all 'pull together'. We consider this further in Chapter 8.

Rewarding effort

- Performance-related pay: payment by results can motivate people, but research shows that workers often suspect that this is a management plot to worsen conditions of employment. Also, commission payments have recently been blamed for encouraging sales teams to push poor products such as endowment mortgages. (Daewoo currently advise that their car sales team do not get commission at all.)
- Employee share ownership: employees will benefit directly by sharing in company profits.

Job security

- If a job is secure and there is an opportunity for career progression then the employee will feel motivated to work hard so as to 'get on'. Much of the success of the Japanese economy has been put down to the fact that the employer could offer a job for life and so expect a high degree of loyalty from the worker.

  As we will see in Chapter 8, the recent UK trend has been towards short-term contracts and outsourcing (contracting out work). There is a danger that this can leave employees insecure and disenchanted.

Case studies

The incentive game

Vic Rosewall runs 'Top Brand Incentives' a firm providing gifts to motivate and reward staff. He believes in giving goodies to everyone in the team, not just the star players. He believes that straight competition for a prize can backfire: 'A dozen reps with one winner means 11 losers...it can have a negative effect...the others lose heart thinking 'It's always that bloke from London who wins the trip to Barbados'.

Mr Rosewall also acknowledges that the performance of many staff does not relate to any figures at all. For this reason he recommends the 'collective carrot'; this means that everyone will encourage everyone else. Gifts range from camcorders to vacuum cleaners to watches to holidays. You can even have a row of grapes in a vineyard with your name on it.

Faith Leigh, editor of *Incentive Today*, believes that gifts are better than money for both the giver and the receiver. Money just gets used for the household bills whilst a firm 'can buy an award for £10–£18 with a perceived value of £500–£1,000', she says.

The possibilities are endless. Where the idea is to foster team spirit then dune buggy racing or war games are a possibility. If it's just a case of cheering up the staff a group of players called 'Murder my Lord?' will bump off the boss over dinner. The problem is that he comes back later dressed as the devil!

Source: Adapted from the *Observer*

Stressful or stimulating?

Employees undertake tremendous responsibilities in the Toyota production system. At each worksite a team of employees designs the standardised work procedures for their own job and strives continuously to find ways to improve those procedures. The team members use *kanban* (cards) to manage the flow of work and to order parts and materials. What is more, they each work to master every job at their worksite so that any member of the team can help or even fill in for any other member of the team.

British workers at the new Japanese car factories of Toyota (Burnaston near Derby) and Nissan near Sunderland find that they are given the authority to manage their own work within multi-skilled teams. The employees are encouraged to suggest improvements to make their work more efficient, a process called kaizen. Undoubtedly this places extra demands on staff, but the belief is that this is stimulating rather than stressful.

In 1990 workers in Toyota plants in Japan suggested nearly two million improvements to the production process. Management listened and 97 per cent of these were implemented.

Source: *The Toyota Production System*, Toyota Motor Corporation

Addendum: Stress the Demon King?

'Stress – today's evil word – is not always the demon king it is made out to be. A certain amount of stress is a necessary, even a beneficial, element in our lives. When the brain registers that a potentially stressful situation exists, we experience a surge of adrenaline, and this in turn can lead to an increase in performance.'

Source: Ursula Markham, *Managing Stress*

John Lewis – working in partnership

John Lewis employs 34,000 people in its 22 department stores and 111 Waitrose supermarkets.

The staff, who are officially described as partners, do not exactly control the company but they do elect half the board. The constitution of the company makes it clear that 'the Partnership's ultimate aim shall be the happiness in every way of all its members'.

All of this seems to be working because in 1995 profits were up 25 per cent.

Since there are no outside shareholders, all of this profit is available for reinvestment in the company and payment of an annual staff bonus – set this year at 12 per cent of salary, or six weeks' pay.

Chairman Stuart Hampson believes that the unique structure and values of the group, including the partnership bonus, has something to do with its success. 'It gives us a great advantage because the partners own the business. The hope is that they participate in it as if it were their own business'.

Source: adapted from *The Guardian*

Activities

1 Which of the management theories can you identify in the case studies above? In each case, how are the management attempting to gain employee co-operation?

2 **How well motivated are you?**

Anyone with responsibility for a group of people must be able to motivate them, i.e. to give them an incentive for doing and completing a task. Some people are easier to motivate than others. A good leader is one who can motivate all individuals in the group.

Complete this check-list for your workplace (this includes a school or college). You should rate each feature on this scale:

1 = very poor, **2** = poor, **3** = good, **4** = excellent.

Before you begin consider how the performance/success of your organisation and the people in it can be measured. Is it quantifiable?

Cleanliness	Deadlines met	Level of interest
Willingness to work	Atmosphere	Participation
Enjoyment	General level of punctuality	Discipline
Sickness*/absenteeism	Attendance	Performance

(*excellent here means no sickness!)

How did your organisation do? Add up the scores you have recorded for each feature:

- 0–15 means **motivation** is non-existent. Something is seriously wrong, for example, are the working conditions satisfactory? Is the organisation about to close? Are the jobs totally boring? Are people under stress? Do workers and management/tutor ever communicate? Can you identify any other reasons?
- 16–25 means **motivation** is poor. Work through the check-list. Are all the scores low? Are there any quite high? Is the problem sickness? Participation? What are the strengths and weaknesses?
- 26–35 means a good level of **motivation**. Can you identify the strengths and weaknesses within your organisation?
- 36+ means a very high level of motivation.

These are the characteristics of a good working environment (36+):

- good atmosphere;
- people want to come to work, they enjoy being at work;
- management/tutors appreciate you and the work you do;
- the staff are well paid and rewarded;
- colleagues work well together;
- there is good career and professional development;
- routine jobs have been extended or changed to include more interesting work through 'job enrichment';
- there are good communication networks and everyone is well informed and involved in the organisation.

3 It has been suggested that many HR managers feel that stress and job insecurity do not prevent people from working efficiently. What do you think? Can stress actually motivate you? (Think about assignment deadlines and mandatory unit tests.)

Absenteeism as a measure of performance

Currently, 200 million working days are lost a year in the UK, costing £9 billion!

Absenteeism of staff can be defined as persistent or regular absence from work without a valid reason. For whatever reason, absenteeism means that people who are not ill do not attend work. If there is a high general level of staff absence then a company might conclude that there is absenteeism. This may take the form of non-attendance but also includes bad time keeping, such as arriving late and leaving early. High rates of absenteeism reduce productivity and can be very expensive for businesses. A number of studies have been made over the last decade which show how various companies have tackled this problem.

Case studies

Fit for the job?

The General Electric Company (GEC) in Cincinnati provided, but did not enforce, a professional programme of fitness and recreation. Employees who did not participate continued with an average absenteeism rate of 8.93 days per annum. For those who did take part absences were almost halved.

Cutting the rate

Sandvik, whose saws are found in DIY shops around the UK, suffered from an absence rate of 25 per cent! In fact Swedish industry has traditionally recorded high rates of absenteeism and this was no worse than their competitors. However, the company recognised that the rate had doubled over the previous 25 years. They set up a committee of three workers and three production managers to see what could be done. Following investigations a programme was implemented including:

- better management–employee communications;
- investigating employee complaints;
- keeping in touch with absent workers;
- improving training and induction programmes.

As a result absence was reduced overall – in one section by as much as 65 per cent!

Review questions

1. A supermarket is about to install bar code readers at its check-out points. What training is needed by the cashier and supervisor?
2. Give three benefits of human resource planning.
3. Why can a high labour turnover cause problems for a business?
4. Suggest four items of information needed for a staffing plan.
5. How might Theory X and Theory Y help you to motivate people?
6. A colleague who is always late is dismissed. Is this fair? Explain your answer.
7. A colleague whom no one likes is dismissed. Is this fair? Explain your answer.
8. What type of problem would be dealt with by a trade union shop steward?
9. How can a refusal to work overtime affect productivity?
10. Give two examples of when ACAS might become involved in an industrial dispute?
11. What are the main duties of employees?
12. What are the key features of the Equal Pay Act? Have its aims been achieved?
13. Why is sex discrimination still prevalent in society?
14. What is the Race Relations Act trying to achieve?
15. Give three ways of motivating people. Mention three theories of motivation in your answer.
16. What should be done before a performance appraisal scheme is introduced?
17. How might the withdrawal of goodwill by workers in a factory affect its operations?
18. What is a Works Council?
19. What would be the most effective way of training teachers – on the job or off the job?
20. What policies could a business adopt to retain its best staff?

Key terms

Human resources
Personnel
Staffing plan
Labour turnover
Recruitment
Selection
Legal requirements
Discrimination
– direct
– indirect
EOC
Equal opportunities policy
Contract of employment
Terms
– express
– implied
Statutory rights
Disciplinary procedure
Dismissal
– fair
– unfair
Appeals procedure
Industrial Tribunals
Reinstatement
Re-engagement
Compensation
Industrial relations
Trade union
Employers' association
Consultation
Negotiation
Industrial disputes
Industrial action
Stike action
ACAS
CBI
TUC
Advisory
Conciliation
Arbitration
Training
Induction
Health and safety training
On-the-job training
Off-the-job training
Training plan
Occupational health service
First aid box
Incentive
Productivity
Appraisal
– closed
– open
The Hawthorne Experiment
The hierarchy of needs
Hygiene factors and motivators
Theory X
Theory Y
Empowerment
The Expectancy Theory
Motivation
Works Councils
Quality circles
Performance-related pay

Assignment 7
Your organisation – human resources

This assignment develops knowledge and understanding of the following element:
4.1 Investigate human resourcing.

It supports development of the following core skills:
Communication 3.1, 3.2, 3.4
Information technology 3.1, 3.2, 3.3

You are required to act on the following memo. You may choose your own organisation or you may select another – perhaps a work placement.

```
Your organisation

To:   Your group

From: Senior Management Team

The management team want your group to carry out an investigation
into selected aspects of the organisation's Human Resourcing
Policy.
```

Terms of reference

We want you to:

1. Explain the roles and responsibility of the human resources department.
2. Identify the expressed and implied terms in a sample contract of employment.
3. Describe the current procedures for staff training and development. How, and by whom, are areas for training and development identified?
4. Identify the ways in which the performance of staff is measured.
5. State the objectives of the organisation. How are the staff motivated to work towards these goals?
6. Is a trade union or a staff organisation recognised, and if so what part does it play?
7. Describe procedures for grievance, discipline and appeals within the organisation.

For each point you should make observations and may make recommendations; give particular emphasis to equal opportunities and staff development.

You should supply all sources of information and attach any relevant documents as appendices.

Notes:

The report must be word processed.

It should be a maximum of eight pages long.

Note that managers are only prepared to give one interview which must be properly booked in advance.

Appendices should include at least:

- a summary of the relevant legislation relating to employment
- a sample contract of employment.

8 Job roles, recruitment and responses to change

What is covered in this chapter

- Job roles and responsibilities within organisations
- Working conditions and practices
- The workplace revolution – reasons for change
- The current debate on human resources management
- Recruitment and selection of staff
- Legal and ethical obligations in

These are the resources that you will need for your Human Resources file:

- job descriptions
- person specifications
- plc annual reports
- curriculum vitae (CVs)
- application forms.

Job roles and responsibilities within organisations

Organisations may have different legal identities, and develop different organisational structures and cultures. These factors have implications for those who work within specific organisations, but nevertheless a number of general roles can be identified.

Shareholders

If the business is a public or private company then it is owned by the **shareholders**. These may be members of the public, other companies who buy into the company (and may eventually take it over), the government, or institutions with funds to invest, such as insurance companies, trade unions or banks.

The shareholders are entitled to attend the Annual General Meeting where they are informed of the annual results and vote to accept the audited accounts. The shareholders also vote to elect the company directors. Sometimes, as in family-owned concerns, the directors may be the only shareholders.

Directors

The directors are elected to run the company on behalf of the shareholders. The directors are said to exercise 'stewardship' over the funds invested in the company by the shareholders and they are accountable to them for their actions. Directors can be removed and replaced by a majority vote of the shareholders and must abide by the regulations set out in the Companies Act of 1985. These include publishing an annual report. The financial details of this are discussed more fully in Chapter 14.

Directors can be executive or non-executive.

- Executive directors are full-time employees responsible for running part of the company's activities such as finance, sales or research and development. They make decisions about the day-to-day running of the company.
- Non-executive directors are advisors brought in because of their particular knowledge and expertise in certain areas of business. These tend to be part-time and may have directorships with several different companies. In the UK some MPs, especially in the Conservative party, have a number of non-executive directorships although they must make their interests public. In the USA such involvement by politicians in business is illegal.

The board of directors is essentially concerned with making company policy and turning this into achievable aims. The kind of policy decisions that will be taken are:

- Where are we now? — shown in the *Annual Report and Accounts*
- Where do we want to go? — shown in the *Corporate plan*
- How will we get there? — the reason for *Strategic decisions*

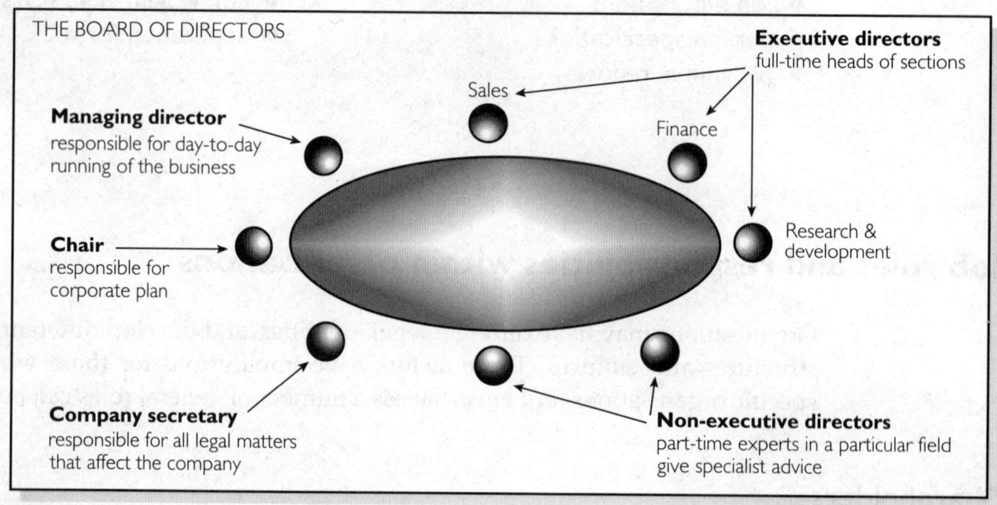

The Managing Director will have valuable business experience and proven ability and is elected by the Board to head the organisation. It is becoming common to adopt the American style of calling the Managing Director the Chief Executive.

The Company Chair is elected by the Board to chair the board meetings and is responsible for strategic decisions. The Chair may have executive status or may leave the day-to-day running to the Managing Director.

The Company Secretary is responsible to the Board for ensuring that all legal requirements are fulfilled. This includes dealings with shareholders, contracts into which the company enters and health and safety issues. The secretary also deals with correspondence associated with these matters.

Not every company will have a full board of directors as shown above. However, there must be at least one director and a Company Secretary.

Case study

Directors' pay

The pay of directors is disclosed in the annual report. The theory is that shareholders will take action if they disapprove. However, the very high pay rises given to directors of the newly privatised public utilities have caused the government to consider legislation to control pay.

The high-earning bosses of the public utilities

1 David Jeffries, chairman of the National Grid. **Annual salary £359,000** (including bonus and relocation expenses). Likely profit on share options £1,788,980.

2 Cedric Brown, chief executive of British Gas. **Annual salary £475,000** (rise of 75 per cent from £270,000 to take in new bonus scheme). But revised package from next year could see salary double to nearly £1 million.

3 Sir Desmond Pitcher, chairman of North West Water. **Annual salary (including performance bonus) £338,000** – plus £22,500 paid into pension fund. (Salary represents rise of 571 per cent since privatisation).

4 Ed Wallis, chief executive of PowerGen: **Pay this year £400,000**. Profits on share options £876,000. Next year – likely profit from share options: £697,000.

5 John Baker, chief executive of National Power. **Annual pay £437,000**. Profits from share options: £713,000. Next year, likely profit from share options: £603,000.

6 James Smith, chairman of Eastern Electricity. **Annual salary (including all payments) £242,000.** Made profits of £466,867 on share options since privatisation of industry.

Source: *The Observer*, March 1995

Equal opportunities in the boardroom?

Mary Baker, who serves on the board of Barclays, the Prudential, Avon and FMI, says, 'A board is always looking for a range of experience from its new executive directors. It is perfectly obvious a woman is going to have had different experiences from a man. A board without any representation from half the human race is going to be unbalanced. But the track record must stand up. You can't go out on the street and take the first woman you find.'

A survey published by the Institute of Policy Studies in November 1991 found that women accounted for only 5 per cent of all UK company directors.

According to *Crawfords Directory of City Connections (1992)* of the 4,000 plus top directors in the country, that is Chair, Chief Executives and Finance Directors, only 20 are women (0.5 per cent of the total) and of these most are Finance Directors.

Activity

1 Look at the directors for all of the companies for which you have the annual reports. What percentage of directors are women? There is usually a photograph!
2 What other posts do the directors hold?
3 Look up directors' pay (emoluments).
4 Look at the 'Statement of Directors' Responsibilities'.

Directorship – challenge or threat?
Company directors have a far higher death rate from stress-related factors than other occupations. Directors have a risk of dying from coronary disease of eight times the average. Risk of death from other stress-related causes is also higher than in other jobs:
strokes (20 times average), duodenal ulcers (five times average) and suicide (seven times average).

Managers

What is the purpose of management?

It is useful to remember where we started. Business organisations exist to satisfy demand for particular goods and services and in order to do this they need resources; the factors of production. Management is concerned with planning, controlling and co-ordinating the acquisition and use of these resources. In medium to large concerns particularly, managers run the business by using people and information.

The term 'managing' comes from the Latin word for hand, as does the word 'manual'. It originally meant 'handling things' but did not originally apply to people. The term 'man management' was introduced by the War Office at the turn of the century.

Levels of management

It is usual to think of management as a series of levels within an organisation; we have already seen this in our organisation charts in Chapter 3. Each level will have specific duties and responsibilities delegated to it by the level above. The top managers in a business are the directors. All other levels in the hierarchy above the operatives perform management functions of some kind.

Figure 8.1 shows the different management activities of each level of the management hierarchy.

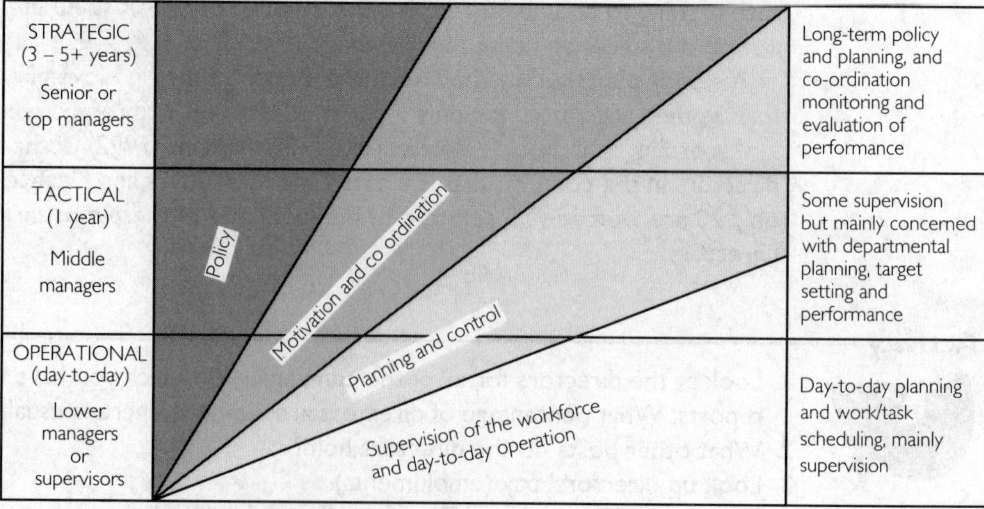

Figure 8.1 Management activities related to management levels

What are the functions and responsibilities of management?

There are many studies which try to identify exactly what it is that managers should do. The first theories were based on an observation of military or engineering principles and were written as a guide to others. The Frenchman, Henri Fayol, himself a coal mining engineer, set out some of the early ideas in 1916. His work, only published in English in 1949, suggested that there were five basic functions of management which would be found to a greater or lesser extent in every organisation regardless of size, objectives, type of activity or legal form.

- **Forecasting** Forecasting is the process of predicting what will happen in the future. It is vital to the success of any organisation that it has an accurate picture of future events in order to make the right decisions when responding to change. A sales forecast, for example, would use past sales data to identify patterns and trends. On the basis of these managers will use their knowledge of the market to identify future trends.
- **Organising** Organising is the process of arranging and being responsible for the work or jobs done by individuals to achieve the organisation's goals and objectives. People can be organised into teams or work groups to perform specific tasks.
- **Commanding** This is the process of leading by giving orders and instructions and expecting them to be carried out. It is an authoritarian approach which equates the workforce to military personnel.
- **Co-ordinating** This means bringing the various jobs and tasks together into one harmonious operation, perhaps to achieve an even flow of work without hold-ups or disruptions. We see in Chapter 13 how the departmental budgets are co-ordinated to produce the master budget.
- **Controlling** This involves directing, inspecting and regulating work. It may mean having to take remedial action. Departmental heads, for example, need to keep within spending budgets.

Today management functions also include:

- **Communicating** Being a good communicator is probably the most important ability needed by a modern manager. Good communications involves understanding and being understood by many groups. A manager will need to negotiate with subordinates, superiors, colleagues, trade unions, government officials and outside agencies.
- **Planning** This is the means by which a forecast is acted upon. A plan is a detailed scheme, method or procedure for achieving an organisation's goals. In Chapter 15 we will look at business planning.
- **Decision making** Although this was implied in Fayol's original five functions of management, it is now the focal point of all management action. Managers are continuously making decisions about what to purchase and where, how much to sell, and so on. The type of decisions that managers are allowed to make often depends on which rung of the management ladder they are on. For example, the Bank Manager of a high street branch will only be able to make loans up to an agreed amount. Anything above this will have to be referred upwards to the Area Manager. The outcome of a disciplinary procedure or a job interview will be a management decision.
- **Motivating** This is the action of getting people to do something because they want to rather than because they are forced to. We have discussed motivation in some detail in Chapter 7.

- **Innovating** This means bringing in new ideas, routines, methods of work, products, materials. Managers innovate whenever they change any of these. In recent years Human Resources managers have introduced quality circles, performance related pay and empowerment (giving employees more responsibility).
- **Creating** Managers need to be imaginative and original. They must be able to approach problems from different perspectives in order to reach solutions. They need to synthesise or combine ideas from other disciplines.
- **Developing** The Manager's role may involve developing people either by direct 'on-the-job' training, or by 'off-the-job ' training at college or elsewhere. Many organisations require their managers to be involved with successive planning, i.e. managers should positively train people so that they are eventually able to take over the managers' jobs. Besides this training function, managers also have a role to play in developing personality.
- **Delegating** This is the process of giving authority to lower level managers to make specific decisions. It is necessary because each manager cannot do all the tasks that need to be done. The Senior Manager needs to ensure that the subordinate can do the work and that the work gets done. Senior managers remain responsible for all delegated work; they 'carry the can'.

Activity

This activity is for discussion. People who know little about music sometimes suggest that an orchestra could play just as well without the conductor at the front. A manager is a bit like a conductor.

a Imagine that the managers in your organisation all went on holiday (or away on a conference) for a year. What would not get done and what difference would this make:
- On the first day?
- After the first week?
- After the first month?
- After the first year?

From this what do you conclude that they do?

b Can you give an example from your organisation of each of Fayol's functions?

Managers as leaders

Managers at every level need to have leadership qualities in order to bring the best out of those for whom they are responsible.

Activities

1. Look up 'lead', 'leader' and 'leadership' in a dictionary and a thesaurus. From your experience of leaders (for example, form/house captains, Cub or Brownie leaders), did they lead 'from the front' (i.e. by example) or 'from the back' (i.e. shout encouragement from behind 'Go on, you can do it!)?
2. Working as a group, brainstorm what you think are the qualities of a good leader.
3. Working on your own, write down which of these qualities you believe you have.
4. Again working on your own, which of these qualities do your friends and colleagues say you have?

How do managers lead?

There are three main ways of looking at what makes a good leader:

- trait theories
- style theories
- contingency theories

Trait theories

Trait theories suggest a list of qualities (traits) that make an effective leader. It is agreed that important qualities are: integrity, enthusiasm, warmth, calmness, 'tough but fair'. However, there are a number of such lists and none is exhaustive.

The particular traits required will vary with the situation and the job in hand. People who are leaders in one situation -situational leaders – will not always be successful in all situations.

Style theories

A list of some of the main styles of leadership that have been identified includes:

- **Autocratic** leaders – these people take all decisions with very little or no consultation. They expect their orders to be carried out without any disagreement or questions.
- **Democratic** leaders – these people take great care to involve all members of the team in discussion. It is a 'we need to find out what everyone thinks' approach. Although the style can work well with a small, highly motivated team, it can fail when the group cannot make a decision and needs real guidance and direction.
- **Consultative** leaders – similar to the democratic approach but instead of allowing the group to make the decision, they do so themselves. This approach can create a high level of motivation with good quality output and results.
- **Laissez-faire** leaders – these intervene as little as possible and allow the group to take control. The group becomes leaderless.
- **Task/activity** leaders – these people concentrate on the job to be done, for example, certain football managers 'take every game as it comes'.
- **People** leaders – these care more about the people they lead, their emotions and feelings. The captain whose side has just lost 7–0 would say 'We tried hard but we were beaten by the better team on the day'.

Various theorists have combined these leadership styles in different ways. First, there is Douglas McGregor's two extremes: the **autocratic leader** (Theory X) and the **democratic leader** (Theory Y) (see Chapter 7).

Second, there is Rensis Likert's four stages (a refinement of McGregor):

- **Stage 1:** authoritarian
- **Stage 2:** benevolent authoritarian
- **Stage 3:** consultative
- **Stage 4:** participative.

A third study is that of Tannenbaum and Schmidt who published a continuum of styles in *How to Choose a Leadership Pattern* (1958):

Freedom for team members

Use of authority by the leader

- ☐ Leader defines limits asks team to make a decision
- ☐ Leader suggests problem gets suggestion makes decision
- ☐ Leader suggests tentative decision subject to change
- ☐ Leader presents ideas invites questions
- ☐ Leader explains decision to group
- ☐ Leader makes decision and informs team

Contingency theories

These theories emphasise what is known as the 'best fit', that is, a different approach to leadership may be necessary to perform different tasks within the same organisation. If we define a leader as someone who is in charge of a group of people then the leadership style will be dependent on a number of factors including:

- nature of the task
- personality of the leader
- group personality.

Activities

1 On this leadership spectrum where would you put your boss (line manager)?

Autocratic — Consultative — Democratic — Laissez-faire

Compare your decision with the rest of the group.

2 Do you feel another style would be more effective, if so which?

3 Do you have the skills to be a manager? The following exercise is sometimes used in management training courses:

Participants are given a glossary of skills and their definitions (Table 8.1). They are then asked to identify which of these skills they have and where they have used them – they must include all areas of their lives.

Try it yourself.

Table 8.1 Skills and their definitions

Skill	Definition
Communicating a written b verbal	The ability to convey and receive information clearly both verbally and in writing.
Decision-making	The ability to arrive at a resolution after consideration.
Information gathering	The ability to gather all necessary information from a wide variety of sources.
Evaluating	The ability to assess amount, value or significance after careful appraisal and study.
Analysing	The ability to identify and examine the components of a situation or structure.
Motivating	The ability to generate a willingness to work, to achieve goals and satisfy needs.
Negotiating	The ability to consult and bargain to achieve agreement or compromise.
Listening	The ability to integrate the physical, emotional and intellectual messages received in search for understanding and meaning.
Delegating	The ability to entrust a task/responsibility to someone and provide the person with the necessary guidelines and information to carry out the task/responsibility.
Taking responsibility	The ability to assume accountability for your own, and sometimes other people's actions.
Organising	The ability to structure, arrange and allocate work effectively.
Planning	The ability to formulate or organise a method by which something is done.
Prioritising	The ability to assess comparative levels of importance or urgency.

4 Arrange an appointment with your manager – it can be your course tutor. Find out what percentage of his or her time is spent on each function. Ask the manger to list the functions in order of importance for him or her. What does he or she think are the most important functions?
5 Try to repeat activity **4** by asking people in different levels of management. Are there any differences? Compare your results with other people in your group.
6 Each member of the group should list the functions of management in their order of importance. These lists should then be compared to achieve an overall ranking.
7 What do these results tell you about yourself, your view of managers and your view of workers?

The supervisor

The supervisor is usually regarded as being the first stage of the management hierarchy of an organisation. Although the role varies between organisations, generally the supervisor is the management person most directly concerned with the workforce and with whom they have the most contact.

A straightforward way of finding out what supervisors do is to look at job adverts and job descriptions. Here are some examples:

Job	Tasks/skills/functions
Cash Control Supervisor Dobsons Ltd	Supervise a small group of staff dealing with cash. Take responsibility for cash records. Communicate with staff.
Purchasing Supervisor Springfield Engineering	Organise the purchasing office which has nine staff. Plan and be responsible for the allocation of work.
Accounts Supervisor Johnson, Smith and Shah	Be responsible for a group of accountancy staff – deputising for the Manager – must be a good motivator.
Insurance Claims Dept Groom and Wilding	Assisting the Manager with the settlement of claims. Must be able to exercise judgement and use initiative.

Notice the key words:
Supervise – staff – responsibility – communicate – organise – plan – allocation of work – deputising – motivator – assisting – judgement – initiative.

Activity

Collect adverts for 'Supervisors', 'Managers' and 'Operatives' (the workers). Note the skills, functions and activities which are associated with each group. Comment on your findings and compare your results.

When we look at job descriptions we will see that channels of communication are identified. A supervisor in a supermarket will communicate as follows.

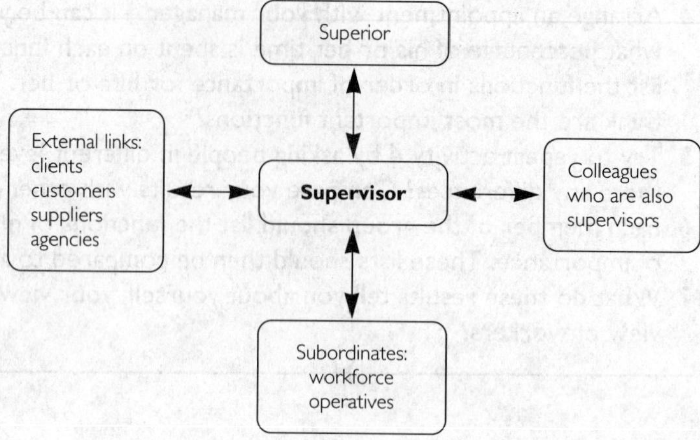

The operative (worker)

The operative is at the base of the triangle in the hierarchy of an organisation and is responsible to a manager, usually a supervisor. In some organisational cultures the operative has a very narrow role and follows a rigid set of tried and tested procedures designed to produce a precise result. In others a high degree of responsibility is given. We will look at two case studies.

Case study

The operative's job (1)

Production lines demanding repetitive behaviour occur not only in manufacturing, but anywhere which demands mass production. This can include offices and fast-food restaurants. Below is a check-list used by management as a means of quality control. It shows clearly what the waiter/waitress is expected to do.

Greeting the customer	Yes	No
1 There is a smile		
2 It is a sincere greeting		
3 There is eye contact		
Taking the order	**Yes**	**No**
1 Counter person is familiar with the menu ticket		
2 Customer gives order only once		
3 Orders of four items or less are memorised		
4 There is suggestive selling		
Assembling the order	**Yes**	**No**
1 The order is assembled in proper sequence		
2 Grill slips are handed in first		
3 Drinks are poured in proper sequence		
4 Proper amount of ice		
5 Cups slanted and finger used to activate		
6 Drinks are filled to the proper level		
7 Drinks are capped		
8 Clean cups		
9 Holding times are observed on coffee		
10 Cups are filled to the proper level on coffee		

Presenting the order	Yes	No
1 It is properly packaged		
2 The bag is double folded		
3 Plastic trays are used if eating inside		
4 A tray liner is used		
5 The food is handled in a proper manner		
Asking for and receiving payment	**Yes**	**No**
1 The amount is stated clearly enough to hear		
2 Denomination received is clearly stated		
3 The change is counted out loud		
4 Change is counted efficiently		
5 Large bills are laid on the till until change is given		
Thanking the customer and asking for repeat business	**Yes**	**No**
1 There is always a thank you		
2 The thank you is sincere		
3 There is eye contact		
4 Return business was asked for		

Activities

1. What is suggestive selling?
2. What do you think about the use of the word 'sincere'?
3. Why are large bills laid on the till until change is given?
4. Many fast food chains are franchises. Why is it particularly important for them to check that the service is standardised?

Operatives as team members

'An individual will only succeed by working in close co-operation with the rest of the group…we have applied the concept of team working to everything that we do. Our organisational design is based upon strong integration of teams focused on meeting customer needs. Through teamwork we seek to realise the full potential of the individual'

Source: National & Provincial Building Society recruiting advertisement

When Henri Fayol developed his management theory to include 14 points, the last one was 'esprit de corps' or teamwork. Some of the studies of motivation, you will remember, showed the benefits which can be derived from effective team operation and engendering a sense of common purpose. It is for this reason that management training involves physical team exercises such as boating, mountain climbing and even war games. It is also the reason why some organisations are keen on recruits successful in team sports.

Case study

The operative's job (2)

The Toyota production process depends upon teams, usually of eight employees, working with a leader. Each has the responsibility and authority to design their own jobs. Working together, the members of the team discover ways to smooth the flow of production, to raise quality and to improve their working conditions.

The production system does not allow for a build up of stock but responds directly to market demand – what is called a 'pull system'. Since the shifts work set times an increase in the sales volume will reduce the time allowed for a team to produce a single unit of output. The time taken to produce one unit is called the 'takt time'. The obvious consequence would seem to be that the teams would need to work harder – but this is not so. It is policy not to increase the individual work loads of employees.

The solution is for teams to sit down and plan changes in procedure that will enable them to meet the new targets. They may modify their systems of work or modify their equipment. Only where this is not sufficient will they take a member from another team for the day.

The employees who move from team to team tend to be those with more experience, who in this way develop their flexibility and assume new responsibilities. It is claimed that the team system brings a spirit of close camaraderie as all members work towards a common goal.

Team spirit on a wider level is developed by the constant appearance of top executives in the workplace. They visit plant production lines, suppliers and dealers to see first hand what is going on, and act on what they see.

Source: Toyota Motor Company, Burnaston, Derbyshire

Activity

Refer back to the section on *Motivation* in Chapter 7. Which theories are at work in the examples above?

Consultants

Consultants will be brought into the business from outside to give specific advice. They are employed for their expertise in particular areas and are usually contracted for a specific job. Examples are:

- work study – planning the most efficient method of manufacture
- systems analysis – designing IT systems specifically for the organisation, for example, systems for accounting, management information (MIS), stock control
- marketing – providing market research.

Consultancy is attractive to firms as it provides specialist solutions whilst allowing the firm to carry on with business as normal. Although fees can be high, the projects are usually short-term and do not warrant recruiting a new member of staff.

In the USA consulting is a major growth area. Top firms are now providing solutions involving inter-disciplinary teams, sometimes of over a dozen people. Increasingly they are seeking larger, longer-term contracts, for example, Bain & Co stayed in McGraw Hill for years overseeing their projects ('hand-holding' to use the jargon).

In his book *'Troubleshooter'* John Harvey Jones, former head of ICI, gives an entertaining account of how a consultant can operate in UK manufacturing industry.

Case study

Employers are so concerned not to fall foul of employment legislation that some consultants are offering intensive training courses (around £150 for the day) on how to sack people legally. The Padgett–Thomson course work-book has headings such as 'What's so hard about goodbye?'.

Advisers

In some ways advisers are similar to consultants. The non-executive directors are brought in for their specialist advice. Eminent scholars perhaps with expertise in certain fields of research are often used in an advisory capacity.

Activities

Look at the advert for a human resources manager on page 302.

1 What level of management do you feel this post is at?
2 Which of Fayol's functions are mentioned (they may have other names)?
3 What link is there with the board of directors?
4 Why do former government ministers become non-executive directors of privatised companies? What do you think about this?
5 Why may a company prefer to bring in a consultant to look at computer systems rather than employ a full-time member of staff?

Working conditions and practices

Working conditions – some recent trends

Permanent (or long-term) contracts may be either full-time or part-time.

Of those in employment 5% of men and 40% of women are in permanent part-time employment. Overall a quarter of employees are now part-time and this is the fastest growing sector of the jobs market. Why is this?

The increasing number of women joining the workforce through economic necessity has increased the demand for flexible employment. The government-sponsored Labour Force Survey into employment trends showed that in the year to summer 1994 only 13% took part-time employment because they could not get a full-time job.

Case study

Sandra Hitching, director of human resources at Kelly Recruitment Services believes that 'There is much more emphasis and awareness of the working mother. Many companies now provide part-time, flexi-time and homeworking which enables mothers – and fathers – to have more balanced lives'.

A case in point is Lynne Turner, a qualified accountant who at 32 is senior finance manager of the Alliance and Leicester Building Society. She is the only woman in senior management working part-time – 3 days a week.

Julian Woodfall, human resources manager at the Alliance and Leister says 'Good people are hard to get, so we took the decision to ensure that part-time employees are not any worse off'. For the past 5 years the society has provided the same pension scheme and pro-rata holiday entitlement for full-time and part-time employees. Banks such as Nat West allow mothers to work only in term time.

European legislation now gives part-time workers the same compensation and dismissal rights as full-time employees.

Temporary (or fixed-term) contracts may be either full-time or part-time. Labour is one of the major costs of an organisation. At a time when labour is plentiful the short-term contract enables firms to employ staff on a flexible basis. As contracts expire staff can be 'shed' without the cost of redundancy. If there is a shortage of labour this policy will be less successful.

It is becoming common for firms to advertise for temporary contracts for management posts at all levels.

Whilst permanent part-time contracts may be ideal for many, the temporary contract may lead to insecurity.

Outsourcing

Outsourcing describes the process of buying in services from outside companies on a contract basis. Compulsory competitive tendering (CCT), where local authorities give services such as refuse collection to the lowest bidder, is part of this.

Flexible working practices

A number of working practices exist apart from the standard 9 to 5, 5-day week.

- **Job sharing:** it is becoming more common for some jobs, particularly in administration, to be shared by two or more employees. A full-time post may perhaps be filled by two workers, one working 2 days and the other 3 days a week. Where a good working relationship occurs it may be possible to vary days to suit individual needs; as long as the job is done the employer is happy. The advantage for the employer is that of employing part-time staff with the reduction in obligations and cost mentioned earlier. The employees benefit from flexibility. The efficient working of this practice can depend upon each of the job-sharers pulling their weight. Problems may arise if one is left to clear up problems caused by the other.
- **Shift work:** many organisations provide a continuous round the clock service. We are all aware of 24-hour access to: telephone services, the police, the fire service, hospitals and some public transport such as night buses. 'Twilight shifts', usually for women working in shops, are now widespread.

  Some manufacturing industries have worked shifts for many years as have the associated service industries of maintenance, transport and distribution. The 'Japanisation' of UK industry has spread the practice to suppliers. Just-in-time (JIT) stock control in which parts are delivered just as they are needed, means that where a manufacturer works shifts then so must the industries from which it draws its components. The CBI announced that many businesses closed down only for a day or so over Christmas 1994, rather than the usual week. In manufacturing this was largely the result of JIT production.

Shift work involves a certain amount of disruption to personal and family life and a number of studies have found that it is not ideal for employees. Usually the shifts are rotated with rest days in between to share the load of 'anti-social' hours.

- **Flexible working hours (flexi-time):** in some organisations employees are allowed, within limits and as long as they work a full week, to vary the time that they start and finish work. There are obvious advantages to the employee who has some control over the working day. This allows for personal arrangements or avoiding the rush hour and perhaps getting cheaper travel as a result. Flexi-time is often used by administrative staff dealing with paper-based work, for example, the accounts section at British Telecom.
- **Annual working hours:** some employers, such as travel agents and accounts departments, experience busy and slack periods. A set number of hours may be worked over the year, but weekly hours are varied to suit demand.
- **Work location:** whilst the idea of 'going to work' is likely to remain the norm, things are changing. There have always been those who are on the move: drivers, the sales team and field researchers for instance. Increasingly employees are able to work from home. For years the rag trade has employed homeworkers to sew garments on piece-rate, but it is new technology that is allowing homeworking for those who traditionally had to go to the office. The buzz word is 'teleworking'. The main growth will be the number of people working at home occasionally, perhaps to complete a particular report.

Case study

Teleworking

- John Ruscoe farms sheep in the Orkneys. Working from home, he also spends $7\frac{1}{2}$ hours per day working as a software designer for ICL.
- British Airways has a 57-strong team in New Delhi. Working in shifts they handle problems in the 20 reservations systems that BA has around the world. The work is performed in India because labour is cheap. As handling information can amount to 25% of a company's operating costs, there is potential for enormous savings in locating the work in developing countries.
- British Telecom has concentrated most of its directory enquiry staff in Scotland, Northern Ireland and the West Country. All operator and 999 calls from the City of London are answered in Margate on the Kent coast, an area with some of the worst unemployment in the UK. BT has also been experimenting with operators working from home.
- IBM France found that its sales force was able to spend 45% more time with its customers when they became a 'remote' workforce linked to the office by telecommunications networks. This meant that less office space was required and also fewer facilities, such as staff canteens.

Teleworking saves the employee the cost and time involved in travelling. It saves the employer money on office space and facilities, and because there is no natural end to the day, people tend to work longer. It saves society congestion on the roads.

Disadvantages for the employee are that the work is always there, the social aspect of work is taken away, and the cost of running the home may go up.

With improvements in international links via satellite, fibre optic cabling and more efficient software the 'information superhighway' is making it possible to perform data processing tasks from anywhere in the world. The World Bank has trailed the idea of security cameras in American shopping malls being monitored by people in Africa.

Activities

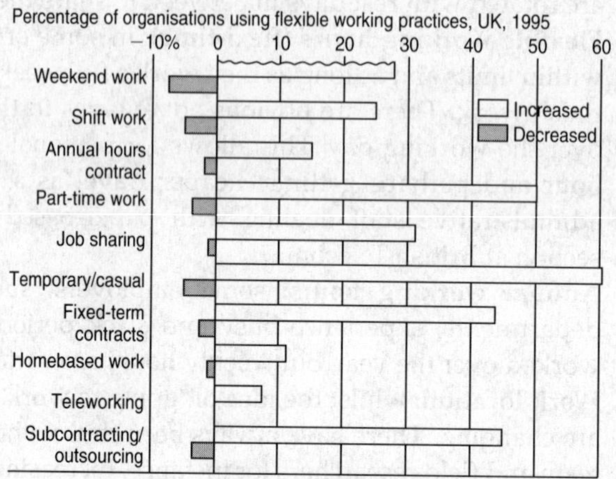

Source: Chris Brewster, Cranfield. Reproduced in the Guardian

1 What does the chart show about UK working practices?

2 Less than 50% of the UK working population has a full-time, long-term contract. Why do you think working practices have changed over recent years?

3 Are there positive benefits to employees from these changes? Give two examples mentioning practices shown in the chart.

The workplace revolution – reasons for change

The document below gives the reasons for change and suggests how this should be introduced.

Why may change be necessary?

Several pressures are acting together to oblige employers to consider introducing change. The main ones at present are:

- increased competition
- customer demand
- demographic and structural changes in the labour market
- threats and opportunities arising from completion of the Single European Market
- changing employee relations.

Employers are responding to these pressures in one or more important ways, for example by:

- introducing new technology
- developing new products
- developing new markets overseas
- introducing 'quality management' and/or 'customer care' programmes
- decentralising and/or restructuring the organisation
- introducing one or more forms of flexibility (see sections on Flexible working practices and Hours of Work).

Dealing with the human factor

The last of the factors above – the human factor – is the one most likely to be neglected, causing stress and resentment amongst the workforce. Positive steps must be taken to foster enthusiasm and commitment at an early stage and throughout the change process. Steps should include:

- ensuring that communications arrangements are effective, that they begin as early as possible and continue throughout the change process
- consulting with employee representatives and, if necessary, involving full time officials
- tapping the resources and ideas of employees through departmental meetings, task forces, working parties etc, especially in relation to job design.
- ensuring that adequate training takes place early enough to develop the necessary skills and competencies.

Through communication, consultation, involvement and training, all those affected can be encouraged to become parties to the change and be willing to try to make it work.

Source: *Management of Change*, ACAS

The workplace revolution – adapting to change

According to the survey below, change is not always managed effectively.

Case study

Rewriting the rules – *The Observer* Business/Gallup Survey (September 1994)

Several thousand managers were asked about the changing nature of their jobs. The survey found that:

- in 70% of organisations restructuring of management had taken place in the previous year
- staff cutbacks and cost-cutting programmes are usual – new managers are brought in if the current ones will not do the job
- jobs are less secure
- organisations are more concerned with cost than with staff development
- job satisfaction is diminishing
- empowerment is regarded cynically as a way of increasing the workload
- performance-related pay (PRP) has a de-motivating effect
  (note: these findings have been confirmed in research by the Institute of Management Studies)
- average weekly working hours are: 42 hours at the office plus 8.5 at home
- 49% had acquired a new career-related skill in the previous 6 months
- 20% have suffered stress-related illness in recent years.

The conclusion is that major changes are occurring in the contract between employer and individual. The old order has been broken up and a new one is not yet established.

Four groups were identified who were adapting differently to recent changes:

made-its: confident senior managers, happy with change because they carried it out

square pegs: traditional middle managers most affected and most unhappy with the changes

rising stars: confident, young and ambitious, they have only ever known change and hope to do well out of it

change leaders: middle managers unsettled by change but prepared to work hard and put it into effect.

Activities

1 Copy the table below and complete the second column.
2 Refer to the results of the Business/Gallup survey above. What do you conclude about the effectiveness of each of the changes? Add your comments in the third column.

Changes	Employer aims	Successful?
Performance-related pay		
Appraisal		
Trend towards part-time working and short-term contracts		
De-recognition of unions		
New working practices including: team-working, quality circles, empowerment, total quality management (TQM)		
Changes	**Government/EU aims**	**Successful?**
Health and Safety legislation		
Equal opportunities legislation		

3 Why do you feel that so many changes to employment conditions have been made in recent years? Do you think that they are desirable for the employees/the employers?

Stress linked to contract jobs culture

Chris Mihill
Medical Correspondent

STRESS at work will become a growing problem over the next 10 years as organisations increasingly hire contract or freelance workers rather than permanent staff, a leading organisational psychologist said yesterday.

"We are entering an era of insecurity which will have implications for all of UK plc. We are entering a freelance culture. We are creating an army out there of contract workers," said Cary Cooper, head of organisational behaviour at the University of Manchester Institute of Science and Technology.

Professor Cooper told an occupational psychology conference at Warwick University, organised by the British Psychological Society: "Within as little as 10 years many white collar professionals will be contract workers with a portfolio of jobs.

But we do not know what will happen to the organisations or to individuals from the point of view of health or productivity."

Some industries, such as the media, already relied heavily on freelances or short-term contract workers and this would become the norm for most businesses, increasingly affecting white collar professionals rather than production line staff, he said. Mr Cooper said the psychological impact of this change on workers had not been studied nor had the implications for the productivity of organisations which employed them. Mr Cooper said excessive stress at work had major effects on health, absenteeism, alcoholism and mental illness, but many managers were not yet convinced that stress was detrimental to productivity.

Many companies which employed stress counsellors did so only for cosmetic reasons. Managers needed to become less autocratic, to manage by reward instead of punishment and to accept that dual-earning families – and two-thirds of women now work – needed more flexible work patterns. There was also a need to train people in marketing themselves as freelance employees.

The recent court case involving stress at work of social work manager John Walker was a landmark decision which would force employers to take the problem seriously.

"Never mind lip service about staff being the most valuable resource, this case was about the duty of care to manage people as human beings," Mr Cooper said. "There are two or three dozen other cases in the pipeline. Firms are going to have to pay, not just talk about these issues."

Source: *The Guardian*, 4 January 1995

Activities

1. According to the article on page 364 what is causing stress to workers?
2. Look at the employment pages in the press. Note the terms offered by the prospective employers. Are there many temporary contracts?
3. 'Milkmen to read gas meters', ran a newspaper headline. What advantage is there for British Gas in subcontracting meter reading?
4. Does your organisation subcontract (security guards, canteen staff perhaps)? What is the advantage of not having these people on the payroll?

The current debate on human resources management

In order to respond to change, organisations need to remain flexible. This means that employees can no longer expect a job for life, and that the jobs they do have will be subject to change. In profitable, well-established organisations that have built up a distinct culture over the years, human resources management is able to perform an effective role in developing the potential of employees to the good of both the employee and the company. Elsewhere human resources management is caught in the middle of the traditional conflict between the needs of the employer and of the employee. Many of the new management initiatives have attempted to reconcile these opposites but in some companies, particularly those newly privatised, employees feel suspicious and confused. As Tom Keenoy of Cardiff Business School has written: 'Employees are to be both self-interested and to work in teams; to reduce costs whilst improving quality; to be flexible (and disposable) while remaining committed; to be enterprising and empowered but endure a seemingly constant process of performance auditing'. The need to be flexible can create a feeling of insecurity.

The human resources section has a difficult job in the 90s. It is an arm of senior management whose policies frequently make employees' lives harder. Yet it needs the employees to trust that this is for the good of all. It is true that in recent years industrial disputes are less frequent, but this may be more to do with reduced trade union power and with job insecurity than with good industrial relations.

Within the personnel profession there is a serious debate as to the way forward. One suggestion is that the name 'Human Resources' may itself be a problem. 'After all you can do a whole lot of things to resources that you cannot do to people' says Dr Ian Cunningham in his book *Wisdom and Strategic Learning* (McGraw-Hill).

Another concern is that there is too much concentration on the short term. This puts pressure on people and is not always in the best interests of the business. Managers on short-term contracts and performance-related pay need results now in order to keep their jobs. They are less likely to put time and investment into research and development or long-term projects which will bring results in some years time.

Assignment 8.1
How does it work?

This assignment develops knowledge and understanding of the following elements:
4.2 Investigate job roles and changing working conditions

It supports development of the following core skills:
Communication 3.1, 3.2, 3.4
Information technology 3.1, 3.2, 3.3

Contact an organisation in your locality which is a company, for example, a bank, supermarket, travel agent or football club. (You may work for one part-time.)

Your tasks

1. Either make an appointment or write to the personnel/human resources section with a view to examining the job roles in that organisation performed by: a given manager, a supervisor, an operative.
   Research the details of the directors – these will be available from Companies' House (see page 744) if not from the company.
   Make a report detailing the roles played in the organisation by these people. (Job specifications and advertisements are often available.)
2. Describe the following: flexi-time, shift-work, job sharing, home working.
   Explain the advantages and disadvantages to both organisation and employee. Does the organisation you have approached use these? For each explain where it is used and give details. For any not used:
   (i) say whether or not it would be possible to use these
   (ii) if it would not be possible, explain why not.
3. Give reasons why working conditions are subject to change. Provide an in-depth explanation for one of these reasons (illustrate from your organisation if appropriate).
4. Produce a plan for implementing the change that you have described. Who would have responsibility for implementing this?

Recruitment and selection of staff

Human resources management is concerned with identifying needs for new staff and recruiting the appropriate people. If it is to be effective this process requires careful planning.

General procedures

Recruitment and selection is carried out as a joint exercise by the managers of the section requiring staff and the Human Resources Department.

Once the vacancy has been identified, the recruitment process consists of the following steps:

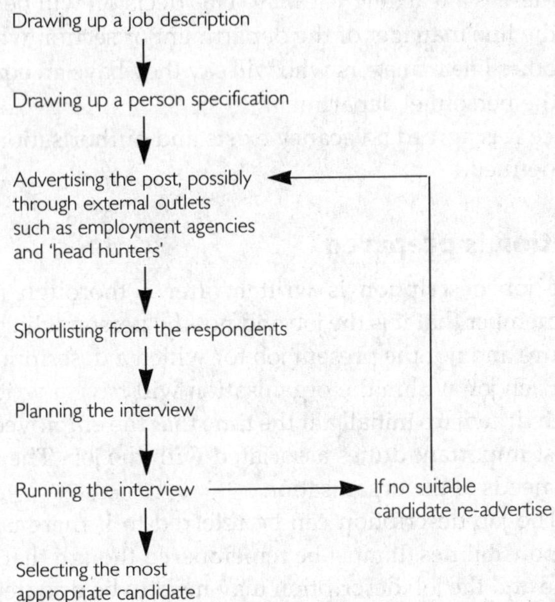

In the rest of this chapter we will look at the recruitment process in detail.

Activity

The Southfleet College of Further Education needs to appoint a new Lecturer in Business Studies. The Lecturer's contract will run from 1 September next, and an appointment will need to be made by the end of May. This is to allow the person appointed to give the required period of notice from her/his present job.

You work for the Personnel Department and have been asked by your manager to co-ordinate the recruitment process. The advertisement, job description and person specification have already been prepared by the Head of Business Studies and approved by your section. The date is 1 March.

Your job is to timetable the recruitment and selection procedure. Give exact dates for each important stage. These dates must be realistic – people need to be given notice as they may travel considerable distances.

Identify the vacancy

Vacancies can occur because people:

- have left the organisation through retirement, or changing jobs;
- have been dismissed;
- have been promoted;
- additional staff are needed for expansion.

Where a person has left a post questions which must be asked are:

- Is the post now needed? This is particularly important when staff resource budgets are tight and cutbacks are being made.

- Should the duties and responsibilities of the post be changed? A vacancy gives the opportunity to re-examine a job. Many jobs change over time because of, for example, new methods of working, changes in the external environment, the introduction of new technology. The decisions as to whether the vacancy exists will normally be made by senior managers, for instance a Head Teacher or Principal will decide if there is a teaching vacancy. This decision will be made after consultation with:
- the line manager of the department or section where the vacancy arose;
- other line managers who will say they have an equally valid claim to any new posts;
- the personnel department.

Once it is agreed a vacancy exists and authorisation is given to fill it then the job must be defined.

The job description is prepared

The job description is written after a thorough job analysis has been undertaken. Remember that it is the job and not the person which is being analysed, and that it is the future and not the present job for which a description is needed.

Each job within the organisation will have a written **job description**. This will have been drawn up initially at the time that the employee was appointed and will set out the most important duties associated with the job. The aim is to make sure that the job fits the needs of the organisation.

The job description can be referred to if there is any dispute about an individual's responsibilities. It must be remembered though that the nature of a job will change over time and the job description may need to be updated periodically.

A job description is shown in Assignment 8.3. It will include:

- job title
- grade
- department/section
- location
- responsible to (manager's title)
- responsible for (staff for whom the post holder is responsible)
- purpose of the job/post – this should show in general terms what the job is about
- duties/responsibilities – this should briefly list the main duties and responsibilities of the post. These may be listed in order of priority, beginning with the most important. This section may be subdivided into types of duties
- qualifications/skills/experience – not always included. Where it does appear it gives only those items that are essential and necessary, for example where a clean driving licence is required, or a salesperson dealing regularly with customers in Poland 'must be able to speak Polish fluently'
- special notes/background, for example, this section could show whether the job is noisy or hazardous or how many people work in the section.
- references to show date compiled and name of compiler – useful when updating.

The person specification is prepared

The **person specification** is a document showing the skills, qualifications, aptitudes and abilities which a person will require in order to successfully perform a particular job in the organisation. It will list those features which are essential and absolutely necessary, and may additionally include other qualities which would be desirable though are not essential.

A person specification is shown in Assignment 8.3. It will include:

1. Physical characteristics – For example, someone joining the Police or Fire Service should be a minimum height with good vision.
2. Experience – Is previous experience absolutely necessary or will training be given?
3. Qualifications – Many jobs require a specific qualification which indicates a level of skill and training, for example, 'Lorry Driver Needed, must have a clean HGV (Heavy Goods Vehicle) licence'. Many skilled craft jobs require a specific qualification. Formal educational and training qualifications may include: GCSE, A level, RSA, BTEC, CGLI, LCCI, NVQ, GNVQ, BA, BSc, MA, MSc, MPhil, PhD. There is also a range of professional qualifications.
4. Aptitude – Put here any special abilities or qualifications that are needed, for example, 'the candidate should be flexible and adaptable, able to work under pressure, but remain calm in this very busy office'. This was part of an advert for a travel booking clerk with a national holiday tour operator.
5. Motivation – You will find phrases such as: Are you 'ambitious', 'a go-getter', 'a self starter, 'able to work on your own'? Do you 'thrive on change and innovation'? Can you 'make your own decisions'? All these have appeared in adverts for people needed to sell financial services.
6. Special circumstances – Perhaps the person will need to spend time away from home, to work unsociable hours or to be prepared to relocate if necessary. Any special circumstances need to be mentioned.

Job descriptions and person specifications do not always follow the same rigid format given above and, depending upon the job in question may not have information under all of the categories that we have listed. On some occasions an employer will send out information to a job applicant that is a combination of the two documents.

Activities

1 Using the headings above prepare a job description for yourself as a student or trainee on this course.

2 If you are at work check your job description and, if appropriate, show how your job has changed by rewriting it.

3 Use the headings above to create a person specification for someone wanting to join your course; or
prepare a person specification for someone applying for your job.

Attracting the right people

Internal vacancies

The organisation may already have the right people with the right skills to do the job, particularly if the training and development programme has been effective. In this case they may appoint internally. This may of course leave a vacancy elsewhere.

Vacancies can be advertised within the organisation by putting advertisements on prominent company notice boards and in company news letters, bulletins and newspapers

The main advantages of making internal appointments are that it is cheap, fast, and avoids many of the problems of training and induction. However, there are disadvantages. Existing staff may feel they have an automatic right to promotion whether or not they are competent. Also without new skills and ideas brought in from outside, an organisation could be resistant to change.

External vacancies

It is usually necessary to make an external appointment and some organisations are compelled to advertise all posts externally. In this case the process must be carefully planned to deliver the appropriate applicants. Advertising, together with the administrative costs of despatching application forms, checking returned forms, shortlisting and interviewing, often with senior staff, can be time consuming and expensive.

A firm will want to be sure that it attracts the right sort of people for the job. If it does not then the whole recruitment process will have to be repeated whilst the business carries on with a staff shortage. There are a number of ways of looking for staff outside the organisation:

- Job Centres, once notified, will do the 'recruiting' by sending suitable people for interview and selection. The service is free and most useful for advertising skilled, semi-skilled, clerical and manual jobs. They also keep registers for professional people.
- Employment agencies are private sector companies whose aim is to make a profit by selling a service. They are found in many high streets.
- Educational establishments such as schools and colleges can be a useful source of potential employees. Companies can either use the centre's careers services directly or participate at careers events.
- Management recruitment consultants are private sector agencies used to recruit senior management. Look at the 'appointments' section of a quality Sunday newspaper where you will find adverts for 'Chief Executive', 'International Marketing Director', etc. These have generally been placed by specialist recruitment companies.
- Sometimes senior staff are recruited directly by executive search consultants often called 'head-hunters'. A firm wishing to engage someone with special qualities for a top position will give the job description to the consultant, who will to seek out possible candidates to approach. The consultant is able to do this by being 'in the know'. Often the 'target' will be working for a rival firm so the approach will be made in confidence. The head-hunter will charge a large commission for a successful appointment but there are no advertising costs. The whole process is similar to that of a football manager looking for a top player.

Getting a head

Lester B. Korn of Korn/Ferry International says 'We are hunters, skilful hunters in search of talented heads'.

In the USA one in five top executive jobs are filled by such firms. The process of head hunting has given rise to a group of 'corporate job-hoppers' who will move from one company to another for an extra few thousand dollars. Top executives get worried if the phone does not ring four times a year; as it suggests that they are no longer in demand.

- Advertising in the press is a common way of attracting staff. With a situation of high unemployment, people are motivated to read advertisements, but there is the need to place these where the 'right' people will see them. This means selecting the right newspaper, magazine or even commercial radio station – and being prepared to pay. The advertisement will need to:

a attract attention and arouse interest among the right people;
b state what is being offered – at least in general terms;
c state what is required by the employer – such as experience, qualifications, ability;
d state what the next step is – how the candidate applies.

Activity

How would the following be recruited:
a a new bass player for a top band?
b a new business studies teacher for a college?
c a stores worker for a builders' merchant?
d a chief accountant?
e head of BBC Radio 4?

Responding to advertisements

There are a number of ways of asking people to respond to an advertisement.

Table 8.2 Responding to advertisement instructions

Possible instruction	What the applicant does
'Send for further details' – here the advertisement itself will give only general details	Writes or telephones and will be sent: the job description; the person specification; an application form; information about the post and organisation (may include an organisation chart, equal opportunities policy and so on).
'Write a letter of application supported by a CV' in this case the advertisement will have given precise details of the job and what is required of the applicant (these will be the job description and person specification in brief)	Writes a letter matching it closely to the requirements of the advertisement and includes a CV highlighting relevant experience as well as general educational information.
'Please send CV'	Some firms want only the CV as this will include all relevant details. No letter of application or supporting statement is required.
Write a letter of application, CVs are not accepted'	Some firms will **not** accept CVs. These can be professionally produced and, whilst not telling untruths do not necessarily reflect the applicant's communications skills.
'Written applications only'	Some firms want to see how applicants write.

Activity

a Look at the advert for Network SouthEast overleaf. Identify where each part of the advert comes from, such as the job description, the person specification and contract of employment.
b Is there evidence of equal opportunities commitment? (What do you notice about the driver in the drawing?)
c Contact your local paper and find the cost of placing adverts of this size in the classified section of the paper.

Train to drive on one of Europe's largest networks.

LONDON/ORPINGTON/DARTFORD AREAS

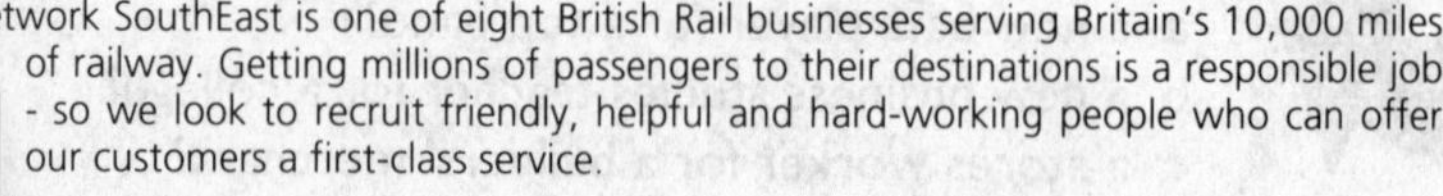

Network SouthEast is one of eight British Rail businesses serving Britain's 10,000 miles of railway. Getting millions of passengers to their destinations is a responsible job - so we look to recruit friendly, helpful and hard-working people who can offer our customers a first-class service.

As long as you're enthusiastic, and we're convinced you're the right person for this responsible job, you won't need formal qualifications. You'll spend two months learning the basic technical and practical skills before accompanying a Train Driver as part of the crew. Then, in about 12 - 18 months, when you've completed the rest of your training, opportunities exist for progressing to driver.

Being a highly safety related job, you'll need to reach our medical standard for which you need to be aged 18-45, and 5'4" - 6'4" tall with weight in proportion. You should also have good hearing and eyesight plus normal colour vision, and although you might still be able to join us if you wear glasses (contact lenses cannot be worn), we'll test your eyesight without them to make sure it's up to the standard we're looking for.

In fact, you'll be required to attend assessment days, so that we can carry out a specially designed programme of psychometric tests - we're extremely selective, and we'll have to make sure you've got the aptitude and potential to become a good Train Driver.

And if you have, you'll enjoy a great package. As well as pay of £153.10 a week, plus London Allowance, we'll offer you generous holidays, free and reduced rate rail travel, an excellent contributory pension scheme and real chances for promotion. After initial training you will be required to work shifts and at weekends.

As women are currently under-represented in this area, they are especially encouraged to apply.

For an application form, phone 0171-928 5151 and quote reference LB18. A limited number of applications will be accepted.

British Rail - working towards equal opportunities.

Reproduced with kind permission from Network SouthEast and Barkers Advertising

The application form

Many, but not all, businesses use an **application form**. The aim is to find out about candidates by asking for information in a structured way. One great advantage of all such forms is that the information can be processed conveniently. Since the right questions are asked the relevant information will be there. It can easily be found and, if necessary, it can be put onto a computerised database with fields set up to correspond with those of the form. The standardisation also means that comparison is easier.

Information normally required on an application form includes:

- personal details – name, address, telephone number, date of birth;
- education and qualifications;
- declaration of a criminal record;
- experience/employment history;

- references – applicants will need to supply names and addresses of usually two referees who will be able to support the candidate's application by confirming that they are of good character and are suitable for the job;
- other information – this allows applicants to write a statement in support of their application. They should state why they are interested in the job and why they feel that they will be able to perform it well. This section also gives the employer a chance to see the style, clarity, tone and use of language in the candidate's writing.

Design of a typical application form An application form must be well designed (see Figure 8.2) and 'user friendly' for both the applicant and the organisation. It must have sufficient space, particularly for surnames and forenames, comply with equal opportunities legislation, be well laid out and easy to read and understand. Remember very few people have perfect vision. In addition it must give sufficient space for people to demonstrate their ability to do the job.

Ideally there should be different forms for different levels and grades of staff. An application form for a part-time, unskilled job should not have a half page for 'qualifications', whereas this may be appropriate for a managerial post.

The form should ideally be of A4 size and no more than four pages long. The spaces should allow for answers to be typed. The present trend for 'small squares' whilst ideal for computer input, makes this very difficult.

An application form is relatively easy to fill in, though it is important to draft out answers in advance. The information provided may form the basis of the contract of employment and incorrect responses may invalidate the contract.

The final section asking for a supporting statement needs thought. It is here that the candidate sells her/himself. If everything else is satisfactory then this is the chance to grab the employer's attention.

When an application form is returned, a covering letter saying that the form is enclosed should be included as a matter of courtesy.

References

A **reference** is a written statement about a person's character and ability by a third party, known as a 'referee'.

An employer will normally require the names of two or perhaps three references. References will only be requested for candidates who are short-listed and are being considered for the post and will then only be read if the candidate is being considered for appointment.

References should always be read with extreme caution, both for what they say and what they leave out. Remember, referees are people whom the candidate has chosen to include and it is courteous to confirm with the referee that his or her name may be used. A referee will not be named if they are going to say anything detrimental about the candidate. For this reason an employer would be suspicious of a candidate who did not include his or her present employer. Occasionally it is actually stated that the present employer must be included. Sometimes a referee may decline saying 'perhaps someone else would be better for you'.

An employer will assume that a referee is honest, but sometimes referees will have their own motives for writing in a particular way. An excellent reference, for example, could be written about a person whom the employer wants to get rid of, while a poor reference might be given about an employee whom the employer wants to keep. It is for this reason that some employers now state that references may be discussed with the candidate.

Application Form

No.

Job applied for:

Where did you hear of this vacancy?

Personal details

Title Mr Mrs Ms Miss

Delete as necessary

Surname

Full First Names

Address

Date of Birth:

Age:

Home Telephone No:

Office Telephone No:

Can we ring you at work?

Do you have a valid driving licence?

Medical details

Do you suffer from any illness which may affect your work? (If Yes please give details below)

References

Please give names and addresses of two people to whom we may apply for references.

Reference 1 (present or last employer)

Name, address and Telephone No:

Reference 2

Name, address and Telephone No:

What is your connection with this person?

May we approach the above individuals without further reference to you? Yes☐ No☐

Availability

When are you free for interview?

When would you be free to take up a new appointment?

New River Housing Association
Pump House Road
Harrogate
North Yorkshire
HG1 2HW

Education and Qualifications

Please give details of your education and qualifications obtained:

Schools/Colleges etc.	From	To	Examinations passed/Qualifications obtained.

Details of any further qualifications obtained or relevant courses attended.

Figure 8.2 Sample application form

Present employment

(Or if now unemployed, details of last employment.)

Name and address:

From: To:

Present salary:

Job title:

Type of business:

Please give a brief description of the job and your responsibilities. Please give your reasons for seeking new employment.

Employment history

Please give details of your previous employment (start from the most recent)

Name and address:	From:	To:	Salary:	Brief description of business and your job:

Other information

Please use this space to explain why you are interested in this position and why you feel able to do the job. We are interested in the type of persor you are as well as your experience and qualifications.
(Please continue on a separate sheet if you wish.)

I declare that the information provided in this application is to the best of my knowledge correct.
I also declare that I am not related to an existing employee of New Islington & Hackney Housing Association.
(Requirement of the 1980 Housing Act.)

Signed__________ Date__________

EQUAL OPPORTUNITY IN EMPLOYMENT - QUESTIONNAIRE

The Association would be grateful if you would answer these questions and tick the appropriate boxes.

1 Post applied for __________

2 Where did you see the post advertised? __________

3 Are you Female ☐ Male ☐

4 Are you a registered disabled person? Yes ☐ No ☐
If Yes please state the nature of your disability

5 How would you describe your ethnic origin?

- Indian Sub-continent (eg Pakistani, Bangladeshi, Indian, Sri Lankan) ☐
- Caribbean ☐
- African ☐
- Asian other (eg Chinese, Vietnamese, Thai, Malaysian) ☐
- British ☐
- European other ☐
- Irish ☐
- Jewish ☐
- Turkish ☐
- Greek Cypriot ☐
- Turkish Cypriot ☐
- Other. Please specify __________
- Combination ☐
- Declined ☐

6 Do you consider youself to be: Black ☐ White ☐ Other ☐ Mixed ☐

7 Date __________

If you do not wish to answer the questions, your application will not be affected

Please return this form with your application, in an envelope marked clearly

New River Housing Association
Pump House Road
Harrogate
North Yorkshire
HG1 2HW

Figure 8.2 (continued) Sample application form

The letter of application

Sometimes there is no application form, candidates are simply invited to write a **letter of application**. This will state that the candidate is applying for the job and give the relevant details of experience and qualifications. It will include a supporting statement saying what qualities are being offered by the candidate and why it is felt that he or she will be an excellent employee.

Such letters require more skill than filling in an application form.

The curriculum vitae (CV)

Some employers ask for a CV. This should be accompanied by a letter of introduction stating which job is being applied for and giving relevant references (see Figure 8.3).

The term **curriculum vitae** means literally 'course of life'; it is the history of a person's achievements. A job applicant will frequently need to send a CV along with the letter of application or the application form.

A carefully produced CV and letter of application is the means by which an applicant for a job will sell themselves to the employer. It is often the first contact with the employer and if it makes no impact then there will be no interview and no job.

The CV should contain relevant factual information without going into details of what a person hopes to do; neither should it be unnecessarily lengthy. It should be geared to the particular job requirements. Word processing makes it possible to adapt the essential facts conveniently but some organisations may ask for the document to be hand written.

The CV should be between one and three sheets long, certainly no longer, though it may contain a note to say that additional information is available if required. It will include:

- **Personal details** Name, address, (including postcode), telephone number, (including STD code), date of birth, correct age, whether male or female (if this is not clear from your name).
- **Education and qualifications** List qualifications with the highest first, where grades are quoted be consistent. Ensure that the employer knows what level the qualifications are.
- **Employment History** List employment in reverse chronological order, the most recent first. Include: the name of the employer and the nature of the business; dates of employment in months and years; summary of main duties and achievements; details of any machines operated; more details about the current post than others and adequately explain any gaps between employment.
- **Other information** Hobbies: make sure you can talk about these if asked, that you actually do them regularly and that they are positive – 'watching television' may not impress; indicate any skills which you have acquired or training associated; mention any responsibility, teamwork or organisational skills involved; balance the interests that you list and do not put in too many.

  Extra information where it is relevant: you may include, for example, languages spoken (if fluent), computer literacy, or a clean driving licence.

Leave out:

- medical details – unless to show that you are now fully fit again;
- reason for leaving employment;
- salary details – unless specifically requested;
- references – unless requested.

Guidelines on presentation

- The CV should be written in your own style.
- It should be free of spelling or grammatical errors and smudges.
- Sentences should be short, but it should not be in note form.
- Avoid gimmicks, these may be eye-catching but do not impress the employer.
- It should be hand-written, if this is requested, otherwise it may be typewritten or word processed.
- Use A4 paper, white or of a pale shade.
- It should be well spaced so as to be clearly read. Styles may vary but layout must be consistent.
- Including a photograph is popular in the USA but is not recommended in the UK.

Give a good impression

- Be seen as a nice person, not bitter, or self-centred, but positive and caring.
- Arouse interest if possible by adding a little flair – at least don't be boring!

Here is an example of a CV with a covering letter.

75c Graceland Road
Salisbury
Wiltshire WS23 7RL

Ms J. McShane
Personnel Department
Sportsworld Films
Wilton
Wiltshire WT1 4JJ
25 March 199-

Dear Ms McShane

I would like to apply for the position of administrative assistant as advertised in the Guardian yesterday.

As you can see from my curriculum vitae I have had 2 years' experience of administrative work in the Civil Service and I have had the opportunity of dealing with a wide range of people on a daily basis. Although I have no specific IT qualifications, I do have the necessary keyboard skills and knowledge of the software that you use.

I am most interested in the situation that you are offering and look forward to hearing from you.

Yours sincerely

William Jamal

William Jamal

CURRICULUM VITAE

WILLIAM JAMAL
75c Graceland Road, Salisbury, Wiltshire WS23 7RL
Tel: 0722 0030
Date of Birth: 25.5.73 Age 21

Qualifications:

June 1991	National Diploma in Business & Finance
June 1989	GCSEs in English Language, English Literature, Mathematics, Art, History, French

Education:	
Sept 89-June 91	Greenwood College of Further Education, Salisbury
Sept 84-June 89	Wallace Road Secondary School, Bristol
Sept 78-June 84	Clifton Street School, Bristol
Employment:	
Aug 91-present	Administrative Officer, Department of Social Security. I have been in this post for just over two years during which I have worked in a range of jobs within the department. These have included visiting the premises of employers with the inspector as well as the work within the section. My current responsibilities involve dealing with queries relating to National Insurance contributions, assessing liability for payments and interviewing members of the public. This demands knowledge, flexibility and tact. In the course of my employment I have gained experience of both manual and computerised office systems. As well as meeting the public I am in frequent contact with other offices within the UK.
Leisure interests:	I enjoy most sports, though I am particularly keen on swimming and cricket. I read a great deal, both novels and poetry; I particularly admire the work of Derek Walcott

Figure 8.3 Example of word processed letter and word processed CV

CV writing agencies

For between £30 and £50 a CV writing agency will produce a CV for you. In this case it is important to make sure that they have all the relevant information, and also to check what they have written.

Activity

There is some evidence that the current trend is away from CVs and towards application forms. Can you think why managers in charge of recruitment may prefer the application form?

The steps in selection

Shortlisting

There may be a large number of applications for a particular job. Not all of the candidates will be suitable and it is inefficient, as well as unfair on these candidates, to interview them all under the circumstances. **Shortlisting** involves working through the initial long list of applicants with the intention of selecting a smaller group – the short list – from which the successful candidate will be chosen

Shortlisting begins with the key people who drew up the person specification using the items on this as the selection criteria and checking each application form, CV or supporting statement against these. This should be a completely impartial process and applications should be judged solely on merit. Even where an applicant is known to the shortlisting panel, perhaps they already work for the organisation, only the quality of the written application should be taken into account.

The mechanics of shortlisting are straightforward; every person's application form must be examined and checked to see if all the criteria have been met. If they have, the person should be shortlisted. If they have not, the person should be rejected. Some employers award points for each criteria on the basis of the quality of the answers.

If there are still too many people a second shortlisting may need to be carried out on the basis of the points procedure.

Equal opportunities legislation must be adhered to whether or not organisations proclaim 'We are an equal opportunities employer'. Applicants who feel that they have been unfairly dealt with may appeal to the industrial tribunal, though it may be difficult to prove that discrimination has taken place.

Testing

In addition to assessing a candidate's application form or CV and giving an interview, many organisations now give some form of test as well. Some examples are:

- Practical work tests – these are given to find out if the candidate really can do the job they claim. Word processing operators, for instance, could be asked to input a test piece to check for speed and accuracy; teachers are often asked to give a demonstration lesson to the interview panel.
- Manual dexterity tests – many jobs, both skilled and unskilled require a high degree of handling skills particularly when any mistake could result in danger or damage. Job applicants may, for example, be asked to change the fuse in an electric plug. Where the job requires using machinery in a routine way then the applicant may be asked to perform the operation several times to ensure that there is no difficulty.
- Medical tests – many jobs require a medical examination to find out if the candidate is fit for the job. This may be a general test or relate specifically to the job. People with sensitive skin may not be able to work with certain materials. Also important is the need to prevent claims for compensation. For instance, a person could claim that their eyes had deteriorated as a result of doing a particular task. If their vision was tested before the job was started a realistic assessment of the claim could be made.
- Intelligence tests – these test a candidate's reasoning ability. You may be familiar with these from your schooldays. Questions might be of the form:
  What is the missing number in this series – 2, 7, 6, 11, 10, 15?
- Psychometric and personality tests – these assess an applicant's attitude and mental ability for doing a particular job, for example, concentration and quick reactions may be significant. Look at the Network SouthEast Advert on page 372.
- Communications and numeracy tests – these are often given to candidates applying for clerical or administrative posts, where these skills are important, although they are sometimes given where their importance is less obvious.

Case study

A testing time

The Post Office's Psychological Services Unit has devised a series of tests. Examples include: add 15 to 92, multiply 19 by 7, subtract £761.82 from £1,115.76.

There is a spelling test and a test in following instructions. One question asks candidates to 'write down the letters VWXYZ with the second and fourth letters interchanged'.

Every year over 100,000 candidates apply to the Post Office. Between a third and a half do not pass the tests.

Psychometric testing was first used in the USA in the 1930s as a means of choosing or promoting staff from senior management downwards. Today 75% of UK organisations who employ over 1000 people use these tests, many of which are bought 'off the peg' from consultants. For such tests to be valuable the tests must be appropriate and the results correctly interpreted.

In October 1994 Anglian Water announced 900 redundancies. The company had used a psychometric test to decide which staff to lay-off. The employees' union Unison claimed that the same test was used for both technical and clerical staff – jobs which need very different qualities. Many occupational psychologists share the concern. To curb abuses, the British Psychological Society has laid down a set of guidelines for training.

Source: Adapted from *The Observer*

Interviewing

An interview is a face-to-face meeting between representatives of the employer and the applicant. It is usually held as the final stage of the recruitment process to decide which of the shortlisted candidates should be employed.

There are two basic types of interview:

- a one-to-one interview where there is one interviewer and one interviewee;
- a panel interview where there are several interviewers and one interviewee.

Careful planning in advance is required:

- The panel should be selected so as to enable a fair hearing for each candidate. Consideration may be given to having male and female interviewers, representatives of different sections of the organisation and staff with equal opportunities responsibilities.
- Questions should be agreed in advance so that each candidate is treated in the same way.
- The selection criteria should be agreed in advance. There may be a marking system for replies.

During the interview:

- The candidate should be helped to feel at ease.
- The panel should listen fairly to the candidate's replies.
- Candidates should be given the opportunity to demonstrate their strengths.
- Where candidates are known to the panel, perhaps because they already work at the organisation, this should not be taken into account at the interview.

'But I've only applied for a part-time clerical assistant's post.'

How should an interview be conducted?

A ten-point plan for a good interviewer

Before the interview:

1 The interviewer should check that the interview arrangements are satisfactory:
- Is the seating adequate?
- Is the lighting satisfactory? Remember it should not shine directly at a person's face.
- Is the room quiet and private? All interviews should be strictly private.
- Has it been ensured that the interview will not be disrupted?
- Has access for candidates with a physical disability been checked?

2 Check through the job description and the person specification. The interviewer must be totally familiar with these as they act as the basis of the interview.

3 Read the application forms again, note any special questions or queries, for instance 'Why did you change school/job in 1991?' or 'What happened between July 1990 and August 1991; you don't appear to have done anything?' – always check dates.

4 Write down the agreed questions that every candidate will have to answer – these are called control questions. This will help the interviewer make comparisons between candidates. They could include:
- Why did you apply for this job?
- Why did you apply to this organisation?
- Why do you think you can do this course?

If it is a panel interview, the members of the panel should agree in advance the sequence and topics to be covered by each interviewer.

Starting the interview:

5 At the beginning of the interview every candidate should be welcomed by name – pronunciation should be checked – and invited to sit down. If water is available it should be indicated. The purpose of the interview should be explained and if there are other panel members these should be introduced.

6 Begin the interview with an 'open' or easy question which should help the interviewees to relax. They will probably be nervous and allowances must be made

for this. Try to avoid asking yes/no questions as the interviewer will get very little information back. Ask something the interviewee can talk about such as 'Can you tell us about the work you did in the accounts section?'
Never ask questions which break the equal opportunities legislation.
(Be prepared to summarise what has been said.)

7 The interviewer should always stay calm and uninvolved and be ready to listen. Be prepared to follow up answers.
'Why did you like working out the trial balance for the company?' or 'Do you enjoy working with figures?' (Could the answer be YES or NO?!)

8 Keep observing the candidate. Watch for body language signals such as:
- the way they sit
- arm and hand movements
- eye movements and eye contact (do they look at you or away from you?)
- voice.

9 At the end of the interview the interviewer should:
- thank the candidate;
- find out if the candidate has any questions or wants to add anything;
- find out when the candidate could start work;
- ask whether the candidate still wants the job;
- tell the candidate how and when they will be told the result of the interview.

After the interview:

10 The candidates should leave feeling that they have had a fair hearing.
Make any notes that might be needed in order to make your decision on which candidate to choose.
Remember an interview is private and all proceedings should be confidential. In other words don't talk about the candidates outside the interview room or to those who are not involved in the process.
Internal candidates who fail interviews should be given the opportunity of a follow-up meeting to explain where they went wrong.

Interviewee techniques

It is vital to prepare for an interview. Remember that you have got this far because of your original application, now it's down to the impression that you make. The object of the exercise is to show you strengths. Points to consider are:

- appearance: you need to reflect the image that the employer is seeking.
- manner: first impressions do count, so wait to be asked to sit down. Speak clearly and look at the panel; ask for clarification if you do not understand a question. Be polite but never be familiar. The panel will be friendly, but it is a formal event.
- achievements: these will already be on your letter, application form or CV. Be prepared to talk positively about these and to expand on what you have written. You should always keep a copy to re-read before the interview. Make your achievements relevant to the job in hand or even a basis for future development.
- personality: your personality will come across – that is the point of an interview. It is natural to be nervous and some allowance will be made; nevertheless the panel will expect you to have made preparations and so be able to answer reasonable questions courteously.
- ambitions: you may be asked 'What do you hope to be doing a year from now?' Be ready for this; ambition shows drive and commitment.

- presence of mind: normally you will be asked to think on the spot about a particular job-related issue. A prospective teacher may be asked 'How would you reflect the school's equal opportunities policy in your lessons?' At this point it helps if you have read the documentation that the employer has sent you! The panel assume that you are genuinely interested in the job and that you will be aware enough of issues to provide an informed answer.
- asking questions: near the end of the interview a panel member will often say 'Do you want to ask us anything?' Have some questions prepared to show that you have thought positively about the job.
- the job offer: 'Are you a serious candidate for this job? If we were to offer you the post would you accept?' You should be ready for this question, especially if you have made a number of other job applications.

Activity

SOFTWARE QUALITY ASSURANCE MANAGER

Milton Keynes

Keystroke plc is a rapidly growing company producing integrated pricing and risk management systems for the financial markets.

The company has maintained expansion throughout the recession and is now seeking a person with suitable skill and experience to take responsibility for software quality at all levels: specification, design, testing, release and maintenance.

The successful candidate will possess:
- organisational ability
- good communication skills
- inter-personal skills
- preferably degree level education.
- general managerial responsibilities.

He or she also needs a minimum of two years' experience of:
- managing software development lifecycles
- project management
- general managerial responsibilities.

Salary will be negotiable depending upon qualification and experience.

If your experience matches our requirements please write in confidence enclosing your full CV and current salary details to:

JEAN MARSHALL
Customer Services Director, Keystroke plc
McArthur Park, Milton Keynes JMK5.

CAN Film Laboratories

require an ASSISTANT EDITOR

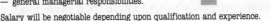

A challenging position has arisen in this unique film production company based at Shepperton, West London.

You will be able to work accurately, to tight deadlines and under pressure, have good communication and organisational skills. The position offers an unrivalled opportunity to understand, empathise with and increase knowledge of the visual arts.

For details and application form, telephone 0181 112 0021.

We are striving to be an equal opportunities employer, and welcome applications from all suitably qualified people regardless of race, gender or disability.

PUMPS OF LONDON
45-47 Well Street, Stepney, London EC1

We require a number of trainees for various departments within this dance shoe manufacturing company. No experience necessary as full instruction will be provided.

We do not operate an ages policy and are willing to interview registered disabled people.

Please supply a handwritten CV to:
Mr Michael Khan, Personnel Manager

Gem Insurance Job Fair
Islington Job Centre
4 Upper Street London N1
Wednesday 30 March 199–

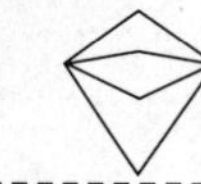

Gem Insurance, one of the UK's leading insurance groups are seeking Home Service Representatives in the Islington Area.

If you would like to know more about the opportunities Gem have, then come along to the job centre on **Wednesday 30 March from 9 a.m.–5 p.m.** On arrival please contact **Janice Gregson** or **Lloyd Woods**.

Gem is a member of Lautro, IMRO and the ABI.

Read each of the job advertisements.

a If you were asked to place these by the employer, which newspaper or magazine would you choose for each one? Give your reasons.
b Pumps of London ask for a CV only. They are not offering further information. Why is this? Is there enough information here to enable you to apply?
c Draw up a person specification for the post at Keystroke plc.
d Prepare suitable interview questions for this post. (Check back against the ten-point plan).

Legal and ethical obligations in recruitment

Business ethics can be defined as 'Moral guidelines for the conduct of business based on notions of what is right, wrong and fair', (Penguin Business Dictionary). People may be pressurised into behaving unethically when seeking profits.

The recruitment process is one of discriminating between applicants, but this must be done on a rational basis. Honesty, fairness and confidentiality are the bywords.

Sometimes firms argue that they must look to their own good, rather than the good of the wider community and it is for these reasons that they prefer not to employ certain people. Race, gender or disability rather than ability becomes important. Much of this is a matter of education. For instance, disabled people on average have a better work attendance than the able-bodied; it appears from recent studies that women are inherently more intelligent than men and so on. Firms may be missing out on opportunities due to prejudice, but where business ethics are in question the law is required to provide a fair framework. We will take two examples.

Equal opportunities

In Chapter 7 we mentioned the legal obligations placed upon employers under equal opportunities legislation. Some employers go beyond the law and provide their own codes of conduct – equal opportunities policies for example.

References

Employers often require a reference from a previous employer. This can be crucial in career terms but may not be accurate. Not all referees behave in an ethical manner and some have their own motives for praising or criticising a leaver. A judgement by the House of Lords has helped, as shown by the following case study.

Case study

Spring v Guardian Assurance plc (July 1994)

Mr Spring's reference stated that 'He is a man of little or no integrity and could not be regarded as honest'. This was the kiss of death to someone in insurance and Mr Spring sued his employer. The Law Lords found that the reference had been negligently compiled and ruled that in future employers must verify the facts before writing a reference.

It may be that references will now become bland and meaningless as employers try not to give offence. If so, firms will need to rely more on their own assessment and recruitment techniques.

Activities

1. What are the incentives for writing a poor employee a glowing reference?
2. Why write a poor reference for a good employee?
3. A firm predicts that unless it cuts costs it will have to close and 'shedding' staff is the only option. The union oppose this.
   a What is the best way of deciding who should go?
   b What ethical issues may arise?

The employee's viewpoint

The lie

THIS YEAR I turned 30, in the midst of a career change. Having working in arts festival fundraising, I had decided to look for a more lucrative job with a City investment bank. But before I had a chance to dust off my power suits and update my CV, several women friends warned me against publicly being over 30; they had found it impossible to make a career move with what some employers view as a terrible stigma. "Drop as many years as you can physically get away with," warned a 32-year-old American friend who, having left a good job in film distribution in the States, worked as a shop assistant here – until she knocked five years off her age.

So, reluctantly, I got out a calculator, started revising my past and worked out all the crucial dates. However, knocking a few years off your life – two, in my case, to get me below the psychologically crucial 30 – is no small undertaking. I found myself preparing for interviews as though I were entering a "How well do you know your CV?" quiz. On the day, I was conscious of sounding a bit too worldly for my shrunken "age". To my horror, in the interview that led to a job offer, they told me I was being hired *in spite of* my being a bit old. Clearly, my strategically adjusted age was crucial to my getting the job.

Source: *The Guardian*

Activities

Study the newspaper article on page 385.

1 Can an employer reject a woman on the grounds of age alone?
2 Why would an employer favour women below 30? Is this reasonable?
3 Should an employer be allowed to choose the best person in their view without hindrance from the law?
4 Is the applicant's approach:
   a justifiable?
   b ethical?

Review questions

1 What are the stages in the recruitment process?
2 What are the stages in the selection process?
3 State two methods for recruiting managers
4 How would you recruit a machine operator?
5 What management style would be most suitable for a co-operative?
6 When would an autocratic style be most effective?
7 What are the responsibilities of directors?
8 Briefly what is the job of middle management?
9 How is information technology encouraging the trend towards 'home-working'? Give two examples.
10 What is flexi-time? How may this benefit: employers? employees?
11 What sort of letter should be sent with a CV?
12 What is the difference between a job description and a person specification?
13 Give two ways in which employers may introduce 'flexibility' into working conditions and practices.
14 What does the contingency theory say?
15 What is meant by 'head-hunting'?
16 Why have employers found it necessary to introduce change into the workplace? Give three reasons.
17 Why is there a trend towards more part-time working?
18 What does 'business ethics' mean?

Key terms

Shareholders
Directors
Managers
Operative
Consultant
Adviser
Superviser
Levels of management
Functions of management

Forecasting
Organising
Commanding
Co-ordinating
Controlling
Communicating
Planning
Decision making
Motivating

Innovating
Creating
Developing
Delegating
Trait Theories
Style Theories
Autocratic leader (Theory X)
Democratic leader (Theory Y)
Consultative leader

Laissez-faire leader
Task/activity leader
People leader
Contingency Theories
Supervisors
Supervisory functions
Operatives
Team work
Flexitime
Teleworking
Advertising
Shortlisting
Testing
Interviewing
Job description
Person specification
Vacancies
– internal
– external
Application form
Reference
Ethical obligations
Legal obligations
Letter of application
Curriculum vitae (CV)
Outsourcing

Assignment 8.2
Are 2CVs reliable?

This assignment develops knowledge and understanding of the following element:
4.3 Evaluate recruitment procedures, job applications and interviews

It supports development of the following core skills:
Communication 3.1, 3.2
Information technology 3.1, 3.3

As an employee of a firm of management consultants you are required to act upon the following memo. You may use your college/school, work experience placement or any other suitable local organisation.

Rice-Porterhouse (Management Consultants) Ltd

To: A Student

From: Mandy Rice

We have been asked by a client to evaluate their recruitment procedures. Would you please visit them to look at the methods they use at present to attract new staff.

In particular we need to know:

1 General recruitment procedures such as:
Who identifies that a vacancy exists?
Who is responsible for recruitment within the organisation?
Where do they advertise vacancies and why is this?
Do they use application forms, CVs, letters of application (or some combination)?

Do they use a panel to interview or one to one? Who sits on interview panels?
Are candidates tested at interview?

Would you ask about the above for posts at two different levels within the organisation?
Presumably there will be some differences in methods used.

2 Is recruitment successful in matching candidates to vacancies, for instance:
Does the organisation find that it is able to attract suitable staff?
Do unsuitable candidates apply?
Do application forms and CVs provide the relevant information?
Are references useful when deciding whether to make an appointment?

3 Would you also find out about contracts of employment, that is:
Are posts offered as permanent full-time, permanent part-time or temporary (fixed-term contract)? What are the reasons for this?
Is the firm making any attempt to introduce flexible working practices? Please explain.

If possible, could you gain the job advertisement, the person specification and the job specification for one post to attach as appendices?

Please form a conclusion as to whether the recruitment procedure is effective at present. Give any suggestions that you feel may be relevant.

Assignment 8.3
Just the job!

This assignment develops knowledge and understanding of the following element:
4.3 Evaluate recruitment procedures, job applications and interviews

It supports development of the following skills:
Communication 3.1

Southfleet College has a vacancy which it wishes to fill. After much discussion the job description and person specification are finalised. These will be sent to interested parties together with the college's standard application form. Since this has a section for a supporting statement a CV is not required.

As all posts must be advertised externally an advertisement is designed and placed in the education section of the daily press.

By the time of the closing date a number of applications have been received; in this assignment you will consider three of these.

The shortlisting panel which is about to meet has set up a grading system. Marks will be awarded for each bulleted item on the person specification – total 12 items – as follows:

Item not covered/inappropriate/unconvincing	0
Item covered but with little explanation	1
Item covered convincingly	2

The relevant paperwork is provided below as follows:

job specification
job description
advertisement
extracts from applications from three candidates showing a summary of relevant details and supporting statements.

Your tasks

1 Split up into teams of three or four. Each team is the shortlisting panel at Southfleet which is to consider the three applications from Mary Jones, Matilda Molenski and Winston Hill. You should work in these groups.

Shortlisting

2 Read the supporting statements and grade them accordingly against the person specification. Use the marking criteria supplied.

3 a How many marks did each candidate get? Check with other groups for consistency.
b Which items were answered the least convincingly?
c Do the marks correspond with your initial impression of the applications?
d Is the grading system satisfactory – can you suggest any improvements?
e Should any of the three definitely not be shortlisted?

Planning the interview

You are to assume that all three candidates will be interviewed:

4 a In the same teams devise a set of four questions which will be asked of every candidate:
- one on equal opportunities
- one on training methods
- one on group working
- one on software.

Make sure that these are relevant to the job and that the candidate should be capable of answering them.

b Devise two more questions designed individually for each candidate:
- one of these will be to allow the candidate to settle down and to speak a little about their experiences;
- the second will be to gain more information/clarification over some matter.

Have supplementary questions ready.

The interview

5 Appoint three people to act the parts of the interviewees.
Each group in turn should now interview one of the candidates in front of the class using the ten-point plan. (You may have to repeat one or more candidates.)
(Provide alternative names, Michael Molenski, Mark Jones, Wendy Hill, if there is a problem!)

Evaluation

The class should evaluate each interview – this is easier if it has been videoed:

6 Was the ten-point plan followed?
Were the questions fair?
How did the various candidates perform?

SOUTHFLEET COLLEGE

Job Description

Post: Computer Applications Support
Grade: Pts 22-25
Reports to: Computing Programme Manager
Faculty/Centre: Academic Services
Department: Learning Resources

1. Purpose of the Post

To assist in the provision of training and support to users of the Learning Centre in the use of microcomputer hardware and DOS/Windows software.
To produce documentation and contribute to the day-to-day running of the Learning Centre, including editing of newsletter.

2. Main Responsibilities

To provide assistance to all Learning Centre users in the guidance and instruction on all present and future computer hardware and software.
To produce documentation from various sources requiring specialist knowledge such as desktop publishing.
To provide day-to-day supervision of student utilisation of the Learning Centre including assisting with student discipline.
To work as part of a team developing learning resource training (Audio Visual, IT, Flexible Open Learning and Library skills).
To be responsible for editing the newsletter and other documentation.
To assist in the development and the operation of the Learning Centre as a multi-media learning resource.

Education and qualifications:

A general education up to GCSE standard and ideally GNVQ advanced or equivalent in a computer-related area.
This Job Description is correct at 1st March 199-. It will, however, be reviewed with you at regular objective setting sessions and may be amended after such consultation to reflect development in or to the job.

SOUTHFLEET COLLEGE
Person Specification

IT Trainer

The following is a list of skills, knowledge and aptitudes required to carry out this job. Paid and unpaid experiences may both be relevant.

Experience:

- Knowledge of micro computers and familiarity with DOS/Windows commercial software.
- Macintosh experience desirable.

Aptitude:

- To have the ability or potential to train users in IT operations.
- To have excellent interpersonal communication skills.
- To think creatively and solve problems.
- To have proven writing skills.
- To have flexibility in approach to work.
- To be able to work as part of a team.
- To be able to prioritise work and meet deadlines in a pressured environment.

Motivation:

- To have an informed understanding of equal opportunities and a commitment to its promotion.
- To show willingness to take responsibility.
- To be motivated to developing a career in training and to keep up to date with new developments.

Special circumstances:

The post holder must be willing to work at all college sites

The post holder would be required to support staff and students during college hours. The Learning Centre is open during the evenings and on some Saturdays therefore flexibility in working hours is necessary.

CUSTOMER FIRST

WANTED – someone interested in developing their career into all aspects of computer applications support and training. The job is challenging and would suit a methodical but flexible mind, but we really want someone who gains satisfaction from relating to people. We don't want a guru – we do want someone who will learn and work in a team.

We support a mixed environment of work stations and PCs with a wide range of commercial software.

- You MUST have proven writing skills as you will be our newsletter and documentation editor.
- You MUST have experience with a wide range of DOS/Windows software in a user-driven environment. Macintosh experience could swing you the job!
- You MUST be motivated to apply today's technology to solve customers' problems.
- You MUST be prepared to train small and large groups.

DOES THIS DESCRIBE YOU?

The college is situated on the edge of Southfleet Great Park on an attractive campus. Appointments on scale between £14K–£17K depending on qualifications and experience. Further information and application forms from the Personnel Officer, Southfleet College, PC486 1BM.

Candidate's name: Winston Hill

Age: 30

Qualifications: BSc(hons) Mathematics, Durham University
Break in employment 1985-1986

Please use this space to say why you are interested in this position and why you feel able to do the job.

In support of my application for the post advertised I would like to supply the following information:

I have been solely responsible for maintaining two networks of PCs at Milton College. Recently I was responsible for upgrading the hardware ready to run Windows software. I am also responsible for rectifying simple faults on a day-to-day basis and calling in the maintenance contractors.

I have been interested in computers since 1983. During this time I have written a number of games programmes which have been published in 'Top Computer'. I own a PC 486 DX machine and regularly communicate by modem with fellow enthusiasts.

Although it is not part of my job description I often assist students who have difficulties with programming and software.

I have experience of a range of machines including a Macintosh.

Signed Winston Hill **Date** 1/4/9-

Candidate's name: Mary Jones

Age: 21

Qualifications: BTEC National Diploma in Computer Studies West Lancs College
No breaks in employment

Please use this space to say why you are interested in this position and why you feel able to do the job.

I would like to supply the following information in support of my application for the Computer Applications Support and Training post.

As you will see from my employment history I have worked for two years with microcomputers at Micro-Train, a small private sector training organisation. Here I was responsible for training various groups of adult-returners and young people on Windows-based software. I have knowledge of Word for Windows 2, WordPerfect, Excel, Lotus 123, Access, Superbase, Pagemaker and Coral Draw. At the Centre students were prepared for a range of external qualifications using these packages often against tight deadlines.

I have had some responsibility for recommending and purchasing new software and attended computer shows to regularly update my knowledge of industry developments. I also subscribe regularly to the trade magazine 'Best PC'. I have recently completed a two-day training course on advanced Access.

At Micro-Train I worked as one of a team of eight full-time workers. I was involved in agreeing financial priorities, curriculum matters and promotional events. Being part of a small team involved such diverse duties as making the tea and liaising with external course moderators.

Although we do not train on Macintosh machines the monthly newsletter which I undertook to produce and edit was put together on an Apple Macintosh situated in the library. So far I have produced eight editions of the newsletter.

At the centre we are committed to developing an equal opportunities policy which we hope to have in place shortly. I have been involved in this.

I believe I have the experience and commitment to work effectively in the team at Southfleet.

Signed Mary Jones **Date** 30/3/9-

Candidate's Name: Matilda Molenski

Age: 18

Employment: none full-time

Qualifications: A level Art, A level Computer Studies (just completed)

In support of my application for the Computer Applications Support and Training post I would like to supply the following information.

As part of my A level course I used a range of computer software on the school network. This included databases, spreadsheets, word processing and desk-top publishing. I also used the system to produce work for my other courses.

I have been active in helping with the publication of the school magazine during my last year at school. This was produced using the desk top publishing package Quark Xpress. The project involved a considerable amount of team co-operation in gathering, writing up, editing and distributing the magazine.

I have attended two spells of work experience whilst in the sixth form. One with an animated computer graphics company in Shepperton, the other with the computer technician in the local college of further education. At the college I spent a certain amount of time helping out in the open learning computer centre and had access to the wide range of computer books and magazines in the library.

At weekends and during holidays I work in the local shopping arcade for 'Budget Booster' where I am now a part-time supervisor. This job requires a number of different skills including handling money, dealing with difficult customers, and working under constant pressure.

The school, and the college where I was placed on work experience both have equal opportunities policies. I feel that all organisations should be committed to equal opportunities.

I would like to develop a career in training and know that I have the motivation to succeed.

Signed: Matilda Molenski **Date:** 29 March 199-

Assignment 8.4
Apply yourself!

This assignment follows on from Assignment 8.3.

It supports development of the following skills:
Communication 3.2, 3.4
Information technology 3.1, 3.3

A problem occurs with the funding at Southfleet College and the appointment cannot be made. Fortunately no one has been appointed to the job.
Time passes ...
After some months the situation is resolved and the College now feels able to re-advertise the job. The advertisement is unchanged except that instead of sending out application forms a CV is requested accompanied by a letter of introduction. These should be hand-written.

Your tasks

1. Apply for the job (assume in doing this that you have satisfactorily finished your present course).
2. Find an advertisement in the press for a job which you think would be interesting and suitable for you when you have finished your course. Produce the word-processed letter of introduction and CV that you would send.
   Telephone for extra details, application form, job description and person specification. If an application form is made available keep this for reference but assume that the application is to be by letter and CV.
3. Summarise the recruitment procedures of the firm, illuminating your report with the sample documents that you have obtained.

UNIT 5 PRODUCTION AND EMPLOYMENT IN THE ECONOMY

9 Production in the economy

What is covered in this chapter

- Production and added value
- Changing patterns of production
- Effects of changing patterns of production
- Government strategies for improving competitiveness of UK industry
- European and international policies
- Comparing the performance of the Uk economy

These are the resources that you will need for your Production and Employment in the Economy file:

- UK and European statistical publications
- databases
- graph paper
- source materials from trade unions and employers' associations
- newspaper and magazine articles.

Introduction

What image do you have of production? Ask your family and friends what images they have. Are their views the same? Do their views depend on their age? Are their images of people working in a factory, chemical plant or steelworks or of people working in a clean high-tech environment or in an office? In this chapter we look at production in business and see how well or how badly the UK is doing compared with its international competitors.

Production and added value

Production is the economic activity needed to manufacture or create products (goods or services) with exchange value, i.e. which people are willing to buy. Cars, computers, films and plays in a theatre can all be produced. Production can take place in the primary, secondary or tertiary sector of the economy (see Chapter 1).

Added value describes the relationship between the costs of the inputs used in production and the value of the outputs. Added value is the difference between the value of the goods or services produced (the total revenue obtained from selling the products) and the cost of obtaining the inputs.

Added value and production

Cost of inputs	Value added by business	Value of outputs
Land, labour, capital	The business adds value to inputs by changing them into outputs	Goods and services

The table below shows the distribution of gross value added by sector for selected countries. Note the importance of the primary sector in Greece, Portugal, Ireland and Turkey.

Country	Primary	Secondary	Tertiary
Belgium	2.1	33.1	68.9
Denmark	4.2	28.5	71.7
Greece	16.3	27.4	56.3
Spain	4.2	36.2	59.6
France	3.5	32.6	68.6
Ireland	8.1	35.8	56.1
Italy	3.8	37.2	67.4
Luxembourg	1.7	39.8	63.7
Netherlands	4.6	34.4	68.1
Portugal	7.3	46.5	62.6
UK	1.5	36.2	66.3
Turkey	17.8	38.1	44.1
USA	2.2	32.2	64.0
Japan	2.4	43.8	53.8

Source: Eurostat

Activity

Draw charts to show the key features of the table. What conclusions can you draw?

Case study

Biscuits!

This example shows how value is added at each stage of the production cycle for biscuits.

Inputs	Value added	Outputs	Sector
Wheat seeds, land	Farmer grows and harvests wheat which is then sold	Wheat	Primary
Wheat	Wheat is ground and milled and sold	Flour	Secondary
Flour and other ingedients	Biscuits are made, packaged and sold	Biscuits	Secondary
Biscuits	Wholesaler stores and sells biscuits	Biscuits	Tertiary
Biscuits	Retailer stores and sells buscuits	Biscuits	Tertiary consumer expenditure

How businesses add value during production

Businesses attempt to add as much value as they can to a product before it is sold in order to tempt people into buying. Here are some ways in which they can do this.

Increasing the productivity of resources used in production

There are three categories of resources or inputs used in production. These inputs or resources are sometimes called **factors of production**.

Input	Costs
Land or natural resources, which includes the earth, minerals and raw materials	Rent and rates: the price of land is determined by the supply and demand and the potential for use, e.g. does it have planning permission? If a business is trying to expand it may be cheaper for it to move, particularly if incentives are available in certain areas
Capital or physical resources, which includes the buildings, plant and machinery used in production	Purchasing capital equipment is expensive. Either the business will have to borrow funds and pay interest on the loan or it will have to plough back profits, so the money cannot be used for anything else (opportunity cost). Businesses which are large borrowers would prefer low rates of interest
Labour or human resources	The cost of employing people is the actual wage plus any 'perks' plus national insurance. Relative to the rest of Europe, the UK is a low-wage economy

Factor productivity

How is labour productivity measured? Every organisation will want to make the best use of its resources by producing goods and/or services at the lowest possible cost. Two measures are widely used in business as a rough and ready guide to measuring and describing **factor productivity**. The first is represented by the formula:

$$\frac{\text{Value of output}}{\text{Number of workers}} = \text{Output for each worker or output per head or productivity per head.}$$

This can be varied by restricting the 'Number of workers' to, for example, sales people or production workers. This will show the productivity of these particular groups.

Another way is to take the value of sales and divide this by the labour costs. Whichever method is chosen, the concept is the same, namely the value/volume of the output is related to the value/volume of the input.

Productivity increases if:

- more output is produced from the same number of resources;
- fewer resources, for example, less labour are used to produce the same or a larger output; this is well demonstrated by the increase in productivity in coal mining.

Sometimes it can be very difficult to interpret these measures of labour productivity. For example:

- if the length of the working day has fallen, the gain in productivity would be under-estimated. If the same output is produced with the same number of workers, then because fewer hours have been used to produce goods, we have a correspondingly lower wage cost;

- the number of workers could be unsuitable as a measure. If labour costs have risen through, for example, overtime working then more money has to be paid to the same number of workers;
- the capital/labour ratio could have changed, for example, more effective machines could have been introduced – this may have been the main cause of the increase of the output;
- the number of people employed could change on a weekly, even daily basis, through absence, retirement, new workers, etc., this may under-estimate the final figure;
- what definition of output is being used? For example, is it gross output or net output, which is referred to? Perhaps, value added (the difference between the cost of the inputs and the selling price), would be a better indicator. This method is used in all the Eurostat data;
- is it the same product? For example, have design or material changes altered the product? Is it better quality? Are we comparing like with like?
- the rate of inflation will affect price and the value. This needs to be accounted for. For example, if prices rise by 10 per cent whilst output stays the same, this would appear as a rise in productivity yet there have been no gains in real terms;
- what happens when there is no physical output? For example, in education, new measures of efficiency have been introduced. These include monitoring the resources, for example, the number of teaching and non-teaching staff used to produce the output, i.e. the number of students who have successfully qualified. The Sheehy Report (Chapter 7) suggested that the police force should be paid on the basis of productivity.

Case study

What affects productivity in a business?

EAL is a large retail chain, similar to 'Do It All' which sells DIY items. It has stores throughout the country and these are usually located on the outskirts of a town. Within each store the customer can walk around and inspect everything on display. Each item has a code/reference number. If the customer decides to purchase an item, this code number is fed into the computer till at the cash desk. This displays whether or not the item is readily available and can be carried away (if you are strong enough to carry it), or if there is a waiting time of *x* number of weeks.

Goods which are not on display, are kept in the warehouse, which is adjacent to the main display area. The stock is stacked on steel shelves which are accessed by fork lift trucks. 'Sales staff', 'check-out till staff' and 'warehouse staff' are strictly separate groups.

These are the main characteristics of the EAL Superstore chain:

1 The display area is largely self service, i.e. it is not labour intensive. This means that very few people are employed to sell goods, therefore, the value of sales per person is quite high. The sales staff are very productive.

2 The computer system provides accurate information about stock and prices, quickly and easily. 'Sales' and 'check-out' staff have instant access to data and do not have to leave the display area. This is a good example of capital replacing labour. The computer tills are labour-saving devices which have improved the level of labour productivity. The introduction of technology into retailing has been a significant factor in improving the level of productivity in this sector of the economy. You will be familiar with other examples, such as bar code readers and computerised tills which print cheques.

3 The fork lift truck in the warehouse area is another example of how technology has helped to improve productivity. Here it has reduced storage and handling costs.
4 The stores are often located in out-of-town areas where they can take advantage of lower building costs because the land is cheaper and pre-fabricated building techniques can be used – there appear to be very few windows! This means the company can build very large premises with sufficient storage and display space to enable it to buy in bulk and reduce its purchase costs. This helps to improve the ratio between resources and output.
5 The way in which staff are managed will directly affect the level of productivity, particularly if they are well motivated. Incentive payments and bonuses are of great help in increasing sales, and are a familiar feature of this type of retail operation.
6 The age, type and quality of the equipment used in the business will significantly affect the productivity of labour. To obtain maximum efficiency, machines need to be fully utilised.

Activity

The suggestion box

The manager in your section believes that productivity can be improved, and asks for suggestions on how this can be done.

a Prepare a notice and leaflets asking people for their ideas.

b Write a memo to your section head outlining one suggestion which you think would improve productivity in your department. You must explain why it would help and it must be cost-effective.

c It may be necessary to change the method of production to improve productivity, for example introducing fork-lift trucks instead of manual handling. What effect would your suggestion have on the employees, the business and the customers?

Substitution between factors of production

The substitution of factors of production refers to a situation in which machines can be used instead of (substituted for) labour and vice versa.

Labour intensive industries

These are industries which use a large amount of labour, compared to the amount of capital (machines, plant and equipment) needed to produce goods or provide services. In **labour intensive industries**, the wage costs form a large proportion of the total costs of production. In Poland, for example, there are many products which are still made largely by hand, such as shoes. In the UK, many tertiary industries such as retailing and personal services are highly labour intensive. When labour is replaced by machines, the machines are called **labour-saving**. Do you believe this trend ought to be encouraged?

Capital intensive industries

These are industries which use a large amount of machinery and equipment and relatively few workers. Their wage costs are only a small proportion of their total costs. For example, in a modern carpet factory you will see very few production workers, compared with a traditional carpet maker, where labour is a much more important element. Many firms have now largely replaced workers with automated production lines. The production of cars, TVs and video recorders, for example, is now almost fully automated.

The ease or difficulty with which machines can be substituted or used instead of people will depend upon:
- the type of product
- the type of production method.

Hairdressing, for instance, is a personal service, and it would be almost impossible to replace a hairdresser with a machine. Generally, the easier it is to substitute or swap machines for labour, the more elastic will be the demand for labour. Therefore, in these cases, a small rise in the wage rate will lead to firms shedding/dismissing labour and using machines instead.

The productivity of the machines and equipment used in the business can be approached in a similar way. Accountants measure productivity by using financial measures of efficiency such as return on capital employed (ROCE, see Chapter 14).

Productivity, efficiency and effectiveness

Productivity is important for every organisation whether it is a manufacturer, wholesaler, retailer, private or public body, charity, sports club or bank. It is defined as the relationship between the output which is produced and the inputs which are used. **Efficiency** measures how well or how badly a business is doing using its existing resources. **Effectiveness** measures what output could be achieved if present inputs were used more intensively.

Methods of production

The method of production is an important factor in determining the amount of added value in a business. A high level of added value can be achieved if there is:
- effective use of labour;
- minimum wastage;
- maximum utilisation of equipment.

Full and effective use of labour might mean employing specialist staff, for instance, should there be sufficient work. There is an increasing tendency to employ people on short-term contracts to allow business 'flexibility'.

Minimum wastage and loss of raw materials calls for detailed control and often computerisation. As we saw when looking at information processing in Chapter 4, companies such as Sainsbury's make full use of computerised stock control systems to analyse flows, minimise delays in ordering and avoid the problems of 'dead stock'.

Finally, machines need to be fully utilised to be profitable. Different forms of organisation of production have evolved to make the most effective use of the workplace. Production methods can be divided into three main types:
- flow production
- batch production
- job production.

A flow production line is a series of linked stages which are needed to produce the final item. The method is the basis for all mass production techniques and requires continuous demand.

A simple flow production process for biscuits might look like this:

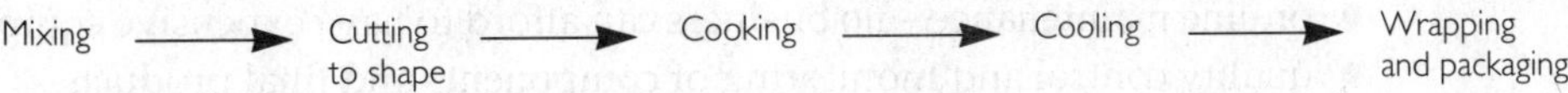

The technique is very useful for producing standardised, identical items when there is a large, permanent and known market demand. Labour tends to be unskilled except for those jobs which involve quality control, checking and monitoring. The machinery and equipment used on assembly lines needs to be very specialised. Most pieces of equipment only perform one task.

When complex flow lines are needed, as for example in the production of motor cars, the key to success is in ensuring that enough components are available at each stage. (See the Toyota case study in Chapter 7.)

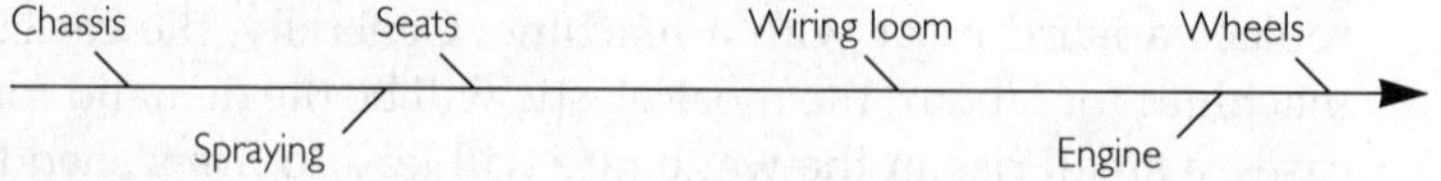

Each line has to be balanced so as to achieve a continuous flow of production.

Batch production can be used when fixed amounts of standard items are required. Batches of biscuits, for example, are produced in response to market demands. Each time a new batch is produced, machines have to be re-set. Cooking times are different for each type of biscuit. Pastry cutters need to change for each shape.

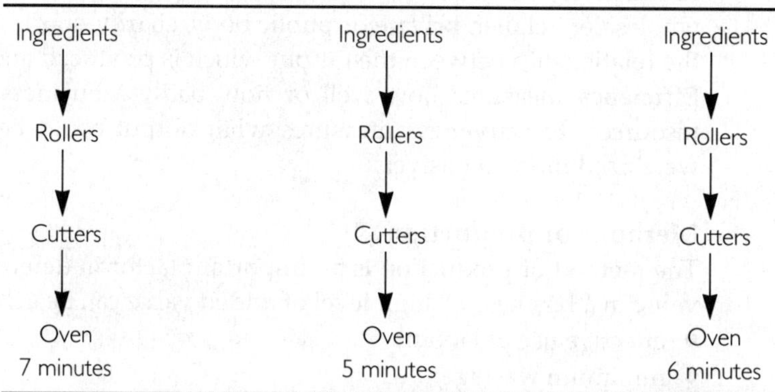

Specialist labour will be needed to set up and re-jig the machinery. Every time machinery has to be re-set it adds to the cost of the product. This is why small orders often cost more to produce per unit, and why discounts may be available on large orders. At one time beer used to be brewed in batches at the same brewery. Today, however, large companies concentrate the production of one brew at a particular brewery.

Job production refers to one-off or special orders for individual items such as a loft conversion, a printing job or an oil painting. This will normally require specialised, highly skilled labour which is expensive. Small companies may be more willing to produce small orders than large companies with expensive production lines. However, one-off jobs can also be very large, the Channel Tunnel is a notable example.

One-off jobs tend to be expensive because there are no economies of scale. The product is designed and made entirely to the client's specification. Compare, for instance, the price of clothes off-the-peg and the same quality made-to-measure.

Large scale production operations require close management and control. Particularly important are:

- scheduling and sequencing of the work.
- on-line maintenance – no business can afford to have expensive equipment lying idle.
- quality control and monitoring of components and final products.

Activity

1 Please use discarded paper for this activity. You may find some near the printer or photocopier. If you recycle waste then this shouldn't create any more.
Split into three groups. Take 50 sheets of A4 paper per group and four coloured pens.
- Group 1 should make 50 identical aeroplanes. Time allowed: 15 minutes.
- Group 2 should make 50 identical aeroplanes with the design on the right on each wing in three colours. Time allowed: 15 minutes

- Group 3 should make 50 identical aeroplanes. 10 with this design on each wing in three colours:

20 with this design on each wing in three colours:

20 with this design on each wing in three colours:

Time allowed: 15 minutes

Brainstorm your results. Which sorts of production did you find the most efficient? Were there any resources lying idle? If you thought about it, how could you make the process more efficient? Should you have quality control?

2 **Photocopying**
You are given a four-page document to photocopy five times. Each completed copy needs to be stapled.

The usual copier has broken down (again) and you have to borrow a small home copier from a colleague. This works well but has no document feeder so that each sheet needs to be carefully placed on the glass.

Decide how you would photocopy the document in the most efficient way. Number the processes below to show the sequence in which you would perform the operation.

Document 1	**Document 2**	**Document 3**	**Document 4**
copy sheet 1	copy sheet 1	copy sheet 1	copy sheet 1
copy sheet 2	copy sheet 2	copy sheet 2	copy sheet 2
copy sheet 3	copy sheet 3	copy sheet 3	copy sheet 3
copy sheet 4	copy sheet 4	copy sheet 4	copy sheet 4
Collate	Collate	Collate	Collate
Staple	Staple	Staple	Staple

Discuss your suggestions. Did you use batch or flow production?

Flow production techniques came in for criticism after their widespread introduction. They were efficient, but could be mindless for workers who were required to perform unsatisfactory, repetitive tasks without ever seeing the end product. This could lead to 'Friday cars'. Some firms have recognised that people work better if they are interested in the task. At Elonex computers, for instance, each computer is assembled entirely by one person.

Efficiency and plant size – the scale of production

Optimum efficiency varies according to the type of product and the production method. Some products such as cars and oil refining have a very large minimum efficient size and production is generally on a very large scale.

Why are some firms small? Why are chemical refineries very large? Why do firms operate at a certain scale or size? As a business grows larger its costs per unit of output, its average costs tend to fall because it becomes more efficient. The term **economies of scale** refers to the advantages which a business gains from being large. This may be due to:

- greater use of specialised labour and equipment thus promoting greater productivity and output;
- the introduction of automatic and new production techniques which might give the firm the opportunity of using 'conveyor-belt' or 'flow' methods of operation, so that staff and machines can be worked to full capacity;
- improved stock and inventory control. Because a firm produces more it does not necessarily mean it has to carry more stock (see the Toyota case study in Chapter 7);
- improved managerial and administrative control;
- the increased size may make it financially more viable, better able to borrow money and more attractive to investors;

Improved stock control prevents costs running away.

- improved methods of working and industrial relations.
- increased bargaining power and an ability to buy resources or distribute the finished article in bulk.
- improved research and development.
- an ability to diversify production and thus spread the risks of a product failure.

These economies which occur solely as a result of the growth of the firm are called **internal economies** of scale and explain why firms are tempted to expand.

However, there is a limit on size. If a manufacturer went beyond the most efficient point then average costs could rise as a result of **diseconomies of scale**. Examples are:

- Administrative complexity may create a situation where decision making may take weeks.
- Machinery and labour may be overworked.
- The source of raw materials could become expensive.
- The market for the product may become saturated due to oversupply.

It is clearly therefore not always an advantage for a firm to be large. Many small firms still exist because:

- of a shortage of land labour and capital;
- of a lack of suitable machines or markets;
- of a need for independence;
- the technical optimum size is small.

Economies which result from the development of the industry or the area in which the business is located are often referred to as **external economies**. The business benefits, not because of its own actions, but because it participates in a general expansion of production within the industry, or area, as a whole. Examples of such economies may include: industry/area promotion or advertising campaigns; improved transport and distribution services;the provision of specialised research and educational facilities. All of these may be achieved by joint industrial spending or through government aid and local authority expenditure, such as TV and newspaper advertising for Milton Keynes, Telford and Swansea (see page 495). Such economies should result in a general improvement in overall costs.

Case study

The UK footwear industry

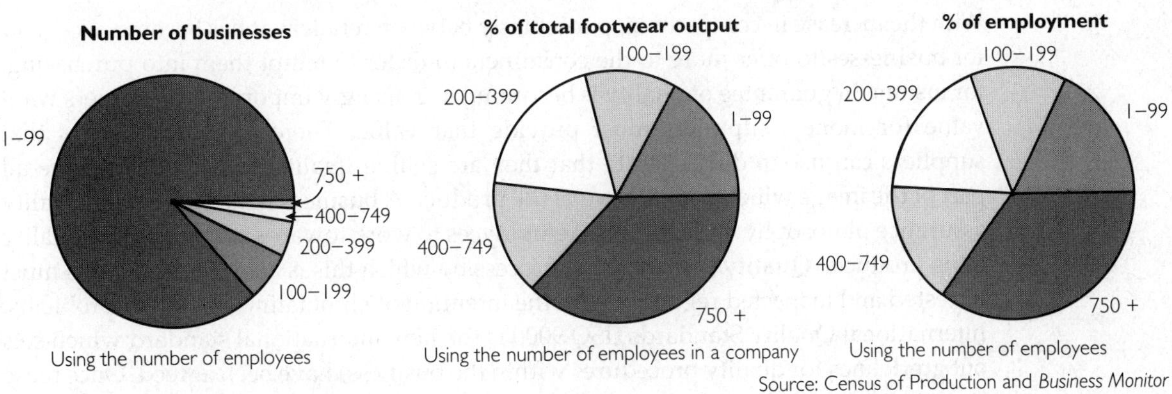

Figure 9.1 Size of the UK footwear business

Figure 9.1 shows the size of UK footwear business. A number of conclusions can be drawn:

- Most businesses (90 per cent) employ between one and 99 employees but these only account for 17 per cent of the total employment.
- The largest proportion of the total output comes from companies employing more than 750 employees.

As new technology is introduced, footwear can be made using assembly line processes. This change tends to increase the size of the business. To take full advantage of the new methods, companies have to be large and it is the big retailers who lead the market. Nevertheless, it is evident from the figures that there is still a considerable market for footwear from small companies.

The market for footwear is driven by the changing tastes and fashion in shoes, but shoe manufacturers tend to follow and not create fashions.

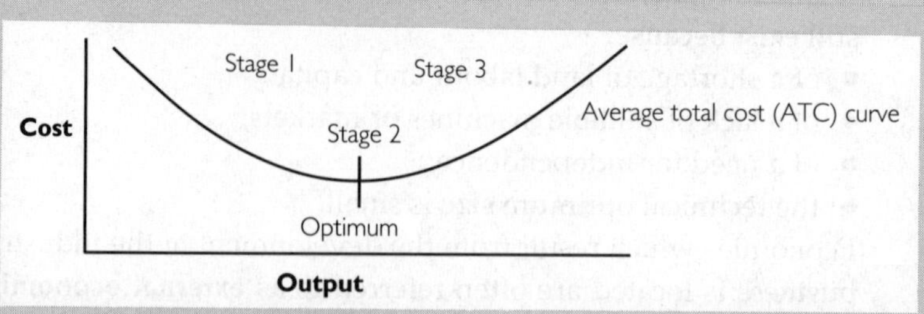

Figure 9.2 An average total cost curve showing how economies and diseconomies of scale affect unit costs

Stage 1 shows decreasing unit costs with economies of scale.
Stage 2 shows the most efficient (optimum) output.
Stage 3 shows increasing unit costs with diseconomies of scale.

Using quality to add value

With the increase in competition, particularly between retailers, it has become necessary for businesses to offer more to the consumers in order to tempt them into purchasing, for instance a guarantee of quality is becoming increasingly important. Customers want value for money; suppliers must provide that value. There are several ways that suppliers can use to demonstrate that they are selling quality products. These are all part of the image which people have of the product. A business which operates a quality assurance philosophy will require all employees to work towards improving the quality of its products. **Quality control** is the process by which this is achieved. Products must be tested and inspected regularly with the intention of eliminating all quality problems. International Quality Standards (ISO 9000 is the new international standard which sets out guidelines for quality procedures within the business) have been agreed. Once these are achieved they allow the business' commitment to quality to be recognised and used in forming and marketing its image of quality (we look at quality symbols on page 44). With increasing international competition from low-cost producers the UK needs to produce high-priced good-quality goods with a high added value in order to be able to compete in overseas markets.

Using marketing and promotion to add value

Marketing is about giving the consumer extra reasons for buying a product (see Chapter 6 for examples of how this can be done). Many customers make the decision about which product to buy on the basis of 'value for money'. This does not always mean the cheapest; indeed many people associate a low price with poor quality. Manufacturers and retailers acknowledge this by offering added extras. For example, 'buy 6, get one free!' The following example shows how far retailers are prepared to go. One month after launching swinging singles nights in 30 of its stores, Asda has announced that a couple who met at one of these nights will be the first to marry in a supermarket. They will stage the ceremony in the aisle, followed by a reception in the supermarket's cafeteria. The Asda marketing director says 'We aim to put theatre and life into retailing by separating ourselves from the pack. We want to prove we offer customers excellent value but with personality thrown in'.

Why businesses aim to add value

Business objectives

We have seen how businesses behave in the market place. To understand this behaviour fully we must recognise that different organisations have different objectives. Indeed the objectives of an organisation may change from time to time with changing market conditions.

Profit maximisation is widely regarded as being the key objective of business. It seems reasonable to suppose that organisations will wish to make the largest profits possible, but observation shows that this is not always the case, at least in the short-term.

Other possibilities are:

- A firm might wish to increase sales so as to become a market leader. To this end it may set a competitive price with which rival firms cannot compete. Ultimately this may maximise profits but the immediate aim might be to put a rival out of business, even if this means making short-term losses to achieve this.
- A firm might wish to establish and maintain a particular reputation, perhaps for quality or sophistication. This would be true of retailers such as Harrods.
- Where there is a distinction between management and ownership as in large companies, the board of directors may well have personal motives for pursuing policies of their own. They may wish to gain publicity and maintain a high profile. This could involve huge outlay, as for example in the sponsoring of major sporting events which might be costly, and unless there are tangible returns, will not maximise profits.
- To meet customer requirements. In order to succeed every business will need to provide customers with what they want, which is the right product, in the right place, at the right price, at the right time. For example, a customer wants to buy a packet of biscuits; what are the requirements?
  - Variety, so a range of biscuits must be on offer;
  - Information, perhaps a list of ingredients on the pack along with nutritional information. Some people for instance are allergic to peanuts and will want to know if any are present;
  - Packaging, this must keep the biscuits clean, fresh and unbroken;
  - A competitive and fair price;
  - Availability in the local shop;
  - Clean hygienic surroundings with goods which are within their 'sell-by' date and are clean and safe to eat.

  This is not an exhaustive list but it does show what people may want and have a right to expect. Customer requirements depend on the type of goods, for example, industrial or consumer, and the type of customer. For more details, see Chapter 1.

Case study

Adding value in the car rental market

Competition is certainly good for the car rental business. Holiday Autos, which has nearly a third of the British holiday hire market in Europe, has just launched a highly competitive new brochure. It specialises in long hire from 3 to 6 days and has undercut all the big firms like Avis, Hertz, Budget and Europacar. It still offers the 'lowest price guarantee' but also gives commission-free currency exchange (commission is charged at 2–3% in the high street) plus half price car parking at airports and highly competitive rates to London airports. 'We are committed to providing every service demanded by the market', said the Holiday Autos chairman.

This example shows clearly why businesses aim to add value to their products. Holiday Autos has found a niche in the market, i.e. the longer hire periods. It has met and undercut the competition, forcing them to respond. It has provided extra reasons for customers to use its cars, i.e. it has met customer requirements. It will earn the profits to rent more cars to earn more profits…

Changing patterns of production

We have looked at the different methods of production. Now we need to see how these are changing.

The external environment – the effect on production and employment

Every business, whether in the public or private sector will be affected by events in the **external environment**, any of which could cause a change in the method of production.

- The **legal** environment – for example, a change in health and safety laws, such as the Electricity at Work Regulations, could mean that more people will be needed for electrical testing.
- The **economic** environment – for example, changes in interest rates and taxation could have either a positive or a negative impact on the business. For instance the decision to tax fuel bills could affect employment in a wide range of occupations.
- The **social** environment – for example, changes in consumers' habits and lifestyles will directly affect the demand for particular products. Some businesses will gain, others will lose. The move towards healthy eating has increased demand for labour in those companies producing health foods, and decreased demand for labour in companies with an unhealthy image. For example, Molins, which makes machines that make cigarettes, is having to rely increasingly on its export market.
- The **design and technological** environment – for example, production methods can change as a result of new technology and materials. The introduction of automated and robotic assembly lines has meant that fewer unskilled workers are needed.
- The **international** environment – for example, the monitor for a computer is made in Taiwan. The demand for workers in Taiwan has increased, but the opportunity cost is the loss of jobs in factories making monitors elsewhere.

- The **political** environment – for example, changes in economic policy introduced through the Budget can have wide-ranging effects on many companies. How will Sunday trading affect employment?
- The **green** environment – for example, is your writing paper made with 'recycled paper' or with paper from 'renewable forests'? The derived demand for workers in both the 'recycled paper' and non-recycled paper industries will change. Are the skills needed to make paper transferable?

Overcapacity and intense international competition in the depressed steel industry was the backdrop for one of the most bitter industrial disputes of 1992. A 22-week strike at Spartan Redheugh in Gateshead occurred when new owners of the company made proposals, some of which would have changed the terms and conditions of its 116-strong workforce, in order to improve competitiveness.

ACAS was involved from the beginning and following 15 meetings in five weeks the dispute was finally settled under a new terms and conditions package which included guarantees that proposed redundancies would be on a voluntary basis.

Source: ACAS Annual Report 1992

In addition, **European** legislation will also be a factor of the external environment. For example, employment policies will be affected by Regulations which apply directly to all Member States or Directives which need ratification by an Act of Parliament, or Decisions which can apply to individual firms. There are currently proposals in Parliament to amend the Regulations on maternity rights, continuity of employment of workers and the deduction of trade union subscriptions.

How will **trade unions** react to new technology? When newspapers tried to introduce computerised printing methods requiring fewer workers, there was considerable industrial unrest.

What affects the way in which organisations respond to external changes?

The way in which a business will respond to changes in its external environment will depend upon:

- The relationship between the demand for the product and the demand for factors of production
- The cost and amount of labour employed in the business
- Whether the change is expected to be permanent, in which case the business will have to adjust its staffing (see the Activity on Human Resources, Chapter 7)
- Whether the change is expected to be temporary, when the company might attempt to 'weather the storm' by keeping the same number of employees
- Whether the change is mandatory, for example, new legislation on health and safety could mean an increase in demand for Health and Safety Inspectors
- Whether the method of production can be changed to include new technology, for example, can machines be swapped for labour?

Use of technology

There have always been problems with introducing new technology into the workplace. Between 1811 and 1816 textile workers were against the mechanisation of the industry because they believed that the introduction of machines would cause unemployment. They formed gangs to wreck the new machinery. These workers were called Luddites after their leader who was nick-named 'General Ludd'. Many were hanged or transported. Today the term is used to describe anyone who is against industrial change or innovation.

Technological change can affect every part of the business, not just the production processes. Examples can be found everywhere: fork lift trucks are used in storage areas, robots are used to spot weld and spray paint cars, bar code readers give itemised till receipts and tell head office what goods have been sold and what stock needs to be ordered. New technology has had a revolutionary impact on the materials used in production and production methods.

Case study

Pizza off, say traditional cheese makers

European makers of Mozzarella cheese (used worldwide as a topping for pizza) are trying to stop a factory being built in Ireland. The factory will use revolutionary new technology which will allow it to produce cheese that can be shredded and frozen immediately. With traditional methods the cheese has to be matured. This is time-consuming and very expensive. 'Trying to keep this technology out of Europe is like trying to keep out Japanese cars', says the chief executive of the new plant.

Innovation and technology

Spies, lovers and examination cheats (reports *The Sunday Times*) now have an opportunity to buy (but not to use, because it is illegal) all the hi-tech gadgets they ever wanted at a new shop in London. Microphone pens and cordless ear pieces mean that a student could ask a friend outside the examination room to supply the right answer to a question!

Activity

With members of your group list:

a as many examples of new technology as you can.

b as many reasons for developing new technology as you can.

Automation

The term automation is used to describe a situation where machines have replaced people for controlling industrial processes. Electronic and computer techniques are used to regulate machines automatically. A good example is the automatic pilot (first tested in 1912) used in most aircraft. A flight plan is fed into the aircraft computer and on-board sensors detect when the plane is not flying on its predetermined route. These sensors then send automatic instructions to parts of the aircraft, for example, the rudder to alter course. Automatic control sensors are used in mining, oil refining and the steel industry, where they are used to detect internal flaws in the steel.

Research shows that in industries which are highly automated the jobs with responsibility are more interesting, stressful, varied and specialised but in return pay more. Working conditions tend to be relatively good compared with those in non-automated industries. The major effect of mechanisation and automation has been to reduce the number of employees required, particularly in manufacturing industry where one machine can now perform the tasks of many workers.

Activity

Make a list of industries which are now automated. For each, state what effect the automation could have on the workers and management.

Contracting out

The term contracting out applies to:

- situations where services, such as school meals, or college cleaning, originally managed and provided by the public sector, in this case the local authority, are now run by the private sector, i.e. they have been contracted or put out to private businesses which now have the contract to carry out the work. Contracting out has been part of the wider process of privatisation designed to reduce the level of government intervention in the economy (see page 429). By 1996 it is estimated that £400 m of services will have been contracted out.
- situations where private businesses arrange for the whole or part of a project to be carried out by subcontractors. The method is very popular in the building and construction trades, for example, where a major company will lead and manage a project but arrange for specialist contractors to complete specific jobs such as the electrical or plumbing work. (If you intend having any building work done, find out if subcontractors are going to be used!)

Computer Aided Design (CAD)

Computer software is increasingly used to help with the design and manufacture of many products. The main advantage of CAD is that designs can be drawn on screen and viewed from many different angles by 'flipping' or 'rotating' the computer image. Different designs can be tested and compared. For example, cars can be tested for drag and wind resistance using computer simulated wind conditions until the most efficient design is found. This technique has meant that the design process is much cheaper and quicker because fewer prototypes need to be constructed. By using stress and strain tests on different materials, designers have discovered that much lighter materials could be used producing a lighter car with better fuel consumption. Information about every component used in the design is immediately available and parts and component lists and drawings can be created and printed quickly. You will have noticed that 'new and improved' models are appearing more often because it is easier to make changes. The information database about the product specification is used to form the basis of the manufacturing process.

Computer Aided Manufacturing (CAM)

Many machines, for example, those used to cut and turn metals, can now be controlled by computer. The instructions for these operations come from the design database which is linked directly to the machine. Changes can be made quickly and easily so batches of components can be made to order. Parts can be standardised and used in many models. The main advantage of CAM has been greater reliability and consistency, although this has only been achieved with the loss of many skilled jobs.

An example of this is the loss of 600 jobs at the Rolls Royce aero engine design centre at East Kilbride in Scotland. A spokesman said that the company needed fewer design engineers because of the efficiency improvements that had come from computerisation of their design work. The cost reductions were necessary to maintain their competitiveness (see page 494).

Just-in-Time (JIT)

This is a very old concept in fresh food retailing and catering, which Japanese business applied to manufacturing. Although JIT methods can affect all aspects of a business, it is usual to think of JIT in a manufacturing context. It can be applied to purchasing, supply and production. Stated briefly, it means only buy supplies when you need them. Here is an example to show what it is and how it works. Look at the diagram on page 402. Under the present system stock (parts and components such as seats and paint) for each stage of the production process would be stored on the site until it was needed. With the JIT method of providing parts and components for stocking the production line, they would only arrive at the assembly line as and when they were needed. Parts are not stocked up in advance and only a minimum amount of stock needs to be kept on the premises.

Advantages of the JIT method

- Less space is needed for storage. This can be very important where land is scarce and/or expensive.
- There is less chance of stock being damaged or deteriorating.
- Storage costs are lower.
- Opportunity costs are lower because capital is not tied up in stock so it can be used to do other things.
- Continuous production is possible when the system runs smoothly.

Disadvantages of the JIT method

- Suppliers need to be totally reliable and will have to co-operate closely with the manufacturer to make the JIT system work.
- Serious problems can occur if supplies are disrupted; some extra stock may be kept to overcome temporary emergencies. A good example of this is the strike by workers at the General Motors plant at Flint in Michigan, USA. The plant makes parts for GM cars throughout the United States. The strike began after GM had 'downsized' (made redundant) a large number of its workforce in an attempt to cut costs. This meant that the remaining workforce had to work much harder to maintain production levels and working conditions deteriorated. The strike began on a Wednesday and by Friday morning most GM plants had to close because of a shortage of parts. What does this tell you about single sourcing and JIT?
- The need to provide a continuous flow of materials requires a very efficient and dedicated management and administration team. Because the JIT system does not provide for back-up stocks, operating the system can be very stressful.

Sourcing

One of the key decisions which needs to be taken by any business is how to source its production or distribution and where to obtain its supplies.

Raw materials, parts   Manufacturer   Wholesaler   Retailer   Consumer

Manufacturers will need to make decisions about the best source of raw materials and/or parts and components. Retailers have to decide whether to buy directly from the manufacturer or to buy through a wholesaler. Consumers also have a choice to make.

Here are three examples of decisions that have to be made:

a Can we make the part or component ourselves or do we have to buy it in from another company? When businesses do decide to buy in parts or components to help the production process, this is called 'contracting out' the work.

b Do we need many suppliers or can we use just one?

c Can we use a local or national supplier, or would it be better to import?

For any decision it is useful to have a set of criteria by which the alternatives can be judged. The cost benefit approach we used in Chapter 2 would be very helpful. Here are some criteria that can be used; you will probably think of others.

- Prices: it should be possible to get cheaper supplies by ordering in bulk from a single supplier and/or by buying locally and/or by ordering regularly from the same supplier.
- Delivery: the main considerations in any decision about delivery are: can the goods be delivered on time, in the right place, to the right person, in the proper condition, in the right quantity? Which supplier is most likely to achieve this? A well established company? A local business? A new entrant to the industry? A small or large company?
- Quality: does the supplier have approved quality control and quality assurance systems? Is the quality consistently of the right standard? Does it always meet the specification that has been laid down and agreed? If there is an outside cleaning contractor at your centre (i.e. this service has been contracted out), there will be a specification for the contract which lays down, for example, the number of times a classroom has to be cleaned each week.
- Reliability: will the goods be delivered as stated on the contract? This is vital when JIT is in operation.
- Control: the ability to have clear lines of communication and decision making with suppliers is vital for a contract to run smoothly. Marks & Spencer, which has very close relationships with its suppliers, rates this feature as being most important when choosing suppliers. Contingency plans need to be available to cover potential emergencies.

Activity

a Use the criteria listed above to create a list of advantages and disadvantages for each of the three choices a, b and c given above.

b What decision would you make in each case? Say why.

Labour flexibility

There are very few production processes which operate at a constant level. Many businesses trade in markets where the demand fluctuates. There will be peaks and troughs in the patterns of work. For instance, the Royal Mail delivers the majority of mail over the Christmas period, Cadbury Schweppes sells most of its chocolate eggs in the period before Easter, and most soft drinks in the summer. Many retail stores sell most of their stock on Saturdays. Most people travel to and from work during the morning and evening 'rush hours'. To cope with such variations in demand, a business requires a flexible workforce. It needs to be able to vary the number of people it employs with more staff working during busy times, for example, shops have a small number of core full-time staff and many part-time staff. When business fluctuates during the day employers often operate flexi-time systems, where workers might work a core time between 10 a.m. and 3 p.m. with their other hours being worked either before or after these times. Many teachers work annual hours with a different number of hours being taught each week depending on the demand. In some businesses it may be necessary for workers to do several jobs, for example stocking shelves and then operating the till. These people will need to be multi-skilled and require extra training.

Activities

1 Make a list of businesses which require temporary staff, part-time staff, staff on flexi-time, multi-skilled or multi-talented staff. Say what work these people might do. Say why these types of staff might be needed (see also page 465).

2 When might demand peak for the following?
- Standard fireworks
- Fred Perry tennis shoes
- Patrick rugby boots
- Hallmark greetings cards

What are the implications for continuity of production?

Mobility of labour

The **mobility of labour** refers to the workers' ability to move from job to job, or area to area.

Occupational (or job-to-job) mobility

The ability to move from one job to another largely depends on the amount of skill, training and experience required for a particular occupation. Mobility is highest when the same job can be done in many industries, for example, the same clerical workers can work for a local authority, a chemical or a construction company. Similarly, brick layers can lay bricks to make houses (construction) or to re-line the inside of a furnace (steel industry). The key question is whether a person possesses skills which can be transferred from one occupation/industry to another.

Mobility will be low either when jobs require a long period of expensive training, or because people possess unique skills and must be retrained whenever they attempt anything else.

The amount of labour mobility is a reflection of the buoyancy of the economy. When the economy is expanding, labour mobility tends to be higher. Can you say why?

Geographical (or area-to-area) mobility

At any one time there could be unemployment in one area and vacancies in another. These labour market imbalances occur either when:

- the supply of labour is greater than the demand, which creates unemployment, or
- the demand for labour is greater than the available supply, which is indicated by vacancies.

One way of overcoming the problem is to provide help for people to move from areas of excess supply, to areas where there are vacancies. The **push and pull theory** invented by geographers to explain the movement of people from rural into urban areas, suggests that people are 'pushed' by unemployment and the lack of job opportunities. They are 'pulled' by the prospect of jobs and 'the big city lights'. For example, during the 1960s there was a major movement of people from North Africa to France, from the Caribbean to the UK, and from Turkey and the former Yugoslavia into Germany, where they were known as 'guest workers'.

Figure 9.3 shows the inter-regional movement of people in the UK. A minus or negative figure means that people have left the region, for example, 4 per cent left the North West (an outflow) while 8 per cent moved into the South West (an inflow).

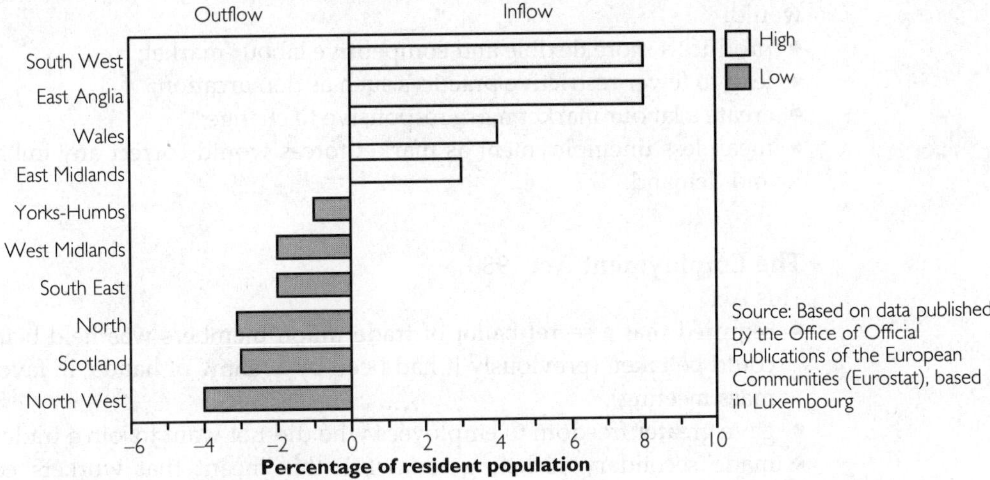

Figure 9.3 Regional migration in the UK

For your own region can you say why people were 'pushed' out, or 'pulled' in?

What affects people's ability to move?

The ability of people to move is mainly affected by their social and economic circumstances.

Reasons for moving	Reasons for staying
Prospects are better	Cannot afford to move – too expensive
Not worth staying	'Our mortgage is bigger than the value of our house'
No family ties, for example, young single people	Family, friends, children's education
Jobs are available for qualified people	No jobs available

Activities

1 **Hold a group discussion on whether it is better to 'take work to the workers', i.e. to build new factories and create job opportunities in areas of unemployment, or 'take workers to the work', i.e. give incentives to people to move away and seek work, even in other countries.**

2 **Construct a chart which shows how long people have been in their present home. Find out whether they would move again! Ask your parent or guardian the same question.**

Employment law and labour flexibility

During the last ten years there has been an enormous increase in the role played by the law in the conduct and regulation of relations between employers and individual employees, trade unions and their members, and between management and trade unions.

The main purpose of the Employment Acts, passed by the Conservative government under Margaret Thatcher as Prime Minister, was to weaken/reform (depending on your point of view) the trade union movement. It was claimed that the legislation would:

- produce a more flexible and competitive labour market;
- lead to fewer restrictive practices such as demarcation;
- create a labour market more responsive to change;
- mean less unemployment as market forces would correct any imbalance of supply and demand.

The Employment Act 1980

This Act:

- required that a secret ballot of trade union members was held before strike action could be taken (previously it had been by a 'show of hands' in favour/against, at a mass meeting);
- gave greater freedom to employees who did not want to join a trade union;
- made secondary picketing unlawful: this meant that workers could not picket anywhere except at their own workplace. (A **picket** is an individual or group, which stands outside the workplace trying to prevent other employees, customers, etc. from entering the premises during a strike.)

The Employment Act 1982

This Act:

- gave further legal protection to people who did not wish to join a trade union;
- made it unlawful for a union to strike, other than for a claim over wages and/or conditions against their employer. Trade unions could otherwise be sued in law.

The Trade Union Act 1984

This Act:

- dictated that secret ballots were needed for union elections at national level;
- ensured that trade unions could be sued over a strike unless it had been agreed by a secret ballot.

The Employment Act 1988

This Act gave union members the power to stop their union from striking if there has been no secret ballot.

The Employment Act 1990

This Act:

- ensured that trade union members who take unofficial strike action against the employer (i.e. a strike not approved by the union as a result of a secret ballot) would be breaking their contracts of employment and could be dismissed;

- stated that a union must disclaim any attempt at unofficial strike action otherwise legal action could be taken against it.

The Trade Union and Labour Relations (Consolidation) Act 1992

This Act brought together a wide range of existing laws relating to the immunities, obligations, and internal government of trade unions and employers' associations. It clarified the status of collective agreements and the regulations concerning industrial action.

What are the effects of this legislation?

The main effects of the legislation appear to have been:

1. Fewer demarcation disputes and a more flexible approach to methods of working, for example, workers have been willing to work in teams and tackle several jobs.
2. Increased levels of productivity.
3. A decrease in the number of days lost through stoppages. (The Miners Strike of 1984 was the exception.)

Case study

Table 9.1 shows the figures for the total working days lost by **industrial stoppages** in 'all industries and services' for 1979–92. The figures for trade union membership are also included.

Table 9.1 Industrial disputes and trade union data

Year	Membership of trade unions (000s)	Working days lost through industrial stoppages	Significant event
1979	13,280	20,470,000	Winter of Discontent
1980	12,940	11,960,000	Employment Act
1981	12,100	4,270,000	
1982	11,590	5,310,000	Employment Act
1983	11,230	3,750,000	
1984	10,990	27,130,000	Trade Union Act
1985	10,820	6,400,000	
1986	10,530	1,920,000	
1987	10,470	3,540,000	
1988	10,370	3,700,000	Employment Act
1989	10,150	4,120,000	
1990	9,950	1,900,000	Employment Act
1991		760,000	Recession
1992		520,000	Recession

Source: *Employment Gazette*

Activity

1 Plot the figures in Table 9.1 on two separate line graphs.
2 Can you comment on the possible effect of the employment legislation?
3 What are the trends in trade union membership and working days lost?
4 Are these trends reflected in your own organisation? Give reasons for your answer.

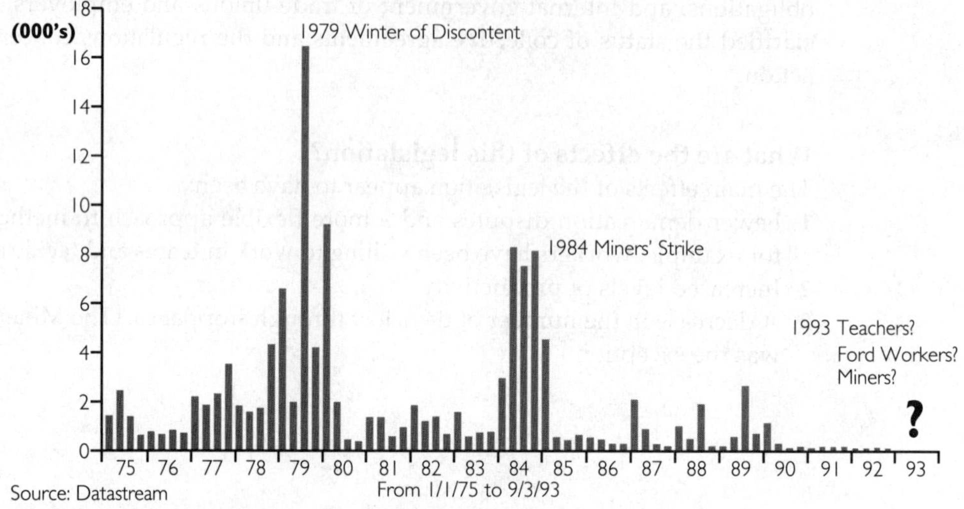

Figure 9.4 UK working days lost in all stoppages – all industries and services

5 Compare the graph of Figure 9.4 with the one you have drawn. Can you spot the mistake on the newspaper version?

Effects of changing patterns of production

Who is affected by changes in the way goods are produced? The biggest impact of any change in patterns of production is felt by the employees and customers. For instance, when supermarkets install bar code readers at check out points workers need to key in less information, customers get itemised bills, the buyers and stock controllers get a computer printout with analysis of the sales and shelf fillers no longer have to put prices on every item. However, as this extract shows, bar codes do not always work in favour of the customer.

Case study

Bar code readers scam prices

An unpublished investigation by the European Commission found that almost 10% of all products sold in supermarkets could be wrongly priced. Here are some examples that were discovered: reduced price labels are not put on properly so that the original higher price is visible and scanned; special offers such as 2 for the price of 1 are sometimes scanned twice.

Activity

When you go shopping, check the shelf price and compare it with the bill price of the products you buy. How do you think that longer shopping opening hours and price cutting between stores have contributed to the mistakes in pricing? The next time you go shopping check your bill!

Effect on employees – human resourcing

Employees are radically affected by changes in methods of production. The organisation's human resource policy may require re-writing. Here are some examples of how working conditions could be affected.

- New working practices could be introduced which require people to work in teams.
- New production processes could involve the use of new machines and patterns of work may be standardised so that people have to work at the same rate as the machines. This can lead to considerable stress.
- Organisations may need reorganising; management structures may need to be changed.
- Cost cutting, 'down-sizing' and redundancies can occur.
- Jobs may be regraded with new job descriptions and people may have to reapply for their own jobs. This can occur when redundancy is threatened and decisions have to be made about who should leave.
- Pay structures may be changed.
- New hours of work may be needed – shift working and Sunday trading may be introduced.
- New contracts of employment could be introduced which reduce the number of full-time permanent posts in favour of part-time or temporary contracts. Most new superstores operate with 20% full-time and 80% part-time staff.

Skill shortages

Skill shortages have become increasingly evident during the 1980s and 1990s as the labour market has changed. The main features now of the labour supply are:

- greater female participation
- fewer young people
- more older workers
- more part-time workers
- greater demand for skills.

As production has become more automated with a large amount of capital equipment being used, the role of workers has changed. Fewer people are required for routine assembly line jobs, and there has been a move away from unskilled manual work into more highly skilled and specialised checking and monitoring tasks. This shift has also been accompanied by a move towards **multi-skilling**, where one worker now does a number of separate tasks. For example, whereas previously it would have needed at least two skilled people to cut (a fitter) and join (a welder) steel pipes, today it is likely that both jobs would be completed by the same person.

Multi-skilling has improved motivation and reduced the number of disputes caused by demarcation (when jobs are strictly separated by the kind of work done by members of different trade unions, such as fitters and welders). This change has occurred in both manufacturing and service industries, and has resulted in a more flexible and adaptable workforce willing to work in teams and accept greater responsibility.

The introduction of new technology has required workers to be trained and educated to deal with the changing conditions. When this training does not take place or insufficient workers are attracted into new jobs, then a **skill shortage** will occur.

Where do skill shortages occur?

1 Small companies tend to have more difficulty than large companies in recruiting skilled workers, possibly because they do not pay enough or there is insufficient internal training.
2 Rapidly growing industries tend to have the most difficulty in recruiting employees, particularly when new production methods or new technologies are developed.
3 The greatest shortfall appears to be in the Engineering and Craft sectors, along with Professional and Technical occupations.
4 Within Europe, countries have different problems, for example, in Greece, companies are short of marketing and clerical staff. Spain, is reporting shortages of staff to work in the tourist industry.

What is not clear is whether the skill shortages experienced by different companies are due to a lack of trained personnel or poor recruitment policies. For example, poor pay and working conditions will deter people from applying. Similarly, many companies do not give enough attention to human resource planning, with the consequence that future skill needs remain unsatisfied.

During the 1990s, it is expected that there will be a continued growth in demand for specialist and highly skilled workers, technicians and scientists, managers and other professionals. However, demand for unskilled workers generally is likely to fall. (There may be localised exceptions when specific projects are undertaken, such as the Channel Tunnel.)

Local forecasts for the demand for skills are often made by the Training and Enterprise Council (TEC) in a particular area.

Case study

Towards the twenty-first century

In this case study there are four exhibits for you to look at. Study them carefully then complete the activities.

Exhibit 1

Here is the prediction made by the South Thames TEC, in Market Assessment Document No. 1, for each of the main sectors represented in its area.

Sector	Demand for skills	No. employed
Business Services	People with degrees, GNVQ Advanced or A levels will always be needed.	27,000
Banking and Finance	Continuing demand for people with managerial and accounting skills. Secretarial skills will also be needed in the area.	12,000
Construction	Continuing demand for carpenters, bricklayers, electricians, etc. Decline in apprenticeships could make it difficult to recruit. The industry relies on untrained casual labour. Likely shortages in technical and managerial jobs.	15,000
Manufacturing	New technology of vital importance particularly for professionals. People need to be updated and re-skilled. Continuing shortage of people with engineering skills and qualifications. Demand for technology-related skills for the printing trades.	22,000

Public Sector	Little prospect of growth, but despite this a continuing shortage of specialists, e.g. solicitors, accountants, computer staff and social workers.	148,000
Retail	New developments are expected, shortage of experienced supervisory staff.	30,000
Sanitary Services	A very competitive market; more health and safety training is required.	16,000
Telecommunications and Postal Services	A completive sector, with continuing demand for high level specialist skills and training.	12,000
Hotel, Catering and Other Services	This sector mirrors the fortunes of the economy; heavily dependent on the tourist trade. Skilled managers and chefs will be needed.	23,000

Source: Adapted From the South Thames TEC Market Assessment Document

Exhibit 2

Skills Gap Returns as Recession Fades!!!

The skills gap is here again says recruitment agency boss – 'six months ago we could have advertised for an accountant at £20,000 and had six good applicants, today you can hardly get one. Its the same with secretarial staff, a post which would have attracted 70 people might today only attract three people. It is fully trained specialists who are most in demand. In large companies managers are more likely to lose their jobs than their contemporaries in smaller firms. The reverse is true of support staff. In the future there is less likelihood of good experienced staff being available.'

Source: Adapted from an article in the *Evening Standard*

Exhibit 3
This is a list of questions from the Lloyds Bank Recruitment Application Form reproduced with kind permission of Lloyds Bank.

4. OTHER EXPERIENCE

This section is concerned with a number of activities involved in working for the Bank. In each case, please state the amount of experience you have had, and if experienced, provide an example(s) to illustrate what the activity involved and what you gained from the experience. You should feel free to draw on any aspects of your life so far – e.g. your school, work, community or home life. ***Continue on a separate sheet if you wish***

Activity	Amount of Experience		
Organising or taking responsibility for other people.	none ☐	some ☐	a lot ☐
Being given sole responsibility for completing a job on time.	none ☐	some ☐	a lot ☐
Making decisions that affect other people.	none ☐	some ☐	a lot ☐
Working with groups of other people as part of a team.	none ☐	some ☐	a lot ☐
Dealing with members of the public.	none ☐	some ☐	a lot ☐

Trying to persuade someone to accept your point of view.	none ☐	some ☐	a lot ☐
Learning about a new subject or developing expertise.	none ☐	some ☐	a lot ☐
Writing and/or checking letters or reports.	none ☐	some ☐	a lot ☐
Collating and checking information, facts and figures.	none ☐	some ☐	a lot ☐

Exhibit 4

Education and Training – a response to skill shortages

'A better trained and educated workforce should be more capable of acquiring new skills and coping with change.'

Activity

Read the case study 'Towards the twenty-first century'. Prepare a short report for your Careers Officer which covers the following points.

a Use the information in the case study to say what skills will be needed during the 1990s and beyond.

b Try and obtain the documents for your local TEC. How do they compare with the one given here, for example, are skill shortages predicted in your area?

c Look at the list of skills required by Lloyds Bank. How does it compare with the Core Skills you have achieved in the GNVQ course?

d What courses should your centre run to train people in the skills they will need?

e What advice would you give to a 14-year-old about to choose options at school?

Effect on customers

Changes are being made to the specification of products all of the time, for example, to the colour, materials, ingredients and physical dimensions. As consumers we are all familiar with the words 'New and improved'. Unfortunately, despite the marketing claims, the changes are frequently neither new or improved having been made solely in the interests of the business and its need to add value. What did Persil Power with added manganese do for your clothes?

Activity

Why you are reading a paperback?

Hardback books are going yellow and falling apart after just a few years of use, says a leading bookseller. The quality is worse than at any time in the last 500 years because of the materials and methods now used to produce books, such as high-acidity paper and glueing of the backs. If better materials were used production costs per book would rise by £1, but the retail price would rise by £6 because of the way publishers calculate prices. Up to £2 of the price of a hardback goes on the outside dust jacket.

a Why do you think that publishers have been using 'shoddy materials'?

b Why is so much money spent on the jackets?

c What do you think would happen to the demand for hardbacks if the price went up with an increase in quality? (Hint:: consider elasticity of demand.)

Effect on suppliers

Relationships with suppliers are never easy especially when the customer, in this case another business (retailer, wholesaler or manufacturer), is changing its method of production. Whenever changes are made to the specification of a product there must be close liaison with the supplier. Good relationships with the supplier are vital if a business is to successfully operate a JIT purchasing and delivery system. Four factors are particularly important.

- There should be as few suppliers as possible, because it is then easier to maintain close working relationships.
- Suppliers must be prepared to deliver smaller quantities of goods more often. When pubs in Kent switched to buying locally produced mineral waters on a need-to-buy basis (to reduce their stockholding costs), the suppliers were forced into delivering twice a week.
- Stable long-term relationships are more likely to lead to a good JIT supplier/customer relationship.
- Suppliers must be totally reliable, willing and able to implement JIT requirements.

Much of the impetus for developing JIT systems has come from the large manufacturing companies which have effectively introduced JIT methods into supplying organisations in order to make their own systems more efficient.

Ways to improve production

Training

Training is a key element in improving production in every organisation. It is about investing in human capital (people). More familiarly, it is the money spent on improving and updating people through education and training.

The quality of the workforce

In the last 20 years, the quality of the workforce in terms of the skills possessed by employees has improved. This means that if the same number of workers is employed, then they should be able to produce a larger output. This is clearly shown by the UK coal industry, where despite severe cutbacks in the number of miners, output has risen substantially.

The usual way to find out the value of a qualification/training, is to compare the earnings of people who have the qualification/training with those without such assets. There is no doubt that a well-trained and educated workforce will cope better with the changes expected in the economy during the next ten years.

Job-related training

Training can be a very expensive process and many companies are reluctant to run their own training programmes preferring instead to poach trained workers from other companies by, for example, offering a more attractive remuneration package.

It is only recently that the UK has recognised that much more needs to be done to improve workforce performance. There are now national policies agreed by the government, employers, training agencies and education organisations. These set targets of achievement for young people and adults, for example:

- By 1997 at least 80 per cent of 16-year-olds should obtain NVQ/GNVQ Intermediate (this is currently 40 per cent).
- By the year 2000 at least 50 per cent should attain NVQ/GNVQ Advanced. This should mean that 50 per cent of the workforce will be trained to this level. (Currently 30 per cent are educated to this level or its equivalent.)

The trends in job-related training

- Over the last five years, the number of employees receiving training related to their job has risen by 80 per cent.
- Younger age groups tend to receive more training.
- The increase in training has been greater for women.
- The most popular form of training is 'off-the-job'.
- Professional people, particularly those working in education and health, get more training than those working in manufacturing industries. Is this wise? Can the UK afford to let its industrial base decline?
- Some 70 per cent of organisations say they have training plans and have allocated budgets.
- Larger organisations tend to provide more training than smaller organisations.
- If you work in Yorkshire and Humberside, you have a better chance of being trained than anywhere else, particularly London which has a relatively poor record.

Activities

1 You work in the Personnel Department of Marion and Lala Ltd, an international fabric and fashion design company. Because you have just successfully completed an Advanced GNVQ you have been asked to write a short report on 'The current pattern of training in the local area – how to improve production'.

a You will need to explain the jargon, for example, what do ET, YT, GNVQ, NVQ and TEC mean? What is a Training Credit and how does the system work?

b Find out what training is offered by the local college. How much does it cost?

c Find out what other local organisations provide training.

d Try and find out what on-the-job training is given by local firms.

Note: Look at the government White Papers, 'Employment in the 1990s' and 'Education and training for the 21st Century', which provided some of the information above.

e Using the information above in trends in job-related training, construct a questionnaire which will help you check the information given there. For example, you could use a question such as:

How many employees are there in the organisation?

1–10	11–49	50–99	100–199	200–499	500+	Please tick
☐	☐	☐	☐	☐	☐	

to find out how big the organisation is. The sizes correspond to small, medium, and large.

2 Then **either;**

If you are in a part-time group, survey your colleagues. (At least one person should have received training in the last six weeks, according to the Employment Department, Labour Force Survey. It is this survey which provides some of the data used by Eurostat the Statistical Office of the European Communities. Because Member States use different definitions it can sometimes be very difficult to make comparisons. Great care must be taken when interpreting data. In the UK, for example, people on government training courses who do not have a regular job are treated as 'employed' for the purposes of the Labour Force Survey.)

or,

If you are at school/college, survey staff to find out what training they have received or will be given.

3 Prepare a short talk suitable for giving to new people starting in your organisation, entitled 'Training in our Organisation'.
If you are in an organisation which does not have training, and 30 per cent do not, try to explain why this is the case.

Research and development (R&D)

European companies are increasingly recognising the advantages of working together in research and development (R&D). The European Union has a large R&D programme which covers a wide range of production, information and communication technologies, industrial and materials technologies, environment and life sciences technologies, energy, human capital and mobility. In addition EUREKA is a separate pan-European initiative to encourage R & D on industry-led market-driven projects. It concentrates on producing hi-tech goods and services which will enable Europe to compete worldwide. (Source: DTI Single Market Fact Sheets).

Most research and development (R & D) expenditure is spent on developing new products, materials and processes with the aim of

- becoming more efficient and/or profitable.
- adding value and beating competitors.

All R & D investment involves taking risks. There is no guarantee of commercial success and the majority of R & D expenditure ends in failure. However, as with any high risk activity, the rewards can be huge. The key to success is to ensure that any invention is protected by patents (see page 95). Gad and Hans Rausing, the Swedish brothers who own the patents for Tetra Pak, the plastic and aluminium coated pack for milk and fruit juice found in every fridge, are now worth over £5,200 million.

During 1993 some £9.1bn was spent on R & D in the UK, 70% of which was spent by the UK corporate sector, 13% by the Government, primarily on defence (nearly 40% down since the end of the 'cold war') and 17% by overseas sources. The top spending industries were pharmaceutical manufacturers (for example Glaxo invested £2.7bn, generating £10.8bn of added value, whilst SmithKline Beecham invested £1.9bn, generating £10.4bn of added value), healthcare operators, engineering and aerospace companies, information technology and electronics.

Activity

Glaxo Un-Wellcome

The Financial Times reported the Glaxo takeover of Wellcome (two of the largest drugs companies in the UK) under the headline 'Savings could reach £600 m with R & D most likely target'. Why are drug companies the biggest spenders on R & D? What effect might a cutback have on employees, customers profits and costs?

Investment in physical capital

When might a business change its level of investment? There are many possibilities, including:

- when a business decides to change the specification of existing products;
- when a business introduces new products in response to market pressures;
- when a business uses new machines.

Investment in **physical capital** refers to the amount and type of investment made in improving, changing and updating the machinery, plant and equipment used in industry. It is about bringing in new technology to help the business. This type of investment is an important reason why productivity and output can grow.

Let us find out how much the UK spends on new physical capital each year. If you refer to the tables for Gross Domestic Product (GDP) in the *Annual Abstract of Statistics* or the *Monthly Digest of Statistics* you will need to find the row entitled Gross domestic fixed capital formation, abbreviated to GDFCF.

Table 9.4 gives the figures for 1969, 1979 1989 in £000 million; this is thousands of millions. All the calculations are based on the prices as they were in 1985. The reason for this is that we can then ignore the effect of inflation and look at real trends in the economy. (For example, if prices doubled but output stayed the same, the UK would appear to be better off, whereas in reality, the same amount of goods are available.)

Table 9.4 Gross domestic fixed capital formation figures in comparison to GDP figures (in £000 million)

	1969	1979	1989
Gross domestic product (GDP)	260.1	331.0	413.3
Gross domestic fixed capital formation (GDFCF)	50.3	56.5	81.0

To find out how much of our wealth (GDP) is spent on renewing and building new plant and machinery, we calculate the GDFCF as a percentage of GDP.

1969	1979	1989
19.34% (37%)	17.07% (31%)	19.6% (32%)

Compare these figures for the UK, with those of Japan which are given in brackets. Japan has always invested more in new capital than the UK.

When we combine this information with figures about the amount of research and development and the number of patents taken out for new products and new methods of working in the UK, we have a possible explanation for why the UK economy has lagged behind that of Japan.

Look at Chapter 4 for more information on new technology and the effect that it has on business and society.

Case study

Japanese companies in Britain – ways to improve production

Since 1984 the number of Japanese companies operating in Britain has grown from 20 to 180. The main reasons for this have been:

- relatively low labour costs, particularly with respect to the 'on costs' such as insurance, associated with employing labour;
- lower taxes on company profits compared to the rest of Europe;
- better communications systems.

Japanese companies can now be found in many industries. Hitachi, for example, make colour television sets in South Wales, but it is in car production that they have made the biggest impact.

Japanese methods and **working practices** have been introduced, and are beginning to affect the way many UK companies now work. The key features of the Japanese management style which are transferable to the UK are:

- A major emphasis on quality 'get it right first time' – every worker is given responsibility to produce quality goods. Individuals are helped by 'quality circles' and 'quality groups' in which the work group are actively involved. The trust and responsibility given to workers improves motivation and creates commitment.
- Developing a well trained and educated workforce.
- Employing people who are willing and able to do a range of jobs (multi-skilling).
- Introducing work teams in which every employee is dedicated to the success of the organisation.
- Creating a working environment in which people are willing to acquire new skills and work for the same company for life. Companies will not want to train their staff if they are going to be poached by other companies.

Activity

Prepare a memo for your section head saying:

a which of the above working practices should be introduced into your business;
b why they should be introduced;
c what difficulties there may be in changing working practices.

Government strategies for improving the competitiveness of UK industry

Supply side economic policies

Supply side economic policies are those designed to change the underlying structure of the economy and improve the ability of markets, businesses and workers to produce goods and services more efficiently. Advocates of supply side policies would support a market-based economy with less government intervention. This is exactly the policy which has been followed by UK governments since 1979.

What policies would be included?

Controlling inflation

How does inflation affect a business? Traditional wisdom/research suggests that inflation will have an immediate but contradictory effect on consumer demand and confidence. Higher prices should mean that people buy less; however, if people think that prices will continue to rise they may well buy more in advance of further price rises. (The example on the following page is often given as an exception to the laws of demand, see page 67.)

Planning and forecasting will become more difficult as conditions change. Generally businesses prefer stable conditions. For instance, if inflation is expected to continue at

Low inflation makes Britain feel so bad

WITHOUT wishing to overstate it, I may have solved the conundrum of the British economy; the mystery of why a combination of circumstances that should be so good feels so flat and uninspiring.

My discovery has nothing to do with tax increases, job insecurity or the fact that the Christmas credit-card bills have just arrived. Nor is it purely because an export-led recovery will only gradually be felt by most of us.

No, the reason is that we do not much like low inflation, and perhaps we never will.

Nor is this a modern phenomenon. When we look back now on the 1950s and 1960s we regard it as a golden age of low inflation and respectable economic growth. But at the time it did not feel so golden. Harold Macmillan's 1957 phrase: "Let's be frank about it; most of our people have never had it so good", (truncated to "you've never had it so good"), was an attempt to buck up a curmudgeonly electorate unconvinced of the merits of a low-inflation, steady-growth world.

Subsequently, economists latched on to the notion that a little bit of inflation was a good thing. It lubricated the wheels of the economy, making it easier to change relative prices and wages, and enabling people to persuade themselves that they were better off. Such thinking was dangerous, and helped usher in the great inflation period of the 1970s and 1980s. But it has its echoes today.

How so? There are the obvious points, notably that an absence of inflation in the price of goods is associated with a lack of asset-price inflation, in particular stagnant house prices.

There is also the familiar "money illusion", whereby people feel better off with a 10% pay rise alongside 8% inflation than when the figures are 4% and 2%, respectively. Michael Portillo, the employment secretary, addressed this theme recently when he said it would require a huge act of statesmanship to persuade people that small pay rises which kept their value were better than larger ones that did not.

Surely, however, both of these are essentially problems of adjustment? Once people have got used to the fact that house prices do not rise by very much they will accept it. Nesting rather than investing then becomes the key motivation for buying a house. And, while acceptance of a stable property market will be slowest in coming to the 1 million households caught in negative equity, it will feed through there eventually too.

Source: *The Sunday Times*, 8 January 1995

say 6% then the business can forecast its expected costs and revenues by using the spot and forward markets. This is better than having variable rates of inflation. Certainty is preferred to uncertainty.

Input costs will rise, for example, there could be increased costs of raw materials, parts and components. Labour costs, i.e. wages, could rise leading to problems over wage negotiations. Energy costs could rise, so industries which are heavily dependent on energy may close down, try to find other sources of supply, or substitute one form of energy for another.

Inflation will have different impacts on borrowers and lenders. Borrowers will tend to gain because the money which they have to pay back will be worth less than its original value. Lenders, however, will be relatively worse off because the money which they get back will be worth less.

How can inflation be controlled? The government's success in controlling inflation largely depends on the cause of inflation. There are two main explanations of how inflation is caused:

- **Keynsians** believe that it is caused by a combination of cost and demand factors namely **cost push inflation,** where increases in input costs are passed on to the consumer as higher prices, i.e. costs push up prices, and **demand pull inflation;** if demand increases when supply is fixed, prices are likely to be forced upwards. If this view is correct, then the best way to control inflation is by a combination of supply side and demand side policies. Supply side policies, such as employment legislation designed to reduce the bargaining power of trade unions and therefore their ability to raise wages, are likely to be most effective in reducing cost-based inflation. Demand side policies, such as cutting government expenditure or raising taxation, should have the effect of reducing the level of aggregate demand.
- **Monetarists**, however, believe that inflation is caused by an excess of money in the economy. Therefore there is no point in applying supply side or demand side regulations and controls. The only solution is to cut the quantity of money in circulation.

Reducing the role of government

One of the main political objectives of government policy has been to reduce the amount of government intervention and government spending. Since 1979 successive Conservative governments have played a smaller role in running the economy. The effects of this policy have been felt in all sectors of the economy.

In education, schools have opted out of the state run system and become grant maintained. Colleges have become self-governing corporations. Hospitals have become trusts. Manufacturing businesses have closed. The private sector is being actively encouraged to finance infrastructure projects such as the high speed rail link to the channel tunnel. The major way in which the objective has been implemented is by privatisation and deregulation.

Privatisation

In the UK **privatisation** really got going in 1979, when the Conservative government sold part of its stake in BP (British Petroleum). The process has continued right through into the 1990s, until now there is little of the 'family silver' left except a few spoons.

Privatisation can mean:

- Selling state, or publicly-owned assets and industries to the private sector. As well as selling off some of the public corporations, the government has sold substantial shareholdings that it acquired in private sector companies. Originally this investment was made either because the government wished to control or to support certain companies. BP (British Petroleum) is an example.
- Transferring public sector services into the private sector – local authorities have been encouraged to put services such as refuse collection 'out to tender'. Recently police forces have contracted out some prisoner escort services to organisations such as Group 4 and discussions are underway to privatise the collection of information at the scene of burglaries and road accidents. It is argued that this will free police time for more vital matters.
- Deregulation – abolishing state controls on the freedom of competition, for example, bus services within cities are now open to private operators.

The process of privatisation has been controversial, but has succeeded in raising enormous one-off sums of money for the government. Many critics have argued, however, that the shares, especially in the early days, were issued too cheaply. The government has so far succeeded in selling: British Airports, British Aerospace, British Airways, British Gas, British Steel, British Telecom, Jaguar, Rolls Royce, Trustee Savings Bank (TSB), and the electricity and water companies, among others.

Activity

Table 9.5 shows the initial share prices of a number of privatised companies. Complete the table by looking up the present values of these shares in a daily paper.

Table 9.5 Privatised companies

Company	Date of privatisation	Share price (p) when privatised	Now
Amersham International	Feb 1982	142	
British Aerospace	Feb 1981	150	
BAA	Jul 1987	100	
British Airways	Feb 1987	65	
British Gas	Dec 1986	50	
British Petroleum	Oct 1979	150	
British Steel	Dec 1988	60	
British Telecom	Dec 1984	50	
TSB	Sep 1986	50	

Why has privatisation occurred?

Supporters of privatisation claim:

- Market forces and private ownership work better than state-run monopolies.
- It will improve the competitiveness of UK industry.
- Competition produces a better allocation of resources and improved services, for example, private bus companies can compete for routes since the deregulation of state-run services and private contractors can compete to provide what were formerly local authority services such as refuse disposal and parks maintenance.
- Central and local government can spend less, so public expenditure can be reduced.
- Private services are more efficient and cost-effective.
- Wider share ownership will encourage people to take a greater interest in the way companies are run. This should make companies more accountable.
- Private companies are more alert to the needs of customers. Plans have been made to split up British Rail for privatisation. The idea is that the different sections will be sold off to be run by new or existing private companies.

Opponents of privatisation claim:

- Competition can lead to wasteful duplication of resources.
- Private companies will not run necessary services unless they are profitable. For example it is unlikely that a private company would maintain important rail services to rural areas, or run off-peak services at their present levels. The company has a responsibility to make profits for its shareholders.
- Private monopolies which have been created, such as the gas, water and electricity companies, use their monopoly to charge high prices. In fact the government did recognise this danger and created watchdog bodies such as OFWAT (water) OFTEL (telecommunications) and OFGAS (gas) to monitor the situation.

- Privatisation has lead to greater unemployment and a worsening of conditions for many workers. BT for example, despite making considerable profits, has reduced staff numbers.
- Small shareholders do not take an active interest in companies and many sold their shares almost immediately.
- The pricing policies which result from attempts to maximise profits leave many people unable to afford essential services.
- Where industries were profitable before they were privatised it is argued that the state, and therefore UK citizens, have been denied the benefits of these profits.

Activity

Read up in the press on recent developments in the plan to privatise British Rail. From what you have read and what you have learnt from this chapter write notes on why you are for or against British Rail staying in the public sector.

You should be prepared to give a four-minute speech putting over your point of view. Don't forget that as well as supporting your own view you should refer to the opposing arguments in order to demolish them.

Making the labour market more competitive

The labour market has been made more competitive by the introduction of employment legislation to reform the trade unions (see page 416). Market forces have become more important and any imbalance in the labour market, such as an excess demand or excess supply of labour should eventually correct itself without the need for the government to intervene. The government policy on unemployment has been to:

- cut direct taxation (income tax) making it more attractive to work;
- reduce welfare benefits, making it less attractive to be unemployed or making work more attractive;
- increase vocational and personal skills by improving education and training and giving retraining incentives, 'so that the unemployed should become more employable'.

These are some of the measures in the 1994 Budget to help the unemployed:

- employers get a National Insurance rebate if they employ people who have been out of work for more than two years;
- work trials: unemployed people are able to try out a new job for three weeks without losing benefits; 150,000 new job opportunities could be expected over the next three years;
- speeding up of family credit so that people got some help with rent and council tax during the first four weeks in a new job;
- making more money available with the Job Finders Grant;
- a Job Match scheme, which helps people build up full-time jobs by putting together a number of part-time jobs;
- unemployment benefit will be called the job seeker's allowance.

The essential difference between this and the Keynsian approach is that the latter would have tried creating jobs through public investment programmes on new infrastructure projects. There is an assumption in the supply side policies that there are jobs available but the unemployed 'do not want them' or are 'not properly trained for them'.

Other supply side policies

Since 1979 the government has introduced many different policy measures in its attempts to change the conditions of supply and so increase the aggregate or total supply of products. An example is making financial markets more competitive, for example, by allowing banks and building societies to compete for business.

Demand side policies

Demand side policies are those which are intended to stimulate, curb, control or direct the level of overall/aggregate demand in the economy. Here are some examples:

- increasing or decreasing the level of government spending. Government spending plans are announced in the yearly Budget. In November 1994 the Chancellor said that the government was going to successively cut public spending over the next five years.
- giving grants and loans to individuals and/or businesses. Since 1990 the government has been particularly concerned to help small businesses.
- attempting to even out the 'booms' and 'slumps' which are part of the trade cycle (see page 34). This is sometimes called demand management.
- changing the levels of direct and indirect taxation. This is done in the Budget (see page 55).
- working with the Bank of England to determine the level and timing of interest rate changes.

See Chapter 1 for further discussion of government policies.

Activity

How fiscal and monetary policies can affect demand

The government will decide which policy instrument to use. Depending on the results it wants to achieve the government can:

1 increase or decrease income tax
2 increase or decrease Value Added Tax (VAT)
3 increase or decrease excise duties
4 work with the Bank of England to increase or decrease the rate of interest.

Create a table like the one below which shows how a change in the tax rates should affect the consumer and the business. We have done one example for you.

Policy change	Effect on consumer	Effect on business
Rise in income tax		
Fall in income tax	People will have more money to spend and a greater incentive to work	Increase in demand for particular products depending on price and income elasticity. Unemployment could be reduced and more people employed
Rise in VAT		
Fall in VAT		
Increase in excise duties		
Decrease in excise duties		
Rise in interest rates		
Fall in interest rates		

A government has these objectives:

a to reduce smoking
b to reduce pollution caused by cars
c to reduce noise in the environment caused by road drills
d to increase the demand for clothing
e to stimulate demand in the housing market.

Which policies could it use to achieve each objective?

Improving international opportunities

In recent years the government has introduced a number of measures to improve the UK's international competitiveness, for example, export information and facilities are provided by the Department of Trade and Industry. The 1994 Budget for instance allocated more funds to the Export Credit Guarantee Department (a form of insurance for UK exporters).

Case study

1994 – a year for privatisation in Europe

In 1994 governments in Europe sold off more than $32 billion worth of state assets. Leading the sell off with the biggest privatisation was France which sold just 38% of Elf Aquitain, the oil and petrol group for $6.1 billion. Meanwhile the partial privatisation of Renault was 10 times over-subscribed. A Renault spokesperson said, 'it is not the job of the state to produce cars and trucks'. France was closely followed by the Netherlands, Italy and Denmark.

Activity

Europe needs to work

One of the last acts of European Commission President Jacques Delors before his retirement in January 1995 (he was succeeded by Jacques Santer, whose first speech hinted that the Commission would be much tougher on the UK) was to launch a new code for business practice in Europe. A group of about 20 of Europe's top companies have so far agreed to try and implement the code, including BP and BT. The group say that businesses should try to prevent redundancies, promote vocational training, help workers find jobs, eliminate discrimination against the long-term unemployed and try to create new jobs.

Is this code trying to influence the supply side or demand side of the economy? Why do you think such a code is necessary?

European and international policies

Britain is now an integral part of Europe. Its trade with the rest of the world has decreased, whilst its trade with Europe has increased.

Free trade versus protectionism

Free trade means that countries can export and import products without restrictions such as tariffs, duties (as in Duty Free Shops) or quotas, which are physical restrictions on the amount which can be exported or imported.

The old duty free allowance meant that an individual could bring into the UK a certain amount of goods, for example, alcohol and tobacco, free of duty. If any extra was brought in, duty (a tax) had to be paid. There was no restriction on the amount, providing people were prepared to pay the duty.

International trade is based on the principle that most countries can produce something better than anyone else. This is called comparative cost advantage. A country should, therefore, export products in which it has a cost advantage and import products where it does not have an advantage.

Advantages of free trade are:

- large-scale production is possible as markets are larger
- consumers have a wider choice and at lower prices.

Protectionism – methods used to restrict imports

Protectionism means that the flow of imports into a country is restricted by its government. Types of **import control** which have been used include:

- import duties which raise the price of imports;
- import quotas which physically restrict the amount of goods coming into a country (import restrictions were for many years put on goods from South Africa). General Agreement on Tariffs and Trade (GATT) has tried to abolish quotas;
- subsidies which help UK businesses compete against overseas producers. These are illegal under EU rules. Japanese industry, however, is still heavily subsidised;
- exchange controls – the supply of foreign currency needed to buy overseas goods is restricted;
- complex import systems. Japan is notorious for having a highly complex system for allowing imports into the country. Many companies have been deterred by the amount of administration involved;
- technical standards. Governments often lay down strict standards which have to be met by overseas producers before their goods are allowed into the country. For example, UK ice cream is not allowed into Europe and UK beer has to be changed before it can be sold in Germany.

The government may want to control imports for any of the following reasons:

- to protect 'infant' industries – new and developing industries need protection if they are to grow and make a contribution in the economy. The question is 'When do they stop growing and therefore need no protection?'
- unfair competition and dumping – if exporters are selling their goods cheaply in the UK then it is argued that UK industry needs protection from such unfair competition;
- to protect employment – bringing in cheap imported goods in favour of UK goods will reduce the demand for the domestic product and cause unemployment. It has been suggested that import controls could have prevented the drastic fall in the UK textile industry which caused massive unemployment in Lancashire;
- strategic industries, such as defence, used to be protected from foreign competition. Agriculture has been protected by subsidies so as to reduce the need for imports. However, British Aerospace (UK) and Matra (France) have discussed whether to merge their missile activities.

World Trade Organisation (WTO)

GATT was an agreement between countries which tried to make rules about international trade. Formed in 1947, it recently met in Uruguay – 'the Uruguay round' to attempt to:

- reduce tariffs, and
- abolish quotas.

The Uruguay 'round' was particularly concerned with trying to create freer trade in agricultural products. There was considerable animosity between the USA and the EU over the latter's heavy subsidies to farmers as part of the Common Agricultural Policy. President Clinton of the USA imposed tariffs on a range of goods from the EU and Japan in protest.

The World Trade Organisation (WTO) is the successor to GATT. It started operating on 1 January 1995 when 'the Uruguay round' finally came into effect. The WTO should have more power to liberalise international trade and investment, and settle international trade arguments. It is a formal legal entity, all of whose rules must be observed by its 120 member governments. It will have tough and speedy mechanisms for dealing with trade disputes. We will have to wait and see how well it does. Its first two years could be tough as it tries to implement the decisions of 'the Uruguay round'.

The EU or SEM (Single European Market) is a free trade area. Since 31 December 1992 there have been no tariffs on goods or services within the EU, so that these goods and services are allowed to move freely. There is a common external tariff which countries outside the EU have to pay to export their goods to the community. Overcoming this tariff was a major reason why Japanese car producers started building cars in the UK. It was also a stumbling block in the GATT talks with the USA.

There has been a great deal of resistance to the SEM from groups such as the French farmers who have reacted violently to imports of agricultural goods from countries such as Britain. There have been a number of incidents in which lorries of imported goods have been taken over and destroyed.

Activity

1 Your section head at High Track, a UK footwear manufacturer, is concerned about falling sales due to competition from 'cheap' imports. There is some local sympathy for the difficulties of your firm as it is a major employer in a depressed area. A conference entitled 'Sole Survivors?' is shortly to be held on the difficulties faced by the industry in general.
You are asked by your superior to write some notes giving the case for protecting your industry from imports. She will attend the conference and wishes to put forward her point of view.

Aim of the European Union

From 1 January 1993 we have a Europe where:

- there are no frontiers or borders between member countries;
- people can move freely and live and work wherever they want within the EU;
- goods can be bought and sold in any country within the EU;

- there should be common or single European decisions on:

social affairs	monetary systems	competition
the environment	foreign policy	health and safety
economic issues	agriculture	taxation, etc.

Almost every part of our lives will be affected.

How the European Union works

The aim of the EU is to have a common market. All the countries should co-operate or work together. Companies should be able to buy and sell goods in any of the member countries. They should not have to pay any duties or taxes when their goods cross a frontier or border (duty free shops could disappear). To help the European Union achieve its aims there are various **European institutions**. Some of these are mentioned below.

The European Commission

This organisation is based in Brussels, the capital of Belgium. It has members or commissioners chosen from different countries. They are supposed to act and think as Europeans. They should not represent the country from which they come.

The European Commission has four main aims. These are to:

- make policies and decisions which cover all community activities;
- get the governments of member countries to agree on policies;
- make sure that the laws of the community are obeyed;
- manage and direct community business.

All EU documents are translated into nine official languages (the United Nations has six). This is very expensive and many translators have to be employed.

The Council of Ministers

All important EU decisions are taken by the Council of Ministers. Each country sends a government minister to the meetings. Membership is not constant and it depends upon what is to be discussed as to who will go. For example, if the discussion is to do with finance then the UK would send the Chancellor of the Exchequer. Ministers will act in the interest of their own countries unlike the European Commission members.

European Parliament

We are represented in the European Parliament by 518 MEPs (Members of the European Parliament). At the time of writing they represent approximately 370 million people. As these MEPs are voted for locally there are many political parties represented. They do not sit by country but in political groups. The European Parliament meets in three centres – Strasbourg, Brussels and Luxembourg. MEPs are elected every five years.

The European Parliament can:

- be consulted by the Commission on new plans;
- decide how the Union is to spend its money (the budget);
- criticise and question the Commission;
- advise the Council of Ministers.

The Court of Justice

The judges who are members of the Court of Justice are free to make decisions in the best interests of the community. They are independent. All laws made by the Council of Ministers must be obeyed in all the member countries and if anyone breaks them they can be taken to the Court of Justice, regardless of any decision which might have been made by a country's own legal system.

Making Community laws

1 The Commission drafts or writes its proposed legislation.
2 The draft is sent to the European Parliament for discussion.
3 It is then passed to the Economic and Social Committee which has a membership of employers, consumers and trade unions.
4 It passes next to the Council of Ministers. If they accept it, the proposal becomes law.

EU competition policy

EU **competition policy** is aimed at ensuring that:

> 'a healthy competitive environment exists throughout a unified European market, for the benefit of all – producers, traders, consumers and the economy in general. The rules seek to prevent enterprises from distorting trade rules or abusing their power in the market place, for instance by price fixing between what ought to be competitors, by agreements on market shares, or by production quotas. They also provide for action to be taken in cases where national governments take measures which favour particular firms by granting them aid or tax advantages. The Commission will apply the rules vigorously.'

Source: *Europe Without Frontiers*, Office for the Official Publications of the European Union.

Regional policy

The Single Market will make some regions more attractive than others, so that economic resources would be likely to move into these areas. Other regions, especially those on the edges of the community could become worse off. The 'Golden Triangle' for development is seen as the triangular area formed by the Ruhr – Brussels – Paris.

It is EU **regional policy** to narrow the gap between rich and poor regions by providing funds to finance social and economic projects. There is, for example, a plaque at Port Talbot station to say that it was partly financed by the European Social Fund. Training for London's 16-year-olds has also been provided by the same source.

Food law

This is a useful example to show how the EU is trying to introduce common standards across the member states with respect to labelling information and permissible additives (E numbers) in foodstuffs. It is the Commission's intention that foodstuffs should be freely available everywhere, but there are still problems.

- The Italian government believes that pasta cannot be called pasta unless it is made entirely of durum wheat, whereas in Germany pasta made with soft wheat is perfectly acceptable. Italian pasta makers do use soft wheat if the pasta is to be sold outside Italy.
- German brewers put additives in beer to be sold outside Germany but no additives are allowed in beer sold within Germany.
- Much UK ice cream cannot be sold in Europe because it has no ice and no cream.

Case study

Taittinger versus Allbev Ltd

Thorncroft Vineyards of Leatherhead in Surrey produce a non-alcoholic traditional fruit drink which they call Elderflower Champagne. This name has been used in traditional recipe books for many years. Recently the company was taken to court by the French Champagne producers, who claimed that the name was misleading and should only be applied to products from the Champagne region of France. Champagne-style drinks are produced in many countries but must be labelled 'methode-champagnoise' to distinguish them from the authentic product.

Perhaps surprisingly, Thorncroft won the case. The court ruled that the name was misleading but that there was no serious intention to misrepresent a product which could never be mistaken for real champagne.

However, in June 1993 the Court of Appeal reversed the judgement, ruling that although champagne sales would not be significantly reduced, the French producers had the exclusive right to use the description Champagne. Thorncroft must now find another name.

Further EU changes involve the standards of hygiene required. Often this means that traditional small-scale producers need to take out existing wooden shelves and replace them with stainless steel at considerable cost.

Case study

The Sharpham Estate near Totnes in Devon is devoted to the production of wholesome food. Since 1980 they have been turning the cream from their 60 Jersey cows into a brie-type cheese sold to local hotels as Sharpham.

EU health rules dictate that the cheese must be made with pasteurised milk, but this will destroy its character. So far a compromise has been reached with the Ministry of Agriculture, Fisheries and Food by which the milk is heated to kill off some, but not all of the bacteria. Heat-treating equipment has cost £10,000, installation £1,000, a water filter £500 and regular testing is £35 each time.

Debbie Mumford, the cheese maker said: 'If this had been my own personal business I couldn't have coped. Fortunately the estate were willing to pay.'

Activities

The introduction of food labelling laws will have a considerable impact on certain UK business.

1 Discuss ways in which UK food manufacturers could be affected by the EU food legislation. Make a case for and against the introduction of such laws.

2 Your library may well have a CD-ROM containing a database of newspaper articles. If so locate articles on issues such as the 'Eurosausage' and the Portuguese carrot.

There has been a fair amount of press coverage about issues such as the legal contents of a British sausage and the carrot which is defined as a fruit for EU purposes. Since jam must contain fruit this allows the Portuguese to continue to make carrot jam. The 'Eurobanana' should have a specified curvature.

The Treaty on European Union

More familiarly known as the **Maastricht Treaty,** this will directly affect the lives of everyone in the UK and influence European decisions well into the twenty-first century. The UK has opted out of several parts of the Maastricht Treaty including:

- the Social Chapter (see Appendix 3)
- the fixing of exchange rates in line with other EU countries
- the move towards a common currency (meaning that the UK can keep its own monetary policy), although a UK spokesperson said 'we are talking'
- the avoiding of excessive budget deficits (meaning that the UK can have a budget deficit)
- having common bank notes throughout Europe.

Where the UK has opted out it will have no voting rights in making those decisions.

Activity

What decision would you make?

At the time of writing the UK has 'opted out', that is, not signed the Social Chapter part of the Maastricht Treaty (along with the sections on Exchange Rates).

Your decision will depend upon your social and economic circumstances rather than your politics. The House of Commons is split over whether the UK should or should not sign.

- Males and females could have a different view. Look carefully at Article 6. Is this positive discrimination in favour of women? Should there be more help for women who want to go out to work?
- Do you favour the 'employee' or the 'employer'? Who do you think is likely to benefit the most?
- Do you think the labour market should be regulated with mandatory legislation?
- Do you think the labour market should be unregulated, i.e. that supply and demand forces are sufficient?
- Do you believe particular groups in the workforce need protection?
- Do you think there should be a minimum wage?
- Would organisations care about health and safety if there was no legislation? What about equal pay?

The Maastricht Treaty is very much a 'live' issue and you will need to follow the news regularly to keep up with developments.

Your group should hold a formal debate. This can be extended to other groups, given suitable accommodation. The proposed motion is 'This House believes that the Social Chapter of the Maastricht Treaty should be welcomed in the UK'. You will need four key speakers. Two who will speak in favour of the motion, and two who will speak against. Copies of the Social Chapter should be available as background reading, and you will find the article in the February 1993 issue of the National Westminster Bank Quarterly Review, very useful.

This activity must be videoed, everyone must have an opinion, and must make a contribution. Everyone will be affected whether in work or full-time education. At the end of the debate, a vote must be taken and the results analysed.

Afterwards, you should write a short article for your local newspaper. This should explain what the Social Chapter is about, and how people in local organisations could be affected. Make sure that the name of your centre is prominently displayed.

Case study

High Track Europe

The SEM will to a greater or lesser extent affect all business including:

- where and how it obtains its resources;
- its method of operation, production and manufacturing;
- the marketing of the finished product.

As a maker of footwear, High Track could be dramatically affected.

High Track SEM check-list

Resources:

- the free movement of people, materials and finance
- supply of labour
- wider sources of finance
- wage levels.

Recruitment and selection of labour:

- Should we advertise in Europe?
- Will high flyers move to European companies?
- Should workers be trained to speak another European language?

Marketing and Distribution:

- Is the product suitable?
- What should be the target market?
- Is the quality up to EU standards?
- What are the trends in Europe and demand for footwear?
- Is there a price threat from Eastern Europe and non-EU countries?

Mergers and take-overs:

- Should we merge with a European manufacturer?
- Should we manufacture in Europe or establish a network of distributors?
- Can we form agreements with other EU markets?
- Who are our European competitors?

Activity

High Track wishes to develop exports to EU countries to take advantage of the SEM. Your manager presents you with the above check-list which she picked up at a conference on 'Britain in Europe'. She asks you for a brief reaction to the following:

1. How do you feel that the coming of the SEM will affect the prospects of your company – can you perhaps see both opportunities and threats that it may bring?
2. Check the exchange rate of sterling against the Belgian franc and German mark.
3. Do you feel that leaving the ERM has affected the chances of UK firms' succeeding in the European market? You will need briefly to explain this.

   Hint: use the information you have collected to show the performance of UK industry.

Industrial strategies

The UK industrial strategy is concerned with improving the productivity and competitiveness of industry, so that 'industry will become leaner and fitter' and better able to compete in world markets. It can include measures to:

1 improve productivity;
2 stimulate competition;
3 provide job opportunities through education and training schemes;
4 prevent take-overs or mergers which are against the public interest;
5 provide incentives to businesses which collaborate on, for example, the development of new technology;
6 curb price rises, for example, BT's price rises are strictly regulated;
7 stimulate regions which are in industrial decline.

We have already seen that many businesses grow by merging with or taking over their competitors, as the following case study demonstrates.

Competing on market share, mergers and take-overs

Case study

You know who – red hot Pepper

Cadbury Schweppes, the UK soft drinks manufacturer, is to take over the American Dr Pepper/Seven Up soft drink companies. The cola and non-cola soft drinks markets are separate. Coca-Cola are market leaders in the highly competitive cola market. It is Cadbury's aim to become the world leader in non-cola drinks.

Whenever possible soft drinks are bottled locally from concentrated syrup provided by the manufacturer. The stages are:

Stage 1 Concentrated syrups made and distributed in bulk by the manufacturer
Stage 2 Local bottling plants where water and fizz are added to bulk syrups
Stage 3 Retailed as cola and non-cola

Many catering outlets now buy the concentrated syrups and add their own water. Can you tell the difference?

Some market share figures are shown in the table below.

US market share of the soft drinks market by brand (1993 % estimates)	US market share by company (1993 % estimates)	The UK cola market (%)
Coca-Cola 19.6	Coca-Cola 32.3	Coca-Cola 42
Pepsi-Cola 16	Pepsi Co 24.1	Pepsi 20
Diet Coke 8.8	Dr Pepper/7-Up 11.4	Sainsbury's 12
Diet Pepsi 6.0	Cadbury Schweppes 5.5	Virgin Cola 8.7
Dr Pepper 5.6	Royal Crown 1.8	Others 17.3
Mountain Dew 4.6	Others 24.9	
Sprite 4.1		
Seven Up 2.9		
Others 32.4		

Activities

1 Draw pie charts to show the share of the US market by brand and by company.
2 Draw a pie chart to show the market share by company after the take-over.
3 Draw a pie chart to show the market share of cola in the UK. Why have Sainsbury's own label and Virgin cola grown so quickly?
4 Give reasons why Cadbury Schweppes considers market share to be so important.
5 Why is bottling done locally?

Some take-overs can be in the best interests of the public, for example, costs may be reduced and there could be an increase in investment. The government can use the Monopoly and Mergers Commission (MMC) to investigate mergers, take-overs and restrictive practices. It is the responsibility of the Office of Fair Trading to take any action needed to fulfil MMC recommendations. UK competition policy is concerned with:

- preventing take-overs or mergers which are against the public interest;
- investigating business practices which it considers to be restrictive and anti-competitive.

These examples show this policy in action. In December 1994 the European Commission imposed fines on 42 companies in the cement industry. They were accused of rigging the market for cement throughout Europe, so that customers had very little choice about who supplied their cement. The cartel had divided up national markets so that there was no cross-border competition. This was directly contrary to EU policy. Blue Circle, one of three British companies involved, was fined £12.3 million.

The Monopolies and Mergers Commission reported on the supply of films to UK cinemas. Its main recommendation was that independent cinema owners were to be given better access to 'big' films with the potential for bringing in audiences. At present the big distributors have tied cinema chains with exclusive arrangements to show only their films.

In 1994 the MMC halted the proposed acquisition by the *Daily Mail* newspaper group of a group of regional newspapers which included the *Nottingham Evening Post*. The MMC said 'It might be expected to operate against the public interest; the increase in regional concentration of ownership was of particular concern because of the possible consequences for free expression of opinion and for diversity of opinion' particularly if some publications were closed.

Activity

Merger mania

Instead of buying existing assets from someone else companies which have spare cash should be increasing capacity through new investment. Mergers usually lead to redundancies and less competition. The UK needs to enlarge its industrial base not reduce it.

Use the examples of mergers given above to create a table showing the possible advantages and disadvantages to the customer and the business in each case.

Comparing the performance of the UK economy

Now that we have looked at the changing patterns of production in the UK economy, we need to put these into the context of world markets and international competitiveness.

Newspaper headlines are continually asking how well or how badly the UK is doing compared with the rest of Europe. There are now 15 member countries of the European Union with a total of over 370 million people (three times as many as Japan, and one and a half times as many as the USA). There are tremendous opportunities for UK industry but equally there are possible threats. How can these opportunities and threats be identified? Every business will need to carry out market research and produce a profile of each market segment, in order to decide where to direct its marketing money.

Sources of information

You will find these sources particularly helpful for this element: the newspapers *The Sunday Times* and *The European*, Eurostat (which covers a wide range of data), OECD individual country reports (there is a very useful statistical appendix at the back of each report, which can be used for making comparisons), *Economic Trends* and the *Employment Gazette*.

Case study

Chinese takeaway – sweet and sour

Remember that different companies will have different views of the same data; it will depend on which business they are in. On the sweet side Unilever (detergents and ice cream) is expanding its operations in China by building a new factory in Shanghai to make Omo and is expanding production of Lux and Lifebuoy. 'We have done extremely well in the last two years' says Unilever's Head of Chinese operations. On the sour side Marks & Spencer's director of retail operations in Hong Kong says 'We have decided against opening a store in China for at least 5 years. To support our high-volume low-margin outlets we need more middle class customers'.

Source: adapted from *The Sunday Times*

What information is needed to make a decision? The following tables show some of the economic data that would be useful.

Who has the highest income per head?

The figures in the first table (taken from Eurostat 1994) show the Gross Domestic Product (GDP) per head (for each member) of the population. GDP per head is the value of the total goods and services produced in one year divided by the number of people in the country. The figures have been standardised to take account of different prices and currencies. In this way they can be directly compared. Where does the UK come?

GDP per head of population

Country	1988	1989	1990	1991	1992
Belgium	12947	14084	15167	16114	17130
Denmark	13650	14430	15380	16581	16812
France	13990	15190	16199	17203	17646
Germany	14589	15740	17078(2)	15817	16777
Greece	6175	6704	6877	7329	7851
Ireland	7997	9006	10291	11120	12029
Italy	12928	13967	14902	15884	16497
Japan	13511	14793	16272	17707	18771
Luxembourg	15312	17350	18413	19639	20538
Netherlands	12534	13709	14829	15502	16061
Portugal	7429	8269	8810	9822	10532
Spain	9187	10098	10927	11972	12121
UK	12986	13912	14566	14701	15422

(2) Break in series owing to the reunification of 3.10.1990

Source: Eurostat 1994

Economic growth and inflation

Questions a business should consider are: How quickly or slowly is the economy growing? Which country is best for our company to export to? Which of our products could be sold?

Annual growth rate and inflation

Country	Average annual rate of growth in GDP for 1987–1992 (%)	Growth in GDP for the 3rd quarter 1994	Inflation: annual change in prices (%)
1 Belgium	2.8	2.5	1.9
2 Denmark	1.1	3.5	2.1
3 Germany	4.7	1.5	2.7
4 Greece	1.8	0	11.9
5 Spain	3.7	−1	4.4
6 France	2.4	1.5	1.6
7 Ireland	5.3	2.2	2.5
8 Italy	2.4	0.7	3.8
9 Luxembourg	3.9	0	2.1
10 Netherlands	2.7	1.7	2.5
11 Portugal	3.5	−0.4	4.8
12 UK	1.6	3.6	2.6
13 Austria	3.5	1.5	3.1
14 Finland	2.3	1.2	1.7
15 Sweden	1	1.4	2.2
16 USA	2.1	3.8	2.7
17 Japan	4.2	0.2	0.5

Sources: Eurostat and *The European*

Note: During 1987–1992 the Irish economy grew the fastest, closely followed by Germany and Japan. Currently the UK is one of the fastest growing economies along with the USA and Denmark. The Mediterranean countries (Greece, Portugal, Italy, Spain) appear to be in decline or growing very slowly and they also have high rates of inflation.

Activity

Write a memo (include charts) to the marketing manager highlighting the main features of the information given above. Say which countries are growing the fastest, which are slowing down and which appear to be beating inflation.

Research and development

Questions to be asked in this area include: How much money is being spent? Is expenditure increasing or decreasing? Are competitors doing more research? Are they developing new products?

Expenditure on research and development (£000)

Country	1991	1992
Belgium	977	1,012.6
Denmark	790	764
France	13,355	12,992
Germany	14,360	14,580
Greece	152	142
Ireland	158	–
Italy	7,028	7,565
Luxembourg	–	–
Netherlands	2,016	2,103
Portugal	252	290
Spain	2,312	2,321
UK	7,238	7,326

Source: *Eurostat*

Activities

1 Here are some figures showing the ownership of household equipment in France (in %). Compare these with the figures for the UK given on page 450. What percentage of your group owns these items?

Household equipment	%
Freezer	71.8
Dishwasher	32.6
Microwave	17.8
Tape recorder	58.4
Personal stereo	36.9
Hi Fi	44.5
Compact disc player	12.3
Video camera	3.5
Photo equipment	51.2
Micro computer	13.0
Motorbike	6.4
Telephone	94.5

2 Write a memo (include charts) to the marketing manager highlighting the main features of the data given on page 445. What have been the trends? Which countries are likely to be our main competitors? Do we need to spend more on research and development?

Investment

Questions concerning investment include: How much is being invested? What are the benefits from a high level of investment? Where is it being invested? How will this affect my business/my sector?

Comparison of investment levels in Europe

Country	% of GDP* used for investment (GFCF)**	% of investment spent on dwellings	% of investment spent on non-residential buildings and civil engineering works	% of investment spent on equipment	% of investment spent on other products
Belgium	19	23	30	43	4
Denmark	15	19	31	50	–
France	20	25	30	37	8
Germany	23	24	29	47	–
Greece	16	23	35	42	–
Ireland	15	24	31	42	3
Italy	19	27	26	44	3
Luxembourg	25	19	38	39	4
Netherlands	20	22	29	48	–
Portugal	27	17	28	44	10
Spain	22	18	46	31	3
UK	15	17	34	44	4

*=Gross Domestic Product **=Gross Fixed Capital Formation
All figures have been rounded to the nearest whole number.
Note: columns 3, 4, 5 and 6 show how the investment is spent.

Source: Eurostat

Activities

1 Write a memo (including charts) to the marketing manager which includes:
   a a list of the countries in order of the % of the GDP used for investment
   b highlights of how each country spends its investment, e.g. Ireland spends 24% on new dwellings.
2 If you worked for a construction company what recommendations would you make?

Inflation

Inflation will affect every business, whether it is selling goods or buying goods. High inflation in the UK will make it difficult to export British goods. UK importers will have to decide where to buy goods.

Changes in the consumer Retail Price Index from 1989 to 1993 (1985=100)

Country	1989	1990	1991	1992	1993
Belgium	107.3	111.0	114.6	117.4	120.6
Denmark	118.1	121.2	124.1	126.7	128.3
France	112.7	116.5	120.2	123.0	123.0
Germany	104.2	107.0	110.7	115.1	119.9
Greece	184.9	222.6	266.0	308.1	352.6
Ireland	113.9	117.6	121.3	125.1	126.9
Italy	123.8	131.8	140.0	147.3	153.8
Luxembourg	105.1	109.0	112.4	115.9	120.1
Netherlands	101.7	104.2	108.4	112.5	114.9
Portugal	151.0	170.9	189.6	206.7	220.0
Spain	128.2	136.8	145.0	153.5	160.6
UK	121.8	133.3	141.1	146.4	148.7

Source: Eurostat

Changes in the food sector price index (1985=100)

Country	1989	1990	1991	1992	1993
Belgium	104.2	107.7	109.4	108.9	108.2
Denmark	111.1	111.4	112.1	114.0	113.7
France	111.9	116.2	119.4	120.1	123.4
Germany	101.3	104.9	108.2	110.8	111.5
Greece	179.5	216.1	259.3	295.8	333.3
Ireland	115.2	116.8	117.7	119.1	118.8
Italy	120.0	127.1	140.2	148.2	150.2
Luxembourg	104.7	108.8	112.1	112.5	111.7
Netherlands	98.1	100.3	103.3	105.5	104.7
Portugal	141.1	158.6	176.4	183.9	185.5
Spain	128.6	136.8	141.2	145.5	145.7
UK	116.3	125.7	132.1	135.0	139.4

Source: Eurostat

Changes in the footwear and clothing sector price index (1985=100)

Country	1989	1990	1991	1992	1993
Belgium	120.6	124.2	129.2	132.8	135.8
Denmark	125.6	126.5	129.6	131.8	132.8
France	188.8	122.4	126.4	129.6	137.9
Germany	106.0	107.5	110.1	113.3	116.4
Greece	206.6	242.1	282.0	321.4	355.4
Ireland	108.3	109.9	111.6	113.9	114.5
Italy	129.7	137.2	144.6	152.2	158.0
Luxembourg	113.4	116.7	120.7	124.8	129.5
Netherlands	95.0	94.1	92.4	93.4	94.7
Portugal	176.1	191.6	215.8	241.8	258.6
Spain	136.2	143.1	150.7	158.4	182.3
UK	113.8	119.1	122.7	123.0	122.1

Source: Eurostat

Activity

Draw line graphs to show the data given on page 447.
Write a memo to the marketing manager highlighting the main features of the data. If you worked for a clothing and footwear or food exporter would your report be any different?

Training

In order to meet the challenge of the SEM, UK business will need to identify the skills required by its workforce. This could involve either training existing staff or recruiting new staff, if necessary from elsewhere. Could you compete?

Activity

How does the UK compare?

The Training Director of your organisation has asked for a report on how training and education in the UK compares with the rest of Europe. You are delighted when you find a table (shown below) based on information published by the Office of Official Publications of the European Communities.

Education and training in Europe

	% share of 18–24 age group in higher education	% share of 14–18-year-olds in full time education	% share of the unemployed in adult training
France	22	83	9
Spain	22	80	9
Belgium	21	93	3
Germany	21	76	16
Denmark	21	78	18
Netherlands	17	91	29
Greece	18	81	3
Italy	16	76	5
Ireland	13	82	2
Portugal	11	60	11
United Kingdom	9	71	7

Note: Data excludes Luxembourg.

Source: Office for Official Publications of the European Communities

This table shows the following:

- in column 2 the percentage share of 18–24-year-olds in higher education in the member states, for example, 22 per cent in France;
- in column 3 the percentage share of 14–18-year-olds in full-time education in the member states;
- in column 4 the percentage share of the unemployed in adult labour market training in the member states.

Write a short report as requested, including charts and noting any significant features. Pay particular attention to how the UK ranks with other member states. Remember, a skilled and well-educated workforce should contribute more to society and business.

Export and import trade

UK exports and imports (£ Millions)

Destination	1979 Exports	1979 Imports	1984 Exports	1984 Imports	1989 Exports	1989 Imports	1994 Exports	1994 Imports
France	3026.6	4015.8	6996.3	5885.7	9542.5	10842.4	6480	7398
Belgium & Luxembourg	1890.6	2272.9	3051.9	3688.1	4889.3	5699.7	3799	3500
Netherlands	3061.3	3442.8	6127	6115.2	6671.4	9617.8	4570	4859
Germany	4217.6	5778.1	7484.2	11088.1	11110.6	20005.3	8482	10925
Italy	1463.1	2478.8	2903.5	3809	4630.6	6707.4	3365	3529
Irish Republic	2544.9	1681.4	3393.8	2635.1	4716.4	4279.5	3363	2811
Denmark	1015.3	1079.6	1195.5	1659.2	1209.2	2236.5	844	1100
Greece	260.1	138	354.3	278.9	571.4	395.1	467	164
Spain	567.3	706.4	1234.3	1603.7	3138	2813.2	2365	1867
Portugal	305.4	338.1	386.4	644.8	915.7	1041.3	580	606
Norway	773.2	1316.9	972.9	3999.4	1057.2	3637.1	849	1854
Sweden	1536.9	1600.2	2893.9	2416.8	2431.9	3747.5	1620	1981
Finland	410.6	792.2	699.5	1248.2	932.2	1893.1	590	1080
Switzerland	1249.2	1835.1	1549.5	2490.1	2246.3	4134.2	1197	2565
Austria	257.3	345.2	320.9	529.5	598.1	934	497	507
Turkey	135.6	65.8	331.4	237.2	434.6	533.7		
Other Countries	323.6	192.1	364.2	262.7	288.9	274.8	753	466
North America	4791.4	6197.2	11416.3	11067.4	14436.7	15929.3	9627	9615
Oil Exporting Countries	3648.1	3212.7	5806.3	2934.2	5832.4	2312.7	2892	1467
TOTAL TRADE, i.e. worldwide	40637	46924.9	70488.3	78967.4	93770.9	121699.2	65273	73247

Surplus balance = Exports > Imports; Deficit balance = Imports > Exports
1994, first two quarters only.

Source: *Monthly Digest of Statistics*

Activity

Write a short article for the local newspaper highlighting the main features of the data given on page 449. What have been the main trends in exports/imports? Which are the UK's main trading partners? The editor loves diagrams! Show the trends as a series of multiple bar charts. What is the balance with each country?

Activity

If you have written each of the memos in the Activities on pages 444–50 you will now have enough material to write a report to the marketing manager. Your report should deal with three major competitors (justify your choice). Carry out a SWOT analysis, i.e. list the strengths, weaknesses, opportunities and threats for each of the three competitors.

Activity

Standard of living

For this activity you will find these publications helpful: *Social Trends, Economic Trends,* Eurostat and OECD reports. Read the article below.

We've never had it so good – so why do we moan?

Since the 1950s Britain has become a land of plenty, and of irrational pessimism, finds **David Smith**

'Let us be frank about it. Most of our people have never had it so good." So said Harold Macmillan in 1957, and "You've never had it so good" became his political slogan for the Conservatives' 1959 election victory. Since then, for fear of ridicule, politicians have been reluctant to offer a hostage to fortune by repeating Supermac's phrase.

But most prime ministers, including John Major today, could legitimately do so. Forget the all-pervading gloom about 1990s Britain and the fact that opinion polls show economic optimism plumbing new depths. On virtually every measure, from after-tax incomes, to ownership of cars and household goods, and the affordability of food and other necessities, it is indeed the case that we have never had it so good.

In 1957, even relatively well-to-do families lived in conditions that would be regarded now as austere. Most homes did not have central heating. A two-bar electric fire was the height of luxury for taking the chill off a bedroom on a winter morning. Lino, rather than fitted carpets, covered the floors. Only a quarter of homes had television sets, with grainy black-and-white pictures, and ownership was concentrated among the better-off.

Just 5% of families owned a fridge, 15% a washing-machine and 14% a car. For those who could afford it, it was a golden age of motoring. Austins, Hillmans and Rileys chugged along uncongested roads. There were 3.7 m cars on the road compared with more than 20 m today.

The contrast with today's typical family is striking. Consumer gadgets that would have been thought of as science-fiction fantasies in the 1950s are now enjoyed by the vast majority.

Today, the home without a colour television is a rarity; they are owned by 99% of families, and some of the other 1% is probably dodging the licence fee. Mintel, the market research company, said in its 1995 Lifestyles report, published last week, that more than a quarter of homes now have three or more televisions; all have a fridge or fridge-freezer, 61% have microwaves, 80% a video recorder, 30% home computers, 43% compact disc players, and so on. Nine-tenths of homes have a telephone, and mobile phone sales to private buyers were one of the hottest consumer areas over Christmas.

The trend continues. "The growth areas for increasing household penetration are dishwashers, microwave ovens, built-in electric ovens, midi and mini hi-fi systems, video cassette recorders and satellite and cable television," said the Mintel report. Last month, despite gloomy pre-Christmas noises from the stores, sales of household goods were at record levels, and up strongly on a year earlier.

Nor is this just a rose-coloured comparison with the low-tech 1950s. Ownership of household durables has increased strongly even since the prosperous mid-1980s, when just 30% of families had video recorders and 10% microwaves. The number of households with dishwashers has risen threefold.

In 1979, when Margaret Thatcher brought the Tories to power, only two-thirds of homes had a colour television and a similar proportion a telephone. Just over 90% had fridges but the freezer age was yet to come. More than half (57%) of families had a car, but the two-car household was unusual; just one in 10. Today, 70% have at least one car, and a quarter of households have two or more.

This miracle of modern prosperity has a down-to-earth economic explanation. In modern industrial economies, technological advances and better production methods produce a year-by-year increase in productivity. Each worker, in other words, is producing more this year than last, and much more than 10, 20 or 30 years ago.

This, in turn, has two related effects. The more productive workers are, the more employers can afford to pay them. Thus, wages tend to rise, both in absolute terms and in relation to prices. Real incomes rise on average by 2% or 3% a year. Compounding this produces, over the long-term, some staggering comparisons. Real incomes per head, after allowing for inflation and taxation, have risen by 136% since 1957, 74% since 1970 and 36% since 1979. The average working man has a take-home salary of £14,000 a year. Had there been no rise in real take-home pay since 1979, that salary would be only £10,300 a year, while the 1957 equivalent, in today's money, was just £5,900.

The implications go beyond ownership of consumer durables. The government's annual Social Trends publication, out this week, will show that it now takes only five minutes of work to produce enough take-home pay to buy a loaf of bread, half what was needed 20 years ago. Just over half-an-hour of work produces enough cash to buy a pound of rump steak, against nearly an hour two decades ago. Both necessities and food traditionally thought of as for special occasions have become much more affordable.

There is a second broad effect of rising productivity and technological advance. It is that consumer durables become cheaper relative to income and, in many cases, in straight cash terms. When colour televisions were relatively new, the average worker needed more than a month's wages to afford one. Today, under half a week's wages is enough.

So why, if we have never had it so good, are we so miserable?

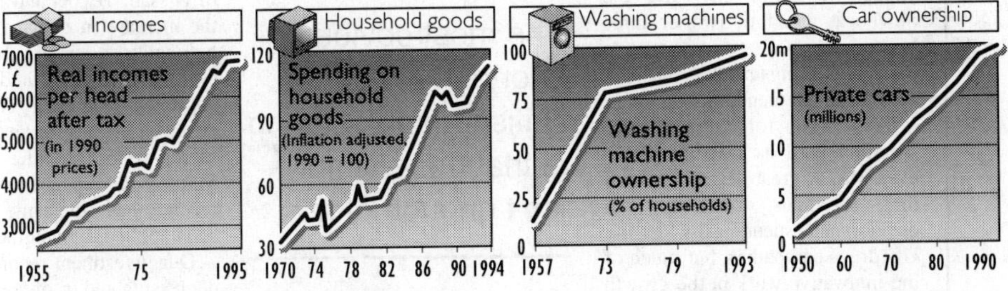

Source: *The Sunday Times*, 22 January 1995

The standard of living is usually measured by taking the figures for the income per head, i.e. Gross National Income divided by the population. However, it can also be useful to compare, for example, the ownership of consumer durables, leisure activities home ownership etc. Write a brief report explaining how the standard of living in the UK compares with its European competitors.

Activity

Look at the article on page 452 and, using the figures in this chapter, suggest different strategies which could be used to improve the competitiveness of specific UK industries. You may find this data helpful. (Hint: look at *Economic Trends*.)

UK competitiveness in trade in manufactures

	1990	**1991**	**1992**	**1993**	**Significance**
Relative export prices	100	101.5	98.3	101	Downward trend shows more competitiveness
Relative profitability of exports	100	98.6	99.7	108	Upward trend shows profitability
Relative producer prices	100	104.3	102.9	95	Falling prices should mean greater profitability
Unit labour costs	100.2	106.1	109.5	93	Falling cost means UK goods should be cheaper to produce

Halting the decline of UK's industrial base

JUST as the big indicators – growth, unemployment, trade, inflation – have been encouraging over the past year or two, so there are some notable successes at a local level.

Of course, there are problems, many of them deep-seated and cultural, which remain to be overcome in industry, and most business leaders are realistic enough to admit that. But the downbeat mood of two or three years ago has given way to cautious optimism that business may be on the mend.

One cause for hope is that Britain is still as ingenious as it ever was. A great deal is made of the enormous research and development spending by the big UK drugs companies, but much of the innovative work in the growth areas of biotechnology and genetics is being carried out on science parks by small start-up firms.

The challenge for an industrialised country, however, is not coming up with the original idea, but knowing how to turn it into a volume business. This is something the UK was supremely good at in the first half of the 19th Century – the only period in our history when finance has been the maidservant of manufacturing – but somehow lost the feel for along the way. When the Germans and the Japanese were building up their consumer goods' industries after the second world war, we were investing in nuclear power stations and Concorde.

There are any number of well-rehearsed reasons for this relative decline, stretching all the way back to Britain's failure to catch the second wave of the industrial revolution in the late 19th Century. Germany and the United States based their rapid growth on electricity and chemicals, while Britain was heavily reliant well into the 20th Century on iron and coal. In addition, our economy is said to be risk-averse, short-termist, suffers from a lack of macro-economic stability, and diverts its best brains away from manufacturing.

The most obvious shortcoming of British manufacturing is that there simply isn't enough of it

Some of these problems are now being addressed. The Bank of England is trying to improve the supply of finance to small firms, the departure from the Exchange Rate Mechanism at the tail-end of a grinding recession provided an ideal set of conditions for growth without inflation, and the Government has realised that, despite what it said in the mid-1980s, a thriving manufacturing base is crucial to economic success.

However, the biggest transformation over the past decade has been the impact of inward investment, with 40 per cent of the total coming to the European Union snapped up by UK. This is by no means an unalloyed benefit, since profits from the UK arms of multinational companies are repatriated, and many foreign-owned factories here tend to be merely assembly plants.

That said, in sectors such as personal computers, where growth in the past two years has been spectacular, and the car industry, inward investment has not only created new jobs in areas of high unemployment, but has had a trickle-down effect on supplier firms. The renaissance of the car components sector would never have happened without the arrival of Nissan, Toyota and Honda, and the increase in demand buttressed by quality agreements between the car manufacturers and a list of approved suppliers. This sort of arrangement has for years been the secret of the retailing success of Marks & Spencer, but only recently have the same disciplines been applied to manufacturing.

Our investment record has been depressing and is, of course, linked to the sluggishness of output growth. But there are three reasons for some optimism. The first is the size and quality of the foreign investment, which has helped halt the long-term decline in Britain's share of world manufacturing exports.

The second is that industry's profitability is stronger than at any time for a quarter of a century. If the Glaxo bid for Wellcome is anything to go by, this money is starting to burn a hole in the corporate sector's pocket. The last time industry was awash with cash – in the mid 1980s –the UK subsequently enjoyed an investment boom.

Lastly, despite the drop in spending on plant and machinery during the recession, industry kept up its investment on training and research and development. Some hard lessons, it appears, have at last been learned.

Source: *The Guardian* 30 January 1995

Pay and benefits in Europe

How do UK workers compare with their European counterparts?

Hours of work

Virtually every country except the UK has statutory legislation which sets out the maximum number of hours a week an employee can work.

For example:
Denmark 37 hpw maximum
France 39 hpw maximum
Germany 48 hpw maximum.

Holidays

Again almost every country has regulations which state the minimum number of paid holidays to which a worker is entitled, for example, Germany has a three week minimum and Denmark has a 30 day minimum. In the UK there is no legislation saying workers are entitled to holidays although the average worker will get between 20 and 25 days.

Minimum wage

Most European countries have a statutory minimum wage, including Greece and Portugal. The UK has no such agreement.

Maternity leave and sick pay

UK workers receive statutory sick pay (SSP). Maternity leave varies between countries; many allow leave for both parents, for example, Denmark allows six months.

Worker participation

With the exception of the UK and Ireland, all European countries have some form of worker participation through Works Councils. Trade union recognition is also variable.

Review questions

1 Define and give three examples of added value.
2 How is labour productivity measured?
3 How can productivity be increased?
4 What are the features of batch, flow and job production?
5 How is efficiency related to the scale of production?
6 Give four ways that business can add value to products.
7 Why do businesses try to add value?
8 How do technology and automation affect production?
9 Explain the uses of CAD and CAM.
10 List the advantages and disadvantages of JIT production and purchasing.
11 What criteria can be used by business when deciding to buy materials?
12 How can a flexible labour force help a business?
13 How has labour law contributed to labour flexibility?
14 How can changing patterns of production affect employees, customers and suppliers?
15 Why can skill shortages occur? How can they be solved?
16 Describe three ways of improving production.
17 Describe the advantages and disadvantages of privatisation.
18 What is the WTO? What are its aims?
19 What are the main aims of the EU? Name three areas of policy.

Key terms

Added value
Labour productivity
Factor substitution
Labour intensive
Capital intensive
Methods of production
Flow production
Batch production
Job production
Scale of production
Technology
Automation
Contracting out
Labour flexibility
Mobility of labour
Employment law
Patterns of production
Improving production
Economies of scale
Ways of adding value
Government strategies
Reducing inflation
Role of government
Privatisation
Supply side policies
Demand side policies
European Union
UK performance
Training
Efficiency
CAD
CAM
Just-in-Time
Sourcing
R and D
Suppliers
Investment
Skill shortages
WTO
Standard of living

Assignment 9 'Update' Part 1

This assignment develops knowledge and understanding in the following elements:

5.1 Analyse production in business
5.3 Examine the competitiveness of UK industry

It supports development in the following core skills:

Communication 3.2, 3.3, 3.4
Application of numbers 3.1, 3.2, 3.3
Information technology 3.1, 3.2, 3.3

You work as a research assistant in the Hurstmead Chamber of Commerce. Every month the Chamber publishes a series called *Market Update*. These cover the major industries which are represented in Hurstmead. Each researcher writes an *Update*. Each assistant has his or her own speciality (it depends on the business they adopted in our introduction – yours is the footwear industry) and in addition chooses one other industry for comparison which always makes up Section F. The researchers usually agree this between themselves.

Hurstmead Chamber of Commerce

1 The update should be word processed and suitable for publication.
2 Only A4 paper must be used.
3 A maximum of 7 sheets of paper is allowed (any extra sheets should be put in an appendix, but do not expect them to be read – business people are always very busy).
4 The Update must contain these sections:

Section A Added value
This section should describe ways in which added value is achieved in a particular business or industrial sector, for example are there special deals, free delivery discounts, etc?

Section B Changes in production and how they affect local business
This should describe examples of changes in production and their likely effects on local businesses (check the innovation and technology sections of the papers).

Section C Ways to improve
Give some hints as to how local businesses could improve, for example training programmes which are available, or technology which could be introduced.

Section D Comparative Performance
Draw charts, graphs and diagrams to show the comparative performance of the UK economy with that of its major competitors. Comment on the major features and say how the business sector could gain or lose.

Section E Strategies and their effects
Select two strategies designed to improve UK industrial competitiveness and show how these could affect the local business or sector, for example you could use the latest budget measures.

5 Always end with something light-hearted; it could be a quote or a funny local news item.
6 Check everything and go to print.

10 Employment trends

What is covered in this chapter

- The workforce
- General trends in employment
- Unemployment
- Labour markets
- Supply of labour
- Wages

These are the resources that you will need for your Production and Employment in the Economy file:

- statistical publications with data on employment and unemployment
- newspaper articles on industrial disputes, wage settlements and employment.

The workforce

Here are the figures for the UK workforce in 1977 and 1994 in thousands:

	1977	1994
Males and females in employment	22,722	21,459
Self-employed persons	1,886	3,282
HM Forces	328	250
Government training schemes		304
Registered unemployed	1,609	2,417
Total workforce	26,545	27,712

The main changes which have taken place between 1977 and 1994 are that:

- Nearly 1 million more people are unemployed.
- Over 1 million more people are classified as 'self-employed'.
- There are over 1 million more people officially in the workforce.
- There are over 1 million less people in employment.
- Government training programmes have been introduced and people on these programmes are counted as being employed.

The size of the labour force is affected by:

- **Population** Changes in the size of the population are affected by the number of births (birth rate) and deaths (death rate). Migration rates, i.e. the movement of people into and out of the country can also be important.
- **Economic activity rates** The **economic activity rate** is the proportion of a particular age group which is in the **labour force**. For example, the activity rates for women and men of working age are 70 per cent and 80 per cent respectively.

General trends in employment

The figures given in Table 10.1 show the distribution of employees in employment, by sex and industry. They will help us to examine some of the major changes which have taken place in the last 20 years or so. Figure 10.1 is a graphical representation of some of the data.

Table 10.1 Employees in employment: by sex and industry

United Kingdom — Thousands

	SIC[1] (1980)	1971	1979	1981	1983	1986	1990	1991	1992
All industries	0–9	22,139	23,173	21,892	21,067	21,387	22,899	22,229	21,758
of which									
Males		13,726	13,487	12,562	11,940	11,744	12,069	11,592	11,253
Females		8,413	9,686	9,331	9,127	9,644	10,830	10,637	10,504
Manufacturing	2–4	8,065	7,253	6,222	5,525	5,227	5,138	4,793	4,589
Services	6–9	11,627	13,580	13,468	13,501	14,297	15,945	15,744	15,644
Other	0, 1, 5	2,447	2,340	2,203	2,042	1,863	1,817	1,692	1,524
Employees in employment by SIC[1] division									
Agriculture, forestry and fishing	0	450	380	363	350	329	298	291	283
Energy and water supply	1	798	722	710	648	545	449	439	403
Other minerals and ore extraction etc	2	1,282	1,147	939	817	729	721	657	635
Metal goods, engineering and vehicles	3	3,709	3,374	2,923	2,548	2,372	2,310	2,139	2,030
Other manufacturing industries	4	3,074	2,732	2,360	2,159	2,126	2,106	1,997	1,924
Construction	5	1,198	1,239	1,130	1,044	989	1,070	962	839
Distribution, catering and repairs	6	3,686	4,257	4,172	4,118	4,298	4,822	4,686	4,605
Transport and communication	7	1,556	1,479	1,425	1,345	1,298	1,382	1,349	1,324
Banking, finance, insurance, etc	8	1,336	1,647	1,739	1,875	2,166	2,744	2,687	2,639
Other services	9	5,049	6,197	6,132	6,163	6,536	6,996	7,022	7,076

[1] Standard Industrial Classification

Source: *Social Trends* (HMSO, 1993)

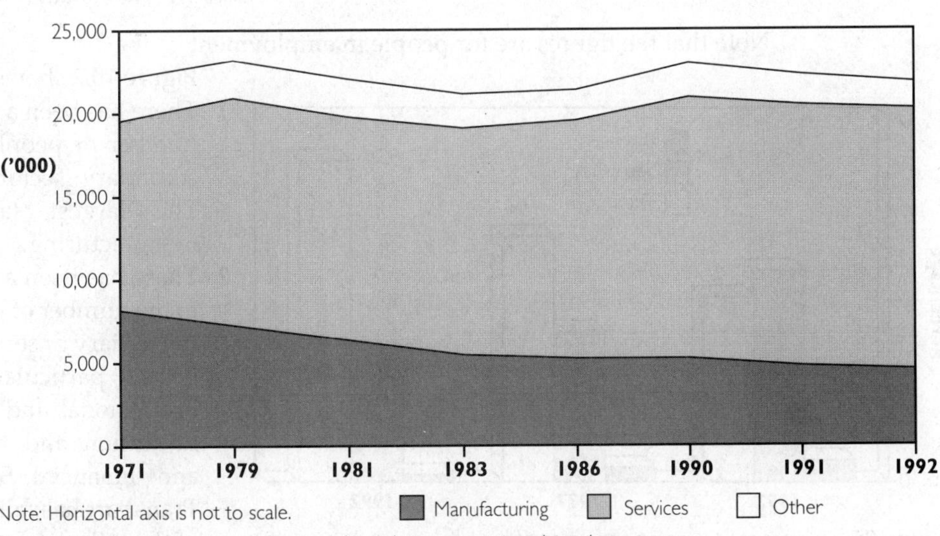

Figure 10.1 Employees in employment by industry sector in selected years

Activities

1 Look at Table 10.1 and answer these questions on your own.
  a What has been the trend in male/female employment?
  b How many people were employed in Metal goods, engineering and vehicles in 1971 and 1992? What has been the percentage change?
  c How many people were employed in Banking, finance, insurance, etc. in 1971 and 1992? What has been the percentage change?
  d What has been the change in Agriculture, etc?

2 Working in pairs choose one SIC (Standard Industrial Classification) division and try and say why the change has occurred. Graph the data shown for your division. Compare the graph with those of your colleagues.

3 Choose an industry which is a major employer in your area. What changes have taken place in the number of people employed within it? How do these changes compare with the national picture? What are the reasons for these changes?

4 Bring the figures up to date. What changes have taken place?

Two major conclusions can be drawn from Table 10.1. First, male employment has fallen whist female employment has risen. Secondly, employment in manufacturing has fallen whilst employment in services has increased (see Figure 10.1).

This can be looked at in another way. By using the particular classification we introduced in Chapter 1 we can see that there has been a significant shift in the number of people employed in the primary, secondary and tertiary sectors of the economy. We have added the 1952 figures below, to give a longer term view. 1952 was just seven years after the Second World War, when the UK still had a manufacturing industry and was an exporter of manufactured goods.

	1952	**1977**	**1992**
Primary	4.5%	3%	1.4%
Secondary	47.0%	33%	23.0%
Tertiary	41.0%	54%	71.0%

R. Bacon and W. Eltis in *Britain's Economic Problem: Too Few Producers*

Note that the figures are for people in employment.

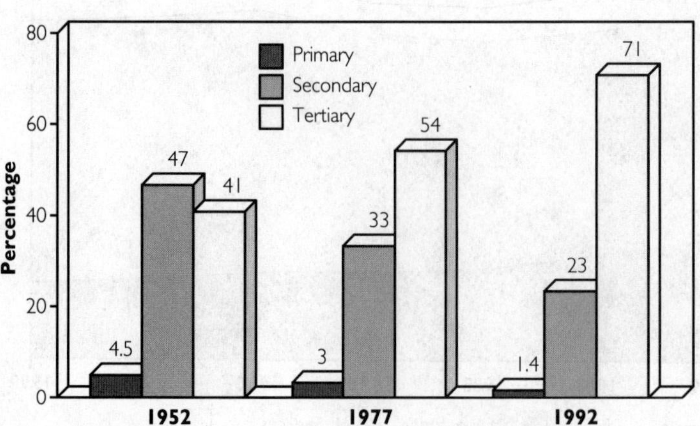

Figure 10.2 Changes in the working population of the UK

Figure 10.2 shows:

1. There has been a dramatic fall in the number of people employed in the secondary sector of the economy. The largest fall has been in manufacturing.
2. There has been a corresponding rise in the number of people employed in the tertiary or service sector. This has been particularly marked in Professional and Scientific Services, Education and Medicine, Housing and Financial Services. However, Transport has fallen with the decline of the railways.

A particular feature of this growth has been the rise in female employment within the **sector**, for example, some 72 per cent of employees in the professional sector are women, many of whom are part-time employees.

The general decline in manufacturing

The decline in the manufacturing sector (**de-industrialisation**) is now causing concern in many European countries. In the UK, for example, 597,000 jobs have been lost since 1988; the majority of which have disappeared since 1990. The greatest decline has occurred in 'traditional industries', for example, textiles, iron and steel, coal mining, shipbuilding, machine tools, metal products and motor vehicles. Much of this has been due to competition from cheaper overseas goods. Because these industries were mainly located in the older industrial areas their decline has caused major structural unemployment in Wales, the North and West Midlands, in particular. These changes have had a significant social and economic impact on many families and communities.

Activity

Read the article 'UK industry in crisis' and answer the following questions.

a Explain the meaning of the terms 'dole queue', 'cutting the dividend', 'laying off workers', 'retrenchment of the last two years' 'swords into ploughshares'.
b What have been the symptoms of the decline in manufacturing industry?
c What has been the government's industrial policy?
d What position did the government take on supporting industry?
e What has been the role of Taiwan?
f Have any manufacturing companies closed in your area? How has this affected your community? (See page 494.)

Trends in Europe

Activity

Look at these figures for the distribution of employees between sectors in the European Union:

	1964	1974	1990
Primary	16%	10%	6%
Secondary	41%	38%	32%
Tertiary	43%	52%	62%

Source: Eurostat

a Show the data above as three pie charts.
b What comments can you make?

The picture for Europe, represented by the figures above, is almost identical to that of the UK. Over the last 30 years there has been a steady shift away from the secondary sector into the service sector. The primary sector, notably Agriculture, has also fallen. France however, still has a significant and vocal farming sector. (Only Japan showed an increase in manufacturing over the same period.) Within Europe the UK has the smallest primary sector of any country; this reflects the high level of output per head in agriculture.

UK INDUSTRY IN CRISIS

THE 5,500 jobs lost last week at three of the UK's leading industrial businesses – British Aerospace, Ford and Vickers – have contributed to another bleak chapter in the recent history of Britain's manufacturing sector.

BAe, the UK's largest manufacturing exporter, set the tone by slumping into the red, cutting the dividend and laying off 3,000 employees with the closure of its historic Hatfield plane-making plant. The grim news was accompanied by the ignominious announcement that emerging nation Taiwan was rescuing BAe's regional aircraft division.

Ford and Vickers' off-shoot Rolls-Royce then reacted to the motor industry's steep recession by cutting 2,500 jobs, while British Coal and Laird added another 900 to lengthening dole queues.

The losses at Ford and RR follow a string of recent cutbacks at Aston Martin, Jaguar, Lotus and truckmaker AWD. The Society of Motor Manufacturers and Traders estimates that 70,000 people have lost their jobs in the industry since the recession began.

Rolls, despite possessing the most prestigious name in the industrial world, has seen sales collapse in the past 18 months and parent Vickers has suffered the humiliation of failing to find a buyer for the company.

Ford has suffered as badly from the recession, which has seen the UK car market shrink by 700,000 vehicles to 1.55 million a year in only three years. The carmaker, perhaps more than others, is heavily dependent on the British market and production capacity is still largely geared to the 1989 UK market levels of 2.3 million vehicles a year. With car sales showing no signs of recovery, Ford first imposed short-time working and has now laid off 1,500.

Overall, Britain's manufacturing industry has been in continuous decline since 1979, with a litany of factory closures, company bankruptcies and staff redundancies. Last week's retrenchment was merely the latest chapter.

Productive capacity has been slashed, new investment has declined by 12 per cent and Britain, once the workshop of the world, now suffers a deficit on trade in manufactured goods for the first time since the Industrial Revolution.

But the most telling statistic lies in the loss of manufacturing jobs, which have declined by 36 per cent to under 4.5 million since 1979. A remarkable 2.6 million people have lost their jobs in industry in just 13 years.

Initially, much of this decline resulted from long-overdue restructuring in the wake of the excesses and inefficiencies of the 1960s and 1970s. But the fear now is that the retrenchment of the past two years, propelled by the worst recession since the war, is causing irreparable damage to the nation's industrial base.

Government policy, particularly the two distinct phases of high exchange rates, contributed heavily to the decline. But perhaps as important, the 1980s and early 1990s have been characterised by the effective withdrawal of the Department of Trade and Industry from the policy-making processes.

Under the stewardship of Industry Secretaries such as Keith Joseph, Cecil Parkinson, Norman Tebbit, Lord Young and Nicholas Ridley, the Government withdrew support for industries like steel, shipbuilding and motors, cut development aid grants to the regions and shifted the emphasis from manufacturing to services.

Equally, successive secretaries of state reinforced the doctrine that competition alone should determine industrial policy. In contrast, many sections of business, including the Confederation of British Industry, were demanding a more interventionist approach, supported by public sector investment in the national infrastructure.

Industry's hopes of a more constructive Government attitude have also been frustrated by the anonymity of Michael Heseltine since he took over at the DTI. Heseltine, by instinct an interventionist, has been conspicuous by his absence from the industrial scene and last week's fresh decline in manufacturing will serve to heighten the puzzlement at this policy vacuum.

The lack of any coherent industrial strategy has been felt most notably by the declining defence manufacturing sector. At least 150,000 jobs have been lost in defence since 1979 and, with the collapse of world-wide spending on arms, there is a pressing need to draw up a coherent 'swords-into-ploughshares' plan, involving the transfer of defence manufacturing capacity into civil industries.

Critics are quick to point out that many other countries have successfully developed their economies with a positive industrial policy. Japan's capital investment per employee during the 1980s, for example, was almost three times that of Britain.

But perhaps the supreme irony is that Taiwan's government-backed aerospace company is rescuing BAe's regional aircraft business.

Aerospace is one of the 10 strategic industries specifically chosen by the Taiwanese government to develop the country's industrial base, while BAe's Hatfield plant, with its unequalled association with British industrial excellence, will probably end up as a DIY superstore stocked with imported screwdrivers.

Source: *The Observer*, September 1992

The trend in self-employment

Self-employment means earning a living in your own business rather than being an employee of someone else. In 1977 7.1 per cent of the workforce was self-employed. In 1994 this had risen to 11.8 per cent of the workforce. This rise has been the largest in any of the European Member States. The largest growth was between 1979 and 1986 which coincided with a large rise in unemployment. People were less able to get paid employment and instead decided to try to become 'their own boss'. In Europe, Greece and Portugal have the highest number of self-employed people.

The shift towards self-employment has been actively encouraged by the government which has provided help and advice through various **small business** schemes. High street banks have also been keen to lend money to help start up new businesses. However, as the interview with the sole trader (page 462) shows, they have been reluctant to continue their support beyond the first year.

Facts about the self-employed

1 The number of males and females in self-employment has grown steadily, however, men out number women by 3 to 1.

2 A significant number of people from ethnic minorities are self-employed, for example, 24 per cent of the total Pakistani/Bangladeshi workforce are in self-employment.

3 Nearly 35 per cent of people in self-employment take on at least one employee.

4 The age profile of self-employed people tends to be older than for the working population as a whole:

Age	Male	Female
15–24	240	40
25–34	610	200
35–44	700	250
45–54	520	180
55–64	310	80
65+	100	30

(All figures are in thousands)

Source: *Labour Market & Skill Trends 1992/93*

Activity

1 To help develop your IT core skills, draw a multiple bar chart of the data above. Why do you think this situation exists?

2 Can you suggest why more people from ethnic minorities tend to be self-employed?

Although people continue to be attracted by the idea of starting their own businesses, and there were over 1,000 new business start-ups per week in April 1993, there are still many problems to be overcome. Here are some of them:

- cost of finance
- cashflow problems
- competition from other firms
- premises costs too high
- shortage of business
- too much official paperwork
- lack of finance
- adverse economic conditions.

Activity

In order to prepare your own business plan you will need to find answers to these problems. Identify those which are in your control.
Hint: Read the case study below first.

Case study

Here is an interview with a sole trader who is self-employed. It contains several hints about how you could tackle the Activity above.

INTERVIEW

With J.C. Appliances, Petts Wood, Kent

Q What business are you in?
A We repair and sell all large domestic appliances.

Q How long have you been in business?
A I started in business about four years ago.

Q Why?
A I had worked in a large company, but I have always wanted to set up on my own.

Q Ambition?
A Yes, it was an ambition.

Q What sort of help did you get?
A The banks were quite keen at first, but they do not help as much as is claimed.

Q What business objectives do you have?
A To give customer satisfaction, and a quality service - really it is about caring for customers, for me it is a quality repair, and I get job satisfaction.

Q What about profit?
A Yes, profits are needed to survive, but they come from providing the service and caring about people. They come second, even third.

Q What about the recession?
A The repairs are doing well, but the new sales are sluggish, people are postponing buying new things unless they have no choice.

Q Why did you set up in this area?
A I know the area, it is a good place, people here want quality service and quality goods.

Q You spotted a 'niche' in the market?
A Yes, people wanted a quality local service, not a national company on the end of a mobile phone which always faded out!

Q How do you get new business?
A We have an ad in Yellow Pages, but it is mostly 'word of mouth' and knowing people. Look, really it's about building a reputation - 'turn up on time, double quick on time, every time'.

Activity

a Carry out an interview similar to the one above with a small-business person. Try to find out about the business objectives, reasons for becoming self-employed and target market.
b What does this interview tell you about these elements?
c Explain the term 'word of mouth'. Why is it important in this case?
d Write up the results of the interview you have carried out.

Self-employment in Europe as a percentage of the total working population

Percentage between	Country
1–10	Germany,Luxembourg, Netherlands, Denmark
11–20	France, Belgium, UK
21+	Spain, Ireland, Italy, Portugal, Greece

Trends in female employment

Look at these figures for male and female employment for the last 40 years:

	Male	Female
1950	13,722	7,035
1977	13,383	9,280
1990	12,076	10,775
1994	10,815	10,644

(Figures are in thousands)

Note: Female employment has risen by 50 per cent. Male employment has fallen by 21 per cent.

The majority of female workers are single, although married women are increasingly entering the labour market. A number of suggestions have been made to account for these trends.

- Changes in economic expectations – households now expect a higher standard of living which can only be achieved with a higher level of household income.
- Changes in social attitudes – the number of female single parents is increasing, therefore there is a greater need for women to work.
- It has become socially more acceptable for women to work – this trend is evident across social groups, although the greatest increase in female activity rates has been in regions where traditionally women have not gone out to work.
- Changes in the types of job available – the growth in the service sector of the economy, which has traditionally employed women, and the decline in the manufacturing sector which has almost exclusively employed men, has given greater opportunities to women.
- Equal opportunities legislation has helped to change social conditions, and improve employment prospects.

Part-time female employment in the EU	
Proportion of the female workforce employed part-time	**Country**
10 per cent	Greece and Portugal
40 per cent	UK and Denmark
60 per cent	Netherlands

Note: Only selected countries are shown to give a general impression

Manual and non-manual employment

Manual labour means physical work which is done by hand, as opposed to mechanical and thinking work, which is **non-manual** or 'white collar' work. In the Standard Occupational Classification, manual jobs are in:
Major Group 5 – Craft and Related Occupations
Major Group 8 – Plant and Machine Operatives
Major Group 9 – Other Occupations, for example, Forestry and Construction labourers.

> 'There has been a gradual rise in non-manual or white collar occupations since 1985. These jobs tend to be concentrated in the service sector which has also expanded. The number of manual jobs has remained stable. These broad trends are expected to continue up to the year 2000 with the main growth area "being for people with Advanced GNVQ and above".'
>
> Quoted in *Labour Market & Skill Trends 1992/93*

Predicted decline in jobs	Predicted growth in jobs
Crafts	Managerial
Skilled Manual	Technical
Unskilled Manual	Professional

It can sometimes be very difficult to classify jobs into manual/non-manual. Some jobs, for example, school caretakers, have both a manual (repairs) and 'white collar' (administration of orders and invoices) aspect to the work.

Generally, the pay and conditions of employment tend to be better for non-manual rather than manual workers.

Activity

a Working in pairs, use a chart similar to this one to classify these occupations: typist, porter, plumber, bus conductor, carpenter, local government officer, chemist, librarian, receptionist, glazier, precision instrument maker, cook, weaver, messenger, kerb layer.
Refer to the Standard Occupational Classification to help you.

	Manual	Non-manual
Skilled	C	D
Unskilled	A	B

A Unskilled Manual
B Unskilled Non-Manual
C Skilled Manual
D Skilled Non-Manual

b Which occupations in your organisation can be classified in this way? Complete a chart similar to the one above. How many people are employed in each category?

Trends in part-time employment

Sixty years ago, the workforce was composed almost entirely of males, the majority of whom would have worked full-time in a secondary, probably manufacturing job. However, with increased competition from overseas, the manufacturing sector has declined. Today almost 50 per cent of the workforce is female, and nearly 6 million of all jobs are part-time. A **part-time** employee, as defined in the *New Earnings Survey*, is one who works less than 30 hours a week (25 or less for teachers), excluding meal breaks or overtime.

Look at the figures below which show part-time employment in Great Britain from December 1992 to December 1994. You should find the full-time figures to complete the table.

Employees in employment (000s)

	Male		Female	
	Full-time	**Part-time**	**Full-time**	**Part-time**
1992 Dec.		1,144		4,844
1993 Mar.		1,112		4,811
1993 Jun.		1,126		4,880
1993 Sept.		1,142		4,869
1993 Dec.		1,162		4,979
1994 Mar.		1,147		4,915
1994 Jun.		1,167		4,957
1994 Sept.		1,169		4,940
1994 Dec		1,216		5,075

Source: *Employment Gazette*

Note: Roughly 1 in 9 males is now employed part-time
Roughly 1 in every 2 working females is part-time

Why has part-time employment risen?

Most of the jobs created in the last ten years have been part-time, because this has suited the needs of business. The majority of these have been for women. Only a small proportion of these jobs has been prompted by the demand for flexible hours/days particularly from people with children of school age. If you survey part-time workers, most of them would prefer to work full-time, but either cannot find a full-time job or cannot find an employer with adequate childcare facilities.

For the employer, the costs of hiring part-time staff can be substantially less than for employing full-time workers, particularly if they are employed for less than 16 hours per week. For example, part-time workers either do not receive or get significantly less sickness pay, holiday entitlement, National Insurance benefits, periods of notice and redundancy payment; but conditions are changing with membership of the EU.

Who is entitled to a redundancy payment?

Redundancy payments are only given to employees – the self-employed and business partners do not qualify. The employee must either have at least two years' continuous service for 16 hours a week or more, or have at least five years' continuous service for eight hours a week or more. Service before the age of 18 does not count.

For each complete year of service, up to a maximum of 20, employees are currently entitled to:

- half a week's pay, for each year of service at age 18 or over but under 22;
- one week's pay, for each year of service at age 22 but under 41;
- one and a half weeks' pay, for each year of service at age 41 or over but under 65.

Generally, the conditions and terms of employment are such as to make it cheaper to employ part-time workers, because the unit wage costs of this group of workers is less. On average an extra 20 per cent is needed to employ a full-time worker. For someone earning £10 per hour, 80 per cent would be money wages and the other 20 per cent would be made up of National Insurance and other employer contributions and costs. Consequently, more part-timers are employed and fewer 'full-timers'. The Burton Group only employ part-time staff.

Although total numbers of employees remain the same, the composition of the work-force is changing. This has affected the communication systems used in business, for example, part-time teachers find it more difficult to attend meetings. Generally, personnel departments have had to re-organise their administration to cope with these changes.

Activities

1 Prepare a brief report which shows:
   a The number of part-time male and female employees in your organisation.
   b The number of full-time male and female employees in your organisation.
   c The changes which have occurred in the last five years, and why these changes have taken place.
2 Choose one other organisation and compare it with your own.
3 How do the figures you have collected compare with those we have given? Give reasons.
4 Draw a graph of the figures we have given on page 465. Can you make a prediction for what might happen over the next two years? What assumptions have you made.

Temporary employment

A **temporary** employee can be employed either full-time or part-time, but does not have a permanent contract of employment. There are particular legal requirements when employing temporary workers but in general they will be on fixed-time contracts.

With fewer jobs available for full-time employees, more people are looking for temporary work. There are several categories of temporary employee.

Temporary full-time

This could mean a person works full-time to replace an existing member of staff who is on maternity leave or long-term sickness leave. In this case, the new employee is 'standing in' or substituting for someone else already in the job, until he or she returns. Here the contract of employment will be temporary.

The definition could also mean a person occupying a job because there is a vacancy waiting to be filled. The post will be temporary, and the person will be on a fixed-term contract, for example, the job will end in three months.

In both cases, the unemployment figures may or may not be reduced. It depends upon whether the temporary person was registered as unemployed.

This short-term cover has advantages for employees who do not wish to commit themselves to longer term permanent employment. It also helps the employer to maintain production/service levels.

Some jobs are only available seasonally, like holiday camps and seaside/winter resorts which only employ people for a fixed period of time. When the contract ends, these people would register as unemployed. This is the reason why unemployment figures tend to be seasonal.

Temporary part-time

This is the familiar 'temp'. Here a person might only work for a few days, on an 'urgent' or 'emergency' job.

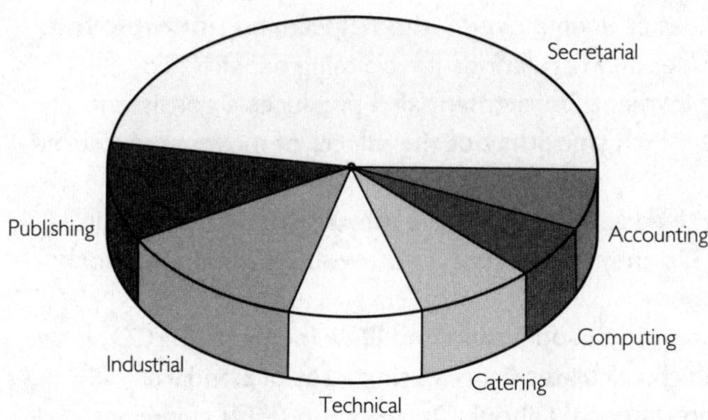

Figure 10.3 The occupation of temporary workers

Some occupations use more temporary workers than others. The main ones, in descending order of importance, are shown in the pie chart (Figure 10.3). This order is continually changing.

People are attracted to temporary employment for two main reasons: either they do not want to be committed to full-time permanent employment, with all its duties and responsibilities under the contract of employment; or they cannot get full-time work, so therefore have to accept temporary work (involuntary temporary work).

Organisations like having temporary workers because:

- they can meet short-term targets;
- some jobs only exist for a short time, for example, the Wimbledon Tennis Championship employs temps for two weeks;
- 'peaks' in the workload can be met without having to employ people permanently;
- temps can be hired quickly;
- there are very few contractual commitments;
- temps are generally cheaper to employ because there are fewer costs to pay – insurance, etc. – than with hiring full-time employees.

Activities

1 Investigate the temporary jobs available in your area. Categorise these according to the Standard Occupational Classification. Why do these jobs exist? Which jobs are the most/least popular? Write a short report on your findings which could be used by the Personnel Department in your organisation.

2 Find out if your organisation uses 'temps'. Why and when does it do this?

Unemployment

Unemployment data

The main secondary source of unemployment data is the *Employment Gazette*, published by the Department of Employment on a monthly basis. This has information for the whole country, regions and local areas. Other tables show the duration of unemployment, the age of the unemployed person, and male or female unemployment.

The figures published are for the number of people registered for employment, i.e. those having no job but who are able and available to work on the day the monthly survey is taken.

Measuring unemployment

In the UK there are two basic methods for measuring unemployment. First, the **claimant count** which uses administrative systems to count those people recorded at government offices as unemployed – the **registered unemployed**. This figure depends on the rules and regulations for claiming benefits. To compensate for this the Employment Department also produces a consistent **seasonally adjusted** series which smooths out the effects of movements caused by administration systems.

The second measure is arrived at by using **The Labour Force Survey**, in which individuals are asked: Do they have a job? If not, would they like to work and what have they done about it?

The Organisation for Economic Co-operation and Development (OECD) is an international organisation which calculates figures using a set of standard assumptions based on the International Labour Organisation (ILO) guidelines. These figures are available in OECD publications for the majority of countries in the world.

There is a continuous debate over the accuracy and reliability of all these figures – do they over-estimate or under-estimate the amount of unemployment? The answer depends on who should or should not be included as unemployed. It will depend on your politics whether you want the figures to be larger or smaller. Your social conscience will decide whether the argument is relevant. But these are some of the issues which form part of the debate. Should people who:

- are unemployed but cannot register to claim benefits be included/excluded?
- are not 'actively' seeking work be included/excluded?
- work part-time on a 'cash in hand' basis but are also registered, be included/excluded?
- can only work part-time because there are no full-time jobs available be included/excluded?
- have just left school and sign on as unemployed be included/excluded?
- are on temporary training courses be included/excluded?
- are on 'short time', i.e. working on less than normal hours be included/excluded?

You should always take great care when:

- comparing unemployment figures over a number of years because the basis for counting could have changed, for example, people on Government Training Schemes are now counted as employed;
- comparing data from individual countries, where again the basis and definition of unemployment could be different. (The same applies to the term 'employment'.) For example, in the USA the figures refer to the whole of the survey week whereas in the UK a person has to be unemployed on the day of the survey; in the USA a person could have been unemployed on any day of the week.

The OECD figures and notes can be very helpful when making international comparisons.

The great debate:

John Maynard Keynes 1883-1946

J. M. Keynes was a major British economist, whose book *The General Theory of Employment Interest and Money* was the basis of macro-economics and examined how the whole economy works. He advocated that a fall in national income, with a shortage of demand for goods and rising unemployment, could be solved by increased government expenditure. His policies, sometimes called Keynsian Economics, dominated UK economic thinking up until the early 1970s. He suggested that because the demand for labour is derived from the consumers' demand for goods and services (see page 474 for more information), then if consumer demand or consumption falls below that needed to achieve full employment, people would be unemployed.

The starting point for his analysis was his assertion that there was a set of conditions at which full employment could be achieved. This would be when the level of output in the economy was equal to the level of demand. He called this the 'equilibrium position', which means the economy would be in balance and there was no need for change.

When, however, people's consumption is below this level, the economy would not be in equilibrium and there would be unemployment. At certain levels of output people are not able to spend enough. Businesses, therefore, are unable to take on workers and unemployment will occur. Keynes's answer to this shortage of demand was to suggest that the government should create the extra demand that was needed by cutting taxation or pumping more money into the economy by 'public works programmes'. This meant government expenditure on schools,and hospitals, etc.

Milton Friedman (1912–) and Monetarism

Monetarism is the economic policy advocated by Milton Friedman, an American economist. It suggests that the country's money supply should be controlled, to keep it in line with its ability to produce goods with the aim of checking inflation. Cutting government expenditure is advocated, and the long-term aim is to return as much of the economy as possible to the private sector, allegedly in the interests of efficiency. Additionally, credit is restricted by high interest rates, and industry is not cushioned against internal market forces or overseas competition (with the aim of preventing 'overmanning', 'restrictive' union practices, 'excessive' wage demands, etc.) Unemployment results, but Monetarists claim, less than eventually occurs if Keynesian methods are adopted.

The theory was ineffectively applied by Edward Heath in the UK in the early 1970s, and from 1979 the Thatcher government attempted a more complete application of monetarism.

Source: *The Hutchinson Encyclopedia*

Activity

Read the article 'UK Industry in crisis' again. Which policies do you think the government has followed in the last three to five years – Keynesian or Monetarist? Which do you favour – the supply side or the demand side?

Trends in unemployment

Seasonally adjusted figures for unemployment in the UK

	Males	Females
1986	2,139	959
1987	1,955	851
1988	1,588	686
1989	1,277	507
1990	1,231	431
1991	1,734	552
1992	2,119	647
1993	2,226	675

Note: All figures are in thousands

Unemployment fell steadily from 1986 until April 1990, when 1,596,000 were unemployed. The most recently available figures for males and females are as follows:

		Males	Females
1994	Jul	1, 979	659
	Aug	1,947	633
	Sept	1,868	586
	Oct	1,848	574
	Nov	1,854	562
	Dec	1,918	585
1995	Jan	1,882	576

Note: All figures are in thousands

Regional distribution of unemployment

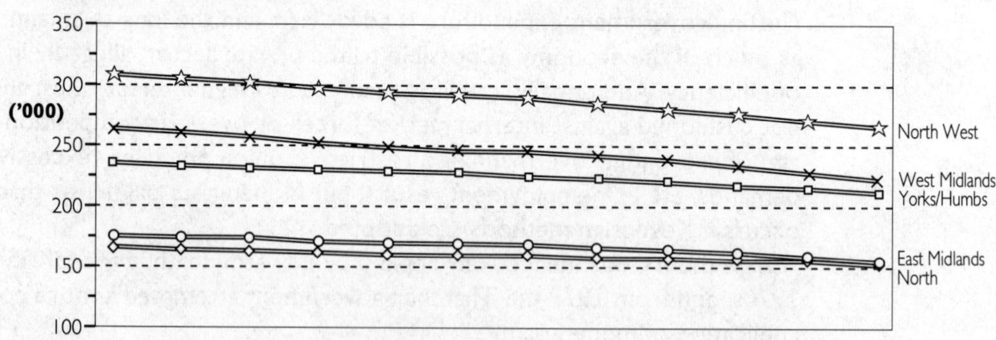

1994	Jan	Feb	Mar	Apr	May	Jun	Jul	Aug	Sep	Oct	Nov	Dec
North	166.7	164.3	162.9	160.9	160.3	159.4	159.5	158.3	157.0	155.6	154.7	152.7
Yorks/Humbs	236.3	233.2	231.0	228.7	227.9	226.6	225.8	223.0	221.1	217.8	215.4	212.3
East Midlands	177.1	175.1	173.8	171.0	170.0	169.5	168.5	166.9	165.5	162.1	158.6	154.7
West Midlands	264.0	260.5	256.0	251.9	248.5	246.4	245.5	242.4	238.8	233.7	228.0	221.5
North West	308.7	304.8	301.0	297.2	294.3	291.9	289.7	284.6	280.9	275.8	270.7	265.2

Figure 10.4 Regional unemployment Source: *Monthly Digest of Statistics*

The February 1993 edition of the *Employment Gazette* gives an excellent account of employment in the UK standard regions. Figure 10.4 shows the trend in **regional unemployment** for the North, Yorkshire and Humberside, East Midlands, West Midlands and the North West. The other regions which are not shown follow the same trends.

Here are the figures showing the unemployment rate in the regions as at October 1994.

Region	Unemployment rate (%)	Region	Unemployment rate (%)
North	11.0	West Midlands	9.1
Yorkshire and Humberside	9.2	North West	9.2
East Midlands	8.4	Wales	9.0
East Anglia	6.8	Scotland	8.8
South East	8.7	Northern Ireland	12.7
South West	8.0		

There have always been variations in the rate of unemployment between regions. Historically, those areas the furthest away from London have had the highest rates. However, recently this picture has changed, although unemployment has been high in all the regions. London and the South East have suffered very badly. Much of this increase was due to the effect of the recession on the service sector, notably financial services. (Note: A chart showing the regional distribution of population is shown on page 241.)

Activities

1 Use the diagram and tables above to show the changes in unemployment in the UK standard regions. Write a short account of the major trends. Can you say why the changes have taken place in your region? (Some of you will have to find the data for the region in which you live!)
2 Choose one other region and compare this with your own. (You will find the publication *Regional Trends* very useful.)
3 Find out the unemployment rate for men and women in your local area. Plot this information on a bar chart. (The *Employment Gazette* should have the information you need.)
4 Update the data given here.

Vacancies

Activity

a Check the local Job Centre, career offices, recruitment agencies, etc. to find the level of vacancies in your local area. How does your local area compare with the region as a whole? Is it better or worse off? (Use the *Employment Gazette* and *Monthly Digest of Statistics*.)

b Plot the figures for 'vacancies' and 'unemployment' for your region and one other region on the same graph. What are the main features of the data? Compare the figures, what conclusions can you draw?

Duration of unemployment

The longer people are out of work, the more difficult it is for them to find employment. Employers appear to prefer hiring either those who have never had employment, or those who have been unemployed for a shorter time. This phenomenon partly accounts for the fact that job creation schemes do not reduce the level of unemployment, but instead increase the size of the workforce. The subsidy given to employers in the 1994 Budget should help to reduce the long-term unemployed, i.e. those who have been unemployed for over 52 weeks.

The length of time for which people are unemployed is related to the level of economic activity and the number of vacancies in the community. Generally, the higher the level of vacancies the more opportunities people have of finding work quickly. During a recession there are likely to be fewer vacancies as demand for labour will be low.

Figure 10.5 shows the duration of unemployment for males and females from 1990 to 1992. This indicates that the length of time for which people are unemployed has increased. These people are the 'long-term unemployed' whom the government is trying to help. Find out the current figures. What are the main changes?

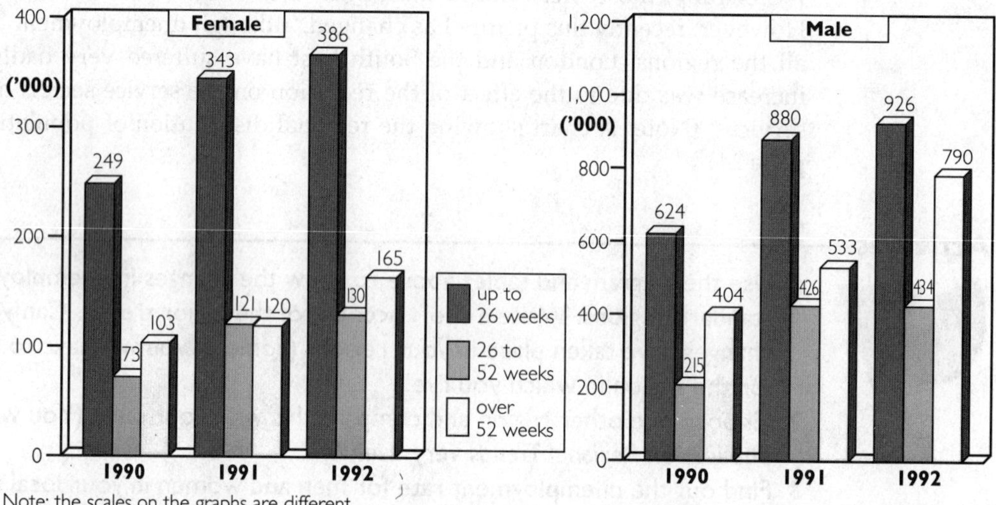

Note: the scales on the graphs are different

Figure 10.5 Duration of female and male unemployment in the UK

Detailed analysis of unemployment figures reveals that four groups of people are most likely to be unemployed for long periods.

Young people

The percentage of young people (defined as 25 and under) who are unemployed fell sharply between 1985 and 1990, from 18 per cent to 9 per cent. This percentage is calculated by:

$$\frac{\text{Number of under 25s unemployed}}{\text{Number of under 25s in the workforce}} \times 100$$

This fall was due mainly to policies introduced by the government, aimed specifically at reducing youth unemployment. School leavers aged 16 had the opportunity to follow subsidised training programmes, which could lead to employment. Both the Youth Opportunity Scheme (YOPS) and the Youth Training Scheme (YTS) were part of this drive to reduce the unemployment figures. Despite these schemes, and since 1990, youth unemployment remains higher than for the workforce as a whole. This is because young people are less likely to be hired, require more training, have less experience, and they are more likely to be fired as lower redundancy payments are generally paid to this group.

People with few or no skills

Unskilled workers are more likely to be unemployed during a recession. They also form the majority of the long-term unemployed. The most likely cause of this is that many unskilled jobs can be done by machines, for example, an automatic dishwasher replaces a 'washer-up'.

Men aged 55 and over

Many men aged 55 and over are now taking early retirement and although they will not receive a state pension, will often get a pension which has been provided in part by their former employer. They are unlikely to be re-employed but might go into self-employment. Many firms use a FIFO – First In First Out – policy when shedding labour, so the oldest employees might go first. The trend towards early retirement is more pronounced in occupations with a high stress level. The majority of people working in the foreign exchange section of banking and financial services are under 40.

Ethnic origin

People from ethnic minorities have a higher probability of being unemployed. When an organisation has an equal opportunities policy, it will usually carry out some form of ethnic monitoring. The purpose of this procedure is to try and ensure that ethnic minorities are fairly represented in the workforce.

Labour markets

There are markets for everything: used cars, used furniture, and stamps can all be bought and sold. But by far the largest is the market for **labour services**. This is the mechanism through which businesses, such as private companies and public corporations can buy labour services and workers can sell their labour services. People are not bought and sold, it is the work they can do or the service that they can provide, which is traded.

Film stars, and pop groups work world-wide, and earn millions of pounds in the **international labour market**. There are **national** labour markets sometimes controlled by government rules and regulations, and there are also **local** labour markets, where there may only be one employer.

Labour is one of the four inputs used by organisations to produce goods and services. It is the factor of production whose reward is wages.

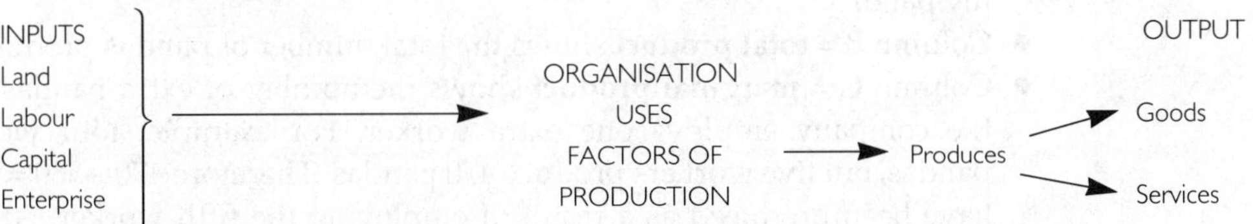

An organisation's demand for labour

If a business produces, for example, children's toys, its demand for workers, the labour, will depend upon the consumer's demand for its toys. This is called a **derived demand**. The labour, workers, are needed not for their own sake, but because they can be used to produce toys. The demand for toy makers is derived or comes from the demand for the output of the business. The consumer will only purchase goods and services, in this case toys, for the satisfaction and pleasure which they give.

Table 10.2 shows how many workers should be employed by a business. It illustrates how we determine how many workers are required by examining the output produced by each worker. The business is a toy company which makes pandas.

Table 10.2 Worker data for a toy company

Number of workers	Total product = Number of pandas	Marginal product = Number of pandas	Marginal revenue product (MRP) in £s	Marginal cost wage rate in £s	Marginal revenue product (MRP) in £s	Marginal revenue product (MRP) in £s
3	240					
		120	360	150 employ	300	600
4	360					
		110	330	150 employ	275	
5	470					
		90	270	150 employ	225	
6	560					
		50	150	150 employ	125	
7	610					
		30	90	150 do not employ	75	
8	640					
Column A	*Column B*	*Column C*	*Column D – MRP when pandas sell at £3*	*Column E – workers have a wage of £150*	*Column F – MRP when pandas sell at £2.50*	*Column G – MRP when pandas sell at £5*

- Column A = number of workers, shows the total number of workers needed to make toy pandas.
- Column B = **total product** shows the total number of pandas produced.
- Column C = **marginal product** shows the number of extra pandas produced when the company employs one extra worker. For example, four workers make 360 pandas, but five workers produce 470 pandas. Therefore 470 – 360 = 110 pandas extra have been produced as a result of employing the fifth worker. At some point, the marginal product could become negative, for example, if the workplace is fairly small (as this one is), extra workers could disrupt production by getting in everyone's way and total production could actually fall. 'Too many cooks spoil the broth!' This tendency for marginal product to decline as extra workers are employed, is sometimes called the Law of Diminishing Marginal Productivity.

- Column D = **marginal revenue product (MRP)**, which is the extra money or revenue which the business obtains as a result of selling the extra pandas that it produces. For example:
  If pandas sell at £3 and marginal product = 120 pandas, then the MRP is the marginal product (number of pandas) multiplied by the selling price (£) = 120 pandas × £3 each = £360.
- Column D gives the extra revenue that could be earned, if this business employed additional people.

We are now in a position where we can answer the question: How many workers should be employed?

Let us say that the current or 'going' wage rate for people in this industry is £150 a week per worker. This is highlighted in Table 10.2 as Column E. On Figure 10.6, we have shown this weekly wage along with the curve showing the marginal revenue product (this is drawn by plotting the MRP figures against the relevant number of workers).

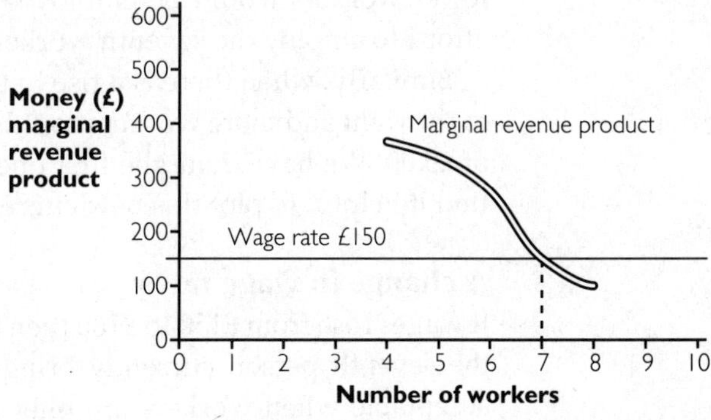

Figure 10.6 Marginal revenue product

Generally, a company should follow guidelines similar to these when hiring workers:

- If the MRP, the extra revenue, is more than the wage rate (the cost of the extra worker) it should employ more workers.
- However, if MRP is less than the wage rate, it should not hire any more workers, i.e. workers cost more to hire than they produce in revenue. For example, when MRP = £90 and the marginal cost wage rate is £150, as in Column E of Table 10.2.
- It should continue to hire workers up until the stage where the MRP = wage rate. In our example when MRP = £150 = the wage rate of £150.

Activity

Liz and Kathy run a small sandwich bar in Borough High Street, a busy shopping area. They want to know whether to employ extra people at a lunchtime, i.e. from 11 a.m. to 2 p.m., at a wage rate of £4.50 per hour.

So far they have calculated these figures on a daily basis.

The price of sandwiches is £1.60 each.

Number of workers	Total sandwiches (product)	Marginal sandwiches (product)	Marginal revenue product (£)
2	540		
3	790	250	400 (£1.60 x 250)
4	990	?	?
5	1,070	?	?
6	1,080	?	?
7	800	?	?

Write a short report advising them what to do. Explain your reasons and include a diagram (this should help to explain things).

Hint: Plot marginal product and marginal revenue product on the same graph.

Changes in demand

What would cause the demand for labour to change in a business? This could be due to any of the following factors.

A change in demand/price of the product

If there is a decrease in the demand for pandas, the price will fall, for example, from £3 to £2.50. The MRP needs to be recalculated using the selling price of £2.50. This has been done in Column F of Table 10.2. The MRP curve would shift to the left (Figure 10.7) and fewer workers would be employed at the wage rate of £150. The business could not afford to employ the seventh worker because the MRP = £125 and the wage is £150.

Similarly, when there is a rise in the price of the product, pandas, the MRP will shift to the right and more workers could be afforded. Try the calculation with a selling price of £5.00. We have done the first one for you in Column G of Table 10.2. You will also find it helpful to plot this new curve. How many people could be employed?

A change in wage rates

If wages rose from £150 to £160 then fewer workers would be employed. In our example the seventh person currently brings in or generates £150 for the business, which is acceptable when workers are only paid £150. However, if the wage was £160, there would be a £10 shortfall. In this case it is likely that fewer workers would be employed.

Conversely, if wages fell, then the company could afford to employ more workers.

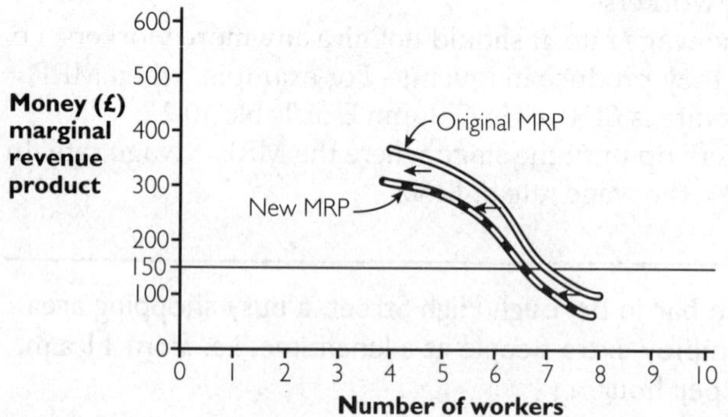

Figure 10.7 Result of a decrease in the demand for pandas

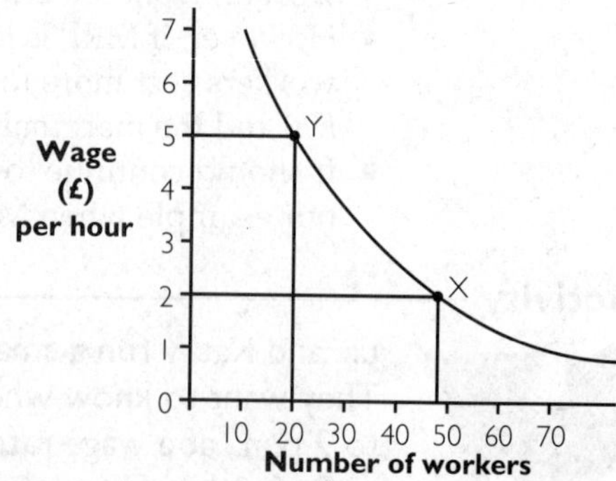

Figure 10.8 Demand curve for labour

Looking at the **demand curve** for labour, and using the information from above we can say that:

- more workers will be employed when wages are low (X);
- fewer workers will be employed when wages are high (Y);
- when wages fall, the demand for workers should rise;
- when wages rise, the demand for workers should fall.

The relationship between the product market and the labour market
An increase in demand for the product will cause a rise in the product's price. This in turn will cause an increase in demand for workers. This relationship is shown in Figure 10.9

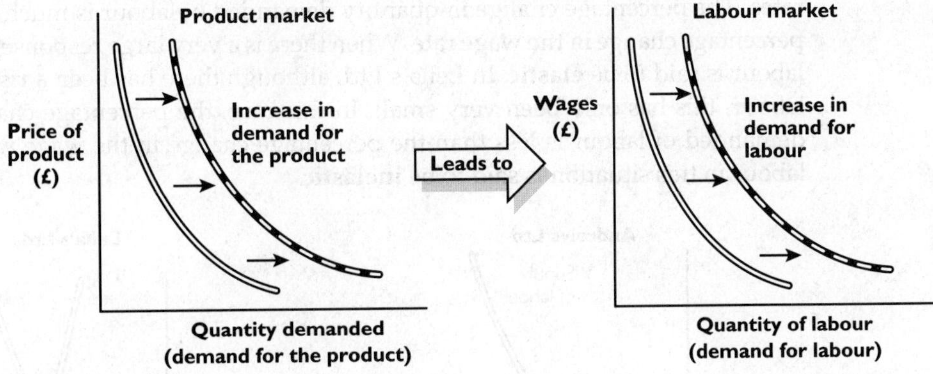

Figure 10.9 Result of an increase in demand for the product

A decrease in demand for the product will cause a fall in the product's price. This in turn will cause a decrease in demand for labour. This relationship is shown in Figure 10.10.

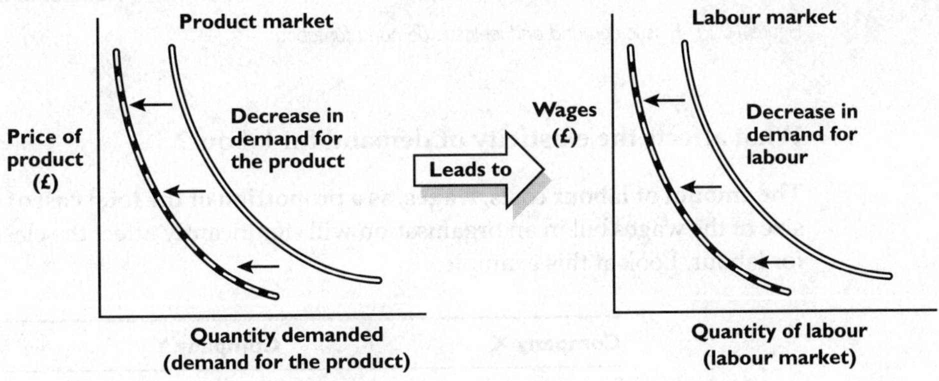

Figure 10.10 Result of a decrease in demand for the product

A change in the method of making the product

A change in either the method of production, or the materials involved could result in the business becoming more efficient. For example, introducing a new machine for fixing the pandas' eyes automatically, could enable more pandas to be produced. This would raise the MRP and could eventually lead to an increase in demand for workers.

The elasticity of demand for labour

The **elasticity of demand for labour** shows how the demand for labour/workers changes as a result of a change in wages. The formula is:

$$\frac{\text{Percentage change in quantity of labour demanded}}{\text{Percentage change in wages}} = \text{Elasticity of demand for labour}$$

To calculate this you will need to know the original wage and the new wage, and the original and new number of workers.

The elasticity of demand for labour shows how demand for labour will respond to a change in its price (wage). Look at the two examples shown in Figure 10.11. In Andrews Ltd there has been a very large rise in demand for labour as a result of the fall in wage rates. The percentage change in quantity demanded of labour is much greater than the percentage change in the wage rate. When there is a very large response, the demand for labour is said to be **elastic**. In Leila's Ltd, although there has been a rise in demand for labour, this has only been very small. In this case, the percentage change in quantity demanded of labour is less than the percentage change in the wage rate. Demand for labour in this situation is said to be **inelastic**.

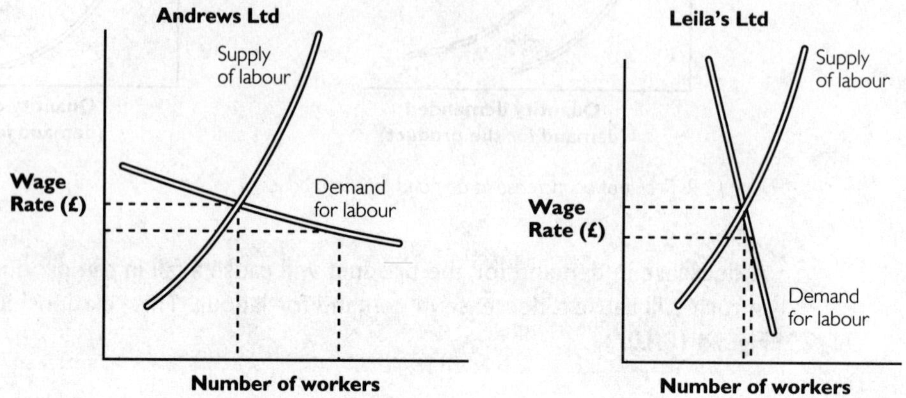

Figure 10.11 Elastic demand and inelastic demand for labour

What affects the elasticity of demand for labour?

The amount of labour costs, wages, as a proportion of the total cost of production The size of the wages bill in an organisation will significantly affect the elasticity of demand for labour. Look at this example:

Company X	Company Y
Total production costs = £1,000,000	Total production costs = £1,000,000
Total labour cost = £800,000	Total labour costs = £200,000
What would happen if wages fell by 5 per cent?	
Wages would fall by 5% x £800,000 = £40,000	Wages would fall by 5% x £200,000 = £10,000

In Company X the fall in wages is more significant than in Company Y. It is likely that the change in the quantity of labour demanded in Company X will be greater than in Company Y. The effect on elasticity is that the bigger the change in the quantity of labour demanded by an organisation, as a result of a change in wages, the bigger will be the elasticity. Generally, the elasticity of demand for labour will be greater in those companies where labour costs are a higher proportion of total costs.

The reaction of consumers to a change in the price of the product Here we are looking at the elasticity of demand for the product (pandas) – see page 68. The formula is:

$$\frac{\text{Percentage change in quantity demanded}}{\text{Percentage change in the selling price}} = \text{Elasticity of demand for the product}$$

When a small change in price leads to a large change in demand, demand is said to be elastic. However, if the same change in price produces a small change in demand, the demand is inelastic.

We know that an organisation's demand for labour (the factor market) depends on the demand for the product, and that a large increase in demand for the product will cause a large increase in the demand for labour. Because of the close relationship between the product market and the labour market, when elasticity of demand for the product is high, then the elasticity of demand for labour is also likely to be high, and vice versa. Big falls in the demand for products are therefore likely to cause big falls in the demand for labour. This is precisely what has happened during the recent recession where the fall in demand for housing and office accommodation, for example, has led to unemployment for construction workers.

Activity

Look at the demand for courses in your college/school. This is also a derived demand. Can you see a relationship between what is happening in the economy and what is happening in education, for example, where industries are declining/expanding, are the education and training courses also declining/expanding?

Activity

1 For each situation below write a set of notes and use diagrams to explain your answer.

- **a** A firm employs two accountants and 94 production workers. What is likely to be the elasticity of demand for each group?
- **b** There has been a substantial fall in the demand for biscuits, primarily for health reasons. What do you expect will happen to the demand for people who work in biscuit factories?
- **c** There is substantial unemployment among UK shipyard workers. Why do you think this has happened? (Hint: you will need to link the product and factor markets.)
- **d** Forde and Jonathan Ltd is a small printing firm making speciality cards. They employ ten workers, but are about to purchase a new labour-saving printing press which will affect productivity and output. What could happen to the employees?

2 Either by using your own organisation or your work experience placement, find out which of the factors below is most important in influencing the demand for managers and unskilled labourers. It would be useful to use a rating scale similar to this one. People could then be asked to rate each factor on the scale of 1 to 6, where 1 represents 'unimportant' and 6 is 'extremely important'.

Consumer demand	1	2	3	4	5	6
Unimportant						Extremely important

- consumer demand
- salary or wage rate
- size of the company
- contribution to output.
- price of the product
- number of managers/labourers
- labour intensive/capital intensive

Supply of labour

In the national economy the **supply of labour** is affected by:

- birth and death rates
- retirement age
- school leaving age
- size of the working population
- willingness to work – the participation rate
- ability to work
- migration – movements of people into and out of the country.

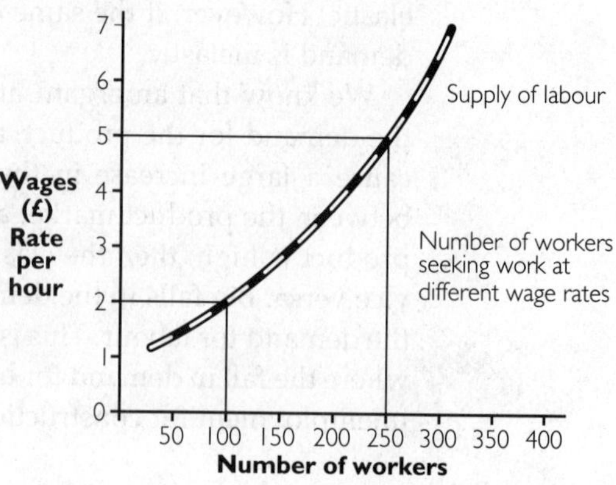

Figure 10.12 The supply of labour

The labour supply for an occupation

The labour supply for an occupation is closely linked to the level of wages that people can receive. Look at Figure 10.12 where it can be seen that the supply of labour rises as the wage rate rises.

The supply would be 100 at a wage rate of £2. This means that 100 workers would be willing to work at this rate. When the wage rate is £5, there would be 250 people seeking work.

There are other reasons – which are often just as important as wages – that attract people to particular occupations.

Fringe benefits

These are non-monetary rewards and can include, for example, company cars for managers and sales executives, or subsidised travel and holiday discounts for people working in travel agencies.

Expected job satisfaction and security

These are often given as reasons why people are attracted to office jobs or the professions. Jobs today are, however, much less secure than ten years ago.

Nature of the job

The working conditions in particular jobs, for example, amount of risk/security, glamour or danger, all have a direct effect on the supply. Some people will be attracted and others deterred by these features. Building sites, refuse collection, libraries, horticulture and the theatre, all attract different kinds of people. What image do you have of people who work in these occupations?

Qualifications and training

Many occupations require a high level of training and/or qualifications, which act as a constraint and limit the number of people able to do certain jobs. For example, once you have completed this course, you will be eligible for jobs not open to unqualified people. Some 60 per cent of the UK working population have fewer qualifications than you will have! If you go on to higher education, then 92 per cent of the working population will be less qualified. People with qualifications have better career opportunities.

Generally, unskilled jobs are not as well paid as skilled jobs, therefore, a change in **wage rates** will have a different effect on the supply of labour to each occupation.

Supply will tend to be elastic for unskilled low-paid work and inelastic for skilled, higher paid work.

Wage rates in competing occupations

The labour market is very competitive, although during a recession it is more likely that potential workers compete for jobs rather than employers compete for labour. Even so, a word processing operator will still seek the best paid employment with the best conditions of work. Companies will need to be aware of market wage rates when setting their own remuneration package.

Activity

Either:

Give three reasons why you were attracted to your present job. Could you work in another company? Could you work in another occupation? Compare your reasons with other people in your group.

Or:

Give three reasons which would tempt you into working in a particular occupation.

Then:

Compile a list of factors which affect the supply of labour to two particular occupations and to two named businesses.

What is the elasticity of supply of labour?

The **elasticity of supply** of labour refers to the extent to which the supply of labour changes in response to a change in wage rates. It is measured by this formula:

$$\frac{\text{Percentage change in the quantity of labour supplied}}{\text{Percentage change in the wage rate}} = \text{Elasticity of supply of labour}$$

Elasticity of supply is affected by the length of time needed for people to obtain training and/or qualifications. Vacancies for professional and highly skilled people can be very difficult to fill in the short term, which is why 'head hunters' operate (see Chapter 7). Long training and intensive education is required. For example, a shortage of teachers now might only be met in several years' time when the current imbalance in the labour market (where demand is greater than the supply) could have disappeared. Therefore, even if wages rise sharply, there will be a time lag before the supply is able to respond. Compare this with unskilled occupations where vacancies can be filled immediately.

What determines the level of wages?

When employers and employees are in a **free bargaining** situation, i.e. neither side has more power than the other (which would happen very rarely) then the market forces of supply and demand are largely responsible for determining the level of wages in a particular industry.

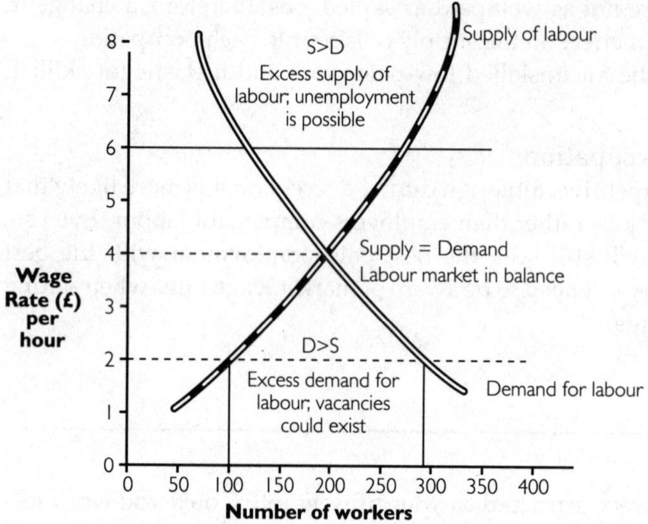

Figure 10.13 How wages are determined when there is free bargaining

Figure 10.13 shows how wages are determined when there is free bargaining. This labour market will be in balance at the wage rate of £4 when the supply of labour equals the demand for labour. At any other wage rate, there will be an imbalance of supply and demand. For example, at a wage rate of £2 per hour few people are willing to work but 290 are demanded. This wage rate is too low to attract the labour that is needed. Market forces will come into play and companies will compete by bidding/pushing up wages so that supply extends and demand contracts, until the supply equals the demand.

However, if wages are currently at £6 per hour there are more people seeking jobs than there are companies willing to employ them. The supply of labour is greater than the demand and there is unemployment. This excess supply means there is a buyer's market, which will pull down the wage rates. Businesses can 'pick and choose' whom they want to employ. Workers already employed will resist this, if possible, by taking industrial action. The London bus drivers strike in April 1993 was an example of this action.

Case study

Bovis Construction

Changes in the demand for labour

Example A – supply and demand for building labourers

How will changes in the demand for labour affect the wage rate? Look at Figure 10.14 which shows the supply and demand for building labourers. The initial wage rate is at W_0 where supply equals demand. Let us assume there is a fall in demand for the product, in this case houses, because there is a recession. The demand for labour decreases because there is less work available. The demand curve for labour will shift

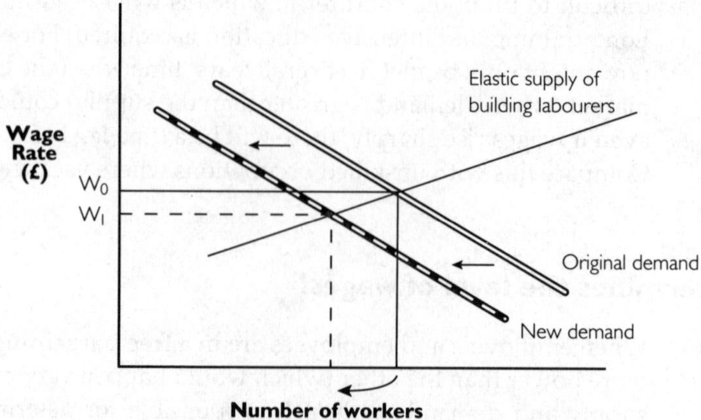

Figure 10.14 Supply and demand for building labourers

to the left (a decrease). The supply of labour is elastic because this is an unskilled job which many people could do. Fewer workers will be employed at a lower wage rate. This will be at W_1, where the new demand curve equals the supply.

Example B – supply and demand for steel fixers and riggers
The initial wage rate for steel fixers and riggers is at W_0 on Figure 10.15, where supply equals demand. When a building project, such as the Channel Tunnel Rail Terminal, at Waterloo in London, is started it will require steel workers. The demand for this group of workers will increase, so the demand curve will shift to the right. The supply of this group of workers is inelastic because it is a highly skilled and specialist job. It will be necessary for the construction company to pay higher wages in order to attract the people it needs. This wage rate is shown at W_1.

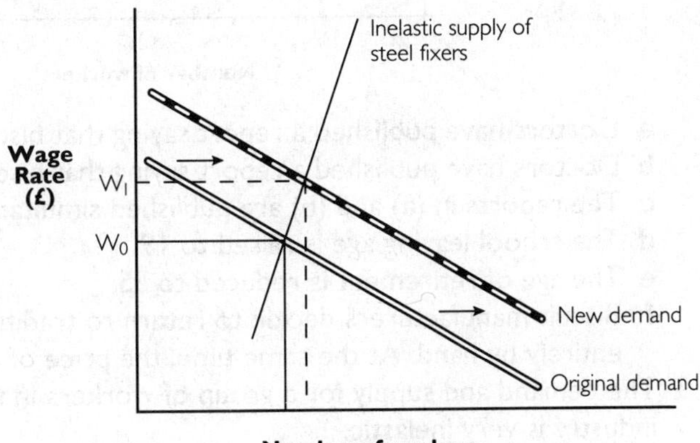

Figure 10.15 Supply and demand for steel fixers and riggers

Activities

1 Draw the supply and demand curves for labour in this industry. What will be the wage rate?

Number of workers demanded	Wage rate	Number of workers supplied
2,400	£2	300
2,120	£4	690
1,780	£6	1,220
1,300	£8	1,530
700	£10	1,870

Show what would happen if the demand for workers rose by 10 per cent.

2 In the diagram on page 484, D_0 and S_0 are the original demand and supply curves for workers in a biscuit factory. D_1 and D_2 are new demand curves. S_1 and S_2 are new supply curves. Initially the industry wage rate is W_0 and the number of biscuit workers employed is QL_0. Each time the starting point is at Z where $D_0 = S_0$. Write short notes saying what will happen in each case giving your reasons.

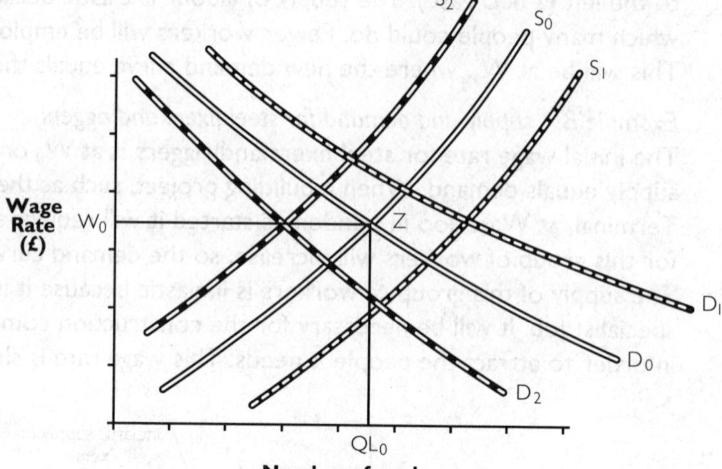

- **a** Doctors have published a report saying that biscuits are very bad for you.
- **b** Doctors have published a report saying that biscuits are very good for you.
- **c** The reports in (a) and (b) are published simultaneously.
- **d** The school leaving age is raised to 19.
- **e** The age of retirement is reduced to 55.
- **f** Biscuit manufacturers decide to return to traditional ways of making biscuits, entirely by hand. At the same time, the price of cakes rises sharply.

3 The demand and supply for a group of workers in the nuclear reprocessing industry is very inelastic.

- **a** Draw the demand curve and supply curve for these workers on the same diagram.
- **b** If the demand for workers increases because the UK has won new contracts to reprocess nuclear waste from other countries, say what will happen to the wage rate.
- **c** If the demand and supply curves were elastic, show how your answer would be the same/different.

The market for skilled and unskilled labour

In each labour market, there are different conditions of supply and demand. Employers and employees have different bargaining strengths. If we take two examples, we can see how these conditions work in the markets for skilled and unskilled labour (see Figure 10.16).

In the market for unskilled labour there is unemployment at the current wage rate of £3, as supply is greater than demand. In the market for skilled labour there are vacancies at the wage rate of £5 because demand is greater than supply.

The vacancies could persist because:

- of the amount and length of training needed to create skilled workers;
- the company is unable to substitute machines for the labour it needs. Could a machine do your job?
- workers may be unable to move to another area to fill vacancies because they cannot afford to;
- the skills that people possess may not be immediately suitable to take other occupations, for example, unemployed steelworkers in Port Talbot could not move to London to fill the vacancies for legal executives.

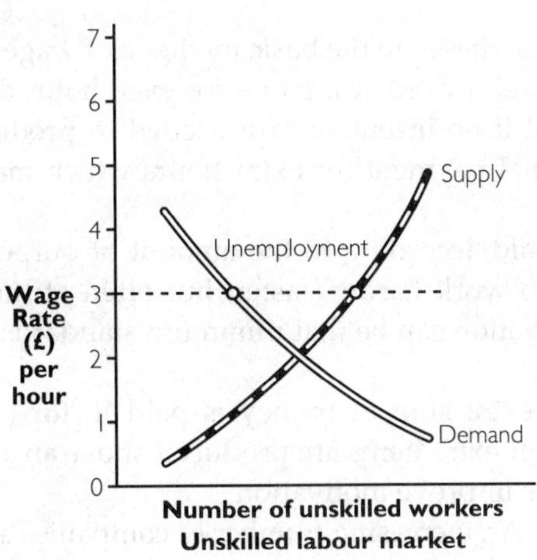

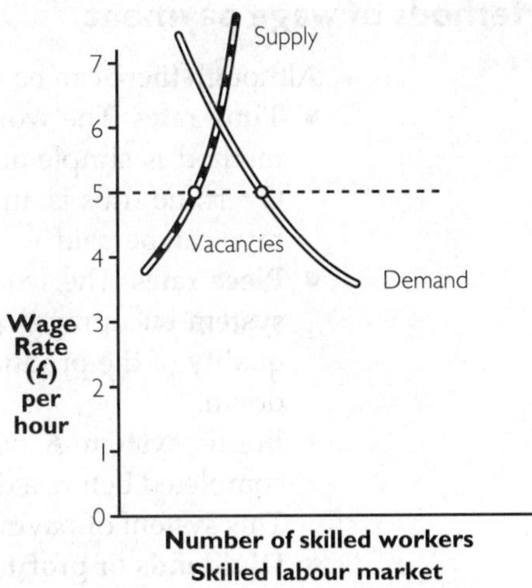

Figure 10.16 The markets for unskilled and skilled labour

Local labour markets

A local labour market is most likely to exist in a small town where a few employers are competing for workers who live within easy access. We call this the **catchment area**. It can vary in size, for instance, in rural areas where public transport is limited, this could be fairly small, and most workers will not expect, or be able to, travel very far. The supply and demand for labour will be limited by the size of the catchment area.

In urban areas, a much bigger pool of labour exists and there are more employers. The catchment area is much bigger therefore it is difficult to think of it as a local labour market, where the supply and demand for labour is restricted.

Where a local labour market does exist, wage rates will all tend to be fairly similar. However, when there are a large number of employers competing for workers in a bigger catchment area, there may be wide differences in the pay and conditions on offer because there will be more opportunities available for employees. The tendency is for the larger firms to offer higher wages because this helps to attract better qualified personnel.

In each area the conditions of supply and demand for labour play a significant part in determining the general or 'going' wage rate.

Wages

Activity

Your group should divide into twos and threes, to carry out a survey of wage rates in the local area. Make a list of the wage rates for as many jobs as possible. Is there much variation? Is it a local labour market? You will need to check Job Centres, employment agencies, the local press, etc. It will help if you look at the New Earnings Survey to check national rates and classify jobs using the Standard Industrial Classification (SIC).

Analyse your findings and present your conclusions as a verbal and written report to the rest of the group.

Methods of wage payment

Although there can be variations, these are the basic methods of wage payment:

- **Time rates** The worker is paid a fixed wage rate for each hour, day or week. The method is simple and useful if no incentives are needed to produce extra output. Overtime (this is an additional payment for extra hours which may be at a higher rate) can be paid.
- **Piece rates** The worker is paid according to the amount of output produced. The system encourages people to work harder/faster, but often at the expense of the quality of the product. A variation can be that minimum standards of work are laid down.
- **Bonus system** A bonus or extra sum of money is paid if, for example, work is completed before a deadline or extra items are produced above an agreed minimum. This system of payment helps improve motivation.
- **Dividends or profit sharing** An increasing number of companies are now involved in some form of worker ownership through company share schemes. The reasoning behind this is that if workers own shares, they are more likely to work for increased profits. Most companies, however, frown on the idea of worker participation at board level, the so-called 'Worker Directors'.

In addition to money wages, many organisations now offer a wide range of non-monetary benefits as part of the total remuneration package (many of which are now subject to taxation). These are sometimes called fringe benefits or 'perks' (a short form of perquisite), defined as an incidental or customary benefit gained from employment. These can include a company car, free medical insurance, free or reduced travel, in-house company discounts, subsidised canteen and social facilities, and 'tips'.

The make-up and payment of wages is often a source of conflict in an organisation. But if the system is clearly understood and carefully administered by the Personnel/Wages Department, many of the potential problems, such as payments being late, under-payment or too many deductions, can be eliminated.

Activity

Either:

Find out – if you can – how people in your group are paid. Why are these methods of payment used in each case?

And/or:

Use brainstorming to list the advantages and disadvantages of each method of wage payment both from the point of view of an employee and an employer.

Wage differentials

Wage differentials are the differences in wage rates that can exist between people working in different occupations or different areas. The term is also applied to the differences in the wages earned by men and women.

Differences in occupational wage rates can be caused by:

1. The conditions of supply and demand for labour. We have already seen how these operate in different markets.
2. Whether the job is dangerous or hazardous, for example, working with nuclear waste.
3. The length of training and qualifications involved, for example, the professions.
4. Whether exceptional ability or unique qualities are needed.
5. Whether the industry is capital or labour intensive. The labour costs of capital

intensive industries tend to be fairly low, therefore higher wages can be paid.

6 The amount of responsibility involved; one example would be an airline pilot.
7 The amount of stress involved. These are supposed to be the most stressful jobs: company director, police officer, miner, pilot, prison officer, construction worker, actor, politician. The least stressful jobs are supposed to be beautician, museum worker, and librarian.
8 The amount of risk involved, for example, insurance companies are wary of insuring construction workers, asbestos workers, boxers, divers and steeplejacks.
9 Whether the supply of labour can be controlled by a trade union or professional association, for example, Equity, the actors' union, and the British Medical Association (BMA). If it can, then wage rates will tend to be higher.
10 The extra earnings available, through perks, and other non-monetary payments, such as discounted airfares for travel agents.

Wage differentials between people doing the same job can be explained by looking at the distinction between an employees' **basic wage** and earnings. The basic wage is the minimum wage that a worker would receive before any additions are made. Whilst **earnings** equals the basic wage plus any payments for overtime, shift working, bonuses, etc.

Activities

1 Give examples of occupations which could come into each of the categories above. Say how wages could be affected in each case, for example, do high-risk jobs necessarily mean higher wage rates?
2 Find out why workers doing the same job, earn different wages. For example, why does a clerical worker at British Steel earn a different wage from a clerical worker with Southwark Council? Why might two clerical workers in the same office 'take home' different pay? Here are some reasons to start you off:
Age of the employee, length of service with the business, pay deductions.

Wage bargaining

Wage bargaining is the process by which the sellers and buyers of labour reach agreement on the wage rate. Before we look at the theory of wage bargaining, there are a number of activities which simulate bargaining, for you to complete.

So far in this chapter our analysis has only shown us how wages are determined when

Activities

In each case below note the process of bargaining you went through. Where did you start from? Who gave way? Did anyone give way? What was the final result? Are both sides satisfied? Who won concessions?

Compare the group results at the end of each session. You will find it helpful if some of these sessions can be videotaped.

1 Your group should divide into pairs. One person should role-play the employer. The other should role-play the employee. You must negotiate an hourly wage rate. The current rate is £3.50 per hour. The employer owns and manages a small shop in your local, fairly depressed neighbourhood or local, prosperous neighbourhood. At the end of this session swap roles and partners.
2 Your group should divide so that two people are employers and everyone else is a worker. One half of the workers should form a trade union.

Employer A – Negotiates separately with each worker. Workers must not reveal how much they have agreed to until the end of negotiations, when they can tell all.
Employer B – Negotiates with the whole group which has formed a trade union.

a What rates of pay were agreed?

b What were the advantages/disadvantages of each method of negotiation to 'employers' and 'employees'?

3 The group should split so that there is one 'employer', who has to recruit a new 'employee'. Everyone else is looking for work. You must negotiate separately. The 'going' or average wage rate in your area is…(you have to supply this figure). At the end of the negotiations, which person has been selected and why?

4 The group should divide so that there is only one person looking for work. Each employer desperately needs an extra employee urgently. What would have happened if the words 'desperately' and 'urgently' were not there? What wage rate was agreed?

5 When these activities are complete, you will need to analyse your findings. Put them into a chart like this:

Employer: Demands or buys labour **Number of employers**	Employee: Supplies or sells labour **Number of potential employees**	**Wage rates** **High**	 **Middle**	 **Low**
I	Many			
I	Few			
I	I			
Few	Many			
Few	Few			
Few	I			
Many	Many			
Many	Few			
Many	I			

Put a tick for the result.

employers (buyers or demanders of labour) and employees (sellers or suppliers of labour) bargain/negotiate freely with each other. In practice, as you have just found out, the bargaining power of employers and employees is not equal.

Look at your analysis of the activities on wage bargaining. It should show that the wage rate is largely determined by the amount of power possessed by each 'side' in the bargaining process. Here are some possible conclusions:

1 Wage rates will tend to be lower when one employer is negotiating separately with individual workers. The buyer has the bargaining power.

2 Wage rates will tend to be higher when many employers are competing for a small number of workers, for example, highly-skilled computer programmers are able to command very high wages. The seller of labour has the bargaining power.

3 When many employers negotiate separately with employees, there will initially be a wide range of wage rates. When everyone has total access to all information, then wage rates tend to be similar.

4 The group that formed the trade union should have been able to negotiate higher wages than those workers who were negotiating separately.

5 Did the employers get together at any time to form an employers' association? In industries where trade unions are weak or non existent and/or employers' associations are strong, wages generally tend to be lower.

Wages in the economy

It is usual in business to place jobs into market groups which are affected by the same external pressures. The market forces which affect computer analysts, receptionists and administration assistants will be different, therefore the wages of each of these groups need to be determined separately. Within a business it may be necessary to adopt different pay structures for each group if it is to succeed in matching its internal needs with changes in the external environment. For example, if there is a shortage of people with computer skills, a very mobile group of workers, the business will have to pay higher salaries in order to attract the staff it needs.

The main problem a business will have is to find out what is the market wage rate for a particular job. What it can do is check the local press for similar jobs, check with other local companies (although they will probably be unwilling to say anything!) or use the New Earnings Survey for national guidelines.

Wage differentials

Table 10.3 Weekly earnings of males and females in manufacturing industries

	£ males	£ females
1988	236.3	138.4
1989	257.3	152.7
1990	282.2	170.3
1991	299.5	184.2
1992	319.8	199.3

Look at Table 10.3; this information is taken from the *Monthly Digest of Statistics*. We can use it to calculate the difference in male and female earnings. For example, in 1988 the average weekly earnings of men in manufacturing industries was £236.30 per week, and £138.40 for women. Women earned 58.6 per cent of a man's wage. The percentage rates of women's wages as compared to men's, over the years, is as follows:

1989 59.3 per cent
1990 60.3 per cent
1991 61.5 per cent
1992 62.3 per cent.

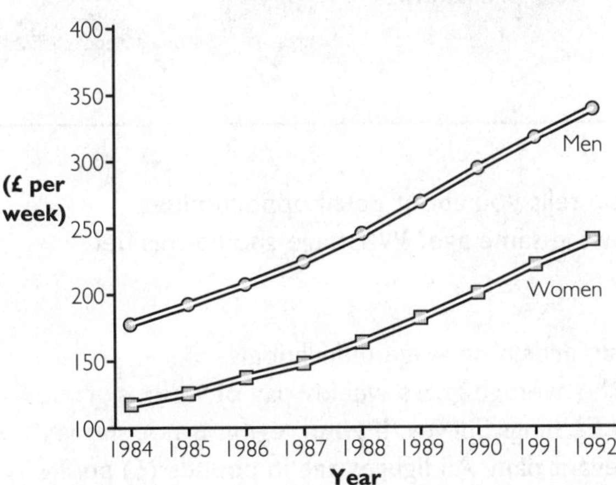

Figure 10.17 Average weekly earnings

You can draw your own conclusions as to when earnings will be the same, i.e. when there will be no **wage differential**. However, you should notice that the hours worked by women are less than men. Although the Equal Pay Act was passed in 1970, there does not appear to have been much progress towards equality.

Figure 10.17 shows the average weekly earnings of men and women from 1984 to 1992. What is the current position?

Why do women earn less than men?

1 Labour turnover tends to be higher for women than men. Women tend to change jobs more often and tend to stay a shorter time with one employer. Therefore, recruitment and training costs are higher than for men. Employers compensate for these higher costs by paying lower wages.

2 Women are more likely to have a higher level of absenteeism than men. Employers, therefore, spend less money on training women, with the result that women tend not to be given as many opportunities for promotion. Because of this, women are more likely to be in lower paid jobs in an occupation. Generally, women are under-represented in middle and top management posts in many organisations. In the more enlightened organisations which have invested heavily in the training of women, this policy has paid off enormously.

3 Women tend to work in different occupations, which are historically lower paid, for example, shops, hotels, pubs and catering. When women do work in industries where the majority of workers are male, for example, metals, engineering, energy and water supply, construction and mining, they tend to be found mainly in catering, secretarial and cleaning jobs.

There were more than 1,000 equal pay cases lodged against the former British Coal, by canteen workers and cleaners, citing surface mine workers or clerical workers as the groups to which they should be compared. An Employment Appeal Tribunal upheld their claim. Equal opportunities legislation has so far had little effect on the economic or social status of women. Forty per cent of women workers have part-time jobs. These tend to be lower paid with few, if any, benefits. The position of many women workers has worsened as a result of the privatisation of many local authority jobs, for example, catering and cleaning posts which were full-time have become part-time and 'term-time only'.

Advel Systems

The company Avdel Systems raised its retirement age for women to 65 from 60 in line with that of male employees, following the European Court of Justice's ruling in Barber v. Guardian Royal Assurance Exchange Group that employers may not apply different pension benefits to men and women. Avdel's employees claim that where discrimination is found to exist, it should be eliminated by equalling pension arrangements at the level of those enjoying the better provisions, and that a lower compulsory retirement age was the better provision.

Source: ACAS Annual Report 1992

Activities

1 Discuss with your group:

a What the Advel Systems' solution tells you about equal opportunities.

b Should men and women retire at the same age? What age should this be?

2 **Wage differentials**

This activity requires you to write an article on wage differentials.

The figures below, which show the average gross weekly pay of various groups of people, are taken from the New Earnings Survey. If your region is not shown, use the same source to get the relevant data. All figures are in pounds (£) per week.

Full-time males on adult rates (£)		
	Manual	**Non-manual**
South East	299.2	483.2
West Midlands	274.2	399.9
South West	271.1	400.0

Full-time females on adult rates (£)		
	Manual	**Non-manual**
South East	204.4	315.5
West Midlands	175.4	253.8
South West	173.4	259.3

Full-time females (£)		
	Manual	**Non-manual**
Aged under 18	112.1	152.2
Aged 40–49	186.4	299.0

Full-time males (£)		
	Manual	**Non-manual**
Aged under 18	111.1	125.7
Aged 40–49	305.4	492.6

Average gross weekly pay of full-time males and females on adult rates

Occupation	**£ Female**	**£ Male**
Biological Scientists	380.4	478.4
Higher and further education	403.7	471.8
Textiles	158.9	241.7

Source: *New Earnings Survey 1994 Part A*

a What can be said about wage differentials between:
- males and females?
- manual and non-manual workers?
- different regions?
- males and females of different ages?

b Suggest reasons why these differentials exist.

c Write up your observations as a short article suitable for publication in your local newspaper.

Trade unions and collective bargaining

In this section we look at various methods of wage determination, paying particular attention to how first trade unions, and then the government, affect wage levels and employment.

The aims of trade unions in the UK are broadly to improve pay, hours and conditions of employment. The major emphasis has always been on improving pay although in most negotiations with employers, there are usually other elements which are regarded as equally important, for example, a reduction in weekly hours, better holiday entitlement, improvements in pension rights, etc.

Addis

Addis, the brush and household goods company based in Swansea, was facing stiff competition from low-cost imports which threatened the survival of the company. The management had proposed a pay freeze, although it was prepared to consider any increase generated by its employees from the introduction of greater flexibility, multi-skilling and other changes to working practices.

The trade unions had put forward a claim that included a substantial increase in pay, a reduction in the working week and an increased holiday entitlement. They also believed the present appraisal scheme was flawed.

ACAS, Wales, arranged conciliation. After two attempts the conciliation was successful when an agreement was reached on multi-skilling. A pay award was made on acceptance of the changes. The link which had existed between appraisal and performance related pay was severed.

Source: ACAS

Traditionally, **collective bargaining**, which is the negotiation between a trade union and an employer or an employer's organisation, over the incomes and working conditions of employees, has been done by three types of unions:

- craft unions, which represent skilled trades people with specific skills;
- industrial unions, which represent workers in an industry;
- general unions, which represent workers across a range of industries.

Normally, full-time national trade union officials, for example, the President, Secretary and Negotiations Secretary, will negotiate with the employer on behalf of all union members. This is equivalent to having one buyer of labour (the employer) and one seller of labour (the trade union). This can result in a conflict of power and strength which both sides are trying to win. A good example of this was the confrontation between the (then) National Coal Board (the employer) and the National Union of Mineworkers (representing all employees) in the 1980s. Following this confrontation there were:

- two unions, the NUM and the Union of Democratic Mineworkers (UDM);
- constant threats of pit closures;
- new employment laws which controlled the ability of trade unions to call strikes and prevented 'unlawful picketing'.

Can trade unions affect the level of wages?

To answer this question, we must distinguish between 'money wages' and 'real wages'. Money wages best describe the basic take home pay of an employee, whereas 'real wages' relate this pay to the goods and services which it will buy. This means that price levels also need to be considered. For example, if take-home pay doubles and at the same time prices double, there has been no change in real wages. People can still only buy the same amount of goods and services as they did previously. However, if money wages rise by more than prices, real wages/income will rise and people will be better off.

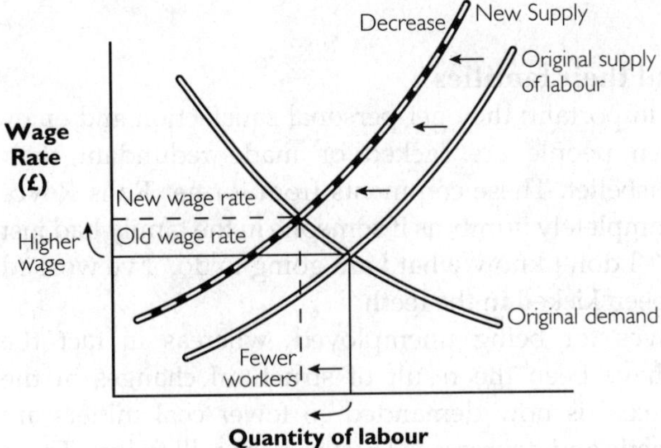

Figure 10.18 Decrease in supply of labour

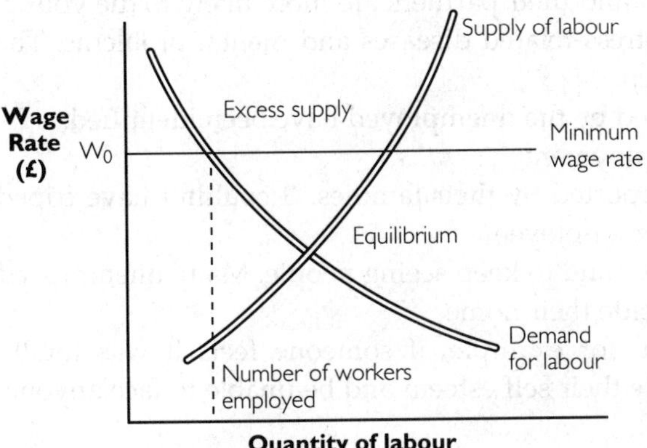

Figure 10.19 Effect of a minimum wage rate

It is highly unlikely that trade union action will have much affect on general price levels, or indeed on the general level of wage rates in the economy. Therefore they can do little, if anything, to change the level of real wages. However, trade union action may affect the wage differentials between occupations/crafts or industries and specific groups could secure wage rises higher than the rate of inflation. For example, some trade unions insist that their members are fully trained and qualified. This will restrict the number of people able to do a particular job and have the effect of decreasing the supply of labour to that occupation. The wage rate will rise but fewer workers will be employed. Figure 10.18 shows how this would work.

Other unions have taken a different approach by negotiating minimum wage rates within an occupation. In the example shown in Figure 10.19, the minimum has been set above the equilibrium level where demand equals supply. The wage rate is at W_0 and supply is greater than demand. Fewer workers are employed than if the wage rate had been negotiated at a lower level, but those in employment get a higher wage. There is now increasing evidence to suggest that both trade unions and government pursue policies on the principle of 'the unemployed don't vote'.

Trade unions will tend to have more power to determine wage levels in those industries where both the demand for the product is inelastic, and the demand for labour is inelastic. In these circumstances it will be possible for unions to negotiate higher wage rates, which in turn could be passed on to consumers as higher prices with only a small reduction in demand for either the product or the labour required to produce it. What would happen if demand for the product is elastic? What would happen if demand for labour is elastic?

Another major factor which will affect the bargaining power of trade unions is the state of the economy. When the economy is expanding and industry is growing rapidly, workers will be in a much stronger position than they would be during a recession, when economic activity is low. It is very difficult for unions or anyone else to push for higher wages when threatened by short-time working or possible redundancy.

Generally, an increase in wages will eventually lead to a fall in employment in most industries.

Trade union influence

Trade unions will have most influence when:	Trade unions will have least influence when:
The economy is growing	The economy is depressed
Demand for the product is inelastic	Demand for the product is elastic
Demand for labour is inelastic	Demand for labour is elastic
Wages are a small part of total costs	Wages form a large part of total costs

Unemployment

Implications for individuals and their families

For many people going to work is important; they get personal satisfaction and enjoy being with their colleagues. When people are sacked or made redundant their immediate reaction is shock and disbelief. These comments from former Rolls Royce workers illustrate the point. 'I feel completely numb, as if someone in the family had just died.' 'I can't believe its happened.' 'I don't know what I am going to do.' I've worked here all my life, I feel as if I've just been kicked in the teeth.'

People tend to blame themselves for being unemployed, whereas in fact the unemployment is most likely to have been the result of structural changes in the demand for the product, e.g. less coal is now demanded so fewer coal miners are needed. People become bitter, apathetic and depressed. They lose the will to live. There are more attempted suicides amongst the unemployed particularly in the first month and after 12 months. The unemployed and their partners are more likely to die young. They are more likely to suffer from stress-related diseases and mental problems. The unemployed visit the doctor more often.

Several causes of the distress suffered by the unemployed have been identified:

- the duration of the period of unemployment
- the extent to which people are supported by their families. 'I couldn't have coped without my family', said one former employee
- the individual's ability to keep active and to keep seeing people. Many unemployed people become too afraid to go outside their home
- the reason for the unemployment, for example, if someone feels it was totally personal they are more likely to lose their self esteem and be unable to face anyone. They lose their self confidence
- being unable to find a new job.

Implications for the local community

The local area can suffer badly if a large local employer closes down making workers redundant. Young people will be unable to find jobs and may have to move away to find work. People will have less money to spend. Shops will shut and may be boarded up. More people will thus become unemployed. This effect is sometimes called the 'reverse multiplier'. The whole area could become depressed. House prices could fall because people can no longer afford to move. People will have a lower standard of living than those in more prosperous areas where employment is high or expanding. Without some form of new investment the area will remain depressed as it becomes less attractive for business to set up or expand. As central government has intervened less in the economy the challenge of attracting new private businesses has been taken up by the borough councils. Here are two examples of councils which have taken positive steps; you will probably find others.

New scheme will help promote jobs and businesses

As part of a new drive to promote jobs in the borough, Bromley Council is to embark on a project to create six workshop spaces in Chislehurst.

The units, ranging from 650 to 940 square feet, will provide space for small firms who have difficulty in finding suitable accommodation.

Under the scheme, vacant shops in local parades will be considered for a range of businesses. If it is successful it could be copied in other parts of the borough.

SWANSEA
BEST RESOURCE PACKAGE FOR
BUSINESS

- ☑ Skilled Labour Forse
- ☑ Grants and Loans
- ☑ Low Overhead Costs
- ☑ Excellent Communications
- ☑ Quality of Life
- ☑ IBA's and Enterprise Zone sites still available

WELCOME TO SWANSEA

I am interested in existing and proposed:

❑ FOOD PARK ❑ FACTORIES ❑ HI-TEC PREMISES
❑ OFFICES ❑ WAREHOUSES ❑ MARITIME UNITS

Name
Company
Position
Address

Tel

ST1 15/1

SWANSEA CENTRE FOR TRADE & INDUSTRY
'A Swansea Bay Partner'

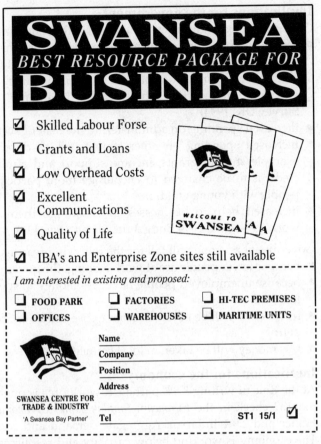

Implications for the regions

Similar effects can be seen across regions. The figures below show regional differences in the standard of living in the UK compared with selected European countries.

Table 10.4 Regional variations in Gross Domestic Product (GDP) per head (European average = 100)

Country/region	GDP per head
Luxembourg	126.1
Netherlands	100.9
Portugal	38.3
UK national average	91.7
North	80.1
Yorks & Humberside	82.5
East Midlands	88
East Anglia	92.3
South East	108.9
South West	88
West Midlands	83.5
North West	97.3
Wales	77.5
Scotland	87.6
Northern Ireland	69.5

Source: Eurostat 1994

Note: Higher figures mean a higher standard of living; only the South East does better than the European average (see page 60 for regional policy). How do these figures relate to unemployment?

Implications for the government

Government expenditure will increase for the following reasons:

- increased spending on unemployment benefit. This is to be renamed Job Seeker's Allowance (JSA) 'and the link between payment and job search activities will be strengthened through a tougher sanctions regime. The new system is expected to encourage more active job search by the unemployed' (Source: OECD Economic Survey UK, 1994)
- increased spending on administering the benefit system
- increased spending on other benefits which depend on the level of income, for example student grants, income support and family credit. The system of family credit is to be changed to encourage more participation in the labour market by people with young children
- increased help to businesses to encourage them to take on more unemployed workers (see the 1994 Budget details on page 431).

Government revenue will fall for the following reasons:

- because fewer people are at work earning, the government will collect less income tax
- because unemployed people have less money to spend, the government will collect less VAT
- less money will be obtained from excise duties on, for example, beer, cigarettes and petrol
- less money will be taken in local council taxes.

Implications for the economy

At the time of writing 8.8% of the UK workforce is unemployed (what is the figure this month? check in the *European, Sunday Times* or *Economist*) compared with 12.6% in France and 2.9% in Japan. Aggregate demand and consumer expenditure is reduced. The economy is working below capacity and resources are not being used effectively. People are our greatest resource, yet with unemployment this resource is being wasted. The economy is losing the goods and services that could have been produced if the unemployed had been at work. The lost output represents the opportunity cost of unemployment, estimated roughly at £8,000 million.

Implications for business

Every business, manufacturer, wholesaler or retailer, will be affected to some extent by unemployment in the community.

1. High unemployment is a sign of recession in the economy and consumer spending will be lower. When incomes are very low spending on consumer durables (particularly electrical goods) tends to be lower, and low-income families tend to spend a higher proportion of their income on necessities such as food, fuel and light. Many businesses can only continue trading by taking lower profit margins and heavily discounting prices.
2. Business costs can be lower, for example, wage costs tend to be relatively stable because employers are in a buyer's market, i.e. there are more people looking for work than there are jobs available. Special grants and loans can be on offer at lower rates (see the Swansea advert on page 495). Buildings and premises costs may be reduced as an incentive for businesses to relocate or expand in a particular area.

   There appears to be a close relationship between unemployment and inflation; generally with high unemployment, inflation is lower.
3. Trade unions tend to have less bargaining power when there is high unemployment, although there are exceptions such as the snap postal strike in January 1995 (see page 492 – do trade unions affect the level of wages?)

4 There may be a need to restructure or reorganise the business to take account of the reduced demand and output whilst maintaining profitability.
5 Payments from customers may be delayed, so the business could experience cash flow problems.
6 The reduction in home demand may push the business into exporting.

Activity

Effects of unemployment

Almost all of the effects of unemployment are negative. There are private and social costs. We can use PEST analysis (Political, Economic, Social, Technical) to examine the different aspects of an issue. This is a useful way of categorising and can be applied to causes and consequences of decisions and actions.

Use PEST analysis to list the effects of high and low unemployment on your local community. You can find out the rate of unemployment for your area by looking at the *Employment Gazette*.

Review questions

1 What have been the main trends in employment in the three industrial sectors?
2 Give two reasons why self-employment has increased.
3 Name three problems faced by the unemployed.
4 Explain why the number of people in full-time employment has fallen.
5 Give two reasons why employers use part-time workers.
6 State three reasons why the employment of females has risen.
7 What are the basic needs of employees?
8 Say why fewer manual workers are employed.
9 Why might a business use temporary workers?
10 What happened to unemployment between 1990 and 1995.
11 Which areas of the UK have been worst affected by unemployment?
12 How does unemployment affect the community?
13 What are the main needs of employers?
14 What affects the demand/supply of labour?
15 Why does a doctor earn more than a nurse?
16 Can trade unions affect the level of wages?
17 What determines the level of wages?
18 Why might wage differentials occur?

Key terms

Economic activity rate
Labour force
Sector
De-industrialisation
Self-employment
Small business
Female/Male employment
Manual/Non-manual
Part-time/Full-time
Temporary
Skilled/unskilled

Unemployment
Claimant count
Labour Force Survey
Registered unemployed
Seasonally adjusted
Regional unemployment
Vacancies
Duration of unemployment
Youth unemployment
Demand for labour
Supply of labour

Wages
Wage payments
Wage differentials
Wage bargaining
Collective bargaining
Industrial stoppages
Market wage rates
Effects of unemployment
– on communities
– on individuals
– on government

Assignment 10
Update Part 2

This assignment develops knowledge and understanding of the following elements:
5.2 Investigate and evaluate employment

It supports development of the following core skills:
Communication 3.2, 3.3, 3.4
Application of numbers 3.1, 3.3
Information technology 3.1, 3.2, 3.3, 3.4

Re-read the introduction to the Update on page 454 to remind yourself of the background to this assignment.

Copies of the Update are given free to local schools, colleges and libraries. Additionally copies are sent to the European towns twinned with Hurstmead. As before, the format of the Updates is now standard and cannot be varied.

HURSTMEAD CHAMBER of COMMERCE
Publication data Version 2

1 The Update should be typed or Word Processed.
2 A4 paper only must be used.
3 The Update must be brief (a maximum of 8 pages).
4 The Update must contain these sections:

Section A: News Update
This consists of a round-up of specialist news items from the local and national press, trade papers and magazines, etc. which are directly relevant to the industry.

Section B: Economic Update
Give the current rate of unemployment, and inflation, in the UK. Show any changes from the previous figures.

Section C: Current Update
For this section you should use diagrams to show national and regional trends in your chosen industry, write brief notes on the major features (you will find the New Earnings Survey and the Employment Gazette particularly helpful)

- the numbers of males and females employed
- the numbers unemployed
- the numbers unemployed in your local area
- current wage rates and hours worked
- part time and full time employment
- wage differentials.

Section D: Update on Europe
Use our standard sources, *Euro Monitor* and *EUROSTAT* to provide the key industry figures. (Employment Gazette and economic Trends also provide comparative figures.)

Section E: Local Update
Say how named local businesses and the local community could be affected by any of the information we are providing.

Section F: Update Briefing
Always begin this section: 'This month we turn the Spotlight on ___________________' (name the industry which must be chosen from a different sector of the economy) then make a comparison between the two industries. Use the *Monthly Digest of Statistics* and the *Employment Gazette* to obtain the information. Do not forget to name the sources; all the businesses in the area rely on Update for its accuracy.

Section G Past Update

Look at employment and wages figures from 5 and 10 years ago. How have they changed?

5 Always end with something light-hearted; it could be a quote or a funny local news item.
6 Check everything and go to print.

11 Financial transactions and record keeping

What is covered in this chapter

- Production and the creation of added value
- The trading cycle
- The distribution of added value
- The money cycle
- Buying and selling procedures
- Business documents used in buying (purchasing) and selling
- Security
- Cash control – recording receipts and payments
- Recording purchases, sales and returns in the day books
- Consequences of incorrect completion of documents

These are the resources that you will need for your Financial Transactions, Costing and Pricing file:

- examples of a range of business documents, including invoices, credit notes, statements of accounts
- examples of documents used by banks, including standing order mandate, bank giro credit slips/paying-in slips, bank statements, cheques, cheque guarantee card (if you have one)

The survival and well-being of a business will ultimately depend upon:

- making a profit, that is, selling the goods or services for more than they cost to produce
- having enough cash when it is needed.

The purpose of this chapter is to look at the cycle of business activity which generates profits and cash flow. We will also look at the documents and record keeping which accompany this.

Production and the creation of added value

Whether they provide goods, such as cars, or services such as window cleaning, all businesses are involved in **production**. A business exists to supply people's needs and wants; it survives where there is an effective demand for the product it sells.

In providing something for which people are prepared to pay, the producer creates wealth in the form of **added value**. This means that the revenue received from business output exceeds the cost of production, so that the business is profitable. A business will continue in production where the profits gained by the entrepreneur represent a worthwhile return on capital invested.

The following are examples of the creation of added value in different sectors of production:

- an oil worker takes goods from nature. The oil is no use to us underground. We are prepared to pay someone to extract it.
- manufacturers increase the value of raw materials or components by converting them into semi-finished or finished goods. Perhaps they turn iron ore into steel, or steel panels into car bodies.

It is important to note the following distinctions:

Finished goods are the final products bought by the consumer, for example a car (though the term can also describe any goods, even semi-finished, which a manufacturer sells, i.e. ex-works).

Semi-finished goods are intermediate products used as components in the production of other goods and services, for example sheet steel.

Work in progress describes goods only partially completed and therefore not yet ready for sale, for example a partly assembled car.

- wholesalers and retailers provide commercial services. They act as intermediaries in the supply chain between the manufacturer and the customer. They are able to buy goods, add a **mark-up** and resell them for a higher price. We are prepared to pay them because they supply services such as: transporting goods, storing them, breaking bulk and displaying them at a location where we are able to buy. Where we do not need these services we may be able to 'cut out the middleman'.
- a solicitor or a doctor will perform direct services for our benefit. We are prepared to pay because we do not have the expertise ourselves.

Here is an example of added value in the supply chain for consumer goods:

The idea of value added is used by the government when levying Value Added Tax (VAT). If each of the transactions above involved VAT it would work like this:

Manufacturer	**Wholesaler**	**Retailer**	**Consumer**
pays £50 materials + £8.75 VAT	pays £150 product + £26.25 VAT	pays £200 product + £35 VAT	pays £250 product + £43.75 VAT
Collects £150 + £26.25 VAT from wholesaler £8.75 reclaimed £17.50 to government	Collects £200 + £35 VAT from retailer £26.25 reclaimed £8.75 to government	Collects £250 + £43.75 VAT from consumer £35 reclaimed £8.75 to government	

The tax collected by HM Customs and Excise is the tax on the added value. In this example, total added value is £200 and total VAT collected by the government is £35.

The trading cycle

For any particular business a trading cycle can be identified. This is the sequence of events through which the business is able to create added value by supplying customer demand for its goods or services. The cycle is illustrated in Figure 11.1.

Notice that the second stage will vary considerably. Depending upon the nature of business it may involve: supplying goods from the warehouse, performing a particular job to the customer's specifications, or manufacturing a new product in a complex production process.

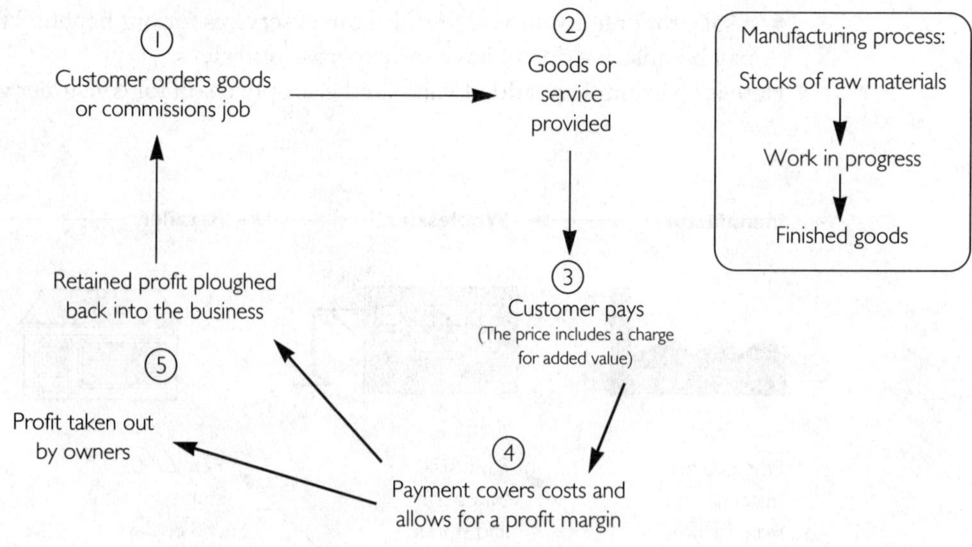

Figure 11.1 The trading cycle

Business profits are reported in the profit and loss account. This will relate to a particular trading period, usually one year, over which the trading cycle will have revolved many times. We will look at financial reports in Chapter 14.

The distribution of added value

The price charged by a business when selling its goods or services will be sufficient to cover its operating costs and allow for a margin of profit. In Chapter 12 we will examine how cost accounting helps a business to determine this price.

Profit is the reward of the owners of the business – those entrepreneurs whose enterprise has brought together the other factors of production. After any taxation due, they may choose either to withdraw the profit or plough it back. In the first case they have the money; in the second case they own a more valuable business.

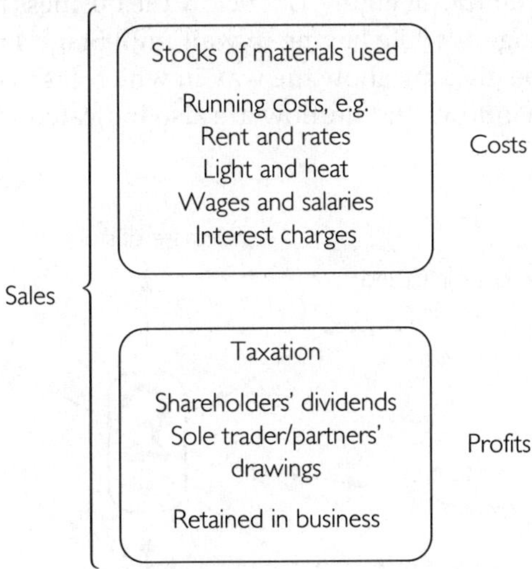

Non-profit-making organisations

Some organisations have no owners who are entitled to benefit personally from the profits; these are said to be 'non-profit making'. Such organisations may have huge funds and may well generate added value; the difference is that everything is ploughed back for future development. Charities and clubs and societies of various sorts are in this sense non-profit-making; the profit is referred to as a 'surplus'. These organisations often have social aims, having been set up to provide a service to their members or to the community. Well-known examples include trade unions, building societies, the co-operative societies, The National Trust and The Automobile Association. There are also many small-scale examples, such as the local sports club or the local history society.

Activities

1 How do the following create added value:
a carpenter; a travel agent; a market trader; a bicycle manufacturer?
For any one of these draw a detailed diagram of the trading cycle to illustrate your answer.

2 Name two non-profit-making organisations not mentioned above. What are any 'profits' used for?

The money cycle

Generating cash flow

Not only does a business need to generate a profit, it must also have sufficient cash available to carry on its day-to-day operations, such as buying stock and paying wages. This is called **working capital**.

Where customers are allowed credit terms, a business will need residual funds or loan facilities to tide it over while waiting for payment. The money cycle illustrates how cash is spent and received over the trading cycle.

In the example in Figure 11.2 below the business has to spend money 'up front' to buy stock at Stage 1, while having to wait until Stage 4 for payment from customers. Stages 1 to 4 in the diagram show the way in which cash is generated through normal trading; other cash inflows and outflow are also indicated.

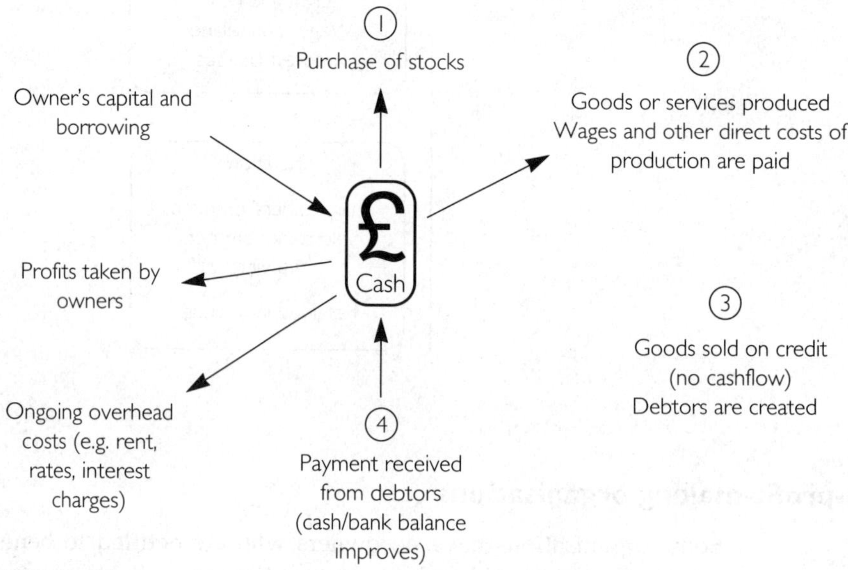

Figure 11.2 The money cycle

The longer the time between Stage 1 (Purchase of stocks) and Stage 4 (Receiving payment) the more likely it is that the business will need further funds to survive. Where loans, overdrafts or new capital are not available then the business may become insolvent (unable to pay its debts).

In Chapter 13 we will look at the need to plan for cash flow so as to anticipate problems such as this. One solution may be to buy stocks on credit so that there is a smaller time between the initial outlay and the receipt of payment.

Case study

Harry the carpenter

Harry is a carpenter who specialises in manufacturing window frames and doors. He works for private households but does most of his work for builders. The most recent contract is for a housing association.

Private households pay cash on completion of a job, while the builders require credit terms. As there is competition, Harry finds that he must accept this situation. He requires full settlement within 30 days of the supply of the goods, though some major customers are often late, knowing that there is little he can do as he is a small business and needs their custom.

Depending upon the size of the job in hand the manufacture can take from a few hours to a week or so. Harry prefers not to carry a large stock of materials and so buys specifically for each contract. He has a reputable business and is allowed 30 days credit by his supplier. Nevertheless he normally pays for materials before he receives payment from his customers.

Activities

1. Identify how Harry's business creates added value.
2. Explain the money cycle and illustrate this as it applies to this business.
3. What other aims could Harry pursue apart from the profit motive?
4. What product does Harry's accountant provide?
5. What is the added value provided by the timber merchant from whom Harry buys (i.e. why is this business able to buy goods at one price and resell the same goods at a higher price)?
6. Housing associations are non-profit making. What is their aim?

Buying and selling procedures

Buying

The procurement function within a business is concerned with ordering stocks so that materials are available as and when required.

It is important that a business obtains good quality stocks on the best possible terms, but some firms are in a better position than others to bargain. For example, the large supermarket chains can dictate terms to their suppliers simply because they place such large orders. They are able to impose conditions about quality (e.g. low fat), production methods (e.g. organically grown), appearance (e.g. no spots on apples), delivery times and credit terms. Such organisations will use specialised buyers to gain the best possible deals. The ultimate example of the buyer requesting a specific product is the creation of 'own brands' such as Virgin Cola or Sainsbury's wine, where products with a distinctive image are created especially for the company.

Small businesses will not be in such a strong position. They cannot gain the lower prices available from bulk-buying and may find, especially in the early stages, that credit terms are not so readily available.

The documents associated with purchasing are examined later in the chapter. Notice that buyers are interested in: price, quality, delivery times, reliability, discounts and terms of payment (for example 30-day credit).

Selling

A business will endeavour to develop a unique selling point, such as a reputation for reliability, service, quality and so on. In a competitive market, however, price will always be an important factor. Ways of increasing sales may therefore include offering discounts and credit terms.

Discounts

The larger organisations again have the advantage. High-volume selling allows for profitability at lower prices, while for the smaller firms discounts may simply represent a loss of income. Sometimes settlement discounts are offered as a 'carrot' to encourage debtors to pay promptly.

Credit

Although it is better if a business can sell for immediate payment, in some trades it may be necessary to offer credit terms in order to secure sales at all. Slow payment by debtors can be a major problem, especially for small businesses. Larger organisations may be less susceptible, not only because they may have larger funds available but also because they have the means of taking legal action against defaulters. Small firms may not be able to afford this. Where credit is offered effective credit control is vital.

Credit control

The flow of money is the lifeline of a business organisation, and any business which needs to extend credit to customers must take care. The NatWest Bank, for example, warns in its *Business Start-up Guide* that it will be difficult to keep debtors to 30-day payment periods.

The following is taken from an article entitled 'Improve Your Cashflow' which was written as a result of the growing problems of non-payment suffered by small businesses. It stresses the importance of tight credit control.

> Bad debt (that is debtors failing to pay) is one of the biggest single causes of business failure. Yet many traders regularly risk their livelihoods simply because they agree to do business without bothering to ensure that they will eventually receive payment. Once your company makes a sale what your customer owes you is your money. The second that money passes from being due to being overdue that money becomes a free loan from you to him... Remember, when a debt has been outstanding for a certain time the interest that you pay to the bank erodes the profit that you would have made on the sale.
>
> There are other hidden costs that are often forgotten:
>
> Loss of interest – money paid on time could have been earning interest.
>
> Loss of discounts – slow payments may prevent you from taking advantage of cash discounts for prompt payment.
>
> Interest charges – slow payment may force you to take on an overdraft.
>
> Collection costs – time and effort spent on debt collection can be expensive.

```
Successful collection of debts is basically a matter of
determination. Here is a five-step routine:
1 Invoice at once and use first-class post.
2 Send a monthly statement to customers.
3 Ten days beyond the due date remind your customer.
4 Ten days later chase. Make a phone call.
5 Follow up the call with a written reminder to the right person.
If payment is not forthcoming the case should be passed to a
collection agency without delay
```

Source: Tony Bushell, General Manager,
Receivable Management Services, Dun & Bradstreet Ltd

For a business keen to break into a new market, or a member of the salesforce trying to win commission for extra sales, it is very tempting to go for sales at all costs, even if this means offering credit without proper safeguards. It is an unwise course to take.

Case study

Lesley Jones trading as Solid Gold Pine

Lesley Jones had visions of selling her hand-crafted wooden toys direct from her workshop in her Welsh cottage and at rural craft fairs. In fact she has found it necessary to sell to retailers in the coastal holiday resorts – all of whom demand credit terms. It seems that her products are not as exclusive as she had thought.

After a lot of hard work Lesley has built up a network of retail outlets, but she does find difficulty in buying in materials while waiting for payment. At last she has been given a large order, but again credit terms are required. Lesley cannot afford to put in a lot of time and materials if she is not going to get paid. What can she do?

The small business adviser at the local enterprise agency gives the following advice on the steps that should be taken as part of a credit control policy.

- Lesley can ask her bank to enquire into the credit status of the new customer. The bank can contact the customer's bank and find out whether there are likely to be problems with repayments. Any decision to offer credit , and if so, what credit limit to set (the maximum amount the customer is allowed to owe), will depend upon the report back.
- If she does go ahead she must be thorough with all invoices and statements. Customers must be made aware when money is due and reminded if they are late.
- She must monitor the balances owed by all debtors and ensure that they are not allowed to exceed their credit limits.
- She can maintain a schedule of **aged debtors** and put pressure upon late payers.
- She could use the banks' factoring service (see Chapter 13). Here the banks will take over the whole business of debt collection for a commission.

Lesley has decided that she will try to manage her affairs by using a computerised accounting package. Not only can such a system produce the business documents, but the accounting entries and stock adjustments can also be made. Additionally the whole monitoring process is helped by the instant availability of various reports about the position of the business and letters reminding customers that they are late. The aged debtors' schedule is one particularly useful report.

Solid Gold Pine								
Account Balances		Financial Controller				Date: 310893		
A/C	Turnover	Credit Limit	Balance	Current	30 days	60 days	90 days	Older
Arfon & Griffiths	2,300.00	1,000.00	250.00	200.00	50.00	0.00	0.00	0.00
Colwyn & Co	3,650.00	1,000.00	550.00	0.00	0.00	500.00	50.00	0.00
Rock Relics Ltd	*5,320.00	500.00	600.00	600.00	0.00	0.00	0.00	0.00
St Davids Crafts	4,200.00	800.00	0.00	0.00	0.00	0.00	0.00	0.00
D Thomas	7,500.00	1,200.00	1,000.00	150.00	750.00	100.00	0.00	0.00
Totals	22,970.00	4,500.00	2,400.00	950.00	800.00	600.00	50.00	0.00

Source: Format used by Sage Sterling's 'Financial Controller' accounting package

Figure 11.3 Example of an aged debtors' schedule as produced by Lesley on her accounting package

An aged creditors' report can be produced in a similar way. This shows whether a business is being slow in paying its suppliers. Some large businesses are slow on purpose, while other businesses find that they do not have sufficient cash. A business that is too slow in paying may find that it is taken to court; it may also find that it is forced in future to pay in cash as its poor credit rating becomes known.

Activities

1 Look at the aged debtors' schedule for Solid Gold Pine and try the following questions:
a Who is Lesley's most valuable customer?
b Why has Rock Relics' account an asterisk (*) against it?
c How do you think that this situation arose?
d What should she do to prevent this happening in future?
e Which debtor(s) should Lesley contact immediately?
f How much does St Davids Crafts owe at the moment?
g Lesley works on terms of 30 days' credit. How much money should she currently be concerned about?
h How is a credit limit set and why is it important?

2 Lesley has just received a further order from Colwyn & Company. Write a letter for Lesley to send in reply. You should explain in this letter why you are writing, what action you wish the customer to take and how you are dealing with the new order they have sent.

The rest of this chapter will look at the business records that need to be kept from day to day. In the following chapters we will see how these records can be used for assessing performance and planning for the future.

Business documents used in buying (purchasing) and selling

It is very common for organisations to buy and sell on credit. That is, they will receive the good or service first and pay at some agreed time in the future.

The table below summarises the documents that will flow between the buyer and supplier.

Buyer	DOCUMENT	Supplier
Example A retailer buying in stock for resale		A wholesaler supplying goods from its warehouse
	ENQUIRY → What do you sell? What does it cost? What are your terms/delivery times?	
←	CATALOGUE (Items available) PRICE LIST (Prices) QUOTATION (Price for custom-made items)	
	PURCHASE ORDER → Lists goods required and requests delivery	
←	ACKNOWLEDGEMENT Confirms that the order has been received and is receiving attention	
←	ADVICE NOTE Indicates when the goods can be expected and advises the buyer to make ready to receive them at this time	
←	DELIVERY NOTE Accompanies goods when they are delivered and requires a signature as proof of delivery	
←	INVOICE Itemises goods delivered and shows the cost and terms of payment	
←	CREDIT NOTE This reduces the charge on an invoice if goods are unsatisfactory	
	There may be a number of transactions in a period. At the end of the period, often after 30 days, the supplier will request payment	
←	STATEMENT OF ACCOUNT Lists all of the transactions and requests the payment due. Often sent on the last day of the month	
	PAYMENT (less any cash discount) → Accompanied by a REMITTANCE ADVICE Payment may be in the form of cash (notes and coins), cheque or credit transfer	
←	REMINDERS Sent if payment is not received	

Worked example

Documents used in credit sales

Big Byte Supplies Ltd is a wholesaler selling computer hardware and software. You work in the sales section where your supervisor is Karen Marsh.

One of your customers is Megadrive Computers, a high street retailer. Until now you have supplied Megadrive with software only; they have proved themselves a reliable customer and you learn that they now propose to sell hardware also.

I ENQUIRY

You receive the following **enquiry**:

MEGADRIVE COMPUTERS
268 Key Street
London E7 4ST
Tel: 0171 888 4444 Fax: 0171 888 3333 VAT Reg No 877 6543 17

1 October 19-4

Big Byte Supplies Ltd
3 Glen Close
London SE1 5SC

Dear Madam/Sir

As you will know we have been a regular customer of yours for nearly two years. During that time you have supplied us with software on credit terms with settlement made on receipt of your monthly statement. I am sure that you will agree that we have proved creditworthy.

We are currently in the process of expanding our range of stock and would be pleased therefore to receive the following from you a.s.a.p.:

Details of prices for printers in the OKAY range.
Details of charges for carriage
Terms and conditions on which the goods are supplied

Yours faithfully

B. Gates

B Gates (Ms)
Purchasing

2 CATALOGUE AND PRICE LIST

You write to Megadrive by return of post:

BIG BYTE SUPPLIES LTD
3 Glen Close
London SE1 5SC

Tel: 0171 666 1111
Fax: 0171 666 1212
VAT Reg: 651 8181 81

2 October 19-4

Ms B Gates
Purchasing Department
Megadrive Computers
268 Key Street
London E7 4ST

Dear Ms Gates

Thank for your enquiry of 1 October.

I am sending our catalogue and price list showing details of OKAY Printers as requested. I can confirm that the following terms can be offered:

Credit of one month as at present. Settlement within 10 days of receipt of statement, strictly net
20% trade discount from list price on all orders
Carriage free on all orders over £1,000, otherwise £25 + VAT
Delivery within 5 working days

I will look forward to receiving your order.

Yours sincerely

K. Marsh

K Marsh
Sales

Enc

BIG BYTE SUPPLIES LTD
3 Glen Close
London SE1 5SC

CATALOGUE

PRINTERS

9 PIN PRINTERS

Cat No	Description
BB9 001	OKAY 280
BB9 002	OKAY 182 80 column
BB9 003	OKAY 320 80 column
BB9 004	OKAY 321 136 Column

24 PIN PRINTERS

Cat No	Description
BB24 500	OKAY 380 80 Column
BB24 600	OKAY 390 80 Column
BB24 700	OKAY 390 Flatbed

LASER PRINTERS

Cat No	Description	Pages Per Minute
BBL 011	OKAY OL 400	4
BBL 012	OKAY OL 810	8
BBL 013	OKAY OL.850 Postscript 2MB	8

BIG BYTE SUPPLIES LTD
3 Glen Close
London SE1 5SC

PRICE LIST
as at 1 September 19-4

PRINTERS

9 PIN PRINTERS

Cat No	Price
BB9 001	£174
BB9 002	£179
BB9 003	£289
BB9 004	£349

24 PIN PRINTERS

Cat No	Price
BB24 500	£179
BB24 600	£389
BB24 700	£529

LASER PRINTERS

Cat No	Price
BBL 011	£449
BBL 012	£845
BBL 013	£1,209

3 PURCHASE ORDER

After a period of time, during which you suspect that Megadrive have been shopping around for a better offer, you receive the following **order**:

MEGADRIVE COMPUTERS
268 Key Street
London E7 4ST
Tel: 0171 888 4444 Fax: 0171 888 3333 VAT Reg No 877 6543 17

5 November 19-4

PURCHASE ORDER
Order No: 4472

Mr K Marsh
Sales Department
Big Byte Supplies Ltd
3 Glen Close
London SE1 5SC

Catalogue Number	Description	Qty	Price
BB24 500	OKAY 380 80 Column 24 pin printer	10	179.00 each
BB24 600	OKAY 390 80 Column 24 pin printer	10	389.00 each
BBL 012	OKAY OL 810 Laser Printer	5	845.00 each

Delivery to: above address

Terms agreed: 20% trade discount
Carriage free
Delivery within 5 working days
Payment within 10 days of monthly statement

B. Gates

B Gates (Ms)
Purchasing

In the same envelope is a cheque. This is accompanied by a remittance advice explaining that the cheque is in full payment for the software purchases made in October.

THE NORTH BANK PLC — 4 November 19-4

Pay: *Big Byte Ltd*

Amount: *Seven hundred and sixty pounds* — £ 760-60

A/c payee

J. Megan
For and on behalf of Megadrive Computers

4 ACKNOWLEDGEMENT

After checking the stock of printers you **acknowledge** receipt of the order and confirm that you can supply the goods on the terms agreed.

BIG BYTE SUPPLIES LTD
3 Glen Close
London SE1 5SC

Tel: 0171 666 1111
Fax: 0171 666 1212
VAT Reg: 651 8181 81

6 November 19-4

ACKNOWLEDGEMENT

Ms B Gates
Purchasing Department
Megadrive Computers
268 Key Street
London E7 4ST

Dear Ms Gates

Reference: Order number 4472

Thank for your order of 5 November for the following:

10	BB24 500	OKAY 380 80 Column 24 pin printer	@ 179.00 each
10	BB24 600	OKAY 390 80 Column 24 pin printer	@ 389.00 each
5	BBL 012	OKAY OL 810 Laser Printer	@ 845.00 each

The matter is receiving our immediate attention and we can confirm that delivery will be on the terms agreed.

Yours sincerely

K. Marsh

K Marsh
Sales

Note: As the delivery time is only 5 working days it may be that an acknowledgement would not be necessary.

5 ADVICE NOTE

You have arranged for delivery with the carrier that you use for delivery purposes. You then send the advice note to tell the customer to be ready to receive the goods on the delivery date.

BIG BYTE SUPPLIES LTD
3 Glen Close
London SE1 5SC

Tel: 0171 666 1111
Fax: 0171 666 1212
VAT Reg: 651 8181 81

ADVICE NOTE
No: 22271

8 November 19-4

Ms B Gates
Purchasing Department
Megadrive Computers
268 Key Street
London E7 4ST

Reference: Order number: 4472   Delivery date: 10 November 19-4 (am)

Qty	Cat No	Description	Unit Price
10	BB24 500	OKAY 380 80 Column 24 pin printer	179.00 each
10	BB24 600	OKAY 390 80 Column 24 pin printer	389.00 each
5	BBL 012	OKAY OL 810 Laser Printer	845.00 each

Delivery by: Road   Delivery address: As above
Items: 25

K. Marsh

K Marsh
Sales

6 DELIVERY NOTE

All of the goods ordered are in stock and have been packed for delivery. The driver is given the **delivery note** shown below made out in triplicate. There are copies for the customer and the carrier as well as for you, the supplier. The driver will not leave the goods until there is a signature confirming delivery. If it is found that some items are missing or there is obvious damage, then the delivery note will be amended to show this before it is signed. Some buyers have their own goods received note.

BIG BYTE SUPPLIES LTD
3 Glen Close
London SE1 5SC

Tel: 0171 666 1111
Fax: 0171 666 1212
VAT Reg: 651 8181 81

DELIVERY NOTE
No: 22271

10 November 19-4

Megadrive (Computers) Ltd
268 Key Street
London E7 4ST

Reference: Order number: 4472   Delivery date: 10 November 19-4 (am)

Qty	Cat No	Description
10	BB24 500	OKAY 380 80 Column 24 pin printer
10	BB24 600	OKAY 390 80 Column 24 pin printer
5	BBL 012	OKAY OL 810 Laser Printer

Delivery by: Road   Delivery address: As above
Items: 25

Goods received as detailed by ________________ signature

________________ please PRINT name

K. Marsh
K Marsh
Sales

Please retain this copy as proof of receipt

7 INVOICE

Now that the goods have been delivered you are able to prepare and send the **invoice** to show the charge for these items. The invoice has the same information as the acknowledgement, the advice note and the delivery note. It is different in that it also includes the total due as calculated under the terms agreed.

BIG BYTE SUPPLIES LTD
3 Glen Close
London SE1 5SC

Tel: 0171 666 1111
Fax: 0171 666 1212
VAT Reg: 651 8181 81

INVOICE
No: 444433

Date/Tax Point
12 November 19-4

Megadrive Computers
268 Key Street
London E7 4ST

Account reference: MEG94
Reference: Order number: 4472

Qty	Cat No	Description	Unit Price	Total Price
10	BB24 500	OKAY 380 80 Column 24 pin printer	179.00	1,790.00
10	BB24 600	OKAY 390 80 Column 24 pin printer	389.00	3,890.00
5	BBL 012	OKAY OL 810 Laser Printer	845.00	4,225.00

Terms: Carriage paid
Strictly net
E and OE

	Sub-total	9,905.00
less	Trade Discount @ 20%	1,981.00
	Total (excl VAT)	7,924.00
add	VAT @ 17.5%	1,386.70
	Total Due	9,310.70

8 CREDIT NOTE

Some days later Megadrive inform you that one of the laser printers is faulty. They send this back to you as requested and on investigation you agree to accept responsibility. You prepare a **credit note** to reduce the amount that the customer will be charged.

BIG BYTE SUPPLIES LTD
3 Glen Close
London SE1 5SC

Tel: 0171 666 1111
Fax: 0171 666 1212
VAT Reg: 651 8181 81

CREDIT NOTE
No: CN255

Date/Tax Point
20 November 19-4

Megadrive Computers
268 Key Street
London E7 4ST

Account reference: MEG94
Reference: Invoice number: 44433

Qty	Cat No	Description	Unit Price	Total Price
1	BBL 012	OKAY OL 810 Laser Printer	845.00 each	845.00

	Sub-total	845.00
less	Trade Discount @ 20%	169.00
	Total (excl VAT)	676.00
add	VAT @ 17.5%	118.30
	Total Credit	794.30

Reason for credit: returned as faulty

9 STATEMENT OF ACCOUNT

There are no more transactions for the month. At the end of November you prepare the **statement of account** and send it to the customer. This shows the following:

- The position of the account at the start of November. Megadrive are an existing customer trading on credit terms. At the start of the month they owed £760.60 from the previous month.
- They paid this amount by cheque on 4 November.
- The invoice sent on 12 November for the goods delivered.
- The credit note sent on 20 November.
- The balance on the account after each of these transactions.

BIG BYTE SUPPLIES LTD
3 Glen Close
London SE1 5SC

Tel: 071 666 1111
Fax: 071 666 1212
VAT Reg: 651 8181 81

STATEMENT OF ACCOUNT

Account Reference: MEG94

30 November 19-4

Megadrive Computers
268 Key Street
London E7 4ST

Date	Details	Debit	Credit	Balance
1 Nov	Balance Brought forward			760.60 Dr
4 Nov	Cheque		760.60	0.00
12 Nov	Goods Invoice 44433	9,310.70		9,310.70 Dr
20 Nov	Credit Note CN 255		794.30	8,516.40 Dr

Balance now due: 8,516.40

Terms: Payment within 10 days of this statement, strictly net

---

REMITTANCE ADVICE

BIG BYTE SUPPLIES LTD
3 Glen Close
London SE1 5SC

Account: Megadrive Computers	Account Ref: MEG/94
Date: 30 November 19-4	Amount Due: £8,516.40

Please enclose this slip with your remittance.

Purchase and sales documents

This example has been looked at from the point of view of the seller, Big Byte Supplies Ltd. In order to see how transactions appear from the purchaser's point of view we need to imagine ourselves in the place of Megadrive Computers.

The documents are the same, it is just a question of who is sending them and who is receiving them; the roles are reversed. Refer back to the flow chart on page 509.

Debit note

Where an invoice is marked E and OE (Errors and Omissions Excepted) the seller is not bound by any mistakes. An undercharge may be corrected by a debit note. In effect this is a further invoice.

Filing the documents

All original documents will be filed. The receiver of the document will file the original document, while the sender will always keep a copy. All documents are numbered and dated so that they can be easily traced when required.

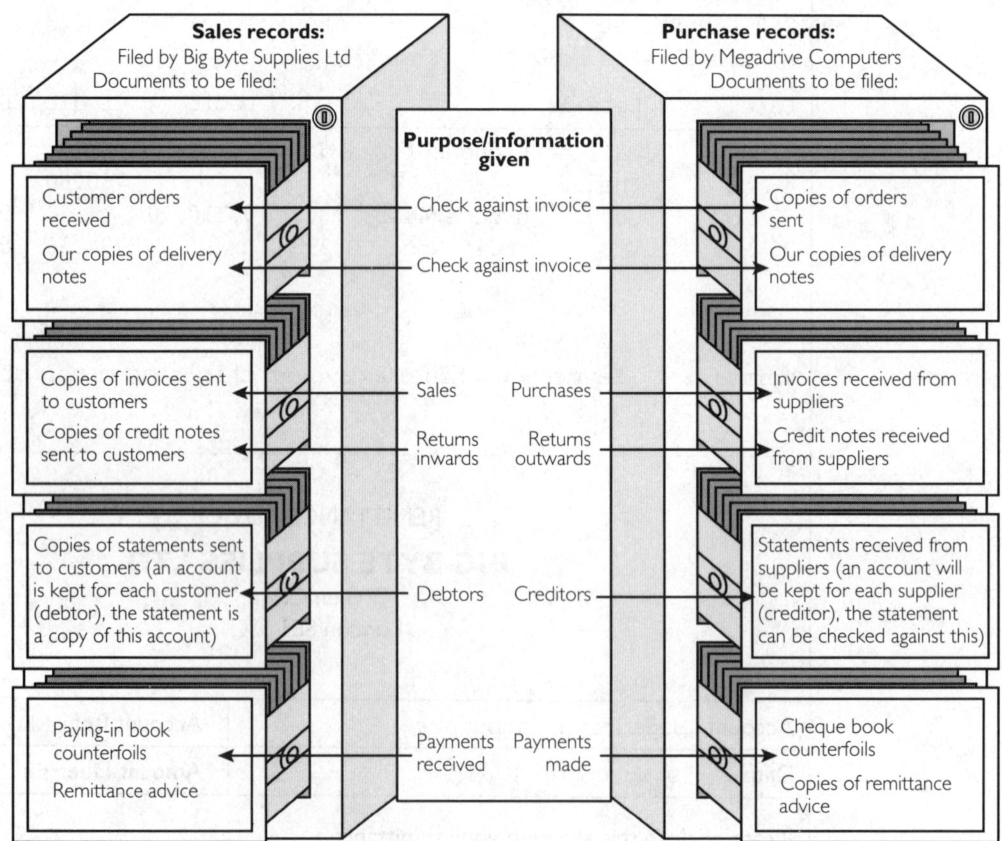

Figure 11.4 Filing the sales and purchases records

Activities

1 Which documents are sent by the buyer and which by the seller?

2 What is the procedure in your college or school for receiving deliveries? Where are deliveries left? Who signs for these?
What sort of discounts are available and why are these given?

3 In the month of December 19–4 further transactions take place between your company (Big Byte) and Megadrive on the conditions already agreed. Remember that Megadrive still owe money for November and that this will be brought forward on to December's statement of account.

4 Dec	Sold to Megadrive	5 BB9 002
		5 BB24 700 Invoice No. 44500
8 Dec	Megadrive sent a cheque in full payment for last November's balance	
12 Dec	1 BB9 002 returned as faulty – broken tractor feed, credit note CN282 sent	
18 Dec	Invoice 44533 sent for sales of 10 BBL011	

Prepare the relevant invoices, the credit note and the statement of account for December.

Discounts

There are two kinds of discount: **cash discount** and **trade discount**.

A trade discount may be offered by one trader to another. This is a reduction in the catalogue (or list) price, usually expressed as a percentage. The trader buying the goods will need to resell them at a profit. This will not be possible if goods are purchased at full catalogue price.

Trade discount is subtracted before the invoice charge is totalled. At no time is the buyer asked to pay the full price.

Cash (or settlement) discount is sometimes offered when goods are sold on credit. The aim is to encourage the buyer to pay on time by offering a reduction in the invoice price for prompt payment. Unlike trade discount, cash discount is conditional, that is, it is only given if the condition of prompt payment is met.

Discount calculations

We have already seen the calculation for trade discount in the worked example. However, the calculation for cash discount is a little more involved.

On the invoice on page 522 Big Byte Supplies Ltd offer their customer Mister Chips a cash discount of 2.5 per cent for prompt payment of the monthly statement.

Since cash discount is not automatic, but is given only for prompt payment, the buyer is initially invoiced for the full value of the goods.

This is only reduced if discount is claimed.

VAT, on the other hand, is calculated on the assumption that, where cash discount is offered, it will always be claimed. It is therefore calculated with a 2.5 per cent reduction from the outset.

The mere fact that cash discount is offered causes VAT to be reduced. This is an unusually kind gesture on the part of the Customs & Excise!

Worked example

Cash discount offered, and cash discount claimed

A customer, Mister Chips Ltd, is offered both trade discount and cash discount. The invoice that is sent is shown below. Notice that the VAT is calculated on the basis that cash discount will be claimed, whereas the goods (excl. VAT) do not have discount deducted.

BIG BYTE SUPPLIES LTD
3 Glen Close
London SE1 5SC

Tel: 0171 666 1111
Fax: 0171 666 1212
VAT Reg: 651 8181 81

Date/Tax Point: 20 January 19-5
Account Ref: CH25

INVOICE
No: 44600

Mister Chips Ltd
1001 Romford Road
Ilford
Essex

Reference: Order number: 564

Qty	Cat No	Description	Unit Price	Total Price
20	BB9 001	OKAY 280 9 pin printer	174.00 each	3,480.00
20	BB24 600	OKAY 390 80 Column 24 pin printer	389.00 each	7,780.00

	Sub-total	11,260.00
less	Trade Discount @ 20%	2,252.00
	Total (excl VAT)	9,008.00
add	VAT @ 17.5%	1,536.99
	Total Due	10,544.99

Terms:
2.5% cash discount for payment within 5 days of statement - otherwise strictly net

Total due this invoice if cash discount is claimed: **£10,319.79**

The amount due if discount is claimed is usually shown for the convenience of the customer. In this case the calculation is:

Goods (excl VAT)	9,008.00 less 2.5%	=	£8,782.80
add VAT	already reduced		£1,536.99
Total due	after cash discount		£10,319.79

The cost of cash discount

Assuming that payment is before 5 February (i.e. within five days of the end of the month), and that cash discount is therefore claimed, the February statement would record the payment as follows:

BIG BYTE SUPPLIES LTD

3 Glen Close
London SE1 5SC

Tel: 0171 666 1111
Fax: 0171 666 1212
VAT Reg: 651 8181 81

28 February 19-5
Account Ref: CH25

Mister Chips Ltd
1001 Romford Road
Ilford
Essex

Date	Details	Debit	Credit	Balance
1 Feb	Balance Brought forward			10,544.99 Dr
4 Feb	Cheque		10,319.79	
	Discount		225.20	0.00
		Balance now due:		0.00

Notice that the cash discount must be shown as a credit item, as it reduces the balance due.

Although cash discount may encourage prompt payment, it can be expensive. In this case it has cost Big Byte Computers £225.20.

A business has to decide whether it is best to give up some income in order to get money promptly or wait a little longer and hope to collect the full amount. The thinking behind allowing cash discount is that it is better to encourage customers to pay rather than to threaten them if they don't.

We will see, when we look at cashflow in Chapter 13, that the difficulty of collecting payments can be a major problem to a business.

Security

Ordering

Within any organisation there will need to be control over the various processes involved in buying and selling. Junior members of an organisation will not be able to order goods without authorisation from a responsible officer. Frequently order forms need to be countersigned by someone in a position of responsibility before they can be processed. This will prevent ordering of unwanted goods or the embarrassing situation of ordering goods without having the funds available to pay for them.

Delivery notes

Goods received must be checked carefully against the delivery note. If goods are signed as received when in fact they were not delivered it is difficult later to prove the truth of the matter.

Invoices

Invoices should not just be paid, but need to be checked both against the relevant order and against the delivery note. This should prevent the payment for goods either not required or not received.

Payments

Special care must be taken with payments.

- Cash is dealt with less frequently these days because it is inconvenient, time consuming, and also because it poses a security problem both to the finances of the firm and to the staff required to handle it.
- Cheques represent a safe method of payment as they are valid only with the signature of certain employees. Normally only the business name will appear on the cheque rather than that of the authorised signatory. Further, a cheque crossed 'a/c payee only' can only be paid into the bank account of the business to which it is made payable. In this case a lost cheque presents no great security problem.
- Credit transfers (bank **giros**) represent safe and convenient ways of transferring money from one bank account to another without the need for cheques.
- Various electronic means of transfer of funds are now available via electronic data interchange (EDI). An example is BACS (Bankers Automated Clearing Services) by which the employer's bank will pay salaries direct to employees' accounts.

In any transactions involving money it is essential that calculations are accurate. The use of computer packages allowing data to be copied rather than input separately on different occasions helps ensure consistency.

A word on calculations

The decimal point

With business documents money will be expressed in pounds and pence. There will therefore be two places of decimals, even if there are no pence:

£24 will be written as 24.00

It is not usual for £s signs to be used before each number, although they are sometimes used for grand totals and do frequently appear at the top of columns. This tends to be the rule in accounting.

Where there are no pounds a zero will appear before the decimal point:

70p will be written as 0.70

There will therefore always be three figures and a decimal point at least. Even zero will be written as 0.00. Have a look at any document to check these rules.

Some examples:

2 = 2.00
2.1 = 2.10
0.5 = 0.50
2.15 = 2.15

Rounding figures for VAT and discounts

Where VAT @ 17.5 per cent and discounts of various amounts are calculated the answers will frequently need to be rounded to achieve two places of decimals. In such cases the rule is to round down.

We simply miss off all figures to the right of the second decimal place. This is not always the nearest number, but it is the rule in documents.

Rounding to the nearest number

VAT and discounts are a special case. Usually we will wish to round not down, but to the nearest number. We may wish to work, for instance, to the nearest 1p or the nearest £. Some of the forecasting that will be carried out in later sections requires this kind of approximation. Here the rule is as follows:

Look at the figure to the right of the last figure that you need:
if it is below 5 just miss it out
if it is 5 or greater, add one to the last figure that you need, for example:

		nearest 1p	nearest £1
2.321	will become	2.32	£2
2.329		2.33	£2
0.5792		0.58	£1

Activities

1 You have a new trainee at your company. Write a memo to explain briefly the following points:

- the difference between cash discount and trade discount
- why your company may offer cash discount, even though it can be expensive
- why it is very important for a driver to get a signature for a delivery note before leaving goods.

2 You work for Pandora's Boxes, West Estate, Grantham, Lincolnshire. Prepare the statement of account for one of your customers, Ms M. Khan of 22 Upper Street, Canterbury, Kent to be sent on 31 January 199–. Details:

1 Jan	Balance B/f, £220 (incl VAT)
4 Jan	Invoice 5515 for goods delivered £880 (incl VAT)
10 Jan	Cheque received from M. Khan £200 (£20 discount has been allowed)
18 Jan	Goods returned as faulty £110 (incl VAT)
25 Jan	Invoice 5772 for goods delivered £420 (incl VAT)

3 Your work for Big Byte Computers in the sales department. You supply a customer, Taurus & Co. Ltd of The Bull Ring, Birmingham, on the following terms:

- 20 per cent trade discount on all goods supplied
- credit of one month
- full settlement on receipt of the monthly statement.

The following transactions took place in May 199–:

1 May	£1,500 owed by Taurus from the previous month		
5 May	supplied to Taurus	5 of BB24 700	Invoice No. 456
	and	10 of BBL 013	
8 May	received from Taurus a cheque for £1,500 in payment for their April account		
16 May	supplied to Taurus	8 of BB9 002	Invoice No. 472
	and	5 of BB24 500	
20 May	Taurus returned 2 of BBL 013 as damaged in transit. Credit Note No. CN 87		

Using the price list in the chapter, complete two invoices, one credit note and the monthly statement of account to show these transactions.

4 Assume that the customer, Taurus & Co. Ltd in question 3 above, was offered 2.5 per cent cash discount for settlement within 30 days.
   a For the invoice dated 16 May (above), recalculate the 'total price' to show the total invoice charge under these terms
   b Calculate the amount that would be paid on this invoice if the cash discount were claimed (you should show all workings).

Recording purchases, sales and returns in the day books

Normally invoices and credit notes will be recorded in monthly day books or journals. These are merely lists showing, for each document:

Date	*Customer/Supplier*	*Invoice No.*	*Total £ (excl. VAT)*	*VAT £*	*Total £*

There is a separate book for sales, purchases, returns inwards and returns outwards. These books are totalled each month.

In Chapter 14 we look at how these totals are transferred to the business accounts.

Cash control – recording receipts and payments

It has been said that the art of business is the art of 'getting paid'. What this really means is that no business can exist for long without cash. In this section we will look at how we can record the inflow and outflow of business cash efficiently.

The meaning of the term 'cash'

Cash can mean literally notes and coins as opposed to cheques. In another sense it simply means immediate payment by whatever means. A cash purchase happens when the customer pays immediately, even if this means using a credit card or writing a cheque (backed by a valid cheque guarantee card) or using some other means such as credit transfer. Similarly cash discount is discount for payment by a certain date, however that payment is made.

Documents used with receipts and payments

The receipt

In accounting a receipt is money received; in common usage it usually refers to a slip of paper acknowledging this payment. Most retail outlets give a printout from the till roll with goods as proof of payment. Some organisations stamp the bill to show payment received, while others will write individual receipts on preprinted sheets which can be purchased from stationers.

Where payment is made through the banking system, the fact that a record will be made by the bank is often regarded as sufficient. Many organisations, because of the cost involved, will only send receipts for postal payments if these are specifically requested.

Remittance advice

Some businesses include a **remittance advice** with their requests for payment. This may take the form of a tear-off slip indicating the amount due, the means of payment and any relevant reference numbers. This avoids the possibility of payments arriving with insufficient means of identification An example is given on page 519.

Banking documents

Paying-in slip Banks issue their business customers with books of paying-in slips to be used when depositing cash or cheques into their bank account. Personal customers, who make fewer deposits, may have a number of slips included in each cheque book. Additionally, single slips are available at bank branches.

The counterfoil, which is stamped by the bank, acts as a receipt for the money deposited. Used paying-in books should be retained for reference purposes.

This system, also known as **bank giro**, can be used to transfer funds to a named account by anyone wishing to do so. It is not restricted to the account holder but can be used as a means of payment by customers.

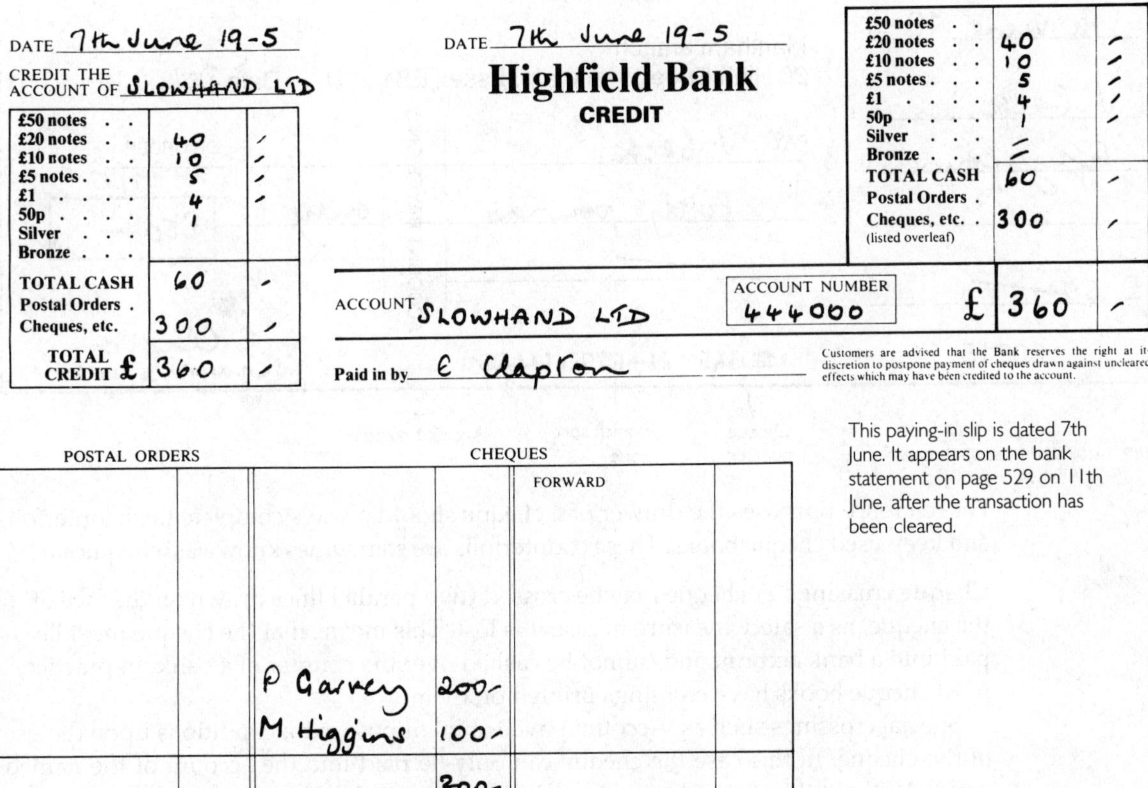

DATE 7th June 19-5

CREDIT THE ACCOUNT OF SLOWHAND LTD

£50 notes		
£20 notes	40	–
£10 notes	10	–
£5 notes	5	–
£1	4	–
50p	1	
Silver		
Bronze		
TOTAL CASH	60	–
Postal Orders		
Cheques, etc.	300	–
TOTAL CREDIT £	360	–

DATE 7th June 19-5

Highfield Bank

CREDIT

£50 notes		
£20 notes	40	–
£10 notes	10	–
£5 notes	5	–
£1	4	–
50p	1	–
Silver	–	
Bronze	–	
TOTAL CASH	60	–
Postal Orders		
Cheques, etc. (listed overleaf)	300	–

ACCOUNT SLOWHAND LTD

ACCOUNT NUMBER 444000

£ 360 –

Paid in by E Clapton

Customers are advised that the Bank reserves the right at its discretion to postpone payment of cheques drawn against uncleared effects which may have been credited to the account.

This paying-in slip is dated 7th June. It appears on the bank statement on page 529 on 11th June, after the transaction has been cleared.

POSTAL ORDERS		CHEQUES		FORWARD	
		P Garvey	200–		
		M Higgins	100–		
			300–		

Figure 11.5 *Example of paying-in slip – front and reverse*

Cheque A cheque is an instruction to the bank from an account holder (the drawer) to pay a named person (the payee) a specified sum of money. The bank will comply as long as the cheque is completed with the correct details and on condition that there are sufficient funds, or overdraft facilities, to meet the payment. If this is not so then the cheque will be dishonoured (not paid). It will be marked 'refer to drawer' and sent back to the account holder. It is said to 'bounce'.

A cheque may only be signed by the authorised signatory. In a private account the name of the **signatory** will be printed on the cheque. Business cheques will have the name of the business only, but the bank will have specimen signatures of those authorised to sign. For security reasons cheques may require more than one signature. In a partnership, for instance, all partners may wish to approve a payment.

Cheque books will be issued to current account holders by banks and building societies. Each organisation will accept cheques drawn on accounts at other organisations, though there will be a period of three or four working days before the cheque is cleared. With building societies this may take longer.

The cheque below is dated 5th June. As it is not presented immediately it appears on the bank statement on page 528 on 14th June.

From a business point of view printed cheque books with numbered cheques are an aid to good record-keeping.

Figure 11.6 Example of cheque

For reference purposes the drawer of a cheque should always complete the counterfoil, and keep used cheque books. These counterfoils are sometimes known as 'cheque stubs'.

Cheque crossings A cheque may be crossed (two parallel lines drawn on the face of the cheque) as a safety measure in case it is lost. This means that the cheque must be paid into a bank account and cannot be cashed over the counter of a bank. In practice, most cheque books have crossings printed on them.

Special crossings such as 'Account payee only' impose extra conditions upon the use of the cheque. In this case the cheque can only be paid into the account of the named payee. Without this it could be endorsed (signed on the back) by the payee to allow it to be paid to someone else's account.

Standing orders and direct debits It is convenient for organisations to both pay, and receive, payment through the banking system without the use of cheques. These two methods may be arranged by filling in a 'mandate' with the relevant instructions and sending it to the bank at which the drawer's account is held.

Standing orders will allow an account holder to instruct the bank to pay stated equal amounts at regular intervals to a named payee. The system is useful where the amount is the same each time, is known in advance and is paid at regular intervals. Insurance premiums, rent and hire purchase payments can be met in this way. For instance the rent may be £200 per month, payable to the landlord on the first of the month until further notice.

Direct debits are similar to standing orders, but here the payee gives the bank permission to pay amounts to a stated payee on demand. In this case the payments need not be at regular intervals and the amount need not be known in advance. This system is useful for variable amounts such as bills for services like the telephone, gas or electricity.

Payees prefer direct debit as it puts them in control. They ask for the amount required when they want it, there is no problem of late payment, and it saves on the expense of processing cheques and sending reminders. For this reason providers of many of the services mentioned put direct debit mandates into their bills to encourage this form of payment. As a precaution it is wise for the payer to put an upper limit on direct debits, so that if bills exceed a certain level the bank will contact them for confirmation before paying.

Although payment is automatic once the system is in operation, the payee will send regular statements to confirm amounts paid. As with cheques, payment will only be made if there are sufficient funds or overdraft facilities available.

Bank statements The bank will keep a record of all of the transactions between itself and the account holder. At agreed intervals a copy of this record, known as a bank statement, will be sent to the account holder.

The statement is compiled in a similar way to the statements of account sent by sellers to credit customers, although in this case the balance shows the state of the bank account, that is, how much money is in it. The final balance figure is perhaps the most important as it shows the account balance at the time the statement was issued.

HIGHFIELD BANK PLC

Bank Statement No.: 61 — Branch: 20 High Street, Markham, Essex EB1 26D

Account Number: 44400 — Tel: 0126 001 9191

Account Title: Slowhand Ltd, 49 White Horse Road, London N11

Date: 30 June 19-5

Date	Details	Withdrawals	Deposits	Balance
1 June	Balance from sheet No. 60			18.20
7 June	00310	41.60		23.40 O/D
	00311	22.25		45.65 O/D
	JB Properties SO	50.00		95.65 O/D
11 June	C-C		360.00	264.35
12 June	00313	41.00		223.35
14 June	00315	50.00		173.35
15 June	Bell Insurance DD	42.50		130.85
	TR		25.75	156.60
18 June	00316	32.35		124.25
	C-C		35.30	159.55
21 June	00314	32.80		126.75
	BK-CH	8.55		118.20
22 June	00312	68.40		49.80
28 June	00317	25.50		24.30
30 June	Balance to sheet No. 62			24.30

Key: SO Standing Order; DV Dividend; C-C Cash &/or Cheques; OD Overdrawn; BK-CH Bank Charges; DD Direct Debit; TR Credit Transfer; AC Automated Cash

Documents shown on pages 527 and 528

Figure 11.7 Example of a bank statement – the latest bank balance is £24.30.

The business should be able to check most of the items on the bank statement against the counterfoils in the cheque book and the paying-in book. Other items such as standing orders and direct debits will need to be checked against payees' receipts.

Bank charges, usually incurred for services arranged or as interest on overdrafts, are imposed by the bank. Similarly, some current accounts pay interest on credit balances. These items usually appear for the first time on the statement. They can be checked against the bank's terms and conditions which will normally be available in the form of a small booklet.

A business will keep its own record of banking transactions in the cashbook thus:

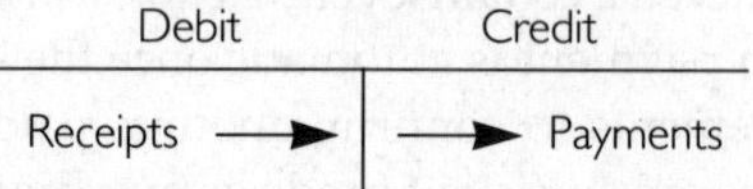

We will look at this in more detail in Chapter 14. See also Figure 11.15 on page 532.

Activity

Study the bank statement and answer the following questions:

a What are the numbers in the details column for 7 June?
b Why do these numbers not run in order throughout the month?
c What happened on 15 June?
d On what dates were cash and cheques paid into the account?
e How much money was in the account when the month began?
f Was the account overdrawn at any time during June? How do you know?
g Assuming that this is the most recent bank statement, what is the current balance?

The cashbook

The reason for having a cashbook is so that money can be easily accounted for without having to go through all of the cheque book and paying-in book counterfoils each time. Nevertheless, simply preparing a cashbook does not guarantee that all is well. It must be checked regularly. Separate columns are used for cash and bank transactions.

The cash balance represents the money held in the business; probably in the cash box, the till or the safe. This money should be counted to see whether it does indeed correspond to the balance on the cash columns. If it does not then we need to find out why. Perhaps we have miscounted, perhaps we have missed an item out or balanced incorrectly. If money is missing questions need to be asked.

The bank balance represents the money held at the bank. We need to check this against the bank statement for the same period. Unfortunately there are a number of reasons why the bank balance in the cashbook may not agree with the bank statement – perhaps cheques paid in have not yet been cleared, or cheques written may not yet have been presented. Other differences may be: bank charges, standing orders or direct debits which are not included in the cashbook. It is necessary to note the differences and try to explain them. This is called **bank reconciliation.**

The cashbook and the bank statement

After studying the cashbook students often ask the question: 'Why does the bank statement show money paid into the bank as a credit and money withdrawn as a debit, while the cashbook shows the opposite?'

The reason is that, like the statements of account, it is simply a matter of whose point of view we look at it from. All documents prepared by the bank, including the bank statement, have been prepared from the bank's point of view. If we deposit money then the bank sees us as a creditor (someone to whom it owes money), hence it regards deposits as credits. If we withdraw money we reduce what it owes us (hence it debits us). If we overdraw then we become a debtor to the bank.

The bank columns in the cashbook work the opposite way round, not because the principles involved are different, but simply because they are our record of the bank. If we pay money in then we see the bank as a debtor (it owes us money), hence we debit it. If we withdraw money then the bank is less of a debtor hence we credit it. If we overdraw then the bank will become a creditor.

The petty cashbook

Sometimes a department will wish to make a small purchase immediately. Perhaps they need to cut a key or pay a taxi fare. Rather than having to request a cheque from the cashier – a process which might take some time and a certain amount of paperwork – it is convenient to have ready cash available.

The usual system is for the cashier to allow the office to have a small cash float for such expenditure. This is called **petty cash** (a corruption of the French word *petit* meaning small). Normally this money will be kept in a lockable petty cash box and will be the responsibility of a member of the office staff. All money must be recorded for security reasons and the officer responsible will keep a petty cashbook for this purpose. There is usually a limit on the expenditure allowed per item.

The imprest system

A common petty cash system involves beginning each period (sometimes a week, sometimes a month) with the same amount of money in the petty cash box. This amount is called the imprest. A decision will be made initially as to how much is a reasonable sum. This will then be provided by the cashier who will record it as an expenditure in the cashbook. At the end of the period the sum spent will be calculated and this exact sum will be requested from the cashier to restore the imprest for the start of the next period.

All items of petty cash expenditure must be authorised by a senior employee who will sign a petty cash voucher.

Petty cash vouchers

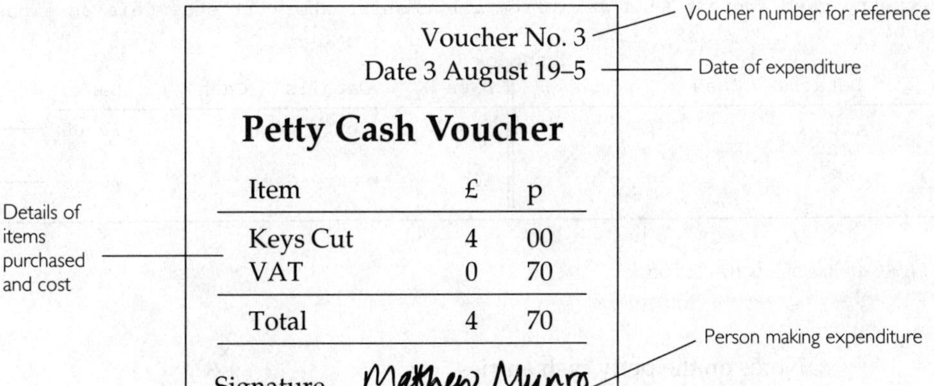

Voucher No. 3 — Voucher number for reference

Date 3 August 19–5 — Date of expenditure

Petty Cash Voucher

Item	£	p
Keys Cut	4	00
VAT	0	70
Total	4	70

Details of items purchased and cost

Signature......Matthew Munro — Person making expenditure

Authorised by... J Smith — Senior member of staff approves expenditure

Figure 11.8 Example of a petty cash voucher

The money will only be released by the petty cashier if these details are supplied. Any receipts obtained will be attached to the vouchers which will then be filed in numerical order.

Writing up the petty cashbook

The rule of recording money received on the debit (left) side and money spent on the credit (right) side applies to the petty cashbook in the same way as it does to the cashbook. Essentially the petty cashbook is concerned with expenditure. Money (the impress amount) is received from the cashier only at the beginning of the week or month and all other transactions for the period record the way in which this is spent.

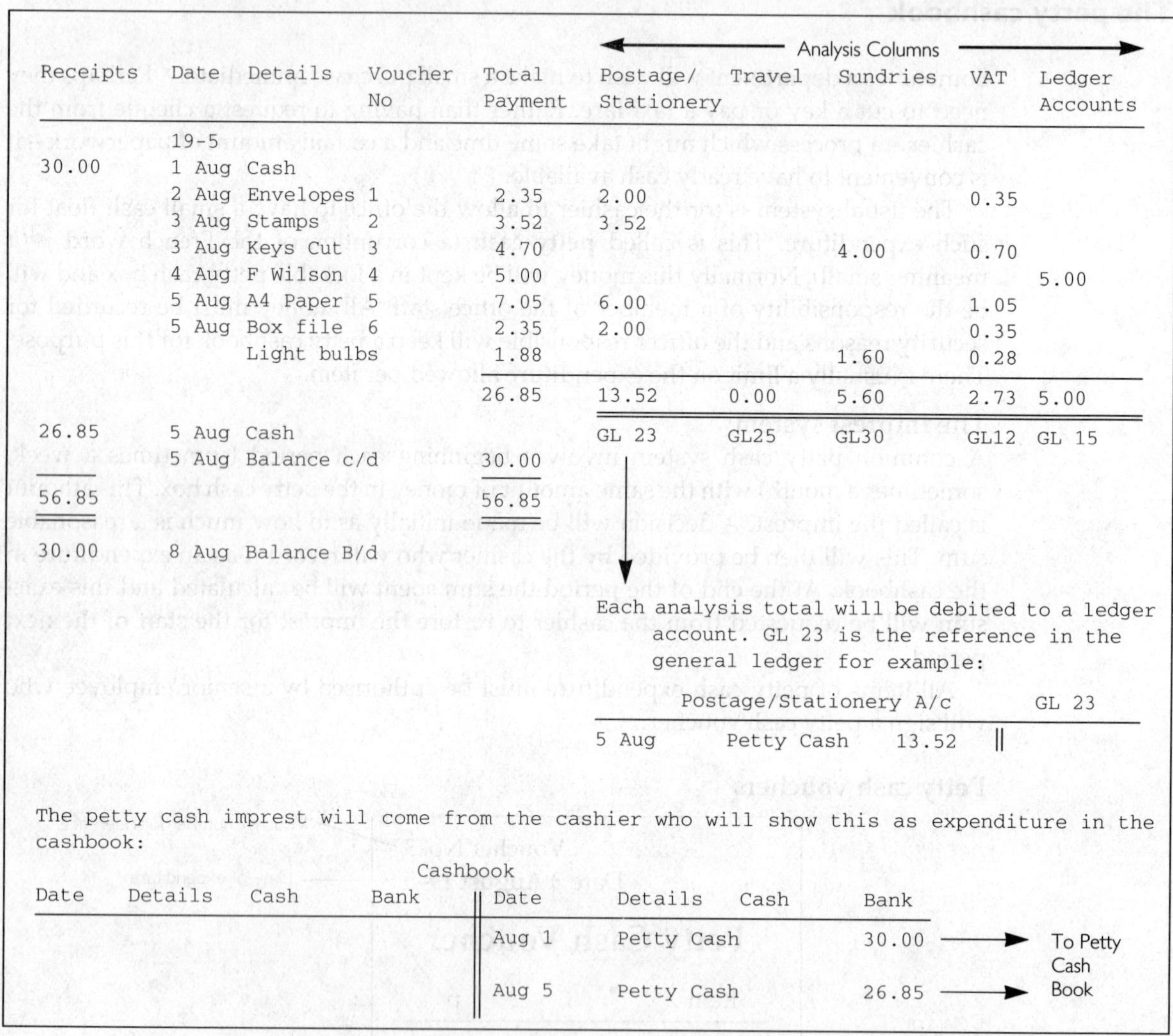

Receipts	Date	Details	Voucher No	Total Payment	Postage/ Stationery	Travel	Sundries	VAT	Ledger Accounts
					← Analysis Columns →				
	19-5								
30.00	1 Aug	Cash							
	2 Aug	Envelopes	1	2.35	2.00			0.35	
	3 Aug	Stamps	2	3.52	3.52				
	3 Aug	Keys Cut	3	4.70			4.00	0.70	
	4 Aug	F Wilson	4	5.00					5.00
	5 Aug	A4 Paper	5	7.05	6.00			1.05	
	5 Aug	Box file	6	2.35	2.00			0.35	
		Light bulbs		1.88			1.60	0.28	
				26.85	13.52	0.00	5.60	2.73	5.00
26.85	5 Aug	Cash			GL 23	GL25	GL30	GL12	GL 15
	5 Aug	Balance c/d		30.00					
56.85				56.85					
30.00	8 Aug	Balance B/d							

Each analysis total will be debited to a ledger account. GL 23 is the reference in the general ledger for example:

Postage/Stationery A/c			GL 23
5 Aug	Petty Cash	13.52	

The petty cash imprest will come from the cashier who will show this as expenditure in the cashbook:

Cashbook

Date	Details	Cash	Bank	Date	Details	Cash	Bank
				Aug 1	Petty Cash		30.00
				Aug 5	Petty Cash		26.85

Figure 11.9 Example of a petty cash book

Notes on the petty cash entries.

Receipts

On 1 August a petty cashbook is set up with an imprest of £30 received from the cashier. This is recorded in the 'Receipts' (debit) column on the left-hand side of the book. The word 'cash' indicates that the money has come from the cashbook.

Total payments
In the first week ending 5 August seven separate items are purchased. These are recorded on petty cash vouchers numbers 1 to 6 (there are two items on voucher number 6). They are entered into the 'total payments' (credit) column on the right-hand side of the book.

Analysis columns
Each item of expenditure is also entered into an analysis column to the right of the total payments column. This enables the accounts department to place each item of expenditure under the correct heading when it is transferred to the main business accounts. The analysis columns used will vary from business to business and will represent those items of expenditure most commonly used in the petty cash expenditure of that particular business.
Columns that are often used include:

- VAT column for VAT registered businesses
  all items in the example, except postage, have VAT on them, currently at 17.5 per cent
- ledger accounts column. Sometimes petty cash will pay for an item not normally paid in this way. As there will not be an analysis column for this type of item it is put into the ledger accounts column under its account name. In the example F. Wilson, a supplier, is paid out of petty cash.

Balancing the account
At the end of the period (the week in this case) the payments are totalled. This total should be cross-checked with the total of the analysis columns.
The cashier is asked to supply money to replace the sum spent of £26.85.
The account is now balanced by subtracting payments from receipts. The balance of £30 is brought down to begin the next week.

The petty cash box
This should, at any point, contain the difference between the imprest received and the sum spent. Before the imprest was restored, for example, it should contain £30 – £26.85 = £3.15. This must be checked and any differences investigated.

Activities

1 You work for the firm of Hughes & Sharp, solicitors, where one of your jobs is to maintain the petty cashbook. The book is kept on the imprest system with a float of £50. There are analysis columns for Postage and Stationery, Travel and General Expenses. (The firm is not registered for VAT.)

You are to enter the following transactions for the month of July into the petty cashbook:

1 July balance B/d of £50
2 July bought stationery for £2.50 voucher number 22
4 July bought envelopes for £1.75
8 July bought glue and tape for £1.60
10 July bought tea and coffee for £3.20
15 July rail fare £5.50
18 July paid window cleaner £10
19 July postage of parcel £4.20
25 July rubber bands and string £2.45

Restore the imprest at the end of the month. Balance the account and bring down the balance at 1 August.

2 **Graham George is responsible for the petty cashbook at Cannon & Co. The book has analysis columns for Postage and Stationery, Travel, Miscellaneous and VAT. Show the entries that he made during the month of April for the following items: The last voucher used before this month was number 56.**

1 April	**balance B/d £35**
4 April	**postage stamps £2.80 (no VAT)**
5 April	**receipt book £2.50 (incl £0.37 VAT)**
9 April	**cleaning materials £3.10 (incl £0.35 VAT)**
12 April	**rail fares £3.00 (no VAT)**
15 April	**entertaining £9.50 (incl £1.41 VAT)**
22 April	**pens and drawing pins £2.82 (incl £0.42 VAT)**
26 April	**bus fare £2.50 (no VAT)**
28 April	**printer ribbon £3.50 (incl £0.52 VAT)**

Restore the imprest on 30 April to £35. Balance the account and bring down the balance to 1 May. Is £35 sufficient or will the imprest need to be increased?

Consequences of incorrect completion of documents

It is of little value recording business transactions if the records are inaccurate. The consequences of inaccurate records are:

- customers may be sent incorrect statements. This causes time-consuming letters of apology and credit notes. There may be a loss of good-will, even a loss of business
- suppliers may be asked to take back goods ordered in error
- cheques incorrectly completed or returned unpaid through lack of funds may cause suppliers to withdraw credit facilities
- if credit limits are ignored bad debts may result as customers build up debts they cannot repay
- incorrect figures that are not detected will ultimately cause errors in financial reports. Errors in sales, expenses and business profits will give misleading management information about business performance. Problems could also arise with the Inland Revenue (tax), and Customs and Excise (VAT).

Avoiding errors

Errors may be avoided by:

- effective systems which can be operated even where the responsible officer is absent
- introducing checking procedures such as asking supervisors to sign petty cash vouchers, getting two signatures on a cheque, producing a trial balance (see Chapter 14), producing a bank reconciliation statement, checking that the cash box contents equal the cash balance on the books
- taking care and using legible handwriting.

Computerised accounting systems minimise the chances of human error by reducing the number of entries required. An integrated package, for example, will transfer the original entries to the relevant accounts automatically. As long as data input is correct there is no problem. Where a mistake is detected, a single correction routine will cancel all related errors. Figure 11.6 shows how sales invoices are recorded in the SAGE Accountant-Plus system.

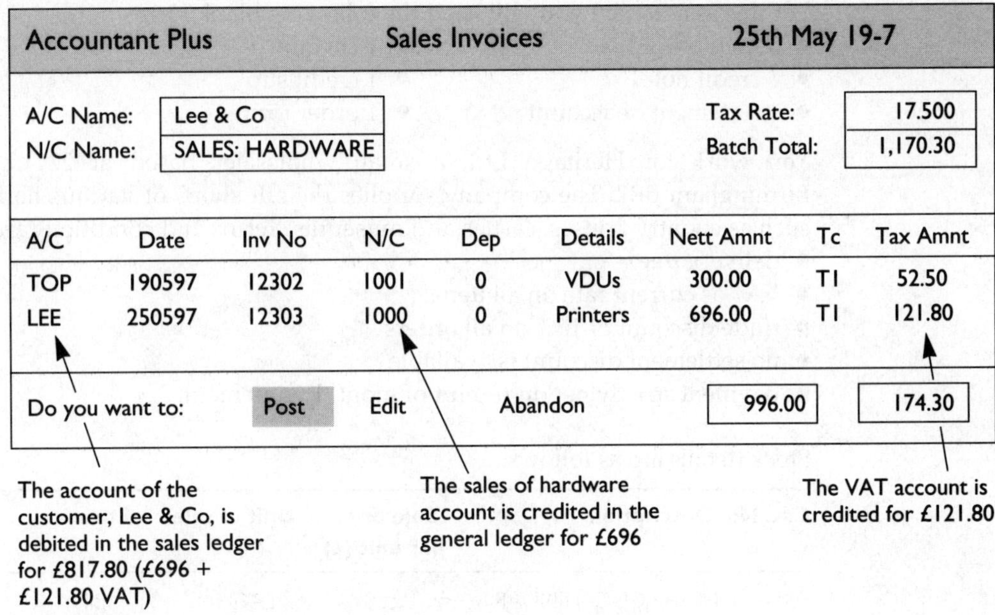

Figure 11.10 The SAGE Accountant Plus system

The procedure for data entry with SAGE is as follows:

- invoices are sorted into batches. Details from each are entered onto a separate line on the daybook screen
- A/C = account reference. The reference LEE tells the package which customer to debit
- N/C = nominal code. The code 1000 tells the package which nominal ledger account to credit
- Tc = tax code. The code T1 tells the package that VAT is at 17.5%. There are other codes for zero-rated items (such as basic food) and non-VAT items.

Assignment 11.1
Heritage Ltd

This assignment develops knowledge and understanding of the following elements:

6.1 Explain added value, distribution of added value and money cycle
6.2 Explain financial transactions and complete supporting documents

It supports development of the following core skills:

Communication 3.2, 3.4
Application of number 3.2

For this assignment you will need the following blank forms:

- 3 invoices
- 1 credit note
- 1 statement of account
- 1 cheque
- 1 credit slip
- 1 order form.

You work for Heritage Ltd, a small wholesaler based at 22 Commercial Way, Birmingham BR2. The company supplies the gift shops of various heritage attractions such as country houses, castles and museums. Terms and conditions are:

- delivery free
- VAT as current rate on all items
- trade discount of 10% on all orders
- no settlement discount is available
- payment strictly net on receipt of monthly statement.

Stock details are as follows:

Cat. No.	Description	Sale price per unit (£)	Unit of sale	Location	Cost price per unit (£)
S001	HERITAGE CALENDAR	2.50	EACH	BIN 1	1.70
S002	HERITAGE NOTEPAD	7.50	BOX (10)	BIN 2	5.45
S003	PEN/PENCIL SET	10.80	EACH	BIN 3	5.40
S004	POSTCARD	1.50	BOX (10)	BIN 4	0.75
S005	EMBOSSED BOOKMARK	16.00	BOX (20)	BIN 5	10.00
H001	GLASS PAPERWEIGHT	4.50	EACH	BIN 6	3.00
H002	WOODEN JIGSAW	3.75	EACH	BIN 7	2.60
H003	PATCHWORK CUSHION	11.50	EACH	BIN 8	9.10
H004	POTTERY VASE	8.25	EACH	BIN 9	5.00
H005	FLOWER PRESS	2.85	EACH	BIN 10	1.90
M001	COUNTRY MINTS	17.50	BOX (10)	BIN 11	13.30
M002	POT POURRI	19.50	BOX (10)	BIN 12	13.85
M003	COUNTRY TEA CLOTH	2.50	EACH	BIN 13	1.25
M004	BEES WAX	2.10	BOX (5)	BIN 14	1.50
M005	WILD HONEY	2.25	EACH	BIN 15	1.12

The transactions listed below took place between Heritage Ltd and a customer, Spa Crafts of 63 Pantile Crescent, Tunbridge Wells, Kent TW2 1OU.

Nov 3 Received order (no SC995) for:
50 of item S001 5 boxes of item S005 10 of item H002
Prepared goods and invoice no H1001

Nov 10 Received a cheque for £920 in settlement for last month's statement

Nov 15 Received order (no SC1001) for:
5 boxes of S004 20 of item H001 20 of item H002
Prepared goods and invoice H1120

Nov 17 Received 5 of item H001 returned as damaged in transit
Prepared credit note C101 after examination of goods

Nov 25 Received order (no SC1008) for:
20 of item S001 10 of item H004 10 boxes of item M004
Prepared goods and invoice no H1230

Your tasks

1 As an assistant at Heritage Ltd you are to prepare all relevant documents to record the transactions with Spa Crafts. When complete you should have: 3 sales invoices, 1 credit note, the customer's statement of account for November.
Note that:
- at 1 November Spa Crafts' account shows that £920 is owed to you
- Spa Crafts have a credit limit of £15 000:

2 It is 8 November 19-6. You are asked to complete an order form (no HL550) for:
50 of item S001 50 boxes of item S002 10 of item S003.
The supplier is: Vic Young Crafts Ltd, 84 The Cut, London SE1 0UT.
Terms: No discounts, VAT on all items at the current rate, carriage free.

3 Assuming that the above order is dispatched to you in full on 10 November 19-6, prepare a cheque payable to Vic Young ready for signature.

4 Prepare a paying in slip on 13 November 19-6 to include:
- the cheque from Spa Crafts received on 10 November
- a further cheque for £250.50 from Old Oak Ltd
- 5 × £5 notes, 2 × £1 coins and 1 × 50p piece received from a cash customer.

5 The latest bank statement is shown below. Calculate the balance after the transactions in Task 3 and 4 above have passed through the system.

NORTH BANK PLC

Bank Statement no: 74 | Branch: 99 The Parade, Birmingham BR2 1DM
Account no: 220644 | Tel: 721 333 444
Account Title: Heritage Ltd, 22 Commercial Way, Birmingham BR2 | Date: 10 November 19–6

Date	Details	Withdrawals Dr	Deposits Cr	Balance
1-Nov	Balance B/f from sheet no 73			1,465.20
2-Nov	18850	880.57		584.63
	18851	720.85		136.22 O/D
3-Nov	CC		2,056.72	1,920.50
5-Nov	18854	480.45		1,440.05
	DD	458.35		981.70
8-Nov	18853	858.50		123.20
9-Nov	BK/CH	17.60		105.60
10-Nov	TR		320.60	426.20
10-Nov	Balance c/f to sheet no 75			426.20

KEY: SO: Standing Order; DV: Dividend; CC: Cash &/or Cheques; O/D: Overdrawn; BK/CH: Bank Charges; DD: Direct Debit; TR: Credit Transfer; AC: Automated Cash

6 Give three possible reasons why, despite there being no errors, the business cash book will usually show a different balance from the business bank statement at any given date.

Supplementary tasks

Your supervisor has asked you write clear explanations on the following for the benefit of a work experience student who will be starting in the office next week.

The importance of documentation

- Explain the purpose of each of the following: sales invoice, delivery note, credit note, customer statement of account.

Security

- Why is it important to maintain an up-to-date running balance on the customer's account? What checks should be made before an order is dispatched?
- An assistant is not allowed to sign the cheque. Why not?
- How could your supervisor check that you have paid money into the bank as requested? Give two ways.
- Your wages are paid directly into your bank account. The letters BACS appear on your payment slip; what do these mean? How does this system benefit your business?

Accuracy

- What could be the consequences for the business of incorrectly completing a sales invoice?
- Draw a diagram of the money cycle as it applies to the transactions between Heritage and Spa Crafts.

Key terms

Statutory	Creditors	Debit
Enquiry	Debtors	Credit
Order	Aged debtors	Balance
Acknowledgement	Aged creditors	Bank reconciliation
Delivery note	Trading cycle	Cheque crossings
Invoice	Added value	Paying-in (giro) slip
Credit note	Money cycle	Credit transfer
Statement of account	BACS	Direct debit
Remittance advice	EDI	Standing order
Tax point	Day books (or journals)	Bank charges
Trade discount	Insolvency	Signatory
Cash discount	Procurement function	Petty cash
VAT	Bad debt	Analysis columns
Credit control,	Cash (different meanings)	Imprest system
Credit limit	Cashbook	Petty cash voucher

Review questions

1 Which document sets out the charge for a consignment of goods delivered?
2 When goods are returned as faulty and the supplier accepts responsibility, which document does the supplier issue?
3 When one trader allows a reduction from the catalogue price to another trader, what is this called?
4 Why will a business sometimes produce a catalogue and price list separately?
5 Is an invoice shown as a debit or a credit entry on a customer's statement of account? Will it increase or reduce the balance due?
6 What is an aged debtor's account?
7 What is a credit limit?
8 Sometimes a partnership may require each cheque to be signed by at least two partners. Why is this?
9 Why are all business documents numbered?
10 What is a bad debt?
11 Why is a cheque crossed?
12 On which side of the cashbook is money received entered?
13 Why is a petty cash voucher used?
14 How can a cashier and a petty cashier check the accuracy of the cash balances that they have calculated?
15 Give three reasons why a bank statement may not agree with the bank balance as shown in the cashbook.
16 What is added value?
17 What does the trading cycle show?
18 What does the money cycle show?
19 What three things may happen to profit?
20 What is insolvency?

Assignment 11.2 Ron Jones Cars

This assignment develops knowledge and understanding of the following elements:

6.2 Explain financial transactions and complete supporting documents

It supports development of the following core skills:

Communication 3.2, 3.4
Application of number 3.2

Ron Jones runs a small car hire business. Much of his custom comes from local businesses and is on credit terms. Recently Ron has got behind with his book-keeping as a result of staff illness and he has asked you to help out. He has left a memo on your desk. Today is 13 December 19–7.

Provided with this assignment are:

- memorandum giving instructions
- today's documents: invoice, credit note, blank cheque, petty cash voucher
- list of December's transactions so far
- sales ledger accounts for M. Jackson and Steel Ltd
- petty cashbook.

Your tasks

1. Comply with Ron's instructions (see the memo opposite).
2. In your reply, which should take the form of a memo to Ron, you should also make reference to the significance of the following:
   M. Jackson, a trader on Roman Road market, has a credit limit of £600
   Ron is not recording VAT on his petty cash expenses
3. The office junior cannot understand why Ron is so worried about the books of the business. He also asks why you cannot sign cheques.
   Write down your replies to these questions giving details.
4. **a** Explain the purpose of each document used in this assignment.
   b Indicate whether each document is associated with sales, purchases, receipts or payments.
   c Explain for each document the consequences of completing it incorrectly.
   d Explain which documents Ron will use when he buys his office supplies (he buys regularly on credit).

RON JONES CARS LTD

MEMORANDUM

To: A Student
From: Ron Jones
Date: 13 December 19-7
Ref: Business records

Thanks for coming to help us out.

I'm afraid we're a bit behind, and the financial year ends on 31st! The cashbook has not been balanced for a while and we haven't done any of the books for December.
Unfortunately I will be out of the office today, but perhaps you could do the following for me:

1 Complete the documents for today's transactions - I've left them in a pile for you.
The cheque is to pay TL Haulage £230.15. If you get this ready I'll come in later this afternoon to sign it. It should catch the post so you can put it through the books
2 Please complete all of the books for December - I've left a list of the transactions for the month so far.
3 Balance all of the books when you've finished and make sure the customer accounts are up to date.
4 Please make a note of anything that needs investigating. I would also appreciate any comments on how our systems could be improved.

RON JONES CARS LTD

VAT Reg No 421 4647 61R

INVOICE

Your Order No: 267
Invoice No: 481

Date: 13th December 19-7

To:
M Jackson
47 Mill Way
Bolton
Lancs

Customer a/c no 23

Quantity	Ref No	Description	Unit Price	Total Price
5 days	1002	Ford Escort	£37.25 per day	
8 days	2009	Ford Transit 35 cwt	£42.35 per day	
13 days		Insurance	£5.50 per day	
255 miles		Excess Mileage	£0.25 per mile	

Total
less Trade Discount @ %
Total
add VAT @ 17.5%
TOTAL £

Terms: Trade Discount 10% on orders over £1,000 otherwise net

Date

£

North Bank plc

19__ 40-09-04

Pay ______ or order

ACCOUNT PAYEE

£

RON JONES CARS LTD

"000430" 40⋯0904: 70277134"

Jones House,
Old Ford Road,
London E3
Tel: 0937 47632/3/4
Telex: 152773

RON JONES CARS LTD

VAT Reg No 421 4647 61R

CREDIT NOTE

Your Order No: 479
Invoice No: 90

Date: 13th December 19-7

To:
Steel Ltd
12-16 Haversham Ind Est
DARTFORD
Kent

Customer a/c no 17

Quantity	Ref No	Description	Unit Price	Total Price
2 days	1012	Ford Sierra	£5.25 per day overcharge	

Total	
less Trade Discount @ 10%	
Total	
add VAT @ 17.5%	
TOTAL £	

Reason for credit note: 2 days charged at incorrect price

Petty Cash Voucher

No. 84

Date 13/12/-7

Item(s) required	Amount £	p
Taxi fare	5	–
TOTAL	5	–

signature J. Harlow   passed by Ron Jones

List of transactions for December — Tom.

Dec 1	Restored petty cash imprest by transferring £22.34 from cash
Dec 2	Invoice number 477 sent to Steel Ltd for hire charge of £344.78 plus VAT
	Paid for paper clips and string from Petty Cash £3.20 (voucher 79)
Dec 4	Bought light bulbs £2.55 and had keys cut £3.65 from Petty Cash (vouchers 80 & 81)
Dec 6	Invoice number 478 sent to M Jackson for hire charge of £45.60 plus VAT
Dec 7	Received a cheque for £312 from Steel Ltd in full settlement of the amount owed from November
Dec 8	Invoice number 479 sent to Steel Ltd for hire charge of £59.60 plus VAT
Dec 11	Paid for window cleaner £7.50 from Petty Cash (voucher 82)
	Sent credit note number 89 to M Jackson for overcharge of £25.50 plus VAT
Dec 12	Invoice number 480 sent to M Jackson for hire charge of £95.25 plus VAT
	Paid £5 to charity from Petty Cash (voucher 83)
Dec 13	Enter up today's documents; sales invoice; credit note; petty cash voucher; cheque

SALES LEDGER (Customer Accounts)

M Jackson

Date	Details	Dr	Cr	Bal
Dec 1	Bal B/f			257.16 Dr

BALANCE NOW DUE £

Steel Ltd

Date	Details	Dr	Cr	Bal
Dec 1	Bal B/f			318.96 Dr

BALANCE NOW DUE £

PETTY CASH BOOK

Receipts	Date	Details	V/N	Payments	Stationery	Postage	Travel	Sundries
7.66	Dec 1	Bal B/f						

12 Costing and pricing

What is covered in this chapter

- Business costs
- Classification of costs by type
- Forecasting costs
- Cost units
- Absorption costing (full or total costing)
- Classification of costs by behaviour
- Marginal costing
- Marginal costing v absorption costing
- The break-even point
  - Break-even graph
  - The margin of safety
  - Profit/volume graph
  - Using a spreadsheet model
  - 'What if?' scenarios
  - Deciding upon production strategy
  - Break-even and the business plan
  - Uses and limitations of break-even
  - The link between costing and pricing
  - The relationship between the financial and the marketing functions

These are the resources you will need for your Financial Transactions, Costing and Pricing file:

- spreadsheet package
- PC
- graph paper

Business costs

What are costs?

Costs can be regarded as the value of the resources which are 'used up' in production. The phrase 'used up' is important, because a business spends money on many items which are not regarded as costs. We can distinguish between:

- revenue expenses: those items such as rent, light and stocks which are consumed on a daily basis. These are costs
- capital expenses: expensive assets which last for a number of years, for example machinery. The purchase of these 'fixed assets' is not regarded as a cost.
  Most fixed assets eventually wear out, but because this takes some time the cost is shared over the life of the asset as **depreciation**. Depreciation is a cost because it recognises value used. Where fixed assets do not depreciate there is no cost.

Accountants and costs

The day-to-day records of the business (the ledger accounts) can be used to provide important information about present performance, and can also be used as a basis upon which to forecast the future.

- The financial accountant will report the past performance of the business to those who have a right to know, the stakeholders. We will look at these reports in Chapter 14.
- The management accountant will provide internal information for the benefit of business managers. This will help them plan for the future, exercise control over the business and make effective decisions.

If we assume that the aim of a business is to make a profit, then there are two main elements which managers can work on:

increasing SALES REVENUE (unit price × quantity sold) controlling COST

In this chapter we will look at how management accountants can calculate costs and use these in making pricing decisions. We will also see that realistic market information is necessary in making such decisions, i.e. we need to know the expected quantity of sales at different prices.

Classification of costs by type

Costs can be classified in a number of ways depending upon how they are to be used. Here we will look at classification by type; later we will look at classification by behaviour.

Types of cost

Direct costs

These are the costs directly associated with the production of a good or service; they arise only because that good or service is being produced. Direct costs consist of:

- **direct materials** – these are the raw materials used in manufacture. For example, wood is a direct material in the manufacture of tables and chairs. For a wholesaler or retailer, direct materials are the stock purchased for resale.
- **direct labour** – this represents the cost of wages paid to those who actually manufacture, assemble or finish the completed item, for example, production workers. Alternatively it is the cost of those actually providing a service.
- **direct expenses** – this is a general heading under which direct costs other than direct materials and direct labour are listed. Examples are royalties paid to the inventor of a product who holds patent rights, hire of machinery used specifically to make a particular product and the cost of production work which is subcontracted out to another business, such as specialist finishing or artwork.

Total direct cost is called **prime cost**.

Indirect costs (overheads):

These are all costs which cannot be classified as direct. They can be subdivided into:

- **manufacturing overheads** (also called production overheads or factory overheads). These are the general costs of running the production process; they cannot be directly identified with any particular goods produced. Included are: indirect labour such as supervisors, general labourers, maintenance and cleaning staff, indirect materials such as cleaning materials, also factory power, rent, light and heat, and depreciation of factory machinery.

- **non-manufacturing overheads** – these include the cost of running the warehouse and the office. They can be sub-divided into:
  administrative costs: salaries of office staff, directors, accountants etc. and office costs including light, heat, rent and rates, depreciation of office equipment.
  sales and distribution costs: salesforce salaries and commission, advertising, carriage out, i.e. wages of drivers, petrol and vehicle maintenance and depreciation.
  finance costs: bank charges, loan and debenture interest and bad debts.

Worked example

Watts Electrical Ltd is a small company producing a single product, the LA Light Bulb. Last year the company produced 125,000 such bulbs. Their costs are shown below:

Cost statement of Watts Electrical Ltd. for the year ending 31 December 19-7

	£	£	£
SALES			400,000
less DIRECT COSTS:			
Materials (£0.64 × 125,000)		80,000	
Labour (£0.72 × 125,000)		90,000	
Royalties (£0.08 × 125,000)		10,000	
Prime cost		180,000	
less OVERHEADS			
Production			
Plant depreciation	5,000		
Maintenance	10,000		
Rent and rates (4/5)	20,000		
Wages and salaries	30,000		
		65,000	
Administration			
Salaries	17,000		
Rent and rates (1/5)	5,000		
Telephone	2,500		
Postage and stationery	1,500		
		26,000	
Sales and distribution			
Advertising	4,000		
Salaries/commission	20,000		
Vehicle expenses	3,000		
Carriage out	1,000		
		28,000	
Finance costs			
Bank interest	700		
Hire purchase interest	300		
		1,000	
TOTAL COST			300,000
PROFIT (Sales – Total cost)			100,000

Notice that:

- if details were not required the cost of the operation could be summarised as:

		£
	Direct cost	180,000
add	Overheads	120,000
	Total cost	300,000

- direct costs can be stated as a cost per unit produced (for example, materials cost £0.64 per unit)
- overheads represent a cost for a time period (for example salaries cost £17,000 p.a.)
- as all units are identical the cost per unit is: £300,000 cost/125,000 units = £2.40 per unit
- some overheads relate to the whole organisation and may need to be apportioned (shared) between two or more functions. In this example rent and rates are apportioned 4/5 factory and 1/5 office.
- grouping of overheads. Management will group overheads so as to give the most relevant information. Possible headings other than those used here include:
  establishment costs – the costs of running the buildings
  employment costs – staff training, National Insurance, canteens, medical/first-aid
  depreciation – sometimes all depreciation is grouped under a single heading. (Some of the business planning guides produced by the clearing banks suggest this.)

Activities

1 Using the figures from Watts Electrical make the following calculations.
  a The inventor wishes to know the percentage royalty paid on sales.
  b The production manager wishes to know:
    (i) the total cost of production for the year (i.e. excluding non-manufacturing overheads)
    (ii) the unit cost of production (remember 125,000 units are produced).

2 a Briefly explain the meaning of the terms capital expense and depreciation.
  b Give three examples of revenue expenses and capital expenses that an airline might have.

3 Z-CALC manufactures a single product, the ZC calculator. The figures below are available at the end of the first financial year ending 30 April 19-6:

Units manufactured	20,000 pa
Direct materials	£0.80 per unit
Direct labour	£1.00 per unit
Factory overheads	£4,000 pa
Administration overheads	£40,000 pa

The calculator was priced at £4.50 per unit and all units produced have been sold.
  a Using Watts Electrical as a guide, you are asked to set out a statement for the year showing:
    - total sales revenue
    - costs itemised as direct and indirect costs
    - the profit.
  b Assuming that all units are identical, calculate the cost per unit.

Forecasting costs

Forecast cost statements use the same general structure as statements used for reporting on past events.

Where a business wishes to forecast its costs it needs reliable data. Forecast figures will come from the following.

Direct materials

- Buyers, who will know the current prices of supplies and whose job it is to negotiate the best terms
- Production department, who will calculate the quantity of raw materials required for a job

> For a particular job or time period:
> direct cost = cost per unit × quantity used

Direct labour

- Personnel section, who will know current wage rates
- Management services (often with the aid of consultants) who conduct work surveys – these determine the optimum times needed for the efficient completion of jobs

> For a particular job or time period:
> direct labour cost = hourly wage rate × hours worked

Overheads

- Past experience with allowances made for differences in inflation, interest rates and production levels.

Standard cost

The expected labour, material or overhead cost per unit achievable under efficient working conditions is called the **standard cost**. Such costs are used as the basis for job estimates and for setting budgets.

Budgets

Budgets are forecasts for a future time peiod. They may be:

- financial, for example sales revenues and costs (in £s)
- quantitative, for example sales and output levels (in units)..

Budgets can be used as targets to aim for (sales) or limits not to be exceded (costs).

Variances

In time budgeted figures will be compared with what actually happens and where differences arise these will be analysed. **Variance** analysis is one of the techniques by which management can control the costs of the business.

Variances may be:

- **unfavourable** (or adverse), that is, actual cost is higher than budgeted cost or actual revenue is lower
- **favourable**, that is, actual cost is lower than budgeted cost or actual revenue is higher.

In Chapter 13 we will examine variances in the cash flow forecast.

Activities

1 JJ Ltd manufacture a single product, 'J-Clean', a new wonder cleaner promoted under the slogan 'It's J for genius!'

a Using the following figures which have been forecast for the six months ending 31 March 19–7 prepare a statement to show:

- sales revenue
- direct costs
- prime cost
- indirect costs (grouped under appropriate headings)
- total costs
- profit.

It is estimated that 100 000 units will be produced and sold.

Sales	£2 per unit
Purchases of raw materials	43p per unit
Direct labour	20p per unit
Direct expenses	5p per unit
Wages and salaries (2/3 factory 1/3 office)	£15,000
Factory power	£2,000
Rent and rates (3/4 factory, 1/4 office)	£8,000
Factory maintenance	£3,000
Light and heat (3/4 factory, 1/4 office)	£4,000
Depreciation of factory machinery	£2,000
Depreciation of vehicles	£1,000

b Calculate the cost of one unit.

2 Melanie Clarke has just set up a small bakery called Crispo Ltd. She supplies local outlets such as restaurants, sandwich bars and delicatessens. The following information is estimated for the first six months of business ending 30 April 19–7:

- Purchases of materials such as flour and yeast used in the baking process total £7,200
- Rates for the period are £1,200 (90% bakery, 10% office)
- Rent for the period is £3,000 (90% bakery, 10% office)
- Depreciation is estimated at: mixing equipment and ovens £400
  computer used for administration £200
- Wages: assistant baker £5,000
  part-time secretary/book-keeper £3,000
- Melanie pays a local firm to make daily deliveries to outlets. Cost will be £3,200
- General administration costs (telephone, stationery etc.) are £400
- Electricity used in the bakery £2,000

a Decide how each of the items will be classified by type (i.e. direct or indirect).

b Produce a clearly itemised statement to show forecast costs for the period. This should include:

- direct costs
- prime cost
- indirect costs (grouped under appropriate headings)
- total indirect cost
- total cost

Case study

Monitoring costs – calculating variances

Pronto Printers are asked to give a business client an estimate for a printing job. The firm base their estimates on standard costs and management have a system for monitoring the accuracy of all estimates.

ESTIMATE FOR JOB NO. 144

	Estimate (based on standard cost)	Actual (actual cost)	Variance
£	£	£	
Direct Materials			
A4 paper	12.00	15.00	3.00 ADV
Printing Plates	18.00	18.00	-
Direct Labour:			
Printing	60.00	56.00	4.00 FAV
Finishing	20.00	36.00	16.00 ADV
PRIME COST	110.00	125.00	15.00 ADV
Overheads Absorbed	140.00	140.00	-
TOTAL COST	250.00	265.00	
PRICE (including 50% mark-up on cost)	375.00	375.00	
PROFIT	125.00	110.00	15.00 ADV

Key FAV = Favourable
ADV = Adverse (unfavourable)

In this case the actual costs have been higher than the estimate. A price of £375 was quoted to the customer who commissioned the job on the basis of this. Whatever the actual costs the customer will pay only the estimated price. As a result of the higher than expected actual costs, the printer will suffer a reduced profit.

Activities

Before answering look back to the section on forecasting costs.

1 Which variances would management be concerned about?
2 Make two suggestions as to why each of the variances above may have occurred.
3 Are all of the adverse variances avoidable?
4 Who is responsible?

Cost units

What is a unit of production?

A unit of production is referred to by accountants as a **cost unit**. This is the basic product or service for which a cost is required. Normally a cost unit is the final product that is sold, but where a product is complex it may be a part of this and where a product is very small it may be a batch.

Examples of cost units are:

Business	Cost unit
Car manufacturer	Car – but broken down into wiring, spraying processes etc., engine, body components, etc.
Tailor	Suit
Solicitor	Consultation
Printer	Job
Football club	Game
Paper manufacturer	Ream (516 sheets)

How do we calculate unit cost?

When calculating the cost of a good or service the producer will usually need to take both price and quantity into account. For example:

material cost = units used × price per unit
labour cost = hours taken × rate per hour

Overheads will need to be apportioned in some way.

Remember that most businesses sell services rather than goods. Here the cost of a job will be based upon unit of service. For example a hairdresser, a systems analyst and a physiotherapist sell their time (in direct labout hours), airlines and coach operators sell passenger/miles.

Activity

Select the correct answers for questions 1–4 from the box below:

1 What is the basic cost unit sold by:
  a your local gas supplier?
  b British Telecom?
  c a solicitor?
2 When your car is serviced your bill consists of parts and labour. What unit of service is the garage selling? (How is the labour section calculated?)
3 In what units does a hotel measure monthly occupancy rates?
4 A railway may need to compare the cost of carrying passengers on two different routes. What units can it use?

Answers (not in order):
labour hours (answers two questions); passenger/miles; guest/nights, call unit, kilowatt hours (kWh)

Absorption costing (also called full or total costing)

Where a cost per unit is calculated to include (absorb) indirect costs as well as direct costs it is called the absorption cost.

Absorption cost = direct cost + indirect cost

How do we calculate absorption cost per unit?

Manufacturing business. Earlier in the chapter (see page 549) we calculated unit cost for Watts Electrical by simply dividing total cost by total production. This was the absorption cost. Remember that:

$$\text{Unit cost} = \frac{\text{direct cost (£180,000) + indirect cost (£120,000)}}{\text{Production (125,000 units)}} = \text{£2.40 per unit}$$

Alternatively, where direct costs are already given as a unit cost these can simply be listed. It is then only necessary to calculate the overhead per unit. For example, for Watts Electrical:

		£	
Direct cost per unit:	materials	0.64	already given
	labour	0.72	
	royalties	0.08	
	prime cost	1.44	
Overhead per unit		0.96	(£120,000 overhead/125,000 units)
Absorption (total) cost per unit		2.40	

Note

- It should be stressed that sharing costs equally between units in this way is only appropriate where a business produces a single, standard product so that each unit really does have an identical cost. (In practice most businesses produce a range of different products which will have different unit costs. For the purposes of this unit, however, it is assumed that manufacturers produce a single product.)
- Sometimes a business is interested specifically in total production cost. In this case absorption cost refers to direct cost + manufacturing overheads (i.e. it does not include non-manufacturing overheads). These businesses will need to set a price that covers administration as well as profit.

Providers of service

Many businesses, for example, a car mechanic or a hairdresser, provide what appears to be a single service. However, these are unlikely to provide an identical car repair or haircut for every customer. The solution is to recognise that what service providers usually sell is their time. If we can calculate the cost of each hour we can calculate the cost of providing a particular service on the basis of the time it takes.

Example: Chris Cross is a plumber who employs one assistant. For the coming year her estimates are:

- overheads £12,000 per annum
- 3,000 direct labour hours (DLH) to be worked
- she pays her assistant £8 per hour.

A job has come in for which she estimates 2 hours labour and £20 raw materials. What is the cost of the job?

Stage 1:
The direct cost is directly related to the job and provides no problem: materials £20, labour 2 hours @ £8.

Stage 2:
Charging for overheads – the recovery rate
Chris must include a charge to cover overheads such as rent, rates and telephone bills. Overheads will be £12,000 this year, but how much of this applies to this job?
The solution is to calculate the overhead cost of each direct labour unit (DLH). We divide the overheads by hours instead of by units:

$$\text{The overhead recovery rate} = \frac{\text{£12,000 Overheads pa}}{\text{3,000 DLH pa}} = \text{£4 per DLH}$$

The overhead in each job is £4 for every DLH worked.
In this case it is £4 per DLH × 2 DLH = £8

Job cost statement	**£**	
Direct cost:		
materials	20	
labour	16	(£8 × 2 hours)
	36	
add overheads	8	(£4 recovery rate × 2 DLH)
Total (absorption) cost	44	

Setting a price (using cost-plus pricing):
Chris aims to make a profit of 25% on cost. The price she charges is therefore:

		£	
	Total Cost	44	COST
add	25% for profit	11	+ PROFIT
	Price charged to customer	55	= PRICE

Although Chris is setting a price in order to make a profit, there are limits. For instance she must be aware of what competitors charge and what customers are prepared to pay. One way in which firms retain their profit margins in a competitive market is by cutting costs rather than raising prices.

The customer's invoice

The calculations above are for Chris' own use. Usually anything other than materials (overheads and profit in this case) will be included in labour. The invoice to the customer will therefore normally include:

Date:	12th December 199–	
Customer	Ms Kay Pinnock 5 Red Hill SE 16 4BMW	
Details of the Job:	To fit new tap	
		£
Charge:	Materials:	20.00
	Labour:	35.00
	Total (excl VAT)	55.00

Process costing and job costing

Process costing

Manufacturers such as Watts Electrical will have a production line turning out identical products. Here the production process is costed so that a unit cost is calculated. This cost will be the same for each unit produced.

Job costing

Where a 'one-off' job is provided, as with Chris Cross, this must be costed as an individual item. Perhaps a customer wants a tailor-made suit or a specially designed machine or an oil tanker. Similarly some trades always perform services for customers on an individual basis. A printer, a mechanic or a funeral director, for example, all work to the individual requirements of their customers. Each job is unique and bears a different cost.

Activities

1 Peak Performance Cycles (PPC) assemble mountain bikes using components bought in from Taiwan. Next year they will produce only one model, the Ranger. Estimated details are:

Unit costs	The Ranger
Direct materials	£50
Direct labour (paid @ £8 per hour)	1 direct labour hour
Estimated production pa	5,000 units

Overheads are estimated at £40,000 pa.

- **a** What is a cost unit for this business?
- **b** Explain why cost per unit can be calculated by simply dividing total costs p.a. by units produced.
- **c** Calculate the total cost of operations for the coming year.
- **d** Set out budgeted cost statement to show the unit cost of the Ranger.
- **e** Calculate the total cost of operations for the coming year.
- **f** The business aims to make a profit of 50% on cost. Set a price for the Ranger.
- **g** There are rumours that Craggs & Co, a competitor, is about to launch a Ranger lookalike model for £90. Explain whether this will affect PPC's pricing strategy.

2 Albert Sparks is an electrician who works an average 30-hour week for 45 weeks in the year. He estimates that his overheads for the coming year will be £5000.

- **a** Calculate the annual number of direct labour hours (DLH) Albert will work next year.
- **b** Use this answer to calculate the overhead recovery rate per DLH.

A contractor has offered Albert an electrical wiring job. Albert estimates that:

- materials will cost him £200 for the job
- the job will take 8 hours
- he costs his time at £10 per hour.

- **c** Set out the budgeted job cost showing the direct cost, indirect cost and total cost of the job.
- **d** Albert aims to make £200 profit on the job. Calculate the price to the customer. Show the invoice (number AS/35) that Albert will give to the customer, Shepherd and Thorn Ltd. Use today's date.

Activities

1 Winston's Wheels, which is located in a new industrial estate in Redcar, deals with general motor repairs and has just opened a crash repair department. Occasionally some of the cars have electrical faults that Winston cannot deal with. In this case he subcontracts the work to an electrical specialist in the next unit.

Budgeted works overheads for the coming year are:

	£
Rent and rates	11,500
Light and heat	5,000
Depreciation	2,500
Insurance: Equipment	2,100
Supervisory salaries	12,000
Cleaning material for washroom	500

All direct labour is paid at £8 per hour.
30 per cent is added to works cost to cover administration and profit.

It is estimated that 12,000 labour hours will be worked during the year.

a Is process costing or job costing appropriate to Winston's business?
b calculate an overhead recovery rate for the year using direct labour hours
c prepare a statement to show the cost of the first two jobs of the year from the details below.

	Job 1	**Job 2**
Customer	**Mr D L Sayers**	**Mr M Chang**
Fault:	Engine misfiring	Dented wing and bonnet, broken lights
Work:	retune fit new plugs and points	Fit new wing and respray
Time (in DLH)	2 hours	8 hours
Parts:	£12	£85
Subcontracted:	none	£35 (trace lighting fault and rewire)

d Draw up the invoices (numbers WW/1 and WW/2) to be given to each customer today. They will show:
- customer details
- description of work done
- parts cost
- labour cost (which will include labour and all other costs)
- subtotal
- VAT
- total due.

2 The Oval Cricket Ball Company is a well-established manufacturing concern run by the May family in Kennington in South London. The company buys in leather, cork, thread and polish, and employs a small workforce to produce a single model of cricket ball called the 'May Ball'. This is distributed to outlets around the country.

The factory and stores take up 75 per cent of the building, the sales and administrative staff work from the office which accounts for the remaining 25 per cent of the space.

Budgeted figures for the year ending 30 June 19–6 are:

Direct costs

leather, thread, cork	£5 per ball
cutting, and sewing, finishing and polishing	£10 per hour
royalty paid to holder of patent	2% per ball (on sales price)

Indirect costs

works supervisor's salary	£15,000 p.a.
rent and rates (to be apportioned 75% factory, 25% office)	£40,000 p.a.
administrative salaries	£30,000 p.a.
finance charges (loans interest and bank charges)	£10,000 p.a.
sales and distribution costs (advertising, sales force salaries)	£30,000 p.a.

Additional information:
Each ball takes half an hour to make
Market research shows that forecast sales are 50,000 units for the year
These sales can be achieved only if a maximum price of £14 per ball is charged to outlets

You are requested by management to:

a produce a budgeted operating statement for the year
b calculate the cost per unit (per cricket ball)
c advise whether it will be profitable to sell at the projected price.

Uses and limitations of absorption costing

Absorption costing is useful in stable conditions where we are fairly certain that we will meet planned production (and sales) levels, or where we are concerned to analyse past results. It also allows a price-fixing business to determine unit cost and to set a profitable price by adding a reasonable level of profit (cost-plus pricing).

However, absorption costing has certain disadvantages when used for forecasting:

- in order to estimate unit cost we need to know what our level of production will be (whether in units or DLH). This is not always easy. Where market conditions are uncertain or where we wish to examine the possibility of extra production, the level of production may be uncertain.
- where prices are market led we cannot simply set a price to give profit. Here we will have to accept the ruling market price and concentrate instead on finding the most profitable level of production.

In such circumstances firms often use an alternative form of costing called marginal costing. For this we need to understand how costs behave as output changes.

Classification of costs by behaviour

As well as classifying costs by type, we can also classify them by behaviour.

It is important when forecasting costs to recognise that not all costs behave in the same way as production levels change.

Variable costs

Variable costs change in proportion to the level of production. The direct costs of materials, labour and direct expenses are usually regarded as variable costs. If we produce more units we need more raw materials and we must pay our direct labour more for the extra time required. Variable costs can be expressed as a cost per unit. For a given level of output:

Variable cost = unit cost x output

Although direct costs are usually assumed to be variable, in practice this is not always so. Labour costs do not always double if production doubles.

Neither employment law nor the labour market will allow us to hire and fire in immediate response to changes in demand (though as we noted in Chapter 4, employers are trying to gain more flexibility by using short-term contracts of employment).

Fixed costs

Fixed costs do not change with the level of production. Most overheads are assumed to be fixed. We will need to pay rent and rates, salaries and finance costs regardless of how much we produce. If we produce more, the rent will not increase, if we close for a holiday the rent will still need to be paid.

It is important to recognise that fixed costs are fixed only over the short term and over a certain range of production. If we take rent as an example:

- Rent may be £5,000 for the year, but next year we will have to pay again.
- The cost of rent is for a certain size of operation. If we get extra orders and need to expand into larger premises then the rent will increase.

Where fixed costs change they do so in leaps. An extra building or an extra supervisor will incur immediate costs. The fixed cost line on Figure 12.2 (page 561) increases in a step-like fashion. In contrast the variable costs display a smooth slope as they change in proportion to production levels.

Semi-variable costs

Semi-variable costs are partly fixed and partly variable. In practice many overheads are semi-variable; they respond to production levels, but do not change in proportion to these levels. Sales and distribution costs may be semi-variable; the sales force would probably be paid a basic salary but with some sort of commission payable for extra sales. The salary is fixed, the commission is variable. A more familiar example is a telephone bill. Here there is a charge for each unit used plus a fixed rental for the use of the equipment.

Semi-variable costs would have a similar appearance on a graph to the total cost line, which is the fixed and variable costs combined.

In order to make forecast costings it is necessary to classify costs as either fixed or variable. Semi-variable costs must therefore be broken down into their fixed and variable components.

Example

The behaviour of fixed and variable costs

The students' union have some spare money and decide to run a free trip to Wales on a 40-seater coach. A ticket to the Swansea arena, costing £5, will be provided for each passenger. The students have already paid out for the coach hire and it is too late to cancel. The costs are:

- Fixed cost (overheads): Coach hire £300
- Variable cost: Arena ticket £5 per head.

For different numbers of students the costs will be:

Student numbers:	0	10	20	30	40	41*	50	60	70	80
	£	£	£	£	£	£	£	£	£	£
Variable Cost (@ £5 per head)	0	50	100	150	200	205	250	300	350	400
Fixed Cost	300	300	300	300	300	600	600	600	600	600
Total Cost	300	350	400	450	500	805	850	900	950	1000
Cost per unit (£)		35	20	15	12.50	19.63	17	15	13.57	12.50

The greater the number of students the less each student will cost. This is because as numbers grow fixed costs are being shared between a greater number. This changes when we reach full capacity, that is, when the bus is full. If we wish to expand the operation (hire another bus) then fixed costs will increase.

*It would be relatively expensive to carry 41 students as a new bus would be required for the extra passenger.

The costs can be illustrated on a graph.

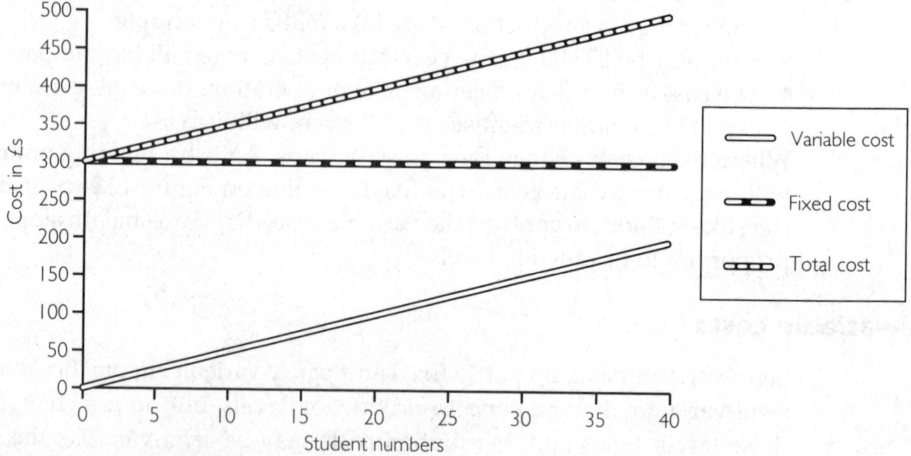

Figure 12.1 Student coach trip to Wales (one coach needed)

In Figure 12.1, the fixed cost (the coach hire) remains at £300 regardless of the number of students.

The variable cost increases at the rate of £5 per student.

The total cost combines the fixed and variable cost. Total cost always begins at fixed cost as this is the only cost at zero output. Thereafter it rises by the amount of the variable cost.

Notice that even if no students go there is a cost of £300.

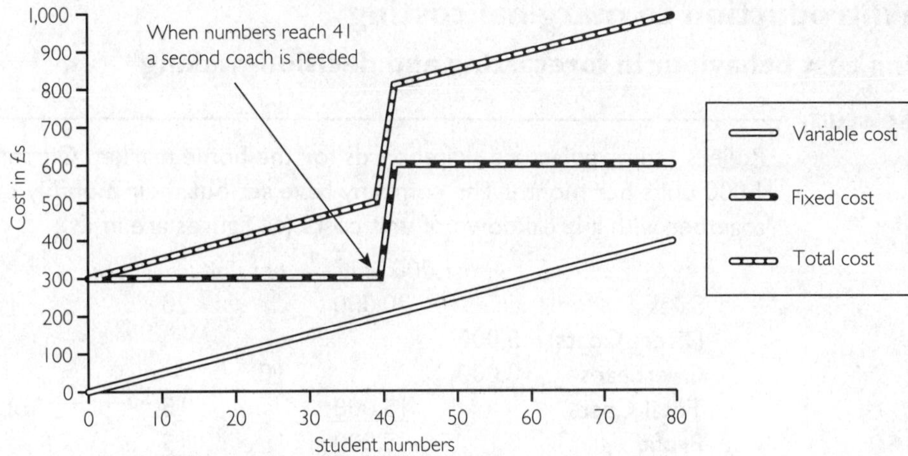

Figure 12.2 Student coach trip to Wales (two coaches needed)

Figure 12.2 shows that once there are more than 40 students, we exceed our present capcity and need to expand operations (hire another coach).

Variable costs still rise in proportion to student numbers, by £5 a student. Fixed costs now step upwards from £300 to £600 when numbers reach 41. Thereafter they will remain at £600 until the second coach is full and a third is required.

Total costs once again combine fixed and variable costs.

Case study

Donald Trump's airline service ran executive shuttle flights between major cities in the USA. As well as providing luxurious facilities he claimed that he would carry every passenger on the flight for which they had booked. If this meant running a plane just for one passenger then he claimed that he would do it.

Trump's business affairs ran into financial difficulties; his shuttle service is now part of US Air.

Activity

1 The students discover that they will after all need to charge for the trip in order to cover costs. No one can afford more than £15 and around 50 students have shown a definite interest; there may be others but you are not sure.
  a Look again at page 560 (cost per unit). How many students should you take?
  b Give clear cost statements to support your conclusions.

2 Why do you think management are interested in knowing which costs are fixed and which are variable?

3 Identify what you consider to be the fixed and variable costs for each of the following:
- The owner of a campsite in Bognor Regis
- A shopkeeper
- An electrician
- A manufacturer of tennis racquets.

An introduction to marginal costing

Using cost behaviour in forecasting and decision-making

Case study

Rollers Ltd manufacture skateboards for the home market. Currently production is at 1,000 units per month. The company have set out their monthly operating budget together with a breakdown of unit costs (all figures are in £s):

		1,000 units		*per unit*	
Sales		20,000		20	
Direct Costs	5,000		5		
Overheads	10,000		10		
Total Costs		15,000		15	← total unit cost
Profit		5,000		5	

Rollers have been pushing hard to break into Europe and finally a salesperson comes up with an order from Paris. The good news is that the order is for 200 boards per month, the problem is that the customer is prepared to pay only £12 per board. Should Rollers Ltd take the offer?

On the face of it, since the unit cost of each board is £15, they would be losing money. However, this is not necessarily so. Remember that the overheads are mainly fixed costs and that these will, by definition, not change if we produce more. We need therefore only worry about the direct costs, which are variable. The new order will have the following effect:

		per unit		*200 units*	
Sales		12		2 400	(£12 x 200)
Direct Costs	5		1,000		(£5 x 200)
Overheads	0		0		
Total costs		5		1,000	
Profit		7		1,400	

The order is profitable.

There are three questions that the firm must ask before going ahead, however.

1 Can it produce the extra skateboards within existing capacity? If not then it will need to expand and fixed costs will rise after all. (Remember the students on the coach!)

2 Will this order affect existing sales? Presumably it will not as it is going abroad. However, if it were for the home market and existing customers heard of it they might also want a reduction in price. The lower price is only possible because the existing customers are covering fixed costs by paying a higher price.

3 Is the profit enough to justify the effort? The answer to this may well depend upon whether there is a better alternative use of resources available.

Point 2 is very important. If everyone pays £12 the business loses out:

		1,200 units	
Sales		14,400	(£12 x 1 200)
Direct Costs	6,000		(£5 x 1 200)
Overheads	10,000		
		16,000	
Loss		(1,600)	

Marginal costing – an explanation

What has happened is that the original (absorption) costing had to take account of the total costs of the operation, including the fixed costs.

The French order is a new factor and is costed by a different method, known as **marginal costing**. The operation is already up and running, and the fixed costs already exist. The only question is whether the income from the new order will exceed the (variable) costs which it involves.

Marginal costing allows us to look at profits over different levels of output and sales, and to decide whether it is worth making extra output. If, as in this case, fixed costs will not vary, they can be ignored. The examination of costs and profits over different levels of output is called cost/volume/profit analysis.

The marginal cost statement is usually set out as follows:

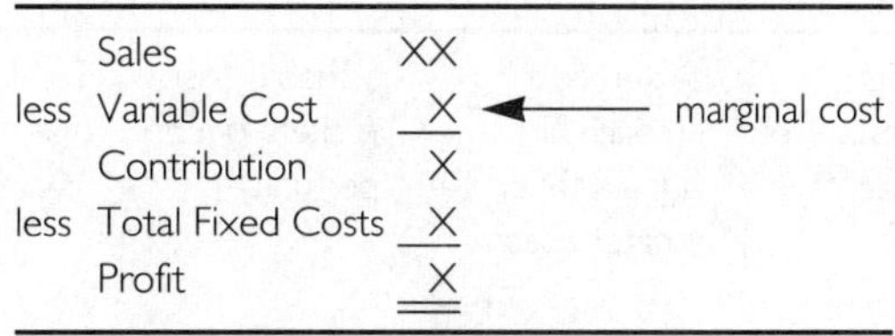

Marginal cost is the cost of making one more unit.
Contribution is: Sales – Variable cost
Contribution initially contributes towards fixed cost. When fixed cost is paid for then contribution becomes profit.

When assessing a project the question to ask is 'Are we better off as a result?' Where fixed costs exist already, a project with a positive contribution is generally seen as worth taking up. It will contribute something to fixed costs and therefore at least cut down the losses. Where a decision is to be taken about setting up a new project, then forecasts will need to show that this will actually be profitable.

Marginal costing versus absorption costing

Marginal costing and absorption costing are useful for different purposes.

Absorption costing shows the total cost of a good or service including overheads. In doing this it enables us to calculate a profitable selling price for each unit. However, since the overheads in an individual unit of production vary for different production levels, absorption costing can only be used if we are able to estimate that level. It can be used to set the budget under normal operating conditions and also to report on past periods.

Marginal costing examines how costs and profits will change over a range of production and is useful for short-term decision-making. It is used when new situations occur or where we wish to set a level of output. Marginal costing will allow us to look at the effect of changes to the budget such as additional orders and to calculate the break-even point.

The break-even point (BEP)

The **break-even point** (BEP) is the level of production and sales at which costs and sales revenues are equal so that there is neither a profit nor a loss. When examining a new project a business will want to know this point as it represents the 'fall-back position' below which it will make a loss. Once the break-even point has been achieved every new sale will bring a profit.

The break-even point can be either calculated or shown graphically.

Example

The students decide that their trip to Wales (see page 560) can only go ahead if they are able to cover costs. They will charge £15 per head and take one 40-seater coach only. The relevant data can be set out in table form:

Units (number of students)	Fixed cost (coach hire @ £300 per 40-seater coach	Variable cost (tickets @ £5 per unit)	Total cost (fixed cost + variable cost)	Sales revenue (@ £15 per unit)	Profit/(loss) (Sales revenue – Total cost)
	£	£	£	£	£
0	300	0	300	0	(300)
10	300	50	350	150	(200)
20	300	100	400	300	(100)
30	300	150	450	450	0
40	300	200	500	600	100

Notice that

- if less than 30 students travel there is a loss
- if 30 students travel the trip will break-even (Cost = Revenue and Profit/(loss) = 0)
- if more than 30 students travel there is a profit.

The break-even graph

The break-even point can be shown by plotting the total cost and sales revenue data on a graph (Figure 12.3). The break-even point is where these lines cut. It is usual also to show the fixed cost line.

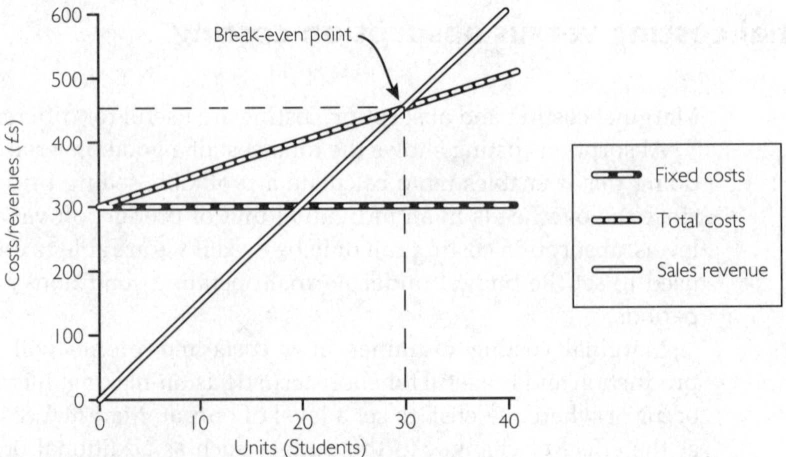

Figure 12.3 Break-even graph for student trip to Wales (also called the cost/volume/profit graph)

The break-even point is shown in two ways:

- on the x axis as 30 units (i.e. 30 seats on the bus sold)
- on the y axis as £450 revenue.

The break-even point can be calculated as follows (notice that it is based on marginal costing techniques):

Stage 1		£ per unit	
	Sales	15	each student pays £15
less	Variable cost	5	£5 is required to pay for the ticket that is provided
	Contribution	10	this leaves £10 to contribute towards the fixed costs

Stage 2 The question is how many £10 do we need to cover the £300 fixed costs?

$$\text{BEP} = \frac{\text{Fixed cost}}{\text{Unit contribution}} = \frac{300}{10} = 30 \text{ units (students)}$$

If we wish to calculate the revenue needed: BEP = 30 seats × £15 = £450

The margin of safety

It would be unwise for the students to go ahead if estimated sales are 30 tickets. All forecasts are liable to be inexact and if they are only one short there will be a loss. It is usual to have a margin of safety, so that a small shortfall will not bring an immediate loss. If, for example, they aim to fill the bus then there is a margin of safety of 10 tickets, or £150. They can fall 10 short of the target and still break even.

The margin of safety is the amount by which the forecast sales exceed the break-even point (Figure 12.4).

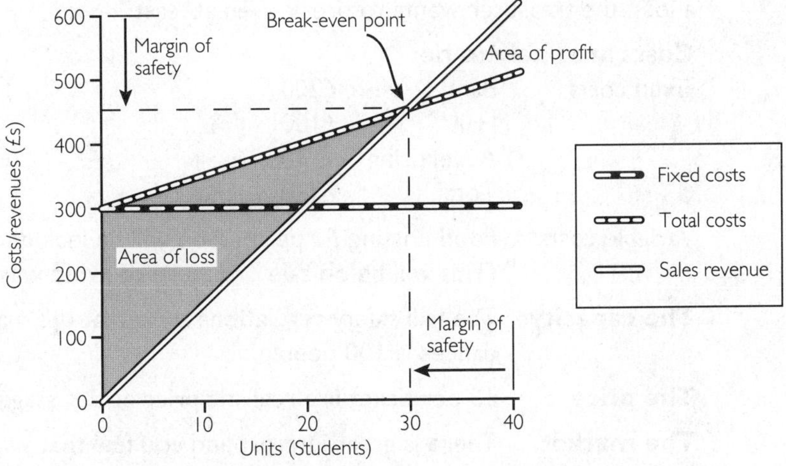

Figure 12.4 Break-even graph for student trip to Wales, showing the margin of safety

Activity

1 Read off the following on the graph:
   a Sales revenue at 10 students; at 25 students
   b Total costs at 10 students; 25 students.
2 What will be the margin of safety if 36 passengers are estimated?
3 What will be the fixed costs if only 1 seat is sold; if 29 seats are sold?

Drawing a break-even graph

The axes:
The x axis (horizontal) represents units produced, or output
The y axis (vertical) represents costs and revenues in £s

The scale:
The x axis extends from zero to the maximum number of units of output
The y axis extends from zero to the cost or revenue at maximum sales, whichever is the higher
The scale for each axis should be rounded up the nearest convenient number where necessary, for example if the maximum revenue is £56,470, then draw the scale up to £60,000

Plotting:
Plot three lines: Fixed cost, Total cost, Total revenue (sales)
Since all lines are straight it is necessary to plot only the first and last point on each line. Joining these two points will produce the line
The two points to plot are: cost or revenue at zero units and cost or revenue at maximum units
The fixed cost line is not strictly necessary but is useful in that it provides the starting point for the total cost line.

Activities

Break dance

You wish to run a student dance to celebrate the end of term break. The aim is to have a good time, rather than to make money. However, you cannot afford to run at a loss; the treasurer wants to break-even at least.

Costs are likely to be:

Fixed costs:	Band	£200
	Hall	£100
	Advertising	£ 30
	Total	£330

Variable costs: Food costing £2 per person will be included in the ticket price. (This will be on sale or return to avoid waste.)

The capacity: The hall safety regulations state that the maximum allowed for dances is 100 people.

The price £5 per ticket is a realistic price at this stage of the year.

The market: There is great interest and you feel that you can fill the hall.

Problem: How many people do you need to break-even?

1 Calculate
  a the unit contribution
  b the break-even point in tickets to be sold
  c the break-even point in revenue required.

2 Explain why the dance should not go ahead as planned.

As you have no intention of abandoning the end of term dance you call a meeting to discuss matters.

The alternatives discussed are:	*Your conclusions are:*
cutting costs – different band, cheaper food, cheaper advertising	all of these are possible
charging more – £5 is the most that people will pay	not possible
find a larger hall – the only other one is far more expensive	not possible

As the band you want is a big attraction you decide not to look for anyone cheaper. After some discussion it is agreed that you can cut the advertising down to £20 by doing some of the work yourselves; you also decide to provide less food per person. Revised costs are: Fixed costs £320; Variable costs £1 per person.

3 Repeat calculations as in **1** above.

4 Calculate the margin of safety:
   a in tickets
   b in revenue.

5 Draw a table of costs, revenues and profits/losses as on page 564. Units will run from 0 to 100 (in 20s).

6 Draw a break-even graph.

Activity

Break dance – cutting your losses

The plan to sell all tickets in advance has not been successful and the weather on the night of the dance is particularly bad. You manage to sell 77 tickets so that despite allowing a margin of safety you have not quite broken even.

At 11 p.m. three students turn up. They are only prepared to pay £2 to come in for the last hour. There is some food left. What do you say?

Remember:
In financial terms, as long as these students pay for their direct costs and provide some contribution you might as well have their money. In this case they each cost you £1, so as long as they pay more than this it is worth it. You will still not break-even, but every little contribution helps to pay the fixed costs. You will at least reduce the loss.

a Complete the figures below.
b Is it worth letting the three students in?
c What are the problems with letting some people in more cheaply than others?

Calculations:	77 tickets	extra 3	80 people
Sales (@ £5)	385		385
Sales (@ £2)		6	6
less Variable Cost @ £1)	?	?	?
Contribution	?	?	?
less Fixed Costs	?		?
Profit/(Loss)	?		?

Marginal costing leads us to the conclusion that, in financial terms, once a project has been set in motion and fixed costs incurred, then any sale with a positive contribution is worth having.

It is the practice of airlines on some routes to allow passengers on to flights more cheaply if they are prepared to wait around at the airport for a flight that is not fully booked. The reductions can be quite substantial, yet these passengers are sitting in identical seats to those who booked earlier and paid substantially more.

What is the thinking behind this?
Are both sets of passengers getting the same product for their money?

'Not bad for a pound!'
The quote was from Oldham Athletic manager Joe Royle after his team had beaten Wimbledon 6–2 in April 1993. In an attempt to draw in more support to help in the fight against relegation the club had reduced some ticket prices to £1.

The marginal cost of a well-behaved fan visiting the ground is zero, hence the club felt that it was a worthwhile experiment which would not only bring in support but would also bring in a little money.

In what way could Oldham have lost out financially by this policy?

Achieving a required profit — an adaptation of break-even

The decision as to whether to proceed with a project will often be based not just on whether it will be profitable but whether the likely profit is sufficient. Venture capitalists, for instance, may require 25 per cent on their capital before supporting a project.

The break-even calculation can be adapted slightly to show the production or revenue required to achieve a desired profit. All we need to do is add the required return to the fixed costs before making our calculation.

In our example of the trip to Wales we may have decided that we wished to make a profit of £50.

In this case: $\dfrac{\text{Fixed cost + required profit}}{\text{unit contribution}} = \dfrac{300 + 50}{10} = 35$ tickets

The Profit/Volume Graph

An alternative to the break-even graph is the profit/volume graph. This is producced from the same table of figures but here the 'units' and 'profit/(loss)' columns are used. The profit/volume graph for the student trip to Wales is shown below:

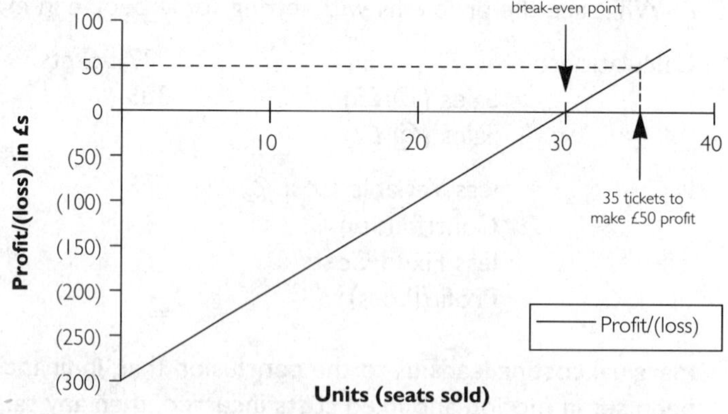

This graph can be used to illustrate profits at different levels of sales. The break-even point is where profit/(loss) is zero.

Activities

1 Arthur King, the proprietor of Camelot Coaches, runs tours to various destinations in the West Country. He currently has only one vehicle, a 50-seater deluxe model. This year he expects to run 50 tours and is in the process of costing one of these.

The Tintagel Tour lasts two days with an overnight stay in a guest house overlooking the cliffs of North Cornwall. The ticket price will include both the cost of accommodation and entrance to Tintagel island.

Projected costs for the tour are:

	Driver	£30 per day (for 2 days)
	Diesel	£70 for round trip
	Entrance to Tintagel island	£4 per person
	Accommodation	£20 per night per person
Additionally:	Coach maintenance, insurance, road tax and administrative costs	£30,000 pa
	(to be apportioned equally between the 50 tours)	

Arthur has found that a realistic price for this tour is £50 per person.

Arthur asks for your help in the following (you may use a spreadsheet model if it is available).

a Identify the fixed and variable costs involved in this tour

b Draw up a table to show the variable cost, fixed cost, total cost, revenue and profit for levels of sales between 0 and 50. Increment the sales in steps of 10.

c Calculate the break-even point for the tour in (i) number of seats to be sold and (ii) revenue.

d Draw a graph to show the break-even point for the tour. Read off (i) the number of seats that need to be sold to break-even, (ii) the revenue that needs to be made to break-even and (iii) calculate the break-even point as a percentage of the total number of seats available. Check your answers with **c** above.

e Assume that Arthur took 45 advance bookings and was prepared to accept a lower price for last-minute bookings in order to fill the coach. What would be the lowest profitable price that he could accept for the five remaining seats?

- Show your calculations and briefly explain your answer
- Explain any problems that could arise with this strategy.

2 If Arthur wished to make a profit of £400 on the tour, how many customers would he need?

a Calculate the answer

b Draw a profit/volume graph to illustrate this.

Assignment 12.1 Expansion in Ashford

This assignment develops knowledge and understanding of the following elements:
6.3 Calculate the cost of goods or services
6.4 Explain basic pricing decisions and break-even

It supports development of the following core skills:
Communication 3.2, 3.3, 3.4
Application of number 3.2, 3.3
Information technology 3.1, 3.2, 3.3

Z-Beds Ltd manufacture a single product, the Z-Bed Deluxe, a new high-tec camping bed guaranteed to give a good night's sleep.

A breakdown of last years figures is given in the opening statement below:

	£	£
Sales		500,000
Raw materials	100,000	
Production-line wages	150,000	
Subcontract work	25,000	
Administration	75,000	
Sales and distribution	60,000	
Finance	40,000	
		450,000
Profit		50,000

Note: 5,000 units were sold during the year.

Forecasts for the coming year indicate the following:

- sales volume will remain at 5,000 units despite a price increase of 5%
- raw material cost will rise by £2 per unit
- wage costs per unit on the production line will remain the same
- sub-contractors are increasing prices by 10% per unit
- There is likely to be a 4% rise in all overhead costs due to inflation.

Your tasks

1 The finance director has asked you to:

- Rewrite the operating statement above showing clearly: direct costs, indirect costs, total cost and profit.
- Draw up alongside this the budgeted operating statement for the coming year
- Calculate the absorption cost per unit for:
  a the past year
  b the coming year
- Attach these figures to a memo giving your comments on any significant differences between the budget and last year's figures. Indicate the percentage change in profit.

2 Draw a break-even graph for next year. Label the break-even point and the margin of safety. Attach a brief comment to explain the usefulness of the information shown.

3 An enquiry has been received from a large wholesaler. This company is prepared to pay £80 per bed for a special order of 1,000 beds. These will be in addition to the estimated 5,000 sales. Z-Beds Ltd have three alternatives:

a The present staff will work overtime to produce the extra beds within the existing premises. Costs will be as for normal production except that labour cost per unit will increase by 50% due to overtime payments.

b An adjoining workshop can be hired together with temporary staff. Direct costs will be as for normal production, extra overheads of £30,000 will be incurred.

c The company can turn down the order as unprofitable.

The marketing director would like the deal to go ahead and has asked you to:

- write an informal report recommending a suitable course of action.
  To support your recommendation you should attach statements to show the financial implications of alternatives (a) and (b).

You should mention additionally:

- any other factors which the company should take into account when considering this order
- why a price below normal production cost may be profitable for special orders.

Using a spreadsheet model to calculate break-even points

The spreadsheet model below can be used to calculate break-even points and the profit and loss at different levels of output. Extra formulae can be copied below row 15 as required.

	A	B	C	D	E	F	G	H	I
1		BREAK -EVEN MODEL							
2									
3	INPUT		Period	Unit		Unit			
4	BOX	Units in	Fixed	Variable		Sales			
5		steps	Costs £	Costs £		Revenue £			
6		20	320	1		5			
7									
8	OUTPUT	Units	Fixed	Variable	Total	Sales	Profit/	BREAK-EVEN POINT	
9	BOX		Costs £	Costs £	Costs £	Revenue £	(Loss) £	units:	=C6/(F6-D6)
10		0	=$C$6	=$D$6*B10	=c10+D10	=$F$6*B10	=F10-E10	£	=I9*F6
11		=B10+$B$6	=$C$6	=$D$6*B11	=c11+D11	=$F$6*B11	=F11-E11		
12		=B11+$B$6	=$C$6	=$D$6*B12	=c12+D12	=$F$6*B12	=F12-E12		
13		=B12+$B$6	=$C$6	=$D$6*B13	=c13+D13	=$F$6*B13	=F13-E13		
14		=B13+$B$6	=$C$6	=$D$6*B14	=c14+D14	=$F$6*B14	=F14-E14		
15		=B14+$B$6	=$C$6	=$D$6*B15	=c15+D15	=$F$6*B15	=F15-E15		

To set up the sheet: enter all formulae as shown and save.

To use the sheet: use the 'Input Box' only

It is necessary to enter only FOUR items of data:

- C6 period fixed costs
- D6 variable cost per unit
- F6 unit sales price
- B6 is used to determine the steps in which the units are spaced. For example:

20 will give: 0 20 40 60 80 100

100 will give: 0 100 200 300 400 500 and so on

The information in the 'Output Box' will be calculated automatically by the formulae shown.

A break-even graph can be produced by highlighting the columns headed 'units' (this is the x axis scale), 'fixed cost', 'total cost' and 'revenue'.

Activities

1 Set up the spreadsheet as above, check that it works and SAVE it under a suitable filename.
2 When you use the sheet from now on always save under a DIFFERENT filename. This will preserve the blank model as a starting point each time.
3 As practice, enter four items of data for the WELSH TRIP (row 6 on the spreadsheet). The table should appear as on page 564 (for this exercise delete row 15 as the coach cannot carry 50 people!).

   Produce a break-even graph like the one on page 564. You will need to highlight the columns headed 'units' (this is the *x*-axis scale), 'total costs', 'fixed costs' and 'sales'. It is more convenient if you can paste the graph below your table on the worksheet.

'What if?' scenarios

Spreadsheets are able to make rapid calculations. For this reason they are useful for looking at the likely consequences of different courses of action.

If we build the spreadsheet on page 571 then we examine alternative scenarios by simply changing the contents of cells: C6, D6 or F6. For example we can ask: what if variable costs rise by 10%? What if a competitor forces us to reduce our prices – can we still make a profit?

In each case the table will instantly display the new figures and the graph will illustrate them. If you have attempted the activity above, experiment by changing the sales and cost figures.

Activity

Break-even and 'what if?' analysis

This activity can be carried out manually though ideally you should use the spreadsheet model.

1 A course is arranged on 'Use of spreadsheet models in forecasting' at a local hotel. The room will cost £500 and the speaker has asked for a fee of £150 for the session. Additional costs include the hire of equipment for £50.

   Each client will be charged £45 for the session which will include coffee and biscuits on arrival and a buffet lunch. The organisers have arranged to pay the hotel £8 per head for providing this. In addition everyone attending will receive free of charge a folder of notes worth £2.

   As there are a limited number of computer workstations available numbers on the course will be limited to 25.

   a Use the spreadsheet to calculate the number of clients required for the course to break-even. Print out the results.

   b Produce and print a break-even chart to accompany your figures

   c Produce a profit/volume graph to show the profit over the possible range of attendance from 0 to 25 people. You will need to highlight the 'unit' and 'profit/loss' columns only.

   d Report the consequences of each of the following in turn and make recommendations, i.e. can we still go ahead? (After each scenario return to the original figures; assume in each case that nothing else changes.)

- What if the folders of notes cost £3 a person?
- What if a rival course is set up with a price of £40 per head? To keep your numbers you must match this price.
- What if you are offered an alternative room for £750 which holds 35 people? If there is demand, should you take this?

Using break-even to decide upon a production strategy – labour intensive v. capital intensive production

Sometimes a business will need to examine the implications of switching from a labour-intensive to a capital-intensive method of production. Cost/volume/profit calculaions can help to answer questions such as: What are the financial implications of investing in new equipment? Is it wise to make such an investment?

Example

The Light Programme Ltd produces a programmable security light suitable for domestic users. A unit price of £30 has been found to be competitive. Market research is currently underway to determine the number of sales that are to be expected for the next year. The company is considering two alternative strategies:

1 Retain the present situation

Under the existing, labour-intensive, production methods estimated costs are:

Variable costs:	£25 per unit
Fixed costs:	£50 000 p.a.
Production capacity:	25 000 units p.a.

2 Proposed option

For next year the company is considering investing in new technology which will transform the production process. The investment required will increase fixed costs (especially finance charges) but more effecient use of labour will result in a reduction in unit cost and increased production capacity. Estimates are:

Variable costs:	£20 per unit
Fixed costs	£150,000
Capacity	30 000 units p.a.

The problem

The company would like answers to the following:

1 What is the break-even point under each of the production methods?
2 How will the new investment affect profitability at different levels of production?
3 What level of sales is needed to make investment in new technology worthwhile?

The solutions

1 The break-even points can be calculated as: $\frac{\text{Fixed cost}}{\text{unit contribution}}$

Present situation: $\frac{£50,000}{£5} = 10,000 \text{ units}$

Proposed option: $\frac{£150,000}{£10} = 15,000 \text{ units}$

Alternatively they are shown on the tables overleaf.

2 Profitability at different levels of production is shown by the following tables.

Present situation	£25	£50,000		£30	
Units	Variable Cost	Fixed Cost	Total Cost	Sales Revenue	Profit/(loss)
0	0	50,000	50,000	0	(50,000)
5,000	125,000	50,000	175,000	150,000	(25,000)
10,000	250,000	50,000	300,000	300,000	0
15,000	375,000	50,000	425,000	450,000	25,000
20,000	500,000	50,000	550,000	600,000	50,000
25,000	625,000	50,000	675,000	750,000	75,000

Proposed options	£20	£150,000		£30	
Units	Variable Cost	Fixed Cost	Total Cost	Sales Revenue	Profit/(loss)
0	0	150,000	150,000	0	(150,000)
5,000	100,000	150,000	250,000	150,000	(100,000)
10,000	200,000	150,000	350,000	300,000	(50,000)
15,000	300,000	150,000	450,000	450,000	0
20,000	400,000	150,000	550,000	600,000	50,000
25,000	500,000	150,000	650,000	750,000	100,000
30,000	600,000	150,000	750,000	900,000	150,000

3 The tables show that at 20,000 units the profit for each option will be the same (£50,000). Below this level the present production method is more profitable, above it the proposed option is more profitable. The cost/profit/volume chart below shows the situation clearly.

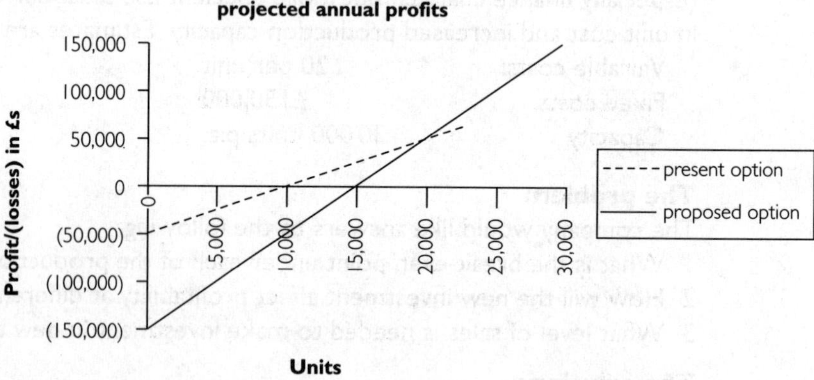

Notice that:

- the profit lines cut at 20,000 units, showing that at this level both options are equally profitable
- at low levels of output the present (labour-intensive) method is more profitable
- at higher levels of output the proposed (capital-intensive) method is more profitable.

Activities

1 What happens to the break-even point if the new investment is made? Why is this?
2 Which option has the greatest potential for profit? Why is this?
3 Should the company invest in new technology if projected sales are 20,001 p.a.? (Remember the margin of safety).
4 What does the chart show about the market conditions in which a firm should invest in new capital equipment? When might it be better to remain labour-intensive?
5 Should the business remain with the present system or invest in new equipment if:
a market research shows 28,000 units p.a. can be sold?
b market research shows that 12,000 units p.a. can be sold?
6 Dot Gratrix runs a small business re-inking typewriter and printer ribbons. The business runs from very cramped premises at present though there are plans for expansion.

Projected monthly costs are:	Rent and rates	£200
	Equipment hire	£ 10
	Light and heat	£ 30
	Postage and packing	£0.60 per ribbon
	Ink	£0.20 per ribbon

Dot charges £2 per ribbon, which is slightly less than her competitors. Potential monthly sales are 1,000. She needs to make £600 profit a month to make all of this worth while. You are asked to provide answers for Dot to the following questions:
a How many ribbons must Dot re-ink each month to break-even?
b Can Dot make earn enough to make the business worth while?
c Suggest one possible way in which profits could be increased.
Dot believes that by investing in better equipment and more suitable premises she could work more efficiently. This will increase her fixed costs to £500 per month, but variable costs will be reduced to £0.50 per ribbon. Sale price and therefore potential market will not change.
Dot also asks you to do the following:
d Plot the projected profit for this new option and the profit for the existing production on the same graph.
e Use the graph to decide the level of sales at which it would become worth while to change to the new option.

Break-even point, multi-product businesses and the business plan

In some situations it is difficult to express the break-even point as the number of units that must be produced (and sold) in order to cover costs. This calculation depends upon knowing contribution per unit and is only easily applied to businesses which sell a single identical product or service. In practice most businesses sell a variety of products or services all with different prices.

For a multi-product business it may be necessary to show the break-even point differently.

Break-even using time

One solution is to calculate the break-even point over a period of time by plotting time on the x axis. The sales line will be cumulative, so that sales for month 1 will be for month 1, sales for month 2 will be month 1 plus month 2 and so on.

Worked example

The Tanner Sandwich Bar sells a variety of food items to staff in local offices Projected figures for the six months January to June are:

- **Sales of £2,000 per month**
- **Variable costs are 50% of sales, that is £1,000 per month.**
- **Fixed costs for the six-month period are estimated at £5,000**

Month	(6 months) Fixed Cost	Cumulative Variable Cost	Cumulative Total Cost	Cumulative Sales (£)	Profit/ (Loss)
Start	5,000	0	5,000	0	(5,000)
Jan	5,000	1,000	6,000	2,000	(4,000)
Feb	5,000	2,000	7,000	4,000	(3,000)
Mar	5,000	3,000	8,000	6,000	(2,000)
Apr	5,000	4,000	9,000	8,000	(1,000)
May	5,000	5,000	10,000	10,000	0
Jun	5,000	6,000	11,000	12,000	1,000

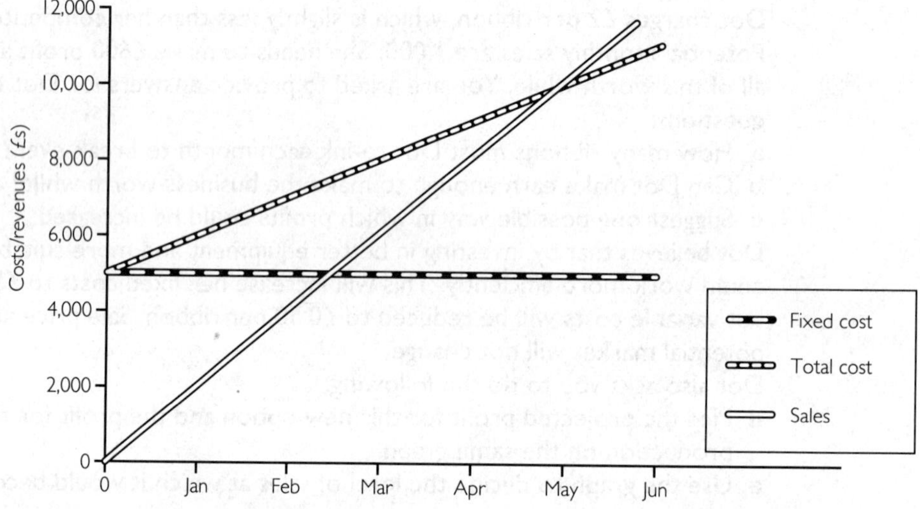

Figure 12.5 Tanner Sandwich Bar

The business will break-even by May when sales turnover reaches £10,000.

Break-even using gross profit margin

The Business Start-Up Guides published by the clearing banks recommend using the gross profit margin to find the break-even point. If we apply this to the Tanner Sandwich Bar it gives the same result as above. The stages are:

Stage 1: Gross profit margin $= \frac{\text{Gross profit*}}{\text{Sales}} \times 100$

*Gross profit = Sales − Direct cost

For the Tanner Sandwich Bar this would be: $\frac{(12{,}000 - £6{,}000)}{£12{,}000} \times 100 = 50\%$

$$\text{Stage 2: Break Even Sales} = \frac{\text{Overheads}}{\text{Gross profit margin}} \times 100$$

For the Tanner Sandwich Bar this would be: $\frac{£5,000}{50} \times 100 = £10,000$

The table would now be:

Sales	Fixed Cost	Variable Cost Sales × GP% (50%)	Total Cost	Sales Revenue	Profit/ (Loss)
0	5,000	0	5,000	0	(5,000)
2,000	5,000	1,000	6,000	2,000	(4,000)
4,000	5,000	2,000	7,000	4,000	(3,000)
6,000	5,000	3,000	8,000	6,000	(2,000)
8,000	5,000	4,000	9,000	8,000	(1,000)
10,000	5,000	5,000	10,000	10,000	0
12,000	5,000	6,000	11,000	12,000	1,000

The graph would be as for Figure 12.5 except that the x-axis would show sales rather than months.

Activity

1 Recycled Cycles is a co-operative which operates under the slogan 'Any colour you like but they're all green!'. They began by stripping down old bicycles, fitting a set of standard new parts and reselling them to the public. The venture has proved so successful that they plan to expand into other items, starting with manual lawn mowers, so that they will no longer sell a single product.

The members of the co-operative, who currently have £20,000 invested in the project, wish you to help them with their forecasts for the coming six months. They have produced the following budgeted costs:

Wages paid to workshop labour £11 per bicycle, £8 per mower
Spare parts and paint £9 per bicycle, £7 per mower
Cost of buying in second-hand items for recycling – £5 per item on average
Salary paid to secretarial staff £5,000
Rent and rates £6,000
Light and heat £1,100
General administrative expenses £ 500
Transport costs £ 900

Budgeted sales are:

420 bicycles average selling price £50
360 lawnmowers average selling price £40

Sales are expected to be shared evenly over the six months.

a Suggest how you might calculate the break-even point.
b Calculate the break-even point in an appropriate form.
c What use to the business is the calculation that you have performed? Mention any limitations of the technique you have chosen.
d The co-operative mention that they would like a 25 per cent return on the capital invested. What return is projected by the figures shown above?

$$\frac{\text{Profit}}{\text{Capital}} \times \frac{100}{1} = \text{Percentage return on capital}$$

What are the uses and limitations of break-even analysis?

The uses of break-even analysis can be summarised as follows:

- to measure profits and losses at various levels of production (and sales). Remember that the term cost/volume/profit analysis is often used to describe this
- to allow the testing of various scenarios by 'what if?' analysis. This is especially effective when a spreadsheet model is used
- to examine the implications of different production techniques such as capital-intensive production v labour-intensive production
- The business plan (see Chapter 15) will usually include a break-even calculation.

Limitations of break-even analysis

- The accuracy of any forecast depends upon the accuracy of the figures used and the further into the future a forecast is made, the less accurate we can expect it to be.
- Break-even analysis assumes a simplified, linear relationship between variable costs and sales. It is assumed that doubling sales will double variable costs, when in practice this may not be true. As we produce more we can take advantage of bulk-buying to reduce unit raw material costs. Equally, direct wages may not change in proportion to production. At least in the short term we cannot simply lay off staff when we have less work and immediately re-employ them as orders pick up.
- Sales income may not, in practice, double as sales volume doubles. We may be prepared to give discounts to large customers.
- The practical implications of all forecasts must be considered. A break-even graph shows that as production exceeds the break-even point, so profits will increase. It is tempting to extrapolate the trend (extend the lines on the graph) and forecast enormous profits at high levels of production. For instance, our dance will break-even at 80 tickets, so why not sell a thousand tickets and make a massive profit? The answer is clear:
  - we have not the capacity (i.e. the hall only holds 100 people)
  - if we are able to expand capacity (i.e. get a larger hall) we will increase our fixed costs and may need to raise large amounts of capital
  - we are assuming that the demand exists. There may not be a thousand people interested.

Break-even analysis is useful within limits. We must recognise that it applies only over a given time period and over a certain range of production. Outside of these limits it can be misleading.

The link between costing and pricing

For a business to be profitable in the long-term, sales revenue must exceed cost. We can distinguish between two different situations:

- Some businesses are **price fixers**. Here management uses absorption costing to calculate the total cost per unit (direct cost and a share of overheads). The sales price is then set as the cost per unit plus the required profit; this is known as cost-plus pricing.

Chris Cross (page 555) was able to set a price of £55 in this way, made up of cost £44, plus £11 profit.

- Some firms are not able to set their own price but are **price takers**, having to accept prices already established in the industry, often because there is strong competition. Here pricing is **market-led**. Since the business cannot set the price the question usually becomes 'How many units do we need to sell at the governing price to make a reasonable profit?' This relies upon marginal costing which concentrates upon how costs behave as more or less is produced.

  The student coach trip (page 561) was based on a price of £15, because this is what the students could afford. The question was 'How many seats to break-even?'

A similar situation may arise where an organisation is up and running and has excess capacity. They gain extra sales by offering special prices. They must ask 'What is the lowest acceptable price that we can take?' The technique used here is called **contribution** (or **marginal cost) pricing**. Generally where there is no better alternative, any sales with a positive contribution will help profits (or at least cut losses). The French order offered to Rollers Ltd (page 562) illustrates this.

The idea is that we only need to consider new costs incurred by the extra work (including any new overheads). Those fixed costs which will exist whether we go ahead or not can be ignored.

Remember that the above strategies are based on the assumption that a business wishes to make profits. In the long-term this is so, although profit maximisation may of itself not be the main aim. (To some companies, as we have seen, market share and reputation may be just as important.)

However, in the short-term a business may have certain specific, limited objectives – staging posts on the way to the long-term objectives. Here a number of pricing strategies may be used which have little to do with costs and profits and everything to do with tactics and manoeuvring in the market. Broadly these are:

Short-term aims	Strategies	Example
Launching a new product	Introductory offers	£49 day trips on Le Shuttle for the launch period only
Promoting an existing product	Special offers	Draught Guinness at £1 a can for a short period
Positioning a product in the market	Premium pricing	Designer perfume or champagne
Increasing or defending market share	Loss leaders	Supermarket turkeys sold below cost at Christmas
	Special offers	£1 for foot passengers on the cross-Channel ferries
Maximising revenue	Skimming (initial high price)	Compact discs
Destroying competitors	Destroyer pricing	Stagecoach (Scottish coach company)

Short-term pricing strategies are discussed in detail in the marketing section in Chapter 6.

Pricing

The relationship between the financial and the marketing function in pricing

We have seen that the finance section performs calculations concerning the relationship between costs, sales, price and profit. Much of the data for this comes from market research conducted by the marketing section. The relationship between finance and marketing can be illustrated as follows:

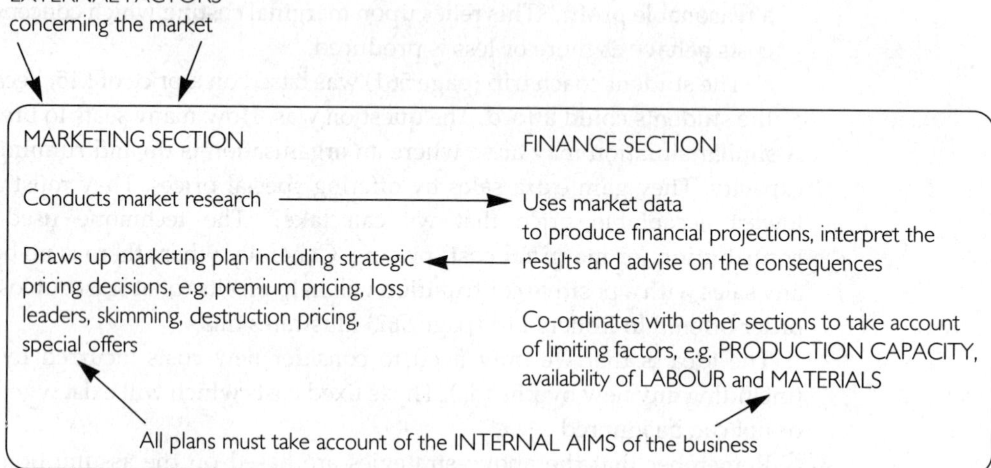
EXTERNAL FACTORS
concerning the market
MARKETING SECTION
FINANCE SECTION
Conducts market research
Uses market data
to produce financial projections, interpret the results and advise on the consequences
Draws up marketing plan including strategic pricing decisions, e.g. premium pricing, loss leaders, skimming, destruction pricing, special offers
Co-ordinates with other sections to take account of limiting factors, e.g. PRODUCTION CAPACITY, availability of LABOUR and MATERIALS
All plans must take account of the INTERNAL AIMS of the business

The marketing section will gain information about:

- the market including: market share, market trends, customers and competitors. It will estimate future demand at different prices.

It will research:

- the product including: who will buy it and what price the market will bear.

It will decide upon:

- the marketing strategy i.e. how the product will be promoted, the price to be charged.

It will be responsible for:

- the salesforce and physical distribution of the product to outlets.

The finance section will use the marketing data to set up forecasts for costs, income and profits, at different prices and for different levels of sales. It can advise on feasibility, for example, When will we break-even? Is the rate of return sufficient? Do we have the necessary financial resources? If the sales fall 10% below the projected level will we have sufficient cash?

Activity

Complete the following

Pricing strategy	Aim	Assumptions (what we need to know)	Used by (e.g. price-takers, price-fixers) In what situation?	Costing strategy (e.g. absorption costing, marginal costing)
Cost-plus pricing				
Market led pricing				
Marginal-cost or contribution				

Key terms

Financial accounting
Management accounting
Direct costs
Prime cost
Indirect overhead cost
Revenue expense
Capital expense
Depreciation
Standard costs
Variances
Favourable variances
Adverse variances
Cost-plus pricing
Market-led pricing
Contribution pricing/Marginal cost pricing
Price-fixers
Price-takers
Cost unit
Unit cost
Unit of production
Unit of service
Overhead recovery rates
Direct labour hours (DLH)
Process costing
Job costing
Variable costs
Fixed costs
Semi-variable costs
Absorption costing/total costing
Marginal costing
Contribution
Break-even point
Margin of safety
Cost/volume/profit analysis
'What-if?' scenario
Capital-intensive production
Labour-intensive production
Excess capacity

Review questions

1 What are the two main types of cost?
2 What is a revenue expense? Give one example.
3 What is a capital expense? Give one example.
4 Give two costs which may be included as part of prime cost.
5 What is a direct cost directly related to?
6 What is another name for indirect costs?
7 What is the estimated cost of a process under normal efficient working conditions called?
8 What is the name given to the difference between the budgeted and the actual figures?
9 How is absorption cost different from marginal cost?
10 Name two variable costs and three fixed costs.
11 What is job costing? Which sort of business might use this?
12 What are semi-variable costs made up of?
13 In marginal costing, what is the term for the difference between sales and variable costs?
14 What does contribution contribute to and when does it become profit?
15 What is a cost unit? Give three examples.
16 What is the break-even point?
17 In which different ways may the break-even point be expressed?
18 If projected sales are 20,000 units and the break even point is 15,000 units, what is the margin of safety? Why is this important?
19 What is cost-plus pricing? Is this based on the marginal or the absorption cost?
20 What is contribution pricing? Is this based on the marginal or the absorption cost?

Assignment 12.2
Hotel La Manche

This assignment develops knowledge and understanding of the following elements:
6.3 Calculate the cost of goods or services
6.4 Explain basic pricing decisions and break even

It supports development of the following core skills:
Communication 3.2, 3.3, 3.4
Application of number 3.2, 3.3
Information technology 3.1, 3.2, 3.3

Ashford in Kent (see the map on page 86) is well placed to take advantage of the growing business traffic between the UK and Europe. It is within easy reach of the Channel Ports of Dover and Folkestone, and is the starting point for Le Shuttle (Eurotunnel's car and freight service). Ultimately the town will have its own major railway station, Ashford International, which will take advantage of the express trains run by European Passenger Services to European cities.

A local consortium is seeking planning permission to build a hotel close to the town, primarily for business customers. Two sites are under consideration and consultants have produced the following financial projections:

Preliminary projected costs/revenues for the first year of operation

	Site A	Site B
Maximum number of guests accommodated per night	100	100
100% capacity pa (in guest/nights) (i.e. 365 nights × 100 guests)	36,500	36,500
Projected occupancy year 1	60%	55%
Revenues:	£	£
Average rate per guest per night (including evening meal)	40.00	40.00
Costs:		
Average cost of evening meal per guest/night	8.75	9.25
Room-staff costs per guest/night	0.55	0.60
Staff costs pa	100,000	100,000
Administration costs pa	240,000	200,000
Advertising costs pa	80,000	80,000
Finance charges pa	Depends on interest rate	

- Long-term loans required: Site A £2 million Site B £1 million. (interest on loans is likely to be between 8% and 15% pa – you are to choose)
- The room rates include an evening meal and are priced so as to compete with rival companies. Research indicates that these are likely to be the optimum prices.
- The cost unit: the hotel is selling accommodation to guests for a night or **guest/nights**.
- Site A will eventually have conference facilities and a gym, but these are not expected to be available in year one.

Your tasks

You have been asked to examine the financial information and present a paper to the next board meeting.

1 Identify each cost as fixed or variable.

2 For each site calculate:

Forecast occupancy level in guest/nights (the number of guest/nights that will be sold in the year according to the consultants' report)

3 **a** Produce a table for each site as follows:

% Occupancy	Units (guest/nights)	Variable cost	Fixed cost	Total cost	Sales revenue	Profit/ (loss)
0						
25						
50						
75						
100						

b Draw a break-even graph for each site for year one.
(Plot cost/income on the *y* axis; plot guest/nights AND % occupancy on the *x* axis.)

c Clearly indicate on each graph:

(i) the break-even point

(ii) the margin of safety (based upon projected occupancy).

d Verify the break-even point by calculation.

4 Produce itemised marginal cost statements for each site to show the forecast profit for Year 1 based on the consultants' figures.

5 If La Manche were to run a special promotion to attract extra custom at weekends, what is the lowest room price per site that they could charge without losing money? (Assume that the evening meal is included.)

6 Produce a worst-case scenario to show what will happen if competition forces prices down to £35 per guest/night.

7 Using all of the information now available write an **informal report** to be presented to your fellow directors at the next board meeting.

The report should assess the financial advantages and disadvantages of each of the proposed sites. You should conclude by recommending the site that you think offers the best prospects for your company.

Presentation of the assignment

Your work should be presented in the form of an informal report (7 above) with **1**, **2**, **3**, **4**, **5** and **6** (above) included as appendices. Refer to these as necessary in the report.

The final report should be word processed. Calculations and graphs should be produced on a spreadsheet.

13 Sources of business finance and budgeting

What is covered in this chapter

- Private sector business organisations
- The need for finance
- The sources of finance
- Security for loans
- The cost of borrowing
- The balance sheet – a statement of assets, liabilities and capital
- Planning for working capital requirements
- Budgets
  - The master budget
- The cashflow forecast
  - The importance of the timing of payments
- Where do the figures come from?
- Feasibility – is the cashflow realistic?
  - Monitoring
- Use of spreadsheets
  - Spreadsheets and 'What if?'
- Sources of finance and the business plan

These are the resources you will need for your Financial Forecasting and Monitoring file:

- literature on financial services, available from high street banks
- business planning/start-up guides, available from high street banks
- a spreadsheet package
- a PC.

Private sector business organisations

Anyone wishing to set up in business will need to decide not only which goods or services they are going to provide, but also which form of business organisation is the most appropriate for them. The amount of finance required will be an important factor in this choice.

The main forms of private sector organisations have been described in Chapter 3; this section compares their ability to raise finance.

Sole trader

This is the easiest form of business to set up. There are no legal fees and there are fewer regulations concerning accounts than with other organisations.

The main financial disadvantage is that, since there is only one owner to contribute capital, there may be limited funds available. Borrowing may also prove difficult except where the owner has personal property which can be used as security for a loan.

Partnership

As a partnership can have between 2 and 20 owners (and for accountants, solicitors and stock exchange members up to 50), more capital is available than for a sole trader. For this reason a sole trader wishing to expand may consider taking on a partner. Similarly it may be easier to borrow money as more security is available.

Both sole traders and partnerships have full (unlimited) liability for all business debts. Borrowing therefore carries a certain amount of risk. In the event of the business being unable to settle its debts the owners will be asked to pay from their private possessions.

Limited company

A limited company must be owned by at least two shareholders but there is no legal limit. It is therefore possible for companies to raise large sums of money through the sale of shares. Any company wishing to raise new capital must, however, have permission (authorisation) from the Registrar of Companies. This is to protect the public from investing in companies which are unsound.

Limited companies are less of a risk to own than other forms of business organisation. The principle of **limited liability** means that, in the event of financial difficulties, the shareholders will lose at most only the capital that they have invested or agreed to invest. The private property of shareholders is safe even if creditors remain unpaid. However, a director who does not act responsibly can be prosecuted by creditors under the 1986 Insolvency Act

Private limited companies may not offer their shares for sale to the general public and for this reason tend to be smaller than the PLCs. Some companies are very small and have the company form of organisation simply to take advantage of limited liability. Nevertheless some private companies raise considerable funds from share issues. Littlewoods, the football pools company, has capital of £2 billion, but remains a private limited company owned by the Moores family.

A private limited company may at some later stage become a PLC in order to raise further money for expansion.

> Amstrad PLC began as a private limited company but became a PLC to fund its expansion into the personal computer market. When intense competition caused the company's shares to lose value, the founder, Alan Sugar, attempted to buy the company back. (Amstrad stands for AM Sugar Trading.)

Public limited companies may offer their shares to the general public and so raise large amounts of capital. A minimum of £50,000 share capital is required before a company can go public, though most PLCs have considerably more than this.

Listed companies are PLCs which have their shares quoted on the **Stock Exchange**. These are the share prices that are displayed in the daily press. The larger companies tend to be PLCs including household names such as Sainsburys, Marks & Spencer, ICI, the high street banks, and the newly privatised businesses such as British Airways and British Petroleum.

To gain a full listing a company must have capital of £700,000, have been trading for 3 years and promise to release at least 25 per cent of shares into public hands.

Not all PLCs have a full stock exchange listing. The **unlisted securities market** (USM) was set up by the Stock Exchange in 1980 to allow smaller companies to 'go public'. This enabled them to raise larger amounts of finance from the general public without the expense of a full listing. It is proposed to rename the market AIM (Alternative Investment Market).

The shareholders

The recent 'privatisation' of companies such as British Airways, British Telecom and the electricity industry has attracted more private shareholders to invest in PLC shares. However, 75 per cent of equities (ordinary shares) are still owned by institutional buyers such as unit trusts, trade unions, pensions funds and insurance companies. In recent years share ownership has proved to be a good investment for these organisations.

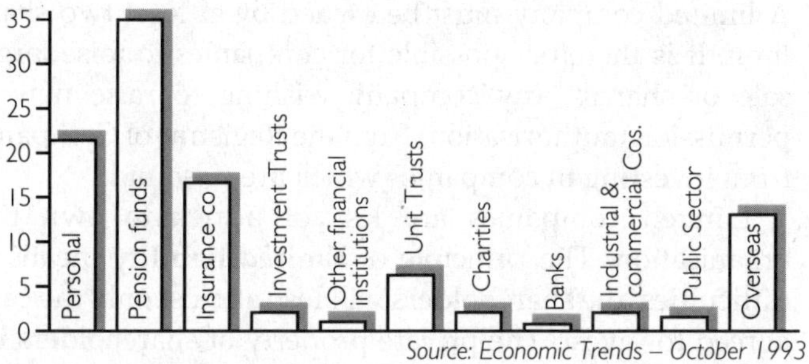

Figure 13.1 The shareholder profile: percentage of UK quoted equities owned by various sectors

Source: *Economic Trends*, October 1993

Shares may be sold by various methods:

- prospectus: Where a new type of share is to be issued a prospectus is prepared showing details of the offer and inviting the general public to invest
- offer for sale: The company sells the shares to an issuing house which then sells on to the public
- a rights issue: The shares are offered to existing shareholders. The issue is made attractive by offering the shares at a reduced price
- a placing: A broker will place new shares with certain investors

Remember it is only the initial sale of the share as a 'new issue' that raises money for the company. When a shareholder sells a share later it is second-hand and brings in money only to the shareholder.

A single share can cost from 1p to a few pounds. Each shareholder can gain financially by:

- reselling the share for a profit. Most shares sold on the stock exchange are 'second hand', although there is a new issues market
- collecting final **dividends** at the end (and sometimes interim dividends half-way through) the financial year. Dividends are the payments made to shareholders by the directors when the company makes profits. The dividend paid is expressed as a payment per share and represents the shareholder's share of profits.

Monitoring the performance of PLCs

Most national daily newspapers will contain a summary at least of the previous day's events on the London Stock Exchange. The 'quality' press will contain a full market report showing the closing prices of the quoted companies.

The FTSE 100 (Footsie) is an index showing the market trend in prices for the top 100 companies listed on the Stock Exchange. It is used to indicate whether in general the market prices are rising or falling.

FTSE 100 ↑ 36.1 at 2829.8

Other similar market indicators are: FTSE 250, FTSE 350, the FT 30 and the FT all share (FT stands for *Financial Times*).

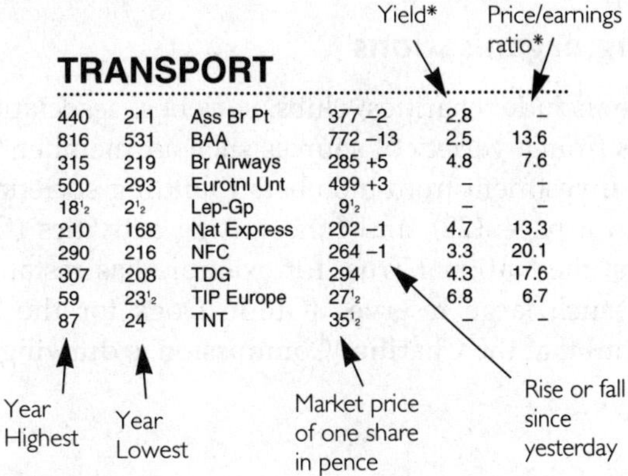

TRANSPORT

440	211	Ass Br Pt	377 −2	2.8	–
816	531	BAA	772 −13	2.5	13.6
315	219	Br Airways	285 +5	4.8	7.6
500	293	Eurotnl Unt	499 +3	–	–
18½	2½	Lep-Gp	9½	–	–
210	168	Nat Express	202 −1	4.7	13.3
290	216	NFC	264 −1	3.3	20.1
307	208	TDG	294	4.3	17.6
59	23½	TIP Europe	27½	6.8	6.7
87	24	TNT	35½	–	–

*Yield and price/earnings ratio are explained on pages 686–7.

The companies listed on the stock market are divided into sections such as: Banks, Electrical, Hotels, Stores, etc. The example shown above is for Transport.

The prices found in the daily press are for the close of dealing on the previous day. When the market is open prices rise and fall continually. Up-to-the-minute prices can be found from databases such as Prestel or by telephoning the various Sharecall services.

Types of share

Preference shares

Preference shares entitle the shareholder to a stated rate of dividend. As the name suggests, preference shareholders are paid dividends before ordinary shareholders and, if a company folds, then the preference shareholders will be paid back before ordinary shareholders.

- Cumulative preference shares: Where profits in one year are insufficient to cover dividend then these dividends are accumulated and paid in following years before other classes of dividend.
- Non-cumulative preference shares: Arrears are not accumulated as above.

Ordinary shares (or equities)

These make up the vast majority of shares in a company and entitle the shareholders to voting rights at the annual general meeting (AGM). There is no stated rate of dividend, rather this is decided by the directors on the basis of annual profits. For this reason they are sometimes called 'risk shares'. In poor years there may be no dividend, but in good years the dividend may be higher than for preference shares.

Companies are able to raise more finance than other forms of organisation but there are a number of disadvantages. The first is that there are legal requirements to fulfil in setting up the company. As a result a company is more expensive to set up than a sole trader or partnership, although the cost may be as little as £100, while some already registered companies can be bought 'off the peg' already set up.

Also, the accounting of a company is less private than for other forms of organisation. Companies are governed by the Companies Act of 1985 (amended in 1989) which states that financial records must be audited and made available to the Registrar of Companies. These records are held at Companies House where they can be inspected by interested members of the general public.

Non-profit making organisations

These include: charities, clubs, societies, associations and trade unions. These acquire funds from a variety of sources such as: members' subscriptions (trade unions and the AA), investment from members (building societies), donations from industry (see the chart on page 122), and fund-raising activities (Oxfam). Many also have commercial wings, the National Trust for example has restaurants and gift shops. Some charities have such large reserves (Guide Dogs for the Blind Association has around £140 million) that the Charities Commission is drawing up guidelines about fund-raising.

Activities

1 Which forms of business organisation would you recommend for the following? Write down a sentence or two in each case to explain your choice (before answering you may wish to reread the relevant section of Chapter 3).
   - **a** Mrs Alice Morecambe who wishes to set up a guesthouse at Blackpool.
   - **b** Sarah Jones and Winston Roberts who wish to set up a sandwich bar to cater for local business trade.
   - **c** A newly qualified solicitor who wishes to set up in business with a colleague.
   - **d** Mary Cox whose family owns a number of apple orchards. She wishes to set up a business to produce and market her own cider.
   - **e** Four teachers decide to leave their jobs and start a business to provide training and consultancy in information technology. Each member is a specialist in different areas: one in CAD (computer aided design), one in spreadsheets and accounts, one in DTP (desk-top publishing) and the other in computer networks.

2 **a** Name five household names which operate as PLCs and five newly privatised companies.
   - **b** Look up yesterday's closing share price for each.
   - **c** Was the price up or down on the previous day? NB Use today's newspaper (prices not available in Monday papers – why not?)

3 Amy Ramesh has £200 of shares in Waterways PLC. She reads in the press that the company is going into liquidation and owes vast sums of money. She is very worried about her position as an owner of the business.

   As a friend studying GNVQ Advanced Business write her a letter to explain exactly what risks she will face.

The need for finance

Any one starting up in business will need finance (money). They should consider two basic questions.

- What do they need the finance for?
- How much will they need?

What is the money for?

Broadly speaking, finance is needed for purchase of assets and for running the business (working capital).

Assets

Before it can begin to operate, a business will need 'start-up finance' in order to acquire certain essential items. A sole trader setting up a small corner shop for example will need premises, shop fittings, some equipment such as a till, possibly a small van and stock to sell. There will also need to be a float of cash for the till and some money in the bank to pay for day-to-day expenditure. These items that the business owns are called assets. They can be subdivided as follows.

Fixed assets These are the 'tools' with which the business works. They are items that may cost a substantial amount but which will last for some time – normally a few years at least. In the example above: premises, delivery van, shop fittings and equipment.

Current assets These are items that will be used from day to day – their value will constantly change. In the example above: stock, cash in bank and cash in hand.

As the business trades there will be no short-term effect on the fixed assets. The value of the current assets, however, will change continually as money is spent and earned, as stock is sold and new stock is bought, and as running costs are paid. The trading cycle in Chapter 11 shows this.

Where a business offers credit a further current asset, debtors, will appear. Debtors are an asset because the value for the goods sold legally belongs to the trader. It is just that for the time being this money remains in the customer's possession. Debtors are a current asset because the debt will be paid shortly – a settlement period of 30 days is common.

Working capital

When the business is up and running it will need to pay various running costs such as heat, light, rent, rates, repairs and wages. It will also need to replenish stocks.

The money required to fund day-to-day operations is called working capital.

How much money will a business need?

The need for funds is affected by a number of factors including the nature of the business and the proposed scale of the operation. A manufacturing concern will, for example, tend to need expensive specialised machinery, while a business providing an information service may need only an office, a computer and a telephone.

> Some businesses need vast sums of money, for example, Eurotunnel, the Anglo–French project which provides a continental rail link beneath the English Channel, had cost an estimated £10 billion by mid-1993. In October 1994, before services began, it owed £8 billion to 220 international banks. Such expensive projects could only be afforded by the issue of shares to the general public.

Activity

1 Consider the following businesses:
- **mobile fish and chip shop**
- **disco available for bookings around the area**
- **window cleaner**
- **farm**
- **bakery.**

a Make a list of the assets that you feel they would need to acquire before they could begin to operate.
b Mark these as fixed and current assets.
c Make an estimate of how much money will be needed to acquire these assets.
d What sort of business organisation would be most likely to enable these funds to be raised?

2 For each of the businesses above, make a list of the running costs they might have.

The sources of finance

Where will the money come from?

In general terms sources of finance fall into two categories:
- finance provided by the owners of the business, known as capital
- finance borrowed from external sources, called liabilities.

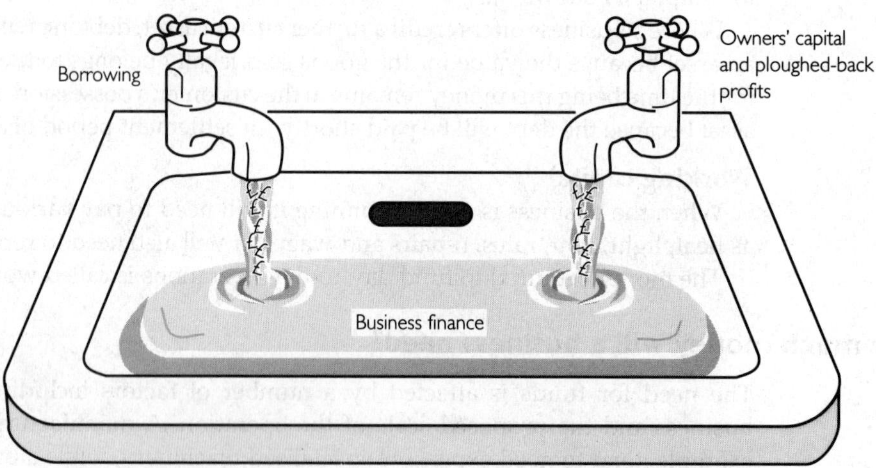

Figure 13.2 Where the money comes from

Capital

The capital invested by the owners is generally considered to be permanent in that it is not due to be repaid by the business after a period of time but will remain as long as the owner is concerned with the business. If a sole trader leaves the business then it will cease unless it is sold to another owner. A leaving partner may have capital returned, though usually a new partner will buy out the partner who is leaving. If a shareholder wishes to regain the money invested in company shares he or she will need to sell the shares to another investor for the current market value. This will not deprive the business of money, although sometimes a business may buy back shares as a means of gaining greater control.

Business profits belong to the owner(s). Where these profits are left in the business, or 'ploughed back', the business gains extra capital. Retained profits are the single most important source of business finance.

Venture capital

Where a small company needs further capital it may seek venture capital. This is money invested in the shares of unquoted companies by wealthy individuals. In bringing in venture capital a business is not borrowing but taking in new owners. Sources include:

- Venture Capital Trusts (VCTs). These are PLCs who rechannel their shareholders' money by reinvesting in small companies seeking finance. The November 1994 Budget sought to encourage this practice by increasing tax relief on profits from VCTs for those individuals holding shares in them for 5 years. The aim is to raise £2.5 billion in 3 years
- Enterprise Investment Scheme – the 'Business Angels'. Here individuals are encouraged, again by tax relief, to invest directly in the shares of small to medium companies. The investor and the company may be brought together through so-called 'marriage bureaux', such as TechInvest, set up by 4 TECs in the North-West, Capital Exchange based in Hereford and the Natwest Angels Service. Total Business Angels investment is thought to be around £2 billion.

Venture capitalists are interested in growth and a high return (25–30 per cent) on their money, but often only for a limited period. They may provide 'pseudo capital' in the form of redeemable preference shares and they may require a degree of control over a business to oversee their investment. Only 3 per cent of funds goes to new business; the rest helps existing companies wishing to expand. A venture capitalist may invest from £30,000 to £500,000.

Although funding is seen as the major problem in setting up a business, there is evidence that many entrepreneurs do not wish to involve others, for fear of losing control.

Liabilities – borrowing

A business may borrow money externally from a number of sources including:

- banks
- finance houses
- building societies
- creditors
- the government.

Banks Services available include:

- Overdraft: The bank may allow the business to overdraw on their current bank account — this may allow day-to-day expenses to be paid at times when the business does not have money available
- Business loan: The bank may advance a business loan for periods of up to ten years. This will allow the purchase of fixed assets or the funding of an expansion of the business. These are items which will provide increased benefits but only over a period of time

- Commercial mortgage: The business may buy premises using a mortgage from a bank. Typically a mortgage will have a repayment period of 25 years
- Debenture: This is a long-term loan to a limited company secured against company assets

Finance houses These are often owned by banks. Services available include:

- Factoring: A **factoring** company will buy the debts of a business, so that rather than waiting for payment the business will have the cash available immediately

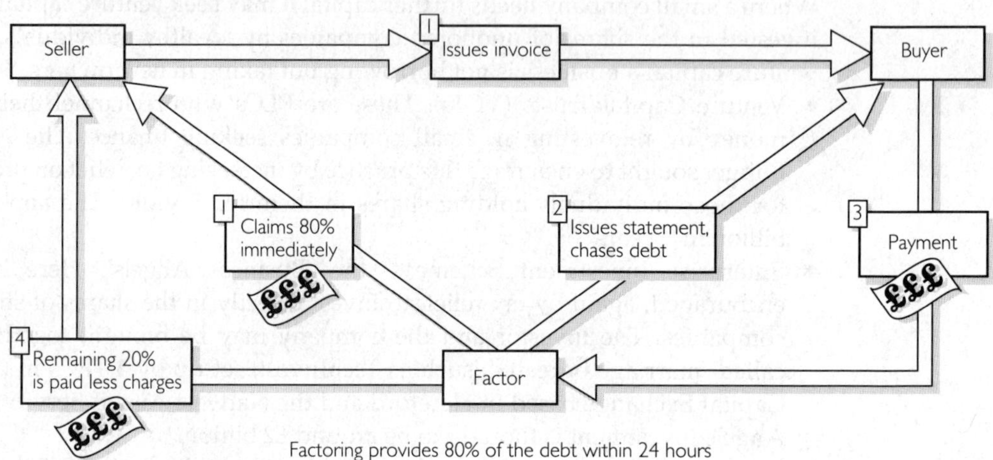

Figure 13.3 How factoring works

- Leasing: Under this arrangement a business pays a rental to secure the use of certain assets such as vehicles or computers. The business does not own the assets but has the benefit of using them without the expense of having to lay out substantial sums of money

  This can help cashflow by allowing a business to acquire expensive assets without having to spend large amounts of its initial capital. It also means that a business is not left with an expensive outdated asset soon after purchase
- Hire purchase (HP): Hire purchase allows a business to acquire an asset by putting down an initial deposit and then paying the balance with interest over an agreed period of time. After the final payment, ownership of the asset passes to the business. Should the business fail to maintain the payments then the asset passes back to the finance company

Building societies The business may buy premises using a mortgage from a building society on similar terms to that offered by a bank. Additionally, since the Building Societies Act, societies can advance funds for other purposes in similar ways to banks.

Creditors The suppliers may allow the business to buy stock on credit, that is they will supply stock now and require payment by some future date, perhaps in a month's time. This is the equivalent to lending money to the business, though in practice the creditor is lending value in the form of goods.

The government and the European Union The government provides a certain amount of financial help to business through the Department of Trade and Industry (DTI) and the Department of Employment often working through the Trading and Enterprise Councils (TECs).

Schemes include:

- Enterprise Allowance, run by TECs
- DTI assistance for new technology development
- long-term loans to small businesses at reasonable rates, as offered by the Scottish Enterprise Development Agency
- the government's loan guarantee scheme
- the European Investment Bank loan support scheme
- various regional development grants.

Other sources are some local authorities who will assist certain projects, and The Prince's Youth Business Trust which will assist young people setting up in business.

Finance of private sector organisations: Summary

Time period	Sole Trader	Partnership	Ltd Co/PLC	Use
Permanent	Owner's Capital	Partners' Capital	New Share issues	Fixed Assets/ Growth
	re-investing profits		build up reserves	
Long-Term (over 10 years)	loans/grants from government agencies			Fixed Assets/ Permanent working capital
	Mortgages from banks/building societies			
			Debentures/ redeemable preference shares	
	Long-term loans			
Medium-Term (3–10 years)			Venture capital	Fixed Assets Increasing working capital
	Medium-Term loans			
	Buying assets on HP/Credit/leasing			
Short-Term (up to 3 years)	buying stocks on credit			stock purchases
	bank overdrafts			stock/wages/ working capital
	Factoring (selling debts at a discount for immediate cash)			" "
	Short-term loans			minor assets
	Hire Purchase			" "

The table on page 593 shows finance as being: permanent, long-term, medium-term or short-term. For balance sheet purposes liabilities tend to be categorised more simply as:

- Long-term liabilities. These are amounts falling due after more than one year, such as mortgages and bank loans. Their purpose is to supplement owners' capital in financing fixed assets. Long-term liabilities are sometimes called 'loan capital'
- current liabilities. These are amounts falling due within one year, such as creditors and bank overdrafts. Their purpose is to supplement income generated from sales in providing working capital for day to day use.

Activity

Here is a sample of answers from a survey into small business start-up funding conducted by the National Federation of Enterprise Agencies (November 1994).

BETTER BUSINESS: SAMPLE SURVEY QUESTIONS

What type of business have you started?

Manufacturing	13
Service	64
Wholesale	1
Retail	12
Other	10

What has been the single most important factor in deciding to set up your own business?

No jobs available	18
Redundancy	27
Good business idea	6
Desire to make money	6
Desire to run your own business	36
More freedom to make decisions	7
Other	0

What has been the largest single constraint in setting up your own business?

Funding	52
Marketing	14
Management skills	7
Premises	7
Advice	5
Training	3
Staff	1
Other	11

Please rank the top three sources of business start up advice and/or practical help

Enterprise agency	60
Bank	9
Friends	9
Relatives	6
Accountant	5
Other	5
TEC	5
DTI	1
Solicitor	0

Are you aware of the Enterprise Investment Scheme?

Yes	32
No	68

If yes, would you use it?

Yes	67
No	15
Don't know	18

What has been the single largest source of funding in starting up your business?

Own money/savings	58
Bank loan	12
Family	12
Other	11
Overdraft	4
Friends	1
Mortgage	1
Venture capital	1

What single factor would have made it easier for you to start up in business?

Grants	28
Easier access to funding	27
Subsidised premises	12
Tax advantages	9
Better advice on planning	7
Preferential bank loans	6
Business angel	2
Other	9

Note:
All businesses surveyed had been started in the previous twelve months.

Write a brief newspaper article summarising the findings of the NFEA survey. The article should be called 'Funding findings'. You should include at least one chart. Give any explanations that you feel are necessary. Make comments as appropriate.

Security for loans

Lenders may need some security for their money. The main question they will ask in considering a loan is 'Will we get our money back?' Frequently, loans are tied to certain business assets and, if none is available, the personal assets of the trader, partners or directors may be used as collateral. At other times a director may give a personal guarantee. Unsecured loans are based on the lender's judgement.

Before granting finance to a new business a bank will usually wish to see that the owner(s) are also willing to risk a fair amount of their own money. If they are not they will want to know why.

Gearing

The term gearing is used to express the relationship between the capital borrowed and that provided by the owner(s). High gearing means a high proportion of capital is borrowed. This can leave a business vulnerable, as loans must be repaid. The gearing ratio is explained on page 659.

The cost of borrowing

The rate of interest is crucial to the business community. Those with capital to invest want high interest rates so as to gain a good return on their money. Those wishing to borrow need the lowest rates possible. Additionally there will be a fee for arranging finance which often needs to be reviewed annually. Charges will vary from bank to bank and interest rates will vary with bank base rate. A loan will probably be at base rate + 4 per cent.

Here are some examples.

- Short-term finance:
  - Overdraft arrangement fee — £80 to £100
  - Overdraft interest charges — 1.5% per month payable quarterly
- Long-term finance:
  The table below was calculated on the EXCEL spreadsheet using the PMT function.

The cost of borrowing over 25 years

Size of loan	9%	9.50%	10%	11%	12%	15%	Rate of Interest
£20 000	168	175	182	196	211	256	Monthly Repayments (£)
	50 400	52 500	54 600	58 800	63 300	76 800	Total Repaid (£)
£50 000	420	437	454	490	527	640	Monthly Repayment (£)
	126 000	131 100	136 200	147 000	158 100	192 000	Total Repaid (£)
£100 000	839	874	909	980	1 053	1 281	Monthly Repayment (£)
	251 700	262 200	272 700	294 000	315 900	384 300	Total Repaid (£)
£200 000	1 678	1 747	1 817	1 960	2 106	2 562	Monthly Repayment (£)
	503 400	524 100	545 100	588 000	631 800	768 600	Total Repaid (£)

The table shows the cost of borrowing various amounts at different interest rates
It is assumed that the length of the loan is 25 years (that of the average mortgage)
It is also assumed that repayments are on a monthly basis
NB in practice the cost of a long-term loan will fluctuate as the interest rate changes

INTEREST RATES—UK HIGH STREET %

Bank inst. acc : 1.0 gross	Building society mortgage : 8.09
Bank base rate : 6.75	Building society inst acc : 4.1+ gross
Bank overdraft : 1.5 per month	Finance House rate : 7.0

Daily interest rates as published in the press

Activities

Return to the answers you gave to the activity on page 590. Select one of the businesses you looked at and undertake the following activities.

1 As financial adviser at the local enterprise agency suggest the most realistic ways in which the business could borrow the capital for their project. Be sure to distinguish between the funds needed for fixed assets and those needed for day-to-day use.

2 What sorts of security would be available for the lenders:

a If the business were new?

b If it were an established business? (Is security always required?)

3 Check the current rates of interest for savers and borrowers by looking at the newspapers or by collecting literature from your local banks or building societies. Are rates currently favourable to borrowers or investors?

The balance sheet – a statement of assets, liabilities and capital

The balance sheet shows the worth of a business at a particular point in time. Essentially it states what assets are owned by the business and where the funds came from to obtain these. Put simply it shows what the business owns, what it owes and what it is worth.

Example

The balance sheet of Syd Southwark shows that he has assets worth £80,000 which were financed by £80,000 worth of liabilities and capital.

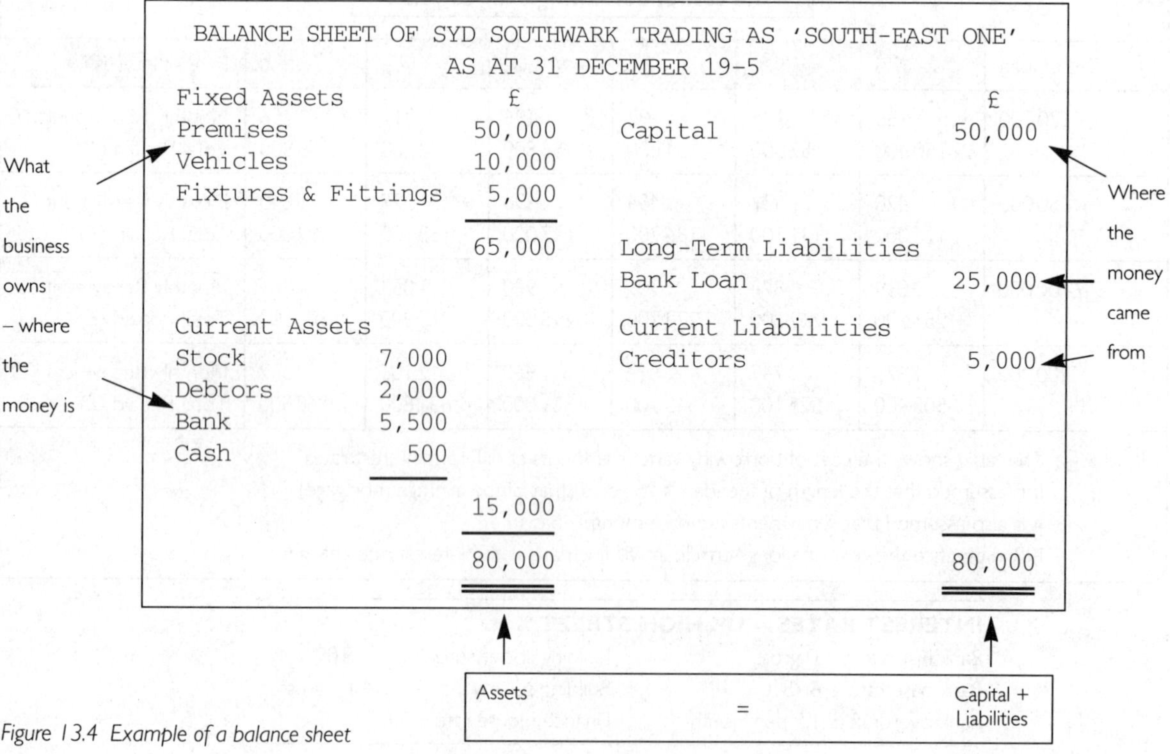

BALANCE SHEET OF SYD SOUTHWARK TRADING AS 'SOUTH-EAST ONE'
AS AT 31 DECEMBER 19-5

		£		£
Fixed Assets				
Premises		50,000	Capital	50,000
Vehicles		10,000		
Fixtures & Fittings		5,000		
		65,000	Long-Term Liabilities	
			Bank Loan	25,000
Current Assets			Current Liabilities	
Stock	7,000		Creditors	5,000
Debtors	2,000			
Bank	5,500			
Cash	500			
		15,000		
		80,000		80,000

Figure 13.4 Example of a balance sheet

The balance sheet presented in vertical format

Although there are a number of possibilities, a balance sheet is usually presented in the vertical format shown below. The grouping of items is:

Assets – **liabilities** (top section) = **capital** (bottom section)

The advantage of this form of presentation is that it clearly shows:

- working capital = current assets – current liabilities. This represents the money available within the business at short notice and is vital to survival
- Capital (including retained profits): this shows what the business is worth to the owner. It is what remains of the assets when the liabilities have been paid.

Other points to notice are:

- the heading. 'As at' indicates that the balance sheet is like a snapshot. It shows the value of the business at a point in time
- the balance sheet, like all other financial statements, is concerned only with the business and not with the private affairs of the owner. This is so even if Syd has put up his private house as security for the bank loan
- the two columns are for convenience and clarity. The left-hand column is used for lists and the right-hand column for the main totals
- items are listed with the longest lasting at the top; that is why premises comes before vehicles in the fixed assets section. This is called the **order of permanence.** NB. In the accounts of a high street bank the items are listed with cash first, because this is what bankers are interested in. This is the **order of liquidity**.

BALANCE SHEET OF SYD SOUTHWARK TRADING AS 'SOUTH-EAST ONE'
AS AT 31 DECEMBER 19-5

		£	£	
	Fixed Assets			
	Premises		50,000	
	Vehicles		10,000	
	Fixtures & Fittings		5,000	
			65,000	
	Current Assets			
	Stock	7,000		
	Debtors	2,000		
	Bank	5,500		
	Cash	500		
		15,000		
less	**Current Liabilities**			
	Creditors	5,000		
	Working Capital		10,000	← Working Capital = Current Assets – Current Liabilities
			75,000	
less	**Long-Term Liabilities**			
	Bank Loan		25,000	
			50,000	← These totals agree because:
				Assets – Liabilities
	Financed by:			
	Capital		50,000	← = Capital

The effect of transactions on the balance sheet

As the business carries on trading items on the balance sheet will change. Below are examples of three transactions and the effects that each will have on the balance sheet:

	Transaction	*Result*
a	Syd spends £500 on more stock	Bank goes down £500 (money spent), stock goes up £500
b	Syd increases the bank loan to buy additional fixtures and fittings for £1,000	Fixtures and fittings up £1,000, bank loan up £1,000
c	All of the debtors pay up	Debtors down £2,000, bank up £2,000

Activities

1 Try each of the transactions above in turn on Syd's balance sheet and total up after each. You will find that the balance sheet always balances. You will notice that each transaction has two effects and that the second complements the first. This is the basis of double-entry book-keeping. (We will consider this in Chapter 14.)

2 Bert Bermondsey, who was recently made redundant, has put all £20,000 of his savings into setting up a small sports shop in South London. So far he has bought some premises for £50,000, with the help of a building society mortgage of £40,000. He has purchased stock for £3,000 and has installed shop fittings worth £5000. He still has £2,000 in the bank.

Bert reminds you that he has a smart car at home which cost him £8,000.

a Draw up his balance sheet as at 30 September 19–5 using the vertical format.
b Explain fully whether the car should be included on the balance sheet.

3 Glastonbury Tours, a small West Country travel agent, has approached you to help with the accounts. The figures available to you are as follows:

- The customers owe £1,200, there is a bank overdraft of £800.
- The business owns a building in the high street which cost £50,000. It also has computer equipment worth £5,000 and office furniture, magazine racks etc. worth £2,000.
- The mortgage on the premises (which has ten years to run) stands at £25,000.

a You are asked to draw up the balance sheet as at 31 December 19–. Use the vertical format.
b Mr Glass, the owner, originally invested all of his savings in the business when he set it up, but wants to know what he is worth now.
c Mr Glass wants to know why debtors are an asset. 'I find them a liability,' he says. 'I'm always having to wait for my money!' Explain as clearly as you can why they may be considered an asset.

4 Buxton Fizz are a new company set up to market mineral water under the slogan 'The Champagne of Derbyshire'. The following figures show their opening financial position:

	£
Capital (invested by shareholders)	120,000
Drilling equipment	80,000
Land and Premises	150,000
Debentures (long-term loan)	50,000
Stocks (of plastic bottles)	12,000
Vehicles	20,000
Cylinders of CO2	10,000
Bank balance	4,000
Creditors	6,000
Mortgage	100,000

a Construct their opening balance sheet on 1 June.

b How can you check that you have prepared the balance sheet correctly?

c When the balance sheet is correct, work out the effects of the new developments shown below and draw up a new balance sheet to include these changes. Make sure that it still balances:

- another £2,000 of bottles are bought on credit
- another £10,000 of shares are sold for cash
- the mortgage is increased to buy more land for £10,000.

Case study

Savoy Hotel plc

The balance sheet on page 600 is taken from the annual financial report of Savoy Hotel plc, a large hotel group. Look at the figures and try the questions below.

1 Redraft the balance sheet as below using totals only. Remember that it should balance.

		£000s	£000s
	Fixed assets		....
	Current assets	....	
less	Current liabilities	....	
	Working capital		....
			....
less	Long-term liabilities		....
			....
	Share capital		....
add	Reserves		....
			....

2 Why are investments classed as fixed assets?

3 Suggest how the company has raised working capital.

4 How much is the Savoy group worth?

5 The ordinary shares originally cost 10p. Look up their present price in today's paper.

Case study

Where did they get the money from?

The figures below are extracted from the balance sheet of The Savoy Hotel plc

Annotation	Item	£000s	Annotation
	Fixed Assets		
Freehold land and buildings	Investment properties	4 500	
Plant and machinery	Tangible assets	76 291	
		80 791	
Funds invested for several years	Investments	23 600	
		104 391	
	Current assets		
Food stocks, cleaning materials	Stocks	7 013	
Debts owed by clients	Debtors	11 007	
	Cash in Hand	1 450	
		19 470	
	less		
	Creditors – amounts falling due within one year		Current liabilities
Short-term loans	Loans and Overdrafts	6 591	
Owed to suppliers,	Creditors	13 312	
Owed to shareholders	Dividends due	2 003	
		21 906	
	Working capital	(2 436)	
	Total assets less current liabilities	101 955	
	less		
	Creditors – amounts falling due after more than one year		Long-term liabilities
Long-term loans	Loans and overdrafts	4 931	
Debentures Mortgages	Creditors	11 315	
Tax due	Other charges	486	
		16 732	
	Net Assets	85 223	
	Financed by:		
27 962 739 Ordinary shares of 10p and 1 306 267 Ordinary shares of 5p	Issued Share Capital	2 861	
Retained profits ploughed back into the business	Reserves	82 362	
	Shareholders' Funds	85 223	

Planning for working capital requirements

Why is working capital important?

Working capital	=	Current assets	–	Current liabilities
		assets which can be quickly turned into cash		the cash which will soon have to be paid

Working capital represents the cash (or near cash) available to the business to finance day-to-day activities. Without this wages cannot be paid, suppliers' statements will not be settled, the mortgage will be in arrears and eventually the business will have to close. Where a business runs short of working capital it is said to suffer cashflow problems.

Current assets are also called 'liquid assets', because they can quickly be turned into cash. Notice that they are listed with the least liquid (stock) first, and the most liquid (cash) last.

Stock	can be sold but it may take some time (even then it may be sold to debtors)
Debtors	usually pay after 30 days
Bank	cheques take three or four days to clear
Cash	instantly available

Note that a manufacturer may have stocks of raw materials and work in progress, as well as finished goods ready for sale.

Cashflow problems may occur because:

- too much is spent on fixed assets
- insufficient stock is sold – rate of turnover is too low
- prices are too low
- costs are too high
- drawings or dividends are too high
- debtors are not paying on time, or bad debts are occurring.

A business can improve cashflow by:

- raising new capital
- 'ploughing back' profits into the business
- raising new loans
- leasing or renting fixed assets instead of buying them
- raising prices (where elasticity of demand allows)
- buying on credit
- selling for cash or using factoring to gain 80 per cent of debtors' money immediately
- cutting costs.

Activities

1 Try each of these situations on the balance sheet of Syd Southwark (page 597) to see the effect on:
- working capital (current assets – current liabilities)
- liquidity (the way in which current assets are made up).

Situation	Working capital up/down?	Liquidity up/down?
a All debtors pay what they owe		
b Syd buys more stock on credit		
c Syd buys more stock for cash		
d Syd spends all the bank balance on new equipment		
e Syd buys new equipment with a long-term loan		
f Syd sells his vehicles and leases them instead		
g Syd puts more of his savings into the business bank account		
h Syd withdraws money from the business for his own private use		

2 Look at the accounts of the Savoy Hotel plc on page 600.
a Comment on the working capital position.
b How could the group increase working capital?
c How did Savoy raise funds for fixed assets?

Budgets

Purposes of budgets

A budget is a plan for a future period based upon forecasts. It can be quantitative (sales of 5,000 bicycles) or financial (£20,000 costs). The budget may act as a constraint upon spending or a target for production or sales.

Types of budget

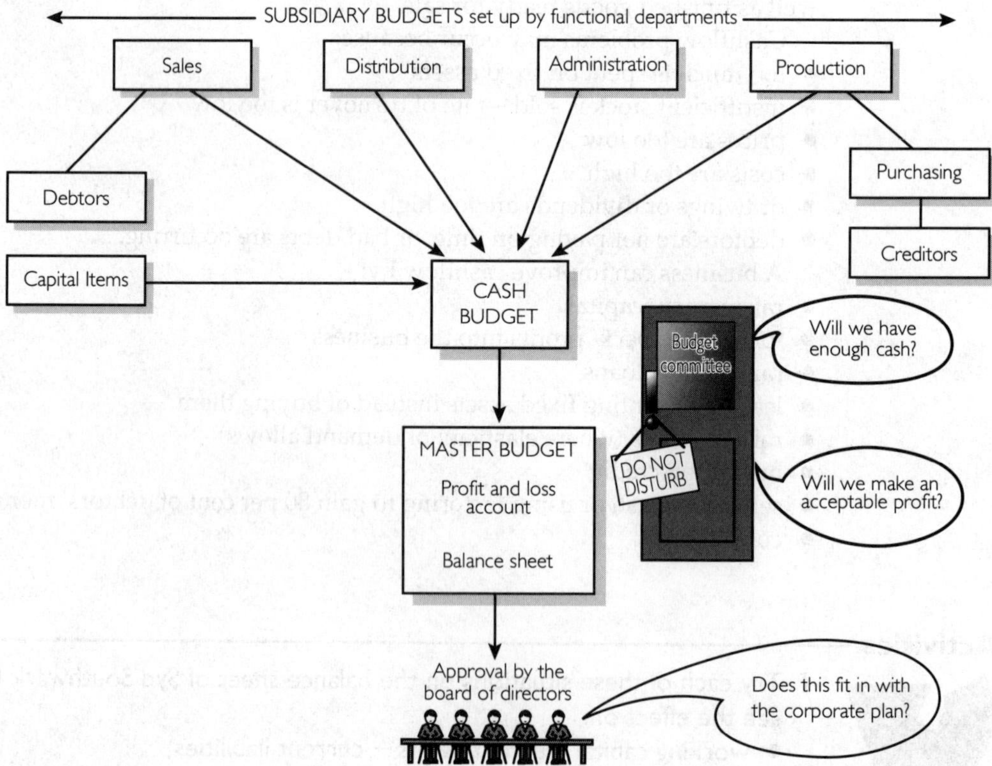

Figure 13.5 The budgeting process

The budgeting process illustrated in Figure 13.5 is the means by which the business formulates its detailed short-term plans for the coming period (probably a year). The firm will already have a corporate plan showing where it is trying to go in the medium to long term (perhaps it wants to be a market leader in ten years' time). This short-term budget shows the immediate steps to be taken towards this longer term goal. It is a detailed plan of action.

Frequently the budget is driven by the sales department which is in touch with market possibilities.

Co-ordination

The subsidiary budgets produced by the various functional departments are brought together at the budget committee for co-ordination. It is important that there is participative budgeting at this stage, that is, departments need to be involved. Heads of departments will resent budgets imposed on them by remote accountants who, they may feel, do not understand their particular problems.

The co-ordinator, possibly the company accountant, will assess the feasibility of the budgets and give advice on whether they are acceptable.

Feasibility – will the budget work?

Questions that might arise at the committee:

- from departmental budgets: Can the production department meet the demand predicted by the sales section? Can the distribution section get goods to outlets to coincide with advertising? What will all of this cost?
- from the cash budget: Will we have sufficient cash to run the operation? Do we need an overdraft? If so, how much and when? Will the bank allow us this much?
- from the master budget: Is there sufficient profit to keep our shareholders happy? What is the return on capital likely to be? Will we be able to fund next year's expansion programme?

Acceptability

The board of directors will need to approve the budget before it is put into operation. They will need to be convinced that the plan is acceptable in terms of company aims and objectives.

Monitoring

If the budget is approved, it will be monitored regularly to ensure that things are going to plan. Managers will look at monthly variances between the budget and the actual performance. Where there are significant differences questions will be asked. Perhaps the budget is unrealistic, perhaps there have been unexpected price rises, perhaps someone is not doing their job.

The master budget

For the purpose of this chapter we will note that the master budget consists of forecasts for:

- the profit and loss account – this is a forecast of the trading position of the business over the period. It compares projected sales with the operating costs incurred in producing these sales
- the balance sheet – this shows the assets, liabilities and capital at the end of the period. We will look at a fully worked example of the budgeting process on pages 667–70, after we have considered profit and loss accounts and balance sheets in more detail.

The Cashflow forecast

The cashflow forecast is an estimate of the cash position of the business over the forthcoming period. It will normally be drawn up for the next 6 or 12 months. It may be part of the budgeting process of an organisation as shown above; in this case it is the cash budget. It will also be part of the business plan drawn up by a new business, or one which is seeking to expand. In this case its use will not be restricted to internal budgeting, it will also be shown to outside agencies such as banks. Unit 8 'Business planning' will require you to include a cashflow forecast in your business plan.

The cashflow forecast is drawn up for three main reasons:

- **as evidence when seeking finance**. A business wishing to arrange an overdraft facility with a bank will wish to show:
  (i) how much it will need to borrow and when
  (ii) that it will ultimately be able to repay.
  Alternatively where a medium or long-term loan is required, perhaps for expansion, then the business will need to show that it will have sufficient funds to pay the instalments as they become due.
- **as a planning tool**. In planning future operations a business will need to know how much finance will be required. It may be necessary to arrange for this in advance. Where a plan indicates that cashflow will be unsatisfactory, there is an opportunity to rethink. Where a number of options are being considered, the cashflow forecast will be an important consideration when making the final decision.
- **as a means of monitoring actual performance against planned performance.** Plans can act as targets: sales income to be achieved and expenses not to be exceeded. Often a cashflow forecast will have two columns per month: one for the budget to be completed at the planning stage and one for the actual figures to be entered as they become known (see page 611). This allows the **variance** between these to be calculated. As with other budgets, management will be concerned to know why significant variances occur. They may ask for instance 'Why are sales less than expected?' or 'Why are expenses more than expected?'

Cash In a cashflow forecast the term 'cash' refers to money received and paid. It will include any payment (cheques, credit transfers as well as cash) which affects the bank account. The cashflow forecast will not include depreciation as this is not a cashflow but merely an accounting adjustment in the books.

Structure of the cashflow forecast

There are three sections in the cashflow forecast.

- Receipts: Details of money expected from various sources
- Payments: Details of money to be spent on various items
- The summary: This is the section at the bottom which compares total receipts with total payments for the month. After taking account of any opening balance it shows the balance of cash available at the end of the month. The exact way in which this section is set out varies slightly from one plan to another, but the format shown in the following example is one that is commonly used.

Worked example

Ben Nevis & Son Ltd

Ben Nevis has set up a small company with his son, Glen, to retail mountain bikes. In the first year he estimates that turnover will be small and there will be no need to register for VAT. All trade will be carried out on a cash basis.

After much careful research into the market and the terms offered by suppliers, Ben has produced a cashflow forecast for the first six months of trading – 1 January to 30 June 19–3.

Cashflow Forecast of...... Ben Nevis & Son Ltd From...1st January...to..30th June..19.-3...

Figures rounded to £s	Jan Budget	Feb Budget	Mar Budget	Apr Budget	May Budget	June Budget	Total Budget
RECEIPTS:							
Cash Sales	1 000	1 000	1 000	2 000	2 000	2 000	9 000
New Capital	8 000						8 000
Total Receipts (A)	9 000	1 000	1 000	2 000	2 000	2 000	17 000
PAYMENTS:							
Cash Purchases	500	500	500	1 000	1 000	1 000	4 500
Directors' salaries	600	600	600	600	600	600	3 600
Wages/salaries	400	400	400	400	400	400	2 400
Vehicle running costs	200	200	200	200	200	200	1 200
Capital items	3 000						3 000
Rent/Rates	200	200	200	200	200	200	1 200
Light/Heat			180			180	360
Telephone/Post			100			100	200
Insurance	300						300
Total Payments (B)	5 200	1 900	2 180	2 400	2 400	2 680	16 760
Net Cashflow (A-B)	3 800	(900)	(1 180)	(400)	(400)	(680)	240
add Opening Bank Balance	0	3 800	2 900	1 720	1 320	920	0
Closing Bank Balance	3 800	2 900	1 720	1 320	920	240	240

Receipts

Payments

Net cashflow for the period (the difference between receipts and payments)

Bank balance at start

Monthly bank balance

Bank balance at the end of the period

His budgeted figures are:

		Jan, Feb, March	April, May, June
Trading	Sales	£1,000 per month	£2,000 per month
	Purchases (£)	£500 per month	£1,000 per month
Capital budget	Opening capital invested in January		£8,000
	Shop fittings purchased in January		£3,000
Profit/Loss	Salaries of Ben and Glen		£600 per month
	Wages of assistant		£400 per month
	Vehicle running costs		£200 per month
	Rent & Rates		£200 per month
	Light & Heat (March and June)		£180 per quarter
	Telephone (March and June)		£100 per quarter
	Insurance paid in January		£300

Note: There will be no money in the bank at the start of January as this is a new business.

Conclusions
The bottom line on the cashflow is the most important as it shows the estimated bank account balance for each month. According to this the company will have to watch the situation very carefully. The bank balance is reducing at an alarming rate and unless some action is taken there will soon be a sizeable overdraft.

Reason
The net cashflow each month appears in parentheses ( ). This means that it is a negative figure. In other words more cash is going out than is coming in.

Solution
Income will need to be increased by selling more or, if possible, increasing prices; alternatively payments will have to be reduced. The expenditure on the shop fittings is a one-off amount, but it is the regular expenses that are the problem. Of these wages especially may need to be looked at (do they need the assistant?).

If you are clear about this, then you understand the basics of cashflow forecasting. The example on page 611 is based on exactly the same principles, but is more complex.

VAT
For the purposes of cashflow we need to include all cash paid and received, including VAT.

VAT in cashflow
All businesses with a turnover exceeding a certain amount (see Appendix 4 for current rates) must register for VAT. This means that they receive a VAT number and must collect VAT at 17.5 per cent on all goods that they sell which are liable for VAT. This is called output tax.

The business will itself have paid VAT called input tax, when it bought goods and services.

Every quarter (three months) the input tax (paid) is deducted from the output tax (collected) and the difference is sent to HM Customs & Excise. Where more VAT has been paid than has been received then a refund of the difference is claimed.

All figures on a cashflow should include VAT.

The VAT return will usually be a payment because as selling prices are higher than buying prices the VAT collected will exceed the VAT paid. Where a refund is claimed VAT will appear in the form of a negative payment rather than income (an item reducing payments).

When we work out profits and losses we will see that VAT is not included at all. This is because it is really neither a profit nor a loss. All that is happening is that VAT that is paid is claimed back, and any surplus is sent to the Customs & Excise.

A business not registered for VAT will not charge VAT on sales, and cannot claim back VAT on payments. To this extent it is worse off.

Remember that VAT will only apply to certain goods and services. It does not, for instance, apply to items such as rail fares, rates, wages and salaries. Neither does it apply to loans. In the March 1993 budget, the government announced their intention to put VAT at 8 per cent on household fuel, which was previously exempt.

The importance of the timing of payments

Even where total income exceeds total expenditure over the period, the timing of payments and receipts may make it necessary to borrow for short-term cash requirements. Page 611 illustrates this.

Problems may occur because of:

- quarterly payments such as gas, electricity and VAT returns
- annual amounts such as rates and insurance which are due in advance
- the need to pay for purchases in advance of sales. A new business may make cash purchases whilst selling on credit
- late payment by debtors
- large outlays on start-up costs and fixed assets.

How long is a month?

Most cashflow formats show the year divided into 12 months. There is no problem here as long as costs and revenues are estimated on a monthly basis. There can, however, be a problem where items such as wages are paid weekly.

Example

Tuesday Welders have taken on a new assistant to help out on a weekly basis.

They estimate that the assistant will be paid £100 per week on average. This is £5,200 per annum (£100 x 52 weeks). If a month is seen as 4 weeks then for each month pay will be estimated as £400 (£100 × 4 weeks).

Over the year this will mean wages of £4,800 only (£400 per month × 12 months). They are underestimating their costs by £400 in the year.

If there are several wage-paid employees then the error becomes quite significant.

Often this problem is resolved by splitting the year into 13 × 4 weekly periods. An alternative is to find an average month by the calculation: weekly cost × 52/12.

Activities

1 The wage bill for Ballast Bros is £700 per week on average. Calculate two ways in which this might be dealt with as a monthly figure on the cashflow forecast.
2 What other items might be paid weekly apart from wages?

Where do the figures come from?

The budgets which provide the figures on a cashflow forecast will be based upon estimates from various sources.

Past experience

An existing business will have past experience to look to. It will, for instance, know the size of last year's heating bill and how much the telephone bill is in a typical quarter. It will also know about sales volumes and any seasonal variations.

Advice

A new business will often need to use someone else's experience. It may consult an accountant, one of the many agencies or the financial adviser at the bank.

Market research

Sales may be predicted on the basis of market research. The selling price may be determined on the basis of cost or by looking at prices of competitors.

Purchases will depend upon stocks required to fulfil sales. The prices will be the best the buyer can achieve.

Payments that are known

Some payments such as business rates, insurance and the costs of certain fixed assets can often be forecast with complete accuracy. In circumstances where agreements have been made, wages and salaries can also be predicted with accuracy, although there may be variations for overtime.

Uncertainties

Costs such as motor vehicle running costs will be estimates based on experience or upon predicted use, but they will be subject to changes in petrol or diesel prices. Similarly interest charges on mortgages and overdrafts will vary with bank base rate. Current interest charges are set out in banking information leaflets and will be used as a basis for estimates, but there is no guarantee that these will not change.

Notice that all figures are rounded to the nearest £, as forecasts can never be correct to the nearest 1p. In some cases, where the sums of money are large, the figures may be rounded to much higher amounts. (An extreme case of rounding up in forecasting is the government's annual budget, for which some figures are summarised in £ billions!)

The rule in all forecasting is to err on the side of caution. Where there is doubt incomes should be estimated at their lowest possible levels and expenses at their highest. If a plan still looks viable in these circumstances then it can be put into operation. If on the other hand a plan predicts financial disaster then changes will need to be made before proceeding.

Solutions to cashflow problems

A business can increase income by increasing profit margins, or by selling more. It can reduce outgoings by cutting costs. Where neither of these is possible, it will need to look to the timing of payments or raising more funds.

An overdrawn balance on a cashflow forecast indicates a shortage of cash at a certain time; an overdraft is not always the best solution to this. The purpose of an overdraft is to tide a business over until the cash comes in.

Where an injection of a sizeable sum is required, perhaps for purchase of new fixed assets, then the bank may suggest a bank loan repayable over a period of time, rather than a large overdraft.

A business which constantly needs to borrow large sums may become over reliant on the bank. If a business is too highly geared, that is, its borrowing is high compared to the owners' capital then it may consider raising extra capital from its owners. This will mean that a partnership may take on an extra partner, or a limited company may gain authorisation to issue more shares. In some cases a business may consider changing its organisation. A partnership, for instance, may become a limited company.

Sometimes it may be sensible for a business to raise capital by selling fixed assets and leasing them instead. Where the business does wish to buy fixed assets then the payments may be spread by means of hire purchase or other credit arrangements.

If the business needs to sell on credit, then it should also try to buy on credit. For a new business this may not be possible until it establishes a reputation as a sound payer. Some businesses suffer from having to buy for cash but sell on credit. Should they wish to expand sales then they would need to lay out a considerable amount of cash on purchases which they would not get back until 30 days (at least) after the goods are sold.

Feasibility – is the cashflow realistic?

Recognising the dangers

A cashflow forecast will often be used as part of a business plan to support an application for a loan or an overdraft. The prospective lender must be convinced that the plan is realistic or it will be rejected.

Research into the success of business plans suggests that they are more likely to be received favourably if they recognise the difficulties that the business is likely to face, rather than pretending that there will be no problems at all. This shows that at least the planner has taken all of the issues seriously. Problems may be as follows:

- **Limiting factors**. It is no use predicting a volume of sales that cannot be achieved, either because it is too optimistic or because the business will be unable to supply that level of demand with its present capacity. For instance, there may be a lack of space, lack of staff or just lack of money. Such restrictions are known as limiting factors and a realistic cashflow must take these into account.
- **Overtrading**. Strangely, a business that attempts to expand rapidly to take advantage of an increased market may put itself out of business. Rapid growth may mean taking on new staff, moving to larger, more expensive premises and buying expensive stocks that may be sold on credit. While the business is waiting for payment the bank overdraft will be rising to an unmanageable size. If the bank decides to 'call in' its loan at this point the business will be unable to pay from the bank account and will have to sell up. This dangerously rapid expansion is called overtrading and is a common cause of business failure.
- **Incorrect forecasting.** A forecast may turn out to be incorrect simply because it is difficult to predict accurately for future periods. Since forecasts are used as a guide for action such errors may turn out to be very costly. A business suddenly finding that it needs to arrange an unexpectedly large overdraft may find itself in difficulties. An existing business asking a bank for finance will normally need to back up any

forecast with audited accounts from the most recent three years, This will give some extra evidence of the ability of the business to perform in the marketplace.

The ultimate danger of incorrect forecasting is that a business may become insolvent through an unforeseen shortage of working capital.

Monitoring

Activity

Monitoring cashflow

The company Hiking & Biking have produced a cashflow forecast for the first 6 months of trading using a sheet provided by their local bank (Figure 13.6).

a **Look at the bottom line. What size of overdraft facility will the company require?**

b **Will the bank be likely to agree to this (assuming that they believe the figures)?**

c **Is an overdraft the best means of funding here?**

d **As the year progresses you are asked to monitor the results. Using either a spreadsheet or a cashflow sheet enter the actual results shown below next to the monthly budget.**

Actual figures:

	Jan	Feb	Mar	April	May	June
Sales (cash)	2 000	3 000	3 000	2 000	4 000	4 000
Cash from debtors (money received)		6 000	6 000	10 000	10 000	11 000
New capital	32 000					
Loans	1 500					
Purchases (cash)	6 000	4 500	4 500	6 000	7 000	7 500
Wages	3 000	3 000	3 000	3 000	3 500	3 000
Professional fees	5 000					
Financial charges	80					
Capital items	15 000	1 000	1 000	1 000	1 000	1 300
Light & heat		400			400	
Telephone			500			500
VAT			(2 718)			2 442

Bank charges 1.5% per month on overdrawn balances (charged next month)
Vehicle running costs: £700 in January thereafter £200 per month
Rent & rates £1 000 per month
Transport/packing 1% of purchases
General expenses as predicted
Insurance nil

e **Calculate the total variances for the period to the right of the totals column. Indicate each as adverse (ADV) or favourable (FAV).**

f **Give one possible explanation for each variance that has occurred. Why is it important to look at variances each month?**

g **Look at the VAT returns. Why is the March figure negative and the June figure positive?**

Cashflow Forecast of...... HIKING & BIKING							From...1st January...to..30th June..19.-4...							
Figures rounded to £s	Jan Budget	Jan Actual	Feb Budget	Feb Actual	Mar Budget	Mar Actual	Apr Budget	Apr Actual	May Budget	May Actual	June Budget	June Actual	Total Budget	Total Actual
RECEIPTS:														
Cash Sales (incl VAT)	2 000		3 000		3 000		2 000		3 000		4 000		17 000	
Cash from Debtors (incl VAT)			6 000		7 000		7 000		9 000		12 000		41 000	
New Capital	32 000												32 000	
Other incl Loans													0	
Total Receipts (A)	34 000		9 000		10 000		9 000		12 000		16 000		90 000	
PAYMENTS:														
Cash Purchases (incl VAT)	4 000		4 000		5 000		6 000		7 000		8 000		34 000	
Credit Purchases (incl VAT)													0	
Drawings/Dividends													0	
Wages/salaries	3 000		3 000		3 000		3 000		3 000		3 000		18 000	
Transport/Packaging	40		40		50		60		70		80		340	
Vehicle running costs	200		200		200		200		200		200		1 200	
Hire/Leasing Repayments													0	
Loan Repayments													0	
Capital items	20 000												20 000	
Rent/Rates	1 000		1 000		1 000		1 000		1 000		1 000		6 000	
Light/Heat			350						350				700	
Telephone/Post					500						500		1 000	
Interest charges													0	
Bank /Finance Charges													0	
Book-keeper													0	
Professional fees	5 000												5 000	
Insurance	2 000												2 000	
VAT					(2 000)						2 520		520	
General Expenses	40		40		50		60		70		80		340	
Total Payments (B)	35 280		8 630		7 800		10 320		11 690		15 380		89 100	
Net Cashflow (A-B)	(1 280)		370		2 200		(1 320)		310		620		900	
Add Opening Bank Balance	0		(1 280)		(910)		1 290		(30)		280		0	
Closing Bank Balance	(1 280)		(910)		1 290		(30)		280		900		900	

Figure 13.6 Cashflow forecast of Hiking & Biking showing columns for monitoring 'actual' performance

Use of spreadsheets

Completing a cashflow forecast manually can be time-consuming. When working manually it is as well to enter all of the data for receipts and payments before attempting any of the calculations. This is because any errors will result in an incorrect bank balance which will carry through from month to month.

It is better, if possible, to use an electronic spreadsheet.

A spreadsheet screen can be set up with text and formulae as in Figure 13.7. When data is entered into the appropriate cell on the worksheet the computer will automatically perform calculations and display the answers instantly. This data can be changed quite painlessly as many times as necessary. The spreadsheet can free us from the tedium of routine calculations and allow us to concentrate on what the data actually mean.

A further advantage is that the information can be displayed graphically in a number of styles. This is particularly effective for presentation purposes.

There are many different spreadsheet packages on the market, but they tend to have similar syntax for entering formulae. The example shown in Figure 13.7 was prepared on the Microsoft package EXCEL. The graphs in Figure 13.8 were produced from selected ranges of data on the sheet used earlier for Hiking & Biking.

Spreadsheets and what if?

A particular advantage of the spreadsheet is that it allows us to examine alternatives.

When we are preparing our financial plans we may wish to compare one set of options with another. Perhaps, for example, we have based our costs on the present rate of interest, but want to know what will happen if rates rise. Can we still succeed if this happens? Perhaps we want to see the effect of a 5 per cent decrease in sales or what will happen if suppliers increase their prices by 2 per cent. Will we run short of cash? This type of enquiry is known as a 'What if?' calculation because we are asking 'What if this happens?' or 'What if that happens?'

Sources of finance and the business plan

In Chapter 15 you will be required to prepare a business plan. Many of the financial aspects of a business plan have been considered in this chapter, in particular:

- the most appropriate form of business organisation
- fixed asset requirements
- working capital requirements
- costs of finance
- security required by the lender.

The cashflow forecast is a crucial element in that it helps in assessing the feasibility of a project and in estimating the requirement for funds.

You may need to refer back to this section when attempting Unit 8 'Business planning'.

	A	B	C	D	E	F	G	H
1	Cashflow Forecast of.........................				From................to..........................19....			
2	Figures rounded	Jan	Feb	Mar	Apr	May	June	Total
3	to £s	Budget	Budget	Budget	Budget	Budget	Budget	Budget
4	RECEIPTS:							
5	Cash Sales (incl VAT)							sum(B5:G5)
6	Cash from Debtors (incl VAT)							sum(B6:G6)
7	New Capital							sum(B7:G7)
8	Other incl Loans							sum(B8:G8)
9	**Total Receipts (A)**	sum(B5:B8)	sum(C5:C8)	sum(D5:D8)	sum(E5:E8)	sum(F5:F8)	sum(G5:G8)	sum(H5:H8)
10								
11	PAYMENTS:							
12	Cash Purchases (incl VAT)							sum(B12:G12)
13	Credit Purchases (incl VAT)							sum(B13:G13)
14	Drawings/Dividends							sum(B14:G14)
15	Wages/salaries							sum(B15:G15)
16	Transport/Packaging							sum(B16:G16)
17	Vehicle running costs							sum(B17:G17)
18	Hire/Leasing Repayments							sum(B18:G18)
19	Loan Repayments							sum(B19:G19)
20	Capital Items							sum(B20:G20)
21	Rent/Rates							sum(B21:G21)
22	Light/Heat							sum(B22:G22)
23	Telephone/Post							sum(B23:G23)
24	Interest charges							sum(B24:G24)
25	Bank /Finance Charges							sum(B25:G25)
26	Book-keeper							sum(B26:G26)
27	Professional fees							sum(B27:G27)
28	Insurance							sum(B28:G28)
29	VAT							sum(B29:G29)
30	General Expenses							sum(B30:G30)
31	**Total Payments (B)**	sum(B12:B30)	sum(C12:C30)	sum(D12:D30)	sum(E12:E30)	sum(F12:F30)	sum(G12:G30)	sum(H12:H30)
32								
33	Net Cashflow (A-B)	B9–B31	C9–C31	D9–D31	E9–E31	f9–F31	G9–G31	H9–H31
34	add Opening Bank Balance		B35	C35	D35	E35	F35	B34
35	**Closing Bank Balance**	B33+B34	C33+C34	D33+D34	E33+E34	F33+F34	G33+G34	H33+H34
36								
37								
38	Notice that the opening bank balance will need to be entered at B34							
39	All monthly receipts and payments will need to be entered in the relevant cells							
40	Answers to calculations will automatically appear in the cells where formulae are indicated							

Note: Before entering formulae, it may be necessary to enter an = sign or a + sign. Check for your spreadsheet.

Figure 13.7 Example of cashflow forecast set up using a spreadsheet

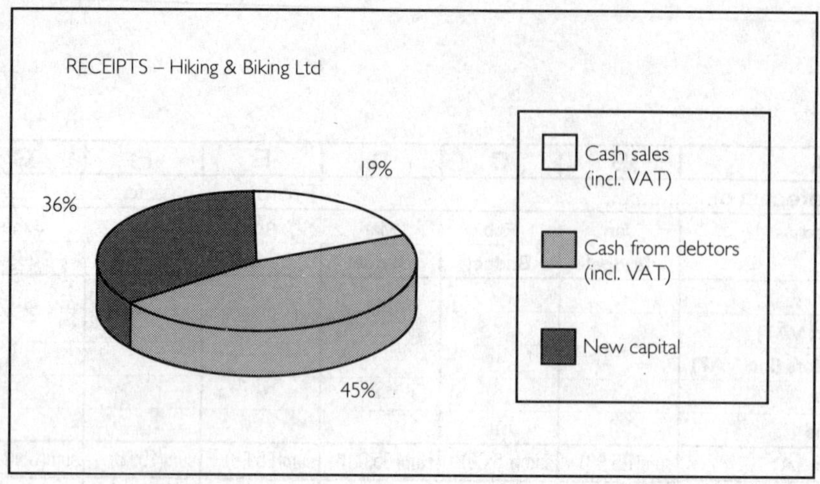

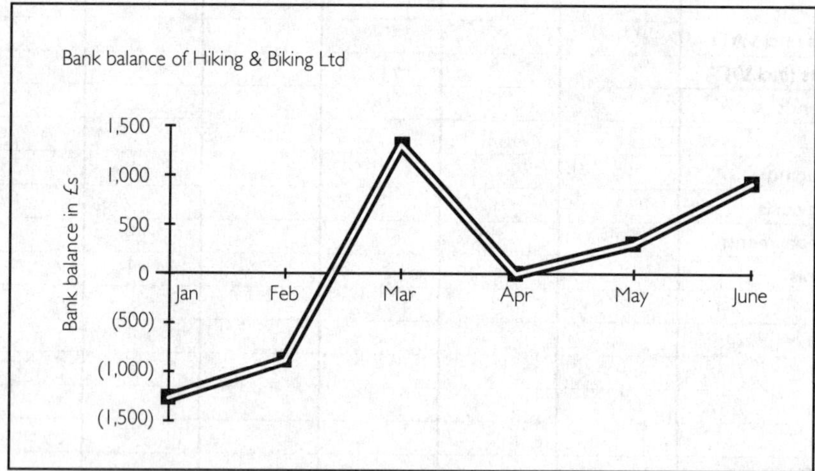

Figure 13.8 Examples of charts produced from a cashflow spreadsheet

Activities

1 a Ask your local bank for a copy of their business plan or start-up guide. Look up the cashflow form that will be provided.

b Compare the cashflow to the one given in this chapter. You may notice that some of the suggested expenses are slightly different. You may also notice that there is a slight variation in the exact method of calculating the bank balance.

c Read the section explaining the importance of the cashflow forecast. Make a note of any additional points that you find useful. This material will be helpful later when you produce your business plan.

d What is the current fee for arranging a business overdraft at your bank? What is the current monthly charge for overdrawn balances?

The following exercises are best performed with the aid of a computer spreadsheet. Where no spreadsheet is available then the bank cashflow forms provided can be used to perform the calculations manually.

2 **a** Load a spreadsheet package and set up a cashflow model as shown on page 613. Enter the formulae shown. Copy the formulae across or down wherever possible, to save time.

b Test that the formulae work by entering simple figures before going on. Remember not to write over the formulae – lock these cells if you know how to.

c Remember to save the file under a suitable name.

d When using the file it will be as well to save each new cashflow under a different name. In this way you will always have the blank original available to start from.

3 Input the figures from Hiking & Biking Ltd into your spreadsheet and save. Check that the closing balances are the same as in the chapter.

Perform the following 'What if' calculations and write down the effect each would have on the overdraft requirement (ignore the effect on VAT). Before each new calculation return to the original figures.

a What if there is a 5 per cent payrise for the workforce from March?

b What if a debtor expected to pay £2,000 in March does not pay until April?

c What if we are able to negotiate one month's credit from our suppliers to begin with purchases in April?

d What if we discover that we have forgotten to enter vehicle road tax and insurance in January – a total cost of £500?

4 Jane Wilton is about to set up in business, initially as a part-time venture, although she intends to go into the project on a full-time basis next year. She has identified a market locally for 'Greenclean', an all-purpose, ozone-friendly, biodegradable household cleaner and has obtained the franchise for her area.

The product will be supplied to Jane at a wholesale price of £1.00 per can. She will work on a mark-up of 200% so as to sell at the manufacturer's recommended retail price of £3.00 per can.

Jane feels that 15,000 units is a realistic sales target for the first year. People use cleaning products throughout the year so she predicts that sales will be steady at 1,250 units per month. All transactions will be on a cash basis for the foreseeable future.

Jane has £3,000 of her own capital and her mother has given her an interest-free loan of £6,000, repayable after three years.

Jane immediately spent £2,000 on fixtures and fittings and £4,000 on equipment for her office. The rest of the money she put into a business bank account. Expenses for the first year, beginning 1 April 19–3 are estimated as follows:

- Rent £4,000 p.a. This is due in advance in April, July, October, January
- Rates £6,000 due immediately
- Light and heat £250 per quarter payable June, September, December, March
- Telephone £200 per quarter payable June, September, December, March
- General administration costs approximately £80 per month
- Insurance £900 payable immediately
- Advertising costs £150 per month on average
- Leasing charges will be £600 per month
- Jane feels that she needs to withdraw £800 per month for living expenses.

Additionally, start-up expenses will be:

- Professional fees for accountancy and legal advice £1,000
- Launch/advertising/promotions £1,500
- Alteration to premises £800

As the small business adviser at Jane's bank, you are to consider the following points.

a What form of business organisation would best suit Jane's needs?
b Draw up an opening balance sheet for the business.
c Draw up a cashflow forecast for the first 12 months and advise Jane of any working capital requirements that she may have
d Jane is interested in buying a car for business purposes. This will cost £5,000. Advise Jane as to the most appropriate means of raising finance for this and explain whether your bank would be prepared to help her.
e Should Jane register for VAT?

Key terms

Listed company
Stock exchange
Unlisted securities market/AIM
Limited liability
Dividends
Preference shares
Ordinary shares (equities)
Registrar of companies
Balance sheet
Fixed assets
Current assets
Current liabilities
Long-term liabilities
Owner's capital
Debenture
Factoring
Leasing
Cashflow forecast
Cash budget
'What if?'
Monitoring
Variance
Working capital
Venture capital
Business angels
Master budget
Subsidiary budget
VAT
Liquidity

Review questions

1 Why will company shareholders not lose their private wealth if a company goes into liquidation?
2 Why might a sole trader take on a partner?
3 To whom must company accounts be sent at the end of the financial year?
4 What is another name for equities?
5 What sort of asset is land?
6 When is the bank account classed as a current liability?
7 If current assets are £10,000 and current liabilities are £6,000, what is the working capital?
8 Which item on a balance sheet represents the value of the business to the owner(s)?
9 What sort of funds are 'permanent'?
10 How does an overdraft appear on a cashflow forecast?
11 How often are VAT returns made to the Customs & Excise?
12 What is the current threshold above which a business must register for VAT? (NB Update this as necessary)
13 What is a budget?
14 What is the heading of the column that is placed against each budgeted column to allow the forecast to be monitored?
15 Some businesses divide their year into 13 periods. Why?
16 What is the name given to the difference between a budget and actual results?
17 What is a subsidiary budget?
18 What is the master budget?
19 What is a business angel?

Assignment 13
Minding your own business

This assignment develops knowledge and understanding of the following elements:

7.1 Explain sources of finance and financial requirements of business organisations
7.2 Produce and explain forecasts and a cash flow for a small business

It supports development of the following core skills

Communication 3.2
Application of number 3.1, 3.2, 3.3
Information technology 3.1, 3.3

You have been left £10,000 by a distant uncle. You have always wanted to run your own business and realise that now is your chance.

Your tasks

You will be required to research information and present a document based upon this research.

1 You will need to assemble the following information.

a Decide what kind of business you wish to set up. Some suggestions are:
- small general retailer
- sandwich service to local offices
- mobile ice-cream seller
- florist
- car tyre fitting.

b Decide on the form of business organisation that you will use and be sure why you have chosen this.

c Identify any local sources of help and advice available to small businesses.

d Decide what assets you will need, how much they will cost and how you will obtain the funds for these.

e Investigate the likely running costs of the business over the first 12 months.

f Make an estimate of the likely sales and purchases that you will make over this period.

2 Using the information that you have assembled produce a document to show the following:
- brief details of your proposed business
- the form of business organisation you will use, with reasons for this choice
- an opening balance sheet to show assets required at the start and how these will be funded (you will need to explain the terms and conditions of any loans)
- a cashflow forecast for the first 12 months of trading, with an assessment of any additional financial needs of the business over this period
- a realistic assessment as to the viability of your plans and how you will monitor progress
- an appendix containing the names and addresses of organisations likely to be of help to you when setting up your business. Briefly indicate the service these offer.

Guidance on presentation

Your work should have a contents page and should be word processed. Wherever possible use applications packages to aid effective presentation.

14 Financial record-keeping, final accounts and monitoring

What is covered in this chapter

- The need for financial record keeping
- The book-keeping system – an overview
- Writing up the books for credit purchases and sales
  - The cashbook
  - The double-entry system of book-keeping
  - Checking the ledger – the final balance
- Final accounts and their purpose
- Sole trader final accounts
- Depreciation of fixed assets
- Bad debts
- Interpretation of accounts – monitoring performance
- Forecast final accounts – cash versus profit
- Partnership accounts
- Final accounts of limited companies
- The cashflow statement
- Published accounts of limited companies
- Business failures
- Accounting standards

These are the resources you will need for your Financial Forecasting and Planning file:

- form 1R28, available from your local Inland Revenue office (see the business section of your local telephone directory)
- published reports from public limited companies, available from companies on request
- business sections from 'quality' newspapers (the Sunday papers have separate business sections which review the main business events of the week).

The need for financial record keeping

A business is unlikely to achieve its aims unless it keeps adequate financial records. These records help in the following ways. First, as an aid to management:

- they allow management to know the present position of the business
- they provide information which will enable management to make decisions for the future
- they provide evidence that can be used when raising finance or valuing the business.

Secondly, they satisfy various **statutory** (legal) requirements:

- requirements of the Companies Acts and Partnership Agreements (discussed later)
- they provide accurate information for assessment of VAT (value added tax), income tax and National Insurance Contributions (NIC).

The book-keeping system – an overview

In Chapter 11 we saw that each financial transaction will be accompanied by a document; you may wish to review this before continuing. Here we will look at business book-keeping: the way in which the details from these documents are recorded in the business accounts.

The diagram below gives an overview of the book-keeping system. So far, we have covered stage 1. In this chapter we will examine stages 2, 3, 4 and 5.

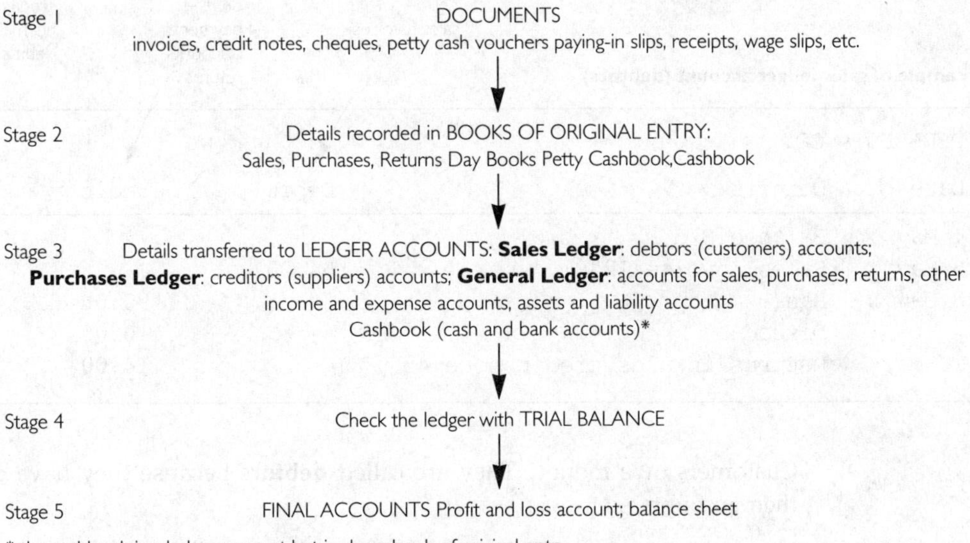

Writing up the books for credit purchases and sales

At some point details from the business documents will need to be entered into the main business accounts, known as the ledger. The ledger accounts are subdivided into three sections:

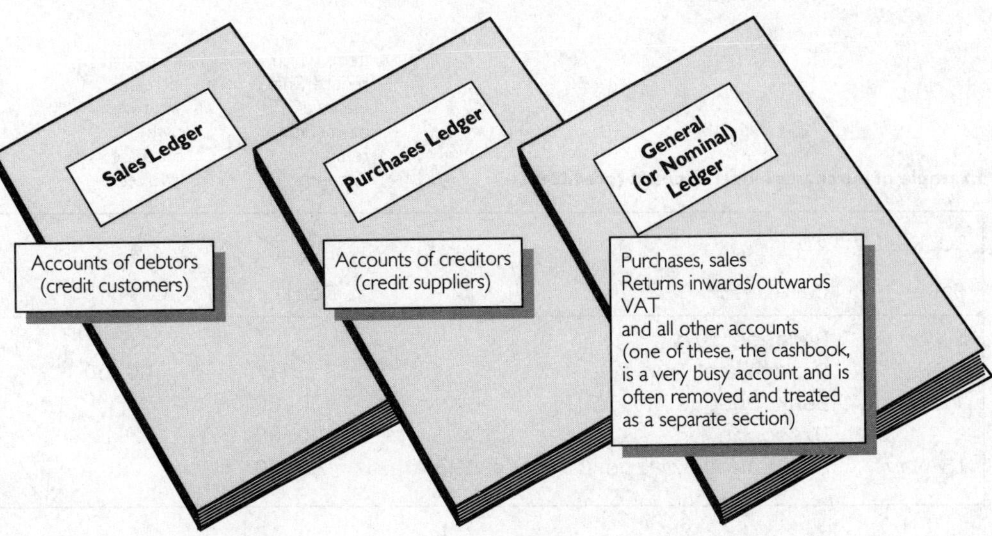

Figure 14.1 The ledger accounts

Writing up the sales ledger – accounts of debtors (customers)

Any trader selling on credit will need to keep an account for each customer or debtor. It looks familiar because the statement of account that is sent to the customer at the end of the month is a copy of a part of this.

Example of sales ledger account (debtors)

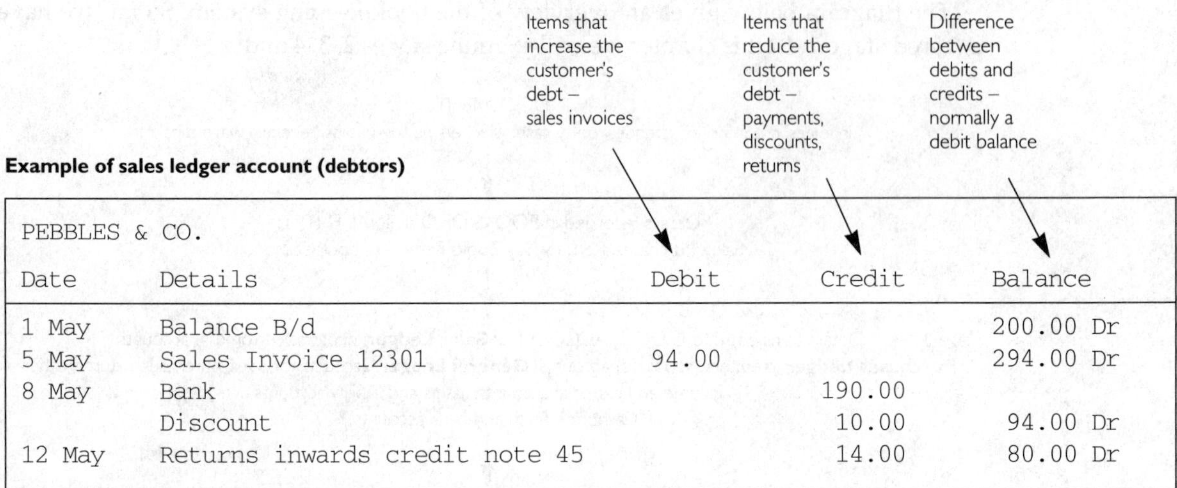

PEBBLES & CO.

Date	Details	Debit	Credit	Balance
1 May	Balance B/d			200.00 Dr
5 May	Sales Invoice 12301	94.00		294.00 Dr
8 May	Bank		190.00	
	Discount		10.00	94.00 Dr
12 May	Returns inwards credit note 45		14.00	80.00 Dr

Customers owe money. They are called **debtors** because they have debit balances in their accounts.

Writing up the purchase ledger – accounts of creditors (suppliers)

A business will also need to know how much it owes to its suppliers. It will receive monthly statements, but it will also keep its own records. The account for each creditor is prepared in a similar way to the debtors' accounts although the entries are the other way round.

Example of purchases ledger account (creditors)

Items which reduce what we owe – payments, returns, discounts

Items that increase what we owe – purchase invoices

Difference between the debits and credits – normally a credit balance

ROCKSALT LTD

Date	Details	Debit	Credit	Balance
1 May	Balance B/d			1,000.00 Cr
3 May	Purchases Invoice 3434		300.00	1,300.00 Cr
7 May	Bank cheque no 12231	900.00		
	Discount	100.00		300.00 Cr
15 May	Returns Outwards Cr Note 123	50.00		250.00 Cr

Suppliers are owed money. They are called **creditors** because they have credit balances.

Writing up the general ledger – recording the purchases, sales and returns

As well as recording debtors and creditors, a business will eventually wish to know its total sales, its total purchases and its total returns for the year. This information comes from the invoices and credit notes.

There are two stages to the process:

1 the details from the documents are entered first into **day books** (or **journals**):

2 each month the day book totals are posted (entered) to the relevant accounts in the **general ledger**. The diagram shows how sales invoices are recorded.

Writing up the books for credit sales

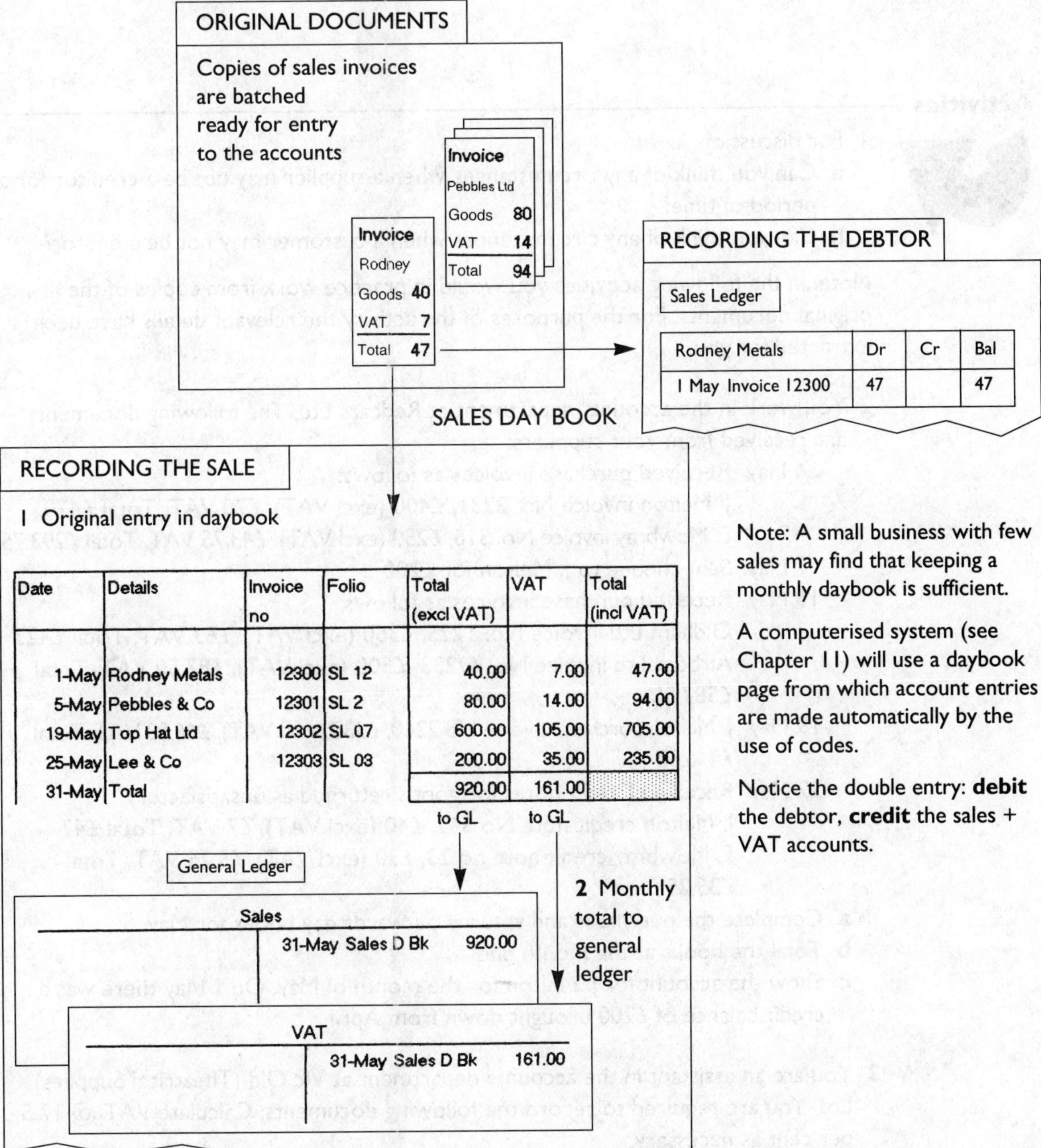

Notes:

1 The invoice details are taken from the supplier's copies of the sales invoices. Where there are a high number of sales these may be collected in batches before being entered.

2 At the end of each month the sales and VAT totals are transferred to the general ledger. The sales total to the sales account and the VAT total to the VAT account.

The purchases, returns inwards and returns outwards day books

The other three day books all have the same format as the sales day book and they all work in exactly the same way.

The whole process for recording purchases, sales and returns is shown on pages 624 and 625.

Activities

1 For discussion:

a Can you think of any circumstances when a supplier may not be a creditor for a period of time?

b Can you think of any circumstances when a customer may not be a debtor?

Note: in the following activities you would in practice work from copies of the original documents. For the purposes of the activity the relevant details have been extracted for you.

2 You work in the accounts department at Redcars Ltd. The following documents are received from your suppliers:

4 May Received purchase invoices as follows:
J. Melton invoice No. 2231, £400 (excl VAT), £70 VAT, Total £470
F. Mowbray invoice No. 316, £250 (excl VAT), £43.75 VAT, Total £293.75

7 May Sent cheque to J. Melton for £200

10 May Received purchase invoices as follows:
Oldham Ltd invoice No. 1225, £360 (excl VAT), £63 VAT, Total £423
Airboat Ltd invoice No. A/233, £500 (excl VAT), £87.50 VAT, Total £587.50

19 May J. Melton purchase invoice No 2260, £380 (excl VAT), £66.50 VAT, Total £446.50

22 May Received Credit notes for goods returned as unsatisfactory:
J. Melton credit note No 542, £40 (excl VAT), £7 VAT, Total £47
F. Mowbray credit note no 23, £30 (excl VAT), £5.25 VAT, Total £35.25

a Complete the purchases and returns outwards day books for May.

b Total the books at the month end.

c Show the account for J. Melton for the month of May. On 1 May there was a credit balance of £200 brought down from April.

3 You are an assistant in the accounts department at Vic Old (Theatrical Supplies) Ltd. You are required to record the following documents. Calculate VAT @ 17.5 per cent as necessary.

6 June Sent sales invoices as follows:
Reputable Reps invoice No. 3100, £500 (excl VAT)
Right Performances invoice No. 3101, £450 (excl VAT)
9 June Received cheque from Reputable Reps for £450
12 June Sent sales invoices as follows:
First Stage Ltd invoice No. 3102, £220 (excl VAT)
Plays for People invoice No. 3103, £800 (excl VAT)
19 June Sent to Reputable Reps sales invoice No. 3104, £80 (excl VAT)
22 June Sent Credit notes for goods returned as damaged:
Reputable Reps credit note No. 40, £20 (excl VAT)
First Stage Ltd credit note No. 41, £15 (excl VAT)

a Complete the sales and returns inwards day books for June.
b Total the books at the month end.
c Show the account for Reputable Reps for the month of June. On 1 June there was a debit balance of £450 brought down from May.

4 Purley Gates Ltd are a wholesaler who supply retailers with garden gates and fences. They trade entirely on 30 days credit. It is your job to deal with the paperwork for purchases and sales, and to write up the daybooks. You will need to calculate VAT on sales as required.
Below are transactions for the month of December:

2 Dec Sent cheque to Postmasters Ltd for £4,750 in full settlement for the £5,000 due (cash discount of £250)
5 Dec Sent sales invoices as follows:
Bentley and Driver £1,500 (excl VAT) Invoice No. 2050
Hawkins Ltd £2,350 (excl VAT) Invoice No. 2051
Wallace Bros £1,840 (excl VAT) Invoice No. 2052
8 Dec Received purchase invoices for supplies delivered:
Postmasters Ltd £2,000 (excl VAT), £350 VAT, Total £2,350. Invoice No. 445
Cheshunt Palings £3,500 (excl VAT) £612.50 VAT, Total £4,112.50. Invoice No. 78
15 Dec Received credit note (no of/123) from The Old Forge for £400 (excl VAT), £70 VAT, Total £470
20 Dec Received returns of damaged goods from Hawkins Ltd, sent Credit note No 450 for £300 (excl VAT), £52.50 VAT, Total £352.50

a Write up all transactions in the relevant day books.
b Transfer the day book totals to the appropriate general ledger accounts.
c On 1 December Purley Gates Ltd owed Postmasters Ltd £5,000. Show the account of Postmasters Ltd for the month of December.
d Bentley & Driver have a credit limit of £5,000. At the start of the month they owed £4,000. What is the purpose of a credit limit, how is it established and what is the immediate problem?
e Write a brief memo for accounts staff suggesting a procedure to prevent this from happening again.

Original documents

5th Nov To: AAA Ltd	Invoice No. 1
2 @ £5	10.00
2 @ £10	20.00
	30.00
VAT @ 17.5%	5.25
TOTAL	35.25

10th Nov To: MM & Co	Invoice No. 2
10 @ £5	50.00
VAT @ 17.5%	8.75
TOTAL	58.75

12th Nov To: JJ Ltd	Invoice No. 3
10 @ £2	20.00
VAT @ 17.5%	3.50
TOTAL	23.50

15th Nov To: JJ Ltd	Credit Note No. 1
1 @ £2	2.00
VAT @ 17.5%	0.35
TOTAL	2.35

20th Nov To: MM & Co	Credit Note No. 2.
2 @ £5	10.00
VAT @ 17.5%	1.75
TOTAL	11.75

Day Books (Journals)

SALES DAY BOOK

Date	Details	Invoice	TOTAL (excl VAT)	VAT	TOTAL
Nov 5	AAA Ltd	1	30.00	5.25	35.25
10	MM & Co	2	50.00	8.75	58.75
12	JJ Ltd	3	20.00	3.50	23.50
30	TOTALS for Month		100.00	17.50	117.50
			Sales A/c	VAT A/c	

RETURNS INWARDS DAY BOOK

Date	Details	Credit Note	TOTAL (excl VAT)	VAT	TOTAL
Nov 15	JJ Ltd	1	2.00	0.35	2.35
20	MM & Co	2	10.00	1.75	11.75
30	TOTALS for Month		12.00	2.10	14.10
			Rets In A/c	VAT A/c	

NOMINAL (GENERAL) LEDGER

SALES

			Nov 30	Monthly Total	100.00

RETURNS INWARDS

Nov 30	Monthly Total	12.00			

VAT

Nov 30	VAT on Rets In	2.10	Nov 30	VAT on Sales	17.50

Sales ledger
(Customers Accounts for Trade Debtors)

AAA Ltd

Date	Details	DR	CR	BAL
Nov 5	Goods Inv 1	35.25		35.25

MM & Co

Date	Details	DR	CR	BAL
Nov 10	Goods Inv 2	58.75		58.75
20	Credit Note 2		11.75	47.00

JJ Ltd

Date	Details	DR	CR	BAL
Nov 12	Goods Inv 3	23.50		23.50
15	Credit Note 1		2.35	21.15

Procedure for recording credit sales and returns

1 Details from Sales invoices entered into Sales Day Book
Details from credit notes entered into Returns Inwards Day Book
2 Day Book totals are posted at month end to General Ledger Accounts
3 Document totals are entered onto customers' accounts in Sales Ledger

Figure 11.7 The day books (journals) showing credit sales

Documents from suppliers

2nd Nov	Invoice 217
J M Supplies	
10 @ £20	200.00
VAT @ 17.5%	35.00
TOTAL	235.00

8th Nov	Invoice 892
LBJ & Co	
5 @ £8	40.00
8 @ £5	40.00
	80.00
VAT @ 17.5%	14.00
TOTAL	94.00

17th Nov	Invoice 310
J M Supplies	
10 @ £12	120.00
VAT @ 17.5%	21.00
TOTAL	141.00

14th Nov	Credit Note 72
J M Supplies	
2 @ £10	20.00
VAT @ 17.5%	3.50
TOTAL	23.50

26th Nov	Credit Note 83
LBJ & Co	
2 @ £5	10.00
VAT @ 17.5%	1.75
TOTAL	11.75

Day Books (Journals)

PURCHASES DAY BOOK

Date	Details	Invoice	TOTAL (excl VAT)	VAT	TOTAL
Nov 2	JM Supplies	217	200.00	35.00	235.00
8	LBJ & Co	892	80.00	14.00	94.00
17	JM Supplies	310	120.00	21.00	141.00
30	TOTALS for Month		400.00	70.00	470.00
			Purchases A/c	VAT A/c	

RETURNS OUTWARDS DAY BOOK

Date	Details	Credit Note	TOTAL (excl VAT)	VAT	TOTAL
Nov 14	JM Supplies	72	20.00	3.50	23.50
26	LBJ & Co	83	10.00	1.75	11.75
30	TOTALS for Month		30.00	5.25	35.25
			Rets Out A/c	VAT A/c	

NOMINAL (GENERAL) LEDGER

PURCHASES

Nov 30	Monthly Total	400.00			

RETURNS OUTWARDS

			Nov 30	Monthly Total	30.00

VAT

Nov 30	VAT on Purchases	70.00	Nov 30	VAT on Rets out	5.25

Purchases ledger

Suppliers' accounts for Trade Creditors

JM Supplies

Date	Details	DR	CR	BAL
Nov 2	Goods 217		235.00	235.00
14	Cr Note 72	23.50		211.50
17	Goods 310		141.00	352.50

LBJ & Co

Date	Details	DR	CR	BAL
Nov 8	Goods 892		94.00	94.00
26	Cr Note 83	11.75		82.25

Procedure for recording credit sales and returns

1 Details from Purchase invoices entered into Purchases Day Book
Details from credit notes from Suppliers entered into Returns outwards Day Book
2 Day Book totals are posted at month end to General Ledger Accounts
3 Document totals are entered into customers accounts in Purchases Ledger

Figure 14.2 The day books (journals) showing credit purchases

The cashbook – recording receipts and payments in the business accounts

The cashier will record receipts and payments in the cashbook. There are often separate columns for:

1 the cash account – to record actual notes and coins received, paid and held by the business

2 the bank account – to record money deposited, withdrawn and held in the business bank account.

Like all accounts the cashbook is two sided. The left-hand or **debit** side records receipts and the **credit** or right-hand side records payments.

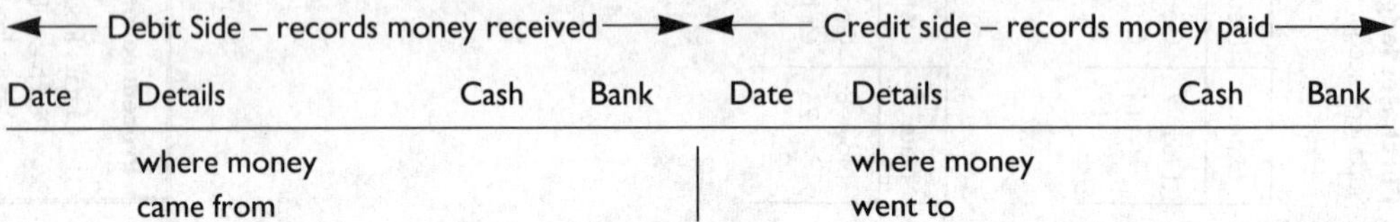

To enter details into the cashbook it is necessary to identify the following points:

- whether the money is received or paid (this determines which side of the book it is entered to)
- the date that the transaction occurred
- details of where the money came from or where it was paid to. This often takes the form of another account name. References such as cheque numbers or account references are often recorded also
- whether it affected the cash account (i.e. money held in the business, perhaps in a cash box or safe) or whether it affected the bank account.

Worked example

Two-column cashbook

Date	Transaction	Workings Cash/Bank	Received/Paid
Jan 1	Opened a business bank account by putting in savings of £2,000 as capital	bank	received
Jan 5	Bought a van for £500 paying by cheque	bank	paid
Jan 10	Withdrew £350 from the bank for use as office cash	bank	paid
	(NB this affects both cash and bank)	cash	received
Jan 12	Bought stock (purchases) for cash £200	cash	paid
Jan 15	Bought stock from a supplier J. Jones £150 on credit NB although this is a purchase it will NOT affect the cashbook until we pay for it!	no effect	
Jan 18	Sold stock for cash £500	cash	received

Jan 19	Paid £300 cash for rent	cash	paid
Jan 20	Sold stock (sales) for £400, received a cheque in payment	bank	received
Jan 25	Bought stationery for office use paying by cheque £100	bank	paid
Jan 28	Wrote a cheque to pay J. Jones for purchases on the 15th	bank	paid

CASHBOOK

Date	Details	Cash	Bank	Date	Details	Cash	Bank
1 Jan	Capital		2,000	5 Jan	Van		500
10	Bank C	350		10	Cash C		350
18	Sales	500		12	Purchases	200	
20	Sales		400	19	Rent	300	
				25	Stationery		100
				28	J. Jones		150
				31	Balances c/d	350	1,300
		850	2,400			850	2,400
1 Feb	Balances B\d	350	1,300				

Notes on the entries

The transaction on 15 January does not involve the movement of money. A purchase invoice would be received but the cashbook only records the movement of money. This happens on 28 January.

The letter C against the entries on 10 January stands for **contra entry**. This means that two entries are made, one opposite the other. The reason is that both the cash and the bank accounts are affected. In this case money is taken from the bank and put into cash.

Where purchases and sales of stock are made (12, 18, 20 Jan) for immediate (cash) payment, then they are detailed as 'purchases' or 'sales', rather than under the name of the customer or supplier. Where payment is finally made for an earlier credit transaction, then the name of the person is used as we are recording a payment to or from a client, not a new purchase or sale.

The closing balances show the state of the cash account and the bank account as a result of the preceding transactions. There is £350 in the cash account and £1,300 in the bank account on 31 Jan.

Balancing the cashbook

An account balance is the difference between the total debits and the total credits on the account. On the cashbook it is the difference between the amount paid in and the amount withdrawn.

You will remember that the balances of the debtors' and creditors' accounts, and the bank statement, were worked on a running balance basis. They were balanced after every transaction. The cashbook is usually balanced on a periodic basis, i.e. it is balanced after a period of time. In the example this happens at the end of the month. It must be stressed that whichever method is used the balance at a particular date will be the same.

Debit and credit balances

The balance always appears first on the smaller side (whichever this is) so as to make the totals equal. It is then brought down to the opposite side – the larger side to start the next period.

A balance brought down to the debit side is called a debit balance. It represents money left – more debits (receipts) than credits (payments). A balance brought down to the credit side is called a credit balance and represents an overdraft – more credits (payments) than debits (receipts).

A bank account can have either a debit or a credit balance, whereas a cash account can never be overdrawn.

The three-column cashbook

Where cash discount is claimed it is useful to record the amount of the discount allowed on sales or received on purchases next to the payment. To achieve this some cashbooks have a third, discount, column on each side.

◄— Debit Side – records money received —► ◄— Credit side – records money paid —►

Date	Details	Discount	Cash	Bank	Date	Details	Discount	Cash	Bank
		£	£	£			£	£	£
	Where money came from (account name)	Discounts allowed to customers				Where money went to (account name)	Discounts received from suppliers		

Worked example

The three-column cashbook

Date	Details	Discount	Cash	Bank	Date	Details	Discount	Cash	Bank
1 Mar	Balances B/d		100	200	2 Mar	Insurance 12350			500
3	Sales			250	3	Willis 12351	8		72
4	Linford	10		190	4	Petrol		15	
5	Bank C		20		5	Cash 12352 C			20
6	Sales		30		5	Burrell 12353	5		95
6	Balance c/d			47	6	Balance c/d		135	
		10	150	687			13	150	687
8 Mar	Balance B/d		135		8 Mar	Balance B/d			47

Notes on the entries

4 March we received £190 from Linford, but allowed £10 discount. Linford has actually cleared a debt of £200

3 March we paid Willis £72 and received £8 discount. We have settled an account of £80

5 March we paid £95 to Burrell and received £5 discount. This has settled an account of £100

Notice that cheque numbers are used to help identify payments

C denotes a contra entry

The discount columns are totalled, but not balanced. They are merely convenient lists. We will see the effects of these on business profits at a later stage

Notice that the bank account is overdrawn by £47 on 8 March. We know this because it has a credit balance, indicating larger payments than receipts.

CASH BOOK

RECEIPTS — Analysis of Receipts

Date	Details	Bank	Overseas	UK	Charter Europe	Long Haul	Leisure Air	Insurance	Hotels
19-Nov	Bal B/d	2 765.20							
22-Nov	Sales	12 056.72	6 500.75	235.12	825.35	728.40	2 200.50	1 441.60	125.00
29-Nov	Sales	11 362.33	5 620.15	187.18	500.20	714.60	2 984.95	1 239.80	115.45
1-Dec	Sales	9 120.17	4 129.20	162.12	481.55	543.82	2 381.62	1 323.56	98.30
4-Dec	Sales	9 143.11	3 900.18	212.34	292.15	498.90	2 512.71	1 492.18	234.65
		44447.53	20150.28	796.76	2099.25	2485.72	10079.78	5497.14	573.40
7-Dec	Bal B/d	12951.69							

PAYMENTS — Analysis of Payments

Date	Details	Bank	Cheque no	Tour Op'tors	Salaries Wages	Post St'nery	Rent Rates	Sundries
19-Nov	Sage Ltd	1 650.57	188550	1 650.57				
20-Nov	Melrose UK	2 720.85	188551	2 720.85				
20-Nov	Petty Cash	30.00	AC					30.00
21-Nov	Fineline	40.68	188552			40.68		
23-Nov	Aerolake	3 420.00	188553	3 420.00				
23-Nov	Melrose UK	1 456.87	188554	1 456.87				
23-Nov	JBJ	4 352.80	188555	4 352.80				
27-Nov	Petty Cash	30.00	AC					30.00
27-Nov	JS Estates	2 470.00	DD				2 470.00	
29-Nov	Sage Ltd	3 426.86	188556	3 426.86				
29-Nov	Petty Cash	30.00	AC					30.00
30-Nov	Aerolake	2 743.65	188557	2 743.65				
30-Nov	Emdale Ltd	175.40	188558			175.40		
30-Nov	Motec Ltd	27.60	188559					27.60
1-Dec	Melrose UK	3 451.70	188560	3 451.70				
2-Dec	JBJ	2 856.10	188561	2 856.10				
4-Dec	Petty Cash	30.00	AC					30.00
4-Dec	Salaries	2 582.76	TR		2 582.76			
4-Dec	Bal c/d	12 951.69						
		44 447.53		26 079.40	2 582.76	216.08	2 470.00	147.60

Figure 14.3 An analysed cash book

Analysed cashbook

It is useful for a business to not only record receipts and payments, but to analyse these into receipts from different sources, and payments on different types of expense. For a small business, or a club or society, such a system may be all that is necessary to provide details of income and expense for management purposes and for the year-end accounts. A large business will need a full system of accounts but may still find analysis columns useful.

The example on page 629 shows an analysed cashbook as used by a retail travel agency. This book has bank columns only as the business does not keep a cash account. At the end of each month the totals of the analysis columns will be transferred to the various income and expenditure accounts in the general ledger.

The cashbook and double-entries

Where a business does not keep an analysed cashbook it will be necessary to transfer entries to the ledger on an individual basis. The double entries will be made as follows:

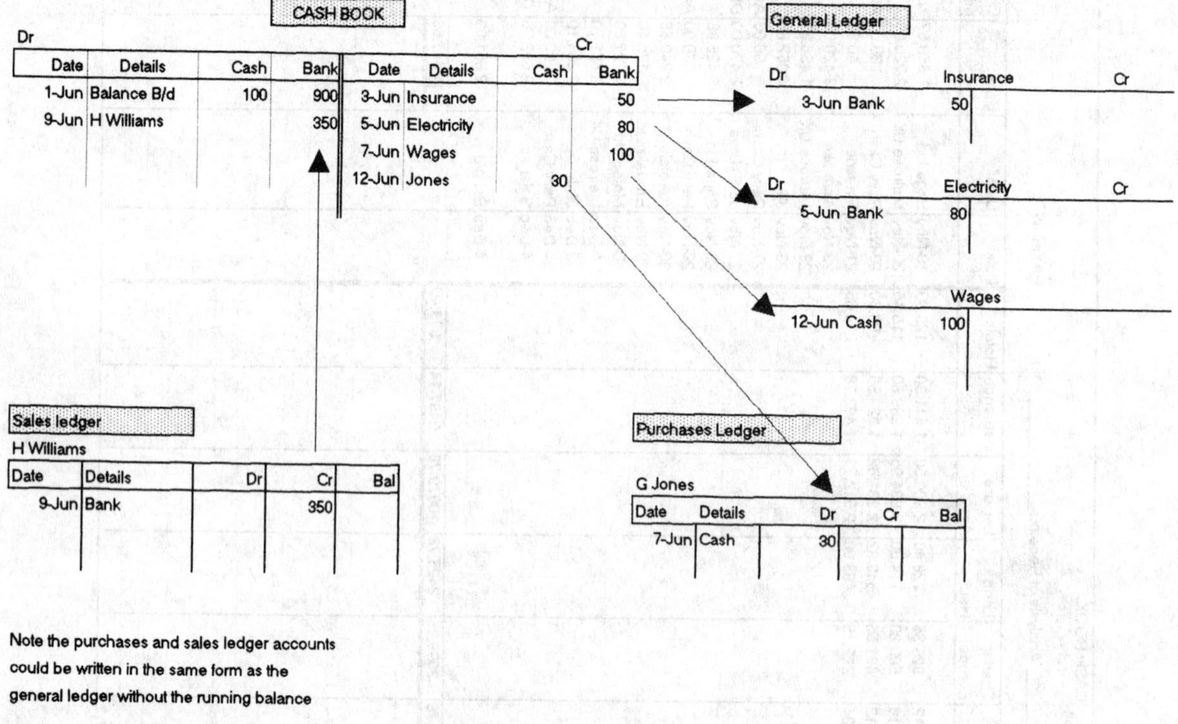

Figure 14.4 Double entry in the ledger

Notice that the credit entries from the cashbook go to the debit of the ledger accounts, while the debit entries of the cashbook go to the credit of the ledger accounts.

Activities

1 Study the example of the three-column cashbook on page 628 and answer the following questions.
   a Is Linford a customer or a supplier?
   b Is Burrell a customer or a supplier?
   c What was the bank balance at the start of the month?
   d Is cash received or paid on 6 March?
   e What was the cash balance at the end of the week?

f Is the £8 discount on 3 March discount allowed, or discount received?
g Is this discount a loss or a gain to your business?
h How would you describe the receipt on 5 March?
i If, on counting the money in the cashbox at 6 March you found that it totalled £130, what action would you take?

2 As cashier for West Stand Ltd, one of your jobs is to enter up the three-column cashbook for December from the following transactions:

Dec 1 Cashbook balances are cash £255, bank £1,740
Dec 3 Sold goods for £35 cash
Dec 4 Purchased goods for £78 cash
Dec 7 Received a cheque from J. Monroe for £88 (this was after £6 discount had been allowed)
Dec 8 Paid A. Hoffman by cheque £349 cheque No. 11120
Dec 10 Paid £15 cash to J. Jones
Dec 15 Sent a cheque to P. Mason for £33, cheque No. 11121. This was in full payment of our account which stood at £40
Dec 22 Received a cheque from B. Ellis for £73
Dec 23 Paid £35 cash to caterers (general expenses) for office party
Dec 28 Settled our account with G. Small, paid £115 by cheque (No. 11122)
Dec 31 We received two cheques from customers: K. Wood £249 and M. Sidhu £200

Balance the book at the end of the month and bring down the balances at 1 January.

3 Due to staff illness you have been asked to write up the cashbook of your employers Park Lane Enterprises. Your firm uses a three-column cashbook. All cash received is placed in a cash box in the office safe.

Mar 1 Cashbook balances are cash £78, bank £5,197 overdrawn
Mar 6 Sent a cheque for £122 (No. 34555) to L. Turner after deducting £8 discount received
Mar 8 Paid cash for purchases of stock of £18
Mar 16 Received a cheque for £244 from N. Marsh Ltd
Mar 17 Paid cash for staff expenses of £33
Mar 18 Received cash from N. Foster for sales worth £48
Mar 20 Paid £20 cash to R. Branston for office cleaning
Mar 21 Received a cheque from JBL Ltd for £333, after allowing £17 discount
Mar 30 Sent cheques to A. Bennett for £208 (No. 34556), Rick Shaw (Transport) Ltd for £490 (No. 34557)
Mar 31 U Sinclair sent us a cheque for £160, this was in full payment of her account which stood at £166

Balance the book at the end of the month and bring down the balances at 1 April. It appears that the cashier will not be back at work next week and you are on annual leave. Write a brief set of instructions for the trainee who will prepare the cashbook next week.

This should mention:

- what the balances at 1 April indicate
- what debit and credit mean
- how the accuracy of the cash account can be checked at the end of the week.

4 You have been made treasurer of the students' union sports club. It is your responsibility to look after the club's money.

The club will arrange matches for a variety of sports by booking local pitches, most of which are owned by the local council, although some are owned by private clubs who are prepared to hire out their grounds. You will need equipment of various types and you eventually hope to buy kit, some reasonable balls and other items such as a first-aid box. There will also be referees to pay.

The club will collect an annual subscription from each member and a match fee of around £2 per player. Additionally there will be fund-raising events such as a Christmas disco and a summer barbecue.

a You decide to open a bank account.

- Obtain information from your local bank about a suitable account. What are the charges involved? What forms do you need to sign, what type of documentation will the bank supply you with?
- Do you have an overdraft facility?
- Are there any bank charges?
- Have a look at receipt books in the local stationers. How much do they cost?
- Is there anything else that you might need?

b Draw up a cashbook – analysed to show different income and expenditure. Record the following items for the first month. It is your policy to pay all cash into the bank as soon as possible. Your new cheque book begins with cheque number 55001.

September 8	Subs received in cash	J. Lake	£10
		J. Cunningham	£10
		M. De Luca	£10
		B. Ene	£10
September 9	More subs from:	N. Townsend	£10 cheque
		R. Landman	£10 cash
	Cheque to Milton CC for hire of pitches		£30
September 12	Game versus Elton Grove		
	Match fees received in cash		£27.50
	Paid referee		£12 cash
September 15	Bought new ball from Vespa Sports paid for by cheque		£18.75
September 18	Collected more subs:		
	cheques from:	B. Birch	£10
		T. Leahong	£10
September 18	Cheque from students union		£50
September 19	Game versus Castle Manor		
	Collected match subs:	cash	£18
		K. Carew	£4.50 cheque
	Paid referee in cash	£12	
	Paid for pitch by cheque made out to CMFC	£25	
September 23	Received late match fees in cash from:		
		T. Leahong	£2.50
		D. Ingle	£2.50
September 25	Subs received from M Zerrougui		£10 cash

c The team manager, who wants to pay for pitches in advance to obtain preferential rates, asks you for a cheque for £45 made out to Tower Astroparks as soon as possible. You are anxious not to get overdrawn so you balance the cashbook to see if the club can afford it.

If you can afford it write a cheque as requested. If not write a memo to the manager, J. Bossley, to explain the situation.

The single-entry system of book-keeping

We may find that for the general ledger books of original entry are sufficient. Certainly, if we drew analysis columns in the cashbook as well as the petty cashbook, then we could total up different types of income and expenditure quite conveniently, and we would have the means to see in detail where our money has come from and where it has gone to.

At the end of the year our accountant would have the necessary information with which to calculate our profit or loss.

The double-entry system of book-keeping

Many businesses adopt a full double-entry book-keeping system. Computerised accounting systems generally require single-entries to be made in the day books and the cashbook as above, but the system then automatically makes double-entries with the help of account codes. The user is able to produce accurate ledger account entries without necessarily understanding how this is done.

It is, however, useful to know something about double-entry book-keeping. In particular it will help you understand the final accounts such as the trading and profit and loss accounts, and the balance sheet that we will look at later.

Rules for double-entry book-keeping

1 The double-entries take place between the ledger accounts. Remember that ledger accounts are always two sided:

DEBIT side			CREDIT side		
Date	Details	£	Date	Details	£
	Debit side RECEIVES – Money or value comes IN			Credit side GIVES – Money or value goes OUT	

Where the running balance format is used for sales and purchase ledger accounts, the principle is the same.

2 Each business transaction must have two effects (a double effect) on the ledger, because if one account gives then another account must receive.
The rule is therefore:

> FOR EVERY DEBIT ENTRY IN ONE ACCOUNT THERE MUST BE A CORRESPONDING CREDIT ENTRY IN ANOTHER ACCOUNT.

The double-entry system simply requires us to look at BOTH sides of every transaction and make the TWO entries each time. If you look back at the entries made in this chapter this is exactly what has happened, although sometimes, for convenience, some of the entries are delayed until the end of the month when we post totals from day books to the ledger.

There is a summary of the procedures that we have followed and the double-entries involved on the following page:

Transaction	**Account Debited** (Account which receives)	**Account Credited** (Account which gives)
Sales on credit	Customer (debtor)	Sales account (at month end)
Purchases on credit	Purchases account (at month end)	Supplier (creditor)
Money received from customer	Cashbook	Debtor
Money paid to supplier	Creditor	Cashbook
Money paid on expenses	expense account (eg electricity)	Cashbook
Petty cash spent	expense account (at month end)	Petty cashbook

Checking the ledger – the trial balance

If in a double-entry system there is a debit entry for every credit entry in the ledger, it follows that the total value of the debit and credit entries should be the same. This fact is used by a book-keeper to check that the ledger is accurate. In practice the book-keeper will use the account balances rather than the totals. Where the trial balance does not balance (where the debit column does not equal the credit column) there is an error on the books.

This list of balances is called the **trial balance**.

Trial Balance as at 31st December 19–:

	£	£
Cash	294.00	
Bank	2883.70	
Petty Cash	40.00	
Debtors	1061.50	
Creditors		178.60
Travel	8.40	
Stationery	5.96	
Light & Heat	157.00	
Wages	280.00	
General Expenses	17.64	
Purchases	460.00	
Sales		2100.00
Returns Inwards	98.00	
Returns Outward		114.00
Discount Allowed	25.00	
Discount Received		9.70
VAT		28.90
Capital		34000.00
Drawings	250.00	
Premises	30000.00	
Office Equipment	850.00	
Total	36431.20	36431.20

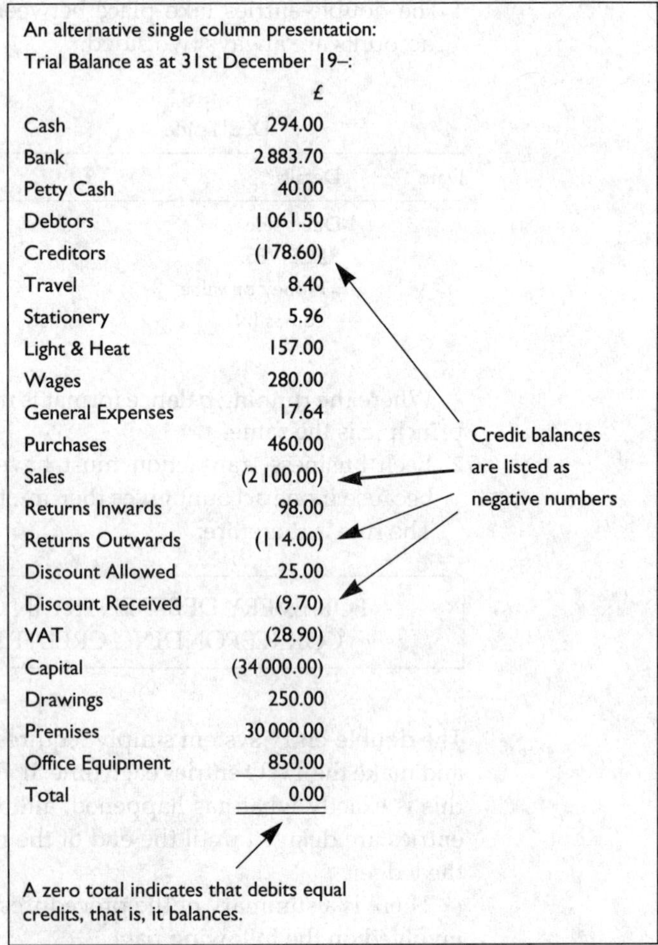

An alternative single column presentation:
Trial Balance as at 31st December 19–:

	£
Cash	294.00
Bank	2883.70
Petty Cash	40.00
Debtors	1061.50
Creditors	(178.60)
Travel	8.40
Stationery	5.96
Light & Heat	157.00
Wages	280.00
General Expenses	17.64
Purchases	460.00
Sales	(2100.00)
Returns Inwards	98.00
Returns Outwards	(114.00)
Discount Allowed	25.00
Discount Received	(9.70)
VAT	(28.90)
Capital	(34000.00)
Drawings	250.00
Premises	30000.00
Office Equipment	850.00
Total	0.00

Credit balances are listed as negative numbers
A zero total indicates that debits equal credits, that is, it balances.

Notice how the trial balance is structured:

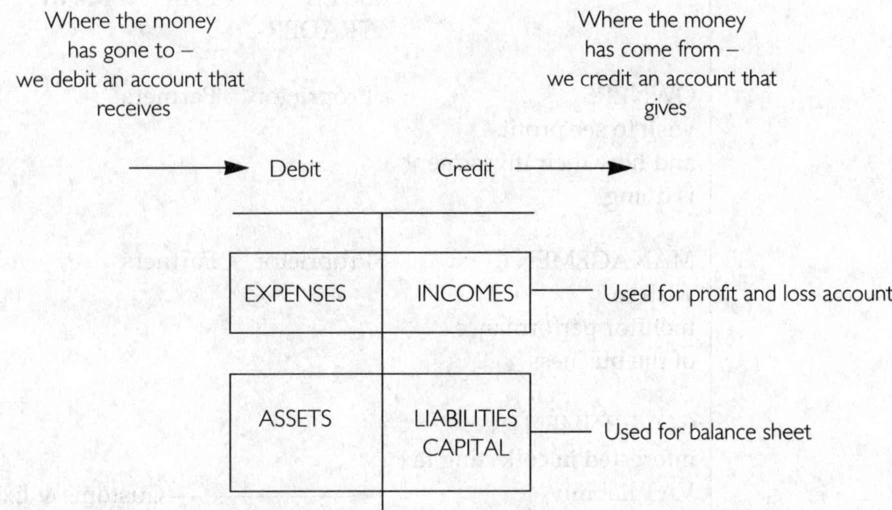

Later in the chapter we will return to the trial balance and see how the figures are used to produce the profit and loss account and the balance sheet.

Final accounts and their purpose

The final accounts of a business are those financial statements produced by a business at the end of a period of trading. In most cases they consist of:

- the **trading account**
- the **profit and loss account**
- the **balance sheet**.

The trading and profit and loss accounts are normally drawn up together and are frequently referred to simply as the profit and loss account. They show the profits or losses over the trading period by comparing value of sales over this time with expenses incurred.

The balance sheet, as we saw in Chapter 13, is a list of the assets, liabilities and capital of the business at a certain date. It shows the *worth, or value, of the business* at this time.

Who needs to see the final accounts?

The final accounts provide financial information about the performance of a business for the benefit of the owners and other interested parties. Those who are thought to have a stake (an interest) in the financial affairs of a business are referred to as stakeholders.

STAKEHOLDERS' REQUIREMENTS	← Stakeholders in different organisations →		
	SOLE TRADER	PARTNERSHIP	LIMITED COMPANY
OWNERS wish to see profits and how their investment is doing	Proprietor	Partners	Shareholders
MANAGEMENT wish to monitor performance of the business	Proprietor	Partners	Directors
GOVERNMENT: interested in collecting tax			
VAT liability	← Customs & Excise →		
TAX on profits	← Inland Revenue →		
	← Income Tax →		Corporation Tax
CREDITORS wish to monitor the safety of their investment	← Bank Building Society Trade Creditors →		
			Debenture holders
EMPLOYEES wish to see the results of their efforts	← no requirement to report →		Accounts made public
THE COMMUNITY See the profits made by organisations whose activities affect the lives of communities	← no requirement to report →		Accounts made public

The requirement to report annually

Each business works to a financial year. This is a 12-month period usually determined by the month in which the business began trading. It will not necessarily run from January to December, but it is just as likely, for example, to begin on 1 May and end on 30 April the following year.

A business is required, for the purposes of taxation, to report its profits or losses at the end of each financial year. In practice this means that a business must keep accurate records and use these to draw up annual final accounts. This is a statutory (legal) requirement. As we shall see, companies are subject to further legal obligations under the Companies Act 1985.

Preparing accounts

Your accountant, if you have one, will draw up your accounts. But whoever prepares them, you are still responsible for their accuracy and for correctly declaring the amount of the profits. The Tax Office will need to be satisfied that the accounts you have supplied show the true results of the business.

Accounts presented to the Tax Office are usually in two parts:

- the Profit and Loss Account which is a summary of the year's trading transactions
- the Balance Sheet shows the 'assets' and 'liabilities' of the business.

As long as your gross business turnover before expenses is below £15,000 for a full year you do not have to prepare detailed accounts to send to the Tax Office. All you have to do is prepare a simple summary showing your turnover, your total business purchases and expenses, and your profits.

You must keep full and accurate accounts from the start. You need to do this whether you draw up the accounts for yourself, have an accountant to do it, or send in a simple summary.

It is a serious offence to understate your profits deliberately. If you cannot give your Tax Office an accurate statement of your profits, they will have to be estimated and you may then have to pay tax on the basis of this estimate. If you consider the estimate is too high, it will be up to you to show that it is. So it is in your interests to keep full and accurate records.

Source: *Starting in Business* IR28 issued by the Inland Revenue (October 1993)

Activity

Look up the telephone number of your local Inspector of Taxes. Ask them to send you a copy of the Inland Revenue guide *Starting in Business* ref IR28. This is written for the general public, is free and will be useful as reference material during your course.

Are final accounts of use to a business?

Although they are largely designed for tax purposes the final accounts can be of use to the business.

- They can be used for securing and maintaining finance. A bank being asked for a loan, for example, will usually ask to see these same accounts. It will want to see the true performance of a business and not some 'dressed up' results. The bank manager knows that the business is unlikely to have overstated its profits to the Inland Revenue.
- The final accounts can be used for monitoring business performance through ratio analysis. We will look at this in detail later in the chapter.
- The figures reported on the accounts may be used as a basis for financial forecasts. Where operations are standard from year to year budgets may be based upon last year's costs plus an allowance for inflation. This is called incremental budgeting.
- Limited companies will distribute summary final accounts to their shareholders in the form of published accounts.

Sole trader final accounts

We will look at sole trader accounts through the case of Sam Saddler, who keeps a small hardware shop. It is the end of his financial year and time to draw up the final accounts. Sam has finished stock-taking and values his unsold stock at £1,000.

Stage 1 The trial balance

Sam has balanced all of his accounts and listed them as a trial balance. Since the debit and credit totals agree he presumes that the accounts are correct.

Trial Balance of Sam Saddler as at 31 March 19-5

		Dr	Cr	
	Sales		10,000	Income
business expenses	Purchases	5,000		
	Rent and rates	1,500		
	Insurance	200		
	Light and heating	800		
	Wages	500		
Opening Stock	Stock at 1 October 1994	2,000		
Fixed Assets	Motor Van	4,000		
	Shop Fittings	6,500		
Taken by owner	Drawings	200		
	Capital		8,000	owed to owner
	Bank Loan		5,000	Long-Term Liability
Current Assets	Bank	2,700		
	Cash	400		
	Debtors	200		
	Creditors		1,000	Current Liability
		24,000	24,000	

Additional Information:
At stock taking the Closing Stock of the business was valued at £1,000

Stage 2 The trading and profit and loss accounts – the calculation of profit

Sam's accountant uses those figures on the trial balance that show *income* and *expense* to draw up a trading and profit and loss account.

The trading and profit and loss account consists of five items:

		£	
	SALES	10,000	– total sales for the period
less	COST OF GOODS SOLD	6,000	– direct cost of these goods
=	GROSS PROFIT	4,000	– the profit on trading
less	EXPENSES	3,000	– overhead costs for the period
=	NET PROFIT	1,000	– the final profit

There are two accounts because there are two measures of profit:
The trading account calculates the gross profit made from trading (buying and selling of stock):

SALES – COST OF SALES = GROSS PROFIT

The profit and loss account calculates the net profit. This is the final profit after running costs (or overheads) have been taken into account:

GROSS PROFIT – EXPENSES = NET PROFIT

In practice it is necessary to work out cost of sales and total expenses. These workings are entered to the left of the main column so as not to obscure the five main items.

The full trading and profit and loss account drawn up by Sam's accountant would be as follows.

Trading and Profit and Loss Account of Sam Saddler for year ending 31 March 19-5

	£	£	
SALES		10,000	
OPENING STOCK	2,000		the calculation
PURCHASES	5,000		for the cost of
	7,000		goods sold is
less CLOSING STOCK	1,000		to the left
COST OF GOODS SOLD		6,000	
GROSS PROFIT		4,000	
less RENT AND RATES	1,500		the individual
INSURANCE	200		expenses are
LIGHT AND HEAT	800		listed to the
WAGES	500		left
		3,000	
NET PROFIT		1,000	

Notice the meaning of the following terms:

- Sales: The total value of stock sold in the period. This refers only to *sales of stock bought for resale* – not to sales of fixed assets, such as an old van, which needs replacing.
- Purchases: The total cost of stock bought in the period. Again this refers only to *purchases of stock for resale*, not to the purchase of assets for use in the business, such as a new filing cabinet.
- Closing stock: The value of unsold stock left at the end of the period.
- Opening stock: The value of unsold stock from last year available when the period started. Stock will normally be valued at cost price
- The heading to the account: Identifies the end of the *trading period over which the profits have been made*. In this case it is a financial year. Sometimes a business will prepare final accounts at intervals within the year, perhaps quarterly. In this case the heading would read as: 'period ending …'.

Cost of goods sold The calculation for cost of goods sold sometimes gives students problems. Remember that cost of goods sold is not necessarily the same as purchases. Most businesses will not sell all that they buy in a particular period. There will normally be opening and closing stock and we must adjust for these.

Sam began the year with stock worth £2,000 left from last year. This year he purchased more goods for £5,000, so that he had £7,000 worth available for sale. He has not sold £1,000 of these – his closing stock. The cost of the goods he actually sold must be £6,000.

Remember that closing stock for one year becomes opening stock for the next year. Though most traders' accounts will show opening and closing stocks, a business in its first year will have no opening stock as there has been no previous year from which it can be carried down.

Expenses

Businesses suffer three types of expense:

- revenue expense
- capital expense
- private expense.

Revenue expenses The profit and loss account lists revenue expenses. These are the overheads, running costs which give short-term benefit but which are *used up* in the trading period. Items which are frequently listed on the profit and loss account include: heat and light, rent and rates, interest charges, petrol, insurance, motor repairs, wages and salaries, advertising.

Capital expenses In Sam Saddler's accounts the shop fittings and motor van are *not* included as expenses for profit and loss purposes. They are certainly expensive items but they will last for longer than the year and are therefore classed as fixed assets. They will appear on the balance sheet as items that the business still owns.

Unlike the insurance, rent and rates which will need to be paid again next year, the fixed assets have not worn out but are still there ready for further use.[1]

Private expenses Drawings represent the money taken out of the business by the owner, Sam, for his own personal use. The profit calculation takes account of business expenses only. Drawings will be shown on the balance sheet.

Drawings versus business expenses

It is true that some people in business run a private car and seem to charge the running costs to the business; others may charge their telephone bill to the business. They are only able to do this if the Inland Revenue has been convinced that the car or the telephone can be justified as a business expense.

11 *Business expenditure*

If you incur any expenditure partly for business purposes and partly for private purposes, you can only claim for the business part.

Examples of expenses which are only partly allowable are rent, rates, lighting and heating bills of premises used partly for business and partly for domestic purposes; also telephone charges where there is both a private and business use of the phone.

Source: *Starting in Business* IR28 issued by the Inland Revenue

[1] Of course fixed assets do eventually wear out and need replacing. The point is that this process happens over a number of years, hence we need to spread the cost. This is called **depreciation**. For the moment we will ignore it, but it will be dealt with in a later section.

Activities

For discussion

1 What do you think is the benefit to a sole trader who is able to claim that she needs a smart car for her business and that most of her petrol, tax, insurance and repair costs are business expenses?

2 How do you think she can persuade the Inland Revenue?

A net loss

Unless a business is selling its stock for less than cost there will usually be a gross profit. However, it is quite possible for running costs on the profit and loss account to be greater than gross profit. In this case the 'profit' will be a negative figure, representing a net loss.

Imagine that Sam's wage bill had been £3,500. His expenses would be higher and he would make a loss:

	GROSS PROFIT		4,000
less	RENT & RATES	1,500	
	INSURANCE	200	
	LIGHT AND HEAT	800	
	WAGES	3,500	
			6,000
	NET LOSS		(2,000)

In accounting, negative figures are normally shown in parentheses (brackets).

Activities

1 Explain what new information a business will obtain from drawing up:
   a a trading account
   b a profit and loss account.

2 What sort of expenses do you think would appear in the profit and loss account of:
   a a hairdresser
   b a sandwich bar
   c a mobile ice-cream seller.

3 On 1 July 19–4 Reg Richards set up in business as a market trader. He extracted the following figures from his books for the six months ending 31 December 19–4:

Sales	25,000
Opening stock	0
Closing stock	2,500
Purchases	12,800
Heating	100
Bank charges	285
Rental	1,000
Petrol	430
Casual wages	620
General expenses	450

a Draw up the trading and profit and loss accounts. Remember to use the correct headings.
b Why is there no opening stock recorded?
c Reg also bought a second-hand van for carrying his stock. Why is this not included as part of his profit and loss account?
d On what date does Reg's financial year end?
e What will happen if Reg is unable to produce his final accounts for the Inland Revenue at this time?
f Make a list of other people who might be interested in Reg's accounts at the end of the first year. Briefly explain each.

4 Justin Case runs an off-licence. The book-keeper has produced the following figures for the first year of trading ending on 30 June 19–7:

Sales	108,715
Purchases	42,504
Rates	12,455
Light and heat	7,423
Interest on loan	2,780
Advertising	5,665
Vehicle expenses	3,821
Wages and salaries	10,450
Stock at 1 July 19–6	12,046
Stock at 30 June 19–7	11,982

a Draw up the trading and profit and loss account for the year
b By what process will the closing stock value have been calculated?
c What effect would an increase in the rate of interest have on Justin's profits? Explain briefly.

5 What might the Inspector of Taxes ask Sam Saddler? (Clue: look at the size of the drawings.)

Stage 3 The balance sheet – the worth of the business

Sam's accountant will also draw up the business balance sheet.

Whereas the trading and profit and loss account deals with the income and expenses on the trial balance, to show profit or loss over the year, the balance sheet uses all of the remaining items, the assets, liabilities and drawings, to show the worth of the business at the end of the year. As the heading indicates the balance sheet is, in effect, a photograph of the affairs of the business *as at* this point in time.

We have already seen the structure of the opening balance sheet for a business in Chapter 13. Sam's business has been trading so he needs also to show the effects of net profit and drawings.

The change in capital indicates the amount due to the *owner* of the business. In the first instance capital is what Sam invested to set the business up. At each year end this figure is updated to include net profits, which are the owner's reward for all the effort and risk involved. Any drawings are subtracted to show that the owner has now removed some capital from the business. The new figure represents the new value of Sam's capital; what the business currently owes to him.

Any net loss will be subtracted from capital.

Balance sheet of Sam Saddler as at 31 March 19-5

	£	£	
Fixed Assets			
Shop Fittings		6,500	
Motor Van		4,000	
		10,500	← Total fixed assets
Current Assets			
Stock	1,000		
Debtors	200		
Bank	2,700		
Cash	400		
	4,300		
less **Current Liabilities**			
Creditors	1,000		
Working Capital		3,300	← Current assets – current liabilities
		13,800	
Less **Long-Term Liabilities**			
Bank Loan		5,000	
Net Assets		**8,800**	← Assets – liabilities = owner's worth
Financed by:			
Capital (at start)		8,000	← Capital as it stood at the start of year
add Net Profit		1,000	← Net profit is the owner's reward
		9,000	
less Drawings		200	← Money withdrawn by the owner
		8,800	← What the owner is worth now

Checking the balance sheet

Sam Saddler's accountant is satisfied that the accounts are correct because the balance sheet balances. If these totals fail to balance then there must be an error and the final accounts must be rechecked.

The balance sheet balances simply as a matter of arithmetic. We began with a trial balance that balanced, and in drawing up the final accounts we have simply rewritten these figures in a different order so as to discover new information such as gross and net profit and the value of the business. Notice *that we have used each trial balance figure once only.*

Sometimes additional figures not yet in the books must be taken into consideration. Closing stock is an example here and we will meet others later. Such *adjustments* must be entered *twice* – once in trading and profit and loss and once on the balance sheet. Closing stock for example appears in the trading account and as a current asset.

Using a worksheet

An accountant may use a worksheet to help in preparing the final accounts of a business. Here each figure on the trial balance is extended into the relevant column to the right, depending upon whether it belongs to the trading account, the profit and loss account or the balance sheet. The column for adjustments is entered first.

Worksheets may have the conventional debit and credit columns within each section or may, as here, be single column, showing debits as positive figures, credits as negative figures and balancing to zero. The final accounts passed to the owner of the business, the Inland Revenue and other interested parties would be presented in conventional form. The worksheet, which is usually drawn up on preprinted stationery, is simply used as an aid to the accountant at the preliminary stage.

The worksheet of Janet Smith – sole trader

The trial balance shown below is in single-column form, balancing to zero. Note: items (i), (ii) and (iii) have double entries, once as a debit (positive) and once as a credit (negative).

Worksheet: Janet Smith as at 31st March 19-5		Adjustments	Trading account	Profit and loss account	Balance sheet
Trial balance:	£	£	£	£	£
Sales	(19,000)		(19,000)		
Stock (at start)	1,000		1,000		
Purchases	10,000		10,000		
Rent	2,500			2,500	
Rates	2,000			2,000	
Insurance	500			500	
Light and heat	700			700	
General expenses	300			300	
Equipment	1,000				1,000
Fittings	500				500
Debtors	200				200
Creditors	(1,000)				(1,000)
Capital	(5,400)				(5,400)
Cash in bank	(600)				(600)
Cash in hand	100				100
Bank loan	(2,000)				(2,000)
Drawings	9,200				9,200
	0				
(i) Stock (at close): assets		3,000			3,000
Stock (at close): cost of sales		(3,000)	(3,000)		
		0			
(ii) Gross profit-balancing figure:			11,000	(11,000)	
			0		
(iii) Net profit-balancing figure:				5,000	(5,000)
				0	0

(i) Closing stock. This is the only adjustment. It is an asset (debit) for the balance sheet and a gain (credit) on the trading account. (Remember that closing stock reduces the cost of purchases.)
(ii) Gross profit is the figure required to balance the trading account to zero. Notice that it becomes a credit (income) when transferred to the profit and loss account.
(iii) Net profit is calculated as the figure required to balance the profit and loss account to zero. Notice that it becomes a liability (negative figure) when transferred to the balance sheet. This is because it is part of capital.

Activity

Redraw the accounts of Sam Saddler (see page 638) in worksheet format. Use a single-column trial balance.

The final accounts of Janet Smith in conventional format

Accounts of Janet Smith Trading as Smith's Stores

Trading and Profit and Loss account of Janet Smith for the year ending 31 March 19-5

Sales		19,000
Opening Stock	1,000	
Purchases	10,000	
	11,000	
less Closing Stock	3,000	
Cost of Stock Sold		8,000
Gross Profit		11,000
less		
Rent	2,500	
Rates	2,000	
Insurance	500	
Light and Heat	700	
General Expenses	300	
		6,000
Net Profit		5,000

Balance sheet of Janet Smith as at 31 March 19-5

	£	£	£
Fixed Assets			
Freezer			1,000
Shop Fittings			500
			1,500
Current Assets			
Stock		3,000	
Debtors		200	
Cash		100	
		3,300	
less **Current Liabilities**			
Creditors	1,000		
Bank (overdraft)	600		
		1,600	
Working Capital			1,700
			3,200
Less **Long-Term Liabilities**			
Bank Loan			2,000
Net Assets			**1,200**
Financed by:			
Capital (at start)			5,400
add Net Profit			5,000
			10,400
less Drawings			9,200
			1,200

Activities

1 Wally Wigan extracted the following figures from his books at 31 December 19–2:

Capital (at start of year)	30,000
Land and Buildings	80,000
Office Equipment	5,000
Bank	4,500
Cash	1,350
Net profit	10,800
Debtors	2,000
Creditors	4,200
Mortgage	60,000
Drawings	5,000
Vehicles	4,000
Closing Stock	3,150

a Prepare the balance sheet at the end of the year.

b If Wally Wigan were to sell the business, how much would he personally receive?

2 Carmen Lam, who runs a motor spares shop, has just completed her first financial year. She has kept careful records and produced a trial balance:

Trial balance of Carmen Lam trading as Carmen Cars as at 30 June 19-5

	Dr £	Cr £
Sales		40,000
Purchases	22,500	
Salaries	14,000	
Electricity and Gas	1,200	
Rent and Rates	2,300	
Equipment	9,000	
Vehicles	5,550	
Debtors	1,240	
Cash at Bank		500
Cash in Hand	50	
Creditors		1,840
Capital		20,000
Drawings	10,000	
Bank Loan		3,500
	65,840	65,840

In addition:
Closing Stock is valued at 3,000

a Draw up the trading and profit and loss account for the first financial year.

b Draw up the balance sheet as at 30 June 19–5.

c Explain why there is no opening stock shown on the trial balance.

d Briefly comment on the state of the bank account.

Other items on the trading and profit and loss account

Carriage, returns and discounts

Carriage

Carriage is a delivery cost.

Carriage inwards is the delivery cost of goods that we have bought. There may be carriage inwards on purchases and on fixed assets.

Some suppliers will charge carriage as a separate item on their invoice, others will give free delivery, while some include carriage in the cost of the goods. In order to be consistent the rule in accounting is:

Where carriage inwards is listed separately add this to the cost of the item being delivered.

Carriage outwards is the cost of delivering the goods that we have sold to our customers. It is regarded as a distribution cost.

Carriage outwards is entered along with other expenses on the profit and loss account.

Returns of stock

Returns outwards (purchases returns) occur when goods that have been purchased prove to be unsuitable or faulty and are returned to the supplier. In effect returned goods have not really been purchased and should not be included in purchases for the year.

On the trading account we subtract returns outwards from purchases to show the real (net) purchases figure.

Returns inwards (sales returns) occur when goods that we have sold to our customers are sent back to us as unsuitable or faulty. The effect is that these goods have not really been sold.

On the trading account we subtract returns inwards from sales to show the real (net) sales figure.

Discounts allowed and received

We saw in Chapter 11 that a business selling on credit may encourage customers to pay on time by offering cash discount for prompt settlement of debts.

Discounts allowed are a *loss* to our business. They represent debts that we will not collect. They are included as an expense on the profit and loss account.

Discounts received are added to gross profit at the start of the profit and loss account. They are a gain.

Other items received

The main income of a business is from sales. However, sometimes other forms of income may need to be shown. These are normally described as items 'received' and include rents received, where premises are sublet, and commissions received. All items received are added to the gross profit at the start of the profit and loss account.

Example

Returns, carriage, discounts and items received in the final accounts

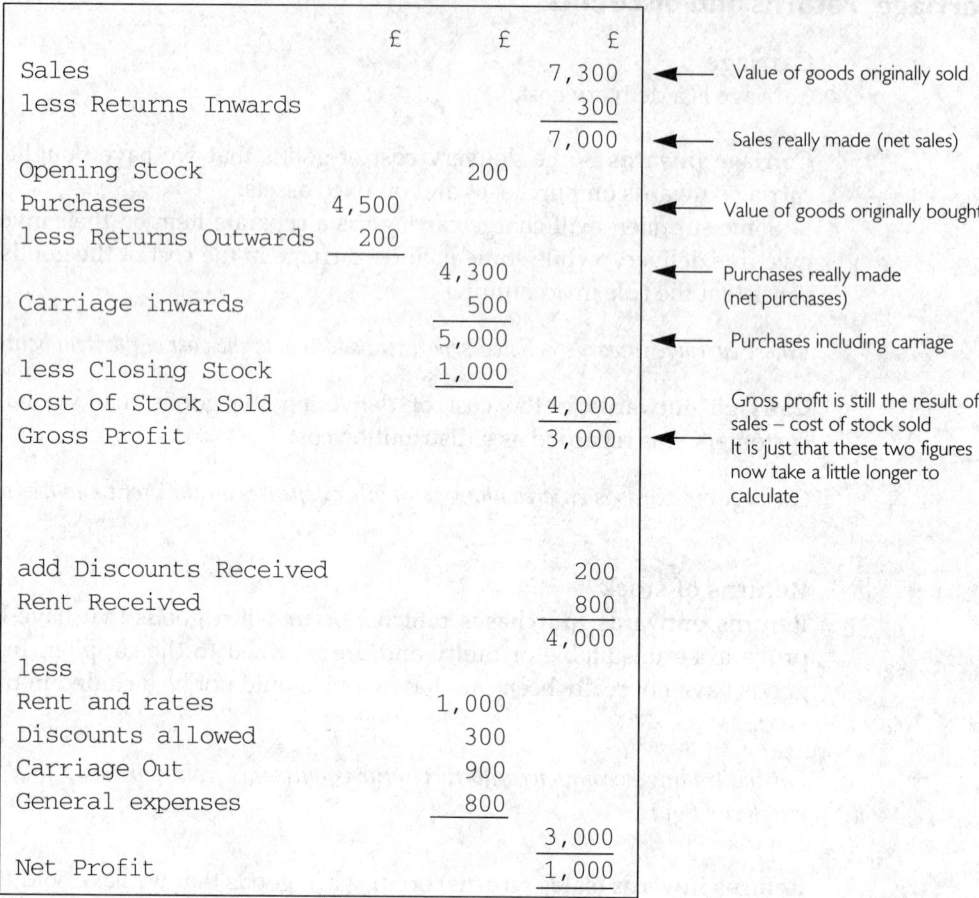

	£	£	£	
Sales			7,300	← Value of goods originally sold
less Returns Inwards			300	
			7,000	← Sales really made (net sales)
Opening Stock		200		
Purchases	4,500			← Value of goods originally bought
less Returns Outwards	200			
		4,300		← Purchases really made (net purchases)
Carriage inwards		500		
		5,000		← Purchases including carriage
less Closing Stock		1,000		
Cost of Stock Sold			4,000	
Gross Profit			3,000	← Gross profit is still the result of sales – cost of stock sold It is just that these two figures now take a little longer to calculate
add Discounts Received			200	
Rent Received			800	
			4,000	
less				
Rent and rates		1,000		
Discounts allowed		300		
Carriage Out		900		
General expenses		800		
			3,000	
Net Profit			1,000	

Notice that a third column might be needed for the subtraction of returns outwards.

Activities

1 Maurice Oxford, a motor mechanic, has just calculated his net profit for the year as £22,000. Unfortunately he has just realised that he has forgotten to include:

- returns inwards of £2,500
- carriage outwards of £850
- discounts received of £1,820.

Calculate what his net profit would be after taking these into consideration.

2 Redraw the trading and profit and loss accounts of Janet Smith (shown on page 645) to include the following:

- Sales returns of £1,000
- £1,800 received by Janet from letting out her basement room to a student
- Cost of delivering sales to customers £1,000
- Discounts which Janet gave to credit customers £450.

Before you begin identify the correct accounting terms for each of the items.

3 Janine Le Havre is the proprietor of Le Cafe Bleu. The book-keeper has just prepared the trial balance for the six months to 31 December 19–6:

Trial balance of The Cafe Bleu as at 31 December 1995	
Sales	75,000
Purchases	30,000
Carriage In	500
Returns In	860
Returns Out	720
Discount Received	520
Discount Allowed	240
Stock	3,500
Salaries	25,000
Electricity and Gas	2,000
Rent and Rates	1,500
Carriage Out	400
Premises	42,000
Equipment	10,000
Vehicles	4,500
Debtors	2,800
Cash at Bank	4,350
Cash in Hand	350
Creditors	3,760
Capital	55,000
Drawings	12,000
Bank Loan	5,000
In addition:	
Closing Stock is valued at £3,000	

a Draw up a trial balance
b Prepare the trading and profit and loss accounts for the period ending 31 December 19–6.
c Prepare the balance sheet as at this date.
d Janine has not registered for VAT. Is there any problem? (Hint see Appendix 4.)

Depreciation of fixed assets

Fixed assets are not written off as expenses in the profit and loss account because, rather than being used up within the financial year they remain useful over a longer period of time. The van we buy this year may cost us £3,000, but it will last for several years. The correct procedure is to recognise that the van is an expense, but that this expense should be shared out over the years of its useful life. We call this annual expense **depreciation**.

Depreciation is a reduction in the book value of a fixed asset due to wear and tear.

Reasons for depreciation include:
- wearing out through use
- decay as a result of age
- obsolescence through changes in fashion or technology.

Activities

1 Can you think of a situation in which land might depreciate? (Think of its uses.)
2 Can you think of any fixed asset that, in your experience, does not depreciate?
3 Can you think of any items which become more valuable as they get older (appreciate)? Why does this happen?
4 What is the tax advantage to a business of writing off assets over as few years as possible? (Hint: Depreciation is an expense.)

How do we calculate depreciation?

In making a provision (allowance) for depreciation we are making an estimate. It is quite possible that two accountants will come to different conclusions about the figures involved, especially if one is working for the owner of a business and the other works for someone interested in buying it!

Depreciation is calculated at the end of the financial year, There are three main methods of arriving at the amount of annual depreciation to be charged:

Method 1 The straight-line method (also called the equal instalment method)
Here we estimate how many years an asset will last (its working life), and how much value it will lose over this time. We then share the loss in value (the depreciation) equally over the life of the asset to find the annual depreciation. The formula used is:

$$\text{annual depreciation} = \frac{\text{estimated loss in value over the life of the asset*}}{\text{the working life of the asset (in years)}}$$

* loss in value is calculated as: cost of the asset – any residual (or scrap) value

Example

We buy a computer system which costs us £4,000.
We estimate that the system will have a useful working life of 4 years after which we can dispose of it for £400.

$$\text{The annual depreciation} = \frac{£4{,}000 - 400}{4} = \frac{£3{,}600}{4} = £900 \text{ per year}$$

Each year £900 will be charged to the profit and loss account.
Each year the value of the asset in the books will be reduced by £900.

Where scrap value is negligible straight-line depreciation is stated as a simple percentage applied to the cost of the asset each year. For example, an asset with no scrap value lasting four years would be depreciated at one-quarter of its value, or 25 per cent a year on cost.

Method 2 The reducing balance method (also called the diminishing balance method)
This method involves deciding upon a set percentage for depreciation each year and applying this to the book value of the asset at the start of the year.

Example

Depreciation on the computer system above is to be provided at 40 per cent per annum on the reducing balance method.

Year 1	balance at start	4,000	
	annual depreciation at 40%	1,600	charged to profit and loss
Year 2	balance at start	2,400	
	annual depreciation at 40%	960	charged to profit and loss
Year 3	balance at start	1,440	
	annual depreciation at 40%	576	charged to profit and loss
Year 4	balance at start	864	
	annual depreciation at 40%	346[1]	charged to profit and loss
	This will never reach a nil value		

[1]To the nearest £

Method 3 The revaluation method

This method is used for assets for which annual depreciation is impossible to predict. For example a herd of cows might produce healthy calves or contract mad cow disease – no-one can tell. In such cases the only method is to revalue each year. In effect, this is similar to an annual stock take for the assets concerned.

It is possible that an asset could appreciate using this method. If so then this would be added to gross profit as a gain.

Entries for depreciation in the final accounts

Once the amount of annual depreciation has been calculated it is recorded in the final accounts as follows:

- In the profit and loss account: the depreciation *for the period* appears as an expense
- In the balance sheet: the depreciation for the period (the profit and loss entry) is added to any previous depreciation on that asset[1] to give total depreciation to date. This is then subtracted from the cost of the asset to give the present book value.

Which method of depreciation do businesses use?

Increasingly the straight-line method is used. Since depreciation is an estimate in any case, it is often seen as sensible to use the easiest method. There are also certain cases where the loss in value is equal for each year. A good example is where a property is bought leasehold, when the lease will have a definite, known lifespan. The using up of the lease is called amortisation (literally meaning death).

The reducing balance method may, on the other hand, reflect more accurately how assets such as vehicles tend to lose value. Anyone who buys a new car knows that more absolute value is lost in the early years when the vehicle is new.

[1] The accumulated depreciation on an asset for all previous years will appear in the credit column on the trial balance

Worked example

Depreciation

Rendell Roofs depreciates fixed assets as:

10% vehicles straight-line, 10% equipment reducing balance

Trial balance of Rendell Roofs as at 31 December 19–6

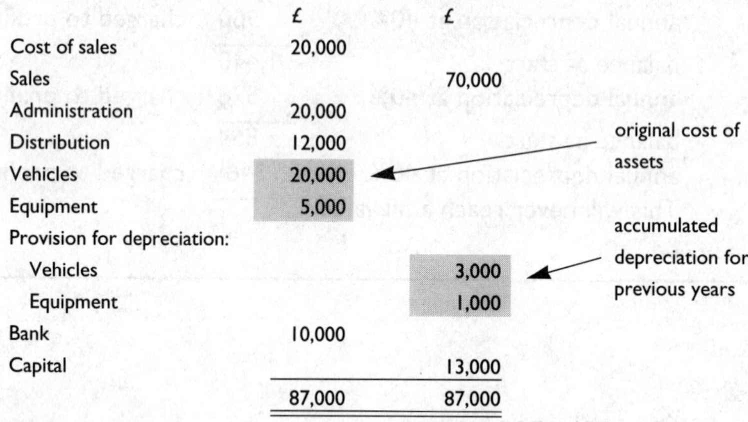

	£	£	
Cost of sales	20,000		
Sales		70,000	
Administration	20,000		
Distribution	12,000		original cost of assets
Vehicles	20,000		←
Equipment	5,000		
Provision for depreciation:			accumulated depreciation for previous years
Vehicles		3,000	←
Equipment		1,000	
Bank	10,000		
Capital		13,000	
	87,000	87,000	

Profit and loss account of Rendell Roofs for period ending 31 December 19–6

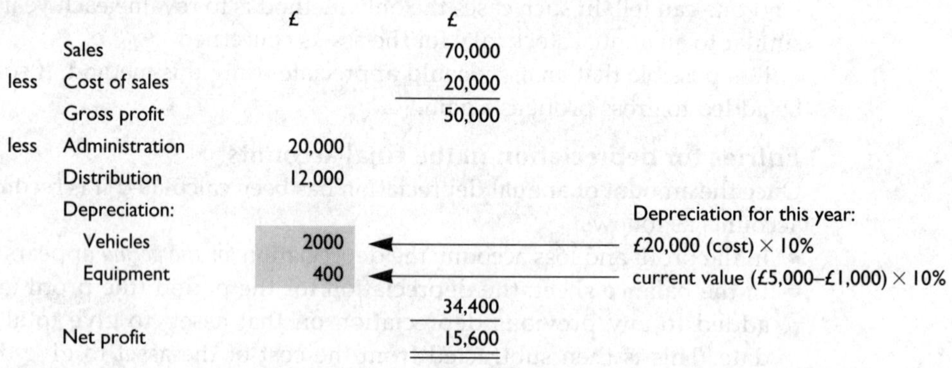

		£	£	
	Sales		70,000	
less	Cost of sales		20,000	
	Gross profit		50,000	
less	Administration	20,000		
	Distribution	12,000		
	Depreciation:			Depreciation for this year:
	Vehicles	2000		← £20,000 (cost) × 10%
	Equipment	400		← current value (£5,000–£1,000) × 10%
			34,400	
	Net profit		15,600	

Balance sheet of Rendell Roofs as at 31 December 19–6

		£ cost	£ depreciation to date	£ net
	Fixed assets			
	Vehicles	20,000	5,000	15,000
	Equipment	5,000	1,400	3,600
				18,600
	Current assets			
	Bank			10,000
				28,600
	Financed by:			
	Capital			13,000
add	Net profit			15,600
				28,600

Activity

1 a The Green Plant Hire Company uses the straight-line method of depreciation. Copy and complete the table below to show the annual depreciation on their fixed assets.

Asset	Cost	Estimated life	Estimated scrap value	Annual depreciation in £s	% depreciation on cost (where no scrap)
Vehicles	£21,000	5 years	£1,000	?	/////////
Machinery	£170,000	8 years	£10,000	?	/////////
Fixtures and fittings	£5,000	10 years	£200	?	/////////
Premises	£120,000	20 year lease	nil	?	?
Furniture	£800	10 years	nil	?	?
Motor Vans	£1,200	4 years	£300	?	/////////
Plant	£85,000	16 years	£5,000	?	/////////

b For which of the above could the useful life be forecast with the greatest accuracy?

2 Long Range Transport provides for depreciation on fixed assets by using the reducing balance method. They ask you to calculate the annual depreciation for the first three years on the following.

a A van bought for £3,000 which will depreciate at 10 per cent p.a.

b A machine bought for £1,500 which will depreciate at 6 per cent p.a. (work to the nearest £).

c If the van was sold after year 3 for £2,500 how would this affect the business profits?

3 Swedish Saunas Ltd have the following entries in their trial balance at 31 December 19–4:

	Debit	Credit
Fixtures and fittings	20,000	
Provision for depreciation on fixtures and fittings		5,000
Computer equipment		
Provision for depreciation	16,000	
on computer equipment		4,000

The company depreciate fixtures and fittings at 25 per cent using the straight-line method and computer equipment at 20 per cent using the reducing balance method.

a Show the entries for depreciation in the profit and loss account for the year ending 31 December 19–4.

b Show the fixed asset section of the balance sheet as at 31 December 19–4.

Bad debts

We have seen that in order to maintain a reasonable level of sales many business need to offer credit to their customers. In Chapter 11 we looked at the risks involved and the need for credit control. Despite their best efforts many businesses continue to suffer from bad debts.

Bad debts occur when a debt cannot be collected. This may happen because:

- A debtor has gone out of business and has no money. There is a particular problem if the debtor's business was a limited company.
- A debtor has died leaving no money.
- A debtor is dishonest and has given false details or changed address.

Whatever the reason, a bad debt is a loss. It may represent goods which are not paid for, services (representing hours) not paid for or possibly sums of money lent that are not repaid.

Entries for bad debts in the final accounts

Bad debts have two effects on the accounts of a business.

- They reduce the debtors. If bad debts appear on the trial balance then this has already taken place.
- They create an account called bad debts. Bad debts are entered as an expense on the profit and loss account. This will cancel out the sales that we have recorded but for which we will not now be paid.

Example

In the year we have written off bad debts to the value of £800.

Gross profit		30,000	
Rent and rates	4,000		
Light and heat	1,500		
Carriage outwards	200		
Depreciation of vehicles	2,500		
Bad Debts (written off)	800		← Bad Debts are an expense on profit and loss
Salaries and wages	15,000		
		24,000	
Net Profit		6,000	

£2.5bn bad debts hit Barclays

Pressure was building in the City last night for a radical boardroom shake-up at Barclays Bank after it plunged into the red for the first time in its history with bad debt write-offs of more than £2.5 billion in 1992. The chief targets of the resignation calls were the chairman and chief executive.

The bank's share price took a 50p nose-dive as astonished investors digested the results. The bank made a loss of £242 million in 1992 with bad debts £1 billion more than in the previous year when profits had been £533 million. Forty per cent of the bad debt write-offs related to loans to the property and construction sector in the 1980s. Many of the businesses in this area have been hard hit by the recession and the fall in property prices. Two large troubled companies to whom Barclays lent were Heron, and Olympia and York – builders of Canary Wharf.

While claiming that the bank would return to profitability in 1993, Andrew Buxton, Barclays' chief executive, said that the level of bad debts was likely to remain high because of the recession.

Source: Adapted from *The Guardian*

As the article shows, bad debt write-offs can easily turn a potential profit into a loss. It is for this reason that management must be very cautious when allowing credit. Of course banks are in the business of giving credit, which is why they must be extremely careful to vet the accounts of businesses to whom they lend.

In Chapter 15 we will look at the preparation of a business plan. One purpose of this will be to persuade a bank manager that we are worth lending money to.

Activities

1 **Read the article on Barclays Bank and answer the following.**

a **Why did the bad debts suffered by Barclays happen?**

b **How do bad debts lead to losses?**

c **From what you have read, do you feel that the bad debts were the fault of Barclays management?**

2 **Jane Winter runs a sports shop trading under the name of Winter Sports. She has just extracted a trial balance and has asked you to help her prepare final accounts for the year just ended.**

Trial Balance of Jane Winter trading as Winter Sports as at 31 December 19-7

	£	£
Sales		380,000
Purchases	330,000	
Sales Returns (In)	5,000	
Purchases Returns (Out)		7,000
Stock at 1 January 19-6	90,000	
Wages and Salaries	30,000	
Rates	6,000	
Telephone	1,000	
Shop Fittings (at cost)	50,000	
Vans (at cost)	40,000	
Provision for depreciation on vans		10,000
Debtors and Creditors	9,800	7,000
Bad Debts	200	
Capital		179,000
Bank	3,000	
Drawings	18,000	
	583,000	583,000

Adjustments to be taken into account at 31 December 19-7:
Closing Stock £100,000
Depreciate shop fittings at 10% per annum and Vans at 20% per annum on cost (i.e. straight-line method)

a **Draw up the trading and profit and loss account for the year just ended.**

b **Draw up the balance sheet as at the year end.**

c **What was Jane's stake in the business at the start of the year? What is it now?**

3 **Mr P. Groves runs a garden centre. He has been in business for some time but the year just ended was the first in which he has offered credit sales. Unfortunately he has suffered from some bad debts.**

Trial balance as at 31 January 19-7

	Debit £	Credit £
stock (at 1 February 19-6)	2,000	
purchases	21,000	
sales		35,000
returns inwards	2,000	
advertising	2,700	
rent and rates	2,200	
insurance	540	
light and heat	760	
bank loan		10,000
discounts received		500
machinery (at cost)	6,000	
premises (at cost)	30,000	
fixtures and fittings (at cost)	8,500	
provision for depreciation:		
machinery		600
fixtures and fittings		500
debtors and creditors	8,400	2,000
bad debts	1,000	
cash in bank	2,500	
cash in hand	400	
capital (at 1 February 19-6)		47,400
drawings	8,000	
	96,000	96,000

The following adjustments also need to be made:
Stock at 31 January 19–7 is valued at £6,000
Depreciation for the year is to be calculated as follows: machinery 5% on cost, fixtures and fittings 5% on cost

a Prepare Mr Groves' final accounts for the year ending 31 January 19–7.
b Write a letter to advise Mr Groves of how he might try to avoid bad debts in the future.
(You may need to refer to Chapter 11.)

Accounting concepts and conventions used when preparing final accounts:

- Going concern – the accountant assumes that the business will continue to operate
- Accruals concept – expenses are to be charged to the period in which they are used up rather than the period in which they are paid
- Consistency – the accounts should be prepared using consistent methods each year, for instance the same method of depreciation
- Prudence – where there is doubt always be pessimistic about profits. For instance make provisions for depreciation.

Interpretation of accounts – monitoring performance

Accounting ratios and percentages

We have seen that final accounts are prepared in order to provide information to interested parties. The level of profit, the size of the turnover (net sales) and the amount of capital can be read off immediately. There are, however, a number of other calculations which may be performed with the figures shown on the final accounts to throw further light on the financial strength of a business.

Since the level of figures will vary from year to year it is useful to have a means of measuring the relationship between the various items on the accounts. For example, increased sales will usually mean increased costs. What we need to know is whether the costs have increased in relation to sales or by a greater or smaller amount. The use of percentages and ratios enables us to draw such conclusions.

Interpretation of accounts is usually more meaningful when performed as a comparison either with other businesses in the same industry or within one business over a period of time. Published company accounts provide the figures of the previous year for exactly this purpose.

Headings under which final accounts may be interpreted are:

- **profitability**
- **liquidity or solvency**
- **gearing**
- **performance or activity**
- **investment.**

Profitability

$$\text{Gross profit \% on sales (or gross profit margin)} = \frac{\text{Gross profit}}{\text{Sales}} \times \frac{100}{1}$$

This should be consistent from year to year unless there has been a change in pricing policy or in the price at which goods are purchased relative to the selling price. A gross profit percentage of 20 per cent would show that for every £1 of sales the business makes 20p in gross profit.

$$\text{Gross profit \% on cost of sales (or mark-up)} = \frac{\text{Gross profit}}{\text{Cost of sales}} \times \frac{100}{1}$$

This is an alternative measure of gross profit. A mark-up of 25 per cent would indicate that for every £1 that the goods cost, 25p is added to arrive at the sales price.

$$\text{Net profit \% on sales (or net profit margin)} = \frac{\text{Net profit}}{\text{Sales}} \times \frac{100}{1}$$

This figure will be influenced by any changes in gross profit percentage. If gross profit percentage is constant any changes in this percentage must be due to a change in the relative level of expenses.

$$\text{Return on capital employed (ROCE)} = \frac{\text{Net profit}}{\text{Capital at start of year}} \times \frac{100}{1}$$

This shows the return (net profit) that the owners have earned on capital invested. This figure may be compared with returns to be earned from other investments such as bank deposits, building societies or the stock market. The owner of a business is risking money and usually working hard. This percentage will show whether all of this effort is worth while; could the owners, for instance, earn more by investing the capital elsewhere and sitting with their feet up?

Sometimes the term 'capital employed' includes all long-term investments, that is capital + long-term liabilities.

Liquidity (solvency) ratios

Liquidity refers to the ability of the business to raise money for day-to-day use. Although profitability is important for the long-term growth and development of a business, in the short term it is lack of liquidity which will cause a business to fold.

$$\text{Working capital (or current) ratio} = \frac{\text{Current assets}}{\text{Current liabilities}}$$

the answer is usually expressed against 1, e.g. 2:1, 3:1

This ratio shows the relationship between current assets (the assets that can be turned into cash fairly quickly) and current liabilities (the amounts that will need to be paid shortly). A ratio of 2:1, that is £2 of current assets to £1 of current liabilities is often quoted as ideal, but this can vary from one type of business to another.

It is important also to look at the make up of the current assets. A business with high stock and debtors' figures, but with a bank overdraft, may still produce a ratio of 2:1. This may hide potential cashflow problems.

A similar measure is the liquid capital ratio (also known as the quick ratio or the acid test ratio):

$$\text{Liquid capital ratio} = \frac{\text{Current assets} - \text{Stock}}{\text{Current liabilities}}$$

Here stock is not included as it is not always very liquid. A business cannot simply turn stock into money because it wishes to; after all this is what a trader is trying to do constantly. The ideal liquid ratio is 1:1, that is, £1 of current assets (excluding stock) for every £1 of current liabilities.

Although shortage of working capital can be disastrous, too high a ratio shows that management is being inefficient in its use of resources. There is no point in keeping large amounts of money in a current bank account, buying an unnecessary amount of stock or letting debtors build up to an unmanageable level. All of these items tie up cash that could be better invested elsewhere. This holds true also at a personal level. We need to have sufficient money at home for day-to-day items, but it would be unwise to have thousands of pounds stuffed in the mattress just in case.

A business can increase working capital by:

- ploughing back profits – this is the best method
- selling fixed assets (and perhaps renting or leasing them instead)
- borrowing money on a medium or long-term basis (can be expensive – depends upon interest rates)
- raising new capital from owners/shareholders
- reducing stock levels.

Gearing

$$\text{Gearing \%} = \frac{\text{External borrowing}}{\text{Capital (shareholders' funds)}} \times \frac{100}{1}$$

This shows the extent to which a business relies upon borrowing. If the figure is over 100 per cent then borrowing exceeds capital. It may be necessary for a business to borrow to finance expansion but this carries risks in the form of high repayments if interest rates are high and the fact that the business is essentially owned by the lender, possibly a bank. If the loan is called in then the business is in trouble and may have to sell up.

Performance ratios (activity indicators)

Rate of stock turnover Turnover refers to the net sales of a business over a period of time. The rate of turnover, on the other hand, is the number of times that average stock is sold during the year.

$$\text{Rate of turnover (or rate of stock turn)} = \frac{\text{Cost of stock sold}}{\text{Average stock*}}$$

$$\text{*Average stock} = \frac{\text{Opening stock} + \text{Closing stock}}{2}$$

Where there is no opening stock the closing stock figure only (not divided by 2) should be used.

Relationship between rate of turnover and profit margin

An industry with a high rate of turnover usually operates on a low profit margin. Indeed, the high rate of turnover is often achieved as a result of the low margin. Supermarkets are an example of this.

A low rate of turnover will mean that a business may need a high margin if it is to survive. For this reason a car showroom will have very high margins. Relatively few cars will be sold, compared with say, items in a supermarket, but each will have a high profit margin.

$$\text{Selling ratio} = \frac{\text{Expenses}}{\text{Sales}} \times 100$$

Percentages may be calculated to show total expenses, or individual expenses per £1 of sales.

$$\text{Debtors' collection period} = \frac{\text{Debtors}}{\text{Credit sales}} \times 365 \text{ days (or 52 weeks)}$$

This shows the time in days (or weeks) that it takes to collect the average debt. The figure can be compared with the industry norm, with last year or with the credit period that has been allowed. This will frequently be 30 days. We have seen that firms are wise to keep a list of aged debtors, showing who owes them money and how old the debt is.

$$\text{Creditors' payment period} = \frac{\text{Creditors}}{\text{Credit purchases}} \times 365 \text{ days (or 52 weeks)}$$

This shows the time in days (or weeks) that it takes to pay the average supplier. It can be compared with the industry norm, with last year or with the credit period that has been allowed. This will frequently be 30 days. It has become common for businesses to delay paying creditors for as long as possible, in the belief that debts should be collected more quickly than creditors should be paid.

In an effort to show a good example to the business world, the government carried out an investigation into the creditor payment record of its own departments at Whitehall. The survey showed that prompt payment of 30-day contracts occurred only 42 per cent of the time in one department. The best payment record was held by the Inland Revenue!

Ratios must be treated with caution

Where ratios show differences in performance we must be clear that these are to do with actual performance. There can be other reasons:

- use of alternative accounting policies may sometimes explain the differences between different businesses
- where the results of a business are compared over a number of years differences can arise because of changes in the value of money.

Worked example

Interpretation of accounts to monitor business performance

Final accounts of KENT BANANAS

Trading and Profit and Loss Accounts

	£000s 19-5	£000s 19-6
Sales Turnover	45	60
Cost of Goods sold	30	41
Gross Profit	15	19
Expenses	8	11
Net profit	7	8

Balance Sheet

	19-5 £000s	19-6 £000s
Fixed assets		
Premises	100	100
Fixtures and Fittings	30	40
	130	140
Current Assets		
Stock	4	3
Debtors	4	5
Bank	2	0
	10	8
Current Liabilities		
Creditors	3	4
Bank overdraft	0	2
	3	6
Working Capital	7	2
	137	142
Long-Term Liabilities		
Bank Loan	36	40
	101	102
Financed by:		
Capital	100	101
add Profit	7	8
	107	109
less Drawings	6	7
	101	102

Interpretation	**19–5**	**19–6**
PROFITABILITY		
Gross Profit Margin	33.33%	31.67%
Mark-up	50.00%	46.34%
Net Profit	15.56%	13.33%
Return on Capital Employed	7.00%	7.92%
ACTIVITY		
Rate of Stock Turnover	7.50 times	11.71 times
Debtors Collection	32.44 days	30.42 days
Creditors Payment	36.50 days	35.61 days
LIQUIDITY		
Working Capital Ratio	3.33:1	1.33:1
Liquid Capital Ratio	2.00:1	0.83:1
CAPITAL STRENGTH		
% Gearing	36.00%	39.60%

Comments:

Turnover has been increased from £45,000 to £60,000 as a result of reducing markup i.e. cutting sales price relative to cost.

Gross profit has increased as a result of this.

Net profit for the year has increased from £7,000 to £8,000 as a result of increased gross profit, but net profit percentage has decreased showing that expenses have not been controlled.

Return on capital employed has grown slightly.

Rate of stock turnover has increased, partly because of a greater sales volume and partly because the business is holding less stock. Debtors' collection and creditors' repayment periods are both steady and satisfactory (assuming credit is of one month).

Liquidity is slightly worrying as the acid test ratio is below 1:1. Perhaps more profit should be retained to build-up reserves.

Gearing is rising but is under control.

Workings for interpretation of accounts
The accounts of KENT BANANAS

Interpretation	**19–5**	**19–6**
PROFITABILITY		
Gross Profit Margin	15/45 × 100 = 33.33%	19/60 × 100 = 31.67%
Mark-up	15/30 × 100 = 50%	19/41 × 100 = 46.34%
Net Profit %	7/45 × 100 = 15.56%	8/60 × 100 = 13.33%
Return on Capital Employed*	7/100 × 100 = 7%	8/101 × 100 = 7.92%
ACTIVITY		
Rate of Stock Turnover	30/4** = 7.5 times	41/3.5 = 11.71 times
Debtors Collection	4/45 × 365 = 32.44 days	5/60 × 365 = 30.42 days
Creditors Payment	3/30 × 365 = 36.5 days	4/41 × 365 = 35.61 days
LIQUIDITY		
Working Capital Ratio	10/3 = 3.33:1	8/6 = 1.33:1
Liquid Capital Ratio	(10-4)/3 = 2:1	(8-3)/6 = 0.83
CAPITAL STRENGTH		
% Gearing	36/101 × 100 = 35.6%	40/102 × 100 = 39.2%

*Using capital at start.
**Closing stock is used here.

Activities

Interpretation of accounts

Final accounts of BOOMERANG

Trading and Profit and Loss Accounts

	19–3	*19–4*
	£000s	*£000s*
Sales Turnover	90	85
Cost of Goods sold	45	40
Gross Profit	45	45
Expenses	25	35
Net profit	20	10

Balance Sheet

Fixed assets		
Premises	140	140
Equipment	39	35
	179	175
Current Assets		
Stock	4	5
Debtors	9	12
Bank	10	9
	23	26

Current Liabilities		
Creditors	6	11
Working Capital	17	15
Net Assets	196	190
Long-Term Liabilities		
Mortgage	72	70
	124	120
Financed by:		
Capital	120	124
add Profit	20	10
	140	134
less Drawings	16	14
	124	120

1 a Produce the following percentages and ratios for Boomerang for the financial years shown:
Gross Profit %, Net Profit %, Return on Capital employed
% Gearing, Working capital ratio, liquid capital ratio
Rate of stock turnover, debtors' collection time creditors' payment time

b Comment on the results of the business under the headings:
Profitability
Liquidity
Gearing
Activity
A period of one month's credit is allowed on sales and purchases

c Mr Cash, the proprietor gave up his £20,000 per year job and sold his house to raise the capital to set up the business in 19–3. Using current interest rates calculate how much better off he would have been if he had stayed at work and invested the money (for 19–3 only).

Trading and Profit and Loss Accounts for period ending 31 March 19-5

	£000s *Sampson Ltd*	*£000s* *Bellhawk*
Sales Turnover	760	945
Cost of Goods sold	380	550
Gross Profit	380	395
Expenses	320	280
Net profit	60	115
less Dividends	40	90
Retained Profits	20	25

Balance Sheets as at 31 March 19-5

	£000s	£000s
	Sampson Ltd	Bellhawk
Fixed assets		
Land & Buildings	920	1,464
Machinery & Vehicle	305	580
	1,225	2,044
Current Assets		
Stock	18	16
Debtors	12	35
Bank	8	1
	38	52
Creditors due within one year		
Creditors	13	22
Working Capital	25	30
	1,250	2,074
Creditors due after one year		
Loans	450	1,010
	800	1,064
Financed by:		
Issued Share Capital	700	1,000
Reserves	100	64
Shareholders' Funds:	800	1,064

2 Your bank has just received the accounts of two clients, Sampson Ltd and Bellhawk. You have been asked to study the figures and comment upon the performance of each.

a Draw up a table of relevant ratios and percentages and comment on performance.

b A high percentage of the sales and purchases of each business is on a cash basis. How does this affect the usefulness of the creditors and debtors repayment figures?

c Write a memo to your superior to accompany your calculations recommending with reasons why you would grant or refuse each company a loan of £200,000.

Assignment 14.1 Castleview

This assignment develops knowledge and understanding of the following element:

7.3 Produce and explain profit and loss statements and balance sheets

7.4 Identify and explain data to monitor a business

It supports development of the following core skills:

Communication 3.2, 3.4

Application of number 3.2,

Information technology 3.1, 3.3

The purpose of this assignment is to give you the opportunity to present sole trader final accounts, and to comment upon their meaning and the underlying principles involved.

Mr B. Shah is a sole trader who sells a variety of goods to passing tourists from his shop in Druid Street. All of the shop customers pay cash but he has recently started a mail order service offering credit terms. Although this has boosted his turnover there is the problem that some of the customers are bad payers. Most give the current recession as their excuse.

Mrs Shah, who works for a local bank, helps keep the business books in her spare time and is confident that the year end figures are correct.

The business began trading on 1 November 19–3 first under the name of Castleview, although you can't actually see the castle from there! Now that the first financial year has ended (on 31 October 19–4) you have been asked for help and advice in preparing the final accounts.

So far you have visited Mr Shah and discussed matters with him. Since then he has collected all relevant financial records and posted them to you with a covering letter (attached) confirming what you have agreed.

You notice that stock taking figures indicate that stock at the 31 October was valued at £17,560 (cost price).

You also recommend:

- depreciation is to be as follows:
  delivery van 20 per cent p.a. (straight-line method)
  fixtures and fittings 10 per cent p.a. (straight-line method).

Your tasks

1 **Read the letter from Mr Shah and comply with his instructions.**
Your answer should take the form of a letter with accounts attached.

- **Prepare a trial balance before you begin the account.**
- **Use suitable ratios to help you answer Mr Shah's questions.**

CASTLEVIEW
Proprietor: B Shah
123 Druid Street Westmere
Tel: 0104–929–6543

Our Ref: GNVQ3/Ass 13.1

Date: 26 November 19–4

To:
A Student
Stone Road
Westmere
W52

Dear Mr/Ms Student

Thank you for coming over to see me the other day. I have considered the matters that we discussed and I am pleased to let you prepare the final accounts for the fee suggested. I have balanced the books and enclose the year-end balances that you require.

I look forward to receiving my completed final accounts as agreed. I would also be grateful if you could indicate how you feel that my business is progressing and I would appreciate any further advice that you may have.

As you know, I have just completed my first year in business so I do not have much experience of accounting. It would help me a great deal if you could explain the following points:

- Is there any way of knowing whether my accounts are accurate?
- Why am I not able to charge the cost of my new delivery van against the first year's profits? (I know people who run their private cars out of their businesses!)
- You mentioned depreciation. Would you please explain what this is?
- Should I register for VAT?
- I realise that the tax man requires me to provide these accounts. Could they be of any benefit to me? What do they show?

I am sorry to rush you but I need to have this information by 9 am tomorrow as I have an appointment with the Inland Revenue in the morning.

Many thanks in anticipation.

Yours sincerely

Brian Shah

B Shah

Enc

Account balances for B. Shah trading as Castleview for year ending 31 October 19-4	
Sales	202,000
Returns Inwards	1,500
Stock at start of year	16,000
Purchases	140,000
Returns Outwards	1,200
Carriage In	2,500
Rates	3,400
Heat and light	3,800
Repairs	1,420
Insurance	2,000
Advertising	950
Telephone	860
Vehicles	3,500
Interest charges	1,450
Vehicle expenses	3,640
Sundry expenses	2,270
Premises	78,000
Fixtures and fittings	5,000
Debtors	6,200
Cash in Bank	1,450
Creditors	8,300
Capital at start of year	32,440
Mortgage	48,000
Drawings	18,000

2 Another client is about to set up as a general retailer. She will operate as a sole trader and has asked your advice on setting up a basic accounting system. Suggest the documents and books that she will need, giving the purpose of each. Add illustrations where possible.

Forecast final accounts – cash versus profit

In Chapter 13 we saw that the business cashflow forecast is concerned only with money paid and money received. We have now seen that the profit and loss account is concerned with something different, that is, period sales (paid for or not) less period costs (paid for or not). Cash and profit are not the same.

The example below shows the cashflow forecast and the master budget for a small to medium enterprise (SME). Ratios have been calculated on the basis of the budgeted figures.

Activity

Park Trading Ltd

Study the information and figures given and then answer the following questions.

1 What is the purpose of a cashflow forecast?
2 Where does the data come from for the various items?
3 Will Park Trading Ltd need an overdraft at any time? If so, in which month(s)? How do you know?
4 Do the forecasts show that the company will be profitable? How do you explain the difference between the cash position of the business and its profitability?
5 If the company were to be sold off at the end of the period how much would the shareholders receive? Which figure shows this?
6 Give one reason why management produces financial forecasts.
7 Are these forecasts part of management accounting or financial accounting?
8 Comment on the liquidity of the business.
9 Park Trading Ltd buys in a computer system for £300. How much does it sell it for?
10 Is the forecast satisfactory? Should any action be taken? Is an overdraft the best way of financing this business? What are the alternatives?

Park Trading Ltd is a wholesaler selling computer hardware. The company has share capital of £300,000 of which £280,000 is to be immediately invested in fixed assets. An overdraft limit of £50,000 has been agreed with the bank.

The budget for the first 6 months is:

Administration	£11,000 per month
Depreciation on fixed assets	25% pa (12.5% for the 6 months)
Sales and distribution	10% of sales value

All sales will be on 1 month's credit.

Initially purchases will be for cash, though by November some will be on credit..

Estimates are:

	Sales	Sales receipts	Purchases	Purchase payments
	£	£	£	£
July	50,000	0	35,000	35,000
August	50,000	50,000	35,000	35,000
September	100,000	50,000	70,000	70,000
October	100,000	100,000	70,000	70,000
November	150,000	100,000	95,000	85,000
December	150,000	150,000	95,000	65,000
Total	600,000	450,000	400,000	360,000
	(1)	(2)	(3)	(4)

At the end of the period debtors will be £150,000 and creditors £40,000.

CASHFLOW FORECAST	July	Aug	Sept	Oct	Nov	Dec	Total
RECEIPTS							
Sales	0	50,000	50,000	100,000	100,000	150,000	450,000 (2)
Share capital	300,000						300,000
Total receipts (A)	300,000	50,000	50,000	100,000	100,000	150,000	750,000
PAYMENTS:							
Purchases	35,000	35,000	70,000	70,000	85,000	65,000	360,000 (4)
Administration	11,000	11,000	11,000	11,000	11,000	11,000	66,000
Sales and distribution	5,000	5,000	10,000	10,000	15,000	15,000	60,000
Fixed assets	280,000						280,000
Total payments (B)	331,000	51,000	91,000	91,000	111,000	91,000	766,000
Opening balance B/f	0	(31,000)	(32,000)	(73,000)	(64,000)	(75,000)	0
add Net cashflow (A-B)	(31,000)	(1,000)	(41,000)	9,000	(11,000)	59,000	(16,000)
Closing balance c/f	(31,000)	(32,000)	(73,000)	(64,000)	(75,000)	(16,000)	(16,000) (5)

The master budget: forecast final accounts of Park Trading Ltd

Forecast trading and profit and loss account for the 6 months ending 31 December 19-

		£000s	£000s		
	Sales		600 (1)		
less	Cost of stock sold		400	50.00%	Mark-up
	Gross Profit		200 (3)	33.33%	Gross margin
	less				
	Depreciation	35		5.83%	expenses as
	Administration	66		11.00%	proportion
	Sales and distribution	60		10.00%	of sales
			161	26.83%	
	Net Profit/(Loss)		39	6.50%	Net profit %

Balance sheet as at 31 December 19-

		£000s	£000s	£000s	
		Cost	Dep	Net	
	Fixed assets	280	35	245	
					Working capital ratio
	Current assets				and Acid test ratio (no stock)
	Debtors		150		2.68:1
less	**Current liabilities**				
	Creditors	40			
	Bank (overdraft)	16 (5)			
			56		
	Working capital			94	
				339	
	As financed by:				
	Share capital (issued)			300	
add	Retained profit			39	13.00% ROCE
				339	(i.e. 26% pa)

Activity

Airwares Ltd

Heath Rowe and Stan Stead are planning to set up a small travel agency to trade under the name of Airwares Ltd. Their cashflow forecast for the first year is shown below together with other relevant notes.

The company will collect money from customers immediately and one month later pay 90% of this to the tour operators, keeping 10% commission.

1. You are to use the forms provided to put together the master budget, that is:
   - Forecast Operating Statement (Profit & Loss Account) for year one
   - Forecast balance sheet as at the end of year one
2. Provide the relevant ratios and percentages indicated on the sheet.
3. Explain why there is such a difference between forecast cash and forecast profit at the end of the year.
4. Comment on the forecasts.
   Will there need to be further borrowing and if so what is the best means of doing this?
   Is the business producing a satisfactory return on capital?
   Will the business succeed?

Cash budget	Jan	Feb	Mar	Apr	May	June	July	Aug	Sept	Oct	Nov	Dec	Total
Airwares Ltd	£	£	£	£	£	£	£	£	£	£	£	£	£
Receipts:													
Sales	25,000	25,000	25,000	90,000	90,000	90,000	35,000	35,000	35,000	16,650	16,650	16,700	500,000
Loans													0
Capital	20,000												20,000
Total receipts (A)	**45,000**	**25,000**	**25,000**	**90,000**	**90,000**	**90,000**	**35,000**	**35,000**	**35,000**	**16,650**	**16,650**	**16,700**	**520,000**
Payments													
Tour operators		22,500	22,500	22,500	81,000	81,000	81,000	31,500	31,500	31,500	14,985	14,985	434,970
Fixed Assets	13,000												13,000
Salaries/wages	2,000	2,000	2,000	2,000	2,000	2,000	2,000	2,000	2,000	2,000	2,000	2,000	24,000
Training													0
Rent/Rates	1,200	1,200	1,200	1,200	1,200	1,200	1,200	1,200	1,200	1,200	1,200	1,200	14,400
Electricity			300			200			200			300	1,000
Insurance	1,500												1,500
Telephone			200			200			200			200	800
Post/stationery	100	100	100	100	100	100	100	100	100	100	100	100	1,200
Advertising	100	100	100	50	50	50	50	50	50	50	50	50	750
Bank charges	500												500
Credit cards	50	50	50	180	180	180	70	70	70	33	33	33	1,000
Accounting												500	500
Sundries													0
Other													0
Total payments (B)	18,450	25,950	26,450	26,030	84,530	84,930	84,420	34,920	35,320	34,883	18,368	19,368	493,620
Balance B/f	0	26,550	25,600	24,150	88,120	93,590	98,660	49,240	49,320	49,000	30,767	29,048	0
add Receipts (A)	45,000	25,000	25,000	90,000	90,000	90,000	35,000	35,000	35,000	16,650	16,650	16,700	520,000
less Payments (B)	18,450	25,950	26,450	26,030	84,530	84,930	84,420	34,920	35,320	34,883	18,368	19,368	493,620
Balance c/f	26,550	25,600	24,150	88,120	93,590	98,660	49,240	49,320	49,000	30,767	29,048	26,380	26,380

Additional information at year end:
creditors £15,030, no debtors, depreciation 10%.

Forecast final accounts (master budget) for Airwares Ltd

Balance sheet as at 31 December 19-

	£	£
Fixed assets		
Equipment		…………
less Depreciation		…………
		…………
Current assets		
Stocks	0	
Debtors	…………	
Bank	…………	
	…………	
less		
Current liabilities		
Creditors	…………	
Working capital		…………
less		…………
Long-term capital		
Bank loan		…………
		…………
Financed by:		
Share capital		…………
Reserves (retained profit)		…………
Shareholders' funds		…………

Operating statement for period ending 31 December 19-

	£	£	£
Sales			…………
less payments			
(to tour operators @ 90%)			…………
Gross profit			
(commission retained @ 10%)			…………
less expenses			
Personnel:			
Salaries	…………		
Training	…………		
		…………	
Establishment:			
Rent/Rates	…………		
Light/Heat	…………		
Insurance	…………		
		…………	
Administration:			
Telephone	…………		
Post/stationery	…………		
Advertising	…………		
		…………	
Financial:			
Bank charges	…………		
Credit cards	…………		
Accounting	…………		
Depreciation:		…………	…………
Total operating costs		…………	…………
Net profit/(loss)			

Gross profit/sales ...... %

% of sales		
Personnel	…………	%
Est'ment	…………	%
Admin.	…………	%
Finance	…………	%
Deprec'n	…………	%
Total	…………	%
Net profit/sales	…………	%
ROCE	…………	%

Working capital Ratio	…………	:1

Partnership accounts

Introduction

A partnership is an association of between 2 and 20 people carrying on in business together with a view to making a profit. We have seen that a business with several partners will be able to raise larger amounts of capital than would be possible for a sole trader.

The fact that the business has a number of owners, all of whom are entitled to share in the profits (and bear the losses) of the business, means that it is sensible to make an agreement about such matters.

The partnership deed

Partners will usually draw up an agreement known as a partnership deed. This sets out:

- capital contributed by each partner
- ratio in which profits (or losses) are to be shared
- rate of interest (if any) to be paid on partners' capital
- rate of interest (if any) charged on partners' drawings
- salaries (if any) to be paid to partners.

If no partnership deed is drawn up then the Partnership Act 1890 is used to settle any disputes. This states that:

- profits (or losses) are to be shared equally
- there will be no interest on capital or drawings
- no salaries are to be allowed
- where more than the agreed capital is contributed by a partner, 5 per cent interest can be paid on the excess.

The accounts

The final accounts of a partnership are similar to those of a sole trader except that as there is more than one owner additional sections cover the sharing of profits and the ownership of capital. There is:

- an appropriation account: a final section of the profit and loss account showing how profits are divided
- a capital account for each partner on the balance sheet: this is not changed by profits and drawings, but is fixed showing the original capital invested
- a current account for each partner on the balance sheet: this shows the profits to which each partner is entitled and any drawings taken.

Worked example

Bing and Singh are the partners in a firm of solicitors. Their partnership deed shows the following:

Capital contributed:	Bing	£15,000
	Singh	£25,000

Share of profits and losses: Bing 2/5
Singh 3/5 (or a ratio of 2:3)

Interest allowed on capital: 10%

Salary: Bing £10,000 (paid in recognition of extra work)

Information for the year ended 31 December 19–4:

The profit and loss account showed that net profit for the year was £50,000

At the start of the year current account balances were:
Bing £2,000 credit (i.e. not all profits in previous years had been withdrawn)
Singh £1,000 debit (i.e. had overdrawn profits in previous years)

Drawings for the year were: Bing £5,000, Singh £10,000

The appropriation account

After the net profit or loss has been calculated in the normal way the appropriation account is drawn up to show how this profit is to be shared out between the partners. Since the partners have drawn up a partnership deed there should be no disagreement about this.

(The appropriation account is part of the profit and loss account of a partnership and is not mentioned in the profit and loss account heading.)

Profit and Loss Account (Appropriation section) for the year ending 31 December 19–4:

	£	£	£
Net Profit			50,000
less Interest on Capital:			
Bing 10%		1,500	
Singh 10%		2,500	
		4,000	
Salary:			
Bing		10,000	
			14,000
			36,000
Balance of Profits Shared:			
Bing 2/5			14,400
Singh 3/5			21,600
			36,000

The Balance Sheet opposite shows only the capital section. The assets and liabilities are as for a sole trader.

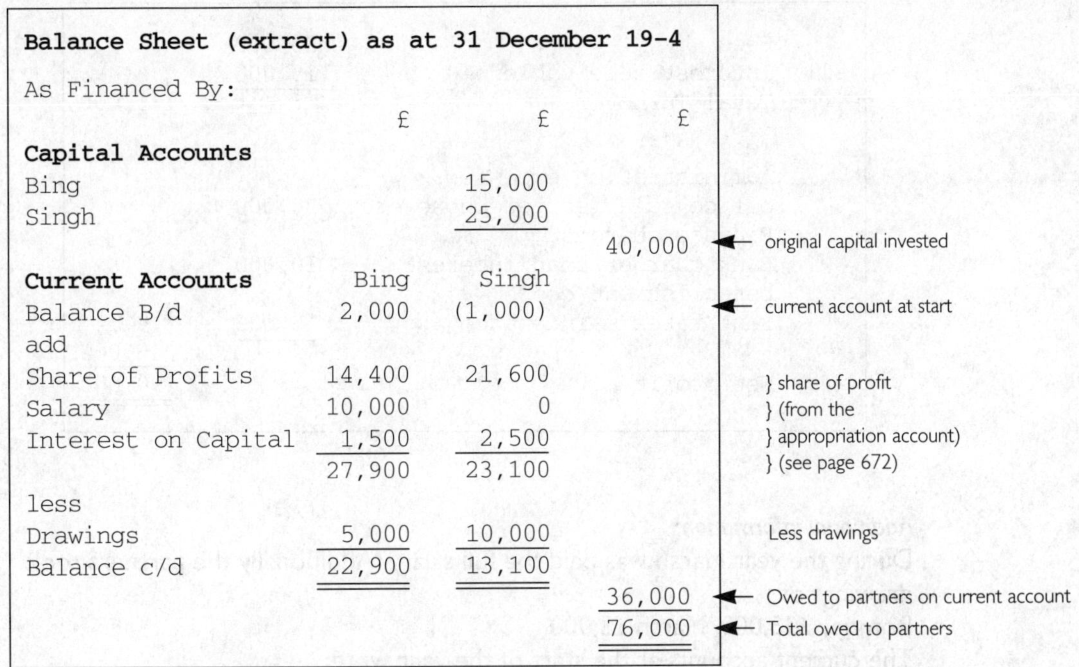

Balance Sheet (extract) as at 31 December 19-4

As Financed By:

	£	£	£	
Capital Accounts				
Bing		15,000		
Singh		25,000		
			40,000	← original capital invested
Current Accounts	Bing	Singh		
Balance B/d	2,000	(1,000)		← current account at start
add				
Share of Profits	14,400	21,600		} share of profit
Salary	10,000	0		} (from the
Interest on Capital	1,500	2,500		} appropriation account)
	27,900	23,100		} (see page 672)
less				
Drawings	5,000	10,000		Less drawings
Balance c/d	22,900	13,100		
			36,000	← Owed to partners on current account
			76,000	← Total owed to partners

Note that capital is usually a credit, indicating that the owner(s) of a business are a form of creditor, that is, the business owes them the money that they have invested.

Above, Singh began the year having a debit balance brought down on current account – this is shown as a negative figure. This means that Singh has drawn out more than his share of profits in previous years. Bing, on the other hand, has withdrawn £2,000 less than the available profits at the start of the year.

Activities

1 Romney and Marsh are a firm of accountants. On setting up the firm the partners contributed capital as follows:

Romney £20,000
Marsh £10,000

The partnership deed indicates that:

- Marsh draws a salary of £15,000 p.a.
- Interest on capital is to be 8% p.a.
- Profits are to be shared in the ratio of 2:1 to Romney and Marsh respectively.

A summary of the profit and loss account for the year ending 30 October 19–5 shows the following:

	Fees	120,000	
add	Interest receivable	15,000	
	Total Turnover		135,000
	less		
	Administration expenses:		
	office salaries/telephone etc.	20,000	
	Finance charges:		
	Bank charges/loan interest	10,000	
	Establishment costs:		
	rent/rates/maintenance	15,000	
			45,000
	Net profit		90,000

Additional information:
During the year Marsh was paid the full salary. Additionally the partners took drawings of:
Romney £25,000, Marsh £3,000
The current accounts at the start of the year were:
Romney £2,000 (credit), Marsh £1,000 (credit)

You are to:
a prepare the appropriation account for the year just ended
b prepare the capital section of the balance sheet to show the partner's capital and current accounts.

2 If Marsh decided to leave the firm, how much would the partnership have to pay him?
3 Redraw the appropriation account for Romney and Marsh as it would appear if there had been no partnership deed.

Final accounts of limited companies

The accounting requirements for UK companies are set out in the Companies Act 1985. In 1989 the Act was amended to bring UK companies into line with directives issued by the European Union. The details are complex but for our purposes the act requires companies to:

- keep accurate accounts of the company's transactions
- prepare final accounts which give a 'true and fair view' of the business' affairs
- provide a summary of this financial information to its members and to lodge a copy of this with the Registrar of Companies at Companies House in Cardiff or in Edinburgh. This summary, known as the published accounts, will be examined in more detail at a later stage.

Further regulations concerning limited company accounts are laid down by the Stock Exchange for PLCs, and also by the Accounting Standards Board. Regulations are necessary because the size of many companies means that their activities affect a large number of people. They also ensure that the directors, who run a company, are made accountable to the shareholders who own it.

In many ways company accounts are very similar to those of sole traders and partnerships. The differences that arise are a result of the difference in ownership. The accounts consist of:

- a trading account
- a profit and loss account – to include an appropriation section
- a balance sheet
- a cashflow statement (applies to large companies only).

The trading and profit and loss accounts of a company are exactly the same as for other forms of organisation, although:

- directors' salaries are charged to profit and loss (directors are employees)
- debenture interest (like all finance and interest charges) are charged to profit and loss.

The appropriation account

After the profit and loss account has been prepared in the normal way the appropriation account is drawn up to show how the directors have decided to allocate the profits. As with a partnership this section is an extension of the profit and loss account.

The profits can either be paid to shareholders (the owners) or retained in the business for future development. In practice the directors often decide to do both. The stages are:

- an estimate is made for corporation tax and this is deducted from net profit
- some of the remaining profit will be allocated to shareholders in the form of dividends. The ordinary dividend will be expressed as so many pence per share, while the preference shares will have a rate of interest already attached to them
- the profit not paid as dividends will be retained in the company and added to the reserves on the balance sheet.

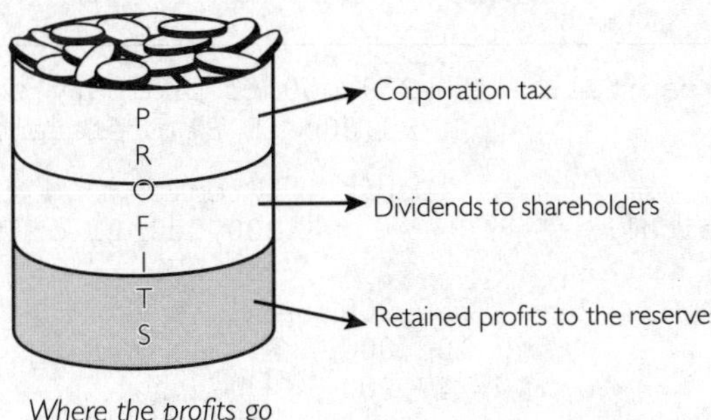

Where the profits go

The balance sheet

This is as for a sole trader except for the capital section. As the company is owned by shareholders so this part is more detailed. It contains the following information.

Authorised capital (also called nominal capital)

This is the share capital that the company is allowed to issue. The registrar of companies must approve any application by the company to issue new share capital. This is listed on the balance sheet for information, but is not added into the totals.

Issued capital (called-up capital)

This is the share capital that the company has actually raised. It may be that not all of the authorised capital has been issued. Perhaps only some of the shares have been made available, or perhaps shares are being paid for by instalments, the method used with the privatisation of companies such as British Gas. Alternatively it may be that the market has not taken up (bought) all of the shares that have been floated. For these reasons the issued capital may be only part of the authorised capital.

Reserves

These are additions to capital other than from the sales of shares. They include:

- general reserve and profit and loss balance – these arise from normal trading activities and are the profits retained in the business and not paid as dividends to shareholders
- revaluation reserve – this is a gain which occurs when an asset, usually property or land, appreciates in value
- share premium account – this is the extra amount (premium) raised on the sale of shares when the market is prepared to pay more than face value. Since issued capital cannot exceed authorised capital, any extra amounts raised are put into this reserve.

All reserves belong to the shareholders:

Issued capital + reserves = shareholders' funds

Loan capital

Long-term liabilities are not part of the shareholders' funds. Debentures are loans, normally secured against company assets, which appear as long-term liabilities.

Worked example

Skyways Ltd completed their financial year on 30 November 19–4. The following details were extracted from their books (the net profit has already been calculated):

	Debit	Credit	
Authorised share capital:		250,000	£1 ordinary shares
		80,000	£1 8% preference shares
Issued share capital:		200,000	£1 ordinary shares fully paid
		80,000	£1 8% preference shares fully paid
Aircraft fleet	330,000		
Debtors	100,000		
Bank	47,000		
Debentures		25,000	
Reserves:		52,000	
Net Profit for the year (pre-tax)		120,000	
	477,000	477,000	

The directors propose:

a) Provision for corporation tax £40,000

b) Final dividends of

The preference dividend (8%)

15% ordinary dividend (or 15p per share)

Profit and loss account of Skyways Ltd (appropriation section) for the period ending 30 November 19-4

		£	£	
	Net Profit		120,000	
	less Provision for corporation tax		40,000	
	Profit after tax		80,000	← Profit available for distribution by the directors
less	Proposed Dividends:			
	preference dividend	6,400		← 8% × £80,000
	ordinary dividend	30,000		← 15% × £200,000
			36,400	← Dividend to be paid to the shareholders
	Retained profit		43,600	← Retained in the business (added to reserves)

Balance Sheet (extracts) of Skyways Ltd as at 30 November 19-4

Fixed Assets			
Aircraft fleet			330,000
Current Assets			
Debtors		100,000	
Bank		47,000	
		147,000	
Less Creditors due within one year			
Proposed dividends	36,400		
Corporation tax	40,000		
		76,400	
Working Capital			70,600
			400,600
Less Creditors due after one year			
Debentures			25,000
			375,600
Financed by:			
Share Capital:			
Authorised: 250,000 £1 ordinary shares			250,000
80,000 £1 8% preference shares			80,000
			330 000
Issued: 200,000 £1 ordinary shares			200,000
80,000 £1 8% preference shares			80,000
			280,000
Reserves:			
			95,600
Shareholders' Equity			375,600

Note that:
Creditors due within one year = current liabilities
Creditors due after one year = long-term liabilities

The directors have proposed:
i) Dividends of £36,400
ii) Corporation tax provision of £40,000.
Until these are paid they will appear as current liabilities.
iii) Reserves = £52,000 + £43,600 retained profit.

Activities

1 A trainee working with you in the accounts department of Cathedral (Publishers) Ltd is unsure about some of the terms associated with company accounts. Copy and complete the table below to help explain to her how these relate to the accounts of sole traders. The first has been filled in already:

Sole trader	Limited company
proprietor	shareholder
drawings	?
income tax	?
?	reserves
?	directors
?	debentures

2 Your company has an issued capital of 50,000 ordinary shares of £1.50 per share. This year profits after tax are £15,000. The directors have proposed an ordinary dividend of 15p per share to be considered at next month's AGM.

a A shareholder, Mrs Queen, who holds 500 shares, has asked you how much she can expect to receive next month. What do you tell her? Can she be absolutely sure that she will receive this amount?

b How much is the total proposed dividend for the year?

c How much do the directors propose to transfer to the company's reserves?

3 Stars & Bars Ltd runs a chain of exclusive 'American style' nightclubs across the UK. The following balances are extracted from the books as at 31 December 19–5:

	£000s	£000s
Sales		785
Returns Inwards	20	
Opening stock	31	
Purchases	302	
Insurance	10	
Wages and Salaries	230	
Reserves		608
Land and buildings	1,100	
Equipment (at cost)	455	
Provision for depreciation on equipment		296
Rent and rates	23	
Debentures		90
Bank	92	
Bad Debts (written off)	5	
Debtors	82	
Creditors		71
Share capital:		
500,000 £1 ordinary shares		500
	2350	2350

Additional information at 31 December 19–5:

- closing stock is valued at £41,000
- depreciation on equipment is to be 20% of cost
- the directors propose to provide for £30,000 corporation tax, and to pay an ordinary dividend of 8p per share.

a You are to draw up the final accounts for the company as at 31 December 19–5.

b Calculate the investment ratios (see pages 686–7). The current share price is £2.25.

4 Rambo (of Romford) Ltd supply computer software. The company has authorised share capital of 40,000 £1 ordinary shares and 5,000 6% preference shares of £2 each.

	£	£
Ordinary share capital		30,000
6% preference share capital		10,000
Vehicles (at cost)	60,000	
Office Equipment	48,000	
Debtors and Creditors	5,100	2,400
Bank	8,700	
8% Debentures		30,000
Purchases and Sales	170,000	360,000
Bad Debts (written off)	700	
Rent and Rates	35,000	
Salaries and Wages	55,000	
Director's fees	40,000	
Repairs and Maintenance	12,800	
General Expenses	2,300	
Debenture Interest	2,400	
Profit and loss account (at 1 January 1996)		2,600
General Reserve		5,000
	440,000	440,000

Additional information as at 31 December 19–7:
Stock was valued at £32,000
Depreciation of fixed assets is to be at 10% on the straight-line method
Corporation tax will be £20,000
The directors have proposed a 10 per cent ordinary dividend and will pay the preference dividend.

a You have to draw up the final accounts for the year ending 31 December 19–7.
b Calculate the investment ratios (see pages 686–7). The current ordinary share price is £2.80.

The cashflow statement

Accounts concentrating solely on profits can give a misleading impression of the state of a business. A large profit, for example, may be achieved by selling goods on credit, but until the customers pay there will be no cash. The immediate survival of a business has more to do with its ability to raise cash and pay its bills, than with making a profit.

The cashflow statement, which has been compulsory for all large companies since March 1993, is an attempt to analyse the actual cash position of the business. It was introduced in the wake of concern that apparently healthy companies were going into liquidation, Asil Nadir's Polly Peck being one of the more spectacular.

The cashflow statement has five main sections which together explain why the cash/bank position of the company has changed. The bottom section checks this. By adding any change to last year's bank/cash balance we should arrive at this year's bank/cash balance.

Worked example

A cashflow statement

This worked example uses a template showing all of the possible items. The parentheses indicate a cash outflow to be subtracted; all other numbers are to be added. In answering the questions which follow it might be useful to construct such a template and complete it as necessary. A spreadsheet is ideal for this.

Always check that the statement is correct by comparing the 'Balance at the end of the year', with the bank/cash balance on the latest balance sheet. In the example £8,000 + £4,000 = £12,000. The bank figure on the latest balance sheet is £12,000, which tallies with the cashflow statement.

THE ACCOUNTS OF OLDBARN LTD for the year ending 31st December 19-5

Profit and loss appropriation account for period ending 31st December 19-5

	£ 000s
Profit (before tax)	30
Corporation Tax	10
	20
Proposed Dividends	15
Retained Profit	5
add bal c/f	2
bal B/f	7

Balance Sheet of Oldbarn Ltd as at:	31st December 19-4			31st December 19-5			*Cashflow calculations*	
	£000s	*£000s*	*£000s*	*£000s*	*£000s*	*£000s*	*£000s*	
Fixed Assets	*Cost*	*Dep*	*Net*	*Cost*	*Dep*	*Net*	change	item
Fixtures & Fittings	20	5	15	20	6	14	1 increase	depreciation
Current Assets								
Stock		15			18		3 increase	stock
Debtors		12			10		2 decrease	debtors
Bank		8			12		4 increase	bank
		35			40			
less Current Liabilities								
Creditors	4			3			1 decrease	creditors
Proposed Dividends	12			15			12	dividends paid
Corporation Tax	9			10			9	tax paid
		25			28			
Working Capital			10			12		
			25			26		
less Long-term Liabilities								
Debentures			7			3	4 decrease	loans
Net Assets			18			23		
Financed by:								
Ordinary Share Capital			16			16	no change	capital
Retained Profits			2			7		
			18			23		

Cashflow statement for the year ended 31st December 19-5

Notes on the 5 sections of the statement:		£000s	£000s	
1) The main source of cash is the normal trading activities of the business. As profit does not equal cash some adjustments need to be made	**Operating Activities:**			
	Net Profit (before tax and interest)	30		
	Depreciation	1		
	(Increase)/Decrease in stocks	(3)		
	(Increase)/Decrease in debtors	2		
	Increase/(Decrease) in creditors	(1)		
	Net cash inflow from operating activities		29	Subtotal (A)
2) This section shows cash from receipts and payments of interest and dividends	**Returns on investments and servicing of finance:**			
	Interest received			
	(Interest paid)			
	(Dividends/drawings paid)	(12)		
	Net cash outflow from returns on investments and servicing of finance		(12)	Subtotal (B)
3) This section shows tax paid during the year NB this is not tax due at the end	**Taxation:**			
	(Corporation tax paid)	(9)		
	Tax paid		(9)	Subtotal (C)
4) This section shows cashflow resulting from the purchase and sale of fixed assets	**Investing activities:**			
	(Payments) to acquire fixed assets			
	Receipts from sales of fixed assets			
This totals all items so far	*Net cash inflow/(outflow) from investing activities*		0	Subtotal (D)
	Net cash inflow/(outflow) before financing		8	Subtotal (E) Total of A to D (above)
5) This section shows cashflows from share capital and loans	**Financing:**			
	Issue of share capital			
	(Repayment) of capital/share capital			
	Increase in loans			
	(Repayment)of loans	(4)		
	Net cash inflow/(outflow) from financing		(4)	Subtotal (F)
The effect of the above on cashflow	Increase/(decrease) in cash		4	TOTAL (G) E + F
This reconciles cash at start with cash at end	**Analysis of changes in cash during the year:**			
	Balance at start of year		8	
	Net cash inflow/(outflow)		4	TOTAL (G) (above)
Should check with balance sheet	**Balance at end of the year**		12	

Activity

1 **a** Prepare the cashflow statement of Winterburn Fuels Ltd as at 30 November 19–6 using the information below.

b Write a letter to accompany the accounts to be sent to the Managing Director, Mr N. Winterburn, 3 Leftonside Road, London N5. In this explain the purpose of the cashflow statement and comment on what it shows about the business.

Profit and loss (appropriation account) for period ending 30 November 19-6

	£000s
Profit (before tax)	70
Corporation Tax	20
	50
Proposed Dividends	30
Retained Profit	20
add bal c/f	15
bal B/f	35

Balance Sheet of Winterburn Fuels Ltd as at:

	30 November 19-5			30 November 19-6		
	£000s	*£000s*	*£000s*	*£000s*	*£000s*	*£000s*
Fixed Assets	*Cost*	*Dep*	*Net*	*Cost*	*Dep*	*Net*
Plant & Machinery	200	10	190	250	20	230
Current Assets						
Stock		55			65	
Debtors		10			21	
Bank		10			18	
		75			104	
less Current Liabilities						
Creditors	8			9		
Proposed Dividends	12			30		
Corporation Tax	10			20		
		30			59	
Working Capital			45			45
			235			275
less Long-term Liabilities						
Debentures			20			20
Net Assets			215			255
Financed by:						
Ordinary Share Capital			200			220
Retained Profits			15			35
			215			255

2 a Prepare the cashflow statement of Matlock Marinas Ltd as at 31 December 19–6.

b Ms Craft, a member of the board of directors, has asked you explain why the company, which is profitable, is finding difficulties in paying its way. Write a letter to her giving an explanation of this point. Give advice as to how the company can improve matters.

Profit and loss appropriation account for period ending 31 December 19-6

	£000s
Profit (before tax)	120
Corporation Tax	40
	80
Proposed Dividends	75
Retained Profit	5
add bal c/f	5
bal B/f	10

Balance Sheet of Matlock Marinas Ltd as at:

	31 December 19-5			31 December 19-6		
	£000s	£000s	£000s	£000s	£000s	£000s
Fixed Assets	Cost	Dep	Net	Cost	Dep	Net
Plant & Machinery	150	20	130	200	30	170
Current Assets						
Stock		58			68	
Debtors		53			95	
Bank		30			0	
		141			163	
less Current Liabilities						
Creditors	8			9		
Proposed Dividends	50			75		
Corporation Tax	30			40		
Bank overdraft	0			15		
		88			139	
Working Capital			53			24
			183			194
less Long-term Liabilities						
Debentures			18			24
Net Assets			165			170
Financed by:						
Ordinary Share Capital			160			160
Retained Profits			5			10
			165			170

Debenture interest paid in 19–6 was £2,000. (NB You will need to adjust the net profit on the cash flow statement to allow for this.)

Published accounts of limited companies

Companies and the disclosure of information

As a business student you will find that there is a problem in obtaining authentic accounting material for study purposes. The reason is that most forms of business are under no obligation to make their affairs public and quite reasonably their owners have no intention of doing so. Limited companies are the exception.

The larger PLCs are quite happy to send out free copies of their latest annual report and accounts (the published accounts), and for practical purposes this is perhaps the easiest way of obtaining 'real' accounting information.

The published accounts

The Companies Act requires each company to disclose a minimum amount of financial information to its shareholders and to all debenture holders. A copy must also be sent to the Registrar of Companies where, on payment of a small fee, anyone who is interested may inspect this.

The shareholders are invited to attend the annual general meeting, or AGM, where the accounts will be presented to the members by the board of directors. Here the main events of the year will be highlighted and items, including the dividends that the directors propose to pay to the shareholders, will be discussed. The accounts must be accepted by the meeting before any proposals can be put into effect.

Companies that are listed on the London Stock Exchange are required to disclose additional information about their activities and to publish an interim, or half-yearly, report.

The annual report and accounts of a PLC usually contains the following:

- profit and loss account
- balance sheet
- cashflow statement (required for certain larger companies)
- notes to the accounts
- auditors' report
- directors' report.

The following is also often given:

- chairperson's statement
- review of activities
- summary of results
- notice of AGM.

Note that the profit and loss account includes a trading account where appropriate and also an appropriation section.

Stewardship and stakeholders

The law is concerned that information is made available by which interested parties can judge how effective the directors have been in managing the resources of the company. In the UK the directors' duties are defined under two headings:

- **stewardship** – this is the duty the directors have for managing the shareholders' money
- **stakeholders** – these are the range of interested parties to whom the directors have a responsibility (see page 636).

Case study

The Gulf War
Conflict between stewardship and duties to stakeholders

The Gulf War began in late 1991 when Saddam Hussein of Iraq invaded Kuwait. The fighting led to difficulties in obtaining oil from the Gulf region with the result that oil prices rose. In Europe the major oil companies responded by increasing their petrol prices.

Critics argued that the petrol sold at these higher prices was old stock that had been bought before the war and that the companies had no reason for charging more. They were accused of acting selfishly against the public interest and of simply taking the opportunity to make extra profits. The companies replied that they had a duty to their shareholders to make the maximum profit possible. By working on behalf of their shareholders (exercising stewardship) the companies were acting against other stakeholders (the community at large). There was a clear conflict of interest.

Similar conflicts exist within the newly privatised electricity, water and gas industries.

The auditors

Since the directors are responsible for the company and it is they who prepare the financial reports, the Companies Act requires that independent external auditors should inspect the accounts on behalf of the shareholders and other stakeholders.

The report is included in the annual report of the company and it is read aloud at the annual general meeting to the shareholders. The purpose of the audit is to see whether or not the accounts present 'a true and fair view' of the finances of the business.

Statement by the Auditors
to the members of Abbey National plc

In our opinion the summary financial statement set out on pages 13 to 15 is consistent with the annual accounts and directors' report of Abbey National plc for the year ended 31 December 1992 and complies with the requirements of section 251 of the Companies Act 1985 and the regulations made thereunder.

Coopers & Lybrand
Chartered Accountants and Registered Auditors
London
1 March 1993

A 'clean' auditors' report

Where auditors are not satisfied with the accounts they can qualify the audit report. Terry Smith in his book *Where were the auditors?* was one of several writers to point out that from 1990 auditors have been far less willing to qualify their reports, thus making incidents like Polly Peck more likely.

Explanation of terms used in published accounts

Comparative figures The present year's figures are accompanied by figures from the previous year for purposes of comparison.

Group accounts Many companies are part of a group of companies controlled by a holding company which is a PLC. Kingfisher, for example, owns Woolworths and Comet. The holding company controls over 50 per cent of the shares of its subsidiaries and is required to publish consolidated accounts showing the position of the group as a whole.

Minority interests These are the assets of the subsidiary companies not controlled by the group.

Extraordinary items These are items which occur outside the ordinary course of business and are not expected to recur frequently. Examples might be the closing down of parts of the operation.

Income from shares in participating interests This includes the group's share of profits or losses in related companies.

Creditors Amounts falling due within one year. These are the current liabilities.

Creditors Amounts falling due after more than one year. These are the long-term liabilities.

Revenue reserves These may be distributed to shareholders. These include the profit and loss balance and the general reserve.

Capital reserves These may not be distributed to shareholders. These include:

- share premium account – this takes any share capital raised over and above the nominal value of the shares when they are issued
- revaluation reserve – if land and buildings are revalued upwards, then the difference between the new and old valuations is put to this reserve.

Investment ratios for limited companies

There are a number of calculations which enable company shareholders to monitor the performance of their investment.

$$\text{Earnings per share (EPS)} = \frac{\text{Net profit} - \text{Corporation tax and preference dividends}}{\text{Number of issued ordinary shares}}$$

This is expressed in pence and is to be found in the published accounts. It is not the dividend that is actually received by the shareholders, rather it is the profit that their shares have earned. The actual dividend paid and the amount retained in the business will be decided by the directors.

A business that retains profits will be building up the value of its shares, as increased reserves increase the value of the company. Some investors want income (dividends), some want capital growth (increase in share value through retained profits).

The EPS is an important figure to a company, since it indicates performance. For this reason there is currently a debate about the way in which it is calculated. The formula above will still apply, but there is a question about the manner in which the figures are achieved.

$$\text{Dividend Yield} = \frac{\text{Dividend}}{\text{Market price of share}} \times \frac{100}{1}$$

This gives the percentage return on the investment in the share. It can be compared with other investments. Remember that some investors want capital growth rather than dividends.

$$\text{Price/Earnings ratio} = \frac{\text{Market price (of ordinary share)}}{\text{Earnings (per ordinary share)}}$$

All figures here are in pence. The resulting figure shows the earnings on the share in relation to the share price. A figure of five would mean that it would take five years at that level of earnings for the share to earn its market value (pay for itself).

Business failures

The use of ratios and percentages to examine business performance can help identify problems before it is too late. Unfortunately in the recession that hit the UK in the early 1990s many firms were unable to survive despite having good management. Small firms were particularly badly hit. A survey carried out by the NatWest Bank listed the main problems of small business (in order of concern) as:

- lack of demand
- high interest rates
- cashflow
- rent and rates
- government regulations.

Insolvency

Businesses and individuals are insolvent if they cannot pay their debts when they are asked to do so. The immediate reason for this may be that the business has a cashflow problem and cannot raise money sufficiently quickly. Insolvency may not necessarily lead to liquidation or bankruptcy as there may be assets which can become available at some point in the future.

If the creditors insist on having debts paid then a legal procedure begins whereby the assets are sold to pay as many of these debts as possible. Inevitably the Inland Revenue (for income tax or corporation tax) and the Customs & Excise (for VAT) are top of the list! The owners of the business are at the bottom.

Under the 1986 Insolvency Act company directors can be personally liable if they do not act in creditors' best interests when a company is at risk.

Bankruptcy

Individuals who are insolvent and required to pay debts are made bankrupt. Since sole traders and partners are personally responsible for their business debts then bankruptcy applies to the owners of these forms of business. This means that after payment of as many debts as the court deems to be reasonable they are discharged and allowed to continue life without debts. Bankrupts may be required to pay off certain debts from future earnings and it may also be difficult for them to begin again in business as their credit rating will now be poor.

Liquidation

In the case of an insolvent company pressed to pay its debts the company is liquidated. That is, it ceases to exist and its assets are sold. Limited liability protects the personal assets of the shareholders.

Receivership (administration)

Where liquidation seems likely, a company or the creditors may call in the receiver. The job of the receiver is to see whether the company can be saved, possibly by some form of reorganisation. If so it will continue to trade after paying off a number of its debts, if not then it will go into liquidation.

The receiver is an independent accountant appointed by a court to look after the running of a company when it is insolvent. The receiver may be appointed at the request of the creditors. The aim is to try to keep the business going.

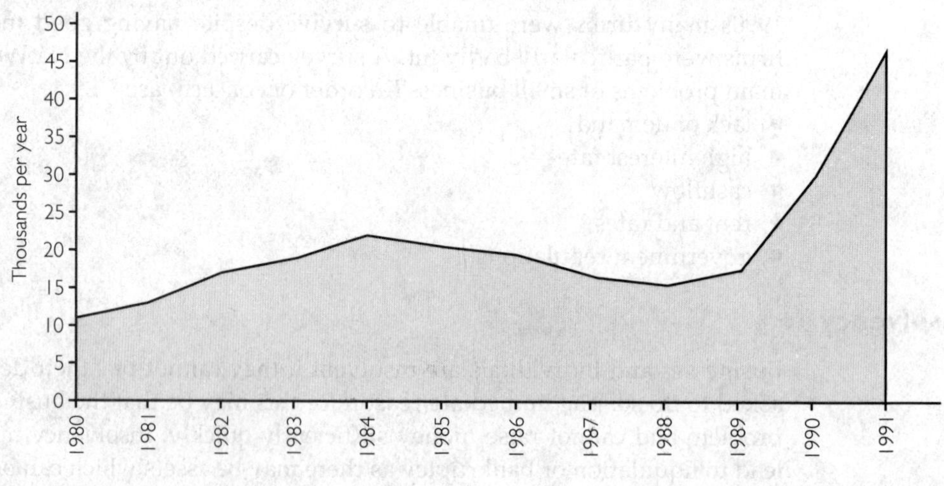

Figure 14.5 Business failures in the UK Source: Dunn and Bradstreet

From 1988 there was a gradual rise in business failures. This trend became severe in the early 1990s when bankruptcies and liquidations ran at 1,000 per week. Small businesses, 'the lifeblood of the economy' according to the government, were particularly badly hit.

Activities

1 Write to the company secretary of a PLC of your choice asking for the latest available copy of the company's published report and accounts. If you already have a report from an earlier activity then use this one.

Some reports have both group and company reports. Use the group report if there is a choice.

Find the profit and loss account and note down the page. Now answer the following questions.

a On what date did the company's financial year end?
b How much is the pre-tax profit?
c What provision has been made for corporation tax?
d How much is the proposed dividend?
e How much is to be retained as reserves?
f Were any interim dividends paid?

2 Turn to the balance sheet, again note down the page. Now answer the following questions.

a What is the size of the authorised capital?
b Has all of this capital been issued? Explain how you know?
c Identify the different reserves maintained by the company and the size of each.

Accounting standards

During the 1960s the accountancy profession came under pressure to impose standards upon its members. There were few reporting requirements at that time and no consistency in the way accounts were drawn up.

The original call for a set of accounting standards came after a series of incidents which showed that the reported accounts of businesses could not be relied upon. In particular the take-over in 1967 of Associated Electrical Industries Ltd (AEI) by the General Electric Company Ltd (GEC) caused a major problem. The accountants at AEI had forecast a profit of £10 million for the year. GEC were influenced by this forecast when they made their successful take-over bid, only to find that in fact a loss of £4.5 million was eventually reported. A sum of £9.5 million of the difference between the forecast figures and the actual loss was put down to 'matters of judgement'.

As a result of this pressure a series of Statements of Standard Accounting Practice, or SSAPs, were drawn up, the first being issued in 1970.

Despite the introduction of these accounting standards there was still no guarantee that company accounts showed the true situation. Ian Griffiths, writing in 1986 in his book *Creative Accounting*, asserted that 'Every company in the country is fiddling its profits...The figures which are fed twice a year to the investing public have all been changed to protect the guilty'. Since this time a number of incidents in the financial world seem to have borne this out, notably the fall of BCCI and Polly Peck. A new series of financial standards (FRS) is now being introduced.

The new accounting standards

The Accounting Standards Board, which came into existence on 1 August 1990, is the body now responsible for setting standards. Examples are:

- SSAP 2 *Disclosure of accounting policies*
  Company accounts should always comply with the four fundamental accounting policies, that is: going concern, accruals, consistency, and prudence concepts. If these have not been followed then this should be noted by the auditors and the reasons for this should be explained.
  Clear explanations of accounting policies should be included as part of the published accounts. This will include the method of depreciation used, whether stock is issued last in first out (LIFO) or first in first out (FIFO) and so on.
- SSAP 9 *Stocks and long-term contracts*
  This states that stock is to be valued at the lower of 'cost and net realisable (market) value.' That is, it will be valued at cost unless current market value is lower.
- SSAP 12 *Accounting for depreciation*
  'To charge a fair proportion of cost (of a fixed asset) to each accounting period expected to benefit from the use of the asset.'
- FRS 1 *Cashflow statements* (applies to all companies except small companies which are not PLCs, banks or insurance companies)
  This shows the increase or decrease in cash over the year, by identifying cash inflows and outflows.
  FRS 3 deals with calculation of earnings per share.

The current situation

The whole question about accounting standards is now out in the open. There will remain certain elements in final accounts that will be matters of judgement, for example the amounts of provisions for depreciation and bad debts, and the valuation of stock. We have seen that accounting profit and cash are not the same thing at all, and it is certainly true that accounts based on the idea of profit allow for some 'creative' reporting.

Key terms

Final accounts	Discounts allowed	FRS
Trading period	Straight-line depreciation	SSAPs
Financial year	Reducing balance depreciation	Profitability
Trial balance	Bad debts	Liquidity
Trading account	Partnership deed	Turnover
Profit and Loss account	Current accounts	Insolvency
Balance sheet	Appropriation account	Liquidation
Revenue expenses	Stakeholders	Bankruptcy
Capital expenses	Stewardship	Accounting Standards Board
Carriage	Auditors	Solvency ratios
Returns	Dividend	Profitability ratios
Depreciation	Annual general meeting (AGM)	Performance ratios
Discounts received	Cashflow statement	

Review questions

1 What are the final accounts?
2 List those people who might wish to see the final accounts of a sole trader?
3 When should a business produce its final accounts?
4 How can a profitable business be short of cash?
5 How do bad debts affect profits?
6 What is the charge for delivery called?
7 When a fixed asset is depreciated by the same amount each year, what method is being used?
8 Name one other method of depreciation.
9 What important items about a business are NOT shown by the accounts? (Hint – The accounts only show what can be valued in money.)
10 Name three matters which may be covered in a partnership deed.
11 Where is the share of profits in a partnership shown?
12 To whom must the published accounts of a limited company be sent?
13 What additional information is shown by the company cashflow statement?
14 What is a dividend?
15 What does AGM stand for? What matters are discussed at this?
16 Give one formula for calculating profitability
17 Give one formula for calculating liquidity
15 What is meant by the terms:
a insolvency?
b bankruptcy?
c liquidity?
16 What is the function of the Accounting Standards Board?

Assignment 14.2 PLC investigation

This assignment develops knowledge and understanding of the following elements:

7.3 Produce and explain profit and loss statements and balance sheets
7.4 Identify and explain data to monitor a business

It supports the development of the following core skills:

Communication 3.2, 3.3, 3.4
Application of number 3.1, 3.2, 3.3
Information technology 3.1, 3.2, 3.3

In this assignment you will study the financial report of a public limited company.

The assignment will enable you to demonstrate an understanding of accounting conventions, financial statements, business objectives and the ways in which wider influences exert an effect on business. You will also use techniques for monitoring business performance.

This is an ongoing assignment which you will need to complete over a period of some weeks. You will need at some stage to compare information with a fellow student and you should plan with this in mind.

You may already have information to hand which may be useful for this assignment.

The instructions are presented in two sections:

1 collection of data
2 presentation of the assignment.

Your tasks

Collection of data

With a friend decide on a line of business in which you are both interested. You should each select a PLC of your choice in this same line of business (the share price of the companies must be listed in the daily press).

From now on you will work independently but at a later stage you will need to compare results.

1 Obtain a copy of the latest available published accounts from your company. If you write to the company then retain a copy of the letter for inclusion in your report.

2 From the published accounts extract the following information* (provide report page numbers for reference and present figures clearly in tabular form):

a From profit and loss account for the past two years:**
turnover
pre-tax profit/(loss)
provision for corporation tax
dividends proposed
retained profits
earnings per share

b From balance sheet for the past two years**, totals for:
fixed assets
current assets
current liabilities (due within one year)
long-term liabilities (due after one year)
Issued Share Capital
Reserves

c From the auditors' report indicate whether the auditors found the accounts to be satisfactory. Mention any qualifications (problems they point out).

d From the notes to the accounts, research details on accounting policies. In particular indicate which methods are used for stock valuation and depreciation.

3 Monitor the PLC for ONE TERM using the daily press. Note down the following once a week (on the same day each time):

a the share price of your PLC as quoted on the Stock Exchange

b the level of the FTSE-100 index.

Clearly tabulate your results. Plot (a) and (b) on separate graphs.***

---

*Where there is a choice use consolidated (group) figures
**Annual accounts will show figures for the year ended AND for the previous year
***Ideally use a spreadsheet package for this

4 Study the press, TV and radio regularly for mention of your PLC or for factors which will influence the industry in which your PLC operates. Remember that some things will affect all industry in general, e.g. changes in government policies, changes in the economy, world events and so on. From the above compile a brief weekly summary of those events which you would consider significant if you were a director of your PLC. NB you should in particular have some idea of reasons for:

a changes in the share price of your company

b changes in share prices in general (as shown by the FTSE-100).

Presentation of the assignment

Present a profile of your chosen PLC containing the following.

a A brief introduction to the company to include:
its size, products/services and position in its industry

b Figures extracted from the published accounts (see 2a and b above) should be accompanied by calculations to show:

- those percentages and ratios for profitability and liquidity (for each year) that are possible with the available figures
- similar results from the other company in the same industry studied by your friend
- a brief comment on the performance of your company based on these calculations.

c Explain what is shown by:

- the profit and loss account
- the balance sheet
- the cashflow statement.

Be sure to distinguish clearly between the uses of each.

d The tables and graphs of share prices (see 3 above). On the graphs you should label the main movements in prices and provide brief explanations by referring to the weekly summary of events.

e The weekly summary of events (see 4 above).

f An appendix which will contain any relevant printed matter to which reference has been made. It should contain at least the PLC report and may also contain any press cuttings and a copy of the letter written to the company secretary requesting the published accounts.

NB No purpose will be served by including material that you do not understand. There will be certain items in all company reports that you are not sure about.

UNIT 8 BUSINESS PLANNING

15 Business planning

What is covered in this chapter

- The business plan for Pot Pourri
- The sales and marketing plan for Pot Pourri
- The world of work – planning for employment and self-employment

These are the resources you will need for your Business Planning file:

- a spreadsheet package
- a word processing package
- a PC
- local newspapers for employment opportunities
- business planning/start-up guides.

In this unit you will use the knowledge and skills that you have developed. You will also need to draw on many of the resources that you have collected throughout the course. Further investigation will, however, be required and relevant addresses can be found in the *Business Planning/Start-up Guide*, available from high street banks, and the *Thomson Directory*, especially the 'Business Advice' section listed under 'Helplines'.

Unit 8 brings together the knowledge, skills and understanding from the other units.

We will use a case study to take you through the process of writing a business plan. There will be activities for you to do at each stage which will help you to collect the information that you will need for your own plan. If you have worked through the activities in the book then you will have some of this information already.

We have used a small pottery business to show how the planning process works. At the end there is a completed business plan and a marketing plan for the pottery as an example of how yours could be presented.

The business plan for Pot Pourri

Scenario – The business idea

Della Clayton has been making pottery for a number of years. She exhibits locally and regularly sells a number of items. Over the years her work has attracted growing interest, and she has recently been offered some contracts to supply local shops and a chain of restaurants with her prize-winning 'Della-ware' six-piece dinner sets.

Della realises that it would not be possible to fulfil these commitments working only in her spare time. However, she has some savings, she has paid off her mortgage and feels that now might be the time to turn her hobby into a full-time occupation.

Activity

What will be the nature of your business?

Ask yourself these questions:

a Will I make a product, like Della, or will I provide a service?

b Will I start a new business or buy an existing business or a franchise?

Many of the household names that we see in the High Street are run under franchise, for example McDonalds and Body Shop. This means that an established business, rather than setting up new branches itself, sells the right to run its operation in a particular area to an independent trader or company.

In return for putting in capital the franchising company provides equipment, expertise and advertising. The new operator, the franchisee, has the advantage of operating under a well-known name with an established reputation. In this way a small business benefits from the economies of scale that come from being part of a large organisation. The franchiser takes a share of the profits without taking a risk and usually has an agreement to provide a certain quantity of stock.

Is Della the right sort of person to set up in business?

After talking things over with friends Della feels that she is the sort of person who will be able to run her own business. She realises that she may not make as much money as if she remained in employment, but is prepared to work hard and is attracted by the idea of being her own boss.

Activity

Are you the right sort of person to run your own business?

a What are your reasons for wanting to run a business?

b What are your strengths, that will help you succeed? In order to identify her strengths and weaknesses Della filled out this checklist. Now fill it in yourself.

Competence checklist for self-assessment:

	Definitely	To some extent	Not at all
Personality			
Have I got a good sense of humour?			
Do I have perseverance?			
Can I handle difficult situations?			
Am I conscientious?			
Do I have initiative?			
Can I make decisions?			
Have I the confidence to see things through?			
Do I have the ambition to succeed?			
Can I organise myself and my time?			
Do I plan ahead?			
Have I imagination to produce new ideas?			
Am I creative?			
Can I solve problems?			

	Definitely	To some extent	Not at all
Meeting people			
Do I enjoy meeting new people?			
Can I deal with difficult people?			
Can I take criticism and advice?			
Do I have tact?			
Do I turn up on time?			
Do I keep my promises?			
Do I listen to other people?			
Communicating			
Can I write business letters?			
Do I enjoy making phone calls?			
Do I listen to other people?			
Do I respect other people's opinions?			
Do I interrupt too much?			
Am I prepared to change my opinions?			
Health			
How many times have I seen the doctor in the last six months?			
Can I take pressure and worry?			
Do I get tired easily?			
Can I work long hours?			
Do I look forward to my three weeks' summer holiday?			
Do I have problems sleeping?			
Do I smoke and drink too much?			
Practical skills			
Can I use a word processing package?			
Can I use an accounting package?			
Am I numerate?			
Can I solve problems which are not routine?			
Can I mend things?			
Do I always have to ask people for help?			
Can I use my work experience?			
Can I use my hobbies?			

Rate yourself on each competence on the scale shown. Notice that 'definitely' is not always the most helpful answer! If you feel that you need extra development in a particular area, identify ways in which you might achieve this.

What sort of business organisation?

Della knows that she is going to produce and sell pottery. She now has to decide which form of business organisation will be the most appropriate to her. There are three possibilities: sole trader; partnership; limited company. Della needs to consider the following points:

- Will she run the business entirely on her own?
- She has some savings but how much more money will she need in order to start up?
- Does she want to keep her business affairs confidential?
- Is she likely to be taking a large risk?
- Is she likely to be owing lots of money?
- Does she need limited liability?
- How large is the operation likely to be?

Della's first thought is that she will work alone on a small scale as a sole trader. She intends to continue to use her existing pottery (a shed in the back garden) and sell only to local outlets. She still thinks that there are possibilities in this, but after speaking to her friend, Devi, who has some contacts in the business world, she now feels that the potential is greater than she first thought. Della is now considering setting up a partnership with Devi who is prepared to bring in her business experience and extra capital.

Their intentions are as follows. Della will produce the pottery to her own designs with the aid of a part-time helper (probably a student with an Advanced level GNVQ) who will be employed in peak periods during the summer holidays. Devi will stay in her present job but will invest some capital, and look after the administration and promotion side. This will include using her contacts to widen the sales base. The business will need larger premises than Della's shed for this more ambitious venture.

The idea of forming a company appealed at first, but the need to comply with so many more rules and regulations put Della off. She does not want to draw up formal documents such as the memorandum and articles of association. A limited company would also have to submit accounts each year to the registrar of companies. For the moment Della prefers to keep her affairs confidential.

In order to set up the partnership Della and Devi had to consider the following issues.

Registration of business

This is not necessary for a partnership.

Choosing a business name

Della and Devi have chosen the name 'Pot Pourri' and they will need to register this. First, however, they need to be sure that it is not already used by another business.

As they are trading under a business name, the partners must show their own names and business address on all business communications. This is a point they need to consider when designing their business stationery.

Devi contacts the Companies Registration Office and obtains a copy of their booklet called 'Business Names – Guidance notes', which contains all that the partners will need to know. In particular it explains that they will have to comply with the Business Names Act.

Income tax and VAT

Business accounts will need to be maintained and presented annually for inspection by the Inland Revenue for income tax purposes. The partners therefore need to set up an efficient financial record-keeping system and have decided that accounts will be maintained on a small business integrated software package. There are many of these on the market and most are quite inexpensive. Sage is the market leader in this field.

The partners will be taxed as private individuals on the profits they receive from the business. This, and the payment of National Insurance, will be their individual responsibility.

As the business wishes to employ a student on a full-time temporary basis in the summer, the partners will need to become familiar with the requirements for the deduction of National Insurance and income tax for employees.

If the turnover is to exceed the set limit per year the business will have to register for VAT with the local Customs & Excise office (see Appendix 4 for current rate).

Partnership agreement

The partners feel it would be wise to have a partnership agreement. Partners are 'jointly and severally' responsible for business debts, meaning that each is responsible for the other. They prepare a summary of the principal terms to enable their solicitor to draw up a formal partnership deed:

Principal terms for the Partnership Agreement for Pot Pourri

Capital to be invested: D. Clayton £4,000
D. Sandesh £8,000

Profit sharing:
D. Clayton to be entitled to a fixed share of the profits to be drawn as a salary at the rate of £1,200 per month.

Subject to the above:
Profits and losses will be shared in the ratio of 2:1 D. Sandesh/D. Clayton

There will be no interest on capital and no interest on drawings

Both partners to have unlimited liability

Roles:	D Clayton to produce and design pottery D Sandesh to provide contacts, administrative support and use of estate car
Security:	The house belonging to D Clayton will be pledged as security for any external finance which is necessary
Decisions:	All business decisions must be unanimous
Cheques:	All cheques to bear signatures of both partners
Death of a partner:	Partners agree that if either dies then the original capital will remain in the business for use by the other for a maximum of 2 years subject to payment of interest on the capital to the estate of the deceased partner at the rate of 10% p.a.
Disputes:	To be resolved by arbitration
Duration of partnership:	Minimum of 3 years; then to continue at will
Retirement:	No retirement during the first 3 years; thereafter a partner may retire on giving 6 months' notice
Alterations:	The partnership agreement can be altered only by mutual consent

Activities

What sort of business organisation will you set up?

1 Draw up a list which shows the strengths and weakness of each of the following as a form of business organisation: sole trader, partnership, limited company.
2 Decide which is the best form of organisation for your business.
3 Choose a business name.
4 Design a logo and appropriate headed stationery for your business using a desk-top publishing package.

The aims and objectives of the business

Della and Devi agree that these would be their aims:

- to provide quality products with quality design
- to establish a reputation in the market for quality at a reasonable price
- to use only natural products
- to get job and personal satisfaction.

Their objective is to make a living by earning more than £30,000 a year in total profit by year 3.

Activity

What are your business aims and objectives?

Make a list of your aims and objectives – don't forget that objectives must be quantified.

Insurance implications

It would be wise for Della and Devi to take out a range of insurance policies. It is possible to insure against almost any risk. However, they cannot insure against making a loss through bad business practice, which is why they are drawing up a business plan.

Insurance premiums – the money which will be paid to the insurance company – can be very high. They will need to balance the cost of premiums against the expected risk. For some items they could decide on self-insurance, that is, they will not insure, but will carry the risks themselves.

The sorts of insurance that are available for their business are as follows.

- Premises – The kiln might set fire to the workshop and damage it!
- Contents – What if the kiln sets fire to some of the stock in the workshop?
- Business interruption – After a disaster, such as a fire, the business may have to remain closed for some time. This insurance will help with the fixed costs – the many bills which will still have to be paid during this time.
- Theft from buildings and vehicles.
- Breakages including goods in transit. Pots are fragile!
- Employer's liability – What if the employee gets injured on the premises?
- Public liability – A customer visiting the workshop may get burnt on the kiln.
- Product liability – What if a customer is hurt by an 'oven-proof' pot exploding?
- Bad debts – What if the customers don't pay?
- Fidelity – What if the helper runs off with the money?
- Personal accident – What if Della breaks her arm on a skiing holiday?

- Legal expenses – These may be needed if the partners are involved in legal action arising from any of the above.
- Motor insurance – Required for the business vehicle.
- Life assurance – For Della and her partner in whom she has an insurable interest.

Some of these insurances are compulsory:

- Premises insurance – The landlord insists that the business insures the property.
- Road traffic insurance – Third-party insurance at least is required by law.
- Employer's liability insurance – This will be necessary for the summer helper.

The partners also choose to insure for contents, breakages, product liability and personal accident. They both already have life assurance.

Della and Devi visit an insurance broker, where they find that the policy offered by McEwan's Insurance Ltd covers all of these risks for one premium of £2,000 a year.

Activity

a Decide on the types of insurance you will need for your business.
b Research the annual premiums for these policies. You may, like Della and Devi, find an insurance company that will offer a package to cover all of your requirements for one premium.

Legal implications – which laws apply?

Della and Devi need to be aware of laws affecting their relationships with consumers, trade customers and suppliers. These are as follows.

- The Supply of Goods and Services Act which states that goods must be of 'satisfactory quality' and 'fit for the purpose for which they are sold'. A pot which is sold as perfect should not be cracked. A pot with a flaw may be sold if advertised as a 'second'. A customer who has the opportunity to check the goods at the time of purchase but does not do so will not be able to complain later. The phrase caveat emptor (let the buyer beware) is the legal term which covers this.
- The Trades Descriptions Act states that goods must not be described incorrectly. The '12-inch dinner plate' should be 12 inches in diameter.
- The Consumer Safety Act protects the consumer from, for example, a pot decorated with a lead-based paint which may be harmful to a child.
- Della and Devi are also customers of their own suppliers. The clay and glaze that they buy should be 'as described' and should be 'of satisfactory quality'. In ordering goods it is important to specify precisely where they are to be delivered. Without such instructions there cannot be a complaint if goods are delivered to inconvenient places. This is particularly important with clay which is very heavy.

Buyer's rights

A buyer who has a complaint because of faulty goods can ask for money to be refunded or for compensation if the goods are kept. Although faulty goods may be exchanged, there is no legal requirement for Della and Devi to do anything other than to refund money. The partners must also remember that they too are buyers and as such they also have these rights.

If goods prove to be faulty soon after purchase, they should take them back to the supplier. Even if the fault is in the manufacture of the product the responsibility is still the supplier's.

Where the supplier will not accept responsibility for unsatisfactory goods the buyer can:

ask for someone in a position of responsibility, such as the manager;

↓

if there is no success then

if the supplier is a branch of a larger organisation, contact head office;

↓

if this fails then

send a solicitor's letter threatening legal action;

↓

as a last resort

consider civil action in the county court, or, depending upon the value of the goods, the small claims court

Legal action may be costly and may not be worth pursuing, though where the claim concerns matters such as trades descriptions, weights and measures, or matters of public health then the authorities will prosecute.

Employment

When the partners take on an employee during the summer months they must ensure that they provide safe working conditions and adequate facilities as laid down in the Factories Acts and the Health and Safety at Work Act.

Activity

Which laws apply to your business?

List the laws that are likely to affect you in your relationship with your customers and suppliers.

Technical matters

Patents and trade marks

Della only uses her own designs so she will not have to pay royalties to other designers. She should, however, copyright these designs so that others cannot use them free of charge.

Since Della wishes to brand her products as 'Della-Ware' – she will need to register this name as a trade mark.

Data protection

If the business holds any personal information on computer about clients or employees (other than pay records and accounts) then it may need to register with the Data Protection Registrar. The partnership will keep computerised accounting records, including lists of customers' names and addresses, and payroll details for their employee. There will be no need to register if information is kept only for these purposes.

Health and safety

The responsibility for health and safety in the workplace is entirely that of the partners. The legislation introduced by the EU means that even as self-employed people they will have to comply. Having a kiln means that they will have to take particular care.

Activity

1 What special health and safety requirements will be necessary for your business?
2 Will you need to register under the Data Protection Act?

The environment

The partners must be aware that when they find suitable premises they will need to:

- obtain planning permission from the local authority to use these for business purposes
- be aware of regulations which might restrict their operations. For example, they will need to consider regulations about noise, pollution, parking and access, delivery times and out of hours working.

Some types of business, such as those dealing in food, gaming, animals, caring and the entertainment business, will need a licence from the local authority before they are able to trade. The pottery does not come into this category.

Activity

Check whether any special regulations apply to your business. In the food industry you will need to be particularly aware. For instance, sandwiches have to be kept in a cold cabinet.

Resources

The resources used by a business are called inputs or factors of production. They are:

- labour – the helper and the partners
- land – the premises
- capital – the physical resources such as the kiln and the financial resources
- enterprise – the entrepreneurs Devi and Della who bring this all together by setting up the business and taking the risks.

Labour – human resources

The two partners will work in the business: Della in designing and potting; Devi in the administration. The trade will peak at certain times of the year, during which they will employ a helper on a temporary contract. They will be responsible for recruitment, selection, training and maintaining the pay records during this period. The employee will be paid £525 per month in line with current earnings for 18 year olds. The helper will work for four months from June to September.

In recruiting staff the firm will need to take full account of the law on equal opportunities and discrimination, and draw up a clear contract of employment.

Land – the premises

Della and Devi will need to decide exactly what they need their premises for, how big they should be and whether the location is important. Cost is also a major factor. The options on acquiring premises are to buy freehold, lease or rent.

The partners did consider renting a unit on an industrial estate in a nearby enterprise zone with special concessions including low rents and rates. Economically this makes sense, as exact location is not important, but Della prefers more peaceful working conditions. They have opted to rent a converted stable/mews which may ultimately provide a more sympathetic environment if they later open a showroom for the public. The rent is £100 per week or £5,200 a year payable in advance in two half-yearly instalments. The business rate will be £1,400 p.a., payable in May.

New legislation concerning the way in which estate agents describe properties meant that the partners wasted less time looking at unsuitable premises.

The landlord has given permission for the necessary non-structural alterations needed to create a working area, a kiln area, storage and office space. Installation of necessary three-phase wiring and safety doors is also approved. The estimated cost will be £3,000, payable immediately. The partners do not own the property and have decided that this will be written off as a cost of their first year of operation.

Activity

1 Make a checklist of features you would require in your business premises
2 List the advantages and disadvantages of acquiring business property by buying, leasing or renting property
3 Identify premises in your area that would be suitable for your purposes
4 Find out the cost of suitable business property in your chosen area.
5 Find out from the local authority the business rates for your intended premises
6 If you are considering buying, then you will require a mortgage. The rate of interest will be an important consideration and you will need to be aware of this.

Capital – meaning here physical resources

The partners will need to consider equipment for the pottery workshops, office equipment, furniture and fittings, and vehicles.

Fixed assets to be acquired To buy and install the potter's wheel, a kiln and other necessary equipment will cost approximately £12,000 (kiln £10,000, potters' wheel £2,000). Specialist tools will cost a further £1,000. The office will need a fax machine, a desk-top computer with appropriate packages for word processing, small business accounts and design. It will also need a small photocopier. The estimated cost of this equipment will be £2,400. A filing cabinet and suitable furniture will cost £600. Total cost will be £16,000 plus VAT.

Vehicles There are a number of options. The supplies will need to be delivered and this will be done by the supplier. The finished goods will need to be transported to the customer. The partners can either ask the buyers to collect, use an independent carrier or deliver themselves. They decide that where the buyer cannot collect they will deliver to avoid the high insurance costs of using an independent carrier.

They will use the estate car that Devi owns and make the necessary arrangements with the insurance company and DVLA at Swansea to enable them to use the vehicle for business and pleasure purposes.

There is no capital expenditure on the vehicle but there will be increased maintenance, depreciation, insurance and fuel costs. An agreement will need to be reached with the Inland Revenue to allow a certain percentage of the car running casts to be treated as a business expense. The estimated cost of running the car allowable against the business is estimated at £2,400 a year or £200 per month.

Activity

Identify and cost the following resources that you will need for your business:

a equipment needed to manufacture goods, for instance, if you are thinking of designing T-shirts you will need printing equipment

b specialised equipment needed to provide a service such as equipment you might need for a mobile disco

c office furniture that is required, for example tables, chairs, shelving, filing cabinets

d any office equipment that is required, perhaps a computer system including printer and applications packages

e vehicle and transport costs.

Stocks This comprises raw materials such as clay, glaze, paints and so on. Della has suggested that they should buy an initial stock worth £2,000. Additionally, stock will be bought in each month sufficient for that month's production. In this way £2,000 of stock will always be in hand to cover emergencies. Storage facilities are good and wastage will be minimal so that the year will end with £2,000 of raw materials closing stock.

Stationery will consist of headed paper, cards, catalogues and price lists, printed forms such as invoices, credit notes and statements of account. An initial cost of £500 is envisaged and thereafter £30 per month.

Packaging will be cardboard boxes and packing materials. These can be bulky, so to save on storage space they will be bought as and when required (JIT). Packaging is vital for fragile goods such as Della's pots.

Activity

If your business makes its own products find out the cost of raw materials. If you are going to trade find out the purchase price of your stock.

Professional services

There are many sources of help and information available to people such as Della and Devi who are starting out in business. Many banks, specialist agencies and government departments are keen to help the 1,000 new businesses being formed every week.

Sources of help, information and advice include:

- local enterprise agencies
- small firms services
- local council (the economic development unit is keen to help new business in the area)
- business start-up scheme which is government funded
- Prince's Youth Business Trust which gives grants and loans to young people starting in business
- Project Fullemploy which provides help to people from ethnic minorities.

Activity

Investigate local sources of help and advice available to your business:
a look up the addresses of local agencies in the telephone directory
b look in the introduction to the business telephone directory which is a mine of information

As well as using these agencies , the partners find it necessary to employ professionals for specific guidance. These include:

- the solicitor – for help with formation of the business including drawing up the partnership agreement. Should they wish to purchase property a solicitor will help with the conveyancing
- the accountant – who will draw up financial reports such as the final accounts for the Inland Revenue, help with VAT returns for Customs & Excise, and provide advice on investment, planning and book-keeping
- the bank manager/bank small business adviser – who will look at their business plan and decide whether or not to allow Devi and Della to borrow money.

Help can also be obtained from management consultants who can advise on the structure and conduct of business operations, and agencies providing advertising and marketing services. Della and Devi are not operating on a sufficiently large scale to require these services.

Market research

The partners realise that they need to carry out more detailed market research as their success in acquiring finance will depend upon this. They decide to check out who their potential customers are and who their competitors are.

They have identified their unique selling point (USP) which is to produce rough earthenware crockery in natural colours catering for the needs of individual customers. Their market will primarily be for quality restaurants, wholefood shops and craft shops. There are no plans to export as yet. Competitors tend to be either large regional companies who do not cater for individual customers or very small potters turning out ornamental items for the tourist market.

The partnership has a contract to supply a chain of restaurants and this, together with estimated supply from individual customers, is the basis for the sales budget. Sales are expected to peak in summer and around Christmas.

Activities

1 Devise a questionnaire consisting of 12 close-ended questions (requiring the answers yes or no) to establish whether or not there is a market for your product.
2 Either from your own research, or from looking at existing businesses of the same type, estimate the sales that you can expect in the first year.

Production and sales budgets

On the basis of their market research Della and Devi estimate sales of units for year 1 as:

Apr	May	June	July	Aug	Sept	Oct	Nov	Dec	Jan	Feb	Mar	Total
45	35	50	65	80	55	45	65	80	30	25	25	600

The partners are a manufacturing concern. They must be sure that they can produce enough dinner sets to satisfy the monthly demand. A production budget is essential to ensure that customers' orders can be fulfilled by the agreed deadlines. It is tempting for a small business to take all orders that come in. Della does not want to turn away business, but she will be working alone and, if she knows that her reputation will depend upon quality and fulfilling her commitments, she must be realistic about the production levels she can achieve. The business plan must take account of limiting factors such as production capacity and the availability of raw materials.

'Overtrading' can result if a business attempts to grow too quickly. That is, to achieve high levels of production quickly, it may spend money it does not have on stock and new equipment only to find that slow payment or bad debts causes cashflow problems. Expansion is better funded from profits at a manageable rate.

Della knows from experience that she can realistically produce 50 units per month. At this rate she could produce the 600 units required in the first year (50 units × 12 months = 600 units). The difficulty is that the goods will not be available when they are needed. This can be seen if a cumulative (year to date) schedule is drawn up showing sales and production totals as the year progresses.

Preliminary sales and production budget

Month	Sales		Production		Closing stock
	Monthly	Cumulative	Monthly	Cumulative	Finished goods
Apr	45	45	50	50	5
May	35	80	50	100	20
Jun	50	130	50	150	20
Jul	65	195	50	200	5
Aug	80	275	50	250	(25)
Sep	55	330	50	300	(30)
Oct	45	375	50	350	(25)
Nov	65	440	50	400	(40)
Dec	80	520	50	450	(70)
Jan	30	550	50	500	(50)
Feb	25	575	50	550	(25)
Mar	25	600	50	600	0
Total for year	600	600	600	600	

The closing stock of finished goods column compares production with sales. This is a negative figure from August to February showing that during these months production is less than sales, meaning that customers' orders cannot be supplied. By March production catches up, but most of the customers will by then have cancelled and gone elsewhere – who wants their Christmas present three months late?

Where demand is seasonal the answer is either to accept fewer orders or to adjust supply. This is why Della intends taking on a student in the summer. The helper will do the fetching, carrying, cleaning up and so on, leaving Della to concentrate entirely on potting. She estimates that with this help she will be able to increase production to 70 units per month. This will allow her to plan to meet demand:

Revised sales and production budget

Month	Sales Monthly	Sales Cumulative	Production Monthly	Production Cumulative	Closing stock Finished goods
Apr	45	45	50	50	5
May	35	80	50	100	20
Jun	50	130	70	170	40
Jul	65	195	70	240	45
Aug	80	275	70	310	35
Sep	55	330	70	380	50
Oct	45	375	50	430	55
Nov	65	440	50	480	40
Dec	80	520	40	520	0
Jan	30	550	40	560	10
Feb	25	575	20	580	5
Mar	25	600	20	600	0
Total for year	600	600	600	600	

The revised production budget is quite satisfactory. The fact that production is at low levels in February and March will allow some time for a short break after all the hard work. Alternatively it means that, if necessary, output can be expanded to meet orders for the next financial year, which by then will be coming in.

Activity

If you are providing a service or producing a product you will need to draw up a production budget to ensure that it is possible for you to satisfy the estimated demand for your product or service.

Financial forecasts

Financial forecasts will help the partners to take decisions and to control their business. As with the production budget, initial forecasts may indicate that present plans will not lead to a satisfactory outcome. In this case adjustments will need to be made. Devi knows from her business experience that producing these forecasts on a spreadsheet will provide the most convenient means of looking at alternatives. As she says 'We can easily set up 'What if?' questions.'

The financial forecasts will show whether the profits are likely to be satisfactory and whether the partners will need to borrow any more funds. Where they show that the business is likely to be successful, the forecasts will give Della and Devi the means of convincing the bank to help them.

A reminder that profit and cash are NOT the same thing

A business may have huge profits but no cash – perhaps because all sales are on credit.

It may have losses but lots of cash, perhaps because it has borrowed a lot, not paid its bills or bought its stock on credit.

As they show different things a business needs both a cashflow forecast and a forecast profit and loss account – often called an operating budget.

The cashflow forecast

Devi and Della need to see whether they will need to borrow any further money at various times in the year. The cashflow forecasts the monthly income and expenses that are predicted. It will show if extra finance such as a medium-term loan or an overdraft facility is required.

The forecast operating budget (trading and profit and loss account)

This will show whether the business can expect to make a profit on the year. Ratio analysis can show whether this is an adequate return on capital invested.

The partners are advised to produce financial forecasts on a monthly basis so that the plans can be monitored regularly as the year progresses. In this way variances can be quickly identified and problems recognised before they become too serious.

Appropriation account

This can be forecast for the end of the year to give the partners some idea of the share of profits that they can expect.

The balance sheet

This forecasts the worth of the business at the end of the first year. It is not always required as part of a business plan. However, it is very useful as it helps to check the accuracy of the other forecasts. If the balance sheet balances then the partners will know that their forecasts are at least arithmetically correct.

Break-even point

It is useful for Della and Devi to know how many units they will need to sell in the year to breakeven. The margin of safety will show how far short of the estimated sales they can fall before they begin to make a loss.

Activity

A vital part of your business plan will be the financial forecasts for your first year. You will need to assemble all of the information that you require for these. This will come from the activities that you have carried out so far.

Start-up guides, produced by banks, provide proformas to help with structuring the accounts. It is convenient to produce forecasts on a spreadsheet as this will allow you to make changes as necessary and experiment with 'What if?' questions.

Remember – be realistic. It is better to know that a business will have difficulties than to try and hide them! This is the point of planning.

The planning process – sequence of activities

Della and Devi have set themselves a target of six months to complete their business plan. They realise that they have a lot to do and must proceed in a logical way in order to meet their deadline. They draw up a Gantt chart which shows the critical path which they must follow throughout the planning process.

Activity

We have now identified the main tasks which you will have to carry out when drawing up your business plan.

Complete the Gantt chart on the following page so as to show the sequence in which you will tackle these activities. You must make sure that you can complete your plan within the deadlines you have been given, so you may need to adjust the time period on the chart to take account of this. You may wish to add other activities.

	Time in weeks									
Activities	1	2	3	4	5	6	7	8	9	10
Self-assessment										
Identify product or service										
Identify form of business organisation										
Identify legal requirements										
Market research										
Check proposal – is it still viable?										
Advertise for staff										
Select staff										
Research premises										
Select premises										
Re-check proposal – is it viable?										
Research equipment										
Select equipment										
Price stocks										
Obtain help and advice										
Draw up financial proposals										
sales budget										
production budget										
cashflow forecast										
profit and loss forecast										
balance sheet										
break-even chart										
Assemble the business plan										

Interview with the small business adviser at the bank

The partners take the plan (overleaf) to the local branch of The North Bank plc. The bank manager is impressed with the figures but wishes to make sure that they are realistic. These are the questions which are asked:

- Are you sure that you can sell this many items?
- Are both partners committed to the enterprise? Devi is investing capital and some expertise but is not actively working in the business. Will she stay if things are more difficult than expected?
- Are the costs based upon up-to-date information?
- Is £1,200 a month a reasonable amount for Della to live on?
- Devi intends to retain her present job and does not require a regular income from the business. Will this continue or will she want drawings during the year?
- Della is working alone for most of the year. In view of this is the production level realistic?
- What happens if Della is ill?
- There is one major contract. What happens if this falls through?
- What about equipment failures?
- Will customers keep to the 30-day credit period?
- Are customers creditworthy? What are procedures for credit control?
- How do the partners see the business progressing?
- Are all of the legal requirements sorted out?

The bank manager is reasonably satisfied but suggests that a new cashflow forecast and operating statement should be worked out for a worst case of a cut in sales of 10 per cent. There is also the difficulty that £24,000 is required immediately as an overdraft while the partners jointly are only investing £12,000. Another appointment is arranged.

POT POURRI

(Personalised dinner sets)

Della Clayton, Devi Sandesh Trading as Pot Pourri
The Wheelhouse, Wateringham H20
Tel: (01010) 820541 Fax: (01010) 820557

Business Plan

The Plan - Table of Contents

1

1 Summary and Objectives

Type of Organisation: Partnership

Business Name: Pot Pourri

Business Address: The Wheelhouse, Wateringham H20

Partners: Della Clayton and Devi Sandesh

People:

Della Clayton

Age:	29
Experience:	Local government finance officer 8 years
Qualifications:	4 O levels, GNVQ Advanced Business
Expertise:	Pottery exhibitions locally, won local design award (Trimnelli Prize) 1990 Sales to local business
Address:	23 Factory Row, Wateringham
Tel:	01010 454545

Devi Sandesh

Age:	32
Occupation:	Commercial designer (freelance)
Experience:	11 years of working on major contracts
Qualifications:	2 A levels, Higher Diploma in Art & Design, Crossley College of Art
Expertise:	Has working relationships with numerous potential business clients
Address:	Roundwood, Warren Place, Penleigh
Tel:	01101 663410

Nature of business and market area:

The business will produce and sell earthenware/ceramic 6-piece dinner sets to the specifications of individual clients. We will work closely with clients to develop designs which are suitable to their image and needs. This plan is based upon a guide price for each dinner set of £140. The summer and Christmas periods are expected to show peak demand.

Our USP will be our emphasis on quality and personal designs which will enable us to secure a niche in the market. We believe that this will enable us to achieve high profit margins which will allow us to concentrate on quality rather than volume.

Sales will be on 30-day credit terms. We have already secured a contract from a chain of local vegetarian restaurants.

The attached cashflow forecast indicates that we will require an overdraft facility of £24,000 for working capital needs for year 1. This will help with start-up costs and will help smooth out delays between expenditure and income as it will initially be difficult to negotiate credit terms with suppliers. This situation will need to be reviewed on an annual basis. We feel that an overdraft will be more appropriate to our needs than a loan as, although a sizeable sum is involved, forecasts show that the business bank account will be in credit after the early months of trading.

2

Security offered to lenders:
Both partners own properties. Della Clayton is willing to offer her home as security for any loans received. Each partner is also prepared to invest a significant sum of capital into the project:

Della Clayton £4,000
Devi Sandesh £8,000

2 Marketing

Market Analysis
We have been offered a contract by a local company to provide dinner sets to their chain of restaurants. Additionally we have carried out a survey of local business. Here are the replies to our key questions:

1 Restaurants
75% said they would consider using quality pottery if it was made locally
70% said they would be interested in a combination of traditional and modern design and priced competitively

2 The retail outlets
45% of gift shops said they would stock our standard lines
45% of craft shops said they would stock our standard line.

Our research, based partly upon firm orders and partly upon market research leads us to expect the following monthly sales:

Sales Budget for year 1:

Month	Sales (units)	
	Monthly	Cumulative
Apr	45	45
May	35	80
Jun	50	130
Jul	65	195
Aug	80	275
Sep	55	330
Oct	45	375
Nov	65	440
Dec	80	520
Jan	30	550
Feb	25	575
Mar	25	600
Total for year	600	600

3

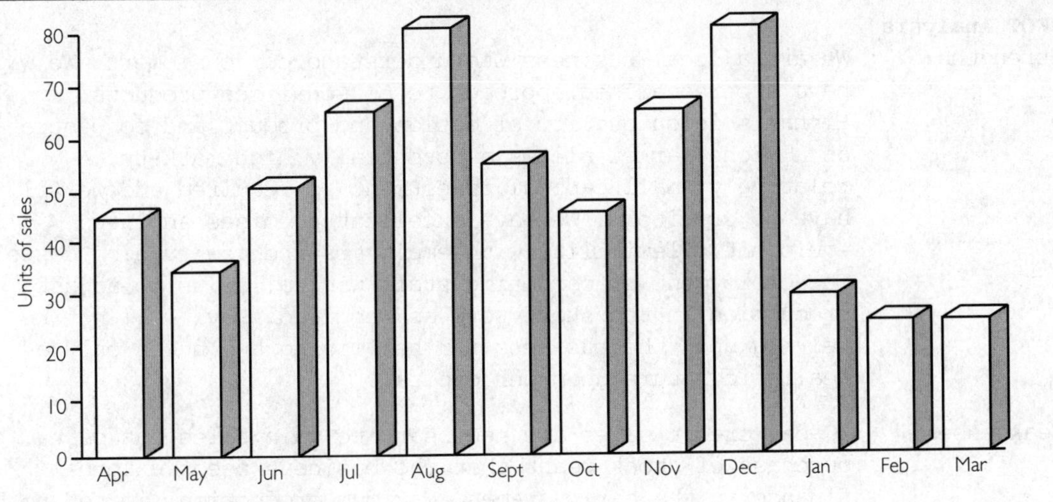

Forecast monthly levels of sales

Customers

We have tried to segment the market according to the type of customer. We expect our customers to be:

1 the chain of vegetarian restaurants for which a contract has been promised
2 the local craft and gift shops
3 one-off contracts for special commissions.

The market is expected to grow by roughly 5% a year. The demand for this type of item is inelastic, the gift and craft market is prepared to pay for quality locally made goods. There will always be a demand for pottery items which are well made and hand crafted.

Competitors

There is only one other pottery business in the immediate area. This, however, mainly sells souvenirs such as pottery animals, ash trays and garden gnomes direct to the customer. The tableware that is generally available from retailers is not a substitute for our goods, which are differentiated by the quality of the designs and the image. We would therefore expect to have a local monopoly with all the benefits this would give us.

Although research indicates that people are willing to pay premium prices for goods which meet their specific needs our prices will be carefully chosen to deter any new entrants coming into the market. We believe that we have found a gap in the tableware market that an operation with our expertise and low costs is equipped to fill.

The product

Our research indicates that present users like our pottery because:

1 it feels good
2 it looks good
3 it is hand made
4 the designs are original and are created specially for the client
5 the items create atmosphere and add style to the surroundings
6 they contribute to the total quality image of our clients.

4

SWOT Analysis

Strengths: We are a local business who understand our customers. We will have a personalised approach to personalised products. Emphasis is on quality of design and product and concentration on a niche market allows a potentially high mark-up. A relatively small capital investment is required and we will have no creditors. We have excellent premises and new equipment, flexibility with employees and low running costs. The employment of part-time staff will allow us to adjust production in the short term as required. Devi will not be relying upon the business for her living and needs only a realistic return upon her capital.

Weaknesses: 30-day credit sales are necessary to gain sales but cash purchase of stock means that the business needs external finance in the early stages. Maximum production limited to 50 units per month with an increase to 70 units possible with temporary help in the summer. There is a reliance on one major contract for high percentage of sales.

Opportunities: According to the Household Expenditure Survey 'meals away from home' are expected to increase. Demand therefore is expected to rise. Few existing quality products of this nature can be obtained locally and no personalised products are available. Premises will allow expansion and possible workshop sales. The current equipment is working with excess capacity. There is always demand among students at the art college for work-experience placements and holiday work in this type of operation.

Threats: The large contract may be terminated. Illness -Della is the sole producer, hence it is necessary to have a good margin of safety. Credit sales mean that there is the possibility of bad debts especially in times of recession. Competitors may enter the market.

For year 1 turnover is estimated at £84,000 (excl VAT) 600 units @ £140

Marketing strategy

The full marketing plan is attached separately. Key points are:

Marketing mix

Price: £140 per unit

Product: High-quality crafted pottery designed to meet clients' needs and expectations

Place : Sales direct to some consumers
Personal selling direct to retailers

5

Promotion: Exhibits at craft fairs and exhibitions
Publicity feature in the local newspaper
Glossy brochure of sample designs
Advertisements in local newspaper
A well-publicised launch with a famous personality
Personal selling and 'word of mouth reputation' advertising
The 'Della-Ware' brand image
Personalised 'mail-shot' to potential clients

An initial budget of £1,200 has been allocated to cover the costs of the launch and mail-shots.

3 Production plan

Dinner sets produced will be to customers' requirements but this will alter the products in terms of style and finish only. There will be no significant difference in resources required to produce individual orders. A unit of production is 1 place setting (6 pieces of pottery).

The production budget has been calculated to ensure that units of finished goods will be available to meet projected sales deadlines. The schedule takes account of the following limiting factors:

(i) maximum production capacity of 50 units per month with Della working alone

(ii) maximum production capacity of 70 units per month in the period June to September when the student helper is employed.

Production budget

Month	Production (units)	
	Monthly	Cumulative
Apr	50	50
May	50	100
Jun	70	170
Jul	70	240
Aug	70	310
Sep	70	380
Oct	50	430
Nov	50	480
Dec	40	520
Jan	40	560
Feb	20	580
Mar	20	600
Total for year	600	600

6

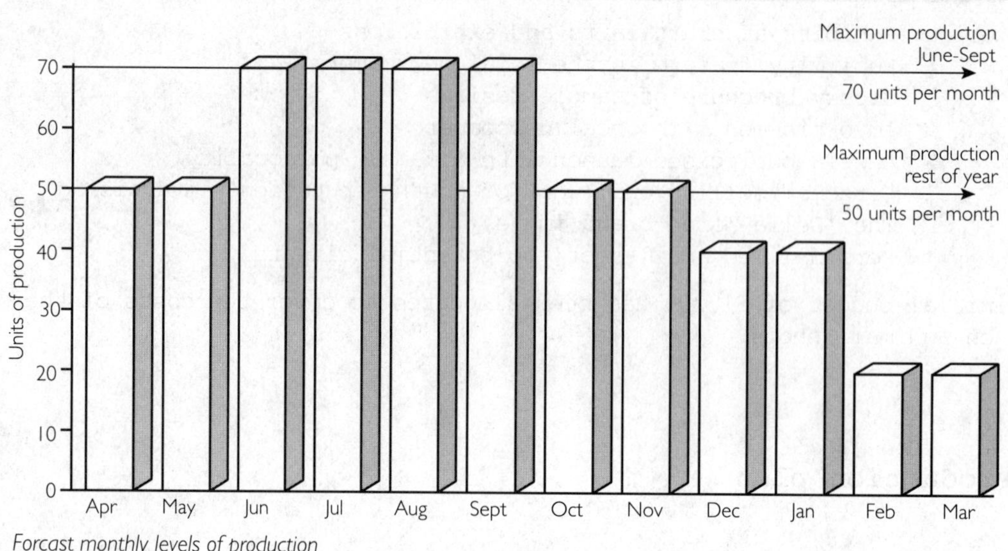

Forcast monthly levels of production

The chart shows that there is excess capacity in the last four months of the year. This will allow for holiday periods, repairs or additional production to start on orders for the new year.

For year 1 forecast raw materials cost will be £30,000 (excl VAT) p.a., i.e. 600 units p.a. @ £50 raw material cost per unit.

Production and sales budgets combined

The chart below shows that the production budget will allow the business to fulfil orders by agreed deadlines. However, because some production will be made in advance there will be a need to have specifications for orders at least a month in advance for most periods of the year.

Month	Sales (units)		Production (units)		Closing stock units) finished goods
	monthly	cumulative	monthly	cumulative	
Apr	45	45	50	50	5
May	35	80	50	100	20
Jun	50	130	70	170	40
Jul	65	195	70	240	45
Aug	80	275	70	310	35
Sep	55	330	70	380	50
Oct	45	375	50	430	55
Nov	65	440	50	480	40
Dec	80	520	40	520	0
Jan	30	550	40	560	10
Feb	25	575	20	580	5
Mar	25	600	20	600	0
Total for year	600	600	600	600	

7

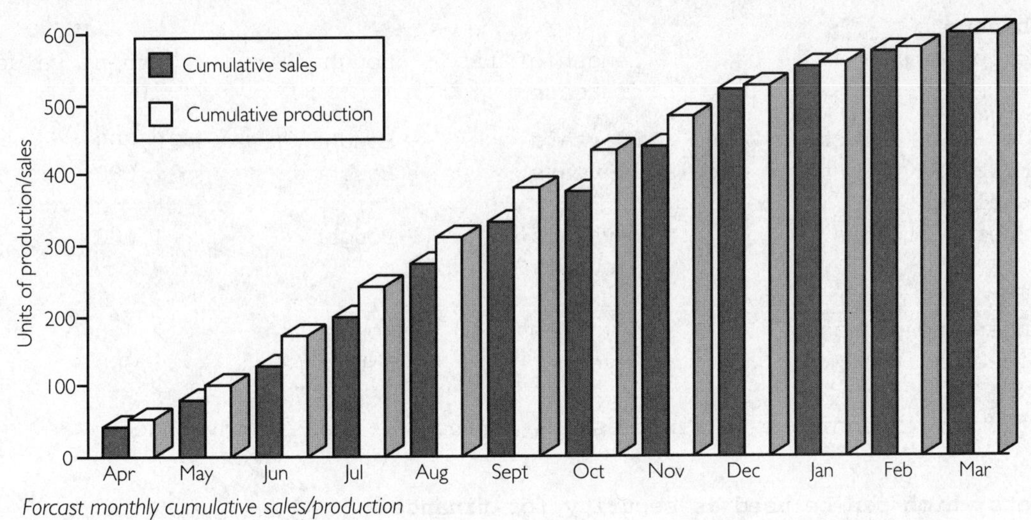

Forcast monthly cumulative sales/production

At each month cumulative production is at least equal to cumulative sales.

4 Resource requirements

Premises:

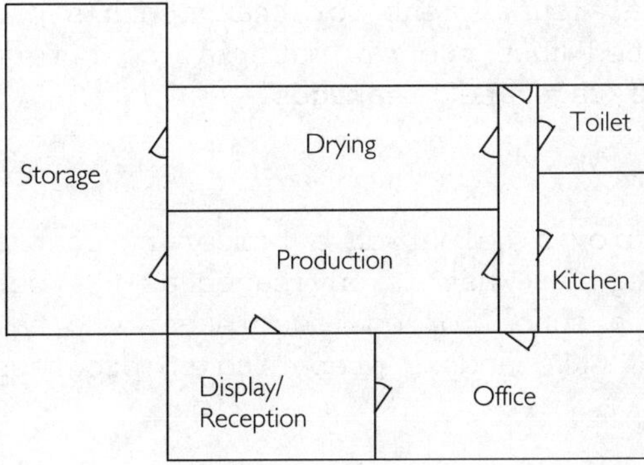

Premises will be rented. Rent will be payable half-yearly in advance at £2,600 per half-year. Rent to be reviewed annually.
The business will be responsible for internal maintenance, the owner will maintain the exterior of the building.

Initial alterations for adaptation of use of premises will be required. This will include sinks, drying and storage areas. The estimated cost payable initially will be £3,000 as the business share of this. This will be written off against profits in year one.

8

Machinery

Description	Length of life or lease	Bought/hired	Current value £
1 'Jet-heat' electric kiln	10 years	Bought	10,000
2 'Multi-rev' Potter's wheels	10 years	Bought	2,000
Specialist tools (shapers, scrapers, brushes etc)	revalued annually	Bought	1,000
Desk-top computer, laser printer and packages	4 years	Bought	2,400
Office furniture	6 years	Bought	600

No further expenditure on fixed assets during the year is envisaged.

Assets which can be used as security for finance

The business has no assets currently, although the estate car owned by D.Clayton will be used for business purposes.

The partners each own personal property with a total value of £160,000.

Raw materials

Raw materials used in manufacturing will consist mainly of clay, glaze and paints.

Materials to the value of £2,000 will be purchased initially. Additionally in each month materials sufficient for that month's production will be bought. It is estimated that the raw material cost for each unit will be £50 after allowing for wastage and breakages.

Labour

It is proposed to employ a helper on a temporary contract for the 4 months from June to September for what is envisaged as the peak period. The post will be suitable for a school or college leaver who has successfully completed an Advanced GNVQ and is preparing to progress into higher education.

5 Financial data and forecasts

Attached are the following as appendices.

Appendix 1

Cashflow forecast showing:	projected total receipts p.a.	£106,588
	projected total payments p.a.	£103,758
	closing balance of	£2,830

9

In order to finance the operations for the first year the business will require an overdraft facility of £24,000. This is mainly due to start-up costs and the need to pay cash to suppliers while selling on 30-day credit. The forecast shows that the overdraft should be cleared after the first 9 months of trading. Thereafter the account should be in credit.

For future periods we would hope to negotiate credit with our suppliers.

Appendix 2
Operating Statement to show monthly profit forecast

Appendix 3
Operating Statement for year 1 (Forecast trading and profit and loss account). This shows that:

Gross profit will be	£54,000
Net Profit will be	£25,342

The return on partners' capital invested (after Della's salary) is:

D Sandesh	7,295/8,000	= 91%
D Clayton	3,647/4,000	= 91%

Forecast year end balance sheet showing net assets of £22,942

Appendices 4 and 5
Break-even point calculations and graph.

At predicted costs and revenues the break-even point will be: 478 units or £66,920

This leaves a satisfactory margin of safety of 20% if D. Clayton's salary is included as a cost.

Appendix 6
Materials and Production Budget

Monitoring and review

The business plan will be used not only as an initial plan but as a working document to facilitate monitoring and review of actual progress.

The budgets will be monitored on a monthly basis by completing the 'actual column' on the cashflow and profit and loss sheets, and comparing these with the budget. Where significant variances are identified then they will be investigated. If it is found that assumptions regarding costs used in preparing the budget are incorrect (for instance the VAT on fuel bills could not have been forecast), then the budget will be recalculated. Where costs are controllable then these will be brought into line.

The budget will serve as a means of setting targets, controlling costs and decision-making.

This business plan was submitted for and on behalf of Pot Pourri by the partners:

Devi Sandesh *Devi Sandesh* Date 5th January 19-4

Della Clayton *Della P. Clayton* Date 5/1/19-4

10

Appendix 1

	A	B	C	D	E	F	G	H	I	J	K	L	M
51													
52	**Cashflow Forecast of..... D Clayton and D Sandesh Trading as POT POURRI**												
53													
54	Figures rounded	Apr		May		June		July		Aug		Sept	
55	to £s	Budget	Actual	Budget	Actual	Budget	Actual	Budget	Actual	Budget	Actual	Budget	Actual
56	RECEIPTS:												
57	Cash Sales (incl VAT)												
58	Cash from Debtors (incl VAT)			7 403		5 758		8 225		10 693		13 160	
59	New Capital	12 000											
60	Other incl Loans												
61	**Total Receipts (A)**	12 000		7 403		5 758		8 225		10 693		13 160	
62													
63	PAYMENTS:												
64	Cash Purchases (incl VAT)	5 288		2 938		4 113		4 113		4 113		4 113	
65	Credit Purchases (incl VAT)												
66	Drawings/Dividends	1 200		1 200		1 200		1 200		1 200		1 200	
67	Wages/salaries					525		525		525		525	
68	PAYE/NI					20		20		20		20	
69	Packaging	45		35		50		65		80		55	
70	Vehicle running costs	200		200		200		200		200		200	
71	Conversion costs (premises)	3 000											
72	Loan Repayments												
73	Capital items (incl VAT)	18 800											
74	Rent/Rates	2 600		1 400									
75	Light/Heat					900						900	
76	Telephone/Post					150						150	
77	Interest charges							1 029					
78	Bank /Finance Charges	200											
79	Advertising/Promotion	1 200											
80	Professional fees	500											
81	Insurance	2 400											
82	VAT					(1 453)						3 063	
83	Stationery	500		30		30		30		30		30	
84	**Total Payments (B)**	35 933		5 803		5 735		7 181		6 168		10 255	
85													
86	Net Cashflow (A-B)	(23 933)		1 600		23		1 044		4 525		2 905	
87	add Opening Bank Balance	0		(23 933)		(22 333)		(22 310)		(21 266)		(16 741)	
88	**Closing Bank Balance**	(23 933)		(22 333)		(22 310)		(21 266)		(16 741)		(13 836)	

Row number	***Cashflow assumptions and explanations:***
all	All cashflow figures should include VAT where it applies For the purpose of this forecast VAT has been added to purchases, sales and capital items only, as these are the most significant.
58	Sales payment is received one month after sale is made
64	Purchases of raw materials are paid in cash. Each month raw materials used are replaced. In April (month one) an extra £2 000 (+VAT) is purchased
68	PAYE/NI here represents the business' contribution to the employee's NI. The employee's deductions come from her/his pay Partners' PAYE/NI is a personal matter and is not included here

11

Appendix 1

	N	O	P	Q	R	S	T	U	V	W	X	Y	Z	AA
51														
52	Period....			Financial year . . . 1st April . . 19–4 . . to . . 31st March . . 19–5 . . .										
53														
54	Oct		Nov		Dec		Jan		Feb		Mar		Total	
55	Budget	Actual	Budget	Actual	Budget	Actual	Budget	Actual	Budget	Actual	Budget	Actual	Budget	Actual
56														
57														
58	9 048		7 403		10 693		13 160		4 935		4 113		94 588	
59													12 000	*
60													0	
61	9 048		7 403		10 693		13 160		4 935		4 113		106 588	
62														
63														
64	2 938		2 938		2 350		2 350		1 175		1 175		37 600	
65													0	
66	1 200		1 200		1 200		1 200		1 200		1 200		14 400	*
67													2 100	
68													80	
69	45		65		80		30		25		25		600	
70	200		200		200		200		200		200		2 400	
71													3 000	
72													0	
73													18 800	*
74	2 600												6 600	
75					900						900		3 600	
76					150						150		600	
77	778						442						2 248	
78													200	
79													1 200	
80											300		800	
81													2 400	
82					3 430						1 260		6 300	***
83	30		30		30		30		30		30		830	
84	7 790		4 433		8 340		4 252		2 630		5 240		103 758	
85														
86	1 257		2 970		2 353		8 908		2 305		(1 128)		2 830	
87	(13 836)		(12 579)		(9 609)		(7 256)		1 652		3 957		0	
88	(12 579)		(9 609)		(7 256)		1 652		3 957		2 830		2 830	

Row number	***Cashflow assumptions and explanations:***
69	Packaging is calculated at £1 per unit sold
77	Interest rates are calculated at 1.5% per month on overdrawn balances. Charged quarterly
82	VAT returns are made each quarter. They are the difference between input and output tax.. VAT is usually a cash outflow as sales value will exceed purchases value. However in June (the first quarter) a refund is claimed as a result of high VAT payments on fixed assets. This is shown as a negative expense.
88	There is an overdraft from April to December. At the year end there is a bank balance of £2 830
Column AA	All totals transfer to the operating budget (without VAT) except those marked *. These transfer to the balance sheet. ***VAT appears on the balance sheet only if amounts are outstanding; here it is assumed to have been paid.

12

Appendix 2

	A	B	C	D	E	F	G	H	I	J	K	L	M	N
103		**Forecast Operating Budget (Profit & Loss account)**												
104		All figures exclusive of VAT	Apr		May		June		July		Aug		Sept	
105		Figures rounded to £s	Budget	Actual	Budget	Actual	Budget	Actual	Budget	Actual	Budget	Actual	Budget	Actual
106	A	**Sales**	6 300		4 900		7 000		9 100		11 200		7 700	
107		Materials purchases	4 500		2 500		3 500		3 500		3 500		3 500	
108		Direct labour	0		0		0		0		0		0	
109		Stock change (increase) or decrease:												
110		Materials	(2 000)		0		0		0		0		0	
111		Finished goods	(250)		(750)		(1 000)		(250)		500		(750)	
112	B	**Cost of goods sold**	2 250		1 750		2 500		3 250		4 000		2 750	
113	C	**Gross Profit (A - B)**	4 050		3 150		4 500		5 850		7 200		4 950	
114	D	**Gross Profit % on Sales**	64.29%		64.29%		64.29%		64.29%		64.29%		64.29%	
115		**less Overheads:**												
116		**Production:**												
117		Wages/salaries	0		0		525		525		525		525	
118		PAYE/NI	0		0		20		20		20		20	
119		Rent/Rates	550		550		550		550		550		550	
120		Light/Heat	300		300		300		300		300		300	
121		Insurance	200		200		200		200		200		200	
122		Depreciation	108		108		108		108		108		108	
123		Premises conversion	250		250		250		250		250		250	
124		**Selling & Distribution**												
125		Packaging	45		35		50		65		80		55	
126		Vehicle Running Costs	200		200		200		200		200		200	
127		Advertising/Promotion	100		100		100		100		100		100	
128		**Administration**												
129		Telephone/post	50		50		50		50		50		50	
130		Depreciation	58		58		58		58		58		58	
131		Professional fees	67		67		66		67		67		66	
132		Stationery	500		30		30		30		30		30	
133		**Finance**												
134		Bank/Finance Charges	17		17		16		17		17		16	
135		Interest charges	359		335		335		319		251		208	
136	E	**Total Overheads**	2 805		2 301		2 858		2 860		2 807		2 736	
137		**Net Profit (C - E)**	1 245		849		1 642		2 990		4 393		2 214	
138	F	Drawings (D Clayton)	1 200		1 200		1 200		1 200		1 200		1 200	
139		Sales required to break-even	6 229		5 445		6 313		6 315		6 233		6 123	
140		(E+F) / D x 100												
141														
142														
143		**Row number**	**Operating budget assumptions and explanations:**											
144		All	All figures are exclusive of VAT											
145		107	Purchases of raw materials are the monthly cost of replacing stocks used. Additionally an initial											
146			stock of £2 000 is purchased in April (month one) for emergencies such as difficulties in supply.											
147		109	Change in stocks is calculated as: opening stock - closing stock.											
148		110	For materials stock change see below appendix 6 (row 10), materials budget											
149		111	For finished goods stock change see appendix 6 (row 19); production budget.											
150			This is valued as: change in stock x unit cost e.g. in April 5 units (decrease) x £50 = (£250)											
151		cell AA141	* Total direct cost (£32 000 materials - £2 000 closing stock) / 600 units produced = £50 per unit.											
152														
153														

13

Appendix 2

	O	P	Q	R	S	T	U	V	W	X	Y	Z	AA	AB	AC	AD
103		For year ending 31st March 19–5														
104	Oct		Nov		Dec		Jan		Feb		Mar		Total			
105	Budget	Actual	Budget	Actual	Budget	Actual	Budget	Actual	Budget	Actual	Budget	Actual	Budget	Actual		
106	6 300		9 100		11 200		4 200		3 500		3 500		84 000			
107	2 500		2 500		2 000		2 000		1 000		1 000		32 000			
108	0		0		0		0		0		0		0			
109																
110	0		0		0		0		0		0		(2 000)			
111	(250)		750		2 000		(500)		250		250		0			
112	2 250		3 250		4 000		1 500		1 250		1 250		30 000			
113	4 050		5 850		7 200		2 700		2 250		2 250		54 000			
114	64.29%		64.29%		64.29%		64.29%		64.29%		64.29%		64.29%			
115																
116																
117	0		0		0		0		0		0		2 100			
118	0		0		0		0		0		0		80			
119	550		550		550		550		550		550		6 600			
120	300		300		300		300		300		300		3 600			
121	200		200		200		200		200		200		2 400			
122	108		108		108		108		108		108		1 300			
123	250		250		250		250		250		250		3 000			
124																
125	45		65		80		30		25		25		600			
126	200		200		200		200		200		200		2 400			
127	100		100		100		100		100		100		1 200			
128																
129	50		50		50		50		50		50		600			
130	58		58		58		58		58		58		700			
131	67		67		66		67		67		66		800			
132	30		30		30		30		30		30		830			
133																
134	17		17		16		17		17		16		200			
135	189		144		109								2 248			
136	2 164		2 140		2 118		1 961		1 956		1 954		28 658			
137	1 886		3 710		5 082		739		294		296		25 342			
138	1 200		1 200		1 200		1 200		1 200		1 200		14 400			
139	5 233		5 195		5 161		4 917		4 909		4 906		66 979			
140																
141									Direct cost per unit				£ 50			
142																

	Row number	Operating budget assumptions and explanations:
143	**Row number**	**Operating budget assumptions and explanations:**
144	108	The direct labour is Della who not a business cost.
145		As a partner her salary is treated as drawings.
146	138	An allowance is made for drawings in the calculation of the break-even sales
147		- the salary is Debbie's only income and the business must cover this
148	115:136	An attempt has been made to position overheads in the months to which they relate.
149		This means that items such as rent are evenly shared over the year whilst others such as
150		the helper's wages and bank charges are allocated to specific months
151	139	Break-even sales (in units). This uses an alternative formula based upon
152		profit margin rather than unit contribution. This is useful where non-standard goods
153		or services are provided. Here all overheads are assumed to be fixed.

14

Appendix 3

Row	AE	AF	AG	AH
1		**Forecast**		
2		**Profit & Loss account for year one**		
3			£	£
4		**Sales**		84 000
5		Raw Materials:		
6		Purchases	32 000	
7		less Closing stock	2 000	
8	(iii)	Direct labour	0	
9		**Cost of goods sold**		30 000
10		**Gross Profit**		54 000
11		**less Overheads:**		
12		**Production:**		
13	(iv)	Wages/salaries	2 100	
14		PAYE/NI	80	
15	(v)	Rent/Rates	6 600	
16	(v)	Light/Heat	3 600	
17	(v)	Insurance	2 400	
18		Depreciation	1 300	
19	(v)	Premises conversion	3 000	
20			19 080	
21		**Selling & Distribution**		
22		Packaging (£1 unit)	600	
23		Vehicle Running Costs	2 400	
24		Advertising/Promotion	1 200	
25			4 200	
26		**Administration**		
27		Telephone/post	600	
28		Depreciation	700	
29		Professional fees	800	
30		Stationery	830	
31			2 930	
32		**Finance**		
33		Bank/Finance Charges	200	
34		Interest charges	2 248	
35			2 448	
36	(vi) ROCE	**Total Overheads**		28 658
37	211%	**Net Profit**		25 342
38		less salary (D Clayton)		14 400
39	(vii) Return			10 942
40	on investment	Share of profits:		
41	91%	D Clayton 1/3	3 647	
42	91%	D Sandesh 2/3	7 295	
43				10 942

Row	AI	AJ	AK	AL	AM
1		**Forecast Balance Sheet as at end of year one**			
2			£	£	£
3		**Fixed Assets**	**Cost**	**Dep**	**Net**
4		Kiln	10 000	1 000	9 000
5		Potter's Wheels	2 000	200	1 800
6		Computer	2 400	600	1 800
7		Office Furniture	600	100	500
8		Tools	1 000	100	900
9			16 000	2 000	14 000
11		**Current Assets**			
12		Stock Raw Materials		2 000	
13	(i)	Debtors		4 113	
14		Cash in Bank		2 830	
15				8 942	
16		less			
17		**Current Liabilities**		0	
18					8 942
19					22 942
21		**As Financed By:**			
22		Capital:	D Clayton		4 000
23			D Sandesh		8 000
24					12 000
25		**Current Accounts**			
26			D Clayton	D Sandesh	
27		Salary	14 400	0	
28		Share of Profits	3 647	7 295	
29			18 047	7 295	
30	(ii)	less Drawings	14 400	0	
31		Balance B/d	3 647	7 295	10 942
32					22 942

Key ***Assumptions and explanations:***

Items are shown on final accounts exclusive of VAT.
This is because VAT paid is reclaimed and surplus VAT collected is sent to Customs & Excise. VAT is therefore neither loss nor gain.
It appears only if due (liability or overpaid (asset)

(i) Debtors owe for goods plus VAT

(ii) It is assumed that the only drawings will be the salary paid to D Clayton

(iii) Della is the only direct labour. Her payment comes in the form of drawings (partner's salary)

(iv) The student helper will be indirect labour i.e. helping but not actually making the pots.

(v) These costs are all assumed to be factory costs

(vi) Return on capital invested = net profit/original capital = 25,342/12,000 x 100

(vii) Partners' return on capital invested = share of profit/capital invested x 100
In Della's case this is the return after salary

15

Appendix 4

The break-even point

Assumptions: Although Della is a partner it is unrealistic to assume that production can continue if she is not paid. Therefore Della's salary is included as part of fixed cost.

		£	
Variable costs:	Raw materials	50	per unit
	Total Variable Cost	50	per unit
Fixed Costs:	Salary	14 400	
	Overheads	28 658	
	Total Fixed Cost	43 058	

Many of the overheads are likely be semi-variable. However, there is insufficient information to enable the fixed and variable elements to be separated. They are treated as fixed for the purposes of this forecast.

BREAK-EVEN POINT

		per unit	
Sales		140	
less variable costs		50	
Unit Contribution		90	
Fixed Costs	=	43 058	478 units per year to Break-Even
Unit Contribution		90	
OR	140 × 478 =		£66 920 turnover required to Break-Even (The variation with cell AA139 on the profit and loss forecast is due to rounding the break-even figure to 478)

MARGIN OF SAFETY

estimated unit sales	600		
less break-even sales	478		
Margin of Safety	122	units or	£17 080 Turnover
That is 122/600 × 100 =	20%	fall off in estimated sales is possible before there will be a loss	

The business will be in profit by the end of December by which time sales will be 520 units

16

Appendix 5 Break-even chart for year one - Pot Pourri

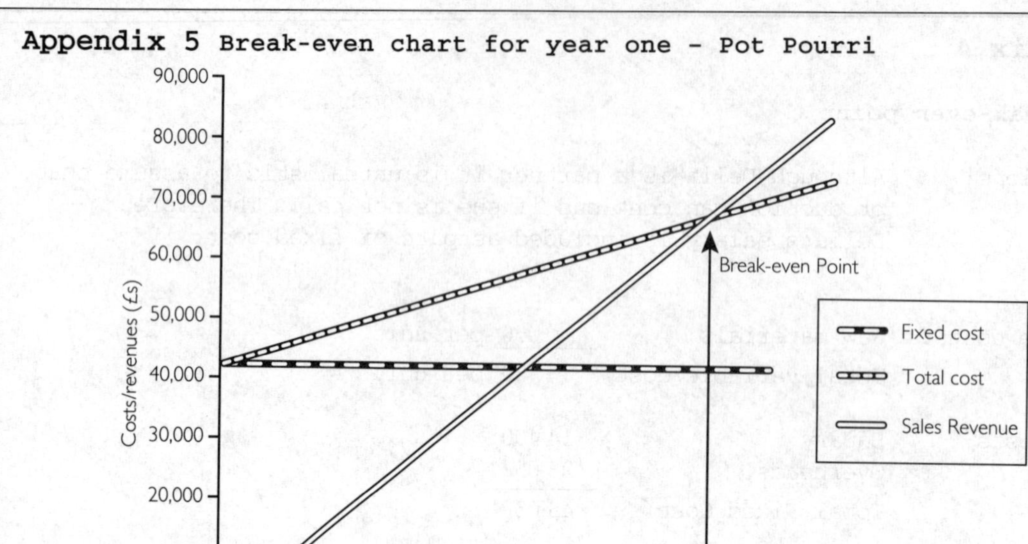

Units produced/sold	Fixed Cost	Variable Cost	Total Cost	Sales	Profit/(Loss)
0	42 458	0	42 458	0	(42 458)
100	42 458	5 100	47 558	14 000	(33 558)
200	42 458	10 200	52 658	28 000	(24 658)
300	42 458	15 300	57 758	42 000	(15 758)
400	42 458	20 400	62 858	56 000	(6 858)
500	42 458	25 500	67 958	70 000	2 042
600	42 458	30 600	73 058	84 000	10 942

Appendix 6 Materials and Production Budgets

	AZ	BA	BB	BC	BD	BE	BF	BG	BH	BI	BJ	BK	BL	BM
1														
2														
3		Apr	May	Jun	July	Aug	Sept	Oct	Nov	Dec	Jan	Feb	Mar	Total
4	**Direct Materials Budget (£)**													
5	Opening stock	0	2 000	2 000	2 000	2 000	2 000	2 000	2 000	2 000	2 000	2 000	2 000	0
6	add Purchases	4 500	2 500	3 500	3 500	3 500	3 500	2 500	2 500	2 000	2 000	1 000	1 000	32 000
7		4 500	4 500	5 500	5 500	5 500	5 500	4 500	4 500	4 000	4 000	3 000	3 000	32 000
8	less Production materials	2 500	2 500	3 500	3 500	3 500	3 500	2 500	2 500	2 000	2 000	1 000	1 000	30 000
9	Closing stock	2 000	2 000	2 000	2 000	2 000	2 000	2 000	2 000	2 000	2 000	2 000	2 000	2 000
10	stock (increase) or decrease	(2 000)	0	0	0	0	0	0	0	0	0	0	0	(2,000)
11														
12	**Production Budget (units)**													
13	Opening stock	0	5	20	40	45	35	50	55	40	0	10	5	0
14	add Production	50	50	70	70	70	70	50	50	40	40	20	20	600
15		50	55	90	110	115	105	100	105	80	40	30	25	600
16	less Sales	45	35	50	65	80	55	45	65	80	30	25	25	600
17	Closing stock	5	20	40	45	35	50	55	40	0	10	5	0	0
18	stock (increase) or decrease	(5)	(15)	(20)	(5)	10	(15)	(5)	15	40	(10)	5	5	0
19	(increase) or decrease	(250)	(750)	(1,000)	(250)	500	(750)	(250)	750	2,000	(500)	250	250	0
20	@ £50 per unit													

17

Activities

1 After reading the business plan write brief notes which would help you answer the small business adviser's questions on page 709.

Be prepared for similar questions about your own business plan.

2 The partners have fortunately prepared their financial data on a standard spreadsheet package. It is therefore easy for them to ask 'What if?' questions by changing the data in specified cells. After reducing the projected sales and production figures by 10 per cent (they subtract 5 units each month) the new figures are printed out. These are on pages 728 and 729.

Look at the revised forecast and prepare answers to the following questions:

a Is the business still profitable?
b Is the overdraft reduced over the year?
c How will the overdraft requirement be affected in terms of:
- amount needed?
- time period for which it is required?

d If fewer goods are now sold, why are the receipts not reduced in April?
e Will the break-even point change?
f The bank manager asked the partners to reduce the sales figures. Why have total payments gone down also?
g Interest rates have not changed so why have interest charges gone up?
h What is to be the effect of the change on each of the partner's prospects?
i Which of the partners will be less happy with the situation?
j Could Devi have invested her £8,000 elsewhere more profitably? (You will need to look at current interest rates to discover the answer to this.)
k Would Della be financially better off if she remained in her job at the local authority earning £20,000 p.a. and investing her savings:
- under the original forecast?
- under the revised forecast?

l Compare the bank balance and the profits for the month of October. How can a profitable business have an overdraft?

3 Perform other 'What if?' calculations using some of the suggestions given below. Return to the original figures after each one.
- Debtors may not pay within 30 days. They take on average 60 days.
- There may be bad debts of £3,500 in August.
- Interest rates might rise by 3 per cent p.a. (by 0.25% per month).
- Raw material costs rise by 10 per cent.
- A new competitor takes 50 per cent of the market.
- Thirty-day credit payment period for purchases is negotiated from October.

Two weeks later...Della and Devi receive a letter confirming that the bank is happy to offer them an overdraft facility of £24,000 with Della's house pledged as security.

Cashflow Forecast of...... D Clayton and D Sandesh Trading as POT POURRI Period..... Financial year . . . 1st April . . 19–4 . . to . . 31st March . . 19–5 . . .

Figures rounded to £s	Apr Budget	Actual	May Budget	Actual	June Budget	Actual	July Budget	Actual	Aug Budget	Actual	Sept Budget	Actual	Oct Budget	Actual	Nov Budget	Actual	Dec Budget	Actual	Jan Budget	Actual	Feb Budget	Actual	Mar Budget	Actual	Total Budget	Actual
RECEIPTS:																										
Cash Sales (incl VAT)																										
Cash from Debtors (incl VAT)			6 580		4 935		7 403		9 870		12 338		8 225		6 580		9 870		12 338		4 113		3 290		85 540	
New Capital	12 000																								12 000	
Other incl Loans																									0	
Total Receipts (A)	12 000		6 580		4 935		7 403		9 870		12 338		8 225		6 580		9 870		12 338		4 113		3 290		97 540	
PAYMENTS:																										
Cash Purchases (incl VAT)	5 288		2 644		3 819		3 819		3 819		3 819		2 644		2 644		2 056		2 056		881		881		34 369	
Credit Purchases (incl VAT)																									0	
Drawings/Dividends	1 200		1 200		1 200		1 200		1 200		1 200		1 200		1 200		1 200		1 200		1 200		1 200		14 400	
Wages/salaries					525		525		525		525														2 100	
PAYE/NI					20		20		20		20														80	
Packaging	40		30		45		60		75		50		40		60		75		25		20		20		540	
Vehicle running costs	200		200		200		200		200		200		200		200		200		200		200		200		2 400	
Conversion costs (premises)	3 000																								3 000	
Loan Repayments																									0	
Capital items (incl VAT)	18 800																								18 800	
Rent/Rates	2 600		1 400										2 600												6 600	
Light/Heat					900						900						900						900		3 600	
Telephone/Post					150						150						150						150		600	
Interest charges							1 048						856						584						2 488	
Bank/Finance Charges	200																								200	
Advertising/Promotion	1 200																								1 200	
Professional fees	500																						300		800	
Insurance	2 400																								2 400	
VAT					(1 733)						2 826						3 194						1 024		5 311	
Stationery	500		30		30		30		30		30		30		30		30		30		30		30		830	
Total Payments (B)	35 928		5 504		5 156		6 902		5 869		9 720		7 570		4 134		7 805		4 095		2 331		4 705		99 718	
Net Cashflow (A–B)	(23 928)		1 076		(221)		501		4 001		2 618		655		2 446		2 065		8 242		1 781		(1 415)		(2 178)	
add Opening Bank Balance	0		(23 928)		(22 851)		(23 073)		(22 572)		(18 570)		(15 953)		(15 298)		(12 852)		(10 787)		(2 544)		(763)		0	
Closing Bank Balance	(23 928)		(22 851)		(23 073)		(22 572)		(18 570)		(15 953)		(15 298)		(12 852)		(10 787)		(2 544)		(763)		(2 178)		(2 178)	

Cashflow forecast – worst case scenario, sales reduced by 10%

Forecast
Profit and loss account for one year

	£	£
Sales		75 600
Raw materials:		
(i) Purchases	29 250	
less closing stock	2 000	
Direct labour	0	
Cost of goods sold		27 250
Gross profit		48 350
(ii) less overheads:		
Production:		
Wages/salaries	2 100	
PAYE/NI	80	
Rent/rates	6 600	
Light/heat	3 600	
Insurance	2 400	
Depreciation	1 300	
Premises conversion	3 000	
	19 080	
Selling and distribution		
Packaging	540	
Vehicle running costs	2 400	
Advertising/promotion	1 200	
	4 140	
Administration		
Telephone/post	600	
Depreciation	700	
Professional fees	800	
Stationery	830	
	2 930	
Finance		
Bank/finance charges	200	
Interest charges	2 488	
	2 688	
Total overheads		28 838
Net profit		19 512
less salary (D Clayton)		14 400
		5 112
Share of profits:		
D Clayton 1/3	1 704	
D Sandesh 2/3	3 408	
		5 112

ROCE
163%

Return on investment
43%
43%

Forecast balance sheet as at end of year one

	£	£	£
Fixed assets	Cost	Dep	Net
Kiln	10 000	1 000	9 000
Potter's wheels	2 000	200	1 800
Computer	2 400	600	1 800
Office furniture	600	100	500
Tools	1 000	100	900
	16 000	2 000	14 000
Current assets			
Stock raw materials		2 000	
Debtors		3 290	
		5 290	
less			
Current liabilities			
Bank (overdraft)		2 178	
			3 112
			17 112
As financed by:			
Capital	D. Clayton		4 000
	D. Sandesh		8 000
			12000
Current accounts			
	D Clayton	D Sandesh	
Salary	14 400	0	
Share of profits	1 704	3 408	
	16 104	3 408	
less drawings	14 400	0	
Balance B/d	1 704	3 408	
			5 112
			17 112

Assumptions and explanations

(i) A reduction in sales also means a reduction in purchases of materials

(ii) Overheads are unchanged except that:
- there will be some reduction in packaging
- the bank interest charges will increase due to the extension of the overdraft.

Operating statement and balance sheet – worst case scenario, sales reduced by 10%

The sales and marketing plan for Pot Pourri

Pot Pourri is a new business and is also small-scale, hence it includes the essential details about its sales and marketing in the business plan. Where the marketing function is very detailed a business will produce a separate sales and marketing plan for consideration. Essentially the aim of this is to:

- help support any applications for finance by setting out the exact requirements and their likely benefits
- set targets for the business to pursue, which may be for some years hence
- provide a yardstick against which performance can eventually be monitored.

It may be that a business has a corporate plan which envisages a development of the marketing strategy over the medium term, perhaps over the next five years. The business, perhaps, wishes to break into a particular market overseas, perhaps it wishes to bring a new generation of products on-line or it may be attempting a dramatic increase in market share. All of this will need careful planning and a carefully designed strategy.

The marketing plan which sets out the strategy may contain the following sections:

- The mission statement/objectives of the business. The plan must be in line with this.
- A SWOT analysis of the current products.
- New products in the pipeline.
- Market research:
  - customer demand
  - competing products
  - competing firms
- Definition of the new strategy.
- The costs and resources required to deliver the new strategy.

The business plan produced by Pot Pourri covers essentially the first year of operation. Although newly formed they have ideas of how they want to progress. They have amplified their marketing plans in a 'sales and marketing plan' which is designed to accompany the business plan. The plan is shown on the following pages.

POT POURRI

(Personalised dinner sets)

Della Clayton, Devi Sandesh Trading as Pot Pourri
The Wheelhouse, Wateringham H20
Tel: (01010) 820541 Fax: (01010) 820557

Sales and Marketing Plan

The Plan - Table of Contents

1

Purposes

The purpose of this marketing plan is to identify sales targets for year 1 and to set out the strategy by which Pot Pourri will meet these. In this respect it is a complement to the business plan already presented. We will also indicate how policy for year one fits into our medium term plans.

In the business plan we have already identified:

- our potential customers
- the competition
- the product image
- some opportunities and threats
- the costs of our operation.

This marketing plan contains the following:

1 The mission statement.
2 A statement of quantifiable objectives.
3 A discussion of the four elements of the marketing mix as they relate to Pot Pourri for the short to medium term
4 Costs of implementing the plan.

1 Mission statement

- The partnership aims to provide a quality service.
- To provide a quality product.
- To establish a reputation for quality and service initially at an area level.
- To establish the presence of the 'Della-Ware' trade mark in the market place.
- Subject to these stated aims the partnership will aim to maximise profits through operations on the present scale.
- To develop quality rather than quantity. The emphasis will be low turnover/high mark-up.

2 Objectives

On the basis of our market analysis, our objectives are:

- to achieve sales of £84,000 in the first year of trading (600 units)
- to repay any overdraft within year 1.

3 The marketing mix

This is discussed under the following headings:

- price
- product
- place
- promotion.

2

Price

Our research (see marketing in the business plan) leads us to expect the following monthly sales:

Apr	May	June	July	Aug	Sept	Oct	Nov	Dec	Jan	Feb	Mar	TOTAL
45	35	50	65	80	55	45	65	80	30	25	25	600

In discussion with potential clients we have ascertained that the best price is £140. Research has indicated that potential sales dropped off quite sharply above this and there was no significant rise with lower prices. This shows that demand is elastic in the higher price range: £140 per unit would seem to be the price to maximise our profits.

Our pottery is custom made and people are more willing to pay higher prices for personalised pieces made to their own specification. Our expected unit costs allow for wastage and breakages to give us the opportunity to experiment with new designs. This gives us a profit margin of around 70 per cent per unit. We have deliberately estimated high costs and believe that in fact they will be lower than this. We have confidence in the quality of our product and feel that there is potential for developing a niche market which will allow for considerable increase in mark-up within the medium term.

We do not intend giving any discounts in the first year of business as there is no indication that this would boost sales. The mark-up figure above does not include direct labour as all products will be made by one of the partners, D. Clayton. However, when the agreed salary is included there is still a significant margin of safety of 20 per cent.

Product

Initially we intend only to sell dinner services as a matter of policy. This we believe will enable us to establish an image as a base for diversification. At a later stage we will widen the range to include other items which may include flower holders, wine goblets and pottery sculptures. These will be of the same high quality with co-ordinated design motifs; they will also bear the distinctive 'Della-Ware' sign.

A special feature of our approach to product design is to involve the client at every stage of the design process, from the rough drawings, through the mock-ups, to the finished article. In this way every client will feel totally happy with the end result.

We are able to use our local knowledge to create a product totally suited to the needs of the client. Ms Clayton's family have lived in Wateringham for nearly 220 years. Our designs for The Ramblers Restaurant which is part of the vegetarian chain for which we have secured our major contract, will for example, be able to show its long history.

The product will enable us to establish our own niche in the market because:

- we have specialised products
- we have local knowledge
- we use personalised designs
- we will use quality materials.

3

Place

Initially we intend to sell within a radius of approximately 50 miles. Sales will be on the following basis:

- direct to some customers such as the vegetarian chain of restaurants with whom we have already had discussions
- direct to selected local retailers
- additional sales can be anticipated at craft fairs, shows and exhibitions within the area.

Where customers cannot collect the goods themselves we will deliver. One day per week will be set aside for this and other administrative purposes. Most of the clients are within easy driving distance.

We are not dependent upon passing trade but potential customers can come to see our workshop which is conveniently situated with easy parking. A future development may well include a showroom on the premises. The workshop is in an idyllic location and there is potential for developing this angle.

Promotion

The business name 'Pot Pourri' has been carefully chosen to appeal to the ABC groups where we would anticipate the majority of our sales to be.

We have produced a brochure of sample designs for mailing to interested parties. Business stationery, letterhead and logo has also been designed to reinforce the image of quality. All pottery will bear the distinctive logo.

Della Clayton's work is already known locally and examples of her work, together with business contact details, are displayed currently in various galleries in the area.

There is to be a feature in the local paper on the launch of the business which will take place on 3 April. This will consist of an open evening at 'The Wheelhouse' by invitation only with a guest-list of local dignitaries and business people who may be potential clients.

Much custom will depend upon reputation and 'word of mouth', indeed since it has become known that the business will now be open for orders there has been considerable interest and a number of enquiries about commissions.

Pot Pourri will exhibit at craft fairs and exhibitions.

The business name and telephone number have been entered in the *Yellow Pages* and *Thomson's Directory*.

We intend to contact all our potential customers personally. Ms Sandesh already has a number of valuable contacts.

All promotion will be geared towards portraying an image of quality.

4 Costs of implementing the plan

Detailed financial forecasts are included in the business plan. These show that at predicted sales levels a profit in excess of £25,000 will be earned in year 1 and that the overdraft will be cleared after 9 months of operation. We consider that this is a conservative estimate of profits as we have made a high estimate for materials costs.

4

The costs of marketing our product will be relatively modest as Devi has many business contacts, and much business will be conducted through word of mouth and reputation. The client base will be relatively small and there is no need for expensive advertising in this niche market. We have identified the following initial costs:

Launch evening	£500
Brochures, business cards, stationery and initial mail-shot to selected customers	£700

Much of the other publicity will be free.

The current size of the operation does not warrant further promotion as maximum production levels will be modest. The business has no short-term plans to expand this, but hopes by reputation to build up an order book of highly specialised commissions.

5

Assignment 15.1
The business plan

This assignment develops knowledge and understanding of the following elements:
8.1 Prepare work and collect data for a business plan
8.2 Produce and present a business plan

It supports development of the following core skills:
Communication 3.1, 3.2, 3.3, 3.4
Application of number 3.1, 3.2, 3.3
Information technology 3.1, 3.2, 3.3

In completing this assignment you may work alone or with a colleague.

You have decided to investigate the possibilities of setting up and running your own business. A distant relative, who approves of this plan, has offered to provide you with an opening capital of £5,000. You will need to borrow any additional funds and you realise that in order to do so you will need to produce a convincing business plan.

Your tasks

You are to investigate a business idea of your choosing, and to prepare a business plan for setting up and running this for the first year. The plan may be used to help convince your local bank manager to lend you extra finance.

This assignment brings together a good deal of what you will have learnt during the course. It can be broken down into the following sections:

Preparation and research

1. Either working independently or with a colleague, decide upon a business idea which you think has potential.
2. Obtain small business information from the various banks. They all produce packs explaining how to set up a plan for a new business and giving valuable information.
3. You will need to carry out a good deal of accurate research into your idea to see if it really is likely to succeed. You should already have a fund of relevant information from earlier activities so use this; do, however, make sure that it is up to date.

   The steps identified in the first section of this chapter will help you to proceed in a methodical way and will provide a checklist of the main aspects that you need to consider. You may also find it useful to refer back to certain sections such as those on marketing, human resources and finance.

   Remember that where you carry out research you should make sure that it is as realistic as possible. For instance your projected sales should be based upon market research. Estimates will be needed for set-up and operating costs, and many of these such as interest charges, rents and business rates can be researched accurately.

The business plan

You should use your research to produce a five-part business plan to show:

- objectives
- marketing plan
- production plan
- resource requirements
- financial support data to include
  cashflow forecast – 12 months
  projected operating statement (profit and loss account) at end of year 1
  projected balance sheet at end of year one
  break-even calculations
  financial assessment of the project.

Details of launch arrangements, sample advertising and publicity material would greatly enhance the package.

Presentation

The final plan should be effectively organised and packaged. It should be word processed, or produced on a desk top publishing package and effectively proof-read before being printed out. The financial projections should be prepared on an electronic spreadsheet.

In addition to the printed plan you should submit a 3.5-in disk containing the WP and spreadsheet files with suitable names. All files should be moved to a relevant sub-directory.

Suggested modes of assessment:

- tutors observe activity
- tutors comment on content of plan
- peer assessment of individual contribution
- self-assessment of individual contribution
- presentation to the bank manager, Prince's Trust or other agency.

The world of work – planning for employment and self-employment

The world of work which you will be entering with your new qualification will expect a lot from you. You will need to be aware of the opportunities and challenges that exist and it is important that you have realistic plans.

Employment or self-employment?

When a firm employs you it is making a considerable commitment. Salaries are one of the main costs a business has to bear, and frequently they represent a fixed cost which must be paid even when business is slack. We have seen that increasingly businesses are concerned to get value for money from their employees, hence the various appraisal schemes, the linking of pay to productivity and the attempts to monitor employee performance. The decision to take on new employees permanently is not taken lightly.

Businesses must now remain 'flexible' if they are to survive and the nature of employment is changing accordingly. Being flexible means, among other things, being able to employ and dismiss staff in response to events. As it can be expensive to make employees redundant, one solution is to engage staff on short-term contracts; an alternative is to subcontract work to self-employed staff.

If you look at the job market you will find that an increasing number of posts are for temporary contracts and virtually all will require some sort of skills update sooner rather than later. As an employee you will need to be adaptable, though where a skill is in demand there can be high rewards – at the time of writing a computer services firm is paying young people £1,600 per week to programme in Visual Basic.

Why work for yourself?

During the 1980s there was a growth of almost 60 per cent in the number of people in self-employment. Often the motivation is:

- possibility of high profits
- the satisfaction of 'being your own boss'.

However, for some people self-employment is a necessary reaction to a changing labour market which can no longer guarantee a job. Since 1979 the Conservative government has been actively seeking to promote the 'enterprise culture'. Unfortunately a large number of the small businesses set up in the 1980s have failed and VAT returns show that half of new businesses do not last five years.

Opportunities for self-employment are provided by ever-increasing specialisation, especially in the service sector. The emergence of short-term contracts and subcontracting of jobs out to tender does mean that endless diverse business opportunities exist. A large business may, for example, bring in outside firms to: clean the office, provide management consultancy, water the office plants, or install the computer network.

Even people who seem to be in employment are frequently self-employed. A hairdresser will frequently rent out space in the shop to another self-employed hairdresser rather than engage an assistant who needs to be paid regardless of the state of trade. Similarly the drivers in a taxi firm will usually be working for themselves, paying the firm a rental for the use of its radio and base.

Working locally

Local employment opportunities vary. Your area may be in a state of change. You may be able to commute to work or realistically you may need to move away. Perhaps you would like to work abroad? You will need to consider the options.

On the other hand much business can be conducted over the telephone from anywhere. Here is a selection from the opportunities page of one of the 'quality' papers:

Start your own import/export agency
No capital, premises or experience required
No risk – work from home

MAKE MONEY FROM HOME
Find out how thousands of people are making substantial incomes working from home
Call for latest free information pack

We need home-based AGENTS in all areas just like you . . . .

Clearly there is an element of risk here and of course payments are all by results.

Activities

Local investigation

1 Identify your area from the map on page 6. Research information about levels and patterns of employment in your area.

2 Look at your own local employment prospects (armed with your GNVQ Advanced in Business). What is available in the local job centre, the local paper and at the careers service which is appropriate to your skills and ambitions?

3 Is there a major employer in your area?

4 Are there recent changes? Perhaps the area is being regenerated by government or EU grants. Do you expect prospects for employment to change in any way?

5 Would you like to work locally, elsewhere in the UK or abroad?

Sometimes a local problem can present an unexpected opportunity, as this newspaper article shows.

'None of this was planned, I didn't research the market, it was just fortunate that it happened.'

PETER Webb once worked for a private contractor who provided plant for British Steel in Corby, Northamptonshire. In 1979 he was made redundant along with thousands of other workers when the steel works closed. He is now managing director of his own civil engineering company called Weldon. His success is entirely due to the closure of British Steel and the chaos which followed.

Not only was the works the town's major employer, but it also created work in the service industries. By 1981 male unemployment was at 30 per cent, and with 70 per cent living in council houses most had to stay. The council pleaded their case with the government and in Europe. The result was that the town was given assisted area status and became the country's first enterprise zone. So far it has received grants totalling £130 million.

Peter and two friends had invested £21,000 in earth-moving equipment which came up for auction, some of which they had previously been working with. The idea was to sell it as quickly as possible, but it soon became clear that it was better to use it to help clear the way for the new industry.

In 1991 the company gained BS 5750 (now European Standard ISO 9002) – the guarantee of quality assurance for all its staff. It carries out an annual training programme for staff and encourages them to learn new skills to enhance their career prospects.

Source: adapted from *The Guardian*

Activities

1 How does a major employer like British Steel generate jobs in the tertiary sector? (A similar effect has happened in Aberdeen with the oil industry; can you mention others?)

2 How can an enterprise zone attract industries to a region such as Corby? What sort of industries would be able to relocate in this way?

Widening horizons

Frequently people need to be prepared to travel to gain a job, either within the UK or abroad. EU employment law has encouraged the free exchange of workers within Europe. Though the language barrier and lack of standardisation of some qualifications still hinders the free flow of labour the completion of the Channel Tunnel is bound to make the UK feel nearer to the continent.

Case study

Driving ambition?

A team of 95 international drivers takes the Eurostar trains across four separate railway systems from Waterloo to Paris or Brussels. All drivers will have passed a four week series of tests designed to prove their concentration, reaction speeds and co-ordination. They also need the ability to learn complex rules as well as a new language.

Drivers receive up to 20 weeks French tuition and spend time 'en famille' in France to help them gain an appreciation of other cultures.

Source: EPS Factsheet no. 20

Working and studying in Europe

A number of recent initiatives have been launched with the aim of encouraging young people to study and work in Europe.

- The Erasmus programme, launched in June 1987, enables young people to spend some time at a university in another member state of the EU. The programme works on an exchange basis and provides special grants and guarantees for around 60,000 students a year.
- The Lingua programmes, set up in 1989, aims to improve foreign language teaching and training in the business world. It also encourages the exchange of teachers and students through projects linking organisations across the EU.
- The Petra programme provides placements and exchanges for young people undergoing training, in employment or seeking employment. The programme is aimed at young people under 28 who do not have a university education. The idea is to give all categories of young people a chance to prepare themselves for a Europe-wide labour market.

Information on the EU can be obtained from: Commission of the European Communities, 8 Storey's Gate, London SW1P 3AT Tel: 973 19 92.

Also: Cardiff Tel: 37 16 31, Edinburgh Tel: 225 20 58, Belfast Tel: 24 07 08, Dublin Tel: 71 22 44.

Practical matters – statutory requirements of employment/self-employment

As an employee you will benefit from understanding the legal requirements of employment. If you become self-employed and especially if you become an employer, this is essential.

Employment law is covered in Chapter 7. Here some practical details relating to income tax, VAT and National Insurance Contributions (NIC) are given. Appendix 4 on pages 752–3 shows the relevant figures at the time of writing. These will vary with the Chancellor's budget in November and you will need to make sure that they are updated.

Personal allowances, the tax return and the code number

Income tax is not based upon gross pay but upon taxable pay. People with the same gross pay may well pay different amounts of income tax, because of their different personal allowances (the amount that they are allowed to earn free of tax).

The basic allowance is given in Appendix 4. The yearly tax return allows additional allowances for dependent relatives, pension fund contributions, subscriptions to professional bodies and some work expenses, such as working clothes (though not travel to work). On the basis of their allowance, everyone is given a personal code number. An allowance of £4,523 a year, for example, would give a code number of 452. The higher the code number, the less tax is due.

When you change jobs, you will be given a form **P45** to take to your new employer. This gives all relevant tax details, including the code number, earnings to date and tax to date for that year. It enables **PAYE** to be deducted at the correct rate.

The tax year

The government's financial year runs from 6 April to 5 April the following year.

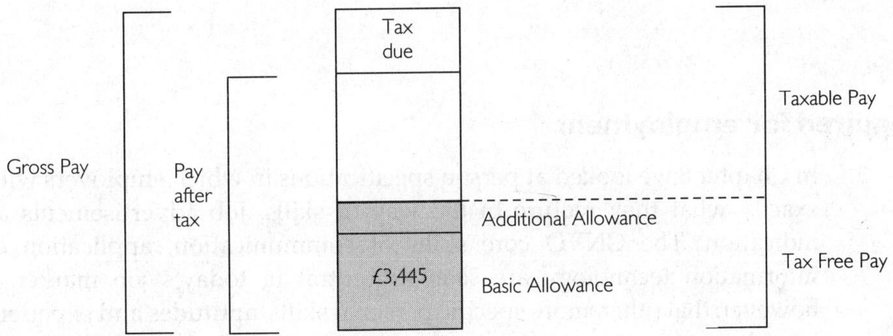

Tax rates

The pay that is not free is called taxable pay. This is taxed at different rates depending upon earnings (see Appendix 4).

The main statutory requirements relating to employees, the self-employed and employers are shown in the tables below and overleaf.

Item	Employee	Self-employed/employer	Forms needed
Income tax – payable to the Inland Revenue		Sole traders and partners provide a statement of profits annually to the Inland Revenue who calculate tax liability on the basis of this	Annual accounts at end of financial year
	Tax deducted at source under PAYE (pay as you earn). Company directors are also taxed as employees	Employers are responsible for correctly calculating, deducting and forwarding the income tax of their employees	P 45 P11 (tax deduction card) Payslip P60

Item	Employee	Self-employed/employer	Forms needed
National Insurance Contributions (NICs) – payable to the Contributions Agency of the DSS (Class 1 and Class 4 are collected by the Inland Revenue with tax)		Self-employed pay a flat-rate Class 2 contribution. Payment is either monthly or quarterly (each 13 weeks). Where profits are above a certain level Class 4 contributions may be due as well	
	Employees pay Class 1 contributions deducted at source from wages/salaries	Employers deduct NICs for each employee from weekly gross pay. There is also an employer contribution per employee (see Appendix 4)	P45 shows National Insurance number P11 records Class 1 NICs Payslip
VAT – collected by HM Customs & Excise		A business must register for VAT (i.e. must charge VAT at present rate) where turnover exceeds the stated limit (see Appendix 4)	VAT return. Returns quarterly or annually (small business)

Skills required for employment

In Chapter 8 we looked at person specifications in which employers will usually set out exactly what they require in the way of skills. Job advertisements also carry some indication. The GNVQ core skills of communication, application of number and information technology are seen as central in today's job market. You may find, however, that other, more specific personal skills, aptitudes and experience are specified in addition.

For some jobs you will be required to take aptitude tests (remember the BR advert on page 372).

Activity

Look again at the advertisements for jobs which you feel will interest you and for which you feel qualified.

What skills do they require? You can usually obtain a person specification by writing or telephoning. This will help you to know employers' expectations.

Skills required for self-employment

The various business start-up guides printed by the clearing banks all begin with a question such as 'Do you have what it takes to work for yourself?'. In our business planning case study Della and Devi considered this problem on pages 695–6. To this list might be added **personal circumstances**, as shown in the table opposite.

Do you have any debts?	If so, it may not be a good idea to start in business just yet – indeed it may not be possible. All businesses need start-up funds. Whilst it is possible to borrow some of these funds, with the support of a good business plan, any bank will also need to see some commitment on the part of the entrepreneur. (S)he will also need to invest some personal capital.
Does your family approve and will they support you?	There will be enough problems without having opposition at home. The business will need all of your concentration and enthusiasm. You will also need support and encouragement.

Activity

If you didn't try the skills checklist before (pages 695–6), try it now. Also consider your personal circumstances. Are you right for self-employment?

Help and advice

There is nothing wrong with asking for advice; indeed many organisations are set up specifically to help with this. The careers service is the most usual avenue. If you are considering setting up in business you will require specialist help.

The Department of Trade and Industry (DTI), which is the government department with overall responsibility for business enterprise, set up a network of 82 TECs (Training and Enterprise Councils) to provide information to businesses in England and Wales. (Subsequently one has folded.) In Scotland a similar service is provided by Local Enterprise Companies and in Northern Ireland by the Department of Economic Development.

Whatever your chosen career path you may find some of the following addresses helpful.

Organisation	Information provided	Booklets	Acts of Parliament
ACAS (Advisory, Conciliation and Arbitration Service) Clifton House, 83-118 Euston Road, London NE1 2RB	Advice for employers. Will mediate in employment disputes	*Employing People*	Acts concerning company law
Accountants (local)	A professional accountant will normally be required to prepare annual accounts. Also gives financial advice	Tax, VAT, investment booklets produced by other bodies	Companies Act Finance Act
Banks (local)	Provide a comprehensive service on all aspects of business planning	Business start-up guides/business plans	Financial Services Act

Organisation	Information provided	Booklets	Acts of Parliament
Chamber of Commerce Citizens Advice Bureau (local)	Local business information Free help and advice on various matters including points of law	Booklets on a range of matters often explaining citizens' rights	
Companies Registration Office, Companies House, Crown Way, Maindy, Cardiff CF4 3UZ Tel: 01222 388588	Company accounts can be viewed. Advice on business names	*Business names – guidance notes*	Companies Act 1985
Customs and Excise (local office)	Advice on VAT	*Should I Be Registered For VAT?*	Finance Act The turnover above which a business must register for VAT is revised annually in the government's November Budget.
Data Protection Registrar, Wycliffe House, Water Lane, Wilmslow, Cheshire SK9 5AF Tel: 01625 535777	Data protection information	Series of booklets on data protection	Data Protection Act 1984
Department of Social Security (local office)	National Insurance Contributions		Finance Act
Department of the Environment	Ultimately responsible for planning permission, though applications are normally dealt with by the local authority	*A step by step guide to planning permission for small businesses*	Environmental Protection Axt
Employment Department, Moorfoot, Sheffield S1 4PQ Tel: 01742 753275	Advice on employment law (also obtainable from local Jobcentre)	Various leaflets on employee rights, trade union membership, redundancy etc.	Employment Protection Acts (1975 and 1978)
Enterprise Agencies (local)	Local help and advice to small businesses	Small business leaflets on start-up, business planning, accounting, marketing, exporting, trade credit, franchising	
Health and Safety Executive (HSE) Baynards House, 1 Chepstow Place, Westbourne Grove, London W2 4TF Tel: 0171 221 0870	Enforces health and safety law in industry. Non-industrial premises (shops and offices) are inspected by the local authority	*Essentials of Health and Safety at Work* (HMSO publication £3.50)	Health and Safety at Work Act 1974 EU Directives
HMSO (Her Majesty's Stationery Office) Tel: 0171 873 0011 (24 hours)	Publishes and sells government publications	Various publications	Publishes Acts of Parliament, British Standards etc.
Inland Revenue (local office)	Income Tax and Corporation Tax details	*Starting in Business (IR 28).* Other leaflets available on self-employment and taxation	Finance Act
Institute of Business Counsellors, PO Box 8, Harrogate, North Yorkshire HG2 8XB Tel: 01423 870025	Advice from counsellors with personal business experience	*Benefits for Business*	

Organisation	Information provided	Booklets	Acts of Parliament
Local Authority	Deals with planning applications, use of premises for business purposes and issues certain licences		Trades Descriptions Act (weights and measures inspectors). Local By-Laws
National Federation of Self-Employed and Small Businesses, 32 St Anne's Road, Lytham St Annes, Lancashire, FY8 1NY Tel: 01253 720911	Represents the interests of small businesses		
Office of Fair Trading, Government Building, Bromyard Avenue, Acton, London W3 7BB Tel: 0171 269 8608	Issues licences for businesses offering credit and hire facilities	*Do you need a Credit Licence?*	Consumer Credit Act 1974
Patent Office, Cardiff Road, Newport, Gwent NP9 1RH Tel: 01633 814 000	Deals with applications for patents, registered designs and trade marks	*Introducing patents – a guide for inventors*	The Patents Act 1977
Prince's Youth Business Trust, 5 Cleveland Place, SW1Y 6JJ Tel: 0171 925 2900	Encourages new business set up by young people. Gives advice and grants		
Solicitor (local)	Will draw up contracts such as partnership deeds, negotiate leases on premises, arrange purchase/sale of premises (conveyancing)	Various leaflets on legal matters	Deals specifically with legal matters – will need to know of all relevant laws
VSO (Voluntary Service Overseas) 317 Putney Bridge Road, SW15 2PG Tel: 0181 780 2266	Arranges voluntary postings overseas for individuals wishing to work on aid projects in developing countries. Provides experience for the individual whilst giving help to developing countries		

Assignment 15.2
Where am I going?

This assignment develops knowledge and understanding of the following elements:
8.3 Plan for employment or self-employment

It supports development of the following core skills:
Communication 3.2, 3.3, 3.4
Information technology 3.1, 3.2, 3.3

Your tasks

1 Write an honest appraisal of your own personal strengths and weaknesses in relation to skills for:
- employment
- self-employment.

2 Consider your ambitions and what you hope to achieve.

3 Produce a realistic personal plan showing time scales, sources of information needed and actions to be taken for you to become either employed or self-employed. This should include details of the kind of employment that you feel is appropriate and any further personal development, skills training and experience that you feel will be required.

Perhaps your long-term goal requires you to go into higher education. In this case you will need to be aware of:
- where the relevant courses are offered
- what results are required for entry
- applications procedures (UCAS forms need to be in by mid-December).

These should be included in your plan.

4 Update your CV and include this with the assignment.

Good luck!

Appendix I

EU Directive 90/270: Minimum requirements for articles 4 and 5 of Employer's Obligation.

1. EQUIPMENT

(a) General Comment

The use of such equipment must not be a source of risk for workers.

(b) Display screen

- The characters on the screen shall be well-defined and clearly formed, of adequate size and with adequate spacing between characters and lines.
- The image on the screen should be stable, with no flickering or other forms of unstability.
- The brightness and/or the contrast between the characters and the background shall be easily adjustable by the operator, and also easily adjustable to ambient conditions.
- The screen must swivel and tilt easily and freely to suit the needs of the operator.
- It shall be possible to use a separate base for the screen or an adjustable table.
- The screen shall be free of reflective glare and reflections liable to cause discomfort to the user.

(c) Keyboard

- The keyboard shall be tilted and separate from the screen so as to allow the worker to find a comfortable working position avoiding fatigue in the arms and hands.
- The space in front of the keyboard shall be sufficient to provide support for the hands and arms of the operator.
- The keyboard shall have a matt surface to avoid reflective glare.
- The arrangement of the keyboard and the characteristics of the keys shall be such as to facilitate the use of the keyboard.
- The symbols on the keys shall be adequately contrasted and legible from the design working position.

(d) Work desk or work surface

- The work desk or work surface shall have a sufficiently large, low-reflective surface and allow a flexible arrangement of the screen, keyboard, documents and related equipment.
- The document holder shall be stable and adjustable and shall be positioned so as to minimise the need for uncomfortable head and eye movements.
- There shall be adequate space for workers to find a comfortable position.

(e) Work chair

- The work chair shall be stable and allow the operator easy freedom of movement and a comfortable position.
- The seat shall be adjustable in height.
- The seat back shall be adjustable in both height and tilt.
- A footrest shall be made available to anyone who wishes one.

2. ENVIRONMENT

(a) Space requirements

The workstation shall be dimensioned and designed so as to provide sufficient space for the user to change position and vary movements.

(b) Lighting

- Room lighting and/or spot lighting (work lamps) shall ensure satisfactory lighting conditions and an appropriate contrast between the screen and background environment, taking into account the type of work and the user's vision requirements.
- Possible disturbing glare and reflections on the screen or other equipment shall be prevented by coordinating workplace and workstation layout with the positioning and technical characteristics of the artificial light sources.

(c) Reflections and glare

- Workstations shall be designed that sources of light, such as windows and other openings, transparent or translucid walls, and brightly coloured fixtures or walls cause no direct glare and, as far as possible, no reflections on the screen.
- Windows shall be fitted with a suitable system of adjustable covering to attenuate daylight that falls on the workstation.

(d) Noise

Noise emitted by the equipment belonging to the workstation(s) shall be taken into account when a workstation is equipped, in particular so as not to distract attention or disturb speech.

(e) Heat

Equipment belonging to workstation(s) shall not produce excess heat which will cause discomfort to workers.

(f) Radiation

All radiation with the exception of the visible part of the electromagnetic spectrum shall be reduced to negligible levels from the point of view of the protection of workers' safety and health.

(g) Humidity

An adequate level of humidity shall be established and maintained.

3. OPERATOR/COMPUTER INTERFACE

In designing, selecting, commissioning and modifying software, and in designing tasks using display screen equipment, the employer shall take into account the following principles:

- Software must be suitable for the task.
- Software must be easy to use and, where appropriate, adaptable to the operator's level of knowledge or experience; no quantitative or qualitative checking facility may be used without the knowledge of the workers.
- Systems must provide feedback to workers on their performance.
- Systems must display information in a format and at a pace which are adapted to operators.
- The principles of software ergonomics must be applied, in particular to human data processing.

Appendix 2

The Data Protection Act 1984

Unfamiliar words or phrases which are used in the Act

Personal data	Information recorded on a computer about living identifiable individuals
Data subject	An individual to whom personal data refers
Data users	People or organisations who control the contents and use of a collection of personal data. A data user will usually be a company, corporation or organisation but it is possible for an individual to be a data user
Computer bureaux	People or organisations who process personal data for data users or who allow data users to process personal data on their computers

Data protection principles

Registered data users must comply with eight principles. Broadly they state that personal data shall:

1 be obtained and processed, fairly and lawfully;
2 be held only for the lawful purposes described in the register entry;
3 be used only for those purposes and only be disclosed to those people described in the register entry;
4 be adequate, relevant, and not excessive in relation to the purpose for which they are held
5 be accurate and, where necessary, kept up to date;
6 be held no longer than is necessary for that purpose or purposes;
7 be surrounded by proper security;
8 An individual shall be entitled:
a At reasonable intervals and without undue delay or expense:
- To be informed by any data user whether he holds personal data of which that individual is the subject;
- To access any such data held by the data user;

b Where appropriate, to have such data corrected or erased.

Exemptions to the Act

The Act does not apply to all personal data:

- Personal data held by an individual in connection with personal, family or recreational purposes.

  This exemption will not apply to an individual who keeps records on behalf of a club, church or voluntary organisation. Then the organisation rather than the individual will be the data user. The individual will not need to register but the organisation may need to do so.
- Information that the law requires to make public.

  For example the Companies Act 1985 requires every registered company to make its registration of members available to public inspection.
- Payrolls, pensions and accounts purposes.

  This exemption does not apply if the data is used for wider purposes for example as personnel records or for marketing purposes.
- National security.

  Exemption at the discretion of the government minister
- Mailing lists are exempt as long as the personal; data only consists of names, addresses and other details needed for distribution such as phone number, fax number etc. The data subject must be asked if they object to the data being held for this purpose.

- Unincorporated members' clubs (e.g. sports clubs which are not registered companies). All the data subjects must be members of the club and must agree to the data being held for this purpose. The personal data about members may only be disclosed in very limited circumstances.

Many of the exemptions are conditional. If the condition is not observed, the exemption does not apply.

The effect of exemptions on those upon whom data is held:

- the personal data is not registered;
- the individual has no right of access to the personal data. However, if access to the data is requested the user must always reply;
- the registrar has no power under the act. However the courts may inspect the data if an individual applies to them suspecting that the data is not exempt.

Powers of the data protection registrar

Every data user who holds personal data must, unless all the data is exempt, apply for registration. The registrar keeps the register of data users and this is open to public inspection.

To register requires completion of an application form and payment of a fee (around £70). An unregistered data user who holds personal data which is not exempt commits a criminal offence. The maximum penalty is an unlimited fine.

Individual rights

- **Subject access right** entitles individuals to a copy of the information which forms the personal data held about them by the data user. Requests for subject access should be made in writing and sent to the data user at the address given in the register entry. The data user may charge a fee for dealing with a subject access request.
- **Right to take action for compensation** – if the individual is damaged by inaccurate personal data or by loss or unauthorised destruction or disclosure of personal data. An application for compensation must be made by the individual to the County Court or High Court . The Registrar cannot award compensation. The term 'damage' includes financial loss and physical injury but does not include distress suffered by the individual.
- **Right to take action** to have inaccurate personal data corrected or erased. The data subject may apply to the County Court or High Court for an order that the data user should correct or erase the data. A Registrar can also order the correction or erasure but the court's powers are wider than the Registrar's. 'Inaccurate' means incorrect or misleading about any matter of fact not an opinion.
- **Right to complain** to the Registrar that any of the Data Protection Principles or any other provision of the Act has been broken. Many individuals prefer to have their complaints investigated by the Registrar rather than incur the expense and trouble of court proceedings.

Appendix 3

Summary of the Agreement on Social Policy concluded between the Member States of the European Union, with the exception of the United Kingdom of Great Britain and Northern Ireland

Article 1

The Member States have these objectives:

- the promotion of employment;
- improved living and working conditions;
- proper social protection;
- discussion between management and labour;
- the development of human resources so as to achieve lasting employment;

whilst taking account of existing differences between Member States.

Article 2

In order to achieve Article 1, Member States will have the support of the European Union in these areas:

- improvement in particular of the working environment to protect workers' health and safety;
- working conditions;
- management/labour information and consultation;
- equality between men and women with regard to labour market opportunities and treatment at work.

It also considers social security and the protection of workers when their employment contract is terminated, i.e. dismissal procedures, without putting a burden on small/medium sized companies.

Article 3

This states that the European Commission will consult with management and labour before, during and after any proposals are made on social policy (i.e. Articles 1 and 2).

Article 4

This states:

- that any agreements made between management and labour at community level can become contracts;
- the European Council can only act on Article 2 if voting is unanimous or there is a qualified majority.

Article 5

The European Commission will encourage co-operation between Member States.

Article 6

This states that there should be equal pay for male and female workers for equal work. Pay, in this context, means earnings, i.e. the basic wage plus any extra cash or benefits. Equal pay without sex discrimination means 'that pay for the same work at piece rates shall be calculated on the basis of the same unit of measurement', and 'that pay for work at time rates shall be the same for the same job.'

Finally, 'this Article shall not prevent any Member State from maintaining or adopting measures providing for specific advantages in order to make it easier for women to pursue a vocational activity or to prevent or compensate for disadvantages in their professional career.'

Article 7

This states that the European Commission should produce a progress report each year.

Declaration 1 which follows Article 7 reinforces the point that small/medium sized employers should not be disadvantaged by the Social Chapter.

Appendix 4

The Budget introduced by Kenneth Clarke, Chancellor of the Exchequer, on Tuesday 29 November 1994

The main points are summarised below. Space is left for you to fill in changes made in future budgets

Income tax

Personal income tax allowance p.a.:

	1995/6	From April 1996
Single person (below age 65)	£3,525	
Additional allowance for married couple or single parent	£1,720	

Taxable income to be taxed at the following rates:

	1995/6	From April 1996
20%	First £3,200	
25% ('the basic rate')*	£3,200 to £24,300	
40%	Over £24,300	

*Dividends for basic rate taxpayers taxed at 20% (to encourage share ownership)

Inheritance tax

	1995/6	From April 1996
Begins at	£154,000	

Corporation tax

Sole traders and partners are taxed upon the annual profits of their business at the rates shown above. Similarly company directors are taxed as employees under the PAYE scheme at these rates. Additionally company profits are subject to corporation tax as follows:

	Year to 31 March 1996	Year to 31 March 1997
25% (small companies' rate)	Up to £300,000 p.a.	
35%	£300,001 to £1,500,000 p.a.	
33% (main rate)	Over £1,500,000 p.a.	

Venture Capital Trusts (VCTs)

From April 1995 there is encouragement for individuals to invest in unquoted trading companies through special VCTs. VCTs are companies quoted on the stock market; they must have at least 70% of their investments in unquoted companies.

Individuals disposing of up to £100,000 p.a. in investments in VCTs are exempt from tax on dividends.

Enterprise Investment Scheme (EIS)

From 28 November 1994 there is relief from capital gains tax of up to 60% for 'Business angels' subscribing to company shares under this scheme.

National Insurance Contributions (NICs)

Class 1 (people in employment):

	1995/6	From April 1996
Weekly earnings	Employee rate:	
Below £59	Nil	
£59–£440	2% of £59 plus 10% of excess	
Over £440	£39.28 per week	

	Employer rate:
Below £59	Nil
£59–£104.99	3%
£105–£149.99	5%
£150–£204.99	7%
£205 and over	10.2%

Class 2 (self-employed):

	1995/6	From April 1996
Flat rate	£5.85 p.w. or £304.20 p.a.	
If profits exceed	£3,310 p.a.	

Class 4 (self-employed):

	1995/6	From April 1996
Rate	7.3% (max. payable p.a. £1,185.52)	
On profits	£6,640–£22,880 p.a.	

From April 1996 there will be a one-year NI 'holiday' for firms taking on long-term unemployed (i.e. those out of work for 2 years). It is hoped to create 5,000 new job opportunities by this measure.

VAT

VAT is at 17.5% on most goods, though some basic goods such as bread and children's clothes continue to be zero-rated.

VAT remains at 8% on domestic fuel (electricity and gas). The planned increase to 17.5% announced in the Budget was abandoned after the government was defeated on this issue.

Registration for VAT: a business must register for VAT when annual turnover exceeds the stated limit. This is reviewed annually.

	1994/1995	From 1 December 1995
Registration is compulsory at	£46,000 p.a.	
De-registration possible at	£44,000 p.a.	

Small firms can choose to pay VAT annually rather than quarterly.

Index